KU-875-476

WITHDRAWN FROM
THE LIBRARY

UNIVERSITY OF
WINCHESTER

KA 0265534 9

THE CULTURE OF POWER
AND
THE POWER OF CULTURE

KING ALFRED'S COLLEGE
LIBRARY

THE CULTURE OF POWER AND THE POWER OF CULTURE

Old Regime Europe 1660–1789

T. C. W. BLANNING

OXFORD
UNIVERSITY PRESS

OXFORD
UNIVERSITY PRESS

Great Clarendon Street, Oxford OX2 6DP

Oxford University Press is a department of the University of Oxford.
It furthers the University's objective of excellence in research, scholarship,
and education by publishing worldwide in

Oxford New York

Athens Auckland Bangkok Bogotá Buenos Aires Cape Town
Chennai Dar es Salaam Delhi Florence Hong Kong Istanbul Karachi
Kolkata Kuala Lumpur Madrid Melbourne Mexico City Mumbai Nairobi
Paris São Paulo Shanghai Singapore Taipei Tokyo Toronto Warsaw

with associated companies in Berlin Ibadan

Oxford is a registered trade mark of Oxford University Press
in the UK and in certain other countries

Published in the United States
By Oxford University Press Inc., New York

© T.C.W. Blanning 2002

The moral rights of the author have been asserted

Database right Oxford University Press (maker)

First published 2002

All rights reserved. No part of this publication may be reproduced,
stored in a retrieval system, or transmitted, in any form or by any means,
without the prior permission in writing of Oxford University Press,
or as expressly permitted by law, or under terms agreed with the appropriate
reprographics rights organization. Enquiries concerning reproduction
outside the scope of the above should be sent to the Rights Department.
Oxford University Press, at the address above

You must not circulate this book in any other binding or cover
and you must impose this same condition on any acquirer

British Library Cataloguing in Publication Data
Data available

Library of Congress Cataloging in Publication Data

Blanning T.C.W.
The Cluture of power and the power of culture: old regime Europe, 1660–1789 /
T.C.W. Blanning.
p. cm.
Includes bibliographical references and index.
1. Europe—Intellectual life—18th century. 2. Europe—Politics and government—18th century. 3. Books and reading—Europe—History—18th century. 4. Philosophy, Modern—18th century. 5. Enlightenment—Europe—18th century. 6. Culture diffusion—Europe—History—18th century. 7. Europe—Social life and customs—18th century. I. Title.

CB411 .B58 2002 2001033864

ISBN 0–19–822745–0

1 3 5 7 9 10 8 6 4 2

Typeset in 10/13.25 JansonText
by Kolam Information Services Pvt. Ltd, Pondicherry, India
Printed in Great Britain
on acid-free paper by T.J. International Ltd, Padstow, Cornwall

To Nicky and Tom

KING ALFRED'S COLLEGE
WINCHESTER
02655349 | 940.25 BLA

PREFACE

During the course of the years that this book has been in gestation I have incurred many debts, not least to the many generations of undergraduates to whom much of it has been exposed in various forms. The knowledge that I badly need the opportunity to articulate ideas for lectures and seminars, to defend them in discussion, and to modify or abandon those which fail to stand up, has always given me immunity to the siren calls from research institutes without students. Of the many postgraduates who have helped this process over the years, I am particularly indebted to Julian Swann, Munro Price, Peter Wilson, Maiken Umbach, Gary Savage, Thomas Ahnert, Verena Westermayr, Andrew Thompson, Mark Berry, Hannah Smith, and Emma Winter. I am also grateful to the numerous institutions which have listened to different parts of the text with varying degrees of attention and approval, notably the German Historical Institutes of London, Paris, and Warsaw, the Modern European History seminar of the University of Cambridge, the faculties of Music and History of Queen's University, Belfast, the University of York, the Anglo-American Conference of Historians, the Free University Berlin, the University of Glasgow, the Society for Court Studies, and the University of the Third Age (the most attentive). Many of my Cambridge colleagues have been generous with their time and wisdom, especially Jonathan Steinberg, Chris Clark, Brendan Simms, Robert Tombs, and Derek Beales. I need hardly add that none of them are responsible for the errors, distortions, and omissions which remain. My greatest debt is recorded in the dedication.

Tim Blanning
Cambridge
January 2001

CONTENTS

PART III – REVOLUTION

LIST OF PLATES

(between pp. 240–241)

KING ALFRED'S COLLEGE
LIBRARY

LIST OF TABLES

Introduction

The Culture of Power and the Power of Culture

OVERTURE

For his lyric tragedy *Zoroastre*, first performed in 1749, Jean-Philippe Rameau wrote what he called 'an overture in place of a prologue', offering the following explanation:

This is the first opera which is performed without a prologue. People were highly astonished by this innovation. Experience has shown that the choice was correct. Time is so valuable in a musical drama, a plot of large dimensions requires such a variety of means within this span; poetry, art, machinery, music and dance must interweave with one another at such fast and diverse tempi that one cannot be too frugal with fractions of seconds and cannot be too strict in the omission of superfluous material.[1]

For a similar reason, 'an overture in place of an introduction' is offered here, or rather 'an overture *as well as* an introduction'. It represents an attempt to deal with a problem faced by the author of any book aimed at an audience wider than just the academic world. An introduction defining the terms, analysing the concepts, explaining the methodology, and discussing the historiography, in the manner apparently obligatory for German monographs, is neither needed nor desired by the great majority. For them, the remainder of this

[1] Jean-Philippe Rameau, *Zoroastre. Tragédie en 5 Actes* (Paris, 1749).

section will provide an outline of what is to be found in the main text. From there they can pass straight to Chapter 1 and the court of Louis XIV. Those interested in discovering the conceptual foundations on which the book is based can remain for the introduction.

This book is a comparative study of the development of political culture in Europe from the late seventeenth to the late eighteenth century. Although there is an occasional glance eastwards and southwards, the focus is chiefly on Great Britain, France, and the Holy Roman Empire. Its central thesis is that during this period a new cultural space developed, which posed new challenges to regimes and their ruling orders. Alongside the old culture, centred on the courts and the representation of monarchical authority, there emerged a 'public sphere', in which private individuals came together to form a whole greater than the sum of the parts. By exchanging information, ideas, and criticism, these individuals created a cultural actor—the public—which has dominated European culture ever since. Many, if not most, of the cultural phenomena of the modern world derive from the 'long eighteenth century'—the periodical, the newspaper, the novel, the journalist, the critic, the public library, the concert, the art exhibition, the public museum, the national theatre, just to list a sample. Of course almost all of these can be found in earlier periods, but it was in the eighteenth century that they came to maturity and fused to trigger what can reasonably be called a cultural revolution. Perhaps most important of all, it was then that 'public opinion' came to be recognized as the ultimate arbiter in matters of taste and politics.

These changes presented regimes with both a challenge and an opportunity. Deft and timely adaptation could bring a healthy flourishing of authority, but a failure to adjust led to a haemorrhage of legitimacy, chronic anaemia and even death, as in the case of the French monarchy. Even the most clear-sighted, such as Frederick the Great of Prussia, found the path that led to stability hard to find and even more hard to stick to. To paraphrase Clausewitz, they found that everything in politics was very simple, but even the simplest thing was difficult.[2] Few had a master plan, and those that did, such as Joseph II of Austria, found that it only made their problems more intractable. With their vision clouded by being denied the advantage of hindsight, sovereigns and their advisers had to grope from one expedient to the next. Yet if it was a difficult task, it was not impossible. Given reasonable intelligence, rulers with access to their subjects' developing concerns should have been able to detect

[2] Carl von Clausewitz, *On War*, ed. and trans. Michael Howard and Peter Paret (Princeton, NJ, 1976), p. 119: 'Everything in war is very simple, but the simplest thing is difficult.'

cultural change. Self-imposed isolation at Versailles anchored the heirs of Louis XIV to a mode of representing kingship which became more moribund with every year that passed. Their more nimble and better-informed British and German colleagues proved able to reinvent themselves as the patriot kings or the servants of the state that the new conditions called for. It was in the public sphere which emerged in the course of the eighteenth century that the work performed today by spin-doctors, image-branders, media consultants, and focus groups became an essential part of the successful politician.

In making a successful transition to modern monarchy, the British and the Prussians were assisted by the prestige conferred by military success. They were the two victors of the Seven Years War, the great world war of the mid-century which made Great Britain the dominant power in the world outside Europe and confirmed Prussia's newly asserted great-power status. The equation must also be turned round: it was just the success of the British and Prussian states in adapting their political cultures which enabled them to achieve success in war. As John Brewer has written, 'States are not just centres of power; they are also centres of authority whose effectiveness depends on the degree of legitimacy that both regimes and their actions are able to command. Broadly speaking, the less legitimacy, the greater the "friction" produced by the conduct of the state and the more resources it has to devote to achieve the same effect.'[3] Those words come from his masterly study of British public finance in the period and reveal a crucial connection between culture and power. In maximizing its fiscal resources and thus its power, the state must create a 'credible commitment' to encourage its taxpayers to make the necessary sacrifices. And in creating the trust which underpins this relationship, the personal culture of the political decision-makers is of cardinal importance.[4] As we shall see, the British and the Prussians followed different paths but arrived at the same goal. The French were starting from the wrong place, with an out-of-date map and so little sense of urgency that they barely moved at all. When the Parisian crowd came to Versailles on 5 October 1789, they found Louis XVI, his family, and his court living in an ossified cultural world from which the spirit had long since departed. It was a museum *avant la lettre*.

Captured by the crowd, who took the King and Queen back to Paris with them on the following day, the royal palace had now become national

[3] John Brewer, *The sinews of power: war, money and the English state 1688–1783* (New York, 1989), p. xx.

[4] Martin Daunton, *The Ransom of Property: The Politics of Taxation in Britain, 1793–1914* (Cambridge, 2001), ch. 1.

property.[5] Of all the manifold failings of the French monarchy in the eighteenth century, the most serious was its inability to sense the growing authority of the nation. This did not spring ready armed from the heads of the revolutionaries in 1789 but had been a long time in the making. Across western and central Europe, the two master nouns of political discourse were 'state' and 'nation'. Louis XIV might well have said *L'État, c'est moi*, but Louis XVI could not say *La Nation, c'est moi*. That was left to the deputies of the Third Estate of the Estates General, who declared themselves to be the 'National Assembly' on 17 June 1789. The alienation between monarchy and nation had been underway at least since 1713, when Louis XIV prompted Clement XI to issue the bull *Unigenitus* against the Jansenists. It became a chasm with the 'diplomatic revolution' of 1756 and was made finally unbridgeable by the Austrian marriage of 1770. Meanwhile, in Great Britain the Hanoverians were slowly, painfully but successfully constructing a new alliance between dynasty and nation, while in Prussia an odd but effective 'state patriotism' was promoted by Frederick the Great.

In what follows, 'culture' is used in the general sense classically defined by Sir Edward Tylor as 'that complex whole which includes knowledge, belief, art, morals, law, custom and any other capabilities and habits acquired by man as a member of society'.[6] No attempt has been made to explore every aspect of this 'complex whole'. Considerations of length and focus have excluded such important aspects as gender and popular culture, and have directed attention to the culture of the elites. For the same reason, not even every aspect of 'high culture' has been given the attention it deserves. Special favour has been shown to music, on the grounds that in the past it has suffered from relative neglect outside strictly musicological studies, but it has a great deal to say about past societies. Political culture has been used in the sense defined by Lynn Hunt, namely 'the values, expectations, and implicit rules that expressed and shaped collective intentions and actions'.[7] Both concepts—'culture' and 'political culture'—have generated a huge and rapidly growing body of literature, but those in search of further exploration of their theoretical aspects will need to look elsewhere.[8]

[5] It is now officially known as the Musée National et Domaine National de Versailles.

[6] Sir Edward Burnett Tylor, *Primitive Culture: Researches into the Development of Mythology, Philosophy, Religion, Language, Art, and Custom* (London, 1871), p. 1.

[7] Lynn Hunt, *Politics, Culture and Class in the French Revolution* (London, 1986), p. 10.

[8] A good place to start is with Lynn Hunt (ed.), *The New Cultural History* (Berkeley, Los Angeles, and London, 1989) and the literature cited and discussed there.

The choice of cultural institution or artefact has also been influenced by the concern with power. This is understood as the power of states to command the obedience of their subjects at home and to assert their interests in the international arena. This is not just a question of military might and the means to finance it, however important they might be. Power depends as much on perception as reality. Even when the emperor's wardrobe is empty, his nudity may be concealed from eyes dimmed by memories of past glory. A strong ruler is made stronger still by skilful projection of his majesty. Writing about Louis XIV, Peter Burke has observed: 'Ritual, art and architecture may all be seen as the instruments of self-assertion, as the continuation of war and diplomacy by other means.'[9] When, in 1679, Louis XIV obliged Frederick William, the Great Elector of Brandenburg, to return to Sweden all the territory conquered during five years of victorious warfare, he did so not by force of arms (there was no French soldier within several hundred miles of the war-zone) but by his aura of authority.[10] It was as much a cultural as a military or diplomatic construct. Indeed, at the height of his powers the 'Sun King' presented a perfect example of a marriage of culture and power. Yet, as we shall see, in the fast-moving world of the long eighteenth century which was just beginning, keeping the two in harmony was an increasingly difficult task. Just over a century later, in 1787, Frederick William's great-great-grandson, King Frederick William II, would exact revenge for his ancestor's humiliation, by coming west to the Dutch Republic to impose his own *pax Borussica* in France's backyard.[11]

REPRESENTATIONAL CULTURE AND THE PUBLIC SPHERE

The conceptual framework underpinning this analysis has been strongly influenced, although not dictated, by Jürgen Habermas's early work, *The Structural Transformation of the Public Sphere*, first published in German in 1962.[12] The

[9] Peter Burke, *The Fabrication of Louis XIV* (New Haven, 1992), p. 65.

[10] The best account of this revealing episode is to be found in Otto Hintze, *Die Hohenzollern und ihr Werk* , 8th edn. (Berlin, 1916), pp. 229–38.

[11] See below, pp. 421–4.

[12] Jürgen Habermas, *Strukturwandel der Öffentlichkeit* (Neuwied am Rhein, 1962); *The Structural Transformation of the Public Sphere: An Inquiry into a Category of Bourgeois Society*, trans. Thomas Burger (Cambridge, 1989). It was translated into French as *L'Espace public: archéologie de la publicité comme dimension constitutive de la société* (Paris, 1978).

influence in the German-speaking world of this volume has been in inverse ratio to its modest size (modest by German standards, that is). It is genuinely difficult to find a German monograph on the period, however specialized and abstruse its contents, which does not contain a reverential reference to Habermas's work. It must surely be the most influential academic dissertation (*Habilitationsschrift*) ever to appear in print. However, although it had important implications for the history of Great Britain and its Empire and even took some illustrative material from British history, its impact on Anglo-American historiography was long delayed by the notorious inability of its practitioners to read any language other than their own. (It is not enough just to know 'a bit of German' to be able to read Habermas in the original. Even native German speakers have difficulty in deciphering his tortuous prose, which gives fresh support for Wickham Steed's old maxim that 'the Germans dive deeper, but come up muddier'). It was not until an English translation was published in 1989 that Habermas was able to colonize the Atlantic world. Since then, Anglophone scholars have certainly been making up for lost time, as studies reflecting his influence have multiplied.[13] As early as 1994 Jeremy Popkin was warning that phrases such as 'the emergence of public opinion' and 'the growth of the public sphere' were hardening into catch-all explanations for the transformations that made the French Revolution possible.[14]

Although the translator of Habermas's book accomplished his thankless task with as much clarity as could be expected, access to *The Structural Transformation of the Public Sphere* remains difficult. It might be helpful, therefore, to summarize the main argument as it affects the argument of this book. There is, of course, plenty more besides in Habermas, not least because he is not writing as a historian. In presenting his macroscopic perspective of European cultural development, his primary purpose is to identify and explain what he regards as the malaise of modern culture and to indicate how it might be rectified. He does this by illustrating and explaining the change in the function of culture from the Middle Ages to the present day. In the process, he provides a socio-historical explanation of 'the culture industry', a phrase first coined by Theo-

[13] There is a helpful list of books and articles dealing with Habermas at both a substantive and a theoretical level in the footnotes of Harold Mah, 'Phantasies of the public sphere: rethinking the Habermas of historians', *Journal of Modern History*, 72 (2000), pp. 151–75. Joan Landes has compared the impact of Habermas's book to Max Weber's *The Protestant Ethic and the Spirit of Capitalism*—Joan B. Landes, *Women and the Public Sphere in the Age of the French Revolution* (Ithaca, NY, and London, 1988), p. 5.

[14] In a review of works by Arlette Farge, Michèle Fogel, and Gudrun Gersmann in *Eighteenth Century Studies*, 28, 1 (1994), pp. 151–2.

dor Adorno and Max Horkheimer in 1944.[15] Habermas also follows them in stressing the essentially political character of culture.[16] At the centre of his analysis is the relationship between what is regarded as public and what is regarded as private. In the Middle Ages, he argues, there was no clear distinction between public and private because there was no clear concept of private property.[17] Those who exercised power—monarchs, nobles, prelates—expressed their status in public in a concrete, non-abstract way, through insignia, clothing, gesture, or rhetoric. Power was both exercised and represented (in the sense of 'being made present') directly: 'as long as the prince and the estates of the realm still "are" the land, instead of merely functioning as deputies for it, they are able to "re-present"; they represent their power "before" the people, instead of for the people.'[18]

This is representational culture. Confined to those who exercise power, it assumes an entirely passive attitude on the part of the rest of the population. It reached its apogee in the courtly, chivalric court-culture of France and Burgundy in the fifteenth century, but it lived on through the early modern period, transforming itself into the baroque. By now, however, representation had become more confined, moving from the streets of the city to the parks and state apartments of the château. In a bourgeois house even the ceremonial rooms are designed to be lived in; in a baroque château, even the living rooms have a ceremonial purpose. Indeed, especially in France, the most intimate—the bedroom—is also the most important and the king was not even left alone when he relieved himself, as the 'groom of the stole' attended to wipe the royal bottom. The sumptuous display of the representational public sphere was not supposed to be recreational or self-indulgent; its purpose was to represent the power of the sovereign before the people. So the sovereign had to be on parade even when he was eating—the people were still allowed to watch. It was only bourgeois banquets which became entirely private.[19]

There was a corresponding change in the role of the nobility during the early modern period, as the decentralized feudal empires made way for centralized absolutist states. In the feudal period, the nobles represented their own power before the people. Indeed it was difficult to say when a noble was a

[15] Peter Uwe Hohendahl, 'Critical theory, public sphere and culture: Jürgen Habermas and his critics', *New German Critique*, XVI (1979), p. 90.

[16] Ibid., p. 89.

[17] *The Structural Transformation of the Public Sphere*, p. 5.

[18] Ibid., p. 8.

[19] Ibid., p. 10. Much of Habermas's historical information is drawn from R. Alewyn, *Das große Welttheater: die Epoche der höfischen Feste* (Hamburg, 1959).

sovereign and vice versa, the king or emperor being only *primus inter pares*. However, the concentration of power in the person of the sovereign in the form of absolutism meant that now the nobles were required to represent not their own power before the people but that of the sovereign.[20] In the course of the eighteenth century, these developments accelerated and intensified, as the feudal powers—prince, Church, and nobility—fell apart in a process of polarization which divided them into their private and public elements. The separation of the privy purse from the state budget, and of institutions of government from the court, the development of a professional bureaucracy and a professional army—all represented what Habermas calls the objectivization of the institutions of public power. Protestantism and/or toleration transferred religion to the private sphere, leaving the Church as just one more public body. Where they survived, the medieval assemblies of the three estates became parliaments.[21] In this way, a clear distinction was established between the public and the private; society was now a private sphere in contradistinction to the state.

Two interconnected developments had dissolved the old order: the exchange of goods and the exchange of information. Together they created a fundamentally different kind of public sphere—the bourgeois. With the rise of capitalism, the seamless web of authority began to fracture and distinct public and private spheres—state and civil society—emerged. It was a process encouraged by related developments within the family, as the separation of the bourgeois family from the work-place and the emergence of a new 'sphere of intimacy' promoted new ideals of love, liberty, and education.[22] While the feudal public sphere had been founded on authority, received passively, the essence of the bourgeois public sphere is rational argument. The bourgeois public sphere can be defined as the medium through which private persons can reason in public. In doing so, they perform the vital function of mediating relations between the essentially separate realms of civil society and the state.[23] Habermas argues not that there was a public mind but that there was a public sphere. What matters about it is not what it contains in terms of ideas or feelings or even its social composition, but the fact that those contents are

[20] Habermas, *The Structural Transformation of the Public Sphere*, p. 10.

[21] Ibid., pp. 11–12.

[22] Ibid., pp. 43–51. On this aspect of Habermas's argument, see also Benjamin Nathans, 'Habermas's "Public sphere" in the era of the French Revolution', *French Historical Studies*, 16, 3 (1990), p. 623 and Dale van Kley, 'In search of eighteenth century Parisian public opinion', *French Historical Studies*, 19, 1 (1995), p. 216.

[23] Thomas McCarthy, *The Critical Theory of Jürgen Habermas* (London, 1978), p. 381.

actively communicated. It is the effort of communication which creates the 'public' and gives it qualities of cohesion and authority quite different from mere aggregates of individuals. In other words, what is so special about this process is the historically unique medium in which political debate now took place: public argument.[24]

Habermas does not suppose that this was a sudden process. Those who established the public sphere were private citizens, not immediately involved in the exercise of power. They did not bid directly for a share of power, rather they undermined the very principle of the existing regime's rule by advocating publicity (*Publizität*) as a principle of control.[25] With the forces of production on their side, it could only be a matter of time before their concept of the public sphere triumphed completely. Long before political victory was achieved, however, the bourgeois succeeded in establishing non-political forms of their new public concept. This they did through cultural media which now became accessible to the public—reading societies, lecture halls, theatres, museums, and concerts.[26] What these various spaces had in common was the sovereignty of rational argument which prevailed in them, outranking the claims of status or wealth. Participants in the institutions of the public sphere were 'mere humans' and the laws of both of the market and the state were suspended.[27]

This in turn was made possible by the same economic forces which began the erosion of the feudal public sphere. Culture was transformed from something which is representational into a commodity which could be desired for its own sake. Cultural industrialization had begun. The more that art objects were produced for the market, the more they escaped from the control of the old patrons—the court, the Church, and the nobles. And the more they became accessible to all, the more they lost their aura, their sacramental character. So for the first time, in the eighteenth century, a reading public developed. One sign of this, among many others, was the replacement of aristocratic patrons by publishers as commissioning agents. The change is

[24] Habermas, *The Structural Transformation of the Public Sphere*, p. 27. There is a particularly good concise definition of what Habermas means by the public sphere in Dena Goodman, 'The public and the nation', *Eighteenth Century Studies*, 29, 1 (1995), p. 1: 'Habermas brought into focus a public sphere of literate men and women, who, through their participation in burgeoning discursive institutions of print and sociability, transformed the social and political landscape of eighteenth century Europe while empowering themselves as autonomous individuals.'

[25] Ibid., p. 28.

[26] Ibid., p. 29.

[27] Ibid., p. 36. See also Wolfgang Jäger, *Öffentlichkeit und Parlamentarismus. Eine Kritik an Jürgen Habermas* (Stuttgart, Berlin, Cologne, and Mainz, 1973), p. 12.

particularly clear, Habermas believes, in the case of music. Until the end of the eighteenth century, all music was tied to the needs of a representational public, confined to three functions: the representation of power, the propagation of Christianity, and the entertainment of aristocrats. The development of the bourgeois public sphere turned music into a commodity, made music accessible to all who could pay, and liberated both composer and performer from the thraldom of representation.[28]

It is from the critical habits and public institutions created in this cultural public sphere of the bourgeoisie that the further development to political criticism occurred. It can be detected for the first time in the economically most advanced country in Europe—Great Britain—around 1700, when forces looking to exert influence on political decision-making appealed to public discussion to legitimate their demands.[29] As part of this development, the old estates-style representation transformed itself into a modern parliament, although it did so painfully slowly in a process lasting the whole century. However, the three decisive moves occurred in the mid-1690s, with the foundation of the Bank of England, the lapse of the Licensing Act in 1695, which abolished pre-censorship, and the first unified cabinet (referring to the Whig cabinet of 1695–8). Harley was the first politician to appreciate the potential of the new situation, followed quickly by Walpole and Bolingbroke, who also appealed to the new bourgeois public sphere.[30]

A cultural public sphere also developed on the continent, but could not progress to the political stage until the capitalist means of production had reached the level achieved by Great Britain after 1688. Public opinion had become politicized in France by the middle of the eighteenth century but, despite such significant pointers as Necker's *Compte rendu*, it could not institutionalize its critical impulse until after the Revolution, for which the public sphere was a central concern.[31] Limping along behind France came the German-speaking regions. Here, the dead hand of absolutism had preserved the barriers between social estates (*Stände*), especially the impenetrable wall which separated the nobility from the bourgeoisie. For their

[28] Habermas, *The Structural Transformation of the Public Sphere*, pp. 39–40. See also Christoph-Hellmut Mahling, 'Zur sozialen Stellung von musikalischem Kunstwerk und Musiker im Wandel vom 18. zum 19. Jahrhundert—eine Skizze', in Rudolf Zeitler (ed.), *Proceedings of the Sixth International Congress of Aesthetics, Uppsala 1968* (Uppsala, 1972), p. 215, which repeats Habermas almost word for word.

[29] Although Habermas does not make this point, public discussion of politics was of course to be found during the crisis of the 1640s and 1650s.

[30] Habermas, *The Structural Transformation of the Public Sphere*, pp. 58–61.

[31] Ibid., pp. 69–70.

part, the bourgeois had been careful to keep their distance from the common people. Consequently, in Germany even more than in France, rational public discourse was confined to the private assemblies of the middle classes. Habermas singles out the reading clubs (*Lesegesellschaften*), which flourished in the second half of the eighteenth century, as a prime example.[32]

For present purposes, it is at this point that Habermas's account begins to move out of range. It may be helpful, however, to sketch in his conclusions, if only to draw attention to the teleological nature of what has gone before. He believes that the emergence of the bourgeois public sphere in the course of the eighteenth century proved to be a false dawn. As Hegel soon spotted, the liberal notion of a universal public sphere was a fiction. In reality it was particular, subjective, and contingent, serving only the interests of the bourgeoisie. That has been demonstrated by subsequent developments—by the degeneration of culture as rational discourse into culture as mindless consumption. This can be seen in the fact that public opinion has become public opinion research, that the meaning of the word 'publicity' has changed from characterizing the public quality of decision-making to denoting the advertisement of commodities, and that the public sphere has shrivelled to become just public relations. In other words, the cultural emancipation of the masses has been a dismal failure. Mass culture has become manipulated culture, its recipients have been degraded as passive consumers. The culture industry is just a prop for the status quo.[33]

This was nothing if not a grand narrative. As Anthony Giddens has commented, Habermas was seeking to become a Marx for our times, changing the world by understanding it.[34] In Germany in the 1960s, especially during the disturbances of 1968 and their aftermath, both his analysis and his programme won wide acceptance on the left. As that false dawn proved to herald not the defeat of the market but its global triumph, Habermas came to seem more like Cassandra than Marx. Increasingly, too, both his conceptual framework and its historical foundations have been criticized. In particular, the use of 'bourgeois' to describe the new public sphere has been found inadequate. The original German word *bürgerlich* is notoriously slippery, as it can be rendered as 'civil' (as in 'civil society'), 'domestic' (as in *Sara Sampson: A Domestic Tragedy*), or even as 'burgher-like' (as in 'the burghers of Nuremberg')

[32] Ibid., pp. 72–3.

[33] Ibid., p. 56. See also McCarthy, *The Critical Theory of Jürgen Habermas*, pp. 382–3 and Hohendahl, 'Critical theory', pp. 90–4.

[34] Anthony Giddens, 'Jürgen Habermas', in Quentin Skinner (ed.), *The Return of Grand Theory in the Human Sciences* (Cambridge, 1990), p. 124.

as well as 'bourgeois'. Behind this problem of translation lies a substantive confusion, for it is never clear whether Habermas's 'bourgeois public sphere' is rooted in class identity.[35] As will be argued in the course of this book, the public sphere which developed in the course of the eighteenth century cannot be described as 'bourgeois' in a social sense, given the high proportion of clergymen and nobles of various types who operated within it. Socially, the public sphere is more like Noah's Ark than a merchantman. All those who wished to flourish in this new metaphorical space had to come to terms with its essentially meritocratic nature. The most heavily handicapped, both institutionally and ideologically, were the clergy, but it is arguable that the Third Estate was obliged to change more radically than was the Second. Nobles had long been mobile and literate and so were relatively well-equipped to handle cultural change. It was the burghers who had most difficulty in changing into bourgeois. When the victims were carted off to the rubbish-tip of history, hidebound aristocrats were certainly prominent in the tumbrils, but they were heavily outnumbered by small-town burghers and conservative peasants.[36]

There is an ideological equivalent to this last reservation. Just as the public sphere was socially heterogeneous, so was it politically multi-directional. It was not an agenda but a space in which all kinds of opinions could be expressed, *including those which were supportive of the status quo*. Yet Habermas presents it as necessarily in opposition, for example:

> The *publicum* developed into the public, the *subjectum* into the [reasoning] subject, the receiver of regulations from above into the ruling authorities' *adversary* [my italics] . . . In our [German] usage this term (i.e., *Räsonnement*) unmistakably preserves the polemical nuances of both sides: simultaneously the invocation of reason and its disdainful disparagement as merely malcontent griping . . . Because it turned the principle of publicity against the established authorities, the objective function of the public sphere in the political realm could initially converge with its self-interpretation derived from the categories of the public sphere in the world of letters.[37]

[35] Benjamin Nathans, 'Habermas's "Public sphere" in the era of the French Revolution', *French Historical Studies*, 16, 3 (1990) p. 622 n. 5.

[36] Christof Dipper, 'Orders and classes: eighteenth century society under pressure', in T. C. W. Blanning (ed.), *The Short Oxford History of Europe: The Eighteenth Century* (Oxford, 2000), pp. 80–5. For a controversial presentation of the French nobility as the leaders of modernization, see Guy Chaussinand-Nogaret, *The French Nobility in the Eighteenth Century* (Cambridge, 1985). On the conservatism of the bourgeoisie, see Hermann Heimpel, 'Das Wesen des deutschen Spätmittelalters', *Archiv für Kulturgeschichte*, 35 (1953), pp. 29–37.

[37] Habermas, *The Structural Transformation of the Public Sphere*, pp. 26–7, 56.

As we shall see, in certain parts of Europe at certain times—notably in France during the second half of the eighteenth century—the relationship between the public sphere and the state was hostile. In most parts of Europe for most of the time, the relationship between the public sphere and the state was amicable and mutually supportive. Indeed, one might well go further and argue that the public sphere was both the creation and the extension of the state. The public sphere was the result of many forces, among them certainly being the increased tempo in the exchange of goods and the exchange of information. Of greater importance, however, were the actions of the state in promoting educational reform, expanding the bureaucracy, and enforcing secularization, to name but three of the most important. In a seminal essay on voluntary associations, Thomas Nipperdey identified what he called 'individualization' (*Individualisierung*) as the crucial element in the formation of modern culture. He argued that the arts and sciences were liberated from their preordained functions in a hierarchically organized society and were made generally accessible (in principle at least). Discussion of the great issues of life and death, for example, was no longer the monopoly of an officially sanctioned Church but free to everyone (in principle at least). In the course of this process, culture became an object of general interest for private citizens, who laid claim to participation in what had previously been an esoteric activity. In short, a public formed. As Nipperdey adds, it was the state itself which did most to accelerate this process by promoting individualism through the notion of undifferentiated citizens, the introduction of legal equality, the abolition of guilds, and so on.[38]

A third major reservation about the Habermas scheme concerns chronology. He argues that the participants in the public sphere voice their criticisms first about culture and then move on to politics:

> Even before the control over the public sphere by public authority was contested and finally wrested away by the critical reasoning of private persons on political issues, there evolved under its cover a public sphere in apolitical form—the literary precursor of the public sphere operative in the political domain. It provided the training ground for a critical public reflection still preoccupied with itself.[39]

This certainly has the ring of probability, as one might well expect members of a nascent public to cut their teeth on soft targets such as novelists or historians

[38] Thomas Nipperdey, 'Verein als soziale Struktur in Deutschland im späten 18. und frühen 19. Jahrhundert', in Thomas Nipperdey, *Gesellschaft, Kultur, Theorie. Gesammelte Aufsätze zur neueren Geschichte* (Göttingen, 1976), pp. 181–2.

[39] Habermas, *The Structural Transformation of the Public Sphere*, p. 29.

before moving on to tougher opposition in the political world. However, a better case can be made for a reverse order. In England there was a flourishing public debate about politics, notably in the 1640s and 1650s, long before a comparable cultural discourse developed. Similarly in France, there was no comparable cultural equivalent to the political polemics unleashed by the Frondes of 1648–53 before the battle between the 'Ancients' and 'Moderns' almost half a century later. The Germans might seem to be the exceptions here, as their reputation for preferring culture to politics is long established. Recently, however, it has been argued with compelling cogency that Habermas was wrong about them too. Ordinary Germans were reading about politics and arguing about politics at least a century before they should have been. In 1695, for example, Kaspar Steiler observed in *The Pleasure and Utility of Newspapers*:

> Lackeys, stable lads, odd-job men, gardeners and porters sit together and chatter about the news in the public prints... So they often think themselves better than the town mayor because they think they know a lot more than he does about matters of state... It is amazing in every town just what a rush there is to the post office on the days when the newspapers arrive; it's even worse than when alms are being handed out.[40]

Many other criticisms have been made of Habermas's book—that he presents an idealized version of public discourse in the eighteenth century, that he neglects the 'plebeian public sphere', that his model is taken from Germany and does not fit England, that he draws too sharp a distinction between state and society, and so on.[41] Nevertheless, when every qualification has been duly registered, the main pillars of his edifice remain. As Margaret Jacob has observed: 'Not everyone accepts all aspects of Habermas' argument, but he deserves the credit for having first made it.'[42] As this book will endeavour to show, once the Marxist residue has been cleared away—the insistence on the 'bourgeois' nature of the public sphere, its allegedly oppositional orientation, and its chronology—what remains provides an illuminating perspective from which to view the political culture of the old regime.

[40] Andreas Gestrich, *Absolutismus und Öffentlichkeit. Politische Kommunikation in Deutschland zu Beginn des 18. Jahrhunderts* (Göttingen, 1994), p. 131. There are many more illustrations of this kind to be found in this very important work.

[41] See for example, the review by Ralf Dahrendorf, 'Zu einer Pathologie der Demokratie', *Frankfurter Hefte. Zeitschrift für Kultur und Politik*, 17 (1962), pp. 781–3.

[42] Margaret Jacob, 'The mental landscape of the public sphere: a European perspective', *Eighteenth Century Studies*, 28 (1994), p. 110 n. 1.

THE NATION

The public sphere was a neutral vessel, carrying a diversity of social groups and ideologies. Depending on the date of its journey, its cargo is usually labelled 'scientific revolution', the 'crisis of the European conscience', or the 'Enlightenment'. These, together with plenty of others, do not have to be thrown overboard, but the argument will be advanced here that room also needs to be found for freight with a less modern or progressive appearance. We shall find, for example, that religion played a major part in mobilizing public discourse and its institutions, including the French periodical press.[43] It was the Jansenist *Nouvelles ecclésiastiques* which claimed to speak with a 'public voice' and in 1732 asserted 'we are not afraid to say that we have the public behind us.'[44] Closely linked to religion was 'nationalism', which claimed a large amount of space in the public sphere, however anachronistic that may sound. The crimes committed in the name of nationality have scarred the twentieth century like no other. As it drew to a close, 'ethnic cleansing' in the Balkans or nationalist terrorism in the United Kingdom, Spain, and the Middle East showed that nationalism has lost none of its destructive power. On every occasion that its obituary has been written, it has risen from its deathbed with renewed vigour. In 1849, in *The Art-work of the Future*, Richard Wagner wrote with his usual confidence: 'Two main stages in the development of mankind lie clearly before us in history—the *racial-national* and the *unnational-universal*. If we are at present looking to the future for the completion of this second stage, we have in the past the closure of the first stage clearly discernible before our eyes.'[45] Just before the outbreak of the First World War, G. Lowes Dickinson wrote: 'the barriers of nationality which belong to the infancy of the race will melt and dissolve in the sunshine of science and art.'[46] Quickly confounded prophecies of this kind could be multiplied at will. The ferocity and longevity

[43] See below, pp. 157–8.

[44] Catherine Maire, *De la cause de Dieu à la cause de la nation: Le Jansénisme au XVIIIe siècle* (Paris, 1998), pp. 227–8. Jansenism also attracted a great deal of international interest—from the Whig press in England, for example.

[45] Quoted in Deryck Cooke, *I Saw the World End* (London, 1979), p. 264.

[46] Quoted in Eric Hobsbawm, *Nations and Nationalism since 1780: Programme, Myth, Reality* (Cambridge, 1990), p. 38. As Noel Malcolm has observed: 'The whole Hobsbawmian enterprise is essentially circular: first it defines the nation in terms that only fit 19th- and 20th-century political conditions, and then it demonstrates that nations were constructed in the 19th and 20th centuries'—Noel Malcolm, 'My country, old or young?', *Sunday Telegraph*, 30 November 1997, p. 13. This is a review of Adrian Hastings, *The Construction of Nationhood: Ethnicity, Religion and Nationalism* (Cambridge, 1997).

of nationalism have been a special puzzle to analysts who believe that the most fundamental source of conflict in human society is not a vertical force such as nationality but a horizontal force such as class: 'Why and how could a concept so remote from the real experience of most human beings as "national patriotism" become such a powerful political force so quickly?' asked a baffled Marxist (Eric Hobsbawm).[47]

One obvious solution to that conundrum, of course, is that a sense of national patriotism is *not* 'remote from the experience of most human beings'. Before we consider that alarming possibility, however, the problem of definition must be addressed. A bibliographical guide to German nationalism published in 1985 included 769 items, many of them of formidable length.[48] An accelerated flow in the meantime has certainly at least doubled that figure, but fortunately the core of the issue can be identified succinctly. The dictionary tells us that 'nationalism' has two meanings: 'devotion to one's nation' and 'a policy of national independence'.[49] That former meaning was helpfully expanded for the eighteenth-century context by Robert R. Palmer when he wrote that what he called the 'larger sense' of nationalism was: 'the idea that a man depends for his well-being, his possession of rights, his hope for self-improvement, his duties and obligations, his faith in a cause for which he is willing to die, not on God, the king, humanity, class, or something vaguely called society, but on his nation or *patrie*'.[50] In other words, nationalism has both a cultural and a political meaning. It is important to stress that these two senses of the word are discrete; they are not two sides of the same coin but are alternatives, usually jingling about in the same pocket—but not always. Virtually all political nationalists will identify the nation as the paramount source of value, but not all cultural nationalists will seek to make cultural and political boundaries coincide. Many Czech nineteenth-century nationalists, for example, did not wish to destroy the Habsburg Empire, while today there are many fervent admirers of Welsh or Scottish culture who do not wish to secede from the United Kingdom. For some cultural nationalists, cultural integrity takes precedence over political unity, as it did for Douglas Hyde, the President of the Gaelic League, who wished to make admission

[47] Hobsbawm, *Nations and Nationalism*, p. 46.

[48] Dieter K. Buse and Juergen C. Dorr, *German Nationalisms: A Bibliographic Approach* (New York and London, 1985).

[49] C. T. Onions (ed.), *The Shorter Oxford English Dictionary, on historical principles*, 3rd edn., 2 vols. (Oxford, 1973), II, p. 1386.

[50] Robert R. Palmer, 'The national idea in France before the Revolution', *Journal of the History of Ideas*, 1 (1940), p. 96.

to the Irish national university conditional on a knowledge of the Irish language.[51]

To accept the view of most modern historians that the essence of nationalism is the 'fusion of culture and polity' (Ernest Gellner) is to put a patch over one eye.[52] To impose too rigid criteria, as Anthony Smith does, for example, when he requires a 'real' nation to be 'a named human population sharing an historic territory, common myths and memories, a mass, public culture, a single economy and common rights and duties for all members' is to put any investigation into lead boots even before the start-line has been reached.[53] Eighteenth-century scholars were more clear-sighted—Johann Christoph Adelung, for example, who defined 'nation' as 'the native inhabitants of a country in so far as they have a common origin and speak a common language, whether they constitute a single state or are divided into several'.[54]

This distinction between cultural and political nationalism is important, because it guards against the long-standing axiom that the appearance of nationalism as a force in European history was a nineteenth-century phenomenon. In a study of national character first published in 1927, Sir Ernest Barker stated firmly: 'The self-consciousness of nations is a product of the nineteenth century.'[55] A representative modern example is Hans-Ulrich Wehler's *Deutsche Gesellschaftsgeschichte*, a distinguished multi-volume history of Germany since the eighteenth century.[56] Wehler identifies nationalism as an attempt to deal with the pressing problems of political legitimation and social integration in a post-revolutionary world. It was a response which proved particularly attractive, he argues, because it was part of an ideology of liberal emancipation and opposition to the status quo.[57] Therein, of course, lies the appeal of this time-schedule: German nationalism is seen to begin as a

[51] John Hutchinson (ed.), *The Dynamics of Cultural Nationalism: The Gaelic Revival and the Creation of the Irish Nation State* (London, 1987), p. 1.

[52] Ernest Gellner, *Nations and nationalism* (Oxford, 1983), p. 13. That nationalism and modernity are intimately and causally connected remains the dominant view in German historiography, judging by the opaque introduction to Jörg Echternkamp's *Der Aufstieg des deutschen Nationalismus (1770–1840)* (Frankfurt am Main and New York, 1998), pp. 13–37. For a more balanced and lucid account, see Hagen Schulze's numerous publications, most recently *States, Nations and Nationalism from the Middle Ages to the Present* (Oxford, 1996), ch. 6.

[53] Anthony D. Smith, 'Nations and their pasts', *Nations and Nationalism*, 2, 3 (1996), p. 359.

[54] Adelung, *Grammatisch-kritisches Wörterbuch*, III, p. 439.

[55] Ernest Barker, *National Character and the Factors in its Formation* (London, 1927), p. 123.

[56] Hans-Ulrich Wehler, *Deutsche Gesellschaftsgeschichte*, 2 vols. (Munich, 1987).

[57] Ibid., I, pp. 544–5. For a restatement of this thesis, see Hans-Ulrich Wehler, 'Nationalismus, Nation und Nationalstaat in Deutschland seit dem ausgehenden 18. Jahrhundert', in Ulrich Herrmann (ed.), *Volk—Nation—Vaterland* (Hamburg, 1996), p. 269.

movement of the left, and then to lose its innocence as its bourgeois creators became ever more inclined to compromise with the old order in the course of the nineteenth century. Pressed from below by the proletariat, lured from above by Prussian military success, they took nationalism with them into the arms of the militarist right. In other words, in its early stages nationalism is allowed only a belated and subsidiary role in a much wider movement of social emancipation. This concern to explain all historical development in terms of horizontal social structure leaves precious little room for a vertical force such as nationalism.

Wehler's is only one of many explanations which make nationalism an integral part of modernization. Eric Hobsbawm, for example, asserts 'the basic characteristic of the modern nation and everything connected with it is its modernity.'[58] According to his timetable, nationalism began in the early nineteenth century as 'purely cultural, literary, folkloric' with no political or even national implications, was then turned into a 'national idea' by pioneering intellectuals, developed into a mass movement with a clear programme, and was then derailed into the virulent forms of fascism in the twentieth century.[59]

Whether following Weber (Wehler) or Marx (Hobsbawm), what all modernization theorists have in common is the belief that nationalism arose as a means of resolving a crisis of legitimation posed by the decay of old forms of authority. Towards the end of the eighteenth century, the old clearly defined groups, based on such specific and concrete identities as estate, specific locality, or dynasty, began to make way for more abstract and impersonal communities based on class and the state. In the celebrated formulation of Ferdinand Tönnies, there was a change from *Gemeinschaft* (communal society) to *Gesellschaft* (associational society).[60] This transition represented the culmination of several long-gestating forces, the most important being increased mobility, the division of labour, specialization of function, the growth of literacy, secularization, centralization, bureaucratization, and the growing belief in activism and criticism fostered by the Enlightenment.[61] As they sensed the ground moving beneath their feet, a growing number of intellectuals looked for more appropriate pillars of support:

[58] Hobsbawm, *Nations and Nationalism*, p. 14.

[59] Ibid., p. 12.

[60] *Gemeinschaft und Gesellschaft* was the title of Tönnies's most important work, published in 1887.

[61] Thomas Nipperdey, 'In search of identity: romantic nationalism', in J. C. Eade (ed.), *Romantic Nationalism in Europe* (Canberra, 1983), p. 9.

This development had the initial result that the educated classes no longer saw the norms of behaviour and the meaning of life as something provided by tradition, but rather as objects for reflection and discussion. Norms were now conveyed primarily in an abstract way, i.e. through language. So the medium by which this reflection and discussion was carried on was language and culture. The educated individual gained his identity and the norms for his behaviour through the culture contained in his own language, through art, literature, philosophy, journalism. That is the reason why culture and one's own language achieved a previously unheard-of importance in the incipient new communication-society. That is the social basis for the rise of romantic nationalism.[62]

Many variations have been played on this theme by analysts of nationalism. In his influential study *Imagined Communities*, Benedict Anderson has argued that nationalism must be understood in terms of the 'cultural systems' out of which—and against which—it arose, especially 'dynastic realm' and 'religious community': 'in western Europe the eighteenth century marks not only the dawn of the age of nationalism but the dusk of religious modes of thought.'[63] This stress on the functional nature of nationalism was taken furthest by Ernest Gellner, whose equally influential *Nations and Nationalism* (1983) made it the very basis of modern life. Nationalism, he argued, has resulted from a dual need to instil in every member of society the same culture: 'Culture is no longer merely the adornment, confirmation and legitimation of a social order which was also sustained by harsher and coercive constraints; culture is now the necessary shared medium, the life-blood or perhaps rather the minimal shared atmosphere, within which alone the members of the society can breathe and survive and produce.'[64] The two most powerful figures in the modern world, the bureaucrat and the entrepreneur, both need this cultural uniformity, the one in pursuit of standardization, the other in pursuit of profit, and both in their application of means–ends rationality. At the root of the modern society they have created is 'its terrible and overwhelming thirst for economic growth',[65] which can only be sustained if all its members receive a common education. In two of the many memorable epigrams which make his book a literary as well as an interpretative classic, Gellner wrote: 'at the base of the modern social order stands not the executioner but the professor' and 'the monopoly of legitimate education is now more important, more central than is

[62] Ibid., p. 10.

[63] Benedict Anderson, *Imagined Communities: Reflections on the Origins and Spread of Nationalism*, rev. edn. (London and New York, 1991), p. 11.

[64] Gellner, *Nations and Nationalism*, pp. 37–8.

[65] Ibid., p. 25.

the monopoly of legitimate violence.'[66] A common culture means a common vernacular culture and it also requires the protection of the state—'As a character in *No Orchids for Miss Blandish* observed, every girl ought to have a husband, preferably her own; and every high culture now wants a state, and preferably its own.'[67] So it is from this visceral urge to make the boundaries of a culture and a polity coincide that nationalism draws its power.

These ingenious explanations certainly have a great deal to be said for them, but not everything. Especially inadequate is their insistence that nationalism is essentially artificial and that nations are 'fictive fabrications' born in the imagination of the deluding or the deluded. Of course nationalists have always recreated a national past to suit their current interests, but—except in a few cases of conscious cynicism—they have not invented that past *ex nihilo*. They have drawn on a stock of images, myths, legends and—yes—verifiable *events* which constitute the national memory. The Germans who revived the memory of 'Herman the German' in the late eighteenth century certainly gave him attributes and loaded him with meanings which had nothing to do with the first century AD. Yet he was not a figment of their imagination. There was a German chieftain (although he was not called Hermann or even 'Arminius') and he did destroy Varus' legions in the Teutoburg forest in AD 9, and Tacitus did describe him as 'unquestionably the liberator of Germany' (*liberator haud dubie Germaniae*). For that reason, history provides the only reliable guide to understanding nationalism and its force: 'Identification with a past is the key to creating the nation, because only by "remembering the past" can a collective identity come into being.'[68]

There is an awkward problem of timing which modernization theories have difficulty in accommodating; indeed, one must agree with the trenchant opinion expressed recently by Adrian Hastings: 'Understanding nations and nationalism will only be advanced when any inseparable bonding of them to the modernisation of society is abandoned.'[69] Both a sense of nationality and a belief that it is important antedate the modern world, however it is defined, by many centuries. In his chronicle of the reign of Louis VI, Abbot Suger

[66] Ibid., p. 34.

[67] Ibid., p. 51.

[68] Anthony D. Smith, 'Memory and modernity: reflections on Ernest Gellner's theory of nationalism', *Nations and Nationalism*, 2, 3 (1996), p. 383. See also the same author's *The Ethnic Origins of Nations* (Oxford, 1986), p. 2.

[69] Adrian Hastings, *The Construction of Nationhood: Ethnicity, Religion and Nationalism* (Cambridge, 1997), p. 9. On the nuances between 'modernists' (such as Hobsbawm) and 'post-modernists' (such as Anderson), see Anthony D. Smith, 'Gastronomy or geology? The role of nationalism in the reconstruction of nations', *Nations and Nationalism*, 1, 1 (1995), *passim*.

recorded that in 1124 the king had appealed to '*tota Francia*' to rally round to protect their nation against the English and German invaders and celebrated his subsequent victory as follows: 'neither in our days nor in far-gone ancient times has France achieved anything more illustrious than this, nor has she with the united forces of her members proclaimed more gloriously the honour of her power than when she at one and the same time triumphed over the Roman emperor and the English king.'[70] Pride taken in the cultural achievements of one's nation can also be found in the High Middle Ages, by Walther von der Vogelweide, for example, who wrote in *c.*1200: 'I have seen many countries, and I liked to observe the best of them . . . [but] German civilization is above all of them. From the Elbe to the Rhine and from there to the frontier of Hungary certainly the best people live whom I have been acquainted with in all the world.'[71] By the late thirteenth century, it has been argued, the word *patria* had acquired a recognizably modern sense, denoting not only national territory but also loyalty to one's fatherland.[72] After citing a number of medieval texts from all over Europe suggesting a clear national consciousness, Halvdan Koht concluded:

There is a striking fundamental uniformity in these varied and simultaneous declarations of national feeling from so many different countries of western Europe, and it must be acknowledged that here are the beginnings of actual nationalism. The common elements of it are evident. Everywhere we observe a juvenile pride in one's own nation as contrasted with others, and the pride is mostly concentrated upon the warlike virtues of the nation, in several cases also upon the superiority of their own civilizations. Thus, this early nationalism includes a hatred or contempt of other nations. Furthermore, the nation is centred in its king, who is the chief of the nation in battle and the visible symbol signifying political unity. The kingdom is the country of everybody, loyalty to the king becomes a national duty and a proof of virtue, and devotion to country (*amor patriae*) becomes not simply patriotism but a real affection for the native land . . . From the beginning of the twelfth century, European nationalism has a continuous history.[73]

No great acumen is needed to spot that what these early manifestations of nationalism have in common is xenophobia, that is to say, national identity is defined not only in terms of a nationality's special virtues but also by

[70] Halvdan Koht, 'The dawn of nationalism in Europe', *American Historical Review*, 52, 2 (1947), p. 266.

[71] Ibid., p. 277.

[72] Mary G. Dietz, 'Patriotism', in Terence Ball, James Farr, and Russell L. Hanson (eds.), *Political Innovation and Conceptual Change* (Cambridge, 1989), p. 181.

[73] Koht, 'The dawn of nationalism in Europe', p. 279.

opposition to the negative characteristics of 'the other'. Fear and hatred of the *furor teutonicus*, for example, helped to foster a sense of nationalism among many on the receiving end of German expansionism.[74] Nor does there appear to have been any progression in this respect: the negative component of nationalism did not fade as its positive functions became necessary to modernization. On the contrary, even if national hatreds wax and wane according to circumstances, they have never gone away. One example from an intermediate period must suffice. In Act I, scene i of Shakespeare's *Henry V*, the bellicose Archbishop of Canterbury urges the king to emulate the exploits of his great-uncle, the Black Prince. Henry replies:

KING HENRY: We must not only arm t'invade the French,
But lay down our proportions to defend
Against the Scot, who will make raid upon us
With all advantages.
CANTERBURY: They of those marches, gracious sovereign,
Shall be a wall sufficient to defend
Our inland from the pilfering borderers.
KING HENRY: We do not mean the coursing snatchers only,
But fear the main intendment of the Scot,
Who hath been still a giddy neighbour to us . . .
A LORD: But there's a saying very old and true: 'If that you will France win
Then with Scotland first begin.'
For once the eagle England being in prey,
To her unguarded nest the weasel Scot
Comes sneaking, and so sucks her princely eggs,
Playing the mouse in absence of the cat,
To tame and havoc more than she can eat.

As we shall see later,[75] this image of the Scots as traitorous opportunists was to have a long life (and indeed is still alive today, having received a fresh transfusion from the general election of 1997). It was not only England's northern neighbours who were pilloried by Shakespeare. In Act III, scene iii of the same play, the garrulous Welshman and the drunken, brutal Irishman made neither the first nor by any means the last of their innumerable appearances in English literature:[76]

[74] Ibid., pp. 269, 277.

[75] See below, pp. 281, 287, 329.

[76] For an exhaustive examination of literary stereotypes, see J. O. Bartley, *Teague, Shenkin and Sawney. Being an Historical Study of the Earliest Irish, Welsh and Scottish Characters in English Plays* (Cork, 1954), *passim*.

FLUELLEN (a Welshman): Captain MacMorris, I think, look you, under your correction, there is not many of your nation—

MACMORRIS (an Irishman): Of my nation? What ish my nation? Ish a vilain and a bastard and a knave and a rascal? What ish my nation? Who talks of my nation?

FLUELLEN: Look you, if you take the matter otherwise than is meant, Captain MacMorris, peradventure I shall think you do not use me with that affability as in discretion you ought to use me, look you, being as good a man as yourself, both in the disciplines of war and in the derivation of my birth, and in other particularities.

MACMORRIS: I do not know you so good a man as myself. So Chrish save me, I will cut off your head.

Both Fluellen and MacMorris are supposed to be fighting in the same army against the common enemy, the French. This is as good an illustration as any of the observation of Anthony Smith, the author of the best of the general studies of nationalism, that too great an emphasis on the modernizing potential of nationalism overlooks its distant origins and ignores its negative impact.[77] He also points out another flaw in modernization theory's interpretation of nationalism—its misunderstanding of the role of religion.[78] At first blush, religion in general, and Christianity in particular, certainly seem to be at odds with an ideology which elevates one particular nation. As we have seen, the apparent coincidence between the 'demystification of the world' (Max Weber) and the rise of nationalism has led analysts as different as Benedict Anderson and Thomas Nipperdey to detect a causal relationship. Yet if the negative aspect of nationalism is taken into account, it can be seen that religion is in fact nationalism's most powerful ally. Very frequently 'the other' which gives a nation a sense of identity is seen as alien partly or even mainly because it is associated with a different religion. Irish nationalism has been intensified by Catholic (and originally also Presbyterian) hostility to Anglicanism; Polish nationalism has been intensified by Catholic hostility to the Lutheranism of the Prussians and the Orthodoxy of the Russians; Greek nationalism has been intensified by hostility to the Mohammedanism of the Turks; Croatian nationalism has been intensified by hostility to the Orthodoxy of the Serbs; and so on. Indeed, there is good biblical support for this view, in the Old Testament's revelation that the children of Israel's conviction of being God's appointed people was accompanied by an equally intense belief that they were surrounded by ungodly enemies. Indeed, eighteenth-century commentators took a close interest in biblical Israel as 'the original nation'.

[77] Anthony D. Smith, *Theories of Nationalism* (London, 1983), p. ix.
[78] Ibid., p. 56.

Awareness of the importance of the other in sustaining nationalism leads necessarily to consideration of the importance of international relations in explaining the phenomenon. If foreign policy does not exercise primacy in this area, it is certainly very important. It is one of the weaknesses of Ernest Gellner's brilliant essay that it treats nationalism as an entirely endogenous phenomenon. He writes, for example, that modern society 'has to be mobile, whether it wishes to be so or not, because this is required by the satisfaction of its terrible and overwhelming thirst for economic growth', but this is an observation which makes better sense if 'economic growth' is replaced by 'state power'.[79] The same substitution could be made with profit whenever he mentions his favourite phrase. The same criticism could be levelled at another distinguished study of nationalism, Liah Greenfeld's *Nationalism: Five Roads to Modernity*, for her account of English nationalism, for example, is almost entirely endogenous. She has a lot to say about the English sense of England being God's nation, but there is only one fleeting reference to Spain and none to France.[80] As will be argued below, a prime force in the generation of nationalism was conflicts between states and the antipathies they engendered. Current events in the post-Soviet states or the Middle East suggest nothing has changed.

The argument that nationalism is a modern invention has also been supported by those who believe that a clear distinction has to be drawn between nationalism and patriotism. The latter is presented as an essentially benign phenomenon, anchored in a love of liberty per se and not to be confused with love of a particular place or people. Moreover, it is held that the two ideologies are directed at quite different targets: 'whereas the enemies of republican patriotism are tyranny, oppression, and corruption, the enemies of nationalism are cultural contamination, heterogeneity, racial impurity, and social, political, and intellectual disunion.'[81] Such a clear-cut distinction can perhaps be sustained at the most rarefied level of the history of ideas, but only by dint of careful selection. The most emphatic exponent of this proposition, Maurizio Viroli, for example, presents John Milton as a representative patriot, for whom 'love of country is a compassionate love of liberty.' But he omits to tell us about Milton's violent antipathy towards 'these murdrous Irish, the enemies of God and mankind . . . the villainous and savage scum of Ireland', or about Milton

[79] Gellner, *Nations and Nationalism*, p. 25.

[80] Liah Greenfeld, *Nationalism: Five Roads to Modernity* (Cambridge, Mass., 1992), p. 86.

[81] Maurizio Viroli, *For Love of Country: An Essay on Patriotism and Nationalism* (Oxford, 1995), pp. 1–2. If nothing else, this book shows that Whig history is very much alive and kicking.

cheering on Oliver Cromwell as he smote hip and thigh the subhuman papistical barbarians who had murdered 154,000 Protestants in Ulster alone (or so Milton believed).[82] Clearly it was one thing to experience compassionate love for English republicans but quite another when it came to 'a Crew of Rebells whose inhumanities are long since become the horrour and execration of all that heare them'.[83]

As we shall see, Milton was neither the first nor the last Englishman to believe that God had selected his nation for special favours. Nor was he alone in thinking that liberty and Protestantism were mutually dependent. 'Patriotism without nationalism'[84] is certainly as possible in theory as it is desirable in practice, but that does not make it anything more than a rarity in reality. The English are not special in this regard. The French Revolution began with the most pacific and cosmopolitanism of intentions, 'declaring peace on the world' in its celebrated renunciation of aggressive war in May 1790. Within three years, the revolutionaries had declared war on most of the rest of Europe, were inflicting devastation on their neighbours on a scale not seen since the Thirty Years War, and were proclaiming the special—the *unique*—virtues of the *la Grande Nation*. As Robespierre told the National Convention in 1794: 'The French people seems to have outdistanced the rest of the human race by 2,000 years; one is tempted to regard it as a different species.'[85] Robespierre also believed that 'the soul of the Republic is the love of the *Patrie*.'[86]

[82] John Milton, *The Works of John Milton*, vol. III *The Reason of Church-government urg'd against Prelacy* (1641), p. 226; vol. VI *Observations upon the Articles of Peace with the Irish Rebels* (1649), pp. 243, 248; vol. VII *Pro Populo Anglicano Defensio*, p. 525; Willy Maley, 'The British problem in three tracts on Ireland by Spenser, Bacon and Milton', in Brendan Bradshaw and Peter Roberts (eds.), *British Consciousness and Identity: The Making of Britain 1533–1707* (Cambridge, 1998), p. 184.

[83] John Milton, *The Works of John Milton*, ed. Freak Allen Patterson 17 vols. (New York, 1931–4). *The Reason of Church-government urg'd against Prelacy* (1641), p. 226; *Eikonoklastes* (1649), p. 188; *Observations upon the Articles of Peace with the Irish Rebels* (1649), p. 248. See also below, p. 287.

[84] This is the title of Viroli's final chapter.

[85] Quoted in T. C. W. Blanning, *The French Revolutionary Wars 1787–1802* (London, 1996), p. 246.

[86] Georges Lefebvre, *The French Revolution from 1793 to 1799* (London, 1964), p. 91.

PART I

Representational Culture

I

Louis XIV and Versailles

The political and cultural transformation which occurred in France during the middle decades of the seventeenth century can be exemplified by a tale of two bedrooms. During the night of 9–10 February 1651, the 12-year-old King Louis XIV was obliged to feign sleep in the Palais Royal, as a mob of rebellious Parisians forced their way into his room to see for themselves that he was still in his capital and still their hostage. Although they then left, it may safely be assumed that the boy-king had been terrified by the experience. Certainly, his political mentors were sufficiently intimidated to make immediate political concessions to the opposition. On the following day, a royal order was signed releasing from custody three of the leaders of the Fronde, as the rebellion was known (*Fronde* means 'sling-shot'), all of them closely related to the king—the prince de Condé, the prince de Conti, and the duc de Longueville. This invasion of the royal bedchamber was as low as the French monarchy was to come in the seventeenth century.

Fifty years later, Louis XIV's bedroom had become the centre of an elaborate ritual which demonstrated the absolute authority of the king over even his mightiest subjects.[1] Architecturally, it had been made the focal point of his

[1] Indeed, 'the state bed was the primary symbol of sovereignty in France'; see Kevin Orlin Johnson, 'Il n'y a plus de Pyrénées: The iconography of the first Versailles of Louis XIV', *Gazette des Beaux Arts*, 97 (1981), p. 30. The bed and the throne were regarded as interchangeable in French royal symbolism; the throne occupied by the king during a royal session of the Parlement of Paris was known as a 'bed of justice' (*lit de justice*), taking the form of five large cushions on which the sovereign reclined rather than sat; Hugh Murray Baillie, 'Etiquette and the planning of the state apartments in baroque palaces', *Archaeologia*, 101 (1967), p. 186.

great new palace at Versailles, the largest, grandest, and most glamorous secular building in Europe. A traveller arriving from Paris first entered an immense open space, bounded to left and right by the stables, big enough to house 12,000 horses and majestic enough themselves to be a royal residence. Entry to the palace proper was through a great railed screen leading into another large space, flanked by buildings occupied by officers of state. At the far end, another screen opened the way to three further courts, each narrower than the last, culminating in the 'Marble Court'.[2] The focal point of the last-named, commanding the central axis of the entire complex, was the king's bedroom. Similarly, from the reverse side of the palace, the central axis runs from the fountain of Apollo as he rises from the sea through the fountain of his mother (Latona), enters the palace façade between the statues of Apollo and Diana (Apollo's sister) and goes from there to the royal bedroom.[3]

It was there that, every morning at the *lever*, the flower of the French aristocracy gathered to wait on their king, as he rose, prayed, performed his bodily functions, chose his wig, was shaved and dressed. The marquis de Saint-Maurice recorded: 'There is no finer sight in the world than the court at the *lever* of the King. When I attended it yesterday, there were three rooms full of people of quality, such a crowd that you would not believe how difficult it was to get into His Majesty's bedchamber'.[4] Every night at the *coucher* the courtiers gathered again, to watch their master feed his dogs, say his prayers, undress, and don his nightgown: 'He said good night with an inclination of his head, and whilst everybody was leaving the room, stood at the corner of the mantelpiece, where he gave the order to the colonel of the guards alone. Then commenced what was called the *petit coucher*, at which only the specially privileged remained. That was short. They did not leave until he got into bed.'[5] No one other than the king ever slept in that bed: if the king needed sex, he went to the bedchamber of the queen or a mistress. Indeed, any woman who

[2] There is a good description of the approach to the palace in Guy Walton, *Louis XIV's Versailles* (Chicago, 1986), ch. I, together with many illustrations and ground plans.

[3] Ralph E. Giesey, 'Models of rulership in French royal ceremonial', in Sean Wilentz (ed.), *Rites of Power: Symbolism, Ritual and Politics since the Middle Ages* (Philadelphia, 1985), p. 59.

[4] Quoted in Jean-François Solnon, *La Cour de France* (Paris, 1987), p. 321. Saint-Maurice was writing about the Louvre in 1667 but his description would have applied equally well to Versailles in 1687 or 1707. He added that there were more than 800 carriages drawn up outside the palace.

[5] W. H. Lewis (ed.), *The Memoirs of the Duc de Saint-Simon*, trans. B. St. John (London, 1964), p. 145.

passed through the royal bedroom in the course of the day was obliged to curtsy in obeisance towards the bed.[6]

The conduct of the *lever*, *coucher*, and other court ceremonies was directed by a rigorous form of etiquette linked to a strict hierarchy. At the equally formal *lever* of the queen, for example, the maid of honour enjoyed the right to pass the queen her chemise, but was obliged to forgo this privilege if a royal princess were present. On one occasion, the unfortunate Queen Marie Thérèse was obliged to stand naked as, first the duchesse d'Orléans and then the even higher-ranking comtesse de Provence arrived to claim the right to transport the royal underwear.[7] The rigid precedence revealed by this episode only served to emphasize the distance which separated the king and his family from his court, for he alone had the power to make exceptions. He alone could indicate by special concession that this or that courtier enjoyed his special favour—or displeasure. It was an asset he exploited with relish and skill, keeping his nobles on their toes as they competed for marks of distinction. When the duc de Saint-Simon angered him by resigning from the army, Louis responded at once, first by going out of his way at the *coucher* to distinguish him (by allowing him to hold the royal candelabra for a few seconds)—and then by ignoring him completely for three years.[8] If Hell is to be denial of the face of God, Heaven in Louis XIV's France was proximity to the king. Such was the verdict of the duchesse d'Orléans after she had been invited to dine with the king and his current mistress, Madame de Montespan:

> That means that I am actually very much in fashion, and the courtiers admire whatever I do, whether it be good or bad... If the courtiers think you are in favour you may do what you like and you are sure of approval, but if they think the contrary, they would hold you up to ridicule, even if you came straight from Heaven.[9]

Louis XIV ruled France for seventy-two years, the longest-reigning monarch in European history. This was partly because he was very much a late arrival, for by the time of his birth his parents had been married for twenty-two childless years. It was partly because his father died when he was only 5; and it was partly because he had been blessed with a particularly robust physical constitution. Yet he was also the author of his own good fortune, for it should

[6] Giesey, 'Models of rulership', p. 60.

[7] Norbert Elias, *The Court Society* (Oxford, 1983), p. 86.

[8] Ibid., p. 89.

[9] To the duchess of Hanover, Saint Germain, 14 December 1674; Gertrude Scott Stevenson (ed.), *The Letters of Madame, The Correspondence of Elizabeth-Charlotte of Bavaria, Princess Palatine, Duchess of Orleans, called "Madame" at the Court of King Louis XIV*, 2 vols. (London, 1924–5), I, p. 29.

be remembered that kingship was not without its risks in early modern Europe. Both Henry III and Henry IV (Louis's grandfather) had been assassinated in 1589 and 1610 respectively, Charles I of England (Louis's uncle) was executed in 1649 and James II (Louis's first cousin) was to be deposed in 1688. After his distressing experience at the hands of the mob in February 1651, Louis took no chances, insisting on very careful protection. He did not move from one room to another in the Louvre without guards first being placed along the corridors and up the staircases, and if he ventured out to attend a religious service in a neighbouring church or chapel, the streets were lined with troops.[10]

More subtly, he cloaked himself in a protective aura none the less effective for being invisible. First at the royal palaces in and around Paris, and then definitively at Versailles, he created a royal culture which not only stabilized his own monarchy but created a model which was followed by most of the rest of Europe. It should never be supposed that the representational culture of the kind which reached its climax at Versailles was an expression of unbounded confidence. On the contrary, the greater the doubts about the stability or legitimacy of a throne, the greater the need for display. There was always a strong undertow of anxiety beneath the smooth surface of courtly confidence. It was a neurosis which found appropriate expression in meticulous attention to detail. The apparently absurd etiquette which attached so much importance to holding the king's candle or fetching the royal chamber-pot was an integral part of this creation. The royal routine was made deliberately and increasingly complex to multiply the opportunities to show who was coming in—and who was going out.[11] As Louis himself pointed out:

> Those people are gravely mistaken who imagine that all this is mere ceremony. The people over whom we rule, unable to see to the bottom of things, usually judge by what they see from the outside, and most often it is by precedence and rank that they measure their respect and obedience. As it is important to the public to be governed only by a single one, it also matters to it that the person performing this function should be so elevated above the others, that no-one can be confused or compared with him; and one cannot, without doing harm to the whole body of the state, deprive its head of the least mark of superiority distinguishing him from the limbs.[12]

Louis also reveals here the essence of royal absolutism—distance. It was by elevating himself so far above the other great magnates of France that he

[10] Baillie, 'Etiquette and the planning of the state apartments in baroque palaces', p. 184.

[11] Roger Mettam, *Power and Faction in Louis XIV's France* (Oxford, 1988), p. 53.

[12] Ibid., p. 117, quoting from Louis's Memoirs.

dispelled any confusion as to where the power to command was located. This was not just a question of coercion. Certainly, he had grasped that the essence of a state was 'a monopoly of legitimate force', as Max Weber famously defined it. It was for that reason that Louis put an end to the private armies which had ravaged France repeatedly for the past hundred years. But he also realized that states were centres of authority as well as power and could be effective only if their coercive capability was recognized as legitimate by their members. It was in pursuit of this legitimacy that he unfolded his grand cultural programme. As Frederick the Great observed admiringly: 'Greedy for every kind of glory, he wanted to make his nation as supreme in matters of taste and literature as it was already in power, conquests, politics and commerce'.[13]

In 1661, the year in which he assumed personal control of government on the death of Cardinal Mazarin, Louis demonstrated his determination to distance himself from his aristocracy by breaking his superintendent of finances—Nicolas Fouquet, marquis de Belle Isle. The latter fell prey to the intrigues of his rival, Jean-Baptiste Colbert, by his own imprudence. By maintaining a private military force on his eponymous island of Belle-Île-en-Mer off the coast of Brittany, Fouquet attracted the charge of treason. By building a great palace at Vaux-le-Vicomte near Paris and patronizing the most celebrated creative artists of the day (La Fontaine, Molière, Louis Le Vau, Nicolas Poussin, André le Nôtre, and Charles Le Brun), he created a court far more glamorous than the king's. 18,000 men toiled on its construction, at a cost of 18,000,000 *livres*.[14] This peacock display allowed his enemy, Colbert, to accuse him of embezzlement and, more seriously, to suggest that he was usurping the cultural role of the king. When Louis attended the lavish festivities mounted there on 17 August 1661, when 6,000 guests dined off silver and gold plate and then attended a play by Molière with sets by Le Brun, followed by a Lully ballet and a gigantic fireworks display, he must have felt like a poor relation. In what was the first major political move of his personal rule, he ordered Fouquet's arrest and imprisonment in a distant Piedmontese fortress. There the disgraced financier festered until his death nineteen years later, an awful warning to any other aspiring Icarus.

[13] Frederick the Great, *Über die deutsche Literatur; die Mängel, die man ihr vorwerfen kann; die Ursachen derselben und die Mittel, sie zu verbessern*, in Horst Steinmetz (ed.), *Friedrich II., König von Preußen und die deutsche Literatur des 18. Jahrhunderts. Texte und Dokumente* (Stuttgart, 1985), p. 96.

[14] Rolf Hellmut Foerster, *Das Barock-Schloß. Geschichte und Architektur* (Cologne, 1981), p. 41.

There could be only one sun in the French firmament and that was the king. Indeed the cult of Apollo and *Le roi soleil* (the Sun-King), was already well under way by this time, his birth on a Sunday being regarded as especially propitious.[15] As early as 1649, at the height of the Fronde, little Louis had been eulogized in a pamphlet as 'this shining star, this radiant sun, this day without night, this centre, visible from all points of the circumference'.[16] Four years later, the victory of the royalist forces in the civil war was celebrated by a lavish ballet at court in which the king himself took the leading role, dressed as Apollo in a fabulous costume and with gilded braids of hair simulating the rays of the sun.[17] In his justification of the event, Cardinal Mazarin argued that so many victories bestowed by Heaven should not only be celebrated by *Te Deums* in churches: 'after such long travail, this winter shall be one long round of festivity.'[18] The association of the sun and the sovereign was as old as antiquity, but Louis and his cultural advisers, led by Colbert, projected the image with a consistency and on a scale never seen before. In his instructions for the Dauphin, dictated in 1661 after the birth of his heir, Louis explained why the sun had been chosen as his favoured symbol:

> by its unique quality,
> by the lustre which surrounds it,
> by the light which it shines on those other stars which surround it like a court,
> by the equal and just distribution of its light which it sheds on all corners of the earth,
> by the good which it brings to all places, creating joy and action in every form of life,
> by its ceaseless motion while appearing constantly at rest,
> by its constant and unchanging course from which it never deviates,
> it is most assuredly the most vital and the most beautiful image of a great monarch.[19]

[15] Friedrich B. Polleross, 'Sonnenkönig und österreichische Sonne. Kunst und Wissenschaft als Fortsetzung des Krieges mit anderen Mitteln', *Wiener Jahrbuch für Kunstgeschichte*, 40 (1987), p. 243.

[16] François Bluche, *Louis XIV* (Oxford, 1990), p. 157.

[17] Marie-Christine Moine, *Les Fêtes à la cour du roi soleil 1653–1715* (Paris, 1984), p. 35. There is a good reproduction of Louis's costume in Peter Burke, *The Fabrication of Louis XIV* (New Haven, 1992), p. 46.

[18] Rudolf Braun and David Guggerli, *Macht des Tanzes—Tanz der Mächtigen. Hoffeste und Herrschaftszeremoniell 1550–1914* (Munich, 1993), p. 135.

[19] Quoted in Ernst H. Kantorowicz, 'Oriens Augusti—Lever du Roi', *Dumbarton Oaks Papers*, 17 (1963), p. 173.

He was as good as his word. In a treatise published in 1679, Menestrier claimed that the royal device now appeared on innumerable artefacts 'as the glorious symbol of the greatness of his reign'.[20] Only the most splendid building in Europe could accommodate a solar system of metaphors. As Colbert informed his master: 'Your Majesty knows that in the absence of brilliant feats of war, nothing does more to signal the grandeur and intelligence of princes than buildings, and all posterity measures them by the yardstick of these superb palaces which they construct during their lifetime.'[21] The result was an equally unprecedented personalization of the monarchy.

The reconstruction of the Louvre, beginning in 1663, and of the adjoining Tuileries, beginning in 1664, created two temples to Apollo, dripping with sun-king imagery. It was at Versailles, however, that the solar imagery was elevated into a cult. When Louis came to the throne, he had several royal palaces from which to choose, three in Paris—the Palais Royal, the Louvre, and the Tuileries—and Vincennes, Saint-Germain-en-Laye, and Fontainebleau in the vicinity of the capital. Versailles was no more than a modest château, built as a hunting-lodge for Louis XIII in 1632–4. Why his son should have decided to make it his main residence and transform it into the biggest palace in Europe will never be entirely clear. Perhaps it was the limitations of the central site for, although adjacent, the three Parisian palaces could not be amalgamated, and remained individually inadequate for a king with Louis's pretensions. Moreover, he never did like living there, perhaps because of the childhood trauma described above, perhaps because he suffered from mild claustrophobia.[22] Probably more important was the consideration that the crowded streets of the capital made it difficult to create a dazzling visual effect. Not even Perrault's east façade of the Louvre can compare with the sight of Versailles as one approaches down the Avenue de Paris (Plate 1). In Paris, the royal palaces had to compete with a host of other grand buildings, ecclesiastical, aristocratic, and municipal; at Versailles, the king's house was *hors concours*. Although the move to Versailles was not completed until 1682, the decision had been announced five years before that. By then, Louis had long

[20] C. -F. Menestrier, *La Devise du Roi justifiée. Avec un recueil de cinq cent devises faites pour Sa Majesté et toute la Maison Royale* (Paris, 1679), quoted in Polleross, 'Sonnenkönig und österreichische Sonne', p. 243.

[21] Antoine Schnapper, 'The King of France as collector in the seventeenth century', in Robert I. Rotberg and Theodore K. Rabb (eds.), *Art and history. Images and their meaning* (Cambridge, 1988), pp. 198–9.

[22] Bluche, *Louis XIV*, p. 57.

ceased to be a Parisian king, for his last stay at the Louvre had been in 1666 and work on modernizing the Tuileries had been cancelled in 1671.[23] Among many other things, the splendour of Versailles confirmed the superior status of the French palace as a model: whereas Italian *palazzi* are blocks, facing inwards to an interior courtyard, with their living rooms shielded from direct sunlight, Versailles and its sucessors are opened towards visitors, leading their eye on a central axis through the *cour d'honneur*.[24]

Yet this does not explain why the other rural residences were not preferred, for arguably they had more to offer in terms of natural assets. The duc de Saint-Simon dismissed Versailles as 'the dullest and most ungrateful of places, without prospect, without wood, without water, without soil; for the ground is all shifting sand or swamp, the air accordingly bad'.[25] Again, one can only speculate, but it seems likely that it was just the thought of turning this unpromising site into a terrestrial paradise which appealed to Louis's imperious nature. His glory could brook no rival, not even from his ancestors. Whatever the reason, he brought to the project a determination so fierce and sustained that all obstacles were overcome. In 1682, the year in which the move of court and government to Versailles was finally completed, the marquise de Scourches observed: 'he loves this house with a passion that is boundless.'[26] So if Le Vau, Mansart, Le Brun, and Le Nôtre—and the rest of the army of architects, painters, and gardeners—must be listed as the creators of the individual components, and if Colbert takes the credit for supplying both the funds and the administrative backbone, only one signature may appear on the total work of art.

The canvas was gigantic. By the time it was fully operational, the court at Versailles numbered some 20,000 people, with approximately 1,000 nobles and 4,000 servants living in the palace complex proper and another 4,000 nobles and their servants living in the town: 'Far from being merely an assemblage of the higher nobility drawn in from the various provinces of the realm, it was a whole society in miniature, with its own priests, soldiers, officials, tradesmen and domestic servants.'[27] And it was also, of course, the

[23] Hélène Himelfarb, 'Versailles, fonctions et légendes', in Pierre Nora (ed.), *Les Lieux de mémoire*, 7 vols. (Paris, 1984), vol. II, *La Nation*, p. 235; William Ritchey Newton, *L'Espace du roi. La cour de France au château de Versailles 1682–1789* (Paris, 2000), pp. 16–17.

[24] Foerster, *Das Barock-Schloß. Geschichte und Architektur*, pp. 26–7.

[25] Lewis (ed.), *The Memoirs of the Duc de Saint-Simon*, p. 132.

[26] Pierre Verlet, *Le Château de Versailles* (Paris, 1985), pp. 132, 142.

[27] Olivier Chaline, 'The Kingdoms of France and Navarre: the Valois and Bourbon courts *c.* 1515–1750', in John Adamson, *The Princely Courts of Europe: Ritual, Politics and Culture under the Ancien Régime 1500–1750* (London, 1999), p. 70. See also Manfred Kossok, *Am Hofe Ludwigs*

seat of government. The presence of all these thousands was informed by a single purpose: the representation and enforcement of the glory of Louis XIV. Many great palaces had been built in the past to advertise the grandeur of their owners, but none had been dedicated in such an exclusive fashion to the elevation of a single individual. The nearest equivalent in terms of size and consistency was the Escorial, the vast palace north of Madrid built by Philip II almost exactly a century earlier. But the Escorial is as much a monastery as a palace, its central axis dominated not by a royal bedroom but by a church of cathedral-like proportions.[28] Although undeniably splendid, the chapel at Versailles is located outside the Cour Royal (the collective name of the three inner courtyards) and was not completed until 1710. Moreover, there are no Christian images in the palace outside the chapel.[29] Iconographically, the centre of Versailles was the 'Salon of Apollo', the throne-room which formed the climax to the sequence of 'grand appartments'. As the painted ceiling depicting 'Apollo in his chariot in company with the seasons' proclaimed, this was a wholly secular shrine. In the unlikely event of anyone failing to make the connection, the meaning of the allegorical complex was spelt out in numerous descriptions of the palace. In the very first, published in 1674, André Félibien told his readers:

> It is well to note that as the sun is the king's device and as poets confound the sun and Apollo, there is nothing in this superb house that is not in rapport with this divinity; therefore all the figures and ornaments to be seen there have not been placed there by chance, but have a relationship either to the sun or to those places where they have been put.[30]

The solar motif was repeated in innumerable ways in the great gardens constructed around the palace, most explicitly in 'Apollo's Chariot' created by Jean-Baptiste Tuby in 1668–70. Situated on the main east–west axis, this colossal group of statuary depicts the Sun God emerging from the ocean to begin his daily journey across the sky. The complexity, sophistication, and

XIV. (Stuttgart 1990), p. 50. By the end of Louis XIV's reign, the town of Versailles had a population of 15,000. It began to grow again when the court returned from Paris in 1723, reaching 70,000 in 1789, by which time it was the seventh largest city in France; Michel Antoine, *Louis XV* (Paris, 1989), p. 233.

28 Even Philip IV's pleasure palace Buen Retiro outside Madrid was placed next to the royal church and convent of San Jéronimo and its gardens contained several hermitage chapels ('retiro' here implying retreat in a spiritual as well as a recreational sense); J. H. Elliott, 'Power and propaganda in the Spain of Philip IV', in Wilentz (ed.), *Rites of Power*, p. 151.

29 Giesey, 'Models of rulership', p. 60.

30 Quoted in Louis Marin, *Portrait of the King* (London, 1988), p. 188.

rectilinearity of the gardens' design proclaimed their patron's mastery of nature. It was Louis XIV himself who wrote the first guide-book, the *Manner in which the Gardens of Versailles are to be shown*, which set down a specific itinerary, so that the effect would be maximized.[31] As Chandra Mukerji has written: 'Versailles was a model of material domination of nature that fairly shouted its excessive claims about the strength of France . . . France was clearly meant to be the new Rome. A few steps into the great formal garden at Versailles provided all that anyone needed to know about the natural authority of the king, the state, and the land of France.'[32]

In the gardens, meteorological considerations limited the media at the disposal of Louis's image-builders, but inside they could use frescoes, paintings, statuary, bas-reliefs, mosaics, and tapestries to celebrate his various achievements: charitable ('The Foundation of the Hôtel des Invalides'), cultural ('Portrait of Louis XIV as Protector of the Academy of Painting and Sculpture'), martial ('Louis XIV on horseback trampling on his enemies and crowned by glory') (Plate 2), political ('Louis XIV taking up personal government'), diplomatic ('Louis XIV bestowing peace on Europe') and sexual ('The baptism of the Grand Dauphin'). The climax was reached in the great Hall of Mirrors, which stretched for seventy-five metres along the entire length of the garden front of the Cour Royal. It was here that the transition from allusive allegory to unconcealed eulogy was made. When consulted in 1679 about the decorative scheme, the royal 'first painter', Charles Le Brun, first thought of depicting his master in the guise of Apollo or Hercules. It was decided higher up, however, that more direct treatment was needed, so in each of the paintings Louis stands at the centre of the composition unconcealed by allegory. Worship of Louis as Sun King made way for worship of Louis in his own persona. No part of government, it was proclaimed, had been neglected by the King's beneficent hand: 'Order restored to finances', 'Patronage granted to the fine arts', 'Navigation re-established', 'Justice reformed', 'Police and public order established in Paris', 'The rage of duelling arrested', and so on.[33] But it was his military achievements which were given pride of place: of the twenty-seven paintings in the Hall of Mirrors, seventeen are devoted to foreign policy, nine of them celebrating victories in the war against

[31] Chaline, 'The Kingdoms of France and Navarre', p. 85.

[32] Chandra Mukerji, *Territorial Ambitions and the Gardens of Versailles* (Cambridge, 1997), pp. 2, 334.

[33] There is a detailed description and analysis of every major painting, not just in the Hall of Mirrors, but in every state-room, in Gérard Sabatier, *Versailles ou la figure du roi* (Paris, 2000), here in chs. 6–9.

the Dutch, concluded in 1678.[34] At one end of the Hall it is the Dutch alliance with France's enemies which is depicted, at the other end it is the Dutch acceptance of a separate peace—or, in other words, there is a progression from provocation to retribution.[35] In between could be found visual depictions of Louis's foreign-policy achievements such as 'The pre-eminence of France recognized by Spain, 1662', 'The war against Spain to defend the rights of the Queen, 1667', 'Franche-Comté conquered for the second time, 1674', and 'The capture of the city and fortress of Ghent in six days, 1678'.[36] At the centre of the whole iconographical scheme stood the decisive moment: 'The King governs by himself, 1661'. This multi-media exercise in glorification included the bust sculpted by Bernini during his otherwise fruitless visit to France in 1665. Everything about this extraordinary figure (perhaps the finest 'swagger portrait bust' ever created), from the set of the king's head to the cloak which swirls over his armour, expresses the vigour, glamour, and self-confidence of the young king.[37]

These were essential qualities if the court were to be made to work. The Bourbon dynasty was barely fifty years old when Louis XIV came to the throne and there were many great French families who regarded him as only *primus inter pares*. Not even the most sumptuous setting could have made him supreme if he had not been blessed with the capacity to command respect. Every contemporary account agreed that he enjoyed this asset in full measure. He compensated for his relatively small stature (he was only 5 feet 3 inches tall)[38] with a dominating personality expressed by deportment, gesture, speech, and simple 'presence'. His natural skill and long training as a dancer had taught him, among other things, how to make an entrance and how to conduct himself in public to maximum effect.[39] Jean-Baptiste Primi Visconti, count of San Maiolo, recorded in 1673 'I went [to Saint Germain] in the month

[34] Christophe Pincemaille, 'La guerre de Hollande dans le programme iconographique de la grande galerie de Versailles', *Histoire, Économie et Société*, 4, 3 (1985), p. 313. See also Joël Cornette, *Le roi de guerre. Essai sur la souveraineté dans la France du Grand Siècle* (Paris, 1993), ch. 8 *passim*. There is a useful key to all thirty ceiling frescoes on p. 245.

[35] Édouard Pommier, 'Versailles, l'image du souverain', in Nora (ed.), *Les Lieux de mémoire*, II, p. 208.

[36] Sabatier, *Versailles*, pp. 308–85.

[37] There is a particularly fine reproduction in Rudolf Wittokower, *Bernini* (London, 1955), plate 97.

[38] Burke, *The fabrication of Louis XIV*, p. 125.

[39] 'The dance class, which Louis XIV took for twenty-five years, turned the dull little prince into a self-assured, self-possessed, totally regal creature'; Régine Astier, 'Louis XIV, "premier danseur"', in David Lee Rubin (ed.), *Sun King: The Ascendancy of French Culture during the Reign of Louis XIV* (Washington, 1992), p. 75.

of February. I caught sight of the king on his way to Mass. Although I had never seen him before and he was lost in a crowd of courtiers, I immediately recognized him. He had a grand majestic air, and by his stature and demeanour you could tell that if he hadn't already been a king, he would have deserved to be one in the eyes of the beholders.'[40] Even one of Louis's sharpest critics, the duc de Saint-Simon, paid the following eloquent tribute: 'Louis XIV was made for a brilliant Court. In the midst of other men, his figure, his courage, his grace, his beauty, his grand mien, even the tone of his voice and the majestic and natural charm of his person, distinguished him till his death.'[41] This priceless asset was also singled out by Voltaire: 'Above all his courtiers Louis rose supreme by the grace of his figure and the majestic nobility of his countenance. The sound of his voice, at once dignified and charming, won the hearts of those whom his presence had intimidated. His bearing was such as befitted himself and his rank alone, and would have been ridiculous in any other. The awe which he inspired in those who spoke with him secretly flattered the consciousness of his own superiority.'[42]

So the court of Louis XIV elevated the king from *primus inter pares* to being both *solus* and *solaris*. But for a French aristocrat, attendance at court was not just submission to a grim instrument of cultural distancing, it was also an opportunity to participate in the most lavish and exciting entertainment to be found in Europe. No one expressed better the general conviction that the royal court was the only place to be than the marquis de Vardes when he told Louis: 'Sire, when one is away from you, one is not just wretched, one is ridiculous.'[43] From the outset, it was made clear that all that was best in aristocratic forms of recreation would become a royal monopoly. All the writers and artists employed by Fouquet[44] passed into the service of the king. To demonstrate just how far a sovereign could outdistance even the mightiest subject when it came to festivity, Louis organized on 5–6 June 1662 a great *Carrousel* (tournament) at the Tuileries which set new standards for extravagant display. Five teams of noblemen dressed as Romans, Persians, Turks, Indians, and Americans jousted, fenced, and tilted, with the *victor ludorum* on each of the two days receiving from the queen a diamond worth 25,000 *écus* and a portrait of the king set in a frame of precious stones.[45] This flamboyant opulence also

40 Quoted in William Beik, *Louis XIV and Absolutism* (Boston and New York, 2000), p. 59.

41 Lewis (ed.), *The Memoirs of the Duc de Saint-Simon*, p. 129.

42 Voltaire, *The Age of Louis XIV*, trans. Martyn P. Pollack (London, 1961), p. 267.

43 Quoted in Solnon, *La Cour de France*, p. 339.

44 See above, p. 33.

45 Moine, *Les Fêtes à la cour du roi soleil*, p. 28; Burke, *The Fabrication of Louis XIV*, p. 66.

enjoyed the endorsement of the Church. In the words of Bishop Bossuet, Louis's tame prelate: 'God forbade ostentation inspired by vanity and the foolish display bred by the intoxication of riches: however, it was also his wish that the courts of kings should be dazzling and magnificent to inspire respect in the common people.'[46]

In fact, it was the nobility rather than the *plebs* which was the main target of Louis's peacock display. When he appeared in a coat encrusted with 14,000,000 *livres*-worth of diamonds, for example, he was demonstrating to his court that no private individual could compete with royal resources.[47] But the courtiers could compete among themselves, constantly outbidding each other in their pursuit of the extravagant fashions set by the king. The colossal expense involved proved to be another instrument of social control, for nobles who spent their revenues on high living at Versailles were nobles with little or nothing left for political intrigue in the provinces. Conspicuous consumption also made most of them dependent on royal largesse. Mme de Maintenon estimated that a single noble at Versailles with a staff of twelve servants would need at least 12,000 *livres* per annum. Only a minority enjoyed that kind of income, the rest could keep afloat only with the financial buoyancy provided by pensions and sinecures.[48] In 1683 1,400,000 *livres* were paid out in royal pensions, a substantial sum representing about 1.2 per cent of total government expenditure but even so a cost-effective investment in social harmony.[49] Control was also exercised in a more direct way through the simple expedient of opening the courtiers' mail in search of anything subversive.[50]

Although the Versailles project was undoubtedly an exercise in political and social control, the familiar image of an emasculated aristocracy pining in its gilded cage is misleading. As the exponents of the 'new court history' have pointed out, not even the court of Louis XIV was a monolith but rather a coalition. To use John Adamson's appropriate metaphor: 'The courtier's firmament contained a constellation, not a single blazing sun'.[51]

[46] Marion, 'Cour', in *Dictionnaire des institutions de la France*, p. 155.

[47] Werner Sombart, *Luxury and Capitalism* (Ann Arbor, Mich., 1967), p. 72.

[48] Etienne François, 'Der Hof Ludwig XIV.', in August Buck, Georg Kauffmann, Blake Lee Spahr, and Conrad Wiedemann (eds.), *Europäische Hofkultur im 16. und 17. Jahrhundert. Vorträge und Referate gehalten anlaßlich des Kongresses des Wolfenbütteler Arbeitskreises für Barockliteratur in der Herzog August Bibliothek Wolfenbüttel vom 4. bis 8. September 1979* (Hamburg, 1981), vol. II, p. 729.

[49] Solnon, *La Cour de France*, p. 363.

[50] Newton, *L'Espace du roi*, p. 18.

[51] John Adamson, 'The making of the Ancien Régime court 1500–1700', in idem, *The Princely Courts of Europe*, p. 17.

Overemphasis on the concept of 'state-building' has obscured the extent to which the court allowed sovereign and courtiers to renegotiate their relationship in a spirit of cooperation, with the former making as many sacrifices as the latter: 'Far from being the cause of the nobles' ensnarement, as was once supposed, service at court generally appears to have been one of the principal means by which aristocratic authority and influence were maintained,' albeit on Louis XIV's terms.[52]

The *Carrousel* of 1662 was also the last major urban festivity of the reign. It was Versailles which now became the representational centre, the first great set-piece being the evocatively named 'Pleasures of the Enchanted Isle' in 1664. At the all-night celebrations held in 1668 to celebrate the end of the war against the Spanish, all the senses of the 600 guests were titillated—by a banquet, a ball, a comedy (Molière's *George Dandin*) and a firework display, all taking place in a park transformed into fairyland by illuminated transparencies.[53] Although made possible by improved lighting, this move to nocturnal festivities also served to distance the leisured world of the court from the round of mundane toil. In an age when workplaces opened at five in summer and six in winter to maximize use of natural light, the courtiers were going home to sleep as lesser mortals were leaving home to work. For the ordinary royal subject, there was a strict division between festive days and working days, between festive spaces and working spaces, but 'in the world of the court, every space is a festive space and every time is a festive time. Court life is totally festive.'[54]

Not even the royal purse was deep enough to sustain too many of the grand occasions, especially when warfare became virtually constant after 1672. In between times, the courtiers were entertained three times a week at the *appartements*, when 'the King, the Queen and the whole royal family descend from their heights to play with members of the assembly,' as the official gazette, the *Mercure Galant*, put it in December 1682.[55] 'Play' in this context meant billiards, cards, and refreshments, as well as the opportunity for the gossip which was the dominant discourse of a society obsessed with precedence and favour. It also meant dancing. The king himself was, by all accounts, a superlative dancer who could out-perform any courtier and hold his own with the professionals. Although he appeared for the last time in a formal ballet

[52] Ibid., p. 15.
[53] Jean-Marie Apostolidès, 'From Roi Soleil to Louis le Grand', in Denis Hollier (ed.), *A New History of French Literature* (Cambridge, Mass., and London, 1989), pp. 315–16.
[54] R. Alewyn, *Das große Welttheater: die Epoche der höfischen Feste* (Hamburg, 1959), pp. 13, 31.
[55] Burke, *The Fabrication of Louis XIV*, p. 91.

in 1669, his continued passion for social dancing ensured that there was no decline in activity. The marquis de Dangeau recorded in his diary that in the six months between 10 September 1684 and 3 March 1685, there were no fewer than seventy royal entertainments involving dancing, including one grand ball, nine masquerades, and fifty-eight *appartements*, or in other words one every two or three days.[56] One must wonder, however, whether even the most dedicated dancer did not weary of such a surfeit, but there was no escape: a royal invitation to the dance was a command. The formal balls especially were strictly regimented affairs, serving more to demonstrate the hierarchical structure of the court and the social disciplining of its members than to allow rhythmic intercourse.[57] Only a small proportion of those attending actually danced; the great majority were spectators. As a contemporary recorded: 'First one must know that no one is admitted to the circle except princes and princesses of the blood, then the dukes and peers and the duchesses, and after these the other lords and ladies of the court, each according to rank.'[58]

Also functional as well as recreational were the *ballets de cour*, lengthy and elaborate combinations of dance, music, verse, and spectacular theatrical effects. In the appropriately orotund words of their most recent historian, they 'responded to a triple aim: to inform the curious; to guide subjects by glorifying the prince—God's image on earth; and to enchant by entertaining a hierarchical but turbulent society by momentarily releasing its aggressiveness and its violence, without forgetting to satisfy an eroticism shared between wanton freshness and gallant precioisity'.[59] Their development mirrored politics. Beginning as private entertainments performed by nobles for nobles, they became representational displays of royal grandeur, performed by professional dancers for the King, with the nobles attending as passive spectators.[60] By 1680 this Italian-bred hybrid developed into distinctively French opera. Ironically, the man mainly responsible was a Florentine, Giovanni Battista Lulli, who in 1660 at the age of 28 became 'Composer of the King's Chamber Music' and the following year 'Music Master of the Royal Family'.

[56] Braun and Guggerli, *Macht des Tanzes—Tanz der Mächtigen*, p. 145.

[57] Ibid., p. 146.

[58] Quoted in Rebecca Harris-Warrick, 'Ballroom dancing at the court of Louis XIV', *Early Music*, 14 (1986), 41.

[59] Marie-Françoise Christout, *Le Ballet de Cour au XVIIe siècle* (Geneva, 1987), p. 8.

[60] Marie-Claude Genova-Green, 'Le ballet de cour en France', in Pierre Béhar and Helen Watanabe-O'Kelly, *Spectaculum Europæum: Theatre and Spectacle in Europe (1580–1750)*, Wolfenbütteler Arbeiten zur Barockforschung, vol. 31 (Wiesbaden, 1999), p. 508.

Marrying the daughter of another senior figure of the royal musical establishment and adopting French nationality, the newly Gallicized Jean-Baptiste Lully encouraged the king to turn his back on the previously dominant Italian school. The last Italian opera to be performed in France for sixty-seven years was Cavalli's *Ercole* in 1662 and in 1666 Louis dismissed his Italian musicians.[61]

To fill their place, he greatly expanded the modest native musical establishment he had inherited, subdivided into the chapel, the chamber, and the stables. Music was omnipresent at Versailles: it was played during the *lever* and the *coucher*, in chapel, at the departure of the hunt, at firework displays, at balls and masquerades, as an aural background to meals, promenades, receptions, and almost every other form of social intercourse, as well as in the more formal context of concerts, ballets, and operas. During Versailles's heyday, more than 200 singers and instrumentalists were engaged in the task of making France the musical arbiter of Europe.[62] The king was only too eager to adopt Perrin's maxim: 'the glory of the King and of France make it unseemly that a nation otherwise invincible should be ruled by foreigners in matters pertaining to the fine arts, poetry and music.'[63]

It was Lully's task to realize the musical objective and in this he succeeded triumphantly. By the time he died in 1687, he had created a distinctively French operatic genre. From the *ballets de cour* of the 1650s and early 1660s, he progressed to writing *comédies-ballets* and *tragédies-ballets* and then, from 1672, the fully fledged *tragédies lyriques*.[64] Their invariable features included a prologue, devoted to singing the praises of Louis XIV, a five-act structure, and subject-matter drawn from classical mythology or (less often) medieval romance.[65] Eschewing the sweet melodies and brilliant singing of the Italian tradition, Lully's prime concern was dramatic dialogue, conducted mainly in the form of melodic recitative, interspersed with short lyrical passages for the expression of especially impassioned moments. These austere exchanges, which can all too easily become monotonous in performance, were interrupted periodically by *divertissements* in the shape of choruses, ballets, and

[61] Robert M. Isherwood, *Music in the Service of the King: France in the Seventeenth Century* (Ithaca, NY, and London, 1973), pp. 133–4.

[62] Solnon, *La Cour de France*, p. 411.

[63] Ibid., p. 412.

[64] James R. Anthony, 'Jean-Baptiste Lully', in Stanley Sadie (ed.), *The New Grove Dictionary of Music and Musicians*, 20 vols. (London, 1980), vol. 11, p. 318; Jérôme de la Gorce, 'L'opéra en France', in Béhar and Watanabe-O'Kelly, *Spectaculum Europæum*, pp. 389–90.

[65] Donald Jay Grout, 'Some forerunners of the Lully opera', *Music and Letters*, 22 (1941), p. 1.

magical stage effects.[66] As any reader familiar with the operas of Rameau, Gluck, Cherubini, Spontini, or Meyerbeer will appreciate, the operatic style codified by Lully was to have a long future.[67] The subject-matter of the libretti was mainly classical (*Cadmus et Hermione*, *Alceste*, *Atys*, etc.), although the opportunities for magical transformation scenes made the epic poems of Tasso and Ariosto popular too (*Roland*, *Armide et Renaud*).

As with the visual expression of Louis XIV's glory at Versailles, the representational significance of these works was made explicit. In the 'Ballet of Psyche or the Power of love, danced by His Majesty on the 16th Day of January 1656', for example, the king entered in the role of 'Spring', accompanied by an adoring party of nymphs chanting:

> Oh how happy we all are
> To see this amorous Spring
> Who radiates such dazzling glory!

'Glory' herself appears later in the work, apostrophizing Louis as her most illustrious manifestation:

> Great King, what is your destiny?
> You who now have the whole world at your feet.

In this pristine world of royal love and royal glory, there is no room for aristocratic rancour or intrigue, so in the fourth *entrée*, the characters representing 'Discord', 'Sorrow', 'Fear', and 'Jealousy' are repulsed when they try to gain admission to the Temple of Love.[68]

As these thinly veiled references to the Fronde demonstrated, the primary purpose of Lully's creations was political. In the 'Ballet of the Seasons' at Fontainebleau on 23 July 1661, just four months after assuming personal control of his kingdom following the death of Mazarin, Louis again appeared

[66] There is an excellent summary of the Lully operatic tradition in Cynthia Verba, *Music and the French Enlightenment: Reconstruction of a Dialogue 1750–1764* (Oxford, 1993), pp. 12–13. Grout's severe verdict on the genre was 'Anyone who plays through the whole score of a Lully opera is likely to emerge from that experience (if he survives it at all) with a confused impression of page upon page of music void of imagination, pale in colour, thin in harmony, monotonous in invention, stereotyped in rhythm, limited in melody, barren of contrapuntal resource and so cut into little sections by perpetually recurring cadences that all sense of movement seems lost in a desert of clichés, relieved all too rarely by oases of real beauty'; 'Some forerunners of the Lully opera', p. 2.

[67] Significantly perhaps, only one of these masters of the 'French style' was French.

[68] *Ballet de Psyché ou De la Puissance de l'Amour, dansé par sa Majesté le 16. jour de Ianvier 1656* (Paris, 1656), pp. 6, 12, 27.

as 'Spring' in the eighth *entrée*: 'The scene which represented Winter is transformed into a garden into which Spring, followed by Laughter, Joy, and Plenty, comes to reign for all eternity.' As Louis demonstrated his skill as a dancer on stage, his aristocratic audience was told:

> The youthful vigour of Spring
> Has chased away bad weather,
> All those mutinous and disordered winds,
> Which in amongst the thick fog
> Caused such fierce squalls,
> Have been banished for ever,
> And Spring has restored to the atmosphere profound peace.
> This season we find so pleasing
> Has sent back to the cold climate of the North
> The Winter which brought us war,
> And has nurtured for our happiness
> The great and immortal flower
> Whose fragrance will be spread throughout Europe.[69]

In this *ballet de cour*, as in the other court presentations, politics and culture combined. In the ninth and final *entrée* of the 'Ballet of the Seasons', the Nine Muses, guided by Apollo and Cupid, came to establish themselves at Fontainebleau, accompanied by the Seven Liberal Arts, together with Prosperity, Health, Peace, and Pleasure. The entire team vowed that it would never leave such a blessed place.[70] To make sure that it did not, Louis XIV continued and greatly extended Cardinal Richelieu's policy of subjecting culture to royal control. Early in 1634, Richelieu had discovered that a group of intellectuals had been holding secret social meetings in Paris. As both a clergyman and a politician, he was especially prone to minding other people's business, so at once he took action to bring this private initiative under state control. Reluctantly sacrificing their independence, the group accepted in return financial sponsorship and the title of Académie Française. The control their new patron sought to exercise was both cultural and political. On the one hand, he charged them with the task of supervising 'the exact rules' of the French language, 'to render it capable of treating the arts and sciences'. On the other hand, he made it clear that the academicians had to be loyal royalists: 'matters political and moral shall be treated in the Academy in conformity with

[69] *Ballet des saisons dansé à Fontainebleau par sa Majesté le 23. Juillet 1661* (*A Paris par Robert Ballard, seul imprimeur du Roy pour la Musique, M.DC. LXI. Avec Privilege de sa Majesté*), p. 18.
[70] Ibid., p. 19.

the authority of the Prince, the state of the government, and the laws of the realm.'[71]

As events were to show, the carrots of financial security and enhanced status were sufficiently alluring to make the coercive stick of government direction unnecessary. The next academy to be founded, that of Painting and Sculpture in 1648, was also derived from a private initiative. This time it was a group of court painters, seeking to escape from the onerous restrictions and artisanal status of the guilds. After a prolonged struggle, they emerged victorious in 1654, with a monopoly of life-drawing and the same rights as their literary counterparts in the Académie Française.[72] The date was significant: it was both the king and his academicians who were the victors of the Fronde. The next move to royal absolutism with the beginning of Louis XIV's sole rule in 1661 also brought an increase in the number of academies. In the same year, the balletomane monarch created the Academy of Dance. In 1663 it was joined by the Academy of Inscriptions and Letters, in 1666 by the Academy of Sciences, in 1669 by the Academy of Music, and in 1671 by the Academy of Architecture. By that time there was no branch of high culture not subject to state control.[73] It was also extended to the fledgling press. In 1663, the historian Eudes de Mézeray was granted permission to publish a literary journal on the grounds that the arts and the sciences enhanced a state's prestige no less than feats of arms and that French intellect was in no way inferior to French valour. But although de Mézeray was authorized to report on innovations in every branch of culture, he was strictly forbidden to venture any opinion on matters of morality, religion, or politics.[74]

The monopoly enforced by the academies ensured that any ambitious and talented artist was obliged to accept state service. Given the scale of Louis XIV's patronage at Versailles and elsewhere, there was also a strong financial incentive to enter the gilded cage. Consequently, almost all the great names of the age—Corneille, Racine, Molière, Lully, Delalande, Couperin, Le Vau, Mansart, de Cotte, Le Nôtre, Le Brun, Mignard, Rigaud, Largillierre,

[71] Timothy Murray, 'The Académie Française', in Hollier (ed.), *A New History of French Literature*, pp. 267–8.

[72] Nikolaus Pevsner, *Academies of Art—Past and Present* (Cambridge, 1940), pp. 85–7; Thomas E. Crow, *Painters and Public Life in Eighteenth Century Paris* (New Haven and London, 1985), pp. 22–8.

[73] As Anthony Blunt observed, Colbert and Louis XIV established 'the closest and most complete State control ever exercised before the present century'; *Art and Architecture in France 1500–1700* (Harmondsworth, 1973), p. 322.

[74] Claude Bellanger, Jacques Godechot, Pierre Guiral, and Fernand Terrou (eds.), *Histoire générale de la presse française*, vol. I: *Des origines à 1814* (Paris, 1969), p. 125.

Girardon, Coysevox—enjoyed an intimate relationship with the state through pensions or appointments. In many ways the most important exceptions—Poussin, Descartes, and Pascal—are more revealing than the rule. First, they did not live to experience the full flowering of the new absolutist culture, dying in 1665, 1650, and 1662 respectively. Secondly, Poussin and Descartes spent most of their adult life outside France. Moving to Rome in 1624, Poussin returned in 1640 on the orders of the king, only to find the commissions he was expected to fulfil—allegories of Cardinal Richelieu—so distasteful that he soon left again.[75] After much restless wandering across the continent, Descartes settled in Amsterdam, taking full advantage of tolerant Dutch culture. It could also be said that Pascal went into self-imposed exile, albeit inside France at the Jansenist convent of Port-Royal. Thirdly, all three of them were important inspirations for the various forms of anti-absolutist counter-culture which developed in the course of the eighteenth century: it has become something of a cliché to say that the neo-classicism which culminated in Jacques-Louis David's 'revolutionary art' was really neo-Poussinism; Cartesian rationality and its methodology of 'systematic doubt' was central to the Enlightenment; Pascal made a powerful contribution to the development of Jansenism, perhaps the most subversive movement of old regime France.[76]

That was all in the future. In the meantime the academies, directed by the firm controlling hand of Colbert, developed a style perfectly designed to represent the glory of Louis XIV. It was secular, rational, imposing, restrained, orderly, and uniform.[77] Above all, the individual genres—visual, musical, balletic, and literary—meshed to form a total work of art. A performance in the gardens of Versailles of a *comédie-ballet* with music by Lully and a text by Molière represented the regime's legitimacy before the great nobles of France in a manner they found irresistible (for the time being). It was also a manner which the rest of France found irresistible. All over the country, it was the style dictated by the centre which prevailed. When commissioning a new building or painting or when organizing a public festivity, provincial patrons sought the

[75] Ibid., p. 282.

[76] Anita Brookner, *Jacques-Louis David* (London, 1980), pp. 44, 64; Wend Graf Kalnein and Michael Levey, *Art and Architecture of the Eighteenth Century in France* (London, 1972), p. 192; Roland Mousnier, 'Les concepts d'"ordre", d'"états", de "fidelité" et de "monarchie absolue" en France de la fin du XVe siècle à la fin du XVIIIe', *Revue Historique*, 502 (1972), p. 295; J. S. Bromley, 'The decline of absolute monarchy', in J. Wallace-Hadrill and J. McManners (eds.), *France: Government and Society*, 2nd edn. (London, 1970), pp. 144–5.

[77] For an excellent description and analysis of the official style in the visual arts, see Blunt, *Art and Architecture in France*, p. 325.

services of an artist associated with the court. Failing that, they obtained metropolitan models for their local artists to imitate.[78] If classicism can be defined as 'the psychological centre of a national culture',[79] then it was during the middle decades of the seventeenth century that French classicism was codified if not created.

The rest of Europe succumbed too, with varying degrees of enthusiasm. The sophistication, self-confidence, and sheer quality of Louis XIV's achievement made most foreign cultures come to seem old-fashioned, dull and—fatal stigma—provincial. Those who could not travel to Versailles to experience its wonders at first hand could make their acquaintance through the numerous descriptions and illustrations which were published. In 1663 Louis instructed Israel Silvestre to engrave 'all his palaces, royal houses, the most beautiful views and aspects of his gardens, public assemblies, Carrousels and outskirts of cities'.[80] This commission initiated a series of magnificent volumes, themselves art objects of high value, which broadcast French culture across the length and breadth of Europe. As Félibien commented: 'it is again by means of these prints that all nations can admire the sumptuous edifices which the king has built everywhere, and the rich ornamentation which embellishes them.'[81] A symbolic moment in the assertion of French cultural supremacy was the failure of Bernini's visit in 1665. Although it yielded the portrait-bust already mentioned, it failed to lead to the reconstruction of the Louvre in the Italian baroque manner. Instead, a French architect was commissioned to design a more austere—and more French—exterior.[82] This episode appears to have marked something of a watershed, as from then on the increasingly self-confident French patrons abandoned Italian architects in favour of natives.[83] By 1682 Ménestrier could claim that the cultural hegemony of Italy was over—it was France that now set the standards in all the arts:

> It is the glory of France to have succeeded in establishing the rules for all the fine arts. During the past twenty years, scholarly dissertations have regulated drama, epic poetry, epigrams, eclogues, painting, music, architecture, heraldry, mottoes, riddles,

[78] Ibid.

[79] T. J. Reed, *The Classical Centre: Goethe and Weimar 1775–1832* (London, 1980), p. 13. As he was writing a history of German literature, Reed wrote 'the psychological centre of a national literature' but his insight applies just as well to a whole culture.

[80] Schnapper, 'The King of France as collector in the seventeenth century', p. 195.

[81] Ibid., p. 196.

[82] François Bluche, *Louis XIV* (Oxford, 1990), pp. 172–4.

[83] Francis Haskell, *Patrons and Painters. A Study in Relations between Italian Art and Society in the Age of the Baroque* (London, 1963), p. 189.

emblems, history and rhetoric. All branches of knowledge are now conducted in our language.[84]

Of all these emblems, it was language which was the most important. In 1685 Pierre Bayle observed from his Dutch exile: 'in future it will be the French language which will serve as the means of communication for all the peoples of Europe,' adding that every educated person wanted to acquire what had become a mark of good breeding.[85] His forecast was confirmed in 1694 by the official journal, the *Mercure Galant*: 'The range of the French language has crossed the kingdom's frontiers. It is confined neither by the Pyrenees, nor by the Alps nor by the Rhine. French is to be heard all over Europe. The French language is spoken at all the courts: the princes and the grandees speak it, the ambassadors write it and high society makes it fashionable.'[86]

Nothing advertised better the cultural hegemony achieved by Louis XIV's France than this peaceful linguistic conquest of the continent. When Louis came to the throne in 1643, French was only one of several competing languages. Either Spanish or Italian could have made as good if not a better claim to be the lingua franca of educated Europe, while Latin still dominated academic discourse. Halfway through his reign it could be claimed that French had become the world language, 'as current among the savages of America as it was among the most civilized nations of Europe'.[87] By the end of the century, the marquis de Dangeau could tell the Académie Française with majestic complacency: 'All our works contribute to the embellishment of our language and help to make it known to foreigners. The wonders achieved by the King have made French as familiar to our neighbours as their own vernacular, indeed the events of these past few years have broadcast it over all the oceans of the globe, making it as essential to the New World as to the Old.'[88] It was a process greatly assisted by the codification of the French language in the great dictionary of the Académie Française, completed in 1694.[89]

84 Quoted in Braun and Guggerli, *Macht des Tanzes—Tanz der Mächtigen*, pp. 123–4.

85 Quoted in Louis Réau, *L'Europe française au siècle des lumières* (Paris, 1951), pp. 3, 18.

86 Ibid., p. 17.

87 By Bouhours in *Entretiens d'Ariste et d'Eugène*, quoted in René Guiet, 'La question de la langue française dans les querelles musicales au XVIIIe siècle', in Caroline. B. Bourland et al. (eds.), *Essays Contributed in Honor of President William Allan Neilson*, Smith College Studies in Modern Languages (Northampton, Mass., 1940), p. 92.

88 Nicole Ferrier-Caverivière, *L'Image de Louis XIV dans la littérature française de 1660 à 1715* (Paris, 1981), p. 371 n. 71.

89 Alain Rey, 'Linguistic absolutism', in Hollier (ed.), *A New History of French Literature*, pp. 373–5.

Several illustrations of the (temporary) validity of Dangeau's boast could be found. The most revealing was the dispute which erupted in 1687 between 'Ancients' and 'Moderns', as the latter dared to claim that the culture of contemporary France was the equal of that of the Greeks and the Romans. In the words of the poem which started it all—*The Century of Louis XIV*, read to the Académie Française by Charles Perrault in February 1687:

> Classical antiquity was always worthy of respect,
> But I never saw it as an object of adoration.
> I regard the Ancients without bending the knee,
> They are great, it is true, but they are men just like us;
> And we can compare without fearing to be unjust
> The century of Louis with that of Augustus.[90]

Wherever he turned in the France of today, Perrault went on, he was overwhelmed by marvellous accomplishments, in the theatre, in literature, in music, and in the visual arts. As for Versailles:

> This is not just a palace, it is an entire city,
> Superb in its grandeur, superb in its substance—
> No, rather it is a world by itself, where all kinds of wonders
> Are brought together from all over the universe...
> What can be found in all antiquity
> To equal their splendour and variety?[91]

In the world of power politics, the decisive revelation of French hegemony came in 1714, the year before Louis's death, when for the first time a Holy Roman Emperor deigned to sign an international treaty (Rastatt) drafted in the French language.[92] With the advantage of hindsight, we can see that the future of French as the world's favoured language was destined to be short, but for most educated Europeans in the eighteenth century its status was unchallenged. Even the Russians now spoke French, noted Coyer in 1779, and thus demonstrated that Leibniz's ambition to create a universal language had now been realized.[93] It was partly on the grounds that the French language had been 'settled by the good writers of the age of Louis XIV', while 'German' was still an aggregate of dialects, that Frederick the

[90] Ibid., p. 366.

[91] Ibid.

[92] Ibid, p. 12. This may have been less the result of French cultural hegemony than of the inability of the French negotiator, the maréchal de Villars, to understand Latin; André Corvisier, *Arts et sociétés dans l'Europe du XVIIIe siècle* (Paris, 1978), p. 21.

[93] G. F. Coyer, *Nouvelles observations sur l'Angleterre par un voyageur* (Paris, 1779), p. 163.

Great justified his decision to use the former for his voluminous literary *œuvre*.[94]

Frederick's admiration of French culture was legendary in France and notorious in Germany. Voltaire reported from Potsdam that one might think oneself in France, for everyone at the Prussian court spoke French and French alone, indeed he had never heard a word of German spoken by the king or his entourage. He concluded: 'our language and our literature have made more conquests than Charlemagne ever did.'[95] Those words were written in 1750, when Prussia and France were still allies. Seven years later, at the battle of Rossbach, Frederick inflicted on his land of cultural allegiance a defeat so total that—according to Voltaire—it represented a humiliation greater than Crécy, Poitiers, or Agincourt.[96] Arguably, it marked the beginning of the end for the old regime.[97]

Rossbach also demonstrated the limits of French cultural hegemony. When it came to exercising control of Central Europe, a Prussian bayonet proved to be more effective than a Lully *comédie-ballet*. Yet it does not disprove the intimate relationship between culture, society, and politics presented in the previous chapter.[98] As we shall see below, the impact of Rossbach and the other Prussian achievements in the Seven Years War produced great fissures in the foundations of French cultural supremacy. No less a person than Goethe observed that: 'The first true and really vital material of the higher order came into German literature through Frederick the Great and the deeds of the Seven Years War'.[99] Before that process can be examined, however, we must turn our attention to the development of representational culture outside France.

94 Réau, *L'Europe française*, p. 23.

95 Ibid., p. 49.

96 Theodor Schieder, *Friedrich der Große: ein Königtum der Widersprüche* (Frankfurt am Main, Berlin, and Vienna, 1983), p. 455.

97 I have discussed this in *The French Revolutionary Wars 1787–1802* (London, 1996), pp. 17, 23.

98 See above, pp. 2–3.

99 *Goethes Werke, hrsg. im Auftrage der Großherzogin Sophie von Sachsen*, 133 vols (Weimar, 1887–1912), XXVII, 104.

2

The Holy Roman Empire and the Habsburg Monarchy

In his treatise on the customs of mankind, Frederick the Great commented on the French cultural conquests of the past hundred years with characteristic asperity (and misogyny):

> The taste for French drama was imported into Germany together with French fashions: enthused by the magnificence which Louis XIV impressed on all his actions, by the sophistication of his court and by the great names who were the ornaments of his reign, all Europe sought to imitate the France it admired. All Germany went there: a young man counted for a fool if he had not spent some time at the court of Versailles. French taste ruled our kitchens, our furniture, our clothes and all those knick-knacks which are so much at the mercy of the tyranny of fashion. Carried to excess, this passion degenerated into a frenzy; women, who are often prey to exaggeration, pushed it to the point of extravagance.[1]

Certainly, examples can be found of German princes great and small imitating Louis XIV, sometimes to comic effect—as in the case of the Prince of Hohenlohe who sought to represent his glory by placing outside his remodelled residence at Weikersheim statues of the four great conquerors of the world: Ninus, Cyrus, Alexander, and Caesar.[2] Only marginally more

[1] *Des mœurs, des coutumes, de l'industrie, des progrès de l'esprit humain dans les arts et dans les sciences*, *Oeuvres de Frédéric le Grand*, 30 vols. (Berlin, 1846–56), I, p. 232.

[2] Heinrich von Treitschke, *Deutsche Geschichte im 19. Jahrhundert*, 5 vols. (Leipzig, 1927), I, p. 19.

convincing was the Elector of Bavaria's staging in 1658 of an elaborate pageant at Munich in conscious imitation of Louis XIV's *Cavalcade* of two years earlier, in the course of which the Elector himself appeared in the guise of the Sun.[3]

It was not just the discrepancy between pretension and reality which made these attempts at self-aggrandisement so reminiscent of La Fontaine's frog.[4] The extravagant courts which mushroomed in the Holy Roman Empire also had a decidedly *parvenu* air, for they were of comparatively recent origin. Even the greatest of them, the court of the Habsburgs, was very much a seventeenth-century creation. It was not until the reign of Ferdinand II (1619–37) that the dynasty abandoned its peripatetic ways and finally came to rest for good in Vienna. In 1519 the imperial court had numbered just 472 and continued to hover around the 500 mark for the next century or so, but then accelerated to soar over 2,000 by the time of Charles VI (1711–40).[5] The inflation can be charted with some precision by counting the number of *Kämmerer* (or 'gentlemen of the bedchamber', that is to say courtiers officially in attendance on the Emperor). When Maximilian I died in 1619, there were only six; in 1566 Maximilian II attended the imperial parliament at Regensburg accompanied by just eight, while Rudolf II made the same journey with twelve in 1594. Then the tally began to mount rapidly, reaching almost a hundred in 1633, 340 in 1678, and 423 by 1705. Charles VI appointed 226 in 1732 alone, so by the time Joseph II began his purge of the court in 1780, there were about 1,500 *Kämmerer*.[6] Apart from anything else, this increase advertised the success of the Habsburgs in making a position at their court attractive to a large and ever-increasing number of the German nobility.

The timing of the rise of the court and its culture in the Holy Roman Empire was determined in large measure by politics. Until 1648 at the earliest, the German princes were preoccupied by struggles with their representative assemblies ('Estates') inside their territories and struggles with the emperor or

[3] Marie-Christine Moine, *Les Fêtes à la cour du roi soleil 1653–1715* (Paris, 1984) p. 168.

[4] 'Une Grenouille vit un Boeuf / Qui lui sembla de belle taille. / Elle, qui n'était pas grosse en tout comme un oeuf, / Envieuse, s'étend, et s'enfle, et se travaille, / Pour égaler l'animal en grosseur, / Disant : "Regardez bien, ma soeur ; / Est-ce assez ? dites-moi ; n'y suis-je point encore ? /—Nenni.—M'y voici donc ?—Point du tout.—M'y voilà ? /—Vous n'en approchez point. "La chétive pécore / S'enfla si bien qu'elle creva. / Le monde est plein de gens qui ne sont pas plus sages : / Tout bourgeois veut bâtir comme les grands seigneurs, / Tout petit prince a des ambassadeurs, / Tout marquis veut avoir des pages.'

[5] Jürgen Freiherr von Krüdener, *Die Rolle des Hofes im Absolutismus* (Stuttgart, 1973), p. 4.

[6] Hubert Ch. Ehalt, *Ausdrucksformen absolutistischer Herrschaft. Der Wiener Hof im 17. und 18. Jahrhundert* (Munich, 1980), p. 39.

their fellow princes outside them. From 1618 until 1648, the Thirty Years War made simple survival the main priority, as Spanish, French, Danish, and Swedish armies inflicted devastation on a scale and of a duration not seen before in Europe. Recovery was slow and painful, interrupted by further French incursions. In the Duchy of Württemberg, a survey conducted in the mid-1650s revealed that the population had fallen by 57 per cent, that one half of all buildings were still in ruins, and that a third of cultivable land was still waste.[7] It says a great deal for the attraction exerted by the French model that the dukes should have sought to emulate it even against this dismal background. As soon as he returned from the wars, Duke Eberhard III (1633–74) began to spend lavishly, on new livery, on silverware, on a new state coach from Metz ('of a kind that is used by the most eminent of princes'), and so on.[8]

Judged by French standards, Eberhard's court was still uncouth, housed in a residence that was more like a castle than a palace and characterized by the excessive drinking and general 'beer and sausages' culture thought by French sophisticates such as Voltaire to be typically German.[9] Even so, there were signs of French influence other than lavish display. In 1664 Eberhard sent the tutor of the ducal pages to Paris to find out what was happening at the cutting edge of European fashion, in 1651 French cuisine made its first appearance, and in 1660 the first of what became an army of French valets arrived to teach the Württembergers how to dress *à la mode*.[10] However, it was when Duke Friedrich Carl assumed control in 1677 as regent for his infant nephew Eberhard Ludwig that French influence really asserted itself. He had given an earnest of his intention by writing the diary he kept during his Grand Tour in the French language.[11]

An engraving of Eberhard III made in the year of his death (1674) depicts 'the bluff old monarch as a benign, though stern father of his people [*Landesvater*]'.[12] He wears his own hair rather than a wig, is set against a plain background and is decorated only by the ducal coat of arms. The style is the man. Friedrich Carl, on the other hand, chose to be represented as an elegant

[7] James Allen Vann, *The Making of a State: Württemberg 1593–1793* (Ithaca, NY, and London, 1984), p. 95; Werner Fleischauer, *Barock im Herzogtum Württemberg*, 2nd edn. (Stuttgart, 1981), p. 17.

[8] Ibid., pp. 56–7.

[9] See below, pp. 241–2. They could draw on a rich store of unflattering stereotypes dating back to Tacitus and confirmed more recently by travellers passing through Germany on the Grand Tour.

[10] Fleischauer, *Barock im Herzogtum Württemberg*, p. 64.

[11] Ibid.

[12] Vann, *The Making of a State*, p. 91.

man of fashion, complete with rosebud mouth and full-bottomed wig, set against a background of swirling drapes, surrounded by symbols of various forms of strength (a sword, a satyr, a lion, an eagle, and Hercules) and accompanied by a bare-breasted personification of Fame trumpeting forth his glory. The paternal image of the *Landesvater* has made way for majesty.[13] The French provenance of this transformation was not in doubt, as life at court was remodelled according to the precepts of Versailles. The unruly drinking bouts favoured in the past were replaced by opera, ballets, and balls. At a *Divertissement à la française* staged by the Regent in 1684, for example, the 8-year-old Duke Eberhard Ludwig was obliged to imitate Louis XIV by dancing the role of Cupid.[14] Württembergers attending the duchy's first *salon*, introduced by Friedrich Karl's prime minister, the French-educated Baron von Forster-Dambenoy, were expected to speak French and be able to talk about the latest French fashions.[15]

Unlike its French model, the Württemberg cultural complex developed in the second half of the seventeenth century cannot have been aimed at the disciplining of the nobles, for the good reason that the duchy had none to discipline. The nobles of the region had established independence from ducal authority in the sixteenth century by making good their claim to be 'Imperial Knights'.[16] In other words, they acknowledged only the Holy Roman Emperor as their sovereign, were not subject to the Duke of Württemberg and were not represented in the duchy's Estates. The latter consisted of two houses, one comprising the fourteen Protestant abbots of the secularized monasteries and the other the representatives of sixty towns.[17] Far from being overawed or seduced by the lavish court unfolded by Friedrich Karl and his successors, the Württemberg burghers were horrified and alienated. As the Regent was also seeking to ally with France to create a standing army, an association was made between Francophilia, despotism, and profligacy every bit as acute as in Stuart England. In 1681, for example, the Estates campaigned for the dismissal of a French governess and a French dancing master, employed to instruct the young duke, on the grounds that they were likely to corrupt their charge with 'loose French morals', 'lascivious

[13] Ibid., p. 140.

[14] Fleischauer, *Barock im Herzogtum Württemberg*, p. 59.

[15] Vann, *The Making of a State*, p. 136.

[16] F. L. Carsten, *Princes and Parliaments in Germany from the 15th to the 18th Century* (Oxford, 1959), p. 3.

[17] F. L. Carsten, 'The causes of the decline of the German estates' in his *Essays in German History* (London, 1985), pp. 119–26.

French ways', 'conversation punctuated with obscene and evil jokes' and 'a style of manners that placed topics of erotic love at the centre of polite discourse'.[18]

As this disapproving but excited obsession with sexuality suggests, a further similarity with contemporary England was the religious flavour of the clash between prince and parliament. The Lutheranism of the Estates deputies, which was being given an increasingly Puritanical edge by the burgeoning Pietist movement, was utterly at odds with the secular hedonism of the Regent's court and what his critics called his 'mocking of the very premises of a legitimate, Christian, German-oriented, non-Machiavellian polity'.[19] For his part, Friedrich Karl took the high ground of absolutism, denouncing the Estates for 'shocking expressions touching his *gloire*.'[20] It was he, however, who lost the struggle, being deposed as Regent in 1693 by the Emperor Leopold I. Although his fate was determined more by the pressures of international conflict, Friedrich Karl's failure demonstrated that representational culture could prove dysfunctional. In the case of Württemberg, it served only to intensify divisions and to make the absolutist ambitions of the Duke that much more difficult to realize. It may well have helped to attract and tame the Imperial Knights of the region, but they represented no political threat anyway. It was the burghers of Stuttgart, Tübingen, and the other towns whose cooperation, or at least acquiescence, was most needed, but they were just the people most alienated by the 'loose and lascivious' French culture of the court and correspondingly more determined to resist its political dimension. As so often in early modern Europe, political opposition supported by religious conviction proved especially tenacious. Unlike the aristocratic targets of Louis XIV's representational culture, the Württembergers did not roll over to have their stomachs stroked. They remained upright, usually seeking cooperation rather than confrontation and often obliged to make concessions, but stubbornly resisting attempts to emasculate the ancient liberties and traditional constitution. They were also successful, prompting no less a person than Charles James Fox to observe later in the century that there were only two

[18] Vann, *The Making of a State*, p. 153.

[19] Ibid., p. 159. At least Friedrich Karl remained notionally a Lutheran. His son, Karl Alexander, who succeeded Eberhard Ludwig when he died without a male heir in 1733, had converted to Catholicism in 1712. Karl Alexander's long-reigning son, Karl Eugen (1737–93), was also a Catholic; Gabriele Haug-Moritz, *Württembergischer Ständekonflikt und deutscher Dualismus. Ein Beitrag zur Geschichte des Reichsverbands in der Mitte des 18. Jahrhunderts*, Veröffentlichungen der Kommission für geschichtliche Landeskunde in Baden-Württemberg, series B (Stuttgart, 1992), pp. 32, 142, 186.

[20] Vann, *The Making of a State*, p. 156.

countries in Europe blessed with true constitutions—Great Britain and Württemberg.[21]

Friedrich Karl might well have rejoindered that the culture he represented had lost the battle but won the war. There was to be no reversion to the simple faith and homespun artefacts of the small-town burghers, for they were increasingly marginalized. Whatever the political disadvantages of the court culture may have been, it certainly increased the distance between the elite and the rest of the population. Perhaps its most graphic manifestation was the difference in dress. As clothes became more elaborate, more expensive, and more French, so were the courtiers increasingly marked off visually. On the one hand, the dukes sent artisans to Paris to learn the latest techniques, such as embroidery, and to buy the latest fabrics; on the other hand they imposed strict limits on what their ordinary subjects might wear. A stream of sumptuary ordinances laid down very precise instructions as to just what various classes might and might not wear. In 1712, for the first time, 'French attire' was confined to the top five groups and denied to all others except native-born French. Even the most exalted members of the aristocracy were denied certain luxury fabrics, which were reserved for the exclusive use of the duke.[22] Some idea of the attention to detail lavished on this social distancing was an ordinance of the same year which confined sleigh-riding to the nobility.

The world of the court and the world of work could not remain wholly separate, even after the former had moved from Stuttgart to the Württemberg version of Versailles at Ludwigsburg, built during the first quarter of the eighteenth century (Plate 7). Indeed, this internal migration created a large new workplace, for the construction of the palace was accompanied by the creation of a new town to service its needs. Moreover, it was a town designed to be in the van of modernity—laid out on rational lines, open to all denominations, and concentrating on urban pursuits conducted on the principle of freedom of trade. It was both a challenge and an affront to Württemberg burghers who relied on the exclusion of non-Lutherans and the restrictive practices of the guilds to preserve their livelihoods.[23] This construction of Ludwigsburg as an island of toleration and enterprise in an ocean of tradition should guard against a natural tendency to view the dukes as representing the old regime and the burghers the new. It was the need to raise the huge sums needed for the

[21] Carsten, *Princes and Parliaments*, p. 5.
[22] Fleischauer, *Barock im Herzogtum Württemberg*, p. 261.
[23] Ibid., p. 167.

new palace, court, and town which prompted the dukes to pursue bureaucratic, fiscal, social, and economic modernization. Although many of the schemes were of short duration, it appears that their efforts did eventually bear fruit, for it was in just the regions they favoured that industrialization flourished in the nineteenth century.[24]

Their primary interest, however, was not industrial but political. Far from being the somnolent hulk of legend, the Holy Roman Empire was an intensely competitive and fluid polity. For princely dynasties able to combine ambition with skill and luck, glittering prizes in the shape of territorial expansion and titular elevation beckoned. Every duke or landgrave aspired to become an elector, and every elector aspired to become a king. For the very greatest princes—Bavaria or Brandenburg—power could be expressed in the most direct and obvious manner, in armed might. For the great majority, however, the main currency of imperial competition was cultural achievement. So the representational display expressed in palaces, academies, opera houses, hunting establishments, and the like was not pure self-indulgence, nor was it deception; it was a constitutive element of power itself. That was why Duke Eberhard Ludwig told his Estates that the castle at Stuttgart was quite inadequate to express a prince's *gloire* and that an entirely new palace was needed. (Their reply that an old-fashioned structure was just the right medium for the old-fashioned princely virtues of duty and piety only indicated how fundamental was the political rift between ruler and representatives.)[25] That was also why Duke Karl Eugen (1744–93) marked his birthday in 1763 with two weeks of balls, banquets, firework displays, operas, ballets, concerts, and hunting, not despite but *because* the Seven Years War had just ended.[26] For the baroque prince, representational display was not self-indulgence, it was his *métier*.[27]

It was also necessary if he were to keep his place on the slippery pole of imperial politics. For all the apparent self-confidence of the great palaces and the brash swagger portraits of their builders, this was a culture with a strong nervous undertow beneath the complacent surface. As we have seen, even Louis XIV and anxiety were born together.[28] How much more was that the

[24] Vann, *The Making of a State*, pp. 176–7, 236–7.

[25] Ibid., p. 173.

[26] R. Alewyn, *Das große Welttheater: die Epoche der Lofircher Feste* (Hamburg, 1959), p. 11.

[27] This is not to suggest that 'cultural competition' was the only means of asserting princely power. A middling state such as Württemberg could also raise an army large enough to enhance its influence in the Empire. This has been demonstrated by Peter Wilson in *War, State and Society in Württemberg, 1677–1793* (Cambridge, 1995), pp. 28, 127–8, 248.

[28] See above, pp. 29, 31–3.

case in central and eastern Europe, where frontiers waxed and waned so rapidly and where opportunity knocked with the same insistence that danger threatened. The troubled decades around 1700 were marked by a surge in palace building, for example, at Nymphenburg and Schleissheim in Bavaria, at Berlin and Charlottenburg in Prussia, at Dresden and Moritzburg in Saxony, at Herrenhausen in Hanover, at Mannheim in the Palatinate, at Wilhelmshöhe in Hessen-Kassel, at Ludwigsburg in Württemberg, and at several ecclesiastical courts, most notably Brühl (Cologne), Bruchsal (Speyer), Mainz, Bamberg, and Würzburg.[29] A particularly fine example of the dialectic between display and anxiety was provided by the rise and fall of the Electorate of Saxony between the middle of the seventeenth and the middle of the eighteenth century, a switchback ride which left in its wake one of the supreme examples of representational culture.

Among many other things, the Saxon experience demonstrated the need for resources. Situated astride the mighty River Elbe and at the crossroads of trade routes from north to south and east to west, the Electorate was probably the richest principality in the Holy Roman Empire. Densely populated by contemporary standards, it boasted two of the major German cities—Dresden, whose population rose from 21,000 in 1700 to over 60,000 by the middle of the century, and Leipzig, whose population increased by more than 50 per cent during the same period to over 30,000.[30] The latter city was the main entrepôt for colonial produce sent from Holland and Hamburg, so to its three great annual fairs came merchants from all over central and eastern Europe, the number from Russia alone multiplying tenfold in the course of the eighteenth century.[31] Textile manufacturing, mining, and agriculture all helped to swell taxable wealth.[32] Saxony had also benefited economically from its status as the home of the Lutheran Reformation, by attracting persecuted co-religionists

[29] Peter Baumgart, 'Der deutsche Hof der Barockzeit als politische Institution', in August Buck, Georg Kauffmann, Blake Lee Spahr, and Conrad Wiedemann (eds.), *Europäische Hofkultur im 16. und 17. Jahrhundert. Vorträge und Referate gehalten anläßlich des Kongresses des Wolfenbütteler Arbeitskreises für Barockliteratur in der Herzog August Bibliothek Wolfenbüttel vom 4. bis 8. September 1979* (Hamburg, 1981), p. 28.

[30] Karlheinz Blaschke and H. Kretzschmar, 'Obersachsen und die Lausitzen', in Georg Wilhelm Sante (ed.), *Geschichte der deutschen Länder: "Territorien Ploetz"*, 2 vols (Würzburg, 1964–71), I, p. 490.

[31] Karl Czok, 'Zur Leipziger Kulturgeschichte des 18. Jahrhunderts', in Reinhard Szekus (ed.), *Johann Sebastian Bach und die Aufklärung* (Leipzig, 1982), p. 27.

[32] Werner Schmidt, 'Das augusteische Zeitalter Sachsens', in Werner Schmidt and Dirk Syndram (eds.), *Unter einer Krone. Kunst und Kultur der sächsisch-polnischen Union* (Leipzig, 1997), pp. 26–7

(especially from neighbouring Bohemia) and by encouraging high rates of literacy through insistence on the need to study the Word.[33]

In short, Saxony enjoyed all manner of geographical, economic, social, and cultural advantages. What it lacked was bulk. In terms of area and population (only about 1,400,000 in 1700),[34] it was only a middling state. In 1696, however, the opportunity arose for massive territorial expansion on the death of John III Sobieski, King of Poland. The Polish-Lithuanian empire he had ruled was comparable in size to the entire Holy Roman Empire, stretching as it did from the River Oder in the west to the Dvina in the east, from the Baltic in the north almost as far as the Black Sea in the south. If its institutions were as primitive as those of Saxony were advanced, the combination of Polish quantity with Saxon quality offered a combination with enormous potential. After a prolonged and intensive diplomatic contest, which need not delay us here, in 1697 Frederick Augustus I, Elector of Saxony, was elected King of Poland, taking the title of Augustus II (Plate 5).

It was one thing to get elected in Poland, quite another to hold on to the prize. In his election campaign, Augustus had been supported by Austria and Russia but opposed by a substantial group of Polish nobles supported and financed by France. To make good his claim he now needed to present himself to his new subjects as a king worthy of the name and thus dispel the notion that he was just a middling German prince imposed by foreign powers. He also needed to persuade his existing population that his elevation was worthwhile, not least because one cost of his election had been conversion to Roman Catholicism. Augustus might well take the view that Poland was worth a Mass, but the overwhelmingly Lutheran Saxons were naturally sceptical.

In pursuit of regal status, Augustus now created a representational court culture which, in terms of both splendour and quality, was arguably 'the most dazzling court in Europe', the authoritative verdict of the peripatetic Baron Pöllnitz in 1729.[35] It was his creation and it did succeed in attracting large numbers of high-born visitors from all over Europe.[36] As Augustus's

[33] Volker Press, *Kriege und Krisen. Deutschland 1600–1715* (Munich, 1991), p. 370.

[34] Schmidt and Syndram (eds.), *Unter einer Krone*, p. 26.

[35] *Mémoires de Charles-Louis Baron de Pöllnitz, contenant les observations qu'il a faites dans ses voyages et le caractère des personnes qui composent les principales cours de l'Europe*, new edn., 3 vols. (Liège, 1734), I, p. 154. The best route to a visual impression of this culture is through the magnificent and numerous illustrations to be found in Schmidt and Syndram (eds.), *Unter einer Krone*.

[36] Dirk Syndram, 'Die Kunst am Hofe Augusts des Starken in Dresden', in Schmidt and Syndram (eds.), *Unter einer Krone*, p. 308.

Grand Tour had lasted two years and included visits to Lisbon, Madrid, Milan, Florence, Venice, Vienna, and—above all—Paris-Versailles, he was well-acquainted with international standards of display.[37] He brought to his projects excellent taste, relentless energy, and a determination to have his own way: there are still hundreds of plans in the Saxon archives marked 'from the hand of the King himself' or 'from an idea of the King'.[38] His most celebrated achievement was also the acme of representational architecture—the Zwinger at Dresden, a large open space surrounded by galleries punctuated by pavilions and expressly designed for courtly display (Plate 6).[39] Here the King-Elector and his nobles performed ritual tournaments as elaborate as they were lavish, proclaiming that this was indeed a court fit for a king.[40] Inside the royal palaces, every decorative art was enlisted to create a world of opulent display worthy of the mightiest monarch. One example must suffice, a creation of the court jeweller Johann Melchior Dinglinger entitled 'The court of the Grand Mogul Aureng Zeb on his birthday'. It was expressly designed to be the most extraordinary work of its kind that ever was, and in that it surely succeeded. On a base of gold and silver roughly one metre square, Dinglinger employed thousands of diamonds, emeralds, rubies, and pearls to depict 132 figures presenting the Grand Mogul with thirty-two gifts of appropriate splendour. The discovery of the secret of porcelain manufacture in 1710 (the first in Europe) and the subsequent development of the manufactory at Meissen gave Augustus a luxury item which spread the fame of his state across Europe, and indeed the world.[41]

This cultural climbing did pay dividends. The clearest sign that Augustus had thrust his way into the first division of European sovereigns came in 1719 when his son and heir, Frederick Augustus, was married to the Habsburg Archduchess Maria Josepha, daughter of the late Emperor Joseph I. To celebrate the occasion, Augustus unleashed the full panoply of his court.

[37] Cornelius Gurlitt, *August der Starke. Ein Fürstenleben aus der Zeit des deutschen Barock*, 2 vols. (Dresden, 1924), I, pp. 22, 34. This first tour, undertaken in 1687, had to be curtailed because of war, but he made good the deficiency in 1693–4 when he made an extended visit to Italy, including Rome and Naples.

[38] Herbert Pönicke, *August der Starke. Ein Fürst des Barock* (Göttingen, 1972), p. 45.

[39] Many excellent illustrations, in the form of both contemporary prints and modern photographs can be found in Karl Czok, *Am Hofe Augusts des Starken* (Leipzig, 1989) and John Man, *Zwinger Palace, Dresden* (London, 1990).

[40] For an excellent and well-illustrated account of the festivities at the court of Augustus, see Helen Watanabe-O'Kelly, *Triumphall Shews: Tournaments at German-speaking Courts in their European Context 1560–1730* (Berlin, 1992), pp. 125–38.

[41] For a good introduction, see Ingelore Menzhausen, *Early Meissen Porcelain in Dresden* (London, 1990).

Two years of preparations, which involved among other things the extension of the Zwinger and the construction of the largest opera house north of the Alps, reached a climax with a full month of festivities to greet the bride and bridegroom on their return from Vienna. The ceremonies can be followed with some precision, for Augustus was careful to have each one recorded in word and image and then broadcast to the world by brochures and engravings. He seized this opportunity to advertise the wealth of his state with both hands. Among the entertainments organized, for example, was a mining festival, at which the main dignitaries were seated in a pavilion shaped like a mountain, while 1,700 miners paraded in a demonstration of every aspect of their industry. At the banquet that followed, the mining motif reappeared in the shape of sugar-mountains placed on the tables, themselves laid out in the shape of the letter 'A' for Augustus.[42] This breakthrough into the first rank of European sovereigns paid a recurring dividend for succeeding generations of the dynasty. Of Augustus II's grandchildren, Maria Amalia married Charles III of Spain; Maria Anna married Maximilian III Joseph, Elector of Bavaria; Josepha married the Dauphin of France, and thus was the mother of Louis XVI; Albert married Maria Christina, daughter of the Empress Maria Theresa, and so became Governor of the Austrian Netherlands; Clemens Wenzeslaus became Prince-Bishop of Freising, Regensburg, and Augsburg and Archbishop-Elector of Trier; and Kunigunde became Princess-Abbess of Thorn and Essen (where she could seek spiritual consolation for having been jilted by Joseph II).[43] This list alone should be sufficient to remind us that dynastic politics could bring material benefits.

Among the highlights of the marriage celebrations of 1719 was a performance of *Teofane*, an *opera seria* by Antonio Lotti, the leading Venetian composer, who had been brought to Dresden expressly for the occasion. Among the all-star cast was the greatest castrato of the day, Francesco Bernardi , better known as 'Senesino'. Among the audience of princes and nobles from all over the Empire, room was found for at least two men capable of appreciating the music, namely Georg Philipp Telemann and Georg Friedrich Händel.[44] *Opera seria* was the representational genre *par excellence*, for it was grand, formal, classical, elitist, hierarchical, and ideally suited to the propagation of an absolutist political message. In the case of *Teofane*, it was conveyed through analogy, for it dealt with the marriage of the great Saxon Emperor Otto II to

[42] The engravings illustrating these episodes are to be found in Czok, *Am Hofe Augusts des Starken*, pp. 101, 108.

[43] See the family tree in Schmidt and Syndram (eds.), *Unter einer Krone*, p. 43.

[44] The immensely elaborate sets by Alessandro Mauro are illustrated in ibid., p. 107.

Theophanu, daughter of the Byzantine Emperor.[45] Baroque kingship was inherently theatrical anyway, so no wonder that *opera seria*'s highly artificial combination of verse, singing, and dancing should have proved so popular with royal patrons.

Undoubtedly the finest *opera seria* composed for the court of Augustus, and indeed one of the finest composed anywhere, was *Cleofide*, with music by Johann Adolf Hasse and libretto by Michelangelo Boccardi. There is a good deal to be learned about the culture it exemplified from the title-page of the libretto distributed to those who attended the first night on 13 September 1731 (Figure 1).

The most striking feature is the size of the type used to display the name of the patron, twice the size of that of the composer, thus advertising that this was an occasion first and foremost to celebrate the grandeur of 'His Majesty by Grace of God' and was taking place only because he commanded it. Moreover, it took place in his own private theatre—in the *Royal Court* Theatre, to which admission was by invitation only: there were no tickets for sale and access was determined solely by the patron. Indeed, the first performance of *Cleofide* had taken place on 17 August and had been an entirely private affair for Augustus, his immediate family, and a few favoured intimates.[46] It was a theatre with an interior dominated by an immense royal box surmounted by a crown and a stage area larger than the auditorium.[47] It was a theatre in which the audience was seated strictly according to rank. It was also a theatre in which applause or disapproval was strictly forbidden unless the king indicated otherwise.

That a man who had been chased from Poland by the Swedes in 1704, and who had returned only by courtesy of the Russian Tsar, should describe himself as 'always great and invincible' says a great deal for his nerve, if not his brazen effrontery. Although of course common to all *opera seria*, the use of the Italian language was also significant. Quite apart from its mellifluous

[45] The best general introduction to *opera seria* is Thomas Bauman, 'The eighteenth century: serious opera', in Roger Parker (ed.), *The Oxford Illustrated History of Opera* (Oxford, 1994), pp. 47–83. This also contains some excellent illustrations of the opera house at Dresden. Reinhard Strohm has pointed out that *opera seria* as the name of the genre did not appear until the late eighteenth century; previously it was known as *dramma per musica*; *Essays on Handel and Italian opera* (Cambridge, 1985), p. 96.

[46] Frederick L. Millner, *The Operas of Johann Adolf Hasse* (n.p., 1979), p. 6.

[47] The best accessible illustration, showing a performance of *Teofane* in progress, is to be found in Parker (ed.), *The Oxford Illustrated History of Opera*, p. 49. The stage measured 890 square metres, which made it larger than most modern stages; Gurlitt, *August der Starke*, II, p. 273.

CLEOFIDE

Drama per Musica

Da rappresentarsi nel Reggio Teatro di Core

Per Commando della Sacra Real Majestà

Di

FEDERICO AUGUSTO

Re delle Polonie, Elettor di Sassonia,

Sempre Grande e Invittissimo

Il mese di Settembre dell' Anno

M DCC XXXI

La Musica è del famosissimo Signor

Giovanni Adolfo Hasse,

detto il Sassone,

Maestro di Capella di S.M. di Polonia, Elettore di Sassonia

Dresda

Presso di Giovanni Conrado Stössel di Corte S.M. di Polonia

Elettorale di Sassonia

CLEOFIDE

Opera

to be performed in the Royal Court Theatre

At the command of His Majesty

By the Grace of God

FREDERICK AUGUST

King of Poland, Elector of Saxony,

Always Great and Invincible

In the month of September of the year

1731

The music is by the most illustrious

Johann Adolf Hasse

known as 'The Saxon'

Master of the Chapel of His Majesty of Poland,

Elector of Saxony

Dresden

Printed by Johann Conrad Stössel, Royal Court Printer

of His Majesty of Poland,

Elector of Saxony

Figure 1. *The title-page of the original libretto of* Cleofide

qualities, it served to distance the aristocratic, classically educated audience from their social inferiors, whose Saxon dialect was deemed unfit for any kind of polite discourse.[48]

Attempting to summarize even the bare essentials of the immensely complex plot of this very long opera, which contains thirty arias and nearly four hours of music, is a formidable undertaking, but necessary if the nature of the genre is to be appreciated. Set in Northern India in 325 BC, it deals with the events surrounding the invasion of Alexander the Great. At the centre is the love between King Poros and Queen Cleofide, rulers of adjacent Indian kingdoms. Defeated but not captured by Alexander, Poros takes the identity of his general, Gandarte. The two constant themes in the labyrinthine plot are Poros' jealousy of Alexander, whom he believes correctly to be a rival for the hand of Cleofide, and Alexander's unswerving magnanimity. No matter how beastly the other characters are to him, he always turns the other cheek. The action takes place at two levels—the personal, based on mistaken identity, for Poros and Gandarte have exchanged identities; and the military, for Poros makes another and equally unsuccessful attempt to defeat the invader. Believing Poros to be dead, Cleofide agrees to marry Alexander in order to bring about peace between the Greeks and the Indians, but secretly resolves to kill herself immediately after the wedding. However, it all ends happily. Poros returns as his true self, Alexander gives back to Poros and Cleofide both their liberty and their kingdoms and bestows his blessing on their marriage. The opera ends amid general rejoicing and unanimous praise for the magnanimous Alexander.

This story had not been tailor-made for Augustus of Saxony. It was adapted from Pietro Metastasio's *Alessandro nell'Italie*, first performed in Rome two years earlier. It is not difficult to appreciate why it might have appealed to its new patron. Alexander, of course, represented the 'always great and invincible' Augustus, behaving with heroic forbearance towards the vanquished Eastern monarch Peter the Great, represented by Poros, and graciously declining the opportunity to add the Russian Empire to Saxony-Poland.[49] If the characters on stage did not all swivel towards the royal box in the final scene when singing 'O Grande! O Magnanimo!' they missed an obvious opportunity to ingratiate

[48] A later and much greater Saxon composer—Richard Wagner—retained a thick Saxon accent throughout his life; Robert W. Gutman, *Richard Wagner: The Man, his Mind and his Music* (London, 1968), p. 26.

[49] Reinhard Strohm, 'Hasse's opera "Cleofide" and its background', in the booklet accompanying the recording of *Cleofide* by William Christie and Capella Coloniensis (Capriccio CD 10 193/96, 1987), p. 31.

themselves with their employer. That Augustus was in reality a client of Peter the Great matters not at all. In the world of representational culture, realism was conspicuous by its absence.

Until relatively recently, the axiom that truth is to be found in realistic representation has impeded appreciation of *opera seria*. As we shall see later in this volume, the romantic revolution in aesthetics created a world diametrically opposed to representational culture. Now that directors feel free to express ideas in any historical setting, or indeed none, and a positive virtue can be made of anachronism, we are better placed to understand works such as *Cleofide* and to take at least the first steps towards rehabilitating Hasse and restoring him to his contemporary eminence. One of the very first German musical journalists, Lorenz Mizler, wrote in 1737:

> Who is it that has received the approbation of a whole nation, a nation that has always been considered as the most knowledgeable about music? Director of Music [*Kapellmeister*] Hasse, a German, is so famous that the Italians prefer him, a foreigner, to all of their local composers. I have been assured that if an opera is to be successful in Italy, then it must be composed by Hasse.[50]

Throughout his career Hasse followed the strict conventions of *opera seria*, which almost invariably began with an overture or *sinfonia* in three sections (fast–slow–fast), consisted almost entirely of *da capo* arias,[51] with very few duets or ensembles, and ended with a rousing chorus to make explicit the opera's central message. The libretto was usually based on a subject taken from classical antiquity, employed six characters—two pairs of lovers, a noble king, and a treacherous general—and ended happily with the pairing-off of the lovers, the exposure of the villain, and the apotheosis of the ruler. This was very much 'singer's opera', with the main emphasis on the ability of each of the principals to demonstrate their mastery in the three styles of Italian singing—*cantabile*, *grazioso*, and *bravura*. Especially in the third section of the *da capo* aria, the singer was not just permitted but encouraged to improvise, embellish, and take risks to dazzle the audience with technical virtuosity.[52] This required a great deal of verbal repetition, which can seem wearisome if not absurd to

[50] Quoted in Millner, *The Operas of Johann Adolf Hasse*, p. 251. Millner includes several other similar tributes from contemporaries.

[51] A *da capo* aria (literally 'from the beginning') is an aria in three parts, the third being a repetition of the first and the second presenting a contrast in tempo and usually in melody.

[52] Dennis Libby, 'Italy: two opera centres', in Neal Zaslaw, *The Classical Era: From the 1740s to the End of the Eighteenth Century* (London, 1989), pp. 17–18; Egon Wellesz and Frederick Sternfeld, *The Age of Enlightenment 1745–1790, The New Oxford History of Music*, vol. VII (Oxford, 1973), p. 8.

modern ears but should not be allowed to obscure the importance of the text. Contemporary aesthetics held that the voice was the only true means of expression and that therefore the prime function of music was to intensify the meaning and expression embodied in the words.[53] The text should not be regarded as a 'libretto' in the nineteenth-century sense; it was a drama and the genre was not called *drama* (or *dramma*) *per musica* for nothing.[54] Members of the audience had every opportunity to verify the contemporary belief that Metastasio was a great poet in his own right, for the house lights were not dimmed and they could follow every word in the text they were handed at the door.

The apparently anomalous character of *opera seria* diminishes, if it does not vanish altogether, when it is placed in its cultural context and its achievements are compared with its intentions. There is little point in criticizing the characters' lack of personality, for classical aesthetics did not believe that giving each character individuality enhanced dramatic impact. Far from seeking the universal in the individual, *opera seria* sought the universal in the universal and so presented generic types.[55] So in *Cleofide* Alexander was made to behave as an emperor ought to behave, not in the style of—say—Macbeth, as a tormented murderer. As the singing of a poetic text was the main medium of the drama, it was natural to employ *castrati* for the male roles, for they combined power with clarity and sweetness with agility. No one in 1731 found it strange that King Augustus, lightly disguised as Alexander the Great, should be represented on stage by a eunuch.[56] As *opera seria* existed primarily to advertise the virtues of the existing social and political order, its ritualistic

[53] Ibid., p. 30.

[54] Stefan Kunze, 'Die opera seria und ihr Zeitalter', in Friedrich Lippmann (ed.), *Colloquium 'Johann Adolf Hasse und die Musik seiner Zeit'* (Siena, 1983), Veröffentlichungen der musikgeschichtlichen Abteilung des Deutschen Historischen Instituts in Rom (n.p., 1987), pp. 5–8.

[55] Libby, 'Italy: two opera centres', p. 27.

[56] A stout—and good—defence of the use of the castrato to depict virile male characters was made by the anonymous English translator of Raguenet's pamphlet comparing French and Italian music, first published in 1702: 'I can't think the Base-Voice more proper for a King, a Hero, or any other distinguish'd Person, than the Counter-tenor, since the Difference of the Voice in Man is merely accidental. And as the Abilities of a Man's Mind are not measur'd by his Stature, so certainly we are not to judge on a Heroe by his Voice: For this Reason I can't see why the part of Caesar or Alexander may not be properly enough be perform'd by a Counter-tenor or Tenor, or any other Voice; provided the Performer, in Acting as well as Singing, is able to maintain the Dignity of the Character he represents'; François Raguenet, *A Comparison between the French and Italian Musick and Operas. Translated from the French, with some remarks. To which is added a critical discourse upon operas in England, and a means proposed for their improvement*, ed. Charles Cudworth (Farnborough, 1968), p. 6.

qualities did not betray a lack of imagination but were intrinsic to the genre. This was revealed by Metastasio when, in reply to an inquiry from the Saxon court about the best way to perform *Demofoonte* (another work set by Hasse), he sent detailed instructions about where the characters were to position themselves on stage, the object being to reveal visually their relative rank.[57] For the same reason, it was entirely appropriate to impose a happy end on what was usually a tangled web of conflict and misunderstanding, often by means of a highly improbable *deus ex machina*, because the main purpose of the work was to demonstrate and commend the eirenic qualities of the sovereign.

Cleofide had the advantage of presenting Augustus as both strong and generous. Those who attended the performance in what was then the largest opera house in Germany (seating around 2,000)[58] could not have doubted that here was a king with both the taste and the resources to mount a spectacle whose magnificence was matched by its quality. Resplendent in the royal box, Augustus certainly looked the part. By the standards of the age he was a tall man (over 5 feet 9 inches), with a massive frame (he weighed around 19 stone) and a commanding presence. Even making allowances for flattery, Louis de Silvestre's magnificent portrait of Augustus in his prime (plate 5) conveys a good sense of the vitality which helped to give him the sobriquet 'the strong'. Anecdotes of his feats of physical strength were legion: that in Spain on the Grand Tour he had caused a sensation at a bullfight by severing the bull's head with one stroke of his sword; that in single combat with a bear he had lost a finger as he tried to tear his opponent's tongue out; that he could break horseshoes with his bare hands; that he had wrestled with a wild boar and killed it single-handed; and so on.[59]

[57] Bruce Alan Brown, 'Maria Theresa's Vienna', in Zaslaw, *The Classical Era*, p. 103. The Metastasio–Hasse team was especially favoured by the rulers of central and eastern Europe for grand occasions. Perhaps the climax of representational art under the old regime came in 1742, following the coronation in Moscow of the Tsarina Elizabeth I. While some monarchs might have been content with a specially commissioned work, Elizabeth went one better and had a theatre built, specially and solely for the occasion. An army of more than 500 artisans ran up a vast wooden structure, said to be capable of holding 5,000 spectators, in just two months. A prologue—'Russia bereaved but comforted'—was followed by a ballet 'Joy of the nations at the appearance of Astrea [i.e. the new Tsarina] on the Horizon and the Restoration of the Golden Age' and then by the main event, *La Clemenza di Tito* by Metastasio and Hasse; Malcolm Burgess, *A Survey of the Stage in Russia from 1741 to 1783, with special reference to the development of the Russian theatre* (unpublished Ph.D. dissertation, University of Cambridge, 1953), pp. 35–41.

[58] Czok, *Am Hofe Augusts des Starken*, p. 97.

[59] Pönicke, *August der Starke*, p. 10.

KING ALFRED'S COLLEGE
LIBRARY

He was even more famous for his sexual prowess. If he did not sire the 365 illegitimate children of legend, he did produce enough to win him the reputation of superhuman potency. The most distinguished of the brood was Maurice de Saxe, the victor of Fontenoy and the most successful French general of the eighteenth century. Once Louis XIV had set the example, it was *de rigueur* for his imitators to take a *maîtresse en titre*, even if only for the sake of appearances. Augustus embraced this French fashion with special enthusiasm, taking his first mistress at the age of 16. Indeed, flaunting his potency was very much part of his style of kingship. At one of the court festivities mounted to mark the visit of Frederick IV of Denmark to Dresden in 1709, for example, the royal visitor was induced to act as coachman to the Countess von Cosel, the current preferred mistress, while Augustus himself served as her footman. The episode was then broadcast by means of an engraving.[60] His generosity to his mistresses was notorious, as titles, palaces, and pensions were showered on them. The same court painter—Louis de Silvestre—was commissioned to paint mistress as well as queen, illegitimate as well as legitimate children.

During the course of his long reign, Augustus the Strong created a representational culture of a quality and splendour unrivalled in the Holy Roman Empire. The Dresden which has come down to us through such pictorial representations as the *vedute* of Bellotto, was as much the personal achievement of Augustus as Versailles was of Louis XIV. Yet the advantage of hindsight tells us that this tremendous structure rested on foundations of sand. After Frederick IV of Denmark had enjoyed the hospitality of Augustus at Dresden, the two monarchs travelled together to Berlin to visit their grim colleague, Frederick William I of Prussia, who despised baroque culture, saved most of his revenue, and spent money only on soldiers. Augustus is reputed to have told Frederick William on a later occasion: 'When Your Majesty collects a ducat, you just add it to your treasure, while I prefer to spend it, so that it comes back to me threefold.'[61] This may have been sound economics and could also have been supported by the parable of the talents, but it did not help Augustus's son and heir, who succeeded as Augustus III in 1733, when he had to face a challenge from Frederick William's son, who succeeded as Frederick II in 1740.

The latter achieved his sobriquet 'the Great' mainly at the expense of Saxony. When Augustus the Strong died, he left his son a superlative cultural centre but also a mountain of debt. He had increased his army to the respect-

[60] Reproduced in Czok, *Am Hofe Augusts des Starken*, p. 87.

[61] Ibid., p. 94.

able total of just under 30,000, but had signally failed to secure Saxony-Poland's great-power status.[62] Frederick William I bequeathed to his son a culture so austere as to be unworthy of the name but an army 81,000 strong which in terms of quality was the best in Europe, supported by a great treasure-chest of 8,000,000 thalers in hard cash, packed in barrels in the cellars of the royal palace in Berlin.[63] At the beginning of the century the Saxon and Prussian armies had been almost exactly the same size, indeed, if anything the Saxon army was rather larger; by 1740 the Prussian army was three times larger and much better trained, equipped, and financed.[64] The series of wars which began in December 1740, when Frederick invaded Silesia, is usually presented as a struggle between Prussia and Austria for the domination of Germany, and rightly so. It was also, however, a struggle between Prussia and Saxony. As the son of Augustus II and an Austrian archduchess, Augustus III had a much sounder claim to Habsburg territory than did Frederick of Prussia. If he had succeeded in adding Silesia to Saxony and Poland, he would have created an unbroken territorial complex reaching from the heart of Germany to the frontiers of Russia.[65] This was one reason why his Prussian rival was so anxious to strike first.

In the first Silesian war of 1740–2, the Saxons had supported Frederick's raid on the Habsburg monarchy, but they deserted him in 1743. So his victory in the second Silesian war of 1744–5 was a Saxon defeat. That was revealed with brutal clarity in 1756 when the third Silesian war (better known in western Europe as the Seven Years War) began. On 29 August Frederick invaded Saxony, hoping to destroy both his immediate target and the Habsburg monarchy further to the south before the dreaded Russian juggernaut could be brought into play the following year. In that he failed, but he did succeed in taking control of Saxony and then milking it for all it was worth. The Saxon army he simply incorporated into his own. The Saxon resources he requisitioned and requisitioned until there should have been nothing left.

[62] Reinhold Müller, *Die Armee Augusts des Starken. Das sächsische Heer von 1730 bis 1733* (Berlin, 1984), p. 8.

[63] Otto Hintze, *Die Hohenzollern und ihr Werk*, 8th edn. (Berlin, 1916), p. 299.

[64] I owe these figures to Dr Peter Wilson of the University of Sunderland.

[65] Peter-Michael Hahn, 'Kursachsen und Brandenburg-Preußen. Ungleiche Gegenspieler (1485–1740)', in *Sachsen und die Wettiner. Chancen und Realitäten* (Dresden, 1990), p. 98. In 1705 Augustus the Strong had written in his own hand a 'Plan in the event of the House of Austria dying out' which envisaged the imperial title passing from the Habsburgs to the Wettins; Monika Schlechte, 'HERCULES SAXONIXUS—Versuch einer ikonographischen Deutung', in ibid., p. 298.

Such was the natural wealth of the country, however, that there was always something to be found by the Prussian foragers. As Frederick himself said, Saxony was like a flour-sack—no matter how hard or often one hit it, a puff of flour would always come out.[66] It can be said with only slight exaggeration that it was the Saxons who financed Prussia's achievement of great-power status, for their involuntary sacrifices financed fully one third of the Prussian war effort.[67]

The end of the Seven Years War in 1763 was also marked by the death of Augustus III and the end of the Polish connection, for Frederick the Great now cooperated with Catherine of Russia to have one of the latter's superannuated lovers (Stanislas Poniatowski) elected as king of Poland. It also marked the end of Dresden as the great German centre of representational culture, for the new Elector was obliged to retrench on every possible front to reduce the mountain of debt created by his two profligate predecessors and the Prussian occupation. The fate of Hasse, 'Il Sassone', was symbolic. He returned to Dresden at the end of the war to find his home in ruins and the opera house devastated. He and his wife (the star soprano Faustina Bordoni) were paid off with two years' salary but no pension. They moved to Vienna.[68] Forty-five years later, the distinguished Prussian composer Johann Friedrich Reichardt reported that complaints from travellers that Dresden was dull compared with Prague or Vienna were well-founded but did not take into account the fact that ever since 1763 the Elector had been struggling to achieve solvency through the strictest possible economy.[69]

The King of France, the Holy Roman Emperor, the Duke of Württemberg, and the Elector of Saxony were all to a greater or lesser extent players in the European states system. Yet representational art was not the prerogative of actual or aspiring great powers. In terms of quality, some of the supreme achievements were the work of very small fry. One example must suffice, but it is a particularly good one (Plate 3). It can best be introduced by the impact it made on one of the greatest minds of the eighteenth century, David Hume, when he visited it in 1748:

66 Günter Vogler and Klaus Vetter, *Preußen von den Anfängen bis zur Reichsgründung* (Cologne, 1981), p. 82.

67 Christopher Duffy, *The Army of Frederick the Great* (London, 1974), p. 130. These are the figures originally compiled by Gustav Schmoller.

68 David J. Nichols and Sven Hansell, 'Johann Adolf [Adolph] Hasse', in Stanley Sadie (ed.), *The New Grove Dictionary of Music and Musicians*, vol. 8 (London, 1980), p. 284.

69 Johann Friedrich Reichardt, *Vertraute Briefe geschrieben auf einer Reise nach Wien und den österreichischen Staaten zu Ende des Jahres 1808 und zu Anfang 1809*, ed. Gustav Gugitz, 2 vols. (Munich, 1915), I, p. 66.

What renders [Würzburg] chiefly remarkable is a Building which surprised us all, because we had never before heard of it, & did not there expect to meet with such a thing. Tis a prodigious magnificent Palace of the Bishop, who is the Sovereign. Tis all of hewn Stone and of the richest Architecture. I do think the King of France has not such a House. If it be less than Versailles, tis more compleat and finish'd. What a surprising thing it is, that these petty Princes can build such Palaces? But it has been fifty years a rearing; & tis the chief Expence of Ecclesiastics.[70]

This compliment was even greater than it seems, for if Hume had returned five years later he would have found the Residenz (as it came to be known) adorned with what by general consent are some of the finest frescoes ever painted.

The Würzburg Residenz exemplifies the characteristically baroque mixture of ambition and anxiety we have noted already. First and foremost, it represented the arrival on the imperial scene of the Schönborns, a family of Imperial Knights who during the late seventeenth and early eighteenth centuries had succeeded in securing election to a remarkable number of ecclesiastical states, including Mainz (twice), Trier, Worms (twice), Würzburg (twice), Bamberg (twice), Speyer, Konstanz, and Ellwangen.[71] Among their numerous architectural achievements, the episcopal palace at Bruchsal and the family seat at Pommersfelden are remarkable enough, but even these are eclipsed by Würzburg. Building began not 'fifty years' before Hume's visit but in 1719, when Johann Philipp Franz von Schönborn was elected prince-bishop. It was fortunate for him that he found in the principality's tiny army a 32-year-old engineering officer who proved to be an architect of genius, arguably the greatest of the German baroque. This was Balthasar Neumann, whose own good fortune was to complete his architectural training just as the ideal patron arrived on the scene.[72]

By the time Hume paid his visit, the exterior was virtually complete but much of the interior decoration remained to be done. The election in 1749 of a

[70] Quoted in Svetlana Alpers and Michael Baxandall, *Tiepolo and the Pictorial Intelligence* (New Haven, 1994), p. 101. The volume contains some magnificent illustrations of the Residenz but a less satisfactory text. Even better illustrations are to be found in Peter O. Krückmann (ed.), *Der Himmel auf Erden. Tiepolo in Würzburg*, 2 vols. (Munich and New York, 1996).

[71] There is an excellent illustration of the success of the family in the shape of a group portrait of eleven Schönborns to be found in the parish church of their seat at Gaibach. It is reproduced in Richard Sedlmaier and Rudolf Pfister, *Die fürstbischöfliche Residenz zu Würzburg*, 2 vols. (Munich, 1923), I, p. 3.

[72] A good and well-illustrated introduction to Neumann's life and work is Max H. von Freeden, *Balthasar Neumann. Leben und Werk*, 2nd edn. (Munich and Berlin, 1963).

Schönborn cousin, Karl Philipp von Greiffenklau (also spelt Greiffenclau), gave the project the necessary final impetus. It was his inspired decision in 1750 to commission Giambattista Tiepolo to paint the frescoes in the grandest of the parade rooms, the Kaisersaal or 'Emperor's Hall'. Its formal purpose was to provide an appropriate setting in which to receive the Holy Roman Emperor, but as that happened on only very rare occasions, in reality it served as the prince-bishop's main assembly room. The patron's choice of subject for the frescoes had a clear programme. The first depicts the marriage of the Emperor Frederick Barbarossa to Beatrice of Burgundy in 1156, at which the Bishop of Würzburg had officiated (Plate 4). As Tiepolo gave the bishop the features of the current incumbent, Karl Philipp's guests could observe the greatest of the medieval German emperors kneeling before their host.[73] The fresco on the other side of the hall, however, revealed that this was more than an exercise in self-glorification. The prince-bishop again has Karl Philipp von Greiffenklau's features, but this time it is he who kneels to Barbarossa, as he is invested with the duchy of Franconia. Uniting the two is a ceiling fresco which shows Beatrice borne across the sky by Apollo to the *Genius Imperii*, a personification of the Holy Roman Empire, sitting on a throne and attended by the *Genius Franconiae*, a personification of Franconia.[74] Greiffenklau was well aware of the dangers which threatened his principality, for during the first Silesian War, Frederick the Great had threatened the then prince-bishop (Friedrich Karl von Schönborn) with secularization if he lent his support to Maria Theresa. So the complementary frescoes in the Kaisersaal were a potent visual reminder of the interdependence of Emperor and Prince-Bishop.[75]

There was no shared glory in Tiepolo's final and greatest contribution to Würzburg—the fresco over the staircase. The German baroque specialized in grand staircases but Würzburg is the acme, a perfect match between architecture and painting. Neumann's structure gave Tiepolo about 600 square metres on which to operate, making the finished product one of the largest paintings in Europe. To analyse the complex iconography of the fresco, whose full title is *Olympus with the four continents of the earth and allegories*, in any detail would easily consume a chapter or even a book. The main object of the exercise is plain enough, however. An important guest would be driven straight into the

[73] There is an excellent illustration in Antonio Morassi, *Tiepolo. His life and work* (London, 1955), plate VII.

[74] Frank Büttner, 'Ikonographie, Rhetorik und Zeremoniell in Tiepolos Fresken der Würzburger Residenz', in Krückmann (ed.), *Der Himmel auf Erden. Tiepolo in Würzburg*, II, pp. 54–5.

[75] Max H. von Freeden, *Das Meisterwerk des Giovanni Battista Tiepolo. Die Fresken der Würzburger Residenz* (Munich, 1956), pp. 41–2.

low-roofed and dimly lit vestibule.[76] As he stepped from his carriage, the light of the staircase stretched ahead. The first image which came into view as he began his ascent was the exotic figure of America, a bare-breasted woman wearing only a feathered head-dress and sitting on a gigantic alligator. Her outstretched arm points to a flag bedecked with a griffon, the Greiffenklaus' heraldic device. As the visitor reaches the half-landing, he sees the full width of the fresco for the first time, as the figures of Asia and Africa come into view. As he turns for the final stage, he is confronted by Europe: against a background of architectural motifs taken from the Würzburg Residenz, Europa sits on her throne to receive her court. The sceptre in her hand and the globe at her feet symbolize European domination of the world. Her continent's cultural supremacy is registered by symbols of Christianity and the arts. She is looking up at a portrait of none other than Bishop Greiffenklau as he ascends towards Olympus, heralded by Fame's long trumpet and escorted by Genius, who bears his coronet. As Mercury rushes to greet the new arrival, Saturn with his symbols of mortality—the scythe and the hourglass—averts his eyes from one so obviously destined to live for ever.[77] That the ruler of a Franconian principality with only about a quarter of a million people[78] should have himself presented as the mightiest ruler of the mightiest continent on earth may seem grotesque, yet the need of the Schönborn clan both to advertise their grandeur and legitimate their rule in the face of danger produced a total work of art of enduring power. For that reason, the last word should go to Michael Levey's eloquent tribute to Tiepolo's achievement:

> Although there seems something a little grandiloquent in a cosmic view which gives such prominence to Carl Philipp von Greiffenklau, ornament of the western world, what his patronage helped to bring into being justifies his claim on the world's attention. There is, thanks to Tiepolo, more than rhetoric to the idea of his fame and glory. An artistic Joshua, Tiepolo has stopped the sun. He has reversed the decline of the *ancien régime* and offered on the Residenz ceiling the most optimistic of

[76] The best guided tour is provided by Peter Krückmann, 'Tiepolo in Würzburg. Fürstbischöfliche Repräsentation und die Kunst der Inszenierung', in Krückmann (ed.), *Der Himmel auf Erden. Tiepolo in Würzburg*, I, pp. 32–42.

[77] Although the best illustrations are to be found in Krückmann's book, the most lucid exposition of the symbolism is to be found in Freeden, *Das Meisterwerk des Giovanni Battista Tiepolo*, pp. 93–7.

[78] The population in 1803, when it ceased to exist as an independent principality, totalled 262,000; Gerhard Köbler, *Historisches Lexikon der deutschen Länder. Die deutschen Territorien und reichsunmittelbaren Geschlechter vom Mittelalter bis zur Gegenwart*, 5th edn. (Munich, 1995), p. 709.

all philosophies, a complete harmony of mankind and nature and art, on a stupendous scale and with a confidence and exhilaration that he never surpassed.[79]

Würzburg, it should be noted, was no pale reflection of a sun which had shone first and brightest at Versailles. The most important artists to work at Würzburg were not French but Germans or Italians, and if Neumann was sent to Paris to consult Robert de Cotte, he was also sent to Vienna to consult Fischer von Erlach and Hildebrandt. Although it is a tribute to the power of Louis XIV's propaganda machine that every European palace built after 1682 should so often be regarded as yet another of his satellites, there were other solar systems. The conviction of French historians such as Louis Réau that 'during this period the true artistic capital of the German-speaking territories was neither Vienna nor Berlin but Paris'[80] reveals a short-sighted inability to detect any line of influence other than that radiating from Versailles. The polycentricity of the Holy Roman Empire was cultural as well as political, as befitted its geographical centrality on the European continent.[81] It absorbed influences from the Netherlands, the Slavonic world, Italy, and Spain, as well as from France. Indeed, the most recent historian of the German courts has identified five categories to introduce order to their wonderful variety: the ceremonial court, the imperial court, the patriarchal court, the sociable court, and the cultural court.[82] Only the first of those can be said to have been influenced directly by Versailles. Moreover, even the most enthusiastic emulators of Louis XIV, such as Augustus the Strong, did not adopt the French model completely and uncritically. It was not French *tragédie lyrique* but Italian *opera seria* that provided the centrepiece of Dresden's representational culture, while its most enduring architectural monument—the wildly exuberant Zwinger—is an aesthetic world away from the restrained classicism of Versailles.

[79] Michael Levey, *Giambattista Tiepolo: His Life and Art* (New Haven and London, 1986), p. 206.

[80] Réau, *L'Europe française au siècle des lumières*, p. 250.

[81] Norman Davies's belief that the centre of Europe is located in 'the suburbs of Warsaw or the depths of Lithuania'—*Europe: A History* (Oxford, 1996), p. 14—can be justified only by reference to the mathematics of latitude and longitude.

[82] Volker Bauer, *Die höfische Gesellschaft in Deutschland von der Mitte des 17. bis zum Ausgang des 18. Jahrhunderts. Versuch einer Typologie* (Tübingen, 1993), pp. 63–73. Cf. Peter Baumgart, 'Der deutsche Hof der Barockzeit als politische Institution' and Renate Wagner-Rieger, 'Zur Typologie des Barockschlosses', both in August Buck, Georg Kauffmann, Blake Lee Spahr, and Conrad Wiedemann (eds.), *Europäische Hofkultur im 16. und 17. Jahrhundert. Vorträge und Referate gehalten anläßlich des Kongresses des Wolfenbütteler Arbeitskreises für Barockliteratur in der Herzog August Bibliothek Wolfenbüttel vom 4. bis 8. September 1979* (Hamburg, 1981), pp. 25, 57–9.

Yet if the triumphalism of the French propagandists—'Paris is to Europe what Greece once was to the ancient world'[83]—was ill-founded in fact, it created a myth which was to prove long-lived. Its longevity was assisted by foreign acknowledgements of French superiority. When Augustus the Strong, for example, instructed his court artist Louis de Silvestre to capture on canvas the moment when the Crown Prince of Saxony was presented to Louis XIV at Fontainebleau in 1714, he was also tacitly recognizing French hegemony.[84] So did those who deplored it—the anonymous German, for example, who lamented in 1689: 'French language, French clothes, French food, French furniture, French dances, French music, the French pox... perhaps there is also a French death! Hardly have the children emerged from their mothers' wombs than people think of giving them a French teacher... To please the girls, even if one is ugly and deformed, one must wear French clothes'.[85] It was a myth that was powerful, but it was also dangerous. So long as it was supported by sufficient cultural achievement to lend it credibility, it could justify both French arrogance and foreign cringing. But once other cultural centres acquired self-confidence, the supportive structure that Louis XIV had provided through his cultural establishments became a serious liability for both monarch and nation.

[83] Louis Réau, *L'Europe française au siècle des lumières* (Paris, 1951), p. 115.

[84] A reproduction of the painting can be found in Karl Czok, *August der Starke und seine Zeit*, 3rd edn. (Leipzig, 1997), p. 95.

[85] Quoted in Adrien Fauchier-Magnan, *The Small German Courts in the Eighteenth Century* (London, 1958), p. 27.

3

The Status of the Artist

Of the many figures with which Tiepolo's great Würzburg fresco teems, none is more prominent than an elegant figure who lolls in a languid posture at the feet of Europa, clothed in a purple military dress-uniform decorated with silver braid. Ignoring the magnificent greyhound which seeks to gain his attention, he stares out haughtily across the staircase. And well he might, for this is Balthasar Neumann, and the staircase was his creation. It was Tiepolo's touching tribute to the man who had given him the ideal space. Tiepolo modestly placed himself at the furthest extremity of the fresco, dressed in working clothes (although he took good care to add a prominent signature and date). The three years he spent at Würzburg with his two sons were certainly remunerative: hired for an initial fee of 10,000 gulden, he was eventually paid 30,000, the staircase fresco being commissioned after his arrival.[1] Moreover, he was housed in the *Residenz* and given the right to sit at the table reserved for those of noble status.

This was nothing less than Tiepolo was used to by this stage in his career, nor was it exceptional. In a culture which placed such a high value on visual representation, painters had long enjoyed a pole position among creative artists when it came to status. The development of individualism in the Italian Renaissance and the sharp competition among patrons lifted painters out of

[1] Svetlana Alpers and Michael Baxandall, *Tiepolo and the Pictorial Intelligence* (New Haven, 1994), p. 103; Werner Helmberger, 'Wo Tiepolo malte. Die Residenz Würzburg vor ihrer Vollendung', in Peter O. Krückmann (ed.), *Der Himmel auf Erden. Tiepolo in Würzburg*, 2 vols. (Munich and New York), I, pp. 49, 54.

the anonymity and handicraft status of the guild tradition. Michelangelo was probably the first to be the subject of a biography during his own lifetime, while Titian was described as the 'first man in Christendom' by the aristocrat who recommended him to a cardinal.[2] Rubens bestrode Europe as diplomat as well as artist and was knighted by Charles I of England, as was Anthony Van Dyck, the first painter to be treated as an equal by the notoriously snobbish English aristocracy.[3] Indeed, the knighting of painters became something of a tradition in England, for they were later joined by Peter Lely (*né* Pieter van der Faes, 1618–80), Godfrey Kneller (*né* Gottfried Kniller, 1649–1723), James Thornhill (1675–1734), Joshua Reynolds (1723–92), Henry Raeburn (1756–1823), and Thomas Lawrence (1769–1830), just to list those artists born before 1800.[4] The funeral of Reynolds was a particularly striking demonstration of the high status he had attained, for after his body had lain in state at Somerset House for several days, his coffin was borne to St Paul's by ten aristocratic pall-bearers—three dukes, two marquises, three earls, a viscount, and a baron. Forty-two mourning coaches attended the cortège, followed by nearly fifty carriages filled with members of the peerage and gentry.[5]

For the same reasons, architects could also enjoy high status, although their necessarily close connection with the technicalities of construction made it more difficult to shake off 'mechanical' associations. On the other hand, their need for a high level of mathematical expertise gave them an academic standing which other artists lacked. Christopher Wren had become Savilian Professor of Astronomy at Oxford and had helped to lay the foundations of the Royal Society before he designed his first building (the chapel at Pembroke College, Cambridge, in 1663). He was the first English architect to be knighted, beginning a hitherto unbroken tradition continued in the eighteenth century by John Vanbrugh (1664–1726), Robert Taylor (1714–88), William Chambers (1726–96), and John Soane (1753–1837). Proximity to the royal patron and the tangible nature of their creations made architects strong candidates for ennoblement across the continent, leading examples being Mansart, de Cotte, Fischer von Erlach, Hildebrandt, Gontard, and Erdmannsdorff. Significantly, it was architects who designed secular buildings for princes who did best. Those who specialized in churches and monasteries

[2] Michael Levey, *High Renaissance* (Harmondsworth, 1975), pp. 59, 66.

[3] Ellis Waterhouse, *Painting in England 1530–1790* (London, 1953), p. 43.

[4] The failure of Hogarth, Stubbs, Gainsborough, and Wright to gain the same accolade demonstrates that merit did not invariably achieve royal recognition.

[5] Ellis Waterhouse, *Reynolds* (London, 1973), p. 36; John Brewer, *The Pleasures of the Imagination: English Culture in the Eighteenth Century* (London, 1997), pp. 288–9.

were much closer to the old craft tradition and enjoyed a correspondingly lower status. Men like Jakob Prandtauer (the builder of Melk), Dominikus Zimmermann (Die Wieskirche), or Johann Michael Fischer (Ottobeuren, Zwiefalten, Diessen) came from a master-mason background and lacked the sophisticated education which might have gained them an *entrée* to court circles.[6] Often they formed extended families of peripatetic designer-craftsmen, notably the *stuccatori* of Wessobrunn or the Dientzenhofer clan of builders from Bohemia.[7] Coming from this milieu did not deprive them of material benefits, nor did it limit their originality—on the contrary—but it did deny them the elevated status of their metropolitan colleagues.

At the other end of the scale from top-flight painters and architects were actors and actresses, especially despised and discriminated against in Catholic countries. In old regime France they were automatically excommunicate for so long as they trod the boards. Even when they were terminally ill there was no escape, for—taking no chances on a last-minute miracle cure—the priest insisted on their abjuring acting for ever before granting absolution and administering the sacraments. According to Baron Grimm, the famous actress Madame Favart adamantly refused to submit to this blackmail even when dying of cancer, only at the very last moment gasping 'O hang it, I renounce'.[8] One who failed to do so in time was Voltaire's close friend, Adrienne Lecouvreur, who was buried at night in unconsecrated ground and without the consolations of the Church. Her fate prompted Voltaire to write a deeply felt and deeply angry tribute. In London, he claimed, she would have been treated with the same dignity as 'the famous actress Mrs Oldfield, buried in Westminster Abbey with almost the same honours accorded to Newton'.[9] His

[6] John Summerson, 'Royalty, religion and the urban background', in *The Eighteenth Century*, ed. Alfred Cobban (London, 1969), p. 82.

[7] Eberhard Hempel, *Baroque Art and Architecture in Central Europe* (Harmondsworth, 1965), pp. 29, 126–33.

[8] F. W. J. Hemmings, *The Theatre Industry in Nineteenth Century France* (Cambridge, 1993), p. 136.

[9] Quoted in Peter Gay, *Voltaire's Politics* (New York, n.d.), pp. 62–3. Anne Oldfield (1683–1730) was certainly given a grand funeral, her pall-bearers being drawn from the nobility and gentry, including Lord de la Warr, Lord Hervey, and George Bubb Dodington. She died both immensely rich and fêted by high society, one of her illegitimate sons marrying Lady Mary Walpole; Joseph Knight, 'Anne Oldfield', in *The Dictionary of National Biography*, vol. 42 (London, 1895), pp. 96–8. However, as usual, Voltaire was being too generous to the English in his anxiety to attack his native country. Until a test case in 1733 allowed a judge to decide otherwise, it was assumed that the Vagrancy Act of 1714 made actors liable to the same penalties as beggars; Paul Langford, *A Polite and Commercial People: England 1727–1783* (Oxford, 1989), p. 48.

chief complaint—that French high society applauded actors on stage but shunned them off it—was echoed sixty years later by the revolutionary actor Fusil, who explained his conversion to republicanism by reference to the treatment he had suffered from aristocratic audiences under the old regime: 'They used to clap us at the theatre because we amused them, but apart from that we were pariahs and bohemians in their eyes. The most trumpery nobleman believed he had the right to insult us and if we dared to issue a challenge, it was prison-cells and fetters for us.'[10]

Musicians fell somewhere in between these two extremes. No less an authority than Aristotle could be invoked in denying them respectability: 'we call professional performers vulgar; no freeman would play or sing unless he were intoxicated or in jest.'[11] If musicians in classical Greece were often slaves, in ancient Persia the performance of music was confined to prostitutes or at least regarded as a degrading activity.[12] Two millennia later, the situation had not improved much. As opera developed out of the theatre, it brought with it much of the latter's lascivious reputation. Female singers had the reputation of being courtesans and indeed often were so. In 1690 Jean-Nicolas du Tralage wrote that most of the women appearing at the Opera were kept by wealthy '*patrons*'. Indeed, the Opera had become a place of assignation: 'In a word, this is where the problems of the Opera began. A seigneur of the court or a rich connoisseur takes pride in having a girl from the opera as a mistress; that is what sets the tone, that has become the fashion: and Opera girls who don't have protectors are regarded as poor creatures indeed . . . So the Academy of Music has become the Academy of Love.'[13] (It need hardly be added that Augustus the Strong of Saxony counted opera singers among his large harem of mistresses.) Male singers enjoyed a different kind of dubious reputation, for the prominent role played by castrati, with their strong but high and sweet voices, brought a disturbing air of erotic ambivalence. Consequently, as François Joseph Fétis put it in an aphorism which paraphrased Voltaire's complaint about the way in which actors were treated, the princes and aristocrats of the old regime 'esteemed music but did not honour musicians'.[14]

[10] Hemmings, *The Theatre Industry in Nineteenth Century France*, p. 139.

[11] Quoted in Dennis McCort, *Perspectives on Music in German Fiction: The Music-fiction of Wilhelm Heinrich Riehl* (Bern and Frankfurt, 1974), p. 23.

[12] Jacques Attali, *Noise: The Political Economy of Music* (Manchester, 1985), p. 12.

[13] J. N. du Tralage, *Notes et documents sur l'histoire des théâtres de Paris* (Paris, 1880), pp. 85–7; cf. John Rosselli, 'From princely service to the open market: singers of Italian opera and their patrons 1600–1850', *Cambridge Opera Journal*, 1, 1 (1989), p. 12.

[14] 'Variétés. De l'éducation sociale en ce qui concerne la musique', *Revue Musicale*, VIII (1830), p. 112.

It was opera which presented such a serious image problem. Writing in the middle of the eighteenth century, a German musician seeking to raise the status of his art asked why there were so few native-born singers and so many Italian imports. He could find some Germans singing for pleasure in the church or in the home, but none in the opera house. This was not just a question of poor pay discouraging training, he asserted, it was more a problem of reputation: 'the behaviour of most people who enter the theatrical profession, and the way they then carry on their life, makes the theatre seem like a seraglio and the home of debauchery... What sort of tone of voice do the clergy and ordinary folk use when speaking the name of an actor? Is it not the tone of censure?' Sadly, he added, they were right to do so, for theatre people met together but did not know each other, lived together but did not love each other, separated but did not miss each other. The remedy he prescribed was as visionary as his diagnosis was eloquent: to select singers whose morals matched their voices.[15]

Association with the Church through religious music did something to deodorize this unsavoury reputation but did nothing to lift its practitioners up the social scale. The primer commissioned by the Empress Maria Theresa for the education of her son Ferdinand contained a table illustrating the social hierarchy, which placed musicians at the very bottom along with beggars and actors.[16] In 1771 she added her own gloss in reply to Ferdinand's request for advice as to whether or not he should employ the 15-year-old musician Wolfgang Amadeus Mozart:

> You asked me whether you should take the young Salzburger into your service. I can't think why you should, for you don't need a composer or any other useless people for that matter. But if you think it will give you pleasure, I shan't stand in your way. I only give you my opinion because I don't want you lumbering yourself with good-for-nothing folk. However, you must certainly avoid giving these people honorary titles as if they were in your service. For it brings service itself into disrepute when these people roam around the world like beggars.[17]

At least one musician, Christian Daniel Friedrich Schubart, believed that members of his profession had only themselves to blame. Reminiscing about his time as organist and director of music at Ludwigsburg after 1769, he

[15] *Fragmente einiger Gedanken des Musikalischen Zuschauers, die bessere Aufnahme der Musik in Deutschland betreffend* (Gotha, 1767), pp. 4–6.

[16] Kurt Blaukopf, *Musik im Wandel der Gesellschaft. Grundzüge der Musiksoziologie* (Munich and Zürich, 1982), p. 118. In a private communication, Derek Beales, who has seen the original, has expressed doubts as to whether the picture in question really bears out this interpretation.

[17] Ibid.

regretted that he had fallen into bad company, wasting his time in wenching and drinking—just like all the other musicians of his acquaintance. Their self-image and social status were also revealed in their collective noun, Schubart added, for they were not referred to as 'virtuosi' or even 'musicians' but were dismissed with contempt as mere 'players' (*Spielleute*). Nothing could have been more humiliating, he lamented, than the Saxon law code, which stated firmly 'players are outside the law (*Spielleute sind rechtlos*),' but he had to concede that sober, god-fearing and well-behaved musicians were 'extremely rare'.[18]

Theatre and music were essential components of representational culture, but their practitioners were all too often censured as immoral and despised as no better than vagrants. Even the allegedly less reprobate painters still suffered from the stigma attached to their origins as craftsmen organized in guilds. As we have seen,[19] artisans could escape to become artists most easily if they enjoyed the support of the state. By deftly exploiting the needs of aspiring absolutism in a period of upheaval, a man such as Charles Le Brun acquired for himself a patent of nobility and for his fellow artists the status of academicians. It proved to be a double-edged victory: if the prize was emancipation from the old guild rules and regulations, the price was subjection to the rules and regulations of the king. This came to be a familiar pattern in Europe. As the secretary of the Academy at Vienna told Prince Kaunitz in 1773: 'It must not only be deeply degrading in general but also detrimental to the impression which foreign visitors receive from the national mentality of a state, if skill in art is restricted by the rules of the guilds.'[20] So eager were the artists to escape from the prison of the guilds that they failed to notice the more elegant bars on the gilded cage they now entered. Only in Italy, it seems, could painters move from handicraft status to full independence without passing through the intermediate stage of state control.[21] It should be added, however, that the degree of control exercised by royal academies varied a great deal, from what was increasingly felt to be excessive *dirigisme* in France to the benign if flaccid *laissez-faire* practised across the Channel. It is not without significance that the 'Royal Academy of Arts in London, for the Purpose of Cultivating and Improving the Arts of Painting, Sculpture and Architecture' was not founded

[18] C. F. D. Schubart, *Gesammelte Schriften und Schicksale*, 8 vols. in 4 (Stuttgart, 1839–40), I, pp. 112–13.

[19] See above, p. 47.

[20] Quoted in Nikolaus Pevsner, *Academies of Art—Past and Present*, (Cambridge, 1940), p. 167.

[21] Ibid., p. 114.

until 1768 and enjoyed a substantial degree of independence from royal control, not least because its public exhibitions were financially so successful.[22]

The same ambivalent route to freedom was also available to the musician. In his autobiography, published in 1755, the virtuoso flautist and composer Johann Joachim Quantz (1697–1773), recounted how he had been born the son of a blacksmith.[23] Only the death of his father when he was 14 launched him on a musical career, for it sent him to be apprenticed to his uncle, who happened to be the town musician at Merseburg in Saxony. In fact the archaic English words 'town wait' would be a better translation of the German *Stadtmusikant*, for to translate that as 'town musician' fails to convey the old-fashioned quality of *Musikant* (as opposed to the modern form *Musiker*). Quantz's uncle, his journeymen, and his apprentices enjoyed a monopoly of music-making in the town, playing at civic functions, in church, and at the modest court of the Duke of Saxony-Merseburg. It was the last of those which widened Quantz's horizons: 'it provided me with no small inspiration, especially as foreign musicians from other courts were often to be heard there.'[24] At Merseburg Quantz learned his craft in the literal sense as a humble apprentice. At 17 he took to the road as a journeyman, attached first to the town musician at Pirna and then to his equivalent at Dresden.

This last move proved to be fortunate, for it gave him the opportunity to transcend the traditional guild-bound world of town waits. Making himself a virtuoso on the transverse flute recently introduced from France, he became the beneficiary of Augustus the Strong's generous patronage. From 1723 until 1727 Quantz toured and studied in Italy at his patron's expense, perfecting his technique as a performer and expanding his range as a composer. It was also through Augustus that he made the acquaintance of Crown Prince Frederick of Prussia, himself a gifted and enthusiastic flautist. Twice a year thereafter, Quantz travelled to Prussia to give Frederick instruction.[25] When his pupil ascended the throne and was able to make him an offer that he and his current employer could not refuse, he entered Prussian service permanently. The terms, as Quantz recorded them in his autobiography, were certainly gener-

22 Ibid., p. 185.

23 'Hernn Johann Joachim Quantzens Lebenslauf, von ihm selbst entworfen', in F. W. Marpurg, *Historisch-kritische Beyträge zur Aufnahme der Musik*, 5 vols. (Berlin, 1754–78), I, 3 (1755), pp. 197–248.

24 Ibid., p. 201. To describe these foreign musicians (by which he meant musicians who were not from Saxony-Merseburg), Quantz used the word *Tonkünstler*—literally 'sound-artists', which has a much more elevated air than *Musikanten*.

25 Peter Schleuning, *Das 18. Jahrhundert. Der Bürger erhebt sich* (Hamburg, 1984), pp. 61–2.

ous: a salary of 2,000 thalers (a level attained in frugal Prussia only by senior civil servants), additional payments for compositions, and two important privileges: he was obliged only to play in the royal chamber ensemble and not in the full orchestra, and only to obey orders when they came from the king.[26] In short, royal patronage—both Saxon and Prussian—had transformed Quantz and his status. Indeed, it was said that Prussia was ruled by Madame Quantz's poodle, for the poodle ruled Madame Quantz, who ruled Herr Quantz, who ruled Frederick the Great, who ruled Prussia.[27]

Guilds in any shape or form were finding life difficult in the eighteenth century, as they were pressed from above by the reforming state and eroded from below by a developing market economy. Yet old habits died hard and attachment to restrictive practices lived on in the professional associations. 'The Society of Musicians' (*Tonkünstler-Societät*), for example, founded in Vienna by the *Kapellmeister* Florian Gassmann in 1771, straddled two musical worlds. On the one hand, it sought to elevate its status by insisting that musicians seeking to join were 'free' (i.e. were not guild-men playing dance music) and also demonstrated its independence by organizing public concerts to finance its widows' and orphans' fund. On the other hand, it always chose a prominent aristocrat as its patron and its president was always the court *Kapellmeister* of the day. There was also a strongly clannish approach reminiscent of the guilds when it came to assessing composers. So when Gluck died, doubts were expressed as to whether the Society should do anything to mark the event because, although he had lived in Vienna for much of his life, he had never been 'one of us'. In 1779 Haydn actively sought admission, seeking to secure his wife's financial future in the event of his premature death, but he withdrew his application when the Society sought to take control of his output. He observed memorably on this occasion: 'I am too sensitive a person to expose myself to the constant danger of being censured: the liberal arts and the sublime science of musical composition cannot tolerate chains imposed by handicraft [*Handwerks-Fesseln*]. Spirit and soul must be free if one is to help the widows and do oneself credit.'[28]

But so great did Haydn's international fame grow that twenty years later the Society made amends, granting him honorary membership at a gala ceremony

[26] 'Hernn Johann Joachim Quantzens Lebenslauf', p. 248.

[27] Schleuning, *Das 18. Jahrhundert*, p. 62.

[28] Eduard Hanslick, *Geschichte des Concertwesens in Wien*, 2 vols. (Vienna, 1869), I, pp. 5–7, 14–15. Mozart also sought to join in 1785, after having performed several concerts for the Society for nothing, but was refused admission when he was unable to find his birth certificate; ibid., I, p. 17.

of expiation presided over by the current patron, Count Kueffstein.[29] Indeed, Haydn's long life (1732–1809) exemplified the forces making for change in a musician's status. When he first went to work for Prince Anton Esterházy in 1769 as *Vizekapellmeister* (assistant director of music), his subordination was carefully spelt out in his letter of employment:

The said Joseph Heÿden [*sic*] shall be considered and treated as a house officer. Therefore his Serene Princely Highness is graciously pleased to place confidence in him, that as may be expected from an honourable house officer in a princely court, he will be temperate and will know that he must treat the musicians placed under him not overbearingly, but with mildness and leniency, modestly, quietly and honestly. This is especially the case when music will be performed before the high *Herrschafft*, at which time said *Vice-Capel-Meister* and his subordinates shall always appear in uniform; and said Joseph Heÿden shall take care that not only he but all those dependent upon him shall follow the instructions which have been given to them, appearing neatly in white stockings, white linen, powdered, and either with pigtail or hair-bag, but otherwise of identical appearance.[30]

So Haydn was not a servant, but he was very much the Prince's man, being at his beck and call and obliged to wear his livery. What distinguished him most sharply from composers of a later generation was his inability to control his own creations. Prince Esterházy paid for the music, so it became his property and his alone:

The said *Vice-Capel-Meister* shall be under permanent obligation to compose such pieces of music as his Serene Princely Highness may command, and neither to communicate such new compositions to anyone, nor to allow them to be copied, but to retain them wholly for the exclusive use of his Highness; nor shall he compose for any other person without the knowledge and gracious permission [of his Highness].[31]

In short, this relationship between patron and composer was more between lord and vassal than between employer and employee. Although the Esterhá-

[29] Ibid., I, p. 16.

[30] H. C. Robbins Landon (ed.), *Haydn: Chronicle and works*, 5 vols. (London, 1976–80), I, p. 350.

[31] Ibid., p. 351. This desire to possess a piece of music all by oneself was by no means confined to the Esterházys. The Prince of Öttingen-Wallerstein wrote to his agent in Vienna in 1788 'Since, as is well known, Jos. Hayden is the greatest composer of symphonies and I am very fond of his music, I should like to receive three new symphonies from him that no one besides me would possess'; quoted in Rebecca Gates-Coon, *The Landed Estates of the Esterházy Princes: Hungary during the Reforms of Maria Theresa and Joseph II* (Baltimore, Md., and London,1994), p. 163.

zys were of relatively recent origin, they had risen very rapidly during the seventeenth century to become the greatest landowners in Hungary with estates divided into thirty-seven lordships covering more than a thousand square miles.[32] The head of the family was almost an independent sovereign, enjoying the right to mint coins, maintain his own army, and pass the death sentence in his courts.[33] As a member of this great household, Haydn was accommodated, clothed, and fed in a manner befitting his place in the Esterházy hierarchy. If he fell ill, he could consult one of the estate's doctors, be treated at one of the estate's hospitals, or even be sent to take the waters at the prince's expense.[34] This was a closed world in which the levelling effects of market forces and the cash nexus had made little impact, as can be demonstrated most clearly by the arrangements made for Haydn's salary in the contract of 1779:

In cash	782 gulden 30 kreuzers
Officer's wine at Esterház	9 kegs
Good genuine firewood at Esterház	6 cords
Wheat	14 litres
Rye	40 litres
semolina	2½ litres
beef	300 pounds
salt	30 pounds
lard	30 pounds
candles	36 pounds
wine	9 kegs
cabbage and beets	1 keg
pork	1 whole pig
good firewood	6 cords
forage	amount necessary for two horses[35]

In short, Haydn enjoyed a high standard of living, despite the modest pecuniary rewards. Moreover, he also lived in three of the most sumptuous

[32] There is an excellent account of the rise of the Esterházys in Harald Dreo, 'Die fürstlich Esterházysche Musikkapelle von ihren Anfängen bis zum Jahre 1766', in *Jahrbuch für österreichische Kulturgeschichte*, I (1971), pp. 80–115. On the estates, see Gates-Coon, *The Landed Estates of the Esterházy Princes*.

[33] János Harich, 'Das fürstlich Esterhazy'sche Fideikommiss', *The Haydn Yearbook/Das Haydn Jahrbuch*, 4 (1968), p. 5.

[34] Karl Geiringer, *Haydn. A Creative Life in Music* (London, 1982), p. 54.

[35] Adapted from ibid., pp. 42–3. There is a great deal of information about the pay and conditions of the musicians employed by Prince Esterházy in Ulrich Tank, *Studien zur Esterhazyschen Hofmusik von etwa 1620 bis 1790* (Regensburg, 1981), *passim*.

residences to be found in the Habsburg monarchy—the Esterházy town palace in Vienna, the ancestral seat at Eisenstadt, and the new summer residence built by Prince Nicholas at Esterháza. Of the last named a traveller recorded: 'with the exception of Versailles, there is perhaps in the whole of France no place to compare with it for magnificence. The castle is very large and filled to bursting with luxurious things. The garden contains everything that human fantasy can conceive to improve or, if you will, undo the work of nature. Pavilions of all kinds stand like the dwellings of voluptuous fairies, and everything is so far removed from the usual human operations that one looks at it as if in the middle of a marvellous dream.'[36] The price of admission to this dream was to serve the representational needs of the Prince. In the early years at least, Haydn seems to have felt no qualms about abasing himself. In 1766 he wrote:

> The most joyous occasion of your name-day (may YOUR HIGHNESS celebrate it in divine Grace and enjoy it in complete well-being and felicity!) obliges me not only to deliver to you in profound submission six new Divertimenti, but also to say that we were delighted to receive, a few days ago, our new winter clothes—and submissively to kiss the hem of your robe for this special act of grace: adding that, despite YOUR HIGHNESS' much regretted absence, we shall nevertheless venture to wear these new clothes for the first time during the celebration of High Mass on YOUR HIGHNESS' name-day. . . . I hope for your favour and grace, YOUR SERENE AND GRACIOUS HIGHNESS', most humble Joseph Haydn.[37]

The divertimenti in question were written to allow the Prince to perform on his favourite instrument, the baryton, a large stringed instrument of the viol family which could be plucked as well as bowed. Difficult and cumbersome, it has survived only because Haydn composed almost 200 pieces for it—and he did so solely because that was what his patron required. It has even been argued that he felt obliged to bring to an end his *Sturm und Drang* period of musical experimentation because his patron found the results too difficult.[38]

The hours Haydn spent writing for the baryton encapsulated his position as a privileged but servile artist. On the one hand he had at his disposal all the resources necessary for high-quality music-making: a numerous, well-equipped, and competent orchestra, an opera company of a similarly high standard, together with a large concert hall and an opera house big enough to seat 500. Although not known today mainly as a composer of opera, Haydn

[36] Ibid., p. 99.
[37] Ibid., p. 126.
[38] Jens Peter Larsen, *Handel, Haydn and the Viennese Classical Style* (Ann Arbor, Mich., 1988), pp. 105–7.

KING ALFRED'S COLLEGE
LIBRARY

himself attached great importance to his numerous works in the genre. To be able to give them no fewer than 203 performances at the Esterháza opera house was a privilege few of his colleagues enjoyed.[39] He also enjoyed the priceless asset of adequate rehearsal time. The story is well-known of how Haydn came to give his Symphony number 45 'The Farewell' its unique last movement, in which each musician falls silent and departs until just two violins remain to play the final notes. This was a subtle (and effective) protest to the Prince on his prolonged stay at Esterháza, which separated the musicians from their wives and families, left behind at the more commodious Eisenstadt.[40] It was also, however, a demonstration of how Haydn benefited from commanding the undivided attention of the musicians he commanded. Not for him the fate of nineteenth-century composers such as Berlioz or Wagner who often had to wait years and to perform the labours of Hercules just to get their music played at all, let alone rehearsed properly. And Haydn was well aware of the paradox that social servitude could bestow artistic freedom:

> My Prince was content with all my works, I received approval, I could, as head of an orchestra, make experiments, observe what enhanced an effect, and what weakened it, thus improving, adding to, cutting away, and running risks. I was set apart from the world, there was nobody in my vicinity to confuse and annoy me in my course, and so I had to be original.[41]

But the world was changing outside the gilded cage of Eisenstadt and Esterháza, and new opportunities—and new risks—beckoned. As we shall see in the next chapter, Haydn was fortunate in being able to exploit the former without falling victim to the latter, in the process enhancing both his wealth and his prestige. When he started his career, he enjoyed what little fame he had because he was part of the Esterházy clientage system; by the time he died, the relationship was reversed.[42] In the long term, it was probably inevitable that he would chafe increasingly at his subordinate status. In particular, the restrictions placed on his freedom of movement by the need to synchronize with the Prince's requirements proved irksome. In 1790 he wrote about

[39] Detlef Altenburg, 'Haydn und die Tradition der italienischen Oper. Bemerkungen zum Opernrepertoire des Esterhazyschen Hofes', in Georg Feder, Heinrich Hüschen, and Ulrich Tank (eds.), *Joseph Haydn Tradition und Rezeption. Bericht über die Jahrestagung der Gesellschaft für Musikforschung Köln 1982* (Regensburg, 1985), p. 84.

[40] The anecdote was in circulation even during Haydn's lifetime; H. C. Robbins Landon and David Wyn Jones, *Haydn: His Life and Work* (London, 1988), p. 112.

[41] Quoted in Lázló Somfai, 'Haydn at the Esterházy court', in Neal Zaslaw (ed.), *The Classical Era: From the 1740s to the End of the Eighteenth Century* (London, 1989), p. 268.

[42] See below, p. 166.

the previous decade: 'I did not know if I was a *Kapell*-master or a *Kapell*-servant... It is really sad always to be a slave... I am a poor creature!'[43]

To be the slave of such a benign and musically gifted autocrat as Prince Nicholas Esterházy was one thing. To be subject to Hieronymus Count von Colloredo, Archbishop of Salzburg, was quite another. The contrasting experiences of the two supreme musicians of the second half of the eighteenth century illustrate well the random quality of life as a creative artist under the old regime. For all his occasional grumbles, Haydn lived and died a loyal and even devoted servant of his patron. Mozart famously did not. The story of his emancipation from Colloredo, deemed by some to be nothing less than 'a declaration of war between the new bourgeois world and the old regime of artistic production',[44] has been told so often through so many different media (most misleadingly by the stage-play and film *Amadeus*) that little more needs to be or can be said. As we shall see in the following chapter, over Mozart's fate has settled a thick layer of myth, which needs to be stripped away.

What does need to be recorded is that he did not find the bars on his particular cage to be gilded in the slightest. In his opinion, his patron was both unappreciative and miserly, conferring neither material benefit nor prestige. He angrily wrote to his father from Vienna in March 1781:

> What you say about the Archbishop is to a certain extent perfectly true—I mean, as to the manner in which I tickle his ambition. But of what use is all this to me? I can't subsist on it. Believe me, I am right in saying that he acts as a *screen* to keep me from the notice of others. What distinction, pray, does he confer upon me? Herr von Kleinmayr and Bönike [archiepiscopal officials] have a separate table with the illustrious Count Arco. It would be some distinction if I sat at that table, but there is none in sitting with the valets who, when they are not occupying the best seats at table have to light the chandeliers, open the doors and wait in the anteroom (*when I am within*)—and with the cooks too![45]

Not unreasonably, Mozart concluded that his employer was trying to treat him like a piece of property. As he went on to complain, in the letter just cited, his request for permission to play at a charity concert of the Society of Musicians,[46] where he would have had the opportunity to win 'the favour of the Emperor and of the public', was turned down flat.[47] Haydn might have

[43] Quoted in Somfai, 'Haydn at the Esterházy court', p. 289.

[44] Giorgio Pestelli, *The Age of Mozart and Beethoven* (Cambridge, 1984), p. 143.

[45] Emily Anderson (ed.), *The Letters of Mozart and his family*, 3rd edn. (London, 1985), pp. 716–17.

[46] See above, p. 85.

[47] Anderson (ed.), *The Letters of Mozart*, p. 718.

composed another 'Farewell' symphony, but Mozart was not Haydn. He was not Haydn because he was a generation younger (born in 1756), had travelled extensively in Europe as a child prodigy, was encouraged in his social aspirations by his ambitious father, and possessed a much less phlegmatic temperament. He kicked hard against the pricks and was duly chastised. In June 1781, after a blazing row about the date on which he should leave Vienna to return to Salzburg, Mozart was ejected from the Archbishop's service in the most literal possible way. In a letter to his father, he described what happened when he went to present a petition to the chief steward, Count Arco:

> Instead of taking my petition or procuring me an audience or advising me to send in the document later or persuading me to let the matter lie and to consider things more carefully—*enfin*, whatever he wanted—Count Arco hurls me out of the room and gives me a kick on my behind. Well, that means in our language that Salzburg is no longer the place for me, except to give me the favourable opportunity of returning the Count's kick, even if it should have to be in the public street.[48]

At least Mozart was then allowed to seek his fortune as a 'free artist'. When Johann Sebastian Bach had tried to resign from the service of the Duke of Saxony-Weissenfels in 1717, he was clapped into prison and was eventually allowed to leave only with the musical equivalent of a dishonourable discharge.[49] This proprietorial attitude towards musicians did not diminish as the century progressed, as the Prussian soprano Gertrude Elizabeth Mara (*née* Schmeling) discovered in 1774. As she recorded in her autobiography, she had received from London the kind of offer German singers could only dream of: 1200 guineas for 12 evenings, plus 200 guineas travel expenses and the proceeds of a benefit concert. At first Frederick the Great gave his permission for her to go, although insisting that her husband stay behind in Berlin as a guarantee that she would return, but then reneged at the last moment. When the couple tried to escape to fulfil the engagement, they were arrested at the gates of Berlin and Signora Mara was imprisoned for ten weeks. Six years later she fell ill, but Frederick refused to allow her to go to a Bohemian spa for a cure: 'But now I began to feel the weight of slavery. Not only was I having to bury my fame and fortune with him [Frederick] but also now my health,' so this time they planned their flight carefully. Describing her emotions on waking up for the first time in the safety of Bohemia, she wrote: 'A magnificent morning

48 Ibid., p. 743.

49 Denis Arnold, *Bach* (Oxford, 1984), p. 16.

awaited my awakening, there was a lawn in front of the house, so I had my tea served there and felt completely happy—*O Liberté!*'[50]

'La Mara' was also the subject of a celebrated anecdote making the rounds in Prussia, which exemplified Frederick's contempt for German culture. When told about her wonderful voice, he is said to have snorted: 'A German singer? I should as soon expect to receive pleasure from the neighing of my horse.'[51] Another version of the same story had him saying: 'I'd rather have the arias of my operas neighed by a horse than to have a German prima donna' and refusing even to hear her, on the grounds that she would have an *accent tudesque*.[52] In fact, 'howled by a dog' would have been a more appropriate metaphor, because La Mara recorded that when eventually she got her audition, she found Frederick sitting on a sofa with General Tauentzien and three Italian greyhounds who at once started howling—as they always did when they caught sight of a woman.[53]

Frederick went out of his way to emphasize his proprietorial, dictatorial attitude to cultural matters in Prussia. As the most authoritative historian of Prussian architecture of the period has remarked, no other absolutist ruler was so directly involved in the details of construction. Hardly a building of importance was erected during his reign without betraying his influence: it was he who decided how, when, and what should be built.[54] As one of his officials concluded at the end of an account of building undertaken at Potsdam during his reign: 'Everything here was done under his direct orders, supervision and execution.'[55] Frederick himself was candid about the self-indulgent character of his lavish building schemes, so sharply at odds with his image of austere dedication to the interests of the state. When on campaign in 1742, for example, he wrote to his secretary Charles Etienne Jordan: 'get fat Knobelsdorff [the architect] to write to me about what is going on at Charlottenburg, in my opera house and my gardens. In these matters I am like a child—these are the dolls I play with'.[56] Significantly, what was most striking about Freder-

[50] O. von Riesemann (ed.), 'Eine Selbstbiographie der Sängerin Gertrud Elizabeth Mara', *Allgemeine Musikalische Zeitung*, X (11 Aug.–29 Sept., 1875), pp. 561, 564, 577.

[51] Percy A. Scholes (ed.), *An Eighteenth-Century Musical Tour in Central Europe and the Netherlands. Being Dr. Charles Burney's Account of his Musical Experiences* (Oxford, 1959), p. 167.

[52] E. E. Helm, *Music at the Court of Frederick the Great* (Norman, 1960), p. 129.

[53] Riesemann (ed.), 'Eine Selbstbiographie', p. 533.

[54] Hans-Joachim Giersberg, 'Friedrich II und die Architektur', in Hans-Joachim Giersberg and Claudia Meckel (eds.), *Friedrich II. und die Kunst*, vol. II (Potsdam, 1986), p. 192.

[55] Hans-Joachim Giersberg, *Friedrich II. als Bauherr. Studien zur Architektur des 18. Jahrhunderts in Berlin und Potsdam* (Berlin, 1986), p. 23.

[56] Ibid., p. 307.

ick's buildings was their representational character. Even the middle-class houses built at Berlin and Potsdam under his direction were all façade—the ground-plans, and with them the *functions* of the buildings (apart from those he lived in himself), were of no interest to him.[57]

This dictatorial attitude was, if anything, even more pronounced in his public musical policies. The same combination of representation and personal self-indulgence recurred. He built one of the largest opera houses in the world, capable of holding more than 2,000 members of the general public, but also treated it as if it were his private theatre. The representational nature of the exercise was underlined on the opening night, attended by all senior military personnel in the capital at the express command of the King. The officers stood in rows in the pit, behind two lines of chairs reserved for the King and his staff.[58] This military motif was persistent: where else but in Prussia could one find a sovereign ordering an opera house to be filled with soldiers before a performance, as a cheap (if malodorous) form of central heating?[59] And where else but in Prussia could one find soldiers being drafted in to bulk out the audience when attendances fell?[60] It was characteristic that Frederick chose not to sit in the royal box but preferred a seat immediately in front of the orchestra pit, so that he could keep a sharp eye on both the stage and the musical director's score.[61] A graphic eye-witness account of what this could involve for the performers was provided by the English musicologist Charles Burney, who visited Berlin in 1772:

> The king always stands behind the *maestro di capella*, in sight of the score, which he frequently looks at, and indeed performs the part of director-general here, as much as of generalissimo in the field . . . In the opera house, as in the field, his majesty is such a rigid disciplinarian, that if a mistake is made in a single movement or evolution, he immediately marks, and rebukes the offender; and if any of his Italian troops dare to deviate from strict discipline, by adding, altering, or diminishing a single passage in the parts they have to perform, an order is sent, *de par le Roi*, for them to adhere strictly to the notes written by the composer, at their peril. This, when compositions are good, and a singer is licentious, may be an excellent method; but certainly shuts

[57] Giersberg, 'Friedrich II. und die Architektur', p. 195.

[58] L. Schneider, *Geschichte der Oper und des Koeniglichen Opernhauses in Berlin* (Berlin, 1842), p. 21.

[59] Riesemann (ed.), 'Eine Selbstbiographie', p. 546.

[60] Leo Balet and E. Gerhard, *Die Verbürgerlichung der deutschen Kunst, Literatur und Musik im 18. Jahrhundert* (Strasbourg, 1936), p. 71.

[61] Dieudonné Thiébault, *Mes Souvenirs de vingt ans de séjour à Berlin; ou Frédéric le Grand, sa famille, sa cour, son gouvernement, son académie, ses écoles, et ses amis littérateurs et philosophes*, 3rd edn., 4 vols (Paris, 1813), II, p. 209.

out all taste and refinement. So that music is truly stationary in this country, his majesty allowing no more liberty in that, than he does in civil matters of government: not contented with being sole monarch of the lives, fortunes, and business of his subjects, he even prescribes rules to their most innocent pleasures.[62]

Even the most imperious of present-day conductors, one suspects, might feel intimidated by Frederick the Great's sharp blue eyes boring into the back of his head. As Thomas Bauman has observed, Frederick's musical regime was 'an astonishing instance of artistic despotism'.[63] He paid the piper and he called the tune, specifying arrangement, key, and tempo into the bargain. As he wrote to his *directeur des spectacles*, Graf von Zierotin-Lilgenau: 'The singers and the musicians are subject entirely to my choice, together with many other objects connected with the theatre, which I order and pay for myself.'[64] Nothing could express better the capricious nature of patronage in an absolutist regime. While Quantz basked happily in the pale sunlight of his sovereign, Elizabeth Mara was treated like a prisoner.

At least Frederick did not resort to physical violence when displeased by faults in tempo or imperfect liaison between orchestra and singers. Yet such was the fate of the members of the numerous serf troupes maintained by Russian magnates. Serf musicians, singers, and actors were bought and sold and, however eminent, were always liable to corporal punishment. One owner, identified in the source only as 'B', prowled in the wings during the performance, berating those on stage with words and gestures. During a performance of *Dido and Aeneas*, he was so incensed by the inadequacy of the leading lady that he rushed on to the stage and slapped her face, adding a good thrashing in the interval.[65] Again, one cannot help but speculate as to what might be the reaction of today's self-regarding thespians to working conditions such as these.

For some lucky serfs, talent could prove a passport to emancipation. Mikhail Matinsky, the author of one of the most successful Russian operas of the eighteenth century—*The St Petersburg Bazaar*—was born as a serf on the estate of Count Yaguzhinsky and for a time played in the serf orchestra of Count Razumovsky. His talents as writer, composer, translator, mathematician, and geographer won him both his freedom and secure employment at the Smolny

[62] Scholes (ed.), *An Eighteenth-Century Musical Tour*, pp. 164, 207.

[63] Thomas Bauman, 'Courts and municipalities in North Germany', in Zaslaw (ed.), *The Classical Era*, p. 242.

[64] Schneider, *Geschichte der Oper*, Beilagen, p. 17.

[65] B. N. Aseyev, *Russky dramatichesky teatr ot ego istokov do kontsa XVIII veka* (Moscow, 1977), p. 304.

Institute in St Petersburg.[66] Fedor and Grigor Volkov, sons of a merchant from Yaroslavl, also showed that the rapidly growing demand for representational culture under the old regime offered an express lane to social advancement in an otherwise ossified society. Such was the fame of the theatre they established in their home town that they were summoned to St Petersburg by the Tsarina Elizabeth in 1752. Her creation of a 'Russian Theatre' at the Golovkin Stone Mansion for them in 1756 marked a watershed in the country's theatrical history.[67] In 1763 her successor, Catherine, made the Volkov brothers nobles and granted them an estate with 700 serfs into the bargain.[68] When Fedor died the same year at the age of 35, a French observer recorded that 'his funeral celebrations matched those of Garrick and the entire nobility was present.'[69]

But for every Matinsky or Volkov who escaped, there were thousands more trapped in degrading subservience. Moreover, in the Russian Empire there was no alternative to employment by the state or a noble for an aspiring artist. In central Europe, the obvious way out of the uncertainty created by capricious patrons was to seek employment with a republic or at least a municipality. That was the advice of one of the earliest writers on the subject, Johann Beer, the librarian of the same Duke of Saxony-Weissenfels who had locked up J. S. Bach for trying to leave his service. In a chapter of his *Musical Discourse* entitled 'On the advantages republics offer over courts in holding on to good musicians', Beer wrote:

> There are numerous courts which at the least disruption reduce their state or merely dismiss their servants so that the court structure is dissolved *vel sua* [by itself]. Therefore, there are many court musicians who are desirous of going to the cities, and who would immediately go there if the municipalities paid as well as the courts.[70]

But that was the rub. The municipalities did *not* pay as well as the courts, nor did they have a high opinion of musicians or any other creative artists for that

[66] Vsevolod' Cheshikhin, *Istoriya russkoy opery (s 1674 po 1903 g.)*, 2nd edn. (St Petersburg, 1905), p. 52. There is some doubt as to whether Matinsky wrote the music as well as the libretto for *The St Petersburg Bazar*; Yu. V. Keldysh, *Russkaya muzyka XVIII veka* (Moscow, 1965), pp. 315–20.

[67] Aseyev, *Russky dramatichesky teatr*, pp. 233–9.

[68] Burgess, *A survey of the stage in Russia*, p. 170.

[69] Antoine François Le Clerc, *Histoire physique, morale, civile et politique de la Russie moderne*, 2 vols. (Paris and Versailles, 1783–5), I, p. 80.

[70] Richard Petzoldt, 'The economic conditions of the eighteenth century musician', in Walter Salmen (ed.), *The Social Status of the Professional Musician from the Middle Ages to the Nineteenth Century* (New York, 1983), p. 176.

matter. Still steeped in the guild mentality, the city fathers knew what they liked, expected value for money, and expected an artist to turn his hand to pretty well anything in the culture line. In short, they were very often if not invariably what a later period came to call 'philistines'.[71] When J. S. Bach moved to Leipzig to become choir-master of St Thomas's church, he found himself obliged to work very hard for a modest salary. In a memorandum submitted to the town council in 1730 he compared the lot of the municipal musicians unfavourably with their colleagues working for Augustus the Strong's court down the road: 'To illustrate this statement with an example one need only go to Dresden and see how musicians there are paid by His Royal Majesty; it cannot fail, since the musicians there are relieved of all concern for their living, free from chagrin, and obliged to master but a single instrument'.[72] If it is perhaps something of an exaggeration to suggest that 'Prince Leopold of Anhalt-Köthen treated Bach as an equal, while the town-council of Leipzig treated him like a serf,'[73] municipal employment did not necessarily represent liberation.

The ideal situation during this period—and indeed any other period—was for a patron to combine munificence with respect and for the artist to feel comfortable with the demands placed on him. It was for this reason that so many French *philosophes* honoured the memory of Louis XIV. D'Alembert, for example, after criticizing the French nobility for neglecting the arts, went on:

> At last Louis XIV appeared on the scene, and the respect he showed for men of letters soon set an example for a nation which was accustomed to taking a lead from its superiors; ignorance ceased to be the cherished birthright of the nobility; now that they were esteemed, knowledge and understanding broke through the barriers which a misplaced vanity had erected for them. Now that it was invigorated by the attention of the monarch, philosophy in particular emerged, albeit slowly, from the sort of prison in which it had been locked up by stupidity and superstition.[74]

Again taking Louis XIV as his model, d'Alembert gave this advice to his fellow intellectuals: 'The only great lords a man of letters should wish to consort with are those he can behave towards and regard as his equals and his friends; all the rest he should avoid.'[75] There was no finer example of a

[71] See below, pp. 173–4.

[72] H. T. David and A. Mendel (eds.), *The Bach Reader* (London, 1966), p. 122.

[73] Peter Rummenhöller, *Einführung in die Musiksoziologie* (Wilhelmshaven, 1978), p. 43.

[74] Jean d'Alembert, 'Essai sur la société des gens de lettres et des grands, sur la réputation, sur les mécènes, et les récompenses littéraires', in *Mélanges de litteraire, d'histoire et de philosophie*, 4 vols. (Amsterdam, 1759), I, pp. 328–30.

[75] Ibid., p. 379.

French beneficiary of royal respect and material support than Jean-Baptiste Lully.[76] Although he signed himself 'Esquire' and described himself as a *gentilhomme Florentin*, he was in fact the son of a miller. Yet he rose to become the musical dictator of France, thanks to the patronage of Louis XIV. In 1672 he was allowed to buy from the bankrupt Perrin his monopoly of operatic performances granted three years earlier. Indeed, the monopoly was reinforced, for henceforth there was a total prohibition on 'singing any piece entirely in music, whether in French verse or other languages, without the permission of the said Sieur Lully, on pain of a fine of 10,000 livres and confiscation of theatres, machines, decorations, costumes and other items'.[77] As he enjoyed royal approval, Lully's fortune was made: one of the best illustrations of the power of Louis XIV in his heyday was the following observation made by Madame de Sévigné in December 1673: 'The king said the other day that if he were in Paris when the opera [*Cadmus et Hermione*] was being played, he would go every day. This word will be worth 100,000 francs to Baptiste [Lully]'.[78] Such was the value of this endorsement that Lully was able to run the Paris Opera at a profit—the only man ever to have done so.[79]

So Lully was not only the most powerful musician in France, he also became immensely rich, living the life of a *grand seigneur* and leaving an estate worth 800,000 *livres*, including five houses in Paris. In 1681 he paid 63,000 *livres* to purchase the honorific office of *secrétaire du roi*, which gave him and his family immediate hereditary nobility.[80] His status also allowed him to escape unscathed when he became involved in one of the most sensational scandals of the reign. In 1685 it emerged that he was a leading member of a homosexual ring, which included such great aristocrats as the comte de Fiesque, the chevalier de Lorraine, and the duc de Vendôme, as well as many poets and musicians. To make matters worse, the denunciation of Lully for debauching his juvenile page came hard on the heels of the exposure of an even higher-ranking group of homosexuals, including a prince of the blood (the prince de Conti) and even one of the king's own illegitimate children (the 16-year-old comte de Vermandois). At a time when sodomy could be punished by the stake,

[76] See above, p. 43.
[77] Isherwood, *Music in the service of the king*, p. 183.
[78] Ibid., p. 189.
[79] Neal Zaslaw, 'Lully's orchestra', in Jérome de La Gorce and Herbert Schneider (eds.), *Jean-Baptiste Lully. Actes du Colloque/Kongressbericht Saint-Germain-en-Laye—Heidelberg 1987* (Laaber, 1990), Neue Heidelberger Studien zur Musikwissenschaft, vol. 18, p. 540.
[80] Anthony, 'Jean-Baptiste Lully', in *The New Grove Dictionary*, vol. 11, p. 317.

Lully was very fortunate to survive, especially as he and his fellow pederasts were also reported to lampoon religion. In the event, he escaped with a stern warning from the king, the loss of his catamite to a religious order, and a great deal of public ridicule (Saint-Evremond wrote a verse depicting Lully as a modern Orpheus, the only difference being that when Lully descended to the underworld, it was a young male criminal he took back with him, leaving Eurydice languishing in chains).[81]

A century later, this combination of respect and material support still represented the ideal form of patronage, as Goethe discovered. Although he had been born (in 1749) and raised in Frankfurt am Main, one of the most populous and dynamic of the self-governing Free Imperial Cities, he found its civic culture restricted and unsophisticated. In 1775 he escaped to the court of a prince, not to a great capital such as Vienna or Berlin but to modest Weimar, most of whose 6,000 inhabitants were wholly dependent on the presence of the Duke of Saxony-Weimar for their livelihood. Although he occasionally chafed at its limitations, he found here conditions so congenial for intellectual pursuits that he remained for the rest of his long life (he died in 1832).[82] Freed from the vulgarizing need to market his writings—but also rescued by his public responsibilities from the mental atrophy induced by incarceration in an ivory tower—Goethe found the ideal balance between leisure and service, independence and responsibility. In May 1789 Goethe wrote a panegyric for his patron, Duke Karl August, which also expressed his belief in the court as the best cultural environment: 'For he has given me what the great rarely grant: affection, leisure, trust, fields, a garden, a house . . . he has been my Augustus and my Maecenas.'[83]

As Goethe wrote those words, the Estates General were gathering at Versailles to begin the dismantling of the old regime in France. So it would be tempting to see his panegyric as a swansong for a doomed order and Goethe himself as an anachronism. Indeed, T. S. Eliot described him 'as about as unrepresentative of his Age as a man of genius can be'.[84] Certainly the future

[81] Henry Prunières, *La Vie illustre et libertine de Jean-Baptiste Lully* (Paris, 1929), pp. 221–9.

[82] There is a particularly intelligent analysis of the relationship between Goethe and Weimar in the best modern study of his life and times—Nicholas Boyle, *Goethe: The Poet and the Age*. Vol. 1: *The Poetry of Desire* (Oxford, 1991), especially ch. 4.

[83] Quoted in ibid., p. 575. As Boyle writes: 'The "panegyric" of 10 May 1789 was Goethe's definitive declaration that a German national culture, the promised land to which the intellectuals of the 1770s had set out, and in which he thought he had lived during his year in Rome, could be permanently established, in Weimar and perhaps in other similar centres, through the patronage of artists by the absolute rulers of feudal principalities'.

[84] Quoted in ibid., p. 7.

seemed to lie with the revolutionary culture of the public sphere. Yet, as we shall see in later chapters, the representational culture of the courts was not killed off by 1789. It proved to be remarkably tenacious, enjoying second and third winds just when it seemed to be collapsing from exhaustion, helped back to its feet by every regime's need to seek legitimation. For the time being, the courtly absolutist culture which had reached its apogee with Louis XIV's Versailles seemed to have run out of steam. In the following section, the focus changes to the forces which had eroded its dominance.

PART II

The Rise of the Public Sphere

4

Communications

FROM VERSAILLES TO PARIS

The closing years of Louis XIV's reign were sombre. The war of the Spanish Succession, which began in 1701, was a chapter of disasters, as enemies old and new stripped the gilt from the ageing king's *gloire*. On the home front, bankruptcy was staved off only by the sharp increase of existing taxes, the introduction of new burdens, and the resort to self-defeating expedients such as the debasement of the coinage, the sale of offices, and the sale of tax exemptions.[1] Nature did her worst too, inflicting epidemics on both humans and cattle (in 1700–1 and 1714 respectively), one of the worst winters of the millennium (1709–10), and repeated harvest failures (in 1710, 1712, and 1713). The combined depredations of these three horsemen of the Apocalypse—war, plague, and famine—reduced the population of France by the end of the reign to its lowest point for three centuries.[2]

At Versailles the confident culture of the palmy days began to crumble. The solid silver furniture was melted down, new building projects were adjourned *sine die*, the balls became less frequent and less gorgeous, even the quality of the artists declined.[3] After marrying his pious mistress, Madame de

[1] William Doyle, *Venality: The Sale of Offices in Eighteenth-century France* (Oxford, 1996), p. 51.

[2] Pierre Goubert, 'La force du nombre', in Fernand Braudel and Ernest Labrousse (eds.), *Histoire économique et sociale de la France*. Vol. II: *Des derniers temps de l'âge seigneurial aux préludes de l'âge industriel (1660–1789)* (Paris, 1970), p. 49; Pierre Goubert, *Louis XIV et vingt millions de français* (Paris, 1966), ch. 4.

[3] Peter Burke, *The Fabrication of Louis XIV* (New Haven, 1992), pp. 109–10.

Maintenon, Louis increasingly turned his attention to the next world, seeking to improve his chances of admission by persecuting those he supposed to be God's enemies on earth. His attack on the Protestants in the 1680s, the Quietists in the 1690s, and the Jansenists in the first decade of the new century certainly gave him the reputation of being the hammer of the heretics, but only served to darken further the atmosphere at court. The last dismal straw was the terrible grief suffered by the king in 1711–12 when he lost in quick succession his son, his grandson, and his eldest great-grandson, to mention only the three most prominent victims of a rash of fatalities to strike the house of Bourbon. High society responded by escaping whenever possible from a palace ruled by religious mania and death to the bright lights of the capital. Increasingly, the road back to Versailles from Paris was crowded in the early hours by carriages bringing the courtiers back after a night out on the town.[4] Long before the old king died in 1715, the court culture he had created at Versailles had lost its appeal.[5] When the duc d'Orléans, who ruled as regent for the infant Louis XV until 1723, set up his court in Paris, he was giving formal recognition to a transfer of cultural authority which had already occurred.

It was given memorable visual expression by one of the great paintings of the century, Watteau's *Gersaint's shop-sign* (Plate 16). Created in the last year of his short life (1684–1721) to hang outside the art gallery of his eponymous friend, this is surely the finest advertisement of any age. Watteau was different. Provincial, lacking formal education, feckless, sensitive, and demanding, he could not be assimilated to the artistic establishment. In the words of Gersaint: 'his disposition was anxious and changeable; he was self-willed; he had a wanton truant wit but his conduct was virtuous.'[6] Unable to serve even the most generous of patrons for long, he preferred the company of actors, fair entertainers, and other raffish groups living on the margins of society. He was particularly attracted to the *commedia dell'arte*, which provided him with the subject-matter of much of his work, including another great masterpiece, the portrait of a clown known simply as *Gilles*.

That Gersaint was one of several contemporaries to write an account of Watteau's life was an indication of the impact he made, both personal and aesthetic. Especially important for future attitudes to art was the recognition of his originality, not as eccentricity to be deplored but as creativity to be

[4] Jean-François Solnon, *La Cour de France* (Paris, 1987), p. 314.

[5] Wend Graf Kalnein and Michael Levey, *Art and Architecture of the Eighteenth Century in France* (London, 1972), p. 201.

[6] Quoted in William Cormack, *The Drawings of Watteau* (London, 1970), p. 7.

admired. Even the hidebound Royal Academy of Painting and Sculpture exempted him from its normal rules, allowing him a free hand in choosing a subject for his *morceau de réception* (the painting required to establish his credentials for admission). Characteristically, Watteau did not bother to avail himself even of this concession until many years had passed. He cared nothing for the Academy and neither sought nor received royal patronage, pension, or title. As Michael Levey has suggested: 'he created, unwittingly, the concept of the individualistic artist loyal to himself, and himself alone.'[7] Not even *The shop-sign of Gersaint* was commissioned, indeed it was Watteau who asked Gersaint for permission to paint it, 'to take the chill off his fingers' following a fruitless journey to London to seek a cure for his tuberculosis.[8] The genre he created—the *fête galante*, with its idealized settings and dreamy eroticism, may seem to modern eyes the quintessence of old regime society, but it also represented an escape route from the representational art of Louis XIV's court. Only if the common but egregious mistake is made of conflating royal absolutism with aristocratic hedonism can Watteau's art be seen as representative of the established order.

The shop-sign of Gersaint is also revealing because of what it was: a sign for a shop in Paris. The paintings on the wall are all commodities and the chief characters are customers. Indeed the shop-sign itself was for sale, serving its original purpose for only a few weeks before being bought by Watteau's patron Jean de Julienne. Its commercial nature was emphasized by its subsequent proliferation in the form of an engraving made in 1732, which was how it came to the attention and then into the possession of Frederick the Great of Prussia.[9] Watteau's familiar technique for imparting an erotic charge to his painting, by juxtaposing the nudes in his paintings with fully dressed observers, does not alter the fact that what is being represented in *The shop-sign of Gersaint* is a commercial transaction. It is not a critique: Watteau was a close friend of Gersaint, was living in his house at the time, and painted this sign as an act of friendship. However, it does depict an important transitional moment, poignantly caught as the woman stepping in from the street pauses to look at the portrait of Louis XIV being packed away. Her companion extends his hand to beckon her on, indicating that there is no point in dwelling on yesterday's man.

[7] Michael Levey, *Rococo to Revolution: Major Trends in Eighteenth Century Painting* (London, 1966), p. 56.

[8] Cormack, *The Drawings of Watteau*, p. 17.

[9] Philip Conisbee, *Painting in Eighteenth-century France* (Oxford, 1981), p. 151; Peter-Eckhard Knabe (ed.), *Frankreich im Zeitalter der Aufklärung* (Cologne, 1985), p. 223.

THE PUBLIC

Gersaint's customers are few in number (and two of them appear to be more interested in the shop-girl than in the pictures), but they represent what was to become an increasingly powerful force in European culture—the paying public. The very concept of 'the public' as an abstraction was in its infancy. In the previous century it had been understood in concrete terms as—say—a theatre audience, that is, a specific group of people, organized hierarchically, defined by the event in question, and passive in its attitude.[10] By the reign of Louis XIV, however, there were some signs of public involvement in the arts. During its first difficult years, the Academy of Painting and Sculpture thought it could strengthen its hand by holding what it called 'public exercises'.[11] The annual exhibitions or Salons decreed by the statutes of 1663 were in fact often postponed, but those that did take place allowed awareness of the existence of a public to be articulated. In 1673, for example, the academicians decided to suspend their normal activities while the Salon was held because 'unfortunate accidents were wont to occur as a result of the *confusion populaire*... and to allow the public freely to move about and satisfy its curiosity'. As this precaution suggests, there was a lively public interest in the visual arts. In 1662, or in other words even before the Salons began, Fréart de Chambray wrote in what was 'probably the first published French work devoted to pictorial aesthetics' (Thomas Crow), entitled *The Idea of the Perfection of Painting*, that 'not only men of letters and those of noble condition, whom we always presume to be the most reflective of people, take an eager interest in painting; even the common man joins in to deliver his opinion and does it so well that painting seems to have become the *métier* of everyone.' Moreover, the academicians were prepared to acknowledge the authority of these lay critics. In 1699, when announcing the resumption of the Salons after a long interval, they stated in the catalogue that they wished 'to renew the former custom of exhibiting their works to the public in order to receive its judgment'.[12]

These were still straws in the wind. Despite Fréart de Chambray's optimism, discussion of the visual arts in France remained the preserve of the few:

[10] Roger Chartier, *The Cultural Origins of the French Revolution* (Durham, NC, and London, 1991), p. 33. Cf. Thomas E. Crow, *Painters and Public Life in Eighteenth Century Paris* (New Haven and London, 1985): 'In discussion of French art before 1747, the term *public* does not normally designate the community of Parisians or Frenchmen, but carries the more restricted sense of a habitual audience for some particular attraction or entertainment.'

[11] Ibid., p. 27.

[12] Ibid., pp. 29, 35, 37.

Hadamart's picture of the Salon of 1699 shows small groups of elegantly dressed members of high society. Moreover, after 1704 the Salons virtually ceased to function for thirty years, with the exception of a minor affair in 1725. It was not until 1737 that they began again on a biennial basis. This time they did not falter, but went from strength to strength, attracting around 15,000 visitors to each Salon in the 1750s and double that number by the 1780s.[13] The detailed printed catalogues, reviews in periodicals, and polemical pamphlets widened the debate still further, thus lending support to Chartier's ambitious conclusion that:

> After 1737, when the Salon became a regular and well-frequented institution, its very existence transferred legitimacy in aesthetic appreciation away from the narrow milieus that up to that point had claimed monopoly (the Royal Academy of Painting and Sculpture, aristocratic and ecclesiastical clients, collectors, and the merchants who sold to them) toward the mixed and numerous public who passed judgment on the paintings hung on the walls of the *Salon carré* in the Louvre.[14]

The official *Mercure de France* anticipated this verdict when it greeted the resumption of the Salons with the words:

> The Academy does well to render a sort of accounting to the public of its work and to make known the progress achieved in the arts it nurtures by bringing to light the work of its most distinguished members in the diverse genres it embraces, so that each thereby submits himself to the judgment of informed persons gathered in the greatest possible number and receives the praise or blame due to him.[15]

In short, by the middle of the eighteenth century, 'the public' had become established as not just *a* legitimate voice in aesthetic appreciation but as *the* most authoritative. La Font de Saint Yenne (usually regarded as the first modern art critic) wrote in 1747: 'It is only in the mouths of those firm and equitable men who compose the Public, who have no links whatever with the artists... that we can find the language of truth.'[16] This was a rise to pre-eminence repeated in other branches of the arts. During the *querelle des bouffons* over the relative merits of French and Italian music during the early 1750s (of which more later),[17] an appeal was made by both sides to the public, 'because it

[13] Chartier, *The Cultural Origins of the French Revolution*, p. 160. 8,000 copies of the catalogue were printed in 1755 and 20,000 in in 1783; Georg Friedrich Koch, *Die Kunstausstellung. Ihre Geschichte von den Anfängen bis zum Ausgang des 18. Jahrhunderts* (Berlin, 1967), p. 150.

[14] Ibid., p. 36.

[15] Crow, *Painters and Public Life*, p. 6.

[16] Ibid.

[17] See below, pp. 357–74.

alone has the right to decide whether a work will be preserved for posterity or will be used by grocers as wrapping-paper' and because the subjectivity of the individual in aesthetic matters can only be corrected 'by the verdict of the public, which is always governed by true feelings and rational opinions'.[18] Perhaps the most eloquent testimony to the force of this new arbiter came from the chief government censor, Malesherbes, who in 1759 wrote in a letter to his father: 'The world of publishing, like all other objects of commerce, is a good to which everyone has the same right and which is susceptible to no favours. The government only watches over it to maintain public order; and to protect the writers' particular interests, it is necessary to establish equal laws. Success alone makes a difference . . . only the public is entitled to judge.'[19]

Acknowledging the authority of the public was one thing; defining it was quite another. One man's enlightened public could all too easily become another man's ignorant mob. For the time being, however, the contrast between the authoritarianism of the royal, aristocratic, or ecclesiastical patron on the one hand and the apparent liberty offered by the objective, abstract public—'a good and generous master', in the view of Oliver Goldsmith[20]—was seductive. No one wrote a more eloquent commitment to the public than Friedrich Schiller, perhaps because he had suffered so much at the hands of an old-style exponent of representational culture, in his case Duke Karl Eugen of Württemberg. In the words of his most acute biographer, Schiller 'was both victim and beneficiary of eighteenth-century absolutism'.[21] He was given an excellent education free, gratis, and for nothing, but at the cost of intellectual slavery. Forced to study medicine at the ducal grammar school against his will, imprisoned for writing his first sensational play—*The Robbers*—and told to confine himself in future to medical treatises, he protested with his feet and ran away. No wonder that two years later, in 1784, he made the following declaration of intellectual independence:

I write as a citizen of the world who serves no prince . . . From now on all my ties are dissolved. The public is now everything to me—my preoccupation, my sovereign and

[18] *Ce que l'on doit dire. Réponse de Madame Foliot à la lettre de Monsieur**** (1753) and [de Rochemont], *Réflexions d'un patriote sur l'opéra françois, et sur l'opéra italien, qui présentent le Parallele du goût des deux Nations dans les beaux Arts* (1754), reprinted in Denise Launay (ed.), *La Querelle des bouffons*, 3 vols. (Geneva, 1973), I, p. 3 and III, p. vii.

[19] Quoted in Jack R. Censer, *The French Press in the Age of Enlightenment* (London, 1994), p. 149. For further examples, see James Van Horn Melton, *Politics, Culture and the Public Sphere in Enlightenment Europe* (Cambridge, 2001).

[20] Quoted in Peter Gay, *The Enlightenment: An Interpretation*. Vol. 2 : *The Science of Freedom* (New York, 1969), p. 62.

[21] T. J. Reed, *Schiller* (Oxford, 1991), p. 6.

my friend. Henceforth I belong to it alone. I wish to place myself before this tribunal and no other. It is the only thing I fear and respect. A feeling of greatness comes over me with the idea that the only fetter I wear is the verdict of the world—and that the only throne I shall appeal to is the human soul.[22]

This sort of wide-eyed declaration was not exceptional. In the previous year, the 17-year-old Viennese composer Josef Weigl had written in the preface of the libretto of his first opera, *Cunning Deceived*: 'May the Gods look kindly on my first-born; and may you, my first and best public, be my divinity!'[23]

Dedication to the public presupposed an awareness on the part of the creative artist that a public existed. It was indeed a common and striking feature of eighteenth-century culture that contemporaries noticed an intensification of public interest. We have recorded already Chambray's absurd claim that 'painting seems to have become the *métier* of everyone.'[24] Yet the extraordinary popularity of the Salons after 1737 certainly suggested that a substantial section of the Parisian population did take a keen interest in contemporary art. Of the many evocative accounts available, the following single example, written in 1785 by Louis de Carmontelle, must suffice:

[The Salon] is a vast theatre where neither rank, favour, nor wealth can reserve a place for bad taste... Paris comes alive, all classes of citizens come to pack the Salon. The public, natural judge of the fine arts, already renders its verdict on the merits of the pictures which two years of labour have brought forth. Its opinions, at first unsteady and tentative, quickly gain stability. The experience of some, the enlightenment of others, the extreme *sensibilité* of one segment, and above all the good faith of the majority, arrive finally to produce a judgment all the more equitable in that the greatest liberty has presided there.[25]

Music had no such obvious point of concentration as an annual exhibition but by way of compensation undoubtedly involved more people more often during the course of the year:

All the Modish World appear
Fond of nothing Else my dear.

[22] Quoted in H. Kiesel and P. Münch, *Gesellschaft und Literatur im 18. Jahrhundert* (Munich, 1977), p. 98.

[23] Otto Michtner, *Das alte Burgtheater als Opernbühne von der Einführung des deutschen Singspiels (1778) bis zum Tod Kaiser Leopold II. (1792)*, Theatergeschichte Österreichs, vol. 3: *Wien* (Vienna, 1970), p. 136.

[24] See above, p. 106.

[25] Quoted in Crow, *Painters and Public Life*, p. 18.

Folks of fashion eager seek
Sixteen concerts in a Week.[26]

This was a verse that appeared in London in 1788 in the comic dialogue *The Musical Courtship*, reflecting the contemporary 'rage for music'.[27] It was the same on the continent. In 1764 a musical lending library was established at Paris because 'music has become almost a universal form of entertainment.'[28] Five years later, in the prospectus for what was probably the first French periodical devoted to music, the *Journal de Musique*, it was firmly stated that everywhere in Europe interest in music had grown to the point that it was now regarded as an essential part of education.[29] Baron Grimm provided confirmation in 1774 when he wrote to the subscribers to his *Correspondance*: 'for two weeks now, it would seem, the only thing one dreams about in Paris is music. It provides the subject-matter for all our arguments and for all our conversations, it is the soul of all our dinner-parties and it would even seem absurd to be interested in anything else.'[30]

The most thoughtful analysis of this sea-change in the musical life of Europe was conducted by the greatest of all the musical periodicals, the *Allgemeine Musikalische Zeitung*, founded in 1798. In a long review of the musical development of Germany during the course of the century that was drawing to a close, the editor argued that during the first fifty years or so, music of a serious kind had been confined to the topmost ranks of society. The ordinary people had been excluded by what he called the 'artificiality' of most church music and the use of the Italian language in the opera house. Public concerts and private music-making were equally rare, while dance music was still too uncouth. Once Frederick the Great had set an example, however, music began to spread, ceasing to be an expensive rarity reared in a hothouse and gradually becoming a popular commodity for everyday consumption. Church music became less austere, opera became more accessible, dance music became more refined, and the growth of instrumental music, especially for wind instruments, allowed many more people to participate actively.

[26] Quoted in Simon McVeigh, *Concert Life in London from Mozart to Haydn* (Cambridge, 1993), p. 1.

[27] Ibid.

[28] Bruno Brévan, *Les Changements de la vie musicale parisienne de 1774 à 1799* (Paris, 1980), p. 80.

[29] *Journal de musique historique, théorique et pratique, sur la musique ancienne et moderne, les musiciens et les instrumens de tous les temps et de tous les peuples* (reprinted Geneva, 1972), p. 1. In his introduction to this reprint, François Lesure discusses the claim of this to be first French musical periodical.

[30] Quoted in Brévan, *Les Changements de la vie musicale parisienne*, p. 35.

Improved printing techniques brought down costs and widened the market for sheet music. As a result, he concluded with satisfaction, music had ceased to be the monopoly of nobles and connoisseurs and had become an integral part of the burgeoning culture of the middle classes.[31]

In short, in western and central Europe at least, the eighteenth century witnessed the emergence of the public as a major cultural force. Although it is a phenomenon much easier to illustrate than to explain, a start can be made by defining its essential characteristics. The public consists of private individuals brought together by the voluntary exchange of ideas to form a whole greater than the sum of its parts. Not only is it independent of the state, it claims a superior status for both quantitative and qualitative reasons: because its numerical strength allows it to claim to be representative of civil society, and because its insistence on free expression and public debate allows it to claim enhanced authority. It is anonymous and unhierarchical, gaining access solely by the capacity to pay for the cultural commodities it consumes. That its discourse is characterized by openness, criticism, spontaneity, and reasoned argument is revealed by cognates such as 'publicity', 'publicize', and 'public opinion'.[32]

LITERACY AND EDUCATION

As another cognate of 'public'—'publish'— demonstrates, the natural medium of the public is the written word. At least until the audio-visual revolution of the second half of the twentieth century, the main means of communication between members of the public was through print. Unable to listen to radio or watch television, unable to reach for the telephone or to link with the Internet, immobilized by slow and expensive transport, the eighteenth-century public had to rely on the pen for escape from isolation. As we shall see, more direct forms of sociability were found in voluntary associations, but even these usually resorted to periodical publications to widen their circle. In other words, the growth of the public presupposes the growth of literacy. When expressed as a negative—that the concept of a public is unknown in illiterate societies—this admittedly does not take us very far (although it is not quite as banal as the truism that 'nomadic tribes do not produce monumental

[31] 'Bemerkungen über die Ausbildung der Tonkunst in Deutschland im achtzehnten Jahrhundert', *Allgemeine Musikalische Zeitung*, 3 (1800–1), pp. 321–5.

[32] Jürgen Habermas, *The structural transformation of the public sphere. An inquiry into a category of bourgeois society* (Cambridge, 1989), pp. 2, 27.

architecture,' offered by Richard Wollheim as a demonstration of the limitations of reductionist sociological theories of art).[33] Nevertheless, it does suggest one important line of inquiry.

Social historians like nothing more than to stress the inadequacy of their evidence and the tentative nature of their (often conflicting) conclusions, but they can at least agree that literacy increased significantly in western and central Europe during the eighteenth century. It was then that the ability to read and write ceased to be the preserve of a small elite and became accepted as a desirable and realizable goal for everyone. During the century between the 1680s and the 1780s, literacy rates in France increased from 29 per cent to 47 per cent for men and from 14 per cent to 27 per cent for women.[34] This statistic becomes more arresting when it is disaggregated on a regional basis. In terms of literacy, there were three Frances: a highly literate north-east, a markedly less literate but progressing south, and a doggedly illiterate 'Atlantic' region stretching from Lower Normandy to the Limousin.[35] In the first of those sectors, north of the cultural divide traced by the celebrated 'Saint-Malo to Geneva line', something approaching mass literacy had been achieved by the outbreak of the Revolution, for most districts had reached a rate of 50 per cent and all exceeded 40 per cent.[36] A growing number of specialized studies provides confirmation. In the Brie to the east of Paris, for example, 73 per cent of male town-dwellers were literate; in Meaux indeed the figure reached 88 per cent.[37]

In the all-important metropolis, statistics are easier to come by and all point to high levels of literacy. For example, in 1789, 90 per cent of male Parisians and 80 per cent of females could sign their wills (although of course only owners of property made wills); 66 per cent of men and 62 per cent of women surviving their marriage partners were able to sign the inventory of their inheritance; the police records of the Châtelet show 62 per cent of men and 16 per cent of women signing their statements; and so

[33] Richard Wollheim, 'Sociological explanations of the arts: some distinctions', in Milton C. Albrecht, James H. Barnett, and Mason Griff (eds.), *The Sociology of Art and Literature* (London, 1970), p. 578 n. 5.

[34] Chartier, *The Cultural Origins of the French Revolution*, p. 69.

[35] Michel Vovelle, 'La sensibilité pré-révolutionnaire', in Ernst Hinrichs, Eberhard Schmitt, and Rudolf Vierhaus (eds.), *Vom Ancien Régime zur Französischen Revolution. Forschungen und Ergebnisse* (Göttingen, 1978), p. 521.

[36] James Collins, *The State in Early Modern France* (Cambridge, 1995), p. 194.

[37] Heinrich Blömeke, *Revolutionsregierung und Volksbewegung (1793–1794). Die 'Terreur' im Departement Seine-et-Marne (Frankreich)* (Frankfurt am Main, Bern, New York, and Paris, 1989), p. 45.

on.[38] The ability to sign a document is more important than it sounds, for it has been argued convincingly by Roger Schofield that, although it may not necessarily be accompanied by an ability to write fluently, it is a good guide to the related ability to read.[39] Not surprisingly, every statistical survey indicates a close correlation between low literacy and low social status, not to mention the feminine gender. However, even plebeian quarters of Paris could boast impressive rates—the Faubourg Saint-Marcel, for example, with 68 per cent, while the historian of the origins of revolutionary radicalism has firmly stated that most Parisians, right down to the humblest porters and water-carriers, could sign their names by 1789.[40]

Elsewhere in western Europe, figures are more difficult to come by, but those available tell the same story. By the middle of the eighteenth century, Scotland had attained 'remarkable, if not total, literacy' with around 65 per cent. The national average for males in England was rather less, at about 60 per cent, although the rate in London, where 92 per cent of bridegrooms and 74 per cent of brides could sign the marriage register, was appreciably higher. The national average for females was about 40 per cent.[41] The Austrian Netherlands (roughly corresponding to present-day Belgium) recorded 61 per cent. Probably the highest national figure was achieved by Sweden, where around 80 per cent of both men and women could read by the middle of the century.[42] The overall figures for German-speaking Europe must be very approximate guesses, but—for what they are worth—they reveal a rising curve from 10 per cent of the adult population in 1700 to 15 per cent in 1770 and 25 per cent in 1800.[43] In fact, these figures may well be an underestimate, for the

[38] Daniel Roche, *Le Peuple de Paris. Essai sur la culture populaire au XVIIIe siècle* (Paris, 1981), pp. 206–9.

[39] R. S. Schofield, 'The measurement of literacy in pre-industrial England', in J. Goody (ed.), *Literacy in Traditional Societies* (Cambridge, 1968), pp. 311–25. This is confirmed by Roger Chartier and Dominique Julia, 'L'école: traditions et modernisation', in *Seventh International Congress on the Enlightenment: Introductory Papers. Budapest 26 July–2 August 1987* (Oxford, 1987), p. 109.

[40] R. B. Rose, *The Making of the Sans-culottes: Democratic Ideas and Institutions in Paris, 1789–92* (Manchester, 1983), p. 19.

[41] John Brewer, *The Pleasures of the Imagination. English Culture in the Eighteenth Century* (London, 1997), p. 167. For a powerful argument that the literacy rate was probably much higher, see Keith Thomas, 'The meaning of literacy in early modern England', in Gerd Baumann (ed.), *The Written Word: Literacy in Transition* (Oxford, 1986), p. 102.

[42] R. A. Houston, *Literacy in Early Modern Europe: Culture and Education 1500–1800* (London, 1988), pp. 43, 140; Chartier and Julia, 'L'école: traditions et modernisation', pp. 109–10.

[43] Horst Möller, *Vernunft und Kritik. Deutsche Aufklärung im 17. und 18. Jahrhundert* (Frankfurt am Main, 1986), pp. 263, 269.

few regional studies available indicate much higher rates. Nor were these success stories confined to such obvious centres of literacy as Berlin (where 94.1 per cent of owner-occupiers could sign their names in 1782).[44] In East Prussia, at the very edge of German-speaking Europe, only about 10 per cent of male adult peasants could sign their names in 1750, but it was a figure which grew to 25 per cent in 1765 and 40 per cent by 1800.[45] The undynamic Electorate of Trier, predominantly agricultural, exclusively Catholic, and ruled by an archbishop, seems as unlikely a candidate for cultural progress as it is possible to imagine. Yet the episcopal visitation records reveal that virtually all parishes boasted a school by the 1780s and most had a dedicated school-house too. The result was a literacy rate which stood comparison with the most advanced parts of Europe: in the electorate's capital, Koblenz, 86.9 per cent of men and 60.4 per cent of women could sign their marriage certificates by the end of the century.[46] Similar levels were achieved in the neighbouring ecclesiastical principalities of Cologne and Mainz.[47] In Baden by the end of the eighteenth century, between 80 per cent and 90 per cent of men and 40 per cent and 45 per cent of women were literate.[48]

This achievement of mass literacy in a region which was not just Catholic but clericalist warns against any attempt to link literacy too closely with Protestantism. Certainly, many of the most literate parts of Europe were mainly Protestant—the Dutch Republic, Lowland Scotland, England, Saxony, and Sweden. Certainly, the emphasis placed by Protestant reformers on the need to gain access to the word of God also put a premium on the ability to read it. Yet the experience of north-eastern France, the Rhineland, Belgium, northern Italy, and even parts of Poland shows that Protestantism is neither a sufficient nor a necessary explanation of mass literacy. Rather it was the need to compete which prompted both Protestants and Catholics to promote education. To paraphrase Rowland Hill (who wondered why the Devil should have

[44] Helga Schultz, *Berlin 1650–1800. Sozialgeschichte einer Residenz* (Berlin, 1987), p. 276.

[45] James Van Horn Melton, *Politics, Culture and the Public Sphere in Enlightenment Europe* (Cambridge, 2001).

[46] Étienne François, 'Die Volksbildung am Mittelrhein im ausgehenden 18. Jahrhundert. Eine Untersuchung über den vermeintlichen "Bildungsrückstand" der katholischen Bevölkerung Deutschlands im Ancien Régime', *Jahrbuch für westdeutsche Landesgeschichte*, 3 (1977), p. 283.

[47] B. Vogler, 'La Rhénanie', in A. Lottin, J. P. Poussou, H. Soly, B. Vogler, and A. van der Woude, *Études sur les villes en Europe occidentale milieu du XVIIe siècle à la veille de la Révolution française*. Vol. II: *Angleterre, Pays-Bas et Provinces Unies, Allemagne rhénane* (Paris, 1983), pp. 44–6.

[48] Harvey J. Graff, *The Legacies of Literacy: Continuities and Contradictions in Western Culture and Society* (Bloomington, Ind., 1987), p. 187.

all the good tunes): why should the heretics have all the good schools? So, in Catholic Europe it was most often missionary orders which took the initiative to improve—or even initiate—popular education. In France, the Sisters of the Holy Infant Jesus and the Christian Brothers, both founded at Rheims, could claim much of the credit for making north-eastern France one of the most literate parts of Europe. It was the founder of the Christian Brothers, Jean-Baptiste de la Salle, aided and abetted by the royal mistress, Madame de Maintenon, who persuaded Louis XIV to issue a decree ordering all children between the ages of 7 and 14 to attend a Catholic school.[49] Moreover, within Protestant countries, it was often dissenters who formed the educational vanguard—Pietists in Germany and nonconformists in England, for example.[50]

In other words, what is rightly regarded as a central characteristic of the modern world—mass literacy—was promoted by the Churches in the service of religion. There were, however, other and more secular forces working towards the same goal. Their intellectual foundation was the view of human psychology advanced by John Locke in his *Essay Concerning Human Understanding* of 1690. In this fundamental text of the Enlightenment, Locke argued against the existence of innate ideas, most notably original sin. Man does not enter the world irreparably handicapped by Adam's indiscretion, rather he is a *tabula rasa*:

> Let us then suppose the mind to be, as we say, white paper, void of all characters, without any ideas; how comes it to be furnished? Whence comes it by that vast store which the busy and boundless fancy of man has painted on it, with an almost endless variety? Whence has it all the materials of reason and knowledge? To this I answer in one word, from experience, in that all our knowledge is founded and from that it ultimately derives itself.[51]

Locke's successors built imposing educational structures on this epistemological axiom. In particular, they concluded that it was vital for the right things to be written on the white paper of the infant mind, as early as possible and with indelible ink. If that could be done, the condition of the human race could be changed. Children currently picked up their habits and prejudices from their elders, so the human race was caught in a vicious circle of brutality,

[49] Collins, *The State in Early Modern France*, pp. 193–4.

[50] On the Pietist contribution to popular education in Prussia, see Klaus Deppermann, *Der hallesche Pietismus und der preußische Staat unter Friedrich III. (I.)* (Göttingen, 1961), p. 173.

[51] John Locke, *An Essay Concerning Human Understanding* (London, 1690), Book 2, ch. 1, para. 2.

ignorance, superstition, vice, and misery. It could be broken only if an educator intervened to open a window to alternative experience which would provide new and better 'materials of reason and knowledge'. As Diderot wrote to Sophie Valland: 'No, dear friend, nature has not made us evil; it is bad education, bad models, bad legislation that corrupts us.'[52] Especially by deists or materialists who rejected the doctrine of original sin, Locke was fêted as a liberator. Voltaire observed that, whereas previous philosophers had written 'the romance of the soul', Locke had written its history: 'Locke laid bare for mankind human reason in the same way that a good anatomist elucidates the parts of the human body.'[53] (It can be conjectured that Voltaire was less enthusiastic about another of Locke's works—*The Reasonableness of Christianity*.)

Many were the private initiatives undertaken in the century that followed to turn Lockean theory into practice. If they were ever to influence more than a tiny proportion of the population, however, state intervention was needed. In fits and starts, this proved to be forthcoming, less because of any disinterested enthusiasm for progressive pedagogy than for good practical reasons. Especially in western and central Europe, the state was making growing demands on its members. It was obliged to do so, as both its domestic and foreign responsibilities expanded. The Reformation left Churches old and new unable to cope with traditional social responsibilities, thus tempting if not forcing secular authorities to expand their portfolios. The increasingly extravagant culture of the courts and the ever-growing incidence, scale, and cost of warfare prompted an urgent search for new sources of revenue.[54] Gradually, the medieval world of decentralized authority made way for the centralization and concentration of power and it was during the eighteenth century that the decisive break occurred. In England, for example, it was some time during the last quarter of the century that the number of revenue officers—14,000 of them by 1782—exceeded the number of clergymen for the first time.[55] It was a process accompanied and encouraged by a revolution in political theory which made sovereignty the central principle of political discourse and the state, as its agent, 'the master noun of political argument'.[56] The chronic instability

[52] Quoted in Peter Gay, *The Enlightenment: An Interpretation*, vol. 2, p. 170.

[53] Voltaire, *Lettres philosophiques ou lettres anglaises*, ed. R. Naves (Paris, 1964), p. 63.

[54] Modern states collect between a third and a quarter of the Gross National Product; in traditional societies, the figure could be as low as 5%; C. E. Black, *The Dynamics of Modernization. A Study in Comparative History* (New York, 1966), p. 14.

[55] Paul Langford, *A Polite and Commercial People: England 1727–1783* (Oxford, 1989), p. 696.

[56] Quentin Skinner, 'The state', in Terence Ball, James Farr, and Russell L. Hanson (eds.), *Political Innovation and Conceptual Change* (Cambridge, 1989), p. 123. See also Kenneth H. F.

inflicted by confessional conflict and civil strife in the sixteenth and seventeenth centuries provoked an authoritarian surge in the shape of the modern concept of the state as 'that agency in society which enjoys a monopoly of legitimate force'.[57]

In pursuit of this monopoly, the sovereign needed assistance from agents able and willing to take the place of clerics, nobles, or guild men. And that involved promoting appropriate educational institutions: 'Since society was being atomized to enhance its creative and productive activities and since to this end the traditional leadership based on status and privilege was being modernized or eliminated altogether, a new elite, that of professionals, had to be shaped.'[58] Moreover, once it was realized that literacy made communication with—and thus control of—the subjects on the receiving end that much easier, a corresponding impetus for popular education was created. In the interests of centralization and the maximization of the state's resources, regional particularism had to make way for standardization—and that could only be achieved by uniform education. It was a point well made in reverse by the conservative Austrian aristocrat, Count Kajetan Auersperg, who told Leopold II in 1790 that in future education should be confined to nobles and that 'the mass of the people must remain stupid and pious.'[59] That he proved to be fighting a losing battle even in the Habsburg monarchy is some indication of the force of the tide lapping around his ankles.

The state proved to be a jealous master. In particular, it denied that education was a responsibility of the Church: 'it is and shall remain for all time a *Politicum*,' as an Austrian decree firmly stated in 1770.[60] In support of this claim, Count Pergen, later to become Joseph II's chief of police, complained that the clergy had abused their control of education by creaming off the most talented children to swell their own ranks, leaving only the mediocre for state service. Henceforth, he concluded: 'the state must seize complete and permanent supervision and direction of schools and education.'[61] This was a view

Dyson, *The State Tradition in Western Europe: A Study of an Idea and Institution* (Oxford, 1980), p. 33 and below, Ch. 6, pp. 185–94.

[57] Ibid., p. 121. This definition of the state is, of course, that of Max Weber.

[58] Marc Raeff, *The Well-ordered Police State: Social and Institutional Change through Law in the Germanies and Russia 1600–1800* (New Haven and London, 1983), p. 128.

[59] Dana Zwitter-Tehovnik, *Wirkungen der Französischen Revolution in Krain* (Salzburg dissertation, 1975), p. 47.

[60] T. C. W. Blanning, *Joseph II* (London, 1994), p. 39.

[61] Helmut Engelbrecht, *Geschichte des österreichischen Bildungswesens. Erziehung und Unterricht auf dem Boden Österreichs*, vol. 3: *Von der frühen Aufklärung bis zum Vormärz* (Vienna, 1984), p. 68.

shared by Frederick the Great, who in 1743 informed the officials in charge of his new province of Silesia that the purpose of education was to produce young people capable of serving their fatherland by providing them with the knowledge necessary for that elemental task.[62] All over Europe indeed, the middle decades of the eighteenth century were marked by a burst of reforms with three objectives in common: the assumption of public responsibility for education; the formation of a new secular cadre of teachers; and the modernization of the curriculum to serve the practical objectives of the state.[63]

High on the list of those objectives was the promotion of the economy. The dependence of state power on taxable wealth was the central axiom of both 'mercantilism' and 'cameralism', which dominated government thinking in the late seventeenth and eighteenth centuries. Gradually it came to be realized that it was not just a question of educating bureaucrats or even merchants and manufacturers but also of modernizing the attitudes of the labour force. If productivity were to be raised, the pre-industrial work ethic, with its disregard for set time-patterns and liking for high days and holidays, had to be replaced by a market culture. Both Prussian and Austrian officials believed that schools had a vital role to play in instilling the discipline required by the factory. This was one reason why the Prussian state gave so much support to the orphanage and other institutions founded at Halle by the Pietists led by August Hermann Franke, for it was there that Prussian children were taught both the techniques of spinning and weaving and the habit of obedience.[64] It was an enthusiasm shared by private entrepreneurs, by the Austrian magnate Count Auersperg, for example, who had the children of his serfs taught not only manufacturing skills but also reading, writing, and arithmetic.[65]

ECONOMIC EXPANSION

The Count was taking advantage of a sustained expansion of the European economy, a 'secular' trend in the sense that it extended over a century and

[62] Otto Bardong (ed.), *Friedrich der Große*, Ausgewählte Quellen zur deutschen Geschichte der Neuzeit. Freiherr vom Stein-Gedächtnisausgabe, vol. 22 (Darmstadt, 1982), p. 108.

[63] Roger Chartier and Dominique Julia, 'L'école: traditions et modernisation', in *Seventh International Congress on the Enlightenment: Introductory Papers. Budapest 26 July–2 August 1987* (Oxford, 1987) p. 107.

[64] James Van Horn Melton, 'Arbeitsprobleme des aufgeklärten Absolutismus in Preußen und Oesterreich', *Mitteilungen des Instituts für österreichische Geschichtsforschung*, 90 (1982) pp. 56–9, 69–70.

[65] Ibid., p. 72.

more. To link the development of a public sphere to economics is not meant to imply subscription to the notion that this is a sufficient or even a necessary causal relationship. Nevertheless, it does seem clear that between the middle of the seventeenth century and the end of the next, Europe became more populous, more urban, and more prosperous, and that this greatly assisted the emergence of the public as a key player in European culture. Adequate discussion of this process would consume without effort at least one substantial volume, so only the bare outlines can be traced here, but it is essential to convey some impression of the scale of the change.

The most dramatic success story was provided by international trade, with the original impetus probably coming from outside Europe. In the last quarter of the seventeenth century, there was a marked upturn in the Iberian Pacific, demonstrated by the customs receipts at Manila and Acapulco, which increased by 2,600 per cent in the fifty years before 1720.[66] Simultaneously, a demographic surge in China created a corresponding demand which attracted growing numbers of British and Dutch merchants. The Chinese gold they brought back to Europe, together with the rapidly expanding output of Brazilian mines, helped to alleviate the chronic shortage of specie and, among other things, allowed the stabilization of European currencies.[67] With European colonial expansion on the move again after a century of stagnation, in North America, the Caribbean, and the Far East, the scene was set for self-sustaining expansion. Between 1740 and 1780 the value of world trade increased by between a quarter and a third; indeed 'The mid-eighteenth century was one of the most remarkable periods of trade expansion in modern history.'[68] In France the volume of foreign trade doubled between the 1710s and the late 1780s, but its value increased five times.[69] The human cost of this great surge is revealed by more chilling statistics: the number of slaves in the French West Indies increased from about 40,000 to about 500,000 in 1789, with the price of each slave quadrupling during the same period.[70]

What this could mean for a community is well illustrated by the fortunes of Bordeaux, which dominated French trade with the West Indies. Between 1717 and 1789 its trade increased on average by 4 per cent *per annum*, its share of

[66] Pierre Léon, *Économies et sociétés préindustrielles*. Vol. II: *1650–1780. Les origines d'une accélération de l'histoire* (Paris, 1970), p. 128.

[67] Ibid., p. 131.

[68] A. Milward and S. B. Saul, *Economic Development of Continental Europe 1780–1870* (London, 1973), pp. 104–5.

[69] J.-C. Asselain, *Histoire économique de la France du XVIIIe siècle à nos jours*. Vol. I: *De l'ancien régime à la première guerre mondiale* (Paris, 1984), p. 55.

[70] Ibid., p. 62.

French commerce increased from 11 per cent to 25 per cent and its population doubled from 55,000 to 110,000.[71] The agronomist Arthur Young recorded in 1787: 'Much as I had heard and read of the commerce, wealth and magnificence of this city, they greatly surpassed my expectations. Paris did not answer at all, for it is not to be compared to London; but we must not name Liverpool in competition with Bordeaux.'[72] Visual evidence of the accuracy of this description can be found by any present-day visitor, for the city's architecture demonstrates that the eighteenth century was its heyday. For all its splendour, the Place Royale is not the most characteristic site, for it was replicated in other French cities. It is the great opera house—the Grand Théâtre—designed by Victor Louis and built between 1772 and 1780, which best exemplifies the Bordeaux boom. What makes it special is not its size, for although it is very large it is not as big as—say—San Carlo in Naples or La Scala in Milan, nor is it the fact that it was free-standing, for Frederick the Great's opera house on Unter den Linden had anticipated this feature by more than a generation. It is different because in effect it is three buildings, incorporating not just a theatre but also a concert hall and a staircase.[73] It is these last two spaces which reveal the arrival of the public as an architectural influence. As we shall see later,[74] it was during the eighteenth century that the public concert established itself as a major musical medium. To identify the staircase as a space of equal importance is less perverse than it might appear, for it was almost as large as the auditorium and (very large) stage put together. It was there to allow members of Bordeaux high society the opportunity to parade before each other in all their finery—to see and be seen. As the architect Victor Louis (and Charles Garnier almost a hundred years later)[75] grasped, in an opera house the audience is as important a performer as the singers on stage. In a royal opera house, such as that of Augustus of Saxony,[76] it was the royal box which was the cynosure; in a public opera house it is the foyer, staircase, and

[71] François Crouzet and J. P. Poussou, 'Économie et société (1715–1789)', in C. Higounet (ed.), *Histoire de Bordeaux*. Vol. V: *Bordeaux au XVIIIe siècle*, ed. François-Georges Pariset (Bordeaux, 1968), pp. 196–7, 325. Daniel Roche in *France in the Enlightenment*, p. 168, gives the population in 1715 as only 45,000.

[72] Quoted in John Lough, *An Introduction to Eighteenth Century France* (London, 1960), p. 73.

[73] Kalnein and Levey, *Art and Architecture of the Eighteenth Century in France*, pp. 338–9. Kalnein rightly identifies the tripartite structure of the theatre but does not offer an explanation of its significance. There is a good ground-plan of the theatre in Michel Florisoone, 'Romantisme et néo-classicisme', *Histoire de l'Art*, vol. III, ed. Jean Babelon (Paris, 1965), p. 911.

[74] See below, pp. 161–81.

[74] Christopher Curtis Mead, Charles Garnier's Paris Opéra (Cambridge, Mass., and London, 1991), p. 119.

[76] See above, pp. 63–4.

other public rooms. Arthur Young certainly grasped the close connection between commerce and culture in the city:

The theatre, built about ten or twelve years ago, is by far the most magnificent in France. I have seen nothing that approaches it... The establishment of actors, actresses, singers, dancers, orchestra, etc. speaks the wealth and luxury of the place. I have been assured that from thirty to fifty *louis* a night have been paid to a favourite actress from Paris... Pieces are performed every night, Sundays not excepted, as everywhere in France. The mode of living that takes place here among merchants is highly luxurious. Their houses and establishments are on expensive scales. Great entertainments, and many served on [silver] plate. High play [gambling] is a much worse thing; and the scandalous chronicle speaks of merchants keeping the dancing and singing girls of the theatre at salaries which ought to import no good to their credit.[77]

Most other French ports also expanded right up to 1789, unaffected by the recession of the 1770s and 1780s. Yet they contained only a tiny fraction of the French population. For most French people, as indeed for most Europeans, it was the related expansion of manufacturing which held out most hope of material improvement. If many historians now cast doubt on the revolutionary nature of the industrial revolution in Great Britain, stressing instead its gradual character, it remains certain that the manufacturing sector did expand significantly in the eighteenth century and that contemporaries were well aware of the fact.[78] British industrialization was precocious by continental standards, especially with regard to mechanization, but it was not unique. Qualitatively, France may well have fallen behind, but in quantitative terms its host of small manufacturers were doing well. If the British produced more coal, cotton, non-ferrous metals, and ships, the French were ahead in woollens, linens, silks, and pig-iron.[79] Indeed, according to Marczewski, in gross terms manufacturing output in France achieved a higher rate of growth than in Great Britain between the first and the last decades of the eighteenth century, the figures being 4.5 times and 3.9 times respectively.[80]

[77] Quoted in Lough, *An Introduction to Eighteenth Century France*, p. 74. Thirty to fifty *louis* amounted to between £315 and £525 in the currency of the day, using Arthur Young's own conversion table reprinted in ibid., p. vi. Rousseau earned 2,000 *livres* (83.3 *louis*) for the first edition of *La Nouvelle Héloïse*, probably the greatest best-seller of the century; ibid., p. 243.

[78] Langford, *A Polite and Commercial People*, pp. 666–72.

[79] François Crouzet, 'England and France in the eighteenth century: a comparative analysis of two economic growths', in R. M. Hartwell (ed.), *The Causes of the Industrial Revolution in England* (London, 1967), p. 152. Crouzet stresses that it was the economic catatstrophe inflicted by the French Revolution which made relative French backwardness irremediable.

[80] Asselain, *Histoire économique de la France*, p. 88.

It is all too easy to overlook industrial growth if attention is concentrated on the great mechanized factories of 'dark satanic mills' notoriety. Even in Great Britain these were the exceptions. In most parts of Europe most manufacturing, especially in the all-important textile sector, took place within a domestic context on a 'putting-out' basis. That is to say, the entrepreneur provided the raw materials (and often also the tools) for working up at home, collecting and paying for the finished products on a piecework basis. During the past generation, economic historians have paid close attention to this phenomenon, calling it 'proto-industrialization', which may be defined as 'the rise and growth of export-oriented domestic industries, which took place all over Europe during the early modern period'.[81] In its heroic historiographical days in the 1970s, 'proto-industrialization' was held responsible for almost every progressive aspect of the European economy in the seventeenth and eighteenth centuries: population growth, the commercialization of agriculture, capital accumulation, the generation of a labour surplus, proletarianization, the replacement of traditional social institutions by markets, and—last but not least—full-blooded industrialization.[82]

More recently, closer examination of these ambitious hypotheses has left the concept of 'proto-industrialization' in tatters. Its most effective critic, Sheilagh Ogilvie, has concluded that: 'no systematic link can be found . . . between proto-industrialisation and changes in the demography, society or economy of early modern Germany between the late medieval and the nineteenth century.'[83] What has been left behind is the realization of just how regional was the pre-industrial European economy and the consequent appreciation of how much change was occurring, albeit in a very uneven pattern. Several 'industrial landscapes' in Germany, for example, met the proto-industrialization criterion of sixty rural industrial producers per 1,000 inhabitants—parts of the Rhineland, Westphalia, Saxony, Thuringia, Silesia, Baden, Württemberg, and Bavaria.[84] The same could be said of parts of the Low Countries, Switzerland, northern Italy, the Habsburg monarchy, and Catalonia. Given the present state of knowledge, no one can say what was the combined effect of this

[81] Sheilagh C. Ogilvie, 'Institutions and economic development in early modern central Europe', *Transactions of the Royal Historical Society*, 6th ser., 5 (1995), p. 1.

[82] The seminal article is F. F. Mendels, 'Proto-industrialisation: the first phase of the industrialisation process', *Journal of Economic History*, 32 (1972), pp. 241–61.

[83] Sheilagh C. Ogilvie, 'Proto-industrialisation in Germany', in Sheilagh C. Ogilvie and Markus Cerman (eds.), *European proto-industrialisation* (Cambridge, 1996), pp. 135–6. See also her article 'Social institutions and proto-industrialisation', in the same collection.

[84] Ogilvie, 'Proto-industrialisation in Germany', p. 133.

manufacturing activity, but that it generated wealth, promoted mobility, and encouraged literacy seems at least very likely.

Its relationship with the striking demographic changes which occurred during the course of the eighteenth century is more problematic. Did the growing number of consumers stimulate manufacturing, or was it rather the increased employment opportunities offered by manufacturing which encouraged procreation? Whether the chicken or the egg is preferred, there is general agreement that after a slow start the population of Europe increased rapidly from around 120,000,000 in 1700 to around 190,000,000 in 1800.[85] The highest rates were recorded in eastern Europe, although the base point was very low and one has every right to be sceptical about assertions that the population of Hungary, for example, quadrupled.[86] But even in the more densely populated parts of western, central, and southern Europe, there was a significant increase in the course of the century: by 36 per cent in France, 63 per cent in Great Britain, 83 per cent in Spain, and around 100 per cent in the Low Countries and western Germany.[87] The reasons for what proved to be an irreversible surge have been debated with all the enthusiasm that is naturally derived from inconclusive evidence. The most judicious conclusion seems to be that of Milward and Saul: 'The most acceptable explanations for the growth of population in most parts of Europe are to be found in non-economic factors—the reduced virulence of epidemics, the relative absence of wars and in the northern regions at least, favourable changes in the climate.'[88]

URBANIZATION

For the purposes of understanding why a public emerged during the same period, it is important to note that almost all towns grew, that most towns grew quickly, and that several large towns became great cities. The population of the Russian empire may well have grown by two or three times in the eighteenth century, but as virtually all of these millions of additional peasants

[85] André Armengaud, 'Population in Europe 1700–1914', in Carlo M. Cipolla (ed.), *The Fontana Economic History of Europe*, vol. III (London, 1970), p. 12. Pierre Léon, in *Économies et sociétés préindustrielles*, vol. II, p. 214 offers a more precise but similar estimate—from 118,000,000 in 1700 to 193,000,000 in 1800.

[86] Goubert, 'La force du nombre', p. 20.

[87] Léon, *Économies et sociétés préindustrielles*, vol. II, p. 214.

[88] Milward and Saul, *Economic Development of Continental Europe*, p. 130.

remained illiterate (only 7 per cent of army recruits were literate in the middle of the *nineteenth* century),[89] they could not form part of a public. It was in the towns that the public developed and it was to the towns that growing numbers of western Europeans were migrating. After a sluggish start to the eighteenth century, the second half saw increasingly rapid and sustained expansion. In England, one in six of the population lived in a town (defined as a community of more than 2,500) in 1700, a proportion which had doubled to one in three by 1800.[90] In German-speaking Europe, the urban share also doubled in the same period, albeit from a lower base (it increased from 12 per cent to 24 per cent).[91] In France, the urban population increased from 16 per cent in 1725 to 19 per cent in 1789.[92]

Moreover, a further qualitative dimension has to be added in the shape of the metropolis, justly hailed by its historian as 'the unique contribution of early modern Europe to urban civilisation'.[93] It was during the eighteenth century that recognizably modern conurbations developed, with Paris growing from around 450,000 under Louis XIV to 700,000 by 1789 and London soaring from 200,000 in 1600 to 675,000 in 1700, 750,000 in 1750, and almost a million by 1800, ten times larger than any other English city: one in six of English men and women spent part of their working life there.[94] In 1700 only ten European cities had populations in excess of 100,000; by 1800 that number had increased to seventeen and five of them exceeded 200,000.[95] These metropolitan centres were much bigger than any other city in their respective countries: London housed 11 per cent of the English population by 1750 and was more than twelve times larger than its nearest rival,

[89] J. N. Westwood, *Endurance and Endeavour: Russian History 1812–1980* , 2nd edn. (Oxford, 1981), p. 101.

[90] Langford, *A Polite and Commercial People*, p. 418.

[91] Michael Erbe, *Deutsche Geschichte 1713–1790. Dualismus und aufgeklärter Absolutismus* (Stuttgart, 1985), p. 26.

[92] Michel Antoine, *Louis XV* (Paris, 1989), p. 232. It is surprising to find the French figures for 1800 lower than those for Germany, and it is possible that Antoine was using a more rigorous definition of a 'town'.

[93] Josef W. Konvitz, *The Metropolis in Early Modern Europe*, unpublished typescript.

[94] Roche, *Le Peuple de Paris*, pp. 19, 22. Estimating the population of Paris with any confidence is made impossible by the large floating population (perhaps as large as 10% of the whole) which drifted in and out of the capital according to the seasonal labour market and the state of the economy. For the population of London in the eighteenth century, see Ian R. Christie, *Wars and Revolutions: Britain 1760–1815* (London, 1982), p. 7, John Summerson, *Georgian London*, rev. edn. (London, 1972), p. 25, and Brewer, *The Pleasures of the Imagination*, p. 28. On the expansion of London, see especially E. A. Wrigley, 'A simple model of London's importance in changing English society and economy 1650–1750', *Past and Present*, 37 (1967), *passim*.

[95] Léon, *Économies et sociétés préindustrielles*, vol. II, p. 228.

Bristol.[96] So they exercised a correspondingly strong centripetal influence on their national cultures. Further east, in the politically fragmented Holy Roman Empire, there could be no such central magnet, but even here two major cities emerged for the first time. Vienna, established as the capital of the Habsburg monarchy only in the middle of the seventeenth century, had barely reached six figures by 1700, but then soared to 175,000 by 1750 and over a quarter of a million by 1800.[97] Vienna's great rival for the cultural leadership of German-speaking Europe—Berlin—achieved even more startling growth, from 10,000 in 1650 to 50,000 in 1700 to 90,000 in 1740 to 132,000 in 1769 to 170,000 in 1800.[98]

Although Berlin went from market town to metropolis in the space of a century, its growth rate was eclipsed by that of St Petersburg, which went from *swamp* to metropolis in the same period, reaching 250,000 by 1800.[99] These two fastest-growing cities in Europe owed their population explosions to the same source—state action. Indeed, St Petersburg would not have existed at all if Peter the Great had not decided to found a new capital there in 1703. If less artificial in conception, Berlin was the beneficiary of equally determined intervention by successive Hohenzollern rulers. That Huguenot refugees made up almost 20 per cent of the city's population in 1720, for example, was due solely to the asylum granted by Frederick William, the Great Elector, following their expulsion from France by Louis XIV.[100] The capital and skills they brought with them certainly helped to develop the city's economy, but in the eighteenth century at least Berlin remained predominantly a royal city. The great majority of its inhabitants relied for their livelihood on the presence of the government and, above all, the enormous garrison, which in 1766 numbered 671 officers, 27,660 other ranks, and around 11,000 civilian dependants.[101] All over the Holy Roman Empire, state intervention combined

[96] Neil McKendrick, 'The consumer revolution of eighteenth century England', in Neil McKendrick, John Brewer, and J. H. Plumb, *The Birth of a Consumer Society: The Commercialisation of Eighteenth Century England* (London, 1982), p. 21.

[97] Günter Düriegl, 'Wien—eine Residenzstadt im Übergang von der adeligen Metropole zur bürgerlichen Urbanität', in Richard Georg Plaschka and Grete Klingenstein (eds.), *Österreich im Europa der Aufklärung. Kontinuität und Zäsur in Europa zur Zeit Maria Theresias und Josephs II. Internationales Symposion in Wien 20.–23. Oktober 1980*, 2 vols (Vienna, 1985), p. 311.

[98] Schultz, *Berlin 1650–1800*, pp. 33, 61, 122, 172, 296.

[99] Sidney Monas, 'St Petersburg and Moscow as cultural symbols', in Theofanis George Stavrou (ed.), *Art and Culture in Nineteenth Century Russia* (Bloomington, Ind., 1983), p. 27.

[100] Horst Möller, *Aufklärung in Preußen. Der Verleger, Publizist und Geschichtsschreiber Friedrich Nicolai* (Berlin, 1974), p. 10.

[101] Manfred Messerschmidt, 'Preußens Militär in seinem gesellschaftlichen Umfeld', in Hans-Jürgen Puhle and Hans-Ulrich Wehler (eds.), *Preußen im Rückblick* (Göttingen, 1980), p. 50.

with the favourable economic developments noted earlier to promote urbanization: by 1800 there were sixty German cities with populations in excess of 10,000 and fifteen of them were over 30,000.[102]

To readers taught to be aware of the problems of over-population, the encouragement given by eighteenth-century states to religious, political, and *especially* economic refugees may seem perplexing. It makes more sense if one takes into consideration the contemporary axiom that the earth's population had been declining steadily since classical times, due to a sequence of natural disasters. A state which could expand its population, it was argued, was a state which both enhanced itself and deprived its rivals. So Frederick the Great announced in his *Political Testament* of 1768 that 'it is the first, most generally valid and truest principle of government that the real force of a state lies in a numerous population' and Joseph II wrote in 1784 with equal emphasis that 'my first priority, on which the political, financial and even military authorities should concentrate all their attention is population, that is to say, maintaining and increasing the number of my subjects. It is from the maximum number of subjects that all the benefits of the state derive.'[103] Especially in under-populated eastern Europe, governments did all they could to encourage immigration and procreation. Although he set a poor example himself, studiously avoiding the marital bed in favour of an all-male court at Potsdam, Frederick told Voltaire: 'I view my subjects like a herd of stags on some noble's estate; their only function is to reproduce and fill the space.'[104]

While long-established cities such as Paris, London, Madrid, or Rome could expand naturally, in central and eastern Europe it was state action that was decisive. This explains in part the shift in the geographical balance of European culture which began in the eighteenth century and gathered further momentum during the next. If a 'large city' can be defined as a city with a population in excess of 20,000, then in 1300 there were more in this category in Spain (16) and Italy (24) than in all the countries north of the Alps put together (37). In the early modern period, however, Spain and Italy experienced a slight decline to 15 and 22 respectively, while northern Europe almost doubled its score to 70.[105]

[102] John Gagliardo, *Germany under the Old Regime 1600–1790* (London, 1991), p. 127.

[103] Quoted in Kiesel and Münch, *Gesellschaft und Literatur im 18. Jahrhundert*, p. 13, and Blanning, *Joseph II*, p. 79.

[104] Quoted in James J. Sheehan, *German History 1770–1866* (Oxford, 1990), p. 67.

[105] Konvitz, *The Metropolis in Early Modern Europe*.

TRAVELLING AND THE POST

Binding these urban centres together was another development that assisted the emergence of the public: the improvement in physical communications. So cheap and various have means of transportation become that it is difficult to imagine a period when most people stayed put or used their legs: when the young Johann Sebastian Bach wanted to hear Buxtehude playing the organ at Lübeck, he had no choice but to walk there—a journey of around 250 miles each way.[106] The great leap made by the railways in the middle of the nineteenth century has obscured the significant progress made much earlier. Two ways forward were found. The first was through state action, with Louis XIV's France setting the pace. The establishment of a central agency supported by the imposition on communities of the obligation to assist road construction (the *corvée royale*) allowed the construction of a network of well-surfaced, wide, and reasonably straight roads to all parts of the kingdom by the eve of the Revolution (Plate 8).[107] The Royal Road Administration's annual budget had increased from 870,000 *livres* in 1700 to 4,000,000 *livres* by 1770, and by 1786 about 9,000,000 *livres* were being spent on highways each year.[108] Many are the qualifications which need to be made about this process: it all took a very long time, the transport of goods lagged behind that of humans, and the network was essentially radial—that is, it favoured communications between Paris and the provinces rather than between provinces. Nevertheless, by the end of the eighteenth century, the quickest form of public transport—the *diligence*—could manage between 40 and 60 kilometres a day, the time taken to reach Lyons from Paris had been halved, and there was not a city in the kingdom which could not be reached from the capital within a fortnight.[109] It has been estimated that by 1780 around 25,000 kilometres of roads had been built or improved.[110] In the Holy Roman Empire, the fragmentation of authority ensured that improvements were much less uniform, but they certainly occurred. In 1784 Friedrich Carl von Moser recalled with nostalgia the good old days when travelling was a leisurely business and

[106] Denis Arnold, *Bach* (Oxford, 1984), p. 4.

[107] Guy Arbellot, 'La grande mutation des routes de France au milieu du XVIIIe siècle', *Annales. Économies, Sociétés, Civilisations*, 28, 3 (1973), pp. 766–7.

[108] Sheilagh Ogilvie, 'The European economy in the eighteenth century', in T. C. W. Blanning (ed.), *The Short Oxford History of Europe*. vol. VIII: *The eighteenth century* (Oxford, 1999), p. 125; Daniel Roche, *France in the Enlightenment* (Cambridge, Mass., 1998), p. 46.

[109] Ibid., p. 55; Léon, *Économies et sociétés préindustrielles*, vol. II, p. 155. Léon concludes that 'C'est vraiment à partir de 1730–1740 que se forme en Europe la route moderne.'

[110] Roger Price, *The Economic Modernization of France* (New York and Toronto, 1975), p. 5.

recorded that a recent journey on a new highway had been so quick 'that I almost lost the faculties of hearing and seeing'.[111] Moreover, travelling was safer as well as quicker: the Abbé de Véri recorded in his memoirs that the establishment of the *maréchaussée* in 1720 brought a ninefold reduction in the number of executions for highway robbery.[112] For the transport of commodities high in bulk but low in value, the expansion of the canal network in the same period was probably more important, especially the linking of the Loire and the Seine in 1692. When added to existing navigable rivers, the construction of 1,000 kilometres of canals created an inland waterway network of around 8,000 kilometres.[113]

This *étatiste* route to a modern communications network was taken by most other continental countries. In Spain, where very little had been done to improve land communications since the days of Charles V, the arrival of the Bourbon dynasty in 1700 introduced a century of change. A comprehensive ordinance in 1718 ordered the construction of a radial system on the French model, to link Madrid with the regions. The pace of construction was raised by a further major initiative in 1749 and especially by Charles III's ordinance of 1767 which created a network of 'royal roads', the first paved highways since Roman times.[114] From the 1780s it was possible to travel by stagecoach from Madrid to Pamplona, Barcelona, Cartagena, Cadiz, and Lisbon.[115] These improvements to the hardware were accompanied by the creation of something approaching a national postal system, which, among other things, allowed newspapers to be circulated throughout the country.[116] If the mule was still the usual alternative to Shanks's pony in 1800, the previous century had witnessed significant improvement.[117]

An alternative to state intervention was found by the British in the 'turnpike trusts', private companies authorized by Acts of Parliament to build or improve stretches of highway and then to charge travellers a toll. Although most

[111] Friedrich Carl von Moser, *Über Regenten, Regierung und Ministers* (Frankfurt am Main, 1784), pp. ix–x. I owe this reference to Derek Beales.

[112] Baron Jehan de Witte (ed.), *Journal de l'abbé de Véri* (Paris, n.d.), p. 83.

[113] Pierre Léon and Charles Carrière, 'L'appel des marchés', in Fernand Braudel and Ernest Labrousse (eds.), *Histoire économique et sociale de la France*. Vol. II: *Des derniers temps de l'âge seigneurial aux préludes de l'âge industriel (1660–1789)* (Paris, 1970), p. 173.

[114] Jaime Vicens Vives, *An Economic History of Spain* (Princeton, NJ, 1969), pp. 561–2.

[115] Richard Herr, *The Eighteenth Century Revolution in Spain* (Princeton, NJ, 1958), p. 131.

[116] Ibid., p. 564.

[117] There is a more bleak assessment in John Lynch, *Bourbon Spain 1700–1808* (London, 1989), pp. 224–5, and in David M. Ringrose, *Transportation and Economic Stagnation in Spain, 1750–1850* (Durham, NC, 1970), *passim*.

were formed during the second half of the eighteenth century, Daniel Defoe was enthusing about their benefits in the 1720s:

And this is a Work of so much general Good, that certainly no publick Edifice, Alms-House, Hospital, or Nobleman's Palace, can be of equal Value to the Country with this, nor at the same time more an Honour and Ornament to it.

The Benefit of these Turnpikes appears now to be so great and the People in all Places begin to be so sensible of it, that it is incredible what Effect it has already had upon Trade in the Counties where the Roads are completely finished...

The Advantage is also inexpressible to all other kinds of Travelling; such as the Safety and Ease to Gentlemen journeying up to *London* on all Occasions, whether to the Term, to Parliament, to Court or on any other necessary Operation.

Also the Riding Post, as well for the ordinary carrying of the Mails, as for Gentlemen, when their Occasions require Speed, is made extremely easy, safe and pleasant, by this Alteration of the Roads.[118]

As a comparison of the turnpike networks in 1740 and 1770 demonstrates, the momentum conveyed by the profit motive was appreciably more powerful than state directives from Paris or Madrid. By 1800 no fewer than 1,600 turnpike trusts had been formed.[119] The result was a dramatic increase in the speed and frequency of journeys undertaken by private individuals—by the public. In 1754 a newspaper advertisement boasted that 'however incredible it may appear, this coach will actually arrive in London four days after leaving Manchester.' Only thirty years later, keen competition on this key route had halved the journey time.[120] Between the 1740s and the 1780s the journey time from London to Birmingham fell from two days to nine hours.[121] So this was an improvement so rapid that contemporaries could see that a fundamental part of human existence—mobility—had undergone a sea change. A good illustration was provided by Richard Graves in his novel *Columnella*, first published in 1779:

Columnella... observed, that the most remarkable phaenomenon which he had taken notice of these late years, in his retirement, was the surprising improvement in the art of loco-motion, or conveyance from one place to another. 'Who would have believed, thirty years ago,' says he, 'that a young man would come thirty miles in a carriage to dinner, and perhaps return at night? or indeed, who would have said, that

[118] Daniel Defoe, *A tour thro' the whole island of Great Britain. Divided into circuits or journeys. Giving a particular and entertaining account of whatever is curious and worth observation*, 4 vols. (London, 1742), III, pp. 249–50. The first edition was published in 1724–6.

[119] Philip S. Bagwell, *The Transport Revolution from 1770* (London, 1974), p. 39.

[120] Ibid., p. 41.

[121] Ogilvie, 'The European economy in the eighteenth century', p. 125.

coaches would go daily between London and Bath, in about twelve hours; which, twenty years ago, was reckoned three good days journey?'[122]

The wealthier and more enterprising also ventured increasingly beyond their own national frontiers. The wars of the eighteenth century were certainly very numerous, only the 1720s being free of major international conflict, but they were far less destructive and disruptive than the great conflicts of the past. While no one in his right mind would have travelled through central Europe for pleasure during the Thirty Years War, the War of the Austrian Succession or the Seven Years War presented little risk. Consequently, at any one time there were tens of thousands of Europeans on the move, meeting each other at markets, fairs, spas, and the great centres of tourism such as Paris, Venice, Rome, or Naples. Although it must have been a very rough guess, Walpole estimated in 1765 that as many as 12,000 Englishmen were visiting the continent each year and that the number was increasing. In fact, that may even have been an underestimate for, according to French customs officials twenty years later, there were 40,000 British visitors to the continent.[123] In August 1786 the *Daily Universal Register* recorded: 'To such an amazing pitch of folly is the rage for travelling come, that in less than six weeks, the list of Londoners arrived in Paris has amounted to three thousand seven hundred and sixty, as appears by the register of that city.'[124]

All literate people could participate in this acceleration of physical communication, even without leaving their homes, by the simple expedient of writing letters. Indeed, an improved postal service was its most generally experienced benefit. Right across Europe, mail was moved more quickly, more often, more reliably, and more cheaply. The office of Imperial Post-Master in the Holy Roman Empire, held as a hereditary privilege by the princes of Thurn and Taxis, was no sinecure. Stimulated by competition from the rival Prussian and Saxon services (with 760 and 140 post offices respectively), they made their name the most commonly displayed in the world today ('taxi') and built up across central Europe a network of postal stations where both messengers and their horses could be changed day and night. This allowed the letter-post to be moved at speeds of between 130 and 150 kilometres per day.[125] If that rate did not accelerate much in the course of the eighteenth century, the postal

[122] Quoted in Paul Langford, *A Polite and Commercial People: England 1727–1783* (Oxford, 1989), p. 404.

[123] Gerald Newman, *The Rise of English Nationalism* (London, 1987), p. 43.

[124] Quoted in Jeremy Black, *The British and the Grand Tour* (London, 1985), p. 1. There are many more very similar observations to be found in this book.

[125] Christof Dipper, *Deutsche Geschichte 1648–1789* (Frankfurt am Main, 1991), pp. 174–5.

network became much denser: it has been estimated that by 1800 no German community was further than half a day's walk from a postal station.[126] In France it was Henry IV's decision in 1603 to allow royal couriers to carry private mail that began the process. By 1763 postal services were sufficiently developed there to allow a M. Guyot to bring out a *Guide des lettres*, devoted solely to the coming and going of the post.[127] In England, Ralph Allen created a national network after 1720, with the result that by the accession of George III in 1760 most major towns were linked with the capital and with each other by an efficient daily mail service.[128] Of course, writing letters was not the invention of the eighteenth century, but it was then that both a quantitative and qualitative change occurred. A simple but eloquent illustration can be found in the fact that many (perhaps even most) of the century's most popular and representative novels—Richardson's *Pamela* (1740) and *Clarissa* (1748), Rousseau's *Julie, ou la nouvelle Héloïse* (1761), Goethe's *The Sufferings of Young Werther* (1774), Fanny Burney's *Evelina* (1778), and Choderlos de Laclos's *Les Liaisons dangereuses* (1782)—were epistolary in form.

If this was fiction which masqueraded as fact, much of the published correspondence between real people was written with one eye on a wider reading public, for collections of letters became a popular genre. Guides to letter-writing and correspondence itself had been published since the sixteenth century, but here again it was the eighteenth century that witnessed a surge of productivity, often of a very high quality. And it owed much to postal improvements. Horace Walpole would not have written 1,600 letters to Madame du Deffand or more than 800 to Sir Horace Mann (whom he did not meet for the forty-four years of their correspondence) if he had not been confident that they would be delivered.[129] Right across Europe (and the Atlantic), the post created a network which ever-increasing numbers of intellectuals could use for the exchange of opinion, information, and gossip. As John Brewer has remarked, 'Correspondence held the Republic of Letters together,' offering among other illustrations the boast of the classical scholar Gisbert Cuper that 'I have a hundred or so volumes of letters, with the responses of Scholars, who honour me with their friendship and

[126] Klaus Gerteis, 'Das "Postkutschenzeitalter". Bedingungen der Kommunikation im 18. Jahrhundert', in Karl Eibl, *Entwicklungsschwellen im 18. Jahrhundert, Aufklärung*, 4, 1 (1989), p. 66.

[127] Dena Goodman, *The Republic of Letters. A Cultural History of the French Enlightenment* (Ithaca, NY, and London, 1994), pp. 18, 140.

[128] Brewer, *Party Ideology*, p. 159.

[129] Peter Cunningham, 'Preface', in idem (ed.), *The Letters of Horace Walpole*, vol. I (London, 1891), p. xxiii.

correspondence.'[130] The medium also influenced the message, for the relative immediacy now available in long-distance intercourse encouraged a more intimate and subjective style. Indeed, Goethe assigned part of the blame for the effusion of sentimental correspondence to the excellence of the Thurn und Taxis postal service.[131]

THE READING REVOLUTION

Born in 1749, Goethe was a major beneficiary of the emergence of a public. If his career looks old-fashioned, in that he entered the service of a prince—the Duke of Saxony-Weimar—in 1775 and never left it, his *entrée* was not gained via the traditional academic or bureaucratic route. He caught the eye of the young Duke's tutor because he was *famous*, a household name among the educated as the author of a best-seller—*The Sufferings of Young Werther*, published the previous year.[132] He described his audience as 'the middling sort [*einen gewissen Mittelstand*] . . . to which belong the people who live in the small towns, of which Germany boasts so many well-situated and well-stocked examples; all the officials great and small to be found there, the artisans, the manufacturers, and especially their wives and daughters, also all the rural clergy'.[133] These were just the sort of people to have benefited from the social and economic changes sketched in this chapter—and they had equivalents all over central, western, and southern Europe. Their most important collective feature, perhaps, was their self-consciousness. The improvement in symbolic and physical communication was so marked that people noticed and began to feel that they were part of a larger public. That contemporary estimates of the increase in reading could only be wild guesses and were almost certainly exaggerations is unimportant; what matters is the fact that they were made. The following brief selection drawn from the German-speaking world could be multiplied without effort:

[130] John Brewer, 'This, that and the other: public, social and private in the seventeenth and eighteenth centuries', in Lesley Sharpe and Dario Castiglione (eds.), *Shifting the Boundaries: Transformation of the Languages of Public and Private in the Eighteenth Century* (Exeter, 1995), p. 12. Cf. the similar verdict of Goodman, *The Republic of Letters*, p. 16.

[131] Nicholas Boyle, *Goethe: The Poet and the Age*. Vol. 1: *The Poetry of Desire* (Oxford, 1991), p. 127.

[132] Ibid., p. 195.

[133] Quoted in Hans-Ulrich Wehler, *Deutsche Gesellschaftsgeschichte*. Vol. I: *Vom Feudalismus des Alten Reiches bis zur defensiven Modernisierung der Reformära 1700–1815* (Munich, 1987), p. 305.

It is quite certain that the number of people reading is getting larger all the time. (Christoph Martin Wieland, 1765)

[There are] readers of books who rise and retire to bed with a book in their hand, sit down at table with one, have one lying close by when working, carry one around with them when walking, and who, once they have begun reading, are unable to stop until they have finished. But they have scarcely finished the last page of a book before they begin looking round greedily for somewhere to acquire another one; and when they are at their toilet or at their desk or some other place, if they happen to come across something that fits with their own subject or seems to them to be readable, they take it away and devour it with a kind of ravenous hunger. No lover of tobacco or coffee, no wine drinker or lover of games, can be as addicted to their pipe, bottle, games or coffee-table as those many hungry readers are to their reading habit. (The Erfurt clergyman Johann Rudolf Gottlieb Beyer)

Sixty years ago the only people who bought books were academics, but today there is hardly a woman with some claim to education who does not read. Readers are to be found in every class, both in the towns and in the country, even the common soldiers in the large cities take out books from the lending libraries. (*Deutsches Museum*, 1780)

Reading has become a necessity for us all. Every private individual of any means will have a little library and anyone who can read will own at least half a dozen books. (Alois Blumauer, 1782)

In no country is the love of reading more widespread than in Germany, and at no time was it more so than at present. Formerly, only an actual scholar bothered with reading, or he who aspired to become a scholar; the rest of our nation made do with the Bible and a few devotional tracts. But now the situation is quite different. Learning has ceased to be the sole possession of a particular calling and—at least at a superficial level—knowledge of it has become a necessity for all educated groups. The works of good and bad writers are now to be found in the apartments of princes, and alongside the weaver's loom, and, so as not to appear uncultivated, the upper classes of the nation decorate their rooms with books rather than tapestries. In the previous century a soldier with a book in his hand would have been the occasion for biting satire, whereas today an officer who is unread is regarded as contemptible;—our mothers dressed the children early and then went about their business, but our daughters spend the mornings reading poems and periodicals, and in the evening wander alone with a novel in their hands. Yes, even the peasants are now to be found in the taverns reading their almanacs to each other. (*Der Weltbürger* [The Cosmopolitan], 1791) (Plate 10)

Writers are the real *men of the nation*, for their direct sphere of activity embraces all Germany; they are being read everywhere, their publications penetrate gradually into even the smallest towns, with the result that daylight begins to glimmer in regions where twenty-five years ago the most profound darkness reigned. (Christoph Martin Wieland, 1791)

But now it really is the case that a new, universal and far more powerful reading fashion than any before has spread not just throughout Germany but over the whole of Europe too, attracting all classes and strata of society, and suppressing almost every other kind of reading matter. This is the reading of newspapers and political pamphlets. It is at present certainly the most widespread reading fashion there has ever been... From the ruler and the minister down to the woodcutter on the street and the peasant in the village tavern, from the lady at her toilet to the cleaning maid in the kitchen, everyone is now reading newspapers. They calculate the hour when the mail will arrive, and besiege the post office in order to be there first when the mailbag is opened... A lady of taste must have read at least the latest pages in *Moniteur*, the *Journal de Paris* or the *Gazette de Leyde* before she goes to her tea circle, and with the company of gentlemen whom this common spirit assembles more assiduously around the tea table and who exchange news in the *Chronique du mois*, the *London Chronicle*, the *Morning Post*, or the two Hamburg newspapers, and those of Frankfurt or Bayreuth; while the smith sits on his anvil and the cobbler on his stool, temporarily laying down his hammer or awl to read the *Strassburger Kriegsbothen*, the *Brünner Bauern-Zeitung* or the *Staats-Courier*, or has his wife read them to him. (K. A. Ragotzky, 1792)

Everyone today reads a newspaper, from the ruler and his ministers right down to the wood-chopper on the streets and the peasant in the village pub, from the lady at her dressing table to scullery-maid in the kitchen. (*Journal der Luxus nd Moden*, 1793) (Plate 11)

Today people are reading in places where twenty years ago no one had any idea about books; not only the academic but also the burgher and the artisan now provide themselves with food for thought by reading. (Heinrich Bensen, 1795)

In Germany never has there been so much reading going on as at present. (Johann Adam Bergk, 1799)

We are now witnessing the phenomenon of a rage for reading gripping sections of the population which in the past read either very little or not at all. Moreover, they read not to instruct or to inform themselves but for entertainment. Such a thing has not been seen in Germany since printing was invented. Where it will all end is not easy to forecast, but it will probably be for the worse. (Lorenz Westenrieder, 1800)[134]

[134] Quoted variously in: Friedrich Sengle, *Wieland* (Stuttgart, 1949), p. 166; Lutz Winckler, *Kulturwarenproduktion. Aufsätze zur Literatur und Sprachsoziologie* (Frankfurt am Main, 1973), p. 24 n. 28.; Alois Blumauer, *Beobachtungen über Österreichs Aufklärung und Literatur* (Vienna, 1782), p. 53; Reinhard Wittmann, 'Was there a reading revolution at the end of the eighteenth century?', in Guglielmo Cavallo and Roger Chartier (eds.), *A History of Reading in the West* (Amherst, Mass., 1999), pp. 305–6; Gerhard Schulz, *Die deutsche Literatur zwischen Französischer*

This development was not peculiar to Germany—indeed, a French dictionary identified *bibliomanie* as 'one of the sicknesses of the century'.[135] It was also a Francophone Swiss—Jean-Jacques Rousseau—who provided the most vivid account of the 'rage for reading' in action:

> Mme La Tribu's famous lending library provided reading of all sorts. Good or bad was alike to me. I did not choose, I read everything with equal avidity. I read at my bench, I read on errands, I read in the lavatory, and was oblivious of myself for hours on end. I read till my head spun, I did nothing but read. My master spied on me, caught me, beat me, and took away my books. How many volumes were torn up, burnt, and thrown out of the window! How many works returned to Mme La Tribu's shelves with volumes missing![136]

In the course of the eighteenth century, at least in western, northern, and central Europe, a combination of material and cultural forces greatly increased both the number of literate people and their self-consciousness. The result was the formation of a collective entity which saw itself as 'the public'—independent, critical, and the ultimate arbiter of cultural (and perhaps even political) matters. How its rise influenced European culture is the subject of the following chapter.

Revolution und Restauration. Vol. I: *Das Zeitalter der Französischen Revolution* (Munich, 1983), p. 44; Kiesel and Münch, *Gesellschaft und Literatur im 18. Jahrhundert*, pp. 156–7; Uwe Puschner, '"Museum" und "Harmonie"—zwei gesellig-literarische Vereine in München im frühen 19. Jahrhundert', in Hans Ottomeyer (ed.) *Biedermeiers Glück und Ende . . . die gestörte Idylle 1815–1848* (Munich, 1987), p. 213.

135 Dominik von König, 'Lesesucht und Lesewuth', in Herbert Göpfert (ed.), *Buch und Leser* (Hamburg, 1977), p. 91.

136 Jean-Jacques Rousseau, *The Confessions*, ed. J. M. Cohen (London, 1953), p. 47. On the development of lending libraries, see James Van Horn Melton, *Politics, Culture and the Public Sphere in Enlightenment Europe* (Cambridge, 2001).

5

Markets

READING AND READERS

The rapid improvement in physical and symbolic communication discussed in the previous chapter led to an equally rapid increase in printed material available. If it really is the case, as Roger Chartier has boldly asserted, that 'after Gutenberg, all culture in western societies can be held to be a culture of the printed word,' it was only in the eighteenth century that this became fully apparent.[1] The great surge at the time of the Reformation, when Martin Luther became the world's first best-selling author, was not sustained. It was the breakthrough to mass literacy noted above that took books out of the study and into the marketplace as a commodity for mass consumption.[2] As London combined size, literacy, and a relatively liberal regime, it was here that commercialization became apparent earliest. In 1725 Daniel Defoe noted that 'Writing . . . is become a very considerable Branch of the English Commerce. The Booksellers are the Master Manufacturer or Employers. The several Writers, Authors, Copyers, Sub-Writers and all other operators with Pen and Ink are the workmen employed by the said Master-

[1] Roger Chartier, 'Print culture', in Roger Chartier (ed.), *The Culture of Print: Power and the Uses of Print in Early Modern Europe* (Cambridge, 1989), p. 1.

[2] The long delay before Gutenberg's invention had a revolutionary effect is an exceedingly interesting topic but cannot be explored here. For trenchant criticism of the view of Marshall McLuhan, Elisabeth Eisenstein, and Michael Giesecke that the effect was almost immediate, see Uwe Neddermeyer's review of the German translation of Eisenstein's book in *Zeitschrift für Historische Forschung*, 27, 3 (2000), pp. 436–8.

Manufacturers.'[3] By the end of the century these 'Master Manufacturers' had expanded their market to embrace a large proportion of the population. As the London publisher James Lackington noted with satisfaction in his diary in 1791:

I cannot help observing that the sale of books in general has increased prodigiously within the last twenty years. The poorer sort of farmers, and even the poor country people in general who before that period spent their winter evenings in relating stories of witches, ghosts, hobgoblins etc. now shorten the winter nights by hearing their sons and daughters read tales, romances etc., and on entering their houses you may see *Tom Jones, Roderick Random* and other entertaining books, stuck up on their bacon-racks etc. If John goes to town with a load of hay, he is charged to be sure not to forget to bring home *Peregrine Pickle's Adventures*, and when Dolly is sent to market to sell her eggs, she is commissioned to purchase *The History of Joseph Andrews*. In short, all ranks and degrees now READ. But the most rapid increase of the sale of books has been since the termination of the late war [1783].[4]

His impression has been supported by British statistics: during the first decade of the sixteenth century around 400 books were published; by the 1630s that total had risen to 6,000, by the 1710s to 21,000, and by the 1790s to 56,000.[5] The publishing industry of Paris, by contrast, limped along in the rear, shackled by government regulation. The limitation on the number of *librairies* authorized to publish books encouraged their privileged owners to concentrate on milking easy profits from luxury editions. As Paris and Versailles boasted what was probably the greatest concentration of wealth in Europe, the huge margins to be made discouraged commercialization.[6] So did the cumbersome censorship. An aspiring author was required to submit his manuscript to the Chancellor, who appointed a censor from his panel to read it. If it were approved, a certificate of *approbation* was sent back to the

[3] Quoted in Albert Ward, *Book Production, Fiction, and the German Reading Public 1740–1800* (Oxford, 1974), p. 61.

[4] James Lackington, *Memoirs of the first forty-five years of the life of James Lackington, the present bookseller, Finsbury Square, London, written by himself. With a triple dedication. 1. to the public. 2. to respectable booksellers. 3. to sordid booksellers*, 10th edn., 'corrected and much enlarged' (London, 1795), p. 243. Part of this extract is quoted in S. H. Steinberg, *Five Hundred Years of Printing*, new edn., revised by John Trevitt (London, 1996), pp. 119–20.

[5] James Raven, Helen Small, and Naomi Tadmor, 'Introduction: The practice and representation of reading in England', in James Raven, Helen Small, and Naomi Tadmor (eds.), *The Practice and Representation of Reading in England* (Cambridge, 1996), p. 5.

[6] Henri-Jean Martin, 'Livre et lumières en France, à propos de travaux récents', in Giles Barber and Bernhard Fabian (eds.), *Buch und Buchhandel in Europa im achtzehnten Jahrhundert* (Hamburg, 1981), p. 19.

Chancellor, who then issued a privilege to a *libraire* granting an exclusive right to publication for a limited period.[7] Even if eventually successful, this process was long and tiresome, as the censorship bureau 'was staffed with stupid and fearful clerks, anxious to please superiors' and always more inclined to choose the safe option of prohibition rather than risk causing offence.[8] No wonder that Voltaire sighed: 'It is easier for me to write books than to get them published'.[9]

Strait was the gate and narrow was the way that led to officially sanctioned publication in old-regime France, but it was not the only route. Such was the pressure of demand that the government felt obliged to turn a blind eye by granting *permissions tacites* to books not thought worthy of official *approbation* but not so offensive as to justify an outright ban. Even less official was a nod and a wink often given to indicate that a technically illegal book would not be prosecuted.[10] As so often, the old regime contrived to have the worst of all worlds, obstinately maintaining an old-fashioned, authoritarian façade while allowing the demolition teams to enter by the back door. The shift of cultural authority to the public signalled by this uneasy compromise was spelt out in 1759 when the most senior of the government censors, Malesherbes, wrote to his father in a private letter:

> The world of publishing as all other objects of commerce is a good to which everyone has the same right and which is susceptible to no favours. The government only watches over it to maintain public order; and for the concerns of the authors' particular interest, it is necessary to establish equal laws. Success alone makes a difference... only the public is entitled to judge.[11]

Liberal sentiments such as these did not mean that the law could be broken with impunity. Some transgressors escaped undetected or at least unpunished, while others felt the full force of the barbaric penal code. It was just the arbitrary and capricious nature of old-regime law enforcement which made it seem so unjust. In October 1768, for example, the second-hand dealer Jean Lécuyer, his wife Marie Suisse, and the grocer's assistant Jean-Baptiste Josse-vand were sentenced to spend three days chained in the stocks. In addition, the

[7] Robert Shackleton, 'Illustrations of the operation of censorship in eighteenth-century France', in ibid., pp. 187–9.

[8] Peter Gay, *The Enlightenment: An Interpretation*. Vol. 2 : *The Science of Freedom* (New York, 1969), p. 75.

[9] Ibid.

[10] Shackleton, 'Illustrations of the operation of censorship', p. 189.

[11] Quoted in Jack R. Censer, *The French Press in the Age of Enlightenment* (London, 1994), p. 149.

two men were to be branded and sent to the galleys for five and nine years respectively, while Marie Suisse was to be imprisoned for five years. Their crime was to have sold three books 'contrary to good morals and religion', namely Holbach's *Christianity Exposed*, Voltaire's *The Man with Plenty of Money*, and an anti-monastic drama *Éricie or the Vestal Virgin*.[12]

The offending merchandise had been imported from Amsterdam, thus revealing another way in which French readers could evade government censorship. Two great waves of immigration—of Walloons from the southern Netherlands during the Dutch revolt of the late sixteenth century and of Huguenots after Louis XIV's revocation of the Edict of Nantes in 1685—had created several large French-speaking communities in the Dutch Republic. Literate, enterprising, and the beneficiaries of a regime more interested in commerce than conformity, they were well placed to cater to the needs of the growing reading public in France. The same was true of other Francophone communities, in Prussian-ruled Cleves or Neuchâtel, for example, or even in Calvinist Geneva. Indeed, it has been argued persuasively that this 'fertile crescent of printing houses which arched around France from Amsterdam to Avignon' was more important as a source of French-language literature than was Paris.[13] Almost all the great works of the French Enlightenment were first published outside France, both a damning indictment of the old regime and not the least important explanation of its eventual collapse.

The French frontier was so long and demand for the forbidden fruit so strong that, even if the customs officials had been models of efficiency and probity, the task of staunching the flow of contraband would have been beyond them. Yet their task was straightforward compared with that of their German colleagues, confronted by the most fragmented polity in Europe. Wisely, most of them did not try to enforce the impossible, with the result that almost anything could be published somewhere in the Holy Roman Empire. This

[12] John Lough, *An Introduction to Eighteenth Century France* (London, 1960), p. 306. Although this excellent book seems to have escaped the attention of recent historians of the book, chapters 7 and 8—entitled 'The writer and his public' and 'Literature and ideas' respectively—contain the best account of their subject available in any language. Not the least of their advantages is the ability of their author to express himself lucidly and cogently, without resort to jargon and without making simple ideas seem immensely complex. It should be noted that the works in question were not pornographic *libelles* from the gutter but were written by members of what we are told we must call the 'high Enlightenment'. On this topic, see below, pp. 413–15.

[13] The phrase is Robert Darnton's, but the argument is developed most fully by Elizabeth Eisenstein in *Grub Street Abroad: Aspects of the French Cosmopolitan Press from the Age of Louis XIV to the French Revolution* (Oxford, 1992), *passim*. Indeed, she is sharply critical of Darnton's approach for its neglect of ideas.

cheering argument in favour of cultural pluralism did not go unnoticed. In 1814 the publisher Friedrich Perthes recalled with nostalgia: 'In practice, Germany enjoyed complete freedom of the press, because what could not be published in Prussia could be published in Württemberg, and what could not be published in Hamburg could be published ten paces away in [Danish-ruled] Altona. No book remained unpublished, none undistributed.'[14] On the other hand, the lack of a national market or even a unified currency impeded development of the German book trade in certain respects. Until late in the eighteenth century, for example, most transactions between book-dealers were carried out on a barter basis at one or other of the main book-fairs held at Frankfurt am Main and Leipzig. Only gradually did the volume of business make cash the accepted medium of exchange, and even more slowly did the multi-functional entrepreneur make way for specialist publishers, printers, and booksellers.[15] By the end of the century, however, something approaching a modern system had developed. In a lecture delivered in 1805, Fichte observed that: 'during the second half of the previous century, reading emerged to supplant other pastimes which were falling out of fashion ... This new need gave rise to a new branch of business, namely the book trade, which sought to sustain and enrich itself by supplying new commodities.'[16]

These general impressions of a revolutionary change in the production of books can be supported by statistical evidence. The most dramatic rates of growth were naturally achieved in those parts of Europe where the base figures were lowest. They could hardly have been lower than in the Russian Empire, where the printing press arrived more than a century after its invention and where fewer than 500 titles (almost all of them devotional) had been produced in the entire seventeenth century.[17] If the number of books published in 1800 was still far below the scores achieved by western Europe, at least there had been a significant increase (see Table 1). The modest annual average can be made to seem rather more impressive if the period is divided into three, for that reveals that the average rose from 29.9 titles between 1725 and 1754 to 139.6 between 1756 and 1775 and to 313.8 between 1776 and 1800.[18]

[14] H. Kiesel and P. Münch, *Gesellschaft und Literatur im 18. Jahrhundert* (Munich, 1977), p. 118.

[15] Ibid., pp. 124–5.

[16] Quoted in Johann Goldfriedrich, *Geschichte des deutschen Buchhandels vom Beginn der klassischen Literaturperiode bis zum Beginn der Fremdherrschaft (1740–1804)* (Leipzig, 1909), p. 247.

[17] Gary Marker, *Publishing, Printing and the Origins of Intellectual Life in Russia 1700–1800* (Princeton, NJ, 1985), pp. 8, 19.

[18] Ibid, pp. 68, 72, 106.

TABLE 1. *Publishing in Russia, 1725–1800*

Years	*Number of books published*	*Annual average*
1725–9	87	17·4
1730–4	127	25·4
1735–9	107	21·4
1740–4	223	44·6
1745–9	177	35·4
1750–4	175	35
1756–60	262	52·4
1761–5	805	161
1766–70	767	153·4
1771–5	958	191.6
1776–80	1198	240
1781–5	1315	263
1786–90	1936	387
1791–5	1865	373
1796–1800	1531	306
TOTAL	11533	153·77

In France, figures are hard to come by, for the official sector accounted for only a limited part of the total output and did not reflect the true state of the book trade, given the large numbers of books produced outside the country for consumption inside it. We have to make do with confident but vague statements that the number of titles increased from 500 in 1700 to more than 1,000 in 1771, or that it 'doubled' between mid-century and the Revolution, or that the number of books published with *permission tacite* increased 'very rapidly' after 1760.[19] It is from Germany that both the most precise and the most arresting data come. It is some measure of the havoc wreaked on the Holy

[19] Daniel Roche, 'Censorship and the publishing industry', in Robert Darnton (ed.), *Revolution in Print: The Press in France 1775–1800* (Berkeley, Los Angeles, and London, 1989), p. 7; Roger Chartier and Daniel Roche, 'Livre et presse: véhicules des idées', in *Seventh International Congress on the Enlightenment: Introductory Papers. Budapest 26 July–2 August 1987* (Oxford, 1987), p. 94; Henri-Jean Martin, 'Livre et lumières en France, à propos de travaux récents', in Barber and Fabian (eds.), *Buch und Buchhandel in Europa im achtzehnten Jahrhundert*, p. 12.

Roman Empire by the Thirty Years War that it was not until 1765 that the level of book production achieved in 1620 was reached once more. It was just in the 1760s, however, that a rapid and sustained increase began, yielding fully two-thirds of the 175,000 titles produced during the eighteenth century.[20] If pamphlets, periodicals, newspapers, and other ephemera are added, it has been estimated that around half a million printed publications reached the German market in the course of the century.[21]

This quantitative transformation of the world of books brought with it a qualitative consequence of equal importance. Because there were now so many more books available, both the readers and the way in which they read changed. When few titles were produced in small and expensive editions, the texts were read again and again, mainly for the purposes of devotion, instruction, and edification. The typical readers were the priests with their breviaries, the lawyers with their handbooks, or the faithful with their Bibles. In short, they read intensively. Once there were thousands of titles available, produced in larger and cheaper editions, new kinds of readers joined in, looking for topical information, practical advice, and recreation, reading books once and then discarding them. In short, they read extensively. This sea change in reading habits was apparent to contemporaries, none expressing it more clearly that Johann Gottfried Pahl, who, in an essay entitled 'Why is the German nation in our period so rich in writers and books?' wrote:

> In times gone by, no one took up reading who was not already a real academic or aspired to become one. The rest of the nation contented themselves with the Bible and a few books of moral instruction. But now the situation is quite different. The various branches of knowledge have ceased to be the possession of a specific estate and at least a superficial knowledge of them is deemed necessary for all educated people... This love of reading, now so widely diffused, has created the need for a large number of new books especially because the new breed of Germans do not read in the manner of their ancestors. The latter used to study carefully the books they took up, read them several times and only put them down once their propositions and arguments had sunk into their very bones. But we have got used to reading in a hurry. We skim through a book, don't go beyond the surface, pull out bits which the table of contents suggests are particularly entertaining, then start yawning and switch to something else, because it is only novelty which stimulates us. And it is this style of reading which is bound to increase the need for a large number of books.[22]

[20] Kiesel and Münch, *Gesellschaft und Literatur im 18. Jahrhundert*, p. 181.

[21] Hans-Ulrich Wehler, *Deutsche Gesellschaftsgeschichte*. Vol. I: *Vom Feudalismus des Alten Reiches bis zur defensiven Modernisierung der Reformära 1700–1815* (Munich, 1987), p. 304.

[22] Quoted in Erich Schön, *Der Verlust der Sinnlichkeit, oder Die Verwandlungen des Lesers. Mentalitätswandel um 1800* (Stuttgart, 1987), pp. 298–9. The importance of this development

The same point was made in verse by George Crabbe in *The Library* (1781):

> Our patient Fathers trifling themes laid by,
> And roll'd o'er labour'd works th'attentive eye;
> Page after page, the much-enduring men
> Explor'd the deeps and shallows of the pen;
>
> Our nicer palates lighter labours seek,
> Cloy'd with a Folio-number once a week;
> Bibles with cuts and comments thus go down,
> E'en light Voltaire is number'd through the town
>
> See yonder, rang'd in more frequented rows,
> An humbler band of Duodecimos;
> While undistinguish'd trifles swell the scene,
> The last new Play, and fritter'd Magazine.[23]

has escaped some historians of the book. In a remarkably obtuse passage, Robert Darnton has criticized Rolf Engelsing's thesis of a change from intensive to extensive reading, but his only counter-argument is the suggestion that readers of the emotional novels of Richardson or Rousseau read with even greater intensity than in the past; Robert Darnton, 'First steps towards a history of reading', *Australian Journal of French Studies*, 23, 1 (1986), p. 12. From this article one can only conclude that he is unable to tell the difference between 'intensively' and 'intensely'. He has returned to the issue in his recent book *The Forbidden Best-sellers of Pre-revolutionary France* (London, 1996), pp. 218–19, but again cannot rise above the level of assertion. His eagerness to dismiss the distinction between extensive and intensive reading appears to derive from his belief that one who reads a large number of publications might be held not to take their message seriously, which of course would undermine his belief that the old regime in France was destroyed by pornographers. For further criticism of this position, see James Van Horn Melton, *Politics, Culture and the Public Sphere in Enlightenment Europe* (Cambridge, 2000) and Reinhard Wittmann, 'Was there a reading revolution at the end of the eighteenth century?' in Guglielmo Cavallo and Roger Chartier (eds.), *A History of Reading in the West* (Amherst, Mass., 1999), p. 286.

[23] Certain favoured texts could still be read intensively, of course, especially those with a didactic purpose. An excellent example was provided by Gabriel Betteredge, the elderly house-steward of Lady Verinder and narrator of the first part of Wilkie Collins's *The Moonstone* (first published in 1868):

> You are not to take it, if you please, as the saying of an ignorant man, when I express my opinion that such a book as *Robinson Crusoe* never was written, and never will be written again. I have tried that book for years—generally in combination with a pipe of tobacco—and I have found it my friend in need in all the necessities of this mortal life. When my spirits are bad—*Robinson Crusoe*. When I want advice—*Robinson Crusoe*. In past times, when my wife plagued me; in present times, when I have had a drop too much—*Robinson Crusoe*. I have worn out six stout *Robinson Crusoes* with hard work in my service. On my lady's last birthday she gave me a seventh. I took a drop too much on the strength of it; and *Robinson Crusoe* put me right again. Price four shillings and sixpence, bound in blue, with a picture into the bargain.

Yet even Betteredge had also read 'a heap' of other books.

It was a mode of reading which both generated and was encouraged by the spread of lending libraries, very much a phenomenon of the eighteenth century (Plate 9). By 1800 it was estimated by the *Monthly Magazine* that there were at least 1,000 in Great Britain. They spread on the continent with comparable rapidity: at the same period there were nine in Leipzig, ten in Bremen, and eighteen in Frankfurt am Main.[24] One reason for the ability—or perhaps 'temptation' would be a better word—to read extensively rather than intensively was the increased use of the vernacular. It was in the eighteenth century that the domination of the printed word by Latin was finally broken. Before 1500 more than three-quarters of all books published had been written in Latin; by 1800 the figure was well below 10 per cent.[25] In France, even pornography was still being published first in Latin in the middle of the seventeenth century, but a decisive shift to the vernacular was apparent by 1700: Henri-Jean Martin's graph shows the percentage of books published in Latin falling from 35 per cent in 1600 to less than 10 per cent by 1700.[26] His colleague, Dominique Julia, states firmly that by the latter date, Latin had ceased to be used as a living language.[27] In German-speaking Europe it lingered longer, but fell sharply after 1700. The titles of books appearing in the fair catalogues reveal the pattern shown in Table 2.[28] This decline of works in Latin took down with it works on theology. Between the early seventeenth century and 1800, four categories of publications (law, medicine, history, and music) were relatively stable in terms of market share and three (theology, philosophy, and fiction) were much more volatile. Of the latter group, theology was the biggest loser and fiction the biggest winner, as the review of the book-fair catalogues in Table 3 demonstrates:[29]

[24] Wittmann, 'Was there a reading revolution at the end of the eighteenth century?', p. 307.

[25] Lucien Febvre and Henri-Jean Martin, *The Coming of the Book. The impact of printing 1450–1800* (London, 1976), p. 249.

[26] The book in question was *L'Académie des dames*, first published in Latin in 1660 and in French in 1680; Robert Darnton, *The Forbidden Best-sellers of Pre-revolutionary France* (London, 1996), p. 86. Henri-Jean Martin, 'Une croissance séculaire', in Henri-Jean Martin and Roger Chartier (eds.), *Histoire de l'édition française*. Vol. II: *Le livre triomphant 1660–1830* (Paris, 1984), p. 95.

[27] Dominique Julia, 'Livres de classe et usage périodiques', in ibid., II, p. 485.

[28] Schön, *Der Verlust der Sinnlichkeit*, p. 38.

[29] This table is based on Kiesel and Münch, *Gesellschaft und Literatur im 18. Jahrhundert*, p. 200.

TABLE 2. *The percentage of Latin titles published in Germany, 1600–1800*

1600	71
1625	61
1637	54
1650	67
1658	60
1673	58
1681	48
1690	37
1700	38
1740	28
1770	14
1800	4

THE NOVEL

Concealed by the blanket term *belles lettres* is the fact that the literary genre which really triumphed in the eighteenth century was the novel. In the German or French languages it is known as *roman*, which reveals that in part it derived from 'romances', fantastic stories of chivalric derring-do, whereas the English form reveals its other parent—the *novella* or short stories for popular reading, often issued in collections. The modern novel, as it emerged in the first half of the eighteenth century, combined realism with substance, thus justifying Mary McCarthy's definition of the novel as 'a prose book of a certain thickness that tells a story of real life'.[30] It was this reproduction of the modern world in a work of the imagination masquerading as factual *reportage* which impressed contemporaries most. The novelist Clara Reeve (1729–1807) expressed this essential characteristic with especial clarity in *The Progress of Romance*, published in 1785:

The Novel is a picture of real life and manners, and of the times in which it is written. The Romance in lofty and elevated language, describes what never happened nor is

[30] Quoted in Ronald Paulson, *Satire and the Novel in Eighteenth Century England* (New Haven and London, 1967), p. 11.

TABLE 3. *Publishing in Germany, 1625–1800*

Subject	1625	1650	1675	1700	1725	1735	1740	1745	1750	1775	1800
Law	7.4	7.0	11.0	8.6	10.6	8.5	12.0	10.7	8.0	6.2	3.5
Medicine	7.5	5.8	8.3	6.0	8.6	5.3	7.6	6.0	8.0	6.5	4.9
History and related disciplines*	12.0	20.0	14.7	16.0	16.8	18.7	16.6	14.2	16.0	16.2	15.7
Music	3.1	3.8	2.2	3.5	0.4	0.8	1.1	1.3	3.7	2.8	3.0
Theology†	45.8	41.4	40.5	43	39.9	40.5	32.9	31.0	28.9	19.9	6.0
Philosophy‡	18.8	16.9	19.8	20.1	20.1	22.6	25.9	30.4	26.7	34.1	39.6
Belles lettres	5.4	5.1	3.5	2.8	3.6	3.6	3.9	6.4	8.7	14.3	27.3

* Deemed to include biography, ancient history, political science, geography, and travel literature.

† This category contains work devoted solely to theology. It should be borne in mind that many works in other categories, such as history and law, were also concerned very much with religious isues.

‡ Deemed to include education, philology, the natural sciences, economics, technology, mathematics, war, commerce, and 'miscellaneous'.

likely to happen.—The Novel gives a familiar relation of such things, as pass every day before our eyes, such as may happen to our friend, or to ourselves; and the perfection of it, is to represent every scene, in so easy and natural a manner, and to make them appear so probable, as to deceive us into a persuasion (at least while we are reading) that all is real, until we are affected by the joys or distress, of the persons in the story, as if they were our own.[31]

Prose fiction of the seventeenth century had been the preserve of gentlemen scholars, expected to be able to understand classical allusions and quotations from Greek, Latin, or French; the fully-fledged novel of the eighteenth century was accessible to all who could read.[32] There is no need to join the endless debate on which work deserves the title of 'the first novel'. In the French language, the accolade usually goes to *La princesse de Clèves*, written by Marie-Madeleine de La Fayette and published anonymously in 1678. It may well be that this intense story of extramarital love was 'the real catalyst of public recognition that a new kind of narrative genre was becoming dominant',[33] but its setting—the mid-sixteenth-century court of Henri II—was too remote and refined to make a major impact on the reading public that existed. It was not until the 1730s, when several best-sellers were published (most notably Prévost's *Manon Lescaut*) that the French novel can be said to have come of age.[34] By that time the lead had been taken by England. The burst of creativity represented by Daniel Defoe's *Robinson Crusoe* (1719), *Moll Flanders* (1722), and *Roxana* (1724); Jonathan Swift's *Gulliver's Travels* (1726); Samuel Richardson's *Pamela* (1740), *Clarissa* (1748), and *Sir Charles Grandison* (1753); Henry Fielding's *Joseph Andrews* (1742), *Jonathan Wild* (1743), and *Tom Jones* (1749); Tobias Smollett's *Roderick Random* (1748) and *Peregrine Pickle* (1751); and Laurence Sterne's *Tristram Shandy* (1760–7) and *A Sentimental Journey* (1768) made the novel the English literary genre *par excellence*.

Of all those works, both the most influential and the most revealing was Richardson's *Pamela*. Such was his concern with realism that he presented himself not as the author but merely as 'the editor' of a collection of letters written by the eponymous heroine. This also accounts in part for the novel's

[31] Ibid., p. 12.

[32] Ward, *Book Production, Fiction and the German Reading Public*, p. 1.

[33] John D. Lyons, '*La princesse de Clèves* is published anonymously', in Denis Hollier (ed.), *A New History of French Literature* (Cambridge, Mass., and London, 1989), p. 350.

[34] S. P. Jones, *A List of French Prose Fiction from 1700 to 1750* (New York, 1939) lists 946 titles for 1700–50, while A. Martin, V. H. G. Mylne, and R. Frautschi, *Bibliographie du genre romanesque français 1751–1800* (London and Paris, 1977) list 2,663 new works and 4,860 reprints for 1750–1800; Knabe (ed.), *Frankreich im Zeitalter der Aufklärung*, p. 158.

great length (about a quarter of a million words), for authenticity demanded that the letter-writer include much apparent trivia and not just the narrative core. However, the simple plot can be quickly summarized: Pamela is a poor but honest, god-fearing girl, who resists her lascivious master's repeated attempts on her virtue, despite experiencing a growing attraction towards him. As the novel's subtitle—*Virtue Rewarded*—suggests, it all ends happily, with the virtuous Pamela savouring the licit delights of the marriage-bed. Although usually regarded as unreadable, it is in fact a gripping story, well worthy of its best-seller status.

It must be conceded, however, that modern readers taking the plunge will be less impressed than were contemporaries by its strong didactic purpose. By making *Pamela* a secular sermon, Richardson was able to overcome the strong reservations felt by many of his readers about the morality of works of fiction. Indeed, he presented this purpose in a preface serving as a manifesto:

> If to *divert* and *entertain*, and at the same time to *instruct* and *improve* the minds of the YOUTH of *both sexes*:
>
> If to inculcate *religion* and *morality* in so easy and agreeable a manner, as shall render them equally *delightful* and *profitable*:
>
> If to set forth in the most exemplary lights, the *parental*, the *filial*, and the *social* duties:
>
> If to paint VICE in its proper colours, to make it *deservedly odious*; and to set VIRTUE in its own amiable light, to make it look *lovely*...
>
> If these be laudable or worthy recommendations, the *Editor* of the following letters, which have their foundation both in *Truth* and *Nature*, ventures to assert, that all these ends are obtained here, together.[35]

In was not in spite of but because of this HEAVY-HANDED emphasis on the MORAL PURPOSE of Richardson's novel that it aroused such a powerful and immediate response across Europe. Translated rapidly into all the major languages, it was also dramatized for theatrical presentation by Nivelle de la Chaussée in France and no less a figure than Goldoni in Italy (as *Pamela fanciulla* and *Pamela maritata*). In Germany, the powerful strain of Pietist religiosity created an especially receptive audience. Christian Fürchtegott Gellert, himself the author of one of the first sentimental novels in the German language (*The Swedish Countess von G****), wrote a panegyric entitled 'On Richardson's portrait', including the fulsome lines:

[35] Samuel Richardson, *Pamela, or Virtue Rewarded*, ed. Peter Sabor (Harmondsworth, 1980), p. 31.

The works which he created time cannot wither,
For they are nature, taste, religion.
Homer is immortal, yet more immortal still for Christians is
The Briton Richardson.[36]

This verdict was echoed by no less an authority than Denis Diderot, who in his *Panegyric of Richardson* gave him the credit for transforming the status of the novel as a literary form: 'Until now, the novel has been thought of as a tissue of inconsequential and frivolous events, the reading of which was dangerous for both one's taste and one's morals. So I would like to find another word to describe Richardson's works, for they elevate the spirit, touch the soul, are imbued with a love of what is good, yet are still referred to as "novels".'[37] The lubricant which allowed Richardson's moral lessons to gain entry to his readers' psyche was sensibility, a readiness to give the emotions priority and to express them without restraint. If not the inventor of a mood which became something of a cult during the middle decades of the eighteenth century, Richardson was certainly a major beneficiary. Although apparently at odds with the simultaneous cult of reason, it was in reality its complement: 'Perhaps the best way to understand the importance given to *sensibilité* is to view it as an emotional force or energy by which people could do the good portrayed by reason'.[38] Pamela herself was something of a role model in this regard, helping to make weeping, shrieking, breast-beating, hair-tearing, and clothes-rending all part of the *sensibilité* repertoire. Any writer able to create a novel in harmony with this responsive chord was sure of a large audience. As the bookseller in Thomas Bridges's *The Adventures of a Bank-Note* (1770–1) claimed: 'a crying volume... brings me more money in six months than a heavy merry thing will do in six years'.[39]

No eighteenth-century volume opened more tear-ducts than *Julie, ou la nouvelle Héloïse: Lettres de deux amants, habitants d'une petite ville au pied des Alpes. Recueillies et publiées par J. J. Rousseau* ('Julie, or the new Héloïse: letters exchanged by two lovers, living in a small town at the foot of the Alps. Collected and published by J. J. Rousseau'). This lachrymose epistolary novel was directly inspired by Richardson but went much further in its range of

[36] Quoted in Sven Aage Jørgensen, Klaus Bohnen, and Per Øhrgaard, *Aufklärung, Sturm und Drang, frühe Klassik 1740–1789* (Munich, 1990), p. 180.

[37] Denis Diderot, 'Éloge de Richardson, auteur des romans de *Paméla*, de *Clarisse* et de *Grandisson*', in *Œuvres complètes. Édition chronologique*, ed. Roger Lewinter (Paris, 1970), p. 127.

[38] Emmet Kennedy, *A Cultural History of the French Revolution* (New Haven and London, 1989), p. 105.

[39] Quoted in Janet Todd, *Sensibility: An Introduction* (London, 1986), p. 88.

social and emotional references. Unlike Pamela or Clarissa, Julie was the daughter of a titled aristocrat; unlike them, she was neither married nor raped by her lover but gave herself gladly to a man of humbler social station; unlike them, she was forced into marriage, albeit to a man of noble character; unlike them, she neither lived happily ever after (Pamela) nor died in misery (Clarissa) but gave her life to save her child. In short, Julie was a heroine of quite a different order. Voltaire may have said that he would rather kill himself than finish it, but dozens of editions and translations showed that he was the one who was out of step with the reading public of Europe. Indeed it was 'probably the record best-seller of the whole of the eighteenth century'.[40]

Yet poor Rousseau, as ever cross-grained and cross-gartered, made only the paltry sum of 2,000 *livres* from *La Nouvelle Héloïse*, the sum paid to him by his Amsterdam publisher for the first edition.[41] From the pirate editions which then flooded the market from all directions he received not a *sou*, *Pfennig*, or penny. It was no better in Germany. Goethe published his first great success, the play *Götz von Berlichingen*, himself, but did not know how to market it, so was left with a huge stock of unsold copies. Yet when the word got around that it was a sensation, the pirates quickly moved in to saturate the market with illicit copies from which the author reaped nothing. Suitably chastened, Goethe turned to a regular publisher with his next offering, the epistolary novel *The Sufferings of Young Werther*. This proved to be even more successful, quickly becoming the German equivalent of *La Nouvelle Héloïse* and the first book in the German language to be an international best-seller. Alas, the small print in Goethe's agreement with Weygand made it hopelessly one-sided and he probably only just made enough to cover his losses on *Götz*.[42] Novelists fortunate enough to live in England did rather better: Henry Fielding, for example, received £183 10s 10d for *Joseph Andrews* (or about 4,400 *livres*), £700 (16,800 *livres*) for *Tom Jones*, and £1,000 (24,000 *livres*) for *Amelia*.[43] But here too writers needed to keep their wits about them if they were to capitalize on their success in the markets. Richardson, Smollett, and Sterne all made good money from their novels, and Gay did well out of *The Beggar's Opera* and even better out of the sequel *Polly*, but Defoe sold his

[40] Lough, *An Introduction to Eighteenth Century France*, p. 243.

[41] Ibid., p. 242.

[42] Reinhard Wittmann, *Geschichte des deutschen Buchhandels. Ein Überblick* (Munich, 1991), p. 162.

[43] Steinberg, *Five Hundred Years of Printing*, p. 156. After 1726 £1 = 24 *livres*; Lough, *An Introduction to Eighteenth Century France*, p. vi.

copyrights for very little; it was his publisher who made a fortune from *Robinson Crusoe*.[44]

Rousseau, Goethe, and Richardson sold tens of thousands of copies, but they did not represent the typical novelist. Long forgotten but at the time more important were the dim galaxies of lesser lights, less concerned to 'investigate the great doctrines of Christianity under the fashionable guise of an amusement', as Richardson expressed his objective in the epilogue to *Clarissa*, than to give the public what they wanted.[45] It was the hack writer turning out novels with both eyes on the market who prompted Goldsmith to complain about 'that fatal revolution whereby writing is converted to a mechanic trade'.[46] It was they who followed the precepts of Mr Fudge in Goldsmith's *The Citizen of the World* (1761): 'Others may pretend to direct the vulgar, but that is not my way: I always let the vulgar direct me; wherever popular clamour arises, I always echo the million.'[47] It was a formula with a long and glittering future. By 1790 the *Monthly Review* could complain that the market was awash with novels:

> Novels spring into existence like insects on the banks of the Nile; and, if we may be indulged in another comparison, cover the shelves of our circulating libraries, as locusts crowd the fields of Asia. Their great and growing number is a serious evil; for, in general, they exhibit delusive views of human life; and while they amuse, frequently poison the mind.[48]

Sheridan observed in 1775 that the circulating library was 'an evergreen tree of diabolical knowledge', while the conservative Swiss bookseller Johann Georg Heinzmann placed the novel on a par with the French Revolution as a cause of human misery: 'For as long as the world has existed, there have been no phenomena so remarkable as the reading of novels in Germany and the Revolution in France. They have evolved more or less simultaneously, and it is not beyond the bounds of probability that novels have been just as much the cause of unhappiness to people in secret as the terrible French Revolution has been publicly.'[49] Lamentations that popularization meant vulgarization were

[44] Terry Belanger, 'Publishers and writers in eighteenth century England', in Isabel Rivers (ed.), *Books and their Readers in Eighteenth Century England* (Leicester, 1982), p. 22. James Van Horn Melton, *Politics, Culture and the Public Sphere in Enlightenment Europe* (Cambridge, 2001).

[45] John Feather, *A History of British Publishing* (London, 1988), p. 96.

[46] Quoted in Raymond Williams, *The Long Revolution* (London, 1961), p. 162.

[47] Quoted in James Raven, *Judging New Wealth: Popular Publishing and Responses to Commerce in England, 1750–1800* (Oxford, 1992), p. 66.

[48] Quoted in ibid., p. 68.

[49] Quoted in James Raven, 'From promotion to proscription: arrangements for reading and eighteenth century libraries', in Raven, Small, and Tadmor (eds.), *The Practice and Representation*

often given an added edge by misogyny, for it was the novel above all which gave women access to literature as both producers and consumers. In the seventeenth century, the subject-matter of baroque drama, whether secular or religious, classical or courtly, poetry or devotional literature, had been predominantly masculine. The eighteenth-century novel's concern with the 'real' world of the here and now, especially with family relationships, both moved women to the centre of attention and allowed them to write about their own experiences.[50] If woman's role in seventeenth-century literature is best symbolized by Milton's daughter taking dictation from her blind father, a hundred years on novelists such as Eliza Haywood, Charlotte Lennox, Frances Brooke, Sarah Fielding, the Minifie sisters, Maria Cooper, Jean Marishall, Phoebe Gibbs, and Maria Edgeworth had established reputations—and sales—the equal of most of their male colleagues.[51] One of the most durable German novels of the eighteenth century was Sophie La Roche's *Die Geschichte des Fräuleins von Sternheim* ('The story of Miss von Sternheim'), while in France, Marie-Madeleine de La Fayette found many successors, among them Françoise de Graffigny, Marie-Jeanne Riccoboni, Marie Leprince de Beaumont, and Anne-Louise Elie de Beaumont.[52]

As most middle- and upper-class women enjoyed more leisure than their menfolk, the multi-volume novels of Richardson or Fielding presented less of a challenge. Certainly book-sellers noticed the growing proportion of female customers and adjusted their stock accordingly. The flamboyant James Lackington, who hung a flag outside his shop in Finsbury Square bearing the message 'The cheapest book-shop in the world', found a couplet to describe the phenomenon:

> Learning, once the man's exclusive pride,
> Seems verging fast towards the female side.[53]

This was something he welcomed and he was quick to defend his customers against the charge that they were interested only in trivial ephemera:

of Reading in England, p. 179; Wittmann, 'Was there a reading revolution at the end of the eighteenth century?', p. 284.

[50] On the new concern with femininity in the eighteenth century, see Dorinda Outram, *The Enlightenment* (Cambridge, 1995), ch. 6.

[51] Raven, *Judging New Wealth*, p. 23.

[52] Jørgensen, Bohnen, and Øhrgaard, *Aufklärung, Sturm und Drang, frühe Klassik*, p. 180; Joan Hinde Stewart, 'Designing women', in Hollier (ed.), *A New History of French Literature*, p. 553.

[53] Lackington, *Memoirs of the first forty-five years*, p. 248.

KING ALFRED'S COLLEGE
LIBRARY

Ladies now in general read, not only novels, although many of that class are excellent productions, and tend to polish both the heart and head; but they also read the best books in the English language, and many read the best works in various languages; and there are some thousands of ladies, who frequent my shop, that know as well what books to choose, and are as well acquainted with works of taste and genius, as any gentlemen in the kingdom, notwithstanding they sneer against novel readers etc.[54]

Lackington was the classic case of an entrepreneur who made a fortune from the new literary market. As he proclaimed in the caption to his portrait, which formed the frontispiece of his autobiography, he was a man 'Who a few years since began business with five pounds and now sells One Hundred Thousand Volumes Yearly'. He did so by the simple but effective expedient of stacking them high and selling them cheap. On entering the trade as a young man, he found that publishers left with large stocks of unsold titles preferred to destroy most and sell a few at the full price. By buying up the remainders and marking them down, he found he was able to open up a new and lucrative market based on low margins but high volume.[55] He was not alone. John Pendred's *The London and Country Printers, Booksellers and Stationers Vade Mecum*, published in 1785, listed nearly 650 businesses in London engaged in thirty-two different occupations connected with book-selling.[56] As the mediator between writer and public, Lackington was proud of his calling: no mere tradesman he, but an agent of culture. It was a view shared by other high-profile book-sellers such as Friedrich Nicolai of Berlin. 'Madame Folio' of Paris, a book-seller of the Place du vieux Louvre, defended her customers in a pamphlet written in the course of the *querelle des bouffons*[57] against the charge that they formed part of *l'imbécile public*:

The voice of the public is the voice of truth, it has always been feared and respected by both the warrior and the man of letters, because the public alone has the incontestable right to decide which actions and which publications deserve the accolade of heroism and immortality respectively; it is the public alone which has the right to judge whether a work will be passed down to posterity or whether it will go straight from the printer to the grocer to be used as wrapping-paper.

You affect contempt for my customers, she went on, but—now expressing herself in verse:

[54] Ibid., p. 251.

[55] Ibid., p. 268.

[56] John Brewer, *The Pleasures of the Imagination. English Culture in the Eighteenth Century* (London, 1997), p. 138.

[57] See below, pp. 357–74.

Lawyers, financiers, and churchmen,
Burghers, physicians and all the people of fashion,
Pay me a visit every day
And the intellect, taste and wit
Of this select body
Are just as good as those of the Academy.[58]

PERIODICALS AND NEWSPAPERS

By buying cut-price books from 'the cheapest book-shop in the world' or Madame Foliot (*sic*), consumers could now read extensively. They could do so to even greater effect by purchasing one of the thousands of newspapers and other periodicals published during the course of the century. Predictably, there is no clear contender for the title of 'first in the field'. If the essence of a periodical publication is its continuous relationship with the reader, then precursors such as the 'relation' or the 'coranto', which can be found as early as the sixteenth century, are disqualified.[59] It was during the early decades of the seventeenth century that the transition from sporadic to regular publication occurred in several parts of western and central Europe. Uncontroversial milestones on the road to a fully fledged periodical press were: in the Low Countries, the regular weekly publication from 1617 of the *Nieuwe Tydinghe* of Antwerp, which had appeared fitfully since 1605; in Germany, the appearance of the *Frankfurter Postzeitung* in 1615; in England, the regular publication of newsbooks in the 1620s; in France, the appearance of the *Gazette de France* in 1631, the *Journal des Savants* in 1665, and the relaunch of the *Mercure français* (which had first appeared as an annual in 1611) as the quarterly *Mercure Galant* in 1672; in Italy, the appearance in Turin in 1645 of the first newspaper with a title—the *Successi del mondo*—untitled news-sheets having been published since the previous decade.[60]

[58] *Ce que l'on doit dire. Réponse de Madame Foliot [sic] à la lettre de Monsieur**** (1753), reprinted in Denise Launay (ed.), *La Querelle des bouffons*, 3 vols (Geneva, 1973), I, pp. 3–4.

[59] Anthony Smith, *The Newspaper: An International History* (London, 1979), p. 9.

[60] Louis Trenard, 'La presse française des origines à 1788', in Claude Bellanger, Jacques Godechot, Pierre Guiral, and Fernand Terrou (eds.), *Histoire générale de la presse française*. Vol. I: *Des origines à 1814* (Paris, 1969), pp. 78–9, 90, 126; Charles Ledré, *Histoire de la presse* (Paris, 1958), p. 27; Giuliano Gaeta, *Storia del giornalismo*, vol. I (Milan, 1966), p. 143; Michael Harris, 'The structure, ownership and control of the press, 1620–1780', in George Boyce, James Curran, and Pauline Wingate (eds.), *Newspaper History from the Seventeenth Century to the Present Day* (London, 1978), p. 83.

By 1700 Pierre Bayle, who since 1684 had published the *Nouvelles de la République des Lettres* ('News of the Republic of Letters') from his exile in Rotterdam, observed that 'The number of *mercures*, and publications which deserved to be classified as such, has multiplied so greatly that it is time to investigate the phenomenon [*qu'on donnât l'histoire*] ... The number of gazettes which are now being published all over Europe is extraordinary.'[61] It was a development clearly visible to the naked eye of contemporary observers. Every generation in the eighteenth century commented on the proliferation of both the number of periodicals and their readers. This developing perception needs to be emphasized, for it also revealed a developing sense of a reading public. From the rich range of illustrations available, the following selection provide a good flavour of the degree of self-consciousness involved:

Lackeys, stable-boys, janitors, gardeners and night-watchmen now get together and talk about the latest news-sheets ... As a result they are more arrogant than the town's mayor, believing they know and understand much more about matters of state than he does. (Kaspar Stieler, *On the Pleasure and Utility of Newspapers*, 1695)

I believe that there is not a nation in Europe today which does not have one or more newspapers. Everyone wishes to be informed about what is going on; indeed it is just those who are removed from power by estate or material circumstances who are often the most anxious for news, and society in general has got so used to the *Gazette* that they would regard its suppression as an occasion for public mourning. (Denis-François Camusat, *Histoire critique des journaux* (Amsterdam, 1734))

Fifty years ago, members of the general public had no interest in political news, but today everyone reads his *Gazette de Paris*, even in the provinces. And although their opinions are quite misguided, they do take an interest in political matters. (Marquis d'Argenson in his journal, 1749)

The taste for journals, for newspapers, for every kind of periodical publication shows no sign of slackening, and far from proliferation being checked by satiation of the market, it expands unchecked. (Meusnier de Querlon, 1774)

Periodicals have become the store-cupboards of human understanding ... anyone seeking information about any kind of subject can seek refuge in this repository with confidence and will certainly not come away unenlightened or dissatisfied ... It is through periodicals that knowledge which used to be the property of academics ... has been brought into general circulation ... The public exposure and censure of many a crime against justice, humanity, scholarship and common sense has had a most beneficial effect on the lower orders, for they have got to know the rights of man, they have been alerted to many an abuse and have learned to appreciate that

[61] Quoted in Trenard, 'La presse française des origines à 1788', p. 159.

much of what they used to think was useful and laudable was in reality foolish, detrimental, and immoral and so have become inclined to change it. A popular and much-read weekly journal can achieve more than all the books and all the laws. (Johann Heinrich Christoph Beutler and Johann Christoph Friedrich Guthsmuths, *A General Register of the Most Important German Periodicals and Weekly Journals*, 1790)[62]

However exaggerated, these observations were more than the wishful thinking of journalists ever anxious to talk up their importance. There is a mass of statistical evidence to demonstrate that the phenomenon they described was real. In the London of the young Samuel Pepys, for example, there was only one daily newspaper—the *London Gazette*—and that consisted mainly of official proclamations. So the diarist's only access to news was the exchange or the coffee-house.[63] It was during the last three decades of the century that the daily press moved from being a rarity to an everyday object of use.[64] The lapse of the licensing system in 1695 then brought a very rapid increase so that by the end of the century no fewer than twenty newspapers were being published every week. Although only one of those appeared each day, by the 1730s there were six dailies and by 1770s there were nine. Evidence of a rise in circulation accompanying this rise in titles can be found in the stamps bought after the imposition of duty in 1712: 2,500,000 in 1712, 7,300,000 in 1750, 9,400,000 in 1760, and 12,600,000 in 1775.[65] In London in 1746, according to one authoritative estimate, 45,000 papers were sold on Saturdays, or double the figure for the beginning of the century.[66] It is next to impossible to guess just what sort of multiplier should be used to establish actual readership. As copies were available in clubs, coffee-houses, taverns, and many other public places, it was clearly much higher than today. In London in 1739 there were 551 coffee-houses, 207 inns, and 447 taverns.[67] Contemporary estimates of the number of

[62] Quoted in ibid., pp. 159, 171–2; Andreas Gestrich, *Absolutismus und Öffentlichkeit. Politische Kommunikation in Deutschland zu Beginn des 18. Jahrhunderts* (Göttingen, 1994), p. 131; Paul Raabe, *Bücherlust und Lesefreuden. Beiträge zur Geschichte des Buchwesens im 18. und frühen 19. Jahrhundert* (Stuttgart, 1984), pp. 106–7.

[63] J. H. Plumb, 'The public, literature and the arts in the eighteenth century', in Michael R. Marrus (ed.), *The emergence of leisure* (New York, 1974), p. 14.

[64] Karl Tilman Winkler, *Handwerk und Markt. Druckerhandwerk, Vertriebswesen und Tagesschrifttum in London 1695–1750* (Stuttgart, 1993), p. 9.

[65] Michael Harris, 'The structure, ownership and control of the press, 1620–1780', in Boyce, Curran, and Wingate (eds.), *Newspaper History*, pp. 83–4, 87–8.

[66] Michael Harris, *London Newspapers in the Age of Walpole: A Study of the Origins of the Modern English Press* (London, 1987), p. 190.

[67] John Brewer, *Party Ideology and Popular Politics at the Accession of George III* (Cambridge, 1976), p. 148. Aytoun Ellis, in *The Penny Universities. A History of the Coffee Houses* (London,

readers per copy ranged from as low as twenty to as high as fifty.[68] It was also much more common for extracts from newspapers to be read aloud to the illiterate. At the beginning of the eighteenth century, Charles Leslie recorded: 'The greatest Part of the *People* do not Read Books, Most of them cannot *Read* at all. But they will Gather together about one that can *Read*, and listen to an *Observator* or *Review* (as I have seen them in he streets).'[69]

In France, tight government regulation placed an artificial check on expansion. Louis XIV's and Colbert's concern with cultural control led to the appointment of sixty censors, a reduction of the number of Parisian printers by a half, and the granting of monopolies to certain favoured publications. News of political matters was confined to the *Gazette de France*, literature to the *Mercure français*, and science to the *Journal des savants*.[70] Dissidents of whatever stripe were obliged to resort to clandestine printing-presses and to risk long terms of imprisonment. Even so, the great success story of the eighteenth century was the Jansenist weekly *Nouvelles ecclésiastiques*, printed on portable presses from 1728 and distributed throughout France by a network of sympathetic clergy. Indeed, according to the most recent historian of the French press, it was the Jansenist dispute of the 1750s which marked the turning-point in French publishing, as periodicals moved from the tedium of celebratory journalism to the reporting of current affairs.[71] There was certainly a major expansion after mid-century, as Jack R. Censer's statistics demonstrate.[72] The circulation of all periodicals quadrupled during the fifty years before the Revolution and the number of titles increased even more rapidly (see Table 4). Although many of these publications were directed to specialist audiences, the most successful can be described as mass organs. Panckoucke's *Mercure de France* enjoyed a circulation of some 20,000 in 1778, the number of actual readers being very much higher, since many subscriptions were shared by several individuals or by institutions such as reading clubs and coffee-houses. So even a relatively modest sixfold multiplier takes the total well into six figures.[73]

1956), p. xiv, states firmly that 'By the end of the seventeenth century the number of coffee houses in London exceeded 2,000,' but gives no source. The total seems improbably high.

[68] Ibid.

[69] Bonamy Dobrée, *English Literature in the Early Eighteenth Century 1700–1740* (Oxford, 1959), p. 6.

[70] Jean-Paul Bertaud, *La Presse et le pouvoir de Louis XIII à Napoléon* (Paris, 2000), p. 23.

[71] Ibid., pp. 25–8.

[72] Jack R. Censer, *The French Press in the Age of Enlightenment* (London, 1994), pp. 7–8.

[73] Simon Schama, *Citizens. A Chronicle of the French Revolution* (New York, 1989), p. 178.

TABLE 4. *French periodicals, 1745–1785*

	Total	Politics	Literary/philosophical	*Affiches de province**
1745	15	5	9	1
1750	21	5	14	2
1755	25	5	16	3
1760	37	12	19	6
1765	37	12	17	8
1770	50	12	22	16
1775	68	13	31	24
1780	73	18	28	27
1785	82	19	39	34

* The *Affiches de province* consisted mainly of advertisements. Although they included some political news, they were mainly concerned with commercial affairs, rates of exchange, the arrival of ships, and local social events.

These French figures were eclipsed east of the Rhine, where expanding literacy[74] and cultural decentralization made Germany the land of the periodical *par excellence* (see Table 5). Of course, many of these new creations were short-lived, justifying the jibe of Schubart that 'it is true that we have many newspapers. They criss-cross our beloved fatherland just as snowflakes criss-cross the sky in an April snowstorm.'[75] Yet their very creation revealed a large and growing demand. It was of long standing. At the end of the seventeenth century there were between fifty and sixty newspapers being published in the Holy Roman Empire, or more than the rest of Europe put together, with a total readership of around a quarter of a million. By 1750 those figures had risen to 100–120 and 1,000,000 respectively and by 1789 to 200 and 3,000,000.[76] Even in Austria, the chief of police had to concede in 1806 that newspapers had become 'a genuine necessity' for the educated classes, anticipating Hegel's celebrated remark that reading the daily newspaper

[74] See above, pp. 113–15.

[75] Christian Friedrich Daniel Schubart (ed.), *Deutsche Chronik auf das Jahr 1774* (reprinted, Heidelberg, 1975), I, 31 March 1774 p. 3.

[76] Martin Welke, 'Gemeinsame Lektüre und frühe Formen von Gruppenbildungen im 17. und 18. Jahrhundert: Zeitungslesen in Deutschland', in Otto Dann (ed.), *Lesegesellschaften und bürgerliche Emanzipation* (Munich, 1981), p. 29.

TABLE 5. *German periodicals, 1700–1790*

Decade	Number of new journals
Up to 1700	58
1701–1710	64
1711–1720	119
1721–1730	133
1731–1740	176
1741–1750	260
1751–1760	331
1761–1770	410
1771–1780	718
1781–1790	1,225
TOTAL	3,494

represented the morning prayers of modern man.[77] If it was an act of worship carried out by an individual in private, it was done with a sense of being part of a wider public, for it was being conducted simultaneously by thousands of others. To heighten this sense of collectivity, editors of periodicals made frequent use of the epistolary form: the first series of the trail-blazing *Spectator* (March 1711–December 1712) published 250 letters. By the middle of the century, critical debate by means of the letter columns between editor and readers or between reader and reader was well established. *The Gazeteer*, for example, received no fewer than 861 letters during the first quarter of 1764, of which 560 were printed at length and 262 more were summarized as 'Observations from Our Correspondents'.[78]

Throughout Europe, the dissemination of periodicals enjoyed a mutually supportive relationship with the coffee-houses that flourished in the same period. Within fifty years of the opening of Christendom's first—in Venice in 1645—coffee-houses had spread across the continent.[79] More respectable than inns, they quickly won acceptance as an important medium for a new kind of public sociability. Writing at the end of the eighteenth century, Johann

[77] Moran, *The Cotta Press*, p. 125.

[78] Brewer, 'This, that and the other', p. 13.

[79] There is an excellent concise account of the spread of coffee-houses in James Van Horn Melton, *Politics, Culture and the Public Sphere in Enlightenment Europe* (Cambridge, 2001), ch. 7.

Pezzl recorded that the first coffee-house in Vienna had been opened in 1683 by a Pole called Koltschitzky, who had served as an Austrian spy during the Turkish siege and was given the concession as a reward. There were now seventy-five in the city, he added, selling not only coffee but also tea, chocolate, lemonade, and alcoholic beverages. Some had special rooms for smoking, billiards, and card- and board-games, while 'for those who have a taste for news, the best-known German, French, Italian and English newspapers are available'.[80] In England, coffee-houses were at first attacked as subversive novelties, encouraging idleness and sedition, but after 1688 they were more likely to be lauded for encouraging rational discussion. Joseph Addison and Richard Steele praised them as 'schools of Politeness', as well they might, for it was through coffee-houses that periodicals such as the *Spectator* and the *Tatler* reached an audience beyond the subscription list.[81] Enterprising coffee-house owners enhanced their business by subscribing to a far greater range of periodicals and newspapers than any private individual could hope to command. From the start, coffee-houses were associated with the exchange and dissemination of news. The very first broadside to be published about them, in 1670, proclaimed:

> You that delight in wit and mirth,
> And long to hear such news
> As comes from all parts of the earth,
> Dutch, Danes, and Turks, and Jews,
> I'll send Ye to a rendez vous,
> Where it is smoking new;
> Go hear it at a coffee house
> It cannot but be true.[82]

Five years later the government drew attention to this aspect by ordering the suppression of coffee-houses as being 'places where the disaffected met, and spread scandalous reports concerning the conduct of His Majesty and his Ministers', although such was the public uproar that the order had to be quickly rescinded.[83] In most continental countries, censorship was stricter

80 Johann Pezzl, *Beschreibung und Grundriß der Haupt-und Residenzstadt Wien* (Vienna, 1802), p. 87.

81 Lawrence Klein, *Shaftesbury and the Culture of Politeness: Moral Discourse and Cultural Politics in Early Eighteenth Century England* (Cambridge, 1994), p. 12.

82 Edward Forbes Robinson, *The Early History of Coffee Houses in England* (London, 1893), p. 150.

83 Bryant Lillywhite, *London Coffee Houses: A Reference Book of Coffee Houses of the Seventeenth, Eighteenth and Nineteenth Centuries* (London, 1963), p. 17.

and police powers greater, but the practice seems to have differed little throughout the eighteenth century. A French visitor to Vienna in 1704 noted that the city was full of coffee-houses in which people came together to read newspapers and to discuss the contents (which makes them sound a good deal livelier than their present-day equivalents); in 1754 Johann Quistorp described the coffee-houses of Leipzig as being like 'a political stock exchange'; while in 1785 Louis Sébastien Mercier wrote that in the Parisian cafés 'the chatter . . . revolves incessantly around the gazette.'[84] Moreover, this was also a space without social hierarchy, for anyone decently dressed and with the price of a cup of coffee could gain admission. Indeed, that was the first rule laid down by a broadside of 1674 in London:

> First, Gentry, Tradesmen, all are welcome hither,
> And may without Affront sit down Together:
> Pre-eminence of Place, none here should Mind,
> But take the next fit Seat that he can find:
> Nor need any, if Finer Persons come,
> Rise up for to assigne to them his Room.[85]

As coffee-houses were also closely linked to the development of the Penny Post and were often the venues for Masonic meetings, public lectures, and scientific demonstrations,[86] they can be said to have exemplified the public sphere.

CONCERTS

However much they developed in the eighteenth century, art exhibitions, novels, newspapers, periodicals, and letters had all existed in the past. It was in music that a wholly new medium emerged, in the shape of the public concert. Such was the rapidity of its rise that by 1800 it had become 'the main medium for music *per se*'.[87] Of all the cultural developments of the period, it appears to be the one most clearly linked to social change: it has been argued that urbanization and commercialization turned music into a commodity that the growing numbers of middle-class Europeans were eager

[84] Melton, *Politics, Culture and the Public Sphere*.
[85] Aytoun Ellis, *The Penny Universities*. The broadside is reproduced in facsimile as the frontispiece.
[86] Lillywhite, *London Coffee Houses*, pp. 21–4.
[87] Eduard Hanslick, *Geschichte des Concertwesens in Wien*, 2 vols (Vienna, 1869), I, p. ix.

and able to purchase. Barred from the opera houses of the courts by their lowly status, they created their own forum, admitting anyone who had the price of admission. In the process, they also liberated the musician. Freed from the representational restraints imposed by princely or ecclesiastical patrons, composers could now invent their own musical forms and languages. The result was the conquest of the musical world by the symphony, the symphony concert, and the concert hall. This apparently natural progression has led many historians to present the rise of the concert as the cultural equivalent of the French Revolution:

The social history of the eighteenth century is essentially the process by which the rising bourgeoisie tore down the barriers and fences which had reserved cultural goods for the feudal elite. The bourgeois then transformed and developed those cultural goods to suit their own needs, thus creating new forms... Both the arena and the victor's rostrum of this bourgeois musical struggle was the public concert. Its organisation, its construction and its extension provide the keys for understanding the musical and cultural advances and contradictions of the eighteenth century.[88]

There is a great deal to be said for this scenario, but not everything. If a public concert can be defined as a musical performance at which there is a clear distinction between performers and audience, and to which the anonymous public is admitted on payment of an entrance fee, then the first took place in London in 1672, when the following advertisement appeared in the *London Gazette*:

These are to give notice, That at Mr. *John Banister's* house (now called the *Musick School*) over against the *George Tavern* in *Whyte Fryers*, this present Monday will be Musick performed by excellent Masters, beginning precisely at 4 of the clock in the afternoon, and every afternoon for the future, precisely at the same hour.[89]

The price of admission was one shilling and sixpence. As Banister had been dismissed from his post as director of Charles II's band of twenty-four violins five years previously, it might indeed be said that public concerts were 'anti-feudal' from their inception.[90] Moreover, the milieu from which Banister's

[88] Peter Schleuning, *Das 18. Jahrhundert. Der Bürger erhebt sich* (Hamburg, 1984), p. 30.

[89] Quoted in Hugh Arthur Scott, 'London's earliest public concerts', in *Musical Quarterly*, 22 (1936), p. 454. The definition of a concert is taken from Heinrich Schwab, *Konzert. Öffentliche Musikdarbietung vom 17. bis 19. Jahrhundert* (Leipzig, 1971), p. 6.

[90] It is not clear whether Banister had been dismissed for criticizing the King's preference for French musicians or for failing to pay the musicians punctually; Scott, 'London's earliest public concerts', p. 454.

concert developed was far removed from the court. Although meriting the title 'first public concert' by virtue of its formal organization and advance advertising, his event was probably little different in practice from the numerous performances which took place in taverns with special facilities and reputations for public music. Samuel Pepys referred to such an institution in his diary entry for 27 September 1665: 'We to the Kings-head, the great Musique-house, the first time I was ever there and had a good breakfast.'[91] Banister also provided music as the accompaniment to drinking, as the lawyer and amateur musician Roger North recorded in his memoirs: 'The room was rounded with seats and small tables, alehouse fashion. One shilling was the price [*sic*], and call for what you pleased; there was very good musick, for Banister found means to procure the best in towne, and some voices to come and performe there.'[92]

Whether it was the excellence of the drink or the music, Banister had found a ready market and his concerts continued in various venues until his death in 1679. By that time his example was being followed by other entrepreneurs. In the year after his death, a group of professional musicians combined to build a concert hall in York Buildings, off the Strand. In his account, North made it clear that the profit motive was uppermost in this successful attempt to emulate Banister:

> The masters of musick finding that money was to be got this way, determined to take the business into their owne hands; and it proceeded so far, that in York buildings, a fabrick was reared and furnished on purpose for public musick. And there was nothing of musick valued in towne, but was to be heard there. It was called the Musick-Meeting; and all the quality and *beau mond* [*sic*] repaired to it.[93]

High society was encouraged to patronize these concerts by the advertisements which were placed in the newspapers, these two facets of the developing public sphere going hand in hand. Typical was the following advertisement which appeared in the *Daily Courant* in January, 1703:

> At the Desire of Several Persons of Quality,
>
> On Thursday the 28th of this Instant *January*, in York Buildings, will be perform'd a Consort of New Vocal and Instrumental Musick, by the best Masters. Wherein the famous *Gasperini* [*sic*] and Signor *Petto* will play several Italian Sonatas. And Mrs

[91] *The Diary of Samuel Pepys*, ed. Robert Latham and William Matthews. Vol. VI: *1665* (London, 1972), p. 242.

[92] Roger North, *Memoires of Musick being some historico-criticall collections of that subject* (1728), ed. Edward F. Rimbault (London, 1846), pp. 111–12.

[93] Ibid., pp. 112–14.

Campion will sing several English and Italian Songs for her own Benefit. Beginning at 8 of the Clock precisely. None to be admitted without Tickets, which are to be had at *White's* Chocolate House in *St. James's street* and the *Spread Eagle* Coffee-House in Bridges-street, near Covent Garden.[94]

Considerable ingenuity was used to attract attention by exploiting to the full the limited typographical resources available: in 1713 an advertisement for a series of subscription concerts in the *Guardian* used four different typefaces, four rows of asterisks, a row of daggers, another row of double daggers, and a final row of Maltese crosses for good measure.[95] The English were in the vanguard of commercialization here, for advertisements for concerts do not appear to been used in Paris until 1725 or in Vienna until 1780.[96]

They owed their advantage not only to London's great size, prosperity, and commercial character but also to the relative liberalism of the political regime. It was the combination of these conditions which prompted 'mercenary teachers, chiefly forreiners', as Roger North complained, to discover 'the Grand Secret, that the English would follow Musick & drop their pence freely, of which some advantage hath bin since made'.[97] Indeed, it was exploited, most spectacularly perhaps by Giovanni Gallini, a Swiss-Italian dancing-master who came to London in the 1750s, built the Hanover Square Rooms, styled himself Sir John Gallini (a papal title) and left the fabulous fortune of £150,000.[98] In fact, anyone possessing the necessary enterprise, capital, and contacts could organize a concert by assembling an orchestra, hiring a hall, and advertising a programme. If that seems self-evident, it should be contrasted with conditions in the only other metropolis of comparable size and wealth—Paris. The cultural monopoly claimed by the absolutist state in France, which we have encountered already,[99] made its presence felt in this quarter too. When the royal musician, Anne-Danican Philidor, had the bright idea of organizing concerts during Lent, when theatres were obliged to close their doors, his first task was to secure the consent of Francine, who had inherited the monopoly of public musical presentation bestowed on his

[94] Hugh Arthur Scott, 'London concerts from 1700 to 1750', *Musical Quarterly*, 24 (1938), p. 200.

[95] Michael Tilmouth, 'Some early London concerts and music clubs 1670–1720', *Proceedings of the Royal Musical Association*, 84 (1957–8), p. 16.

[96] Michel Brenet, *Les Concerts en France sous l'ancien régime* (Paris, 1900; reprinted New York, 1970), p. 119; Hanslick, *Geschichte des Concertwesens in Wien*, I, p. xiv.

[97] Tilmouth, 'Some early London concerts and music clubs 1670–1720', pp. 13–14.

[98] Robert Elkin, *The Old Concert Rooms of London* (London, 1955), p. 92; Thomas B. Milligan, *The Concerto and London's Musical Culture in the Late Eighteenth Century* (Epping, 1983), p. 1.

[99] See above, pp. 46–9.

father-in-law, Lully, by Louis XIV.[100] It cost Philidor 10,000 *livres* a year and a promise not to perform operatic music, or indeed any vocal music with texts in the French language.[101] Such was public demand, however, that when launched in 1725 his *Concerts Spirituels* were a resounding and lasting success. Nevertheless, the restrictions imposed by the old regime's love of cultural control almost certainly impeded the development of French music.

In both London and Paris, music was commercialized further by its sale in forms other than concerts—as instruments, as scores (both manuscript and printed), as works of theory, and as instruction. In 1699 the raffish journalist Edward Ward described a stroll past St Paul's Cathedral (where, characteristically, he and his companion paused to admire the 'Smutty Prints' on display in the print-shops): 'We walk'd a little further, and came amongst the Musick-shops, in one of which were so many Dancing-Masters Prentices, Fidling and Piping of *Bories* and *Minuets*, That the Crowd at the door could no more forbear Dancing into the Shop, than the Merry Stones of *Thebes* could refuse capering into the Walls, when Conjur'd from Confusion, into order, by the Power of *Orpheus*' Harmony.'[102] It was through shops such as these that the link was made between creators and consumers, by means of sheet music. Although music had been printed since the fifteenth century and had reached an early peak at Venice in the late sixteenth century, it was not until the eighteenth century that a significant market formed across the continent. In particular, it was only after 1700 that the long-known technique of printing music by engraving became widespread, thus allowing much more complex scores to be printed more cleanly, cheaply, and quickly. London led the field, soon joined by Paris from the 1740s and Vienna from the 1770s.[103] It was also in London in the second half of the seventeenth century that John Playford and his son Henry brought modern business practices to bear on music publishing, going beyond mere printing to assembling a catalogue of scores, and then advertising, promoting, and distributing its contents.[104]

During the course of the next century entrepreneurs emerged all over Europe, seeking out talented composers and putting them in contact with consumers, to the benefit of all three parties. The best example of what

[100] See above, p. 97.

[101] Brenet, *Les Concerts en France sous l'ancien régime*, p. 117.

[102] Edward Ward, *The London Spy for the month of March 1699* (London, 1699), p. 3.

[103] D. W. Krummel and Stanley Sadie (eds.), *Music Printing and Publishing* (London, 1990), pp. 95, 98.

[104] D. W. Krummel, 'Music publishing', in Nicholas Temperley (ed.), *The Romantic age 1800–1914*, The Blackwell History of Music in Britain, vol. 5 (Oxford, 1988), p. 46.

publishing could mean for a composer was provided by Joseph Haydn. His original contract with Prince Esterházy, dated 1 May 1761, made it clear that the music he composed was for his patron only:

5to. The said *Vice-Capel-Meister* shall be under permanent obligation to compose such pieces of music as his Serene Princely Highness may command, and neither to communicate such new compositions to anyone, nor to allow them to be copied, but to retain them wholly for the exclusive use of his Highness; nor shall he compose for any other person without the knowledge and gracious permission [of his Highness].[105]

Haydn's periodic visits to Vienna, his correspondence with other musicians across Europe, and the growing public demand for high-class music ensured that this restriction could not have been rigorously enforced, even if his benign employer had attempted to do so. His symphonies were being published in Paris in pirated editions as early as 1764 and were appearing on the programmes of public concerts there from 1776.[106] When the contract was renewed in 1779, the restrictive clause was dropped, leaving the way open for Haydn to take his talents to market. As Daniel Heartz has suggested, if Haydn did not break with the old world of princely patronage as abruptly as Mozart, he did take active steps to establish a closer relationship with the general public. These included plans for foreign travel, the soliciting of subscriptions from connoisseurs, and the commissioning for sale and distribution of engraved versions of his flattering portrait by Johann Ernst Mansfeld.[107] He was assisted greatly by the almost simultaneous founding of the Viennese music-publishing house of Artaria (still in business today). It was to Artaria that he sent most of his major compositions in the years that followed, although he was careful to cultivate contacts with other English, French, and German publishers.[108] So he was already established as an international star long before his visits to London in 1791–2 and 1794–5. Indeed, a London newspaper had lamented in 1785 that:

[105] H. C. Robbins Landon (ed.), *Haydn: Chronicle and works*, 5 vols. (London, 1976–80), I, p. 351.

[106] Brenet, *Les Concerts en France sous l'ancien régime*, p. 309; Giorgio Pestelli, *The Age of Mozart and Beethoven* (Cambridge, 1984), p. 114.

[107] Daniel Heartz, *Haydn, Mozart and the Viennese school 1740–1780* (New York and London, 1995), pp. 400–2.

[108] H. C. Robbins Landon and David Wyn Jones, *Haydn: His Life and Music* (London, 1988), p. 183. The importance of a publisher in helping a creative artist to retain independence has not diminished; the Marxist poet and playwright Bertolt Brecht resided in East Berlin after his return from exile, but he insisted on choosing a West German publisher (Suhrkamp)—and an Austrian passport.

There is something very distressing to a liberal mind in the history of *Haydn*. This wonderful man, who is the Shakespeare of music, and the triumph of the age in which we live, is doomed to reside in the court of a miserable German prince, who is at once incapable of rewarding him, and unworthy of the honour... Would it not be an achievement equal to a pilgrimage, for some aspiring youths to rescue him from his fortune and transplant him to Great Britain, the country for which his music seems to be made?[109]

In the event, kidnapping proved unnecessary. A flattering invitation, conveyed in person by the impresario Salomon, supported by the lure of London's fabled riches, prompted Haydn to make the long journey at the end of 1790. Arriving on the first day of the new year, he found a musical environment quite different from the Esterházy court. Bewildered by the hubbub of 'this endlessly huge city of London', he was even more overwhelmed by the warmth of his public welcome. He wrote home: 'My arrival caused a great sensation throughout the whole city, and I went the round of all the newspapers for three successive days. Everyone wants to know me. I had to dine out six times up to now, and if I wanted, I could dine out every day.'[110] Lionized by English society, from the King and Prince of Wales down, Haydn also made very large sums of money: within six months he was able to remit nearly 6,000 gulden to Austrian banks (i.e. between five and six times his annual salary from Prince Esterházy).[111] According to his contemporary and first biographer, Griesinger, his two visits to London yielded a net profit of 15,000 gulden.[112]

Haydn's fame and fortune in London also provides a good illustration of how the commercialization of an art form could influence its content. This was not so much a question of artistic resources as of patronage. At the Esterházy palace of Eisenstadt, Haydn had at his disposal a magnificent concert hall appreciably *larger* than the Hanover Square Rooms, the venue of the Salomon concerts in London and designed to hold 800 people (although capable of accommodating twice that number).[113] Much more important was the relative size of the orchestras he wrote for. At Eisenstadt and Esterháza in the 1770s,

[109] Ibid., p. 175.

[110] Ibid., p. 229.

[111] Ibid., p. 237. It is impossible to estimate Haydn's salary precisely because a good deal of his remuneration was paid in kind; ibid., pp. 118–19.

[112] Ibid., p. 252.

[113] Ground plans of the concert hall at Eisenstadt, the music room at Esterháza, the Hanover Square Rooms, and the concert hall attached to the King's Theatre in the Haymarket can be found in Michael Forsyth, *Buildings for Music: The Architect, the Musician, and the Listener from the Seventeenth Century to the Present Day* (Cambridge, Mass., 1985), p. 39. The music room at Esterháza was about one half the size of the Hanover Square Rooms.

Haydn was writing symphonies for three first and three second violins, one viola, one cello, one double bass, one bassoon, two oboes, and two horns—fourteen players in all.[114] As each one of these was a permanent charge on the princely exchequer, even as rich a magnate as Prince Esterházy could not afford a larger band. Yet in London an impresario such as Salomon could draw on a much larger pool of professional musicians, hiring them by the season or even by the concert, and so was able to provide Haydn with an orchestra of between fifty and sixty.[115] Significantly, it was only in the other great European metropolis—Paris—that such forces could be matched on a regular basis.

Yet even this discrepancy does not wholly explain the striking stylistic development revealed by the symphonies Haydn wrote for Paris and London in 1784–5 and 1791–5 respectively. A popular explanation is that it was a sense of writing for a large public which spurred Haydn on to greater things:

> The London public of the last decade of the century deserves part of posterity's gratitude for eliciting the expansion of expressive boundaries in Haydn's last twelve symphonies. The music reflects the atmosphere of *fin-de-siècle* London: assured, disputatious, intriguing eccentric, open-minded yet sensitive. Haydn respected and nurtured his public, they, by adulation, encouraged him to a degree and in a manner no other city could have done (and certainly no individual) to further his propensity for musical argument and entertainment.[116]

This is certainly a plausible hypothesis and can be supported by references to Haydn's frequent and fervent expressions of gratitude to his admiring London audiences. If sustained, it would reinforce the belief that 'both the arena and victor's rostrum of the bourgeois musical struggle was the public concert.'[117] Yet it may be doubted whether this was the whole story, either in the particular case of Haydn or more generally.

The sort of reductionist theory which encapsulates the musical history of the eighteenth century with a phrase such as 'the bourgeois asserts himself'[118] sees the artist responding to social conditions. From this perspective, it is the forces of production that lead, by creating a market, turning cultural artefacts

[114] 'A note for volume ten of the Haydn symphonies', recording by Derek Solomons and L'Estro Armonico, CBS Masterworks, M3T 4211.

[115] For information on the size of orchestras in the eighteenth century, see Schleuning, *Das 18. Jahrhundert*. p. 144 and Henry Raynor, *A Social History of Music from the Middle Ages to Beethoven* (London, 1972), pp. 304–5.

[116] Landon and Wyn Jones, *Haydn*, p. 271.

[117] See above, p. 162.

[118] This is the subtitle of Schleuning, *Das 18. Jahrhundert. Der Bürger erhebt sich*.

into commodities and allowing—compelling—creative artists to make the appropriate response. As we have seen, there is much to be said for this, but it fails to accommodate the plethora of evidence which suggests that many artists believed they were free agents, working not in the world of commerce but in an autonomous realm of free creativity. Even if they were deluded, and their cherished liberty was nothing more than false consciousness, it is a dimension that demands to be taken seriously. It is a caveat which might be issued to many present-day historians in search of twenty-first-century precursors, especially in the consumer-spending and leisure industries.

With specific reference to concerts, it is remarkable how many were organized not with a view to making profit but to making music. John Banister charged an admission fee, but Thomas Britton, the equally celebrated early promoter, did not, financing his concerts from his earnings as a 'small coal merchant'.[119] Indeed, the very origins of concerts can be traced to informal groups of musicians meeting in taverns as *Convivia musica* or *Collegia musica* to practise and improve their art, enjoying drink and tobacco at the same time.[120] Attracted by the novelty, other customers then drifted into the room set aside for the musicians, stayed to listen, began to return on a regular basis and to call for their favourite pieces, and so gradually a more formal concert with a set programme began to emerge. This pattern can be detected in a number of German cities during the first quarter of the eighteenth century—in Frankfurt am Main, Hamburg, Lübeck, and Leipzig, to name just the more important.[121]

What these four cities had in common was their commercial character, a bond which certainly lends weight to the association of the rise of concerts with the rise of the bourgeoisie. It was particularly clear at Leipzig, the great entrepôt at the crossroads of central Europe, which enjoyed a new lease of life in the eighteenth century with the rapid expansion of Russian markets. Merchants sat on the board of the association which organized the city's musical life, responding to increased demand like good entrepreneurs by increasing the number of concerts during the three great trade fairs held in the city each year. This was a cosmopolitan world, famously apostrophized by Goethe in

[119] Elkin, *The Old Concert Rooms of London*, p. 26.

[120] Richard Schaal, 'Konzertwesen', *Die Musik in Geschichte und Gegenwart*, 17 vols. (Kassel, Basle, London, New York, 1949–86), VII, col. 1588.

[121] Balet and Gerhard, *Die Verbürgerlichung der deutschen Kunst*, p. 38. They date the concerts in Leipzig from 1743 but in fact they dated back at least to the arrival of Telemann in the city in 1701 and probably further still; see Alfred Dörffel, *Geschichte der Gewandhausconcerte zu Leipzig vom 25. November 1791 bis 25. November 1881* (Leipzig, 1884), p. 2.

Faust as 'Little Paris' and by Lessing as 'a place where one can see the whole world in microcosm'.[122] On 25 November 1781, almost exactly a century after the first *Collegium musicum* had been established, a splendid new concert hall was opened in the former clothiers' hall, whose German name—*Gewandhaus*—has given its name to a symphonic tradition that has lasted until the present day.[123]

In many other places, however, it was not the middle classes who took the initiative in organizing concerts but the nobility. This should not be surprising: only the use of exclusive social categories derived from a Marxist model can obscure the heavy participation by the privileged orders in the construction and expansion of the public sphere. Moreover, it was aristocrats just as much as bourgeois who were the beneficiaries of this new cultural space, for they now had the opportunity to emancipate themselves from both the hegemony previously exercised by the court and the isolation of their rural estates. Of course, the degree of noble involvement reflected the social structure of any particular society. In Russia, where what little commercial enterprise existed was located mainly in the countryside,[124] it was total. The first concert there was given by the twelve German musicians accompanying the Duke of Holstein on a visit he made in 1721–2.[125] This new form of recreation was then copied by native nobles as part of their westernizing experience. The recruiting of Italian instrumentalists to form a court orchestra by the Tsarina Anna in the 1730s encouraged the trend. By the mid-1740s, advertisements were appearing in the *St Petersburg Gazette* for concerts organized by nobles. In 1748, for example, Prince Gagarin announced that the public would be admitted to a concert 'in the Italian, English and Dutch manner' to be held in his palace. Songs would be sung in Italian, Russian, English, and German, tickets would cost one rouble each, and anyone decently dressed would be admitted, with only 'drunks, servants, and loose women' excluded.[126] These 'musical Wednesdays' of Prince Gagarin became a regular part of the capital's musical scene.

The concert culture of Russia had a special flavour deep into the nineteenth century. Perhaps its most striking peculiarity was the popularity of orchestras

[122] Karl Czok, 'Zur Leipziger Kulturgeschichte des 18. Jahrhunderts', in Reinhard Szekus (ed.), *Johann Sebastian Bach und die Aufklärung* (Leipzig, 1982), p. 26.

[123] Dörffel, *Geschichte der Gewandhausconcerte*, pp. 19–20.

[124] Richard Pipes, *Russia under the Old Regime* (Harmondsworth, 1977), p. 198.

[125] A. M. Sokolova, 'Kontsertnaya zhizn', *Istoriya russkoy muzyki*, vol. III (Moscow, 1985), p. 244.

[126] Ibid., p. 247.

consisting of serfs. Even quite modest landowners had serfs trained as musicians, putting them to work in the fields or in the house by day. This was a sensible investment, for not only were the serf musicians available to entertain the family in the evening, they also represented a marketable asset and could be sold on if necessary. No matter how great their skill and resulting fame, they remained at the disposal of their current master. Probably untypical but certainly symbolic was the great whip kept hanging in the wings of his private theatre by Count Kamensky, with which he beat performers in the interval if they had not lived up to expectations.[127]

Corporal punishment of musicians was unknown at the other end of Europe, in relatively commercialized England, but aristocratic control was certainly familiar. The professional musicians may have been to the fore in promoting concerts but they were anxious to confine their clientele to high society and it was their noble patrons who determined what should be played and when. Writing in 1728 about the last quarter of the previous century, the first historian of London concert life—Roger North—recognized that: 'nothing advanced musick more in this age than the patronage of the nobility, and men of fortunes, for they became encouragers of it by great liberallitys, and countenance to the professors. And this was made very publick by a contribution amongst them, to be given as a premio to him that should best entertain them in solemne consort.'[128] That did not change appreciably as the eighteenth century progressed: when the concert promoters announced in their advertisements that they were addressing 'the Nobility and Gentry', they meant what they said. So the most authoritative account of concert life in England in the second half of the eighteenth century concludes: 'It should not be thought that commercial modes of organisation . . . implied a bourgeois cultural leadership . . . Modern musical taste was undoubtedly formed by aristocratic patrons in the fashionable end of town.'[129] With individual concerts priced at half a guinea and subscription to a series costing five guineas, only the affluent could afford to attend the most prestigious events. The hierarchy among London concerts that developed was summarized by *The Morning Post* in 1789 as: 'The HANOVER-SQUARE [Professional

[127] B. N. Aseyev, *Russky dramatichesky teatr ot ego istokov do kontsa XVIII veka* (Moscow, 1977), p. 304.

[128] North, *Memoires of Musick*, p. 117.

[129] McVeigh, *Concert Life in London from Mozart to Haydn*, p. 6. Cf. his later observation that 'Modern concert life was not a bourgeois creation, and concert life only expanded into the City in later emulation, in the same way as the bourgeois bought gentility in the form of pianos and daughters' lessons'; ibid., p. 53.

Concert]—QUALITY. The TOTTENHAM-STREET [Concert of Ancient Music]—GENTRY. The FREEMASONS'-HALL [Academy of Ancient Music]—PEOPLE. And the ANACREONTIC [Society]—FOLKS'.[130]

As this list suggests, there were plenty of opportunities for middle-class Londoners to attend concerts. Just one year earlier, *The Times* commented that 'Music is everywhere the rage—it has spread from the West to the East, and a very elegant concert was given a few evenings ago at a butcher's near Leadenhall-market . . . *Three-penny* concerts in a Hay-loft, and *Six-penny* concerts, at a common Public-house, are proofs that the rage for music is extending from the highest to the *lowest* classes of society.'[131] As this indicates, what was described as a 'concert' in late eighteenth-century England often bore little resemblance to what is understood by the word today. When Joseph Haydn came to London in 1791 he did not perform in a hay-loft or join in a sing-song in a pub, he went to the Hanover Square rooms to be fêted by 'the Nobility and Gentry'. The concerts organized by the 'Concert of Ancient Music' were patronized by the cream of English society, including King George III, who occupied a special box and determined whether or not there should be applause. In 1786 the directors of this organization were the Marquis of Carmarthen, the Earls of Exeter, Sandwich, and Uxbridge, the Viscounts Dudley and Fitzwilliam, Lord Grey de Wilton and two baronets.[132] Nor can the middle-class people who attended the threepenny or sixpenny concerts be described as 'bourgeois' in a Marxist sense. What is conspicuously absent from contemporary accounts is any suggestion that merchants, manufacturers, or financiers were to the fore in promoting or attending concerts. On the contrary, when the first series of subscription concerts was launched in the City of London in 1818, a musical periodical remarked that 'we could never be brought to understand why the solid opulence of trade should not admit the same opportunities for intellectual cultivation' and described the 'mercantile classes' as 'an almost entirely new class of protectors of music'.[133]

In continental Europe the aristocratic element was even more dominant. The earliest concerts in France were private affairs, financed by subscription and confined to a small group of courtiers. Such were the concerts organized by Madame de Prie, who found sixty friends prepared to contribute 400 *livres* each per season.[134] Patronized by the Regent, the duc d'Orléans, and meeting

[130] Ibid., p. 11. [131] Quoted in ibid., p. 34.
[132] Elkin, *The Old Concert Rooms of London*, pp. 84, 86. [133] Ibid., p. 21.
[134] Brenet, *Les Concerts en France sous l'ancien régime*, p. 160.

in a room at the Louvre, these concerts were as far removed from the bourgeois public sphere as it is possible to imagine. The only music accessible to the public was to be heard in the gardens of the Tuileries once a year, on the eve of the Feast of Saint Louis. This was very much part of the old representational culture, complete with music by Lully, a firework display, and a ritual appearance by the King.[135] The form of Philidor's *Concerts Spirituels*,[136] with their admission by ticket and advertisements in the press, pointed the way towards greater public participation, but in practice they were dominated by high society. Indeed, in 1734 they were taken over by the Royal Academy of Music.[137] The only possible link between the Parisian concert scene and the world of commerce was to be found in the involvement of several *fermiers généraux*, the fabulously wealthy financiers who leased from the Crown the right to collect certain forms of indirect taxation. They included the two greatest single individual patrons of music in eighteenth-century France—Pierre Crozat and the sumptuously named Alexandre-Jean-Joseph Le Riche de La Poplinière (1692–1762). Among many other achievements, the latter made a decisive and sustained contribution to the success of Rameau's career.[138] However, this group can be designated 'bourgeois' only if the ownership and exploitation of capital is made the sole criterion of membership (in which case many of the oldest nobles of France would have to be included too). Although often plebeian in origin, the farmers-general wanted nothing more than assimilation with the aristocratic elite. So they bought patents of nobility and lubricated the penetration of their daughters into high society with dowries so generous that even the haughtiest peer of France forgot the word *mésalliance*. In the provinces too, concerts were organized by the academies that sprang up during the early part of the century (Bordeaux 1707, Lyon 1713, Marseille 1717, Nantes 1727, and so on). These institutions invariably sought an aristocratic patron, often the governor of the province, and were dominated by the local *notables*.[139]

In the German musical world, the concerts of the self-governing Free Imperial Cities such as Hamburg and Frankfurt am Main were soon overshadowed by the princely capitals. A correspondent from Hamburg informed

[135] Ibid, p. 169.

[136] See above, p. 164.

[137] Brenet, *Les Concerts en France sous l'ancien régime*, p. 193.

[138] Cuthbert Girdlestone, *Jean-Philippe Rameau: His Life and Work* (London, 1957), p. 473.

[139] Jean Quéniart, 'Les formes de la sociabilité musicale en France et en Allemagne (1750–1850)', in Étienne François (ed.), *Sociabilité et société bourgeoise en France, en Allemagne et en Suisse 1750–1800* (Paris, 1986), pp. 137–40.

KING ALFRED'S COLLEGE
LIBRARY

the readers of Cramer's *Magazin* in 1784: 'Some concerts do take place here, but they are neither public nor as important as those in Berlin, Leipzig, and Vienna. Moreover, they only just manage to hold their heads above water by means of subscriptions.'[140] It is a natural mistake to assume that because Hamburg was a large commercial city, its cultural arrangements were progressive. On the contrary, the conservative Lutheran piety of the city elders meant that there could be no concerts on a Sunday (elsewhere in Germany *the* day) and the restrictive practices of the still powerful guilds ensured that only their members could perform music in public. That the guild musicians lacked the technique to play new music did not matter.[141] Things were no better in Frankfurt am Main, then as now the financial capital of Germany but also a byword for cultural conservatism. No less a witness than the city's most famous son—Goethe—complained about the 'narrow and slow-moving' burgher culture which, as he told his mother after his move to princely Weimar, would have driven him mad if he had stayed any longer.[142] At the beginning of the nineteenth century, travelling musicians such as Louis Spohr were still complaining about the city's meanness and philistinism.[143]

It was not from these cultural backwaters that musical innovation would come, nor even from relatively lively Leipzig. The development of instrumental music, and especially the symphony, owed far more to Mannheim (capital of the Elector of the Palatinate), Eisenstadt (the residence of Prince Esterházy), Salzburg, Berlin, and Vienna. In these residential cities, whose social and economic *raison d'être* was the presence of the court, the public consisted mainly of state employees, most of whom were noble and very few of whom were 'bourgeois' in any sense of the word. It comes as no surprise, for example, to discover that in Berlin, the membership of the 'Association for the Performance of Music' (*Musikübende Gesellschaft*) had a military and bureaucratic flavour. Its membership list in 1755 was as follows:

Georg Christoph von Arnim, Lieutenant
Georg Friedrich von Oppen, Major
Johann Adolf Ernst von Winzingerode, Cavalry Captain

[140] Hanslick, *Geschichte des Concertwesens in Wien*, I, p. 56.
[141] Ibid., I, p. 57.
[142] Goethe to his mother, 11 August, 1785, in *Goethes Werke*, hrsg. im Auftrage der Großherzogin Sophie von Sachsen, 133 vols (Weimar, 1887–1912), V, pp. 178–81. Dieter Borchmeyer, 'Die literarische Kultur Weimars', in Viktor Zmegac (ed.), *Geschichte der deutschen Literatur vom 18. Jahrhundert bis zur Gegenwart*, vol 1, pt. 1, 2nd edn. (Königstein im Taunus, 1984), p. 260. Cf. Boyle, *Goethe: The Poet and the Age*, vol. 1, p. 248.
[143] Clive Brown, *Louis Spohr: A Critical Biography* (Cambridge, 1984), p. 124.

Friedrich Carl Count von Schlieben, Captain
Philip Bogislav von Heyden, Captain
Christoph Wilhelm von Schwerin, Lieutenant
Johann Abraham Caps, Civil Servant
Carl Leveaux, Merchant and Banker
Paul Jeremias Bitaubee, no profession listed
Friedrich Wilhelm Riedt, Court musician
Georg Friedrich Reinbeck, Civil Servant
Philip Sack, Cathedral Organist
Johann Gabriel Seyffahrt, Court musician
Gottlob Friedrich Pauli, Civil Servant.[144]

These were the full members; the concerts were also attended by 'gentlemen and ladies of rank'. Concert life in Berlin had begun as an initiative taken by one of Frederick the Great's musicians, Johann Gottlieb Janitsch, who organized private events for amateur performers and connoisseurs when he moved to the city with his newly crowned employer in 1740.[145]

As so often, the capital of the Habsburg monarchy limped along in the rear of European developments but, in its lumbering way, then proceeded to make a contribution more important than any other. According to Eduard Hanslick, there were no public concerts in Vienna before the accession of Maria Theresa in 1740.[146] Even after the Austrian version of the *Concerts Spirituels* had been launched in 1745, they remained even more closely tied to the regime than in France, for they were dependent on the court theatres or the riding school for a venue (there was no dedicated concert hall in Vienna until 1831).[147] The organizers repaid the compliment handsomely by making their concerts as representational of monarchical glory as anything to be found at Louis XIV's Versailles. Philipp Gumbenhuber, the assistant director of ballet in Vienna, recorded in 1758, for example, that the *Concerts Spirituels* were 'graced with a transparent decoration representing the protection that the august House of Austria has always accorded the arts'. This was replaced on 26 February by a 'Temple with transparent golden ornaments, in the middle of which was depicted, to the acclamations of the people, the celebrated Fame, Crown, and Name of our Sovereigns'. The third and last decoration appeared on 12

144 F. W. Marpurg, 'Entwurf einer ausführlichen Nachricht von der Musikübenden Gesellschaft zu Berlin', *Historisch-kritische Beyträge zur Aufnahme der Musik*, 5 vols. (Berlin, 1754–78), I, 5 (1755), pp. 402–4.

145 Ibid, I, 2 (1754), p. 155.

146 Hanslick, *Geschichte des Concertwesens in Wien*, I, 3.

147 Mary Sue Morrow, *Concert Life in Haydn's Vienna: Aspects of a Developing Musical and Social Institution* (Stuyvesant, NY, 1988), pp. xvii, 38.

March: 'a grand new transparent representing Telemachus conducted by Minerva, dressed in his armour, advancing on a carpeted path toward the Temple of Immortality, from which he is shown from afar the marks of honour and glory that await him; also seen are the pitfalls of Pride, Envy and other Vices, or monsters that oppose his passage. From this well-known symbol is recalled the Idea of what one should expect from a young Hero when he is conducted by Wisdom.' Everyone appreciated that the 'young Hero' was the Archduke Joseph, heir to the throne.[148] The first association for the organization of concerts—the Society of Musical Artists—was less aristocratic but could hardly be described as 'bourgeois' in any progressive sense. On the one hand, it tried to enhance the status of musicians by excluding anyone who played dance music, on the other hand it was first and foremost a friendly society with many of the old guild attitudes. It denied Mozart membership, for example, simply because he could not find his birth certificate and thus prove the legitimacy of his birth.[149] As we have seen, Haydn declined an invitation to join, on the grounds that the Society was dominated by a 'handicraft' mentality.[150]

Musically much more important were the private concerts staged in the aristocratic palaces. Particularly important were the Friday concerts given by Prince Joseph Friedrich von Sachsen-Hildburghausen in the Palais Rofrano. The court composer Giuseppe Bonno was hired by the prince to act as musical director for the concerts, which were given throughout the winter for the nobility.[151] If only the greatest magnates could afford to maintain their own orchestras on a permanent basis, many more could form ensembles when the need arose from the large pool of freelance musicians living in the capital.[152] The high level of musical education enjoyed by the Viennese nobles made them unusually receptive to innovative music of high quality. Their ability to appreciate—and willingness to pay for— it were at least partly responsible for the rapidity with which Haydn, Mozart, and Beethoven developed their art. During his first year as a freelance musician in Vienna, Mozart gave concerts at the residences of Countess Thun, Count Cobenzl, Prince Galitzin, and the Archduke Maximilian Franz (Joseph II's brother). As he proudly told his father, 'If you really believe that I am detested at Court and by the old and new aristocracy, just write to Herr von Strack, Countess Thun, Countess

[148] Heartz, *Haydn, Mozart and the Viennese School*, p. 52.
[149] Hanslick, *Geschichte des Concertwesens in Wien*, I, p. 17.
[150] See above, p. 85.
[151] Heartz, *Haydn, Mozart and the Viennese School*, p. 46.
[152] Hanslick, *Gesehichte des Concertwesens in Wien*, I, p. 38.

Rumbeck, Baroness Waldstätten, Herr von Sonnenfels, Frau von Trattner, *enfin*, to anyone you choose.'[153] A year later he wrote of Prince Galitzin: 'I am engaged for all his concerts. I am always fetched in his coach and brought to his house and treated there most magnificently.'[154] Beethoven was also indebted to the good taste of the Viennese nobles. It was in the palace of Prince Lichnowsky, for example, that his violin concerto, fourth symphony, fourth piano concerto, and the *Coriolan* and first *Leonora* overtures were first performed.[155]

These noble connoisseurs also played a crucial role in promoting the success of the other main vehicle for new music—the 'academy' or 'benefit concert' mounted by a composer-performer acting as his own impresario. It was Mozart's success in attracting noble support for his subscription concerts that got him off to a flying start in the capital. The list of 176 subscribers was nothing less than 'a roll call of the higher nobility, with room left over for luminaries of the lesser nobility and state bureaucracy'.[156] Fifty per cent were from the high nobility, 42 per cent from the lesser nobility, and only 8 per cent from the bourgeoisie.[157] The extent to which he depended on noble patronage is revealed by the calendar of his appearances in February and March 1784, which he sent to his father:

> Thursday, February 26th, at [Prince] Galitzin's
> Monday, March 1st, at [Count] Johann Esterházy's
> Thursday, March 4th, at Galitzin's
> Friday, March 5th, at Esterházy's
> Monday 8th at Esterházy's
> Thursday 11th at Galitzin's
> Friday 12th, at Esterházy's
> Monday 15th, at Esterházy's
> Wednesday 17th, my first *private* concert
> Thursday 18th, at Galitzin's
> Friday 19th, at Esterházy's

[153] Mozart to his father, 22 December 1781, Emily Anderson (ed. and trans.), *The Letters of Mozart and his family*, 3rd edn. (London, 1985), p. 789. Also quoted in Maynard Solomon, *Mozart: A Life* (London, 1995), p. 287.

[154] Mozart to his father, 21 December 1782, Anderson (ed.), *The Letters of Mozart* p. 832. Also quoted in Volkmar Braunbehrens, *Mozart in Vienna* (Oxford, 1991), p. 134.

[155] Joseph Kerman and Alan Tyson, *The New Grove Beethoven* (London, 1983), p. 44.

[156] Solomon, *Mozart*, pp. 291–2. A complete list can be found in Anderson (ed.), *The Letters of Mozart*, pp. 870–2.

[157] Neil Zaslaw, *Mozart's Symphonies: Context, Performance Practice, Reception* (Oxford, 1989), p. 376.

Saturday 20th, at Richter's
Sunday 21st, my first concert *in the theatre*
Monday 22nd, at Esterházy's
Wednesday 24th, my second *private* concert
Thursday 25th, at Galitzin's
Friday 26th, at Esterházy's
Saturday 27th, at Richter's
Monday 29th, at Esterházy's
Wednesday 31st, my third *private* concert
Thursday April 1st, my second concert *in the theatre*
Saturday 3rd, at Richter's.[158]

'Richter' was Georg Friedrich Richter, also a piano virtuoso, who was giving his own series in Trattner's room on the Graben and had invited Mozart to join him. The concerts Mozart called *private* were the subscription concerts, 'private' in the sense that they were exclusively for his benefit.

In other words, whether Mozart was performing in palaces or public rooms, the audience consisted mainly of nobles. It was with them in mind that he wrote the symphonies, serenades, vocal works, and—above all—the piano concertos that made up his programmes. As his copious correspondence with his father during these years makes clear, he kept eyes and ears fixed firmly on what his customers wanted. In this context it is worth recalling the sage insight of Paul Bekker that both the musician and society are involved in the creative process and that the latter's role is not confined to reception and reproduction. Musical form does not consist only of a sound-pattern as recorded by the composer on the stave. In that form it is inert matter: to come alive, it requires perception. That in turn depends on the milieu in which it is performed and it is only when the two—music and milieu—relate to each other that the finished art form emerges. Moreover, this relationship is not between active creator and passive recipient: on the contrary, both are engaged in creative interaction and depend on each other.[159] Wilhelm Furtwängler was making the same sort of point when he wrote, in an essay on ancient music in 1932, that a truly authentic performance would need not only the correct instrumentation but also the right kind of space and, above all, the right kind of mentality on the part of the audience.[160] In relation

[158] Ibid, pp. 869–70.

[159] Paul Bekker, *Das deutsche Musikleben* (Berlin, 1919), pp. 3–5.

[160] Kurt Blaukopf, *Musik im Wandel der Gesellschaft. Grundzüge der Musiksoziologie* (Munich and Zürich, 1982), p. 104.

to Mozart, if it would be pushing the argument too far to classify Mozart's work as 'aristocratic', it would certainly make more sense than to call it 'bourgeois'.[161]

The other great privileged order of old regime Europe—the Church—also made a powerful contribution to the development of concerts. This came in the form of the oratorio, which derived from the spiritual exercises performed at the Congregatio dell'Oratorio in Rome, founded by St Philip Neri in the late sixteenth century.[162] By the middle of the seventeenth century, the performance of sacred texts in the vernacular, accompanied by music, was well established in Italy and was spreading into Austria. In Protestant Germany it was grafted on to a long-standing Lutheran tradition of the *historia*, a musical setting of biblical stories, to emerge as a distinct genre by 1700. Its decisive penetration of the secular musical world came in 1732 when Handel's 'Oratorio or Sacred Drama' *Esther* was first performed in public at the Crown and Anchor Tavern in the Strand and then at the King's Theatre in the Haymarket, hitherto the great centre of Italian opera in London.[163]

The immediate and durable popularity of Handel's oratorios added a new dimension to concert life, first in London and then elsewhere in Europe. This success cannot be explained simply in terms of the brilliance of Handel's music. The new genre also satisfied a social need by making public music-making respectable. The oratorio was edifying, lending itself admirably to the raising of money for charity, so it overcame the old association of listening to music in public with ale-house 'musique rooms' or dance halls. Handel's turn from composing *opera seria* with Italian libretti for the aristocratic patrons of the King's Theatre to oratorios in the English language looks like a classic case of an entrepreneurial response to a fast-growing middle-class market. Yet his audience does not appear to have changed as much as one might have expected. The high cost of mounting an oratorio meant that high admission prices excluded all but the most affluent. In 1737 the periodical *Common Sense* complained that 'every Body knows his [Handel's] Entertainments are calculated for the Quality only, and that People of moderate Fortunes cannot pretend to them, although, as Free *Britons*, they have as good a Right to be

[161] For a recent example of the view that Mozart was a bourgeois revolutionary, see Nicholas Till, *Mozart and the Enlightenment: Truth, Virtue, and Beauty in Mozart's Operas* (London, 1995).

[162] Howard E. Smither, 'Oratorio', *The New Grove Dictionary of Music and Musicians*, ed. Stanley Sadie, 20 vols (London, 1980), vol. 13, p. 657. This account is a great deal more readable than the same author's authoritative but indigestible multi-volume *A History of the Oratorio*.

[163] Donald Burrows, *Handel* (London, 1994), pp. 165–6.

entertained with what they do not understand as their Betters.'[164] The aristocratic patrons remained deeply involved in attending and promoting oratorios, never more so than on the occasion of the great 'Handel Commemoration' of 1784 held in Westminster Abbey and the Pantheon. Organized by Viscount Fitzwilliam, Sir Watkin Williams Wynn, Bart., and Jonah Bates (Commissioner of the Victualling Office), attended by the King, several members of the royal family, and many peers of the realm, the concerts served only to demonstrate the continuing cultural leadership of the aristocracy. Of the 389 subscribers to the Ancient Concerts from which the initiative stemmed, more than a third were peers, baronets, or knights.[165] As the most authoritative account of the affair concludes: 'Concert life was quite clearly not a bourgeois creation but required an already established aristocratic culture which was expanded by emulation by the middle class.'[166]

Oratorios became a permanent feature of concert programmes across Europe. Their importance lay not just in the respectability they brought to the genre but also to the change in attitude they inculcated in concert-goers. Perhaps because the early concerts were so closely connected to taverns, audiences continued to behave in a relaxed fashion long after they had moved to proper music-rooms, arriving late, moving around during the performance, chatting to their neighbours, and so on. An oratorio which proclaimed the truth of religion and the equally important truth of the greatness of the British nation had to be approached in a quite different frame of mind. As an observer of the Handel Commemoration recorded: when George III led the audience (or should it rather be called a congregation?) in standing for the Hallelujah Chorus, it was a demonstration of 'national assent to the fundamental truths of religion'.[167] Here we see the beginning of a phenomenon with a long and distinguished future: the sacralization of art. It was detected in 1778 in Fanny Burney's novel *Evelina, or The History of a Young Lady's Entrance into the World*,

[164] Quoted in Burrows, *Handel*, p. 194; part of this passage is also quoted in Ruth Smith, *Handel's Oratorios* (Cambridge, 1995), p. 36.

[165] William Weber, 'The 1784 Handel Commemoration as political ritual', *Journal of British Studies*, 28, 1 (1989), p. 48.

[166] Anna Verena Westermayr, *The 1784 Handel Commemoration: The Conduct and Interpretation of a Spectacle* (unpublished Cambridge M.Phil. dissertation, 1996), p. 16. William Weber's influential article—'The 1784 Handel commemoration as political ritual', *Journal of British Studies*, 27 (1989) pp. 43–69—contains much of value but exaggerates the extent to which the Commemoration was dominated by party politics.

[167] Westermayr, *The 1784 Handel Commemoration*, p. 42. It is likely that the practice of standing was initiated by George II at the first London performance in 1743; Richard Luckett, *Handel's Messiah: A Celebration* (London, 1992), p. 175. I am indebted to Prof. Derek Beales for this reference.

when the eponymous heroine described a visit to the Pantheon (where part of the Handel Commemoration was to be staged in 1784):

About eight o'clock we went to the Pantheon. I was extremely struck with the beauty of the building, which greatly surpassed whatever I could have expected or imagined. Yet, it has more the appearance of a chapel, than of a place of diversion; and, though I was quite charmed with the magnificence of the room, I felt that I could not be as gay and thoughtless there as at Ranelagh [pleasure gardens], for there is something in it which rather inspires awe and solemnity, than mirth and pleasure.[168]

However, there was still some way to go before concerts could be listened to in the sepulchral hush required by modern audiences, for Evelina went on:

There was an exceedingly good concert, but too much talking to hear it well. Indeed I am quite astonished to find how little music is attended to in silence; for though everybody seems to admire, hardly any body listens.[169]

CONCLUSION

As the example of Europe's concert culture has shown, a public sphere did indeed develop in the eighteenth century, but it was not essentially or even mainly 'bourgeois'. *Sub specie æternitatis* it might be said that the period witnessed the beginning of a transfer of cultural power from the nobility to the middle classes, but any suggestion that the latter had 'triumphed' is, at the very least, a premature verdict. It would make as much sense to argue that it was the nobles who had made the most of the emancipatory opportunities provided by the public sphere. Freed from the constraints of the representational court culture epitomized by Versailles, they found that their education, material resources, and enterprise fitted them well for competition in the meritocratic world which was now opening up. The average European noble in the late eighteenth century enjoyed a cultural diet which was much more varied, much more satisfying, and much more useful than the meagre fare force-fed to his ancestors. Those who could adapt found that a much richer world—in both a material and a metaphorical sense—opened up for them.

The same could be said of creative and performing artists. The dependent culture fostered by the representational world of the courts could bring

[168] Frances Burney, *Evelina, or The History of a Young Lady's Entrance into the World*, ed. Margaret Anne Doody (London, 1994), p. 116.

[169] Ibid., p. 117.

security, wealth, and even status, but it also involved subservience to the patron, whether individual or institutional. Entering the public sphere as a freelancer could be a liberating experience, but—as we shall see later—it could also lead to poverty, insecurity, and a new kind of tyranny—the philistinism of the general public. This dialectic could be resolved only by retaining the material resources of the established order but using them not to represent the glory of the patron but to celebrate the glory of *art*. When this sacralization was achieved, the artist could become the high priest of the modern world, elevated above patron and public. As the eighteenth century drew to a close, the process was well under way and was about to receive a massive impetus from the French Revolution. As the next chapter will show, this great upheaval, which affected every part of Europe, did not come like a clap of thunder in a clear sky, but was a specifically French reaction to a general European phenomenon—the emergence of nationalism.

PART III

Revolution

6

The Rise of the Nation

FROM PERSON TO CONCEPT: 'THE KING IS DEAD, LONG LIVE THE STATE!'

In his pamphlet of 1691, *The Sighs of France in Chains*, the Protestant pastor Pierre Jurieu bitterly complained:

In times gone by, there was talk only of the interests of the state, of the needs of the state, of the preservation of the state. But to speak in this way today would be literally to commit the crime of high treason. The King has taken the place of the state ... The King is now everything and the state is nothing any more ... He is the idol to whom whole provinces, the high and the mighty as well as the lowly, towns, finances—in short, everything—are sacrificed.[1]

Including Jurieu himself, he might have added, since he had been forced to flee France together with some 200,000 of his co-religionists, victims of Louis XIV's Catholic zeal.[2] He might also have summarized his account of the King's usurpation of the state with Louis's most famous saying: *L'état, c'est moi*. There could be no better illustration of the power of political myth than this encapsulation of absolutism. It does not matter that there is no reliable evidence that Louis ever said '*L'état, c'est moi*.' Nor does it matter—much—that it is not an accurate summary of his political principles. In the *Mémoires* he wrote for the guidance of his eldest son, he made it amply clear that he did *not* regard himself

[1] Marcel Marion, 'État', in *Dictionnaire des institutions de la France aux XVIIe et XVIIIe siècles* (Paris, 1923; reprinted 1968), p. 215.

[2] François Bluche, *Louis XIV* (Oxford, 1990), p. 406.

as the absolute owner of his dominions. On the contrary, he stressed that he was merely 'the trustee of the public assets' (*dépositaire de la fortune publique*), which he was obliged to administer as 'a wise steward'. In his treatise *On the Royal Profession* (*Sur le métier du roi*) of 1679 he was even more explicit on the paramount claims of the state: 'The interest of the state must come first... When one looks to the state, one is really working for oneself. The welfare of the former secures the glory of the latter. The ruler who makes the state content, prestigious and powerful also promotes his own glory.'[3] Moreover, the King of France was not absolute in the sense of being able to do anything he liked for, if his sovereignty was perfect and indivisible, his power was restricted by the obligation to heed the laws of God, the laws of natural justice, and the 'fundamental laws' of the land. The French monarchy may have been absolute but it was not despotic.[4]

Perhaps it was not despotic in theory, but practice was a different matter. When Louis waged victorious wars against the Spanish or Austrian Habsburgs and reaped rich rewards in the Netherlands, Alsace, and Franche-Comté, it was possible to believe that the interest of the state was indeed coming first. But when he fought a long, exhausting, and inglorious war to place his grandson on the Spanish throne, it was the Bourbon dynasty rather than the French state which appeared to be at the top of his agenda. On the home front, when he decreed in 1673 that in future the Parlements should register royal edicts before making any comment, when he revoked the Edict of Nantes in 1685, or when he declared in 1714 that his illegitimate sons were eligible to succeed him, he placed himself above the law. Most important of all was the cult of kingship promoted so assiduously at Versailles and discussed in the first chapter of this book. Never before had sovereignty been so personalized, so no wonder that any more general concept such as the state was swamped. So *L'état, c'est moi* would be the perfect motto for the cultural complex designed to elevate him above all other mortals. For that reason, Jurieu's charge must be upheld.

Jurieu died in exile in 1713, when it seemed that Louis XIV's style of kingship was setting the tone not only for France but all Europe. In the words of Voltaire, 19 years old when Louis died, the reign had been 'the most

[3] Fritz Hartung, 'L'état c'est moi', *Historische Zeitschrift*, 169 (1949), p. 18. Cf. Carl Hinrichs, 'Zur Selbstauffassung Ludwigs XIV. in seinen *Mémoires*', in Gerhard Oestreich (ed.), *Preußen als historisches Problem* (Berlin, 1964), p. 300.

[4] Roland Mousnier and Fritz Hartung, 'Quelques problèmes concernant la monarchie absolue', in *Relazioni del X. Congresso Internationale di Scienze Storiche*, vol. IV (Florence, 1955), pp. 6–7.

enlightened age the world has ever seen', in the course of which 'a general revolution took place in our arts, minds and customs, as in our government, which will serve as an eternal token of the true glory of our country.'[5] Yet even as he wrote those words in 1738, the 'cunning of history' (Hegel) was demonstrating the instability of the personalized kingship Louis XIV had created. So single-minded had been its pursuit that the dialectical need for its antithesis was correspondingly intense. It quickly became apparent that the personal absolutism he had created was only one staging-post on the route to the modern state. Just fifty years after the Sun King's death, the observation of Pierre Jurieu quoted above was almost exactly reversed by the Abbé Veri when he wrote: 'The commonplaces of my youth like "serve the King" are no longer on the lips of Frenchmen... Dare one say that for "serve the King" we have substituted "serve the State", a word which, since the time of Louis XIV, has been blasphemy?'[6]

The temporary quality of Louis's victory was obscured by a misunderstanding of its nature. To contemporaries, it looked as though he had triumphed in his own cause but, with the advantage of hindsight, we can see that he was only the instrument of a greater and more impersonal force: the idea of the state. Although its origins can be traced back to the Greeks, in its modern form this was a relatively new concept. It may have been born out of a need to respond to the expansion of the European economy and the strains imposed by commercialization on traditional social relationships. That was certainly the view of Marxist-Leninist historians such as Perry Anderson, who saw the absolutist state as 'the new political carapace of a threatened nobility... whose permanent political function was the repression of the peasant and plebeian masses at the foot of the social hierarchy'.[7] Attractive in its simplicity, this was too much at odds with the absolute monarchs' preoccupation with *reducing* the power of their nobles to be entirely cogent. Much more persuasive has been the argument of Quentin Skinner advanced in his classic study *The Foundations of Modern Political Thought*.[8] He demonstrates that the main elements of the

[5] Voltaire, *The Age of Louis XIV* (London, 1961), pp. 1–2.

[6] Simon Schama, *Citizens: A Chronicle of the French Revolution* (New York, 1989), p. 103. A rather different version of this quotation is to be found in J. McManners, 'The revolution and its antecedents', in J. Wallace-Hadrill and J. McManners (eds.), *France: Government and Society*, 2nd edn. (London, 1970), p. 175: 'Today, hardly anyone dare say in Parisian society, *I serve the king*... You'd be taken for one of the chief valets at Versailles. *I serve the state* is the expression most commonly used.'

[7] Perry Anderson, *Lineages of the Absolutist State* (London, 1974), pp. 18–19. Anderson quotes similar views from Christopher Hill and Louis Althusser.

[8] 2 vols. (Cambridge, 1978).

modern concept of the state were gradually acquired between the late thirteenth and late sixteenth centuries:

> The decisive shift was made from the idea of the ruler 'maintaining his state'—where this simply meant upholding his own position—to the idea that there is a separate legal and constitutional order, that of the State, which the ruler has a duty to maintain. One effect of this transformation was that the power of the State, not that of the ruler, came to be envisaged as the basis of government. And this in turn enabled the State to be conceptualised in distinctively modern terms—as the sole source of law and legitimate force within its own territory, and as the sole appropriate object of its citizens' allegiances.[9]

During those three centuries, three crucial axioms were formed: first, politics came to be regarded as a discrete realm, independent of theology; secondly, the supreme authority in any polity came to be regarded as independent of any international agency such as the Papacy or Holy Roman Empire; and thirdly, that authority also claimed a monopoly of legislation and allegiance within its borders.[10] This long process had been given a sharp impetus by the Reformation. This was partly due to Luther's need to fill the jurisdictional vacuum created by his rejection of the Catholic Church by elevating the power of the secular authorities in secular matters. He made the following precepts of St Paul the most quoted of all biblical texts:

> Let every soul be subject unto the higher powers. For there is no power but of God: the powers that be are ordained of God.
>
> Whosoever therefore resisteth the power, resisteth the ordinance of God: and they that resist shall receive to themselves damnation.
>
> For rulers are not a terror to good works, but to the evil. Wilt thou then not be afraid of the power? (Romans 13: 1–3)

The absolute denial of any right of political resistance which he founded on this text was then given added cogency by the intense and prolonged period of civil strife that followed—and appeared to have been caused by—the spread of religious dissent. It was in the midst of the 'French Religious Wars' that Jean Bodin published *Six Books of a Commonweal* in 1576, in which he derived from the concept of the state the allied principles of non-resistance and absolute sovereignty.[11] Many more years of upheaval, culminating in the Frondes of 1648–53,[12] were needed before theory could be translated into practice. As

[9] Quentin Skinner, *The Foundations of Modern Political Thought*, I, pp. ix–x.
[10] Ibid., II, p. 349. [11] Ibid., II, p. 286. [12] See above, pp. 29–30.

we have seen in Chapter 1, Louis XIV was to be the instrument. Almost simultaneously, Bodin's theory of sovereignty was taken still further by Thomas Hobbes in *Leviathan*, first published in 1651, two years after the execution of Charles I. Although a royalist, Hobbes stressed that allegiance should be paid not to the person who exercised sovereignty but to the sovereignty inherent in the state.[13] Indeed, shortly after completing *Leviathan* he returned to England from his French exile and made his peace with the new regicide regime.

Although fiercely criticized, not to say vilified during the course of his long life (1588–1679), the future lay with Hobbes's *étatiste* authoritarian discourse. By the eighteenth century the new terminology had won general acceptance and 'the state' was firmly established as the 'master-noun of political argument' right across Europe.[14] Moreover, it was a state with an expanding agenda. As power came to be concentrated, so were the traditional intermediary bodies marginalized, their assets expropriated, and their tasks reassigned to the central authorities. If not all of them suffered the terminal fate of the monasteries in Protestant countries, the days of the polycentric state were clearly numbered. Noble clientage systems, provinces, municipalities, trading companies, guilds, universities, and, above all, the Church were pushed to one side by the relentless march of Leviathan. Even in Catholic countries ruled by personally pious monarchs his footsteps were plain to see. At the heart of the educational reforms in the Habsburg monarchy under Maria Theresa (1740–80), for example, was the principle that education must cease to be part of the Church's domain (an *ecclesiasticum*) and become the responsibility of the state: 'it is and shall remain for all time a *Politicum*.'[15] To point out that corporate groups independent of the Habsburg state continued to provide what schooling there was (and most other social services too) does not matter, for 'once the world of ideas has been revolutionised, reality cannot hold out for long'

[13] Quentin Skinner, 'The state', in Terence Ball, James Farr, and Russell L. Hanson (eds.), *Political Innovation and Conceptual Change* (Cambridge, 1989), p. 124.

[14] Ibid., p. 123. Even in the polycentric Holy Roman Empire, the concept was well established by the late eighteenth century. In his trail-blazing dictionary Johann Christoph Adelung emphasized that 'Der Staat' was both 'abstractum' and 'concretum', giving as examples of the former meaning 'to talk against the state', 'a crime against the state', 'for the good of the state'; Johann Christoph Adelung, *Grammatisch-kritisches Wörterbuch der hochdeutschen Mundart, mit beständiger Vergleichung der übrigen Mundarten, besonders aber der Oberdeutschen*, rev. edn., 4 vols. (Vienna, 1807–8). The first edition of his dictionary was published between 1774 and 1786.

[15] T. C. W. Blanning, *Joseph II* (London, 1994), p. 39. See also above, pp. 117–18.

(Hegel).[16] The same reply can be given to all the other reservations which might reasonably be made about the actual performance of the early modern state elsewhere in Europe.

It was not just a question of filling the vacuum. Decision-makers at the centre began to adopt a more positive view of the state's function. A domestic policy confined to containing religious strife and restraining over-mighty subjects was no longer deemed adequate. In the words of Marc Raeff: 'in the course of the seventeenth century, and with accelerated dynamic force, the legislation acquired a positive cast; its aims no longer were to restore and correct abuses and defects but rather to create new conditions, to bring about changes and introduce innovations.'[17] This was part of the more general intellectual change which can still be called the 'scientific revolution'. If no one now believes with Alexander Pope that 'Nature and Nature's laws lay hid in night, God said "Let Newton be!" and all was light,'[18] there was clearly a fundamental change in the mind-set of educated Europeans in the course of the sixteenth and seventeenth centuries, which led towards secular rationalism.[19] Once it was accepted that the earth and the cosmos were governed by the same natural laws and that these laws could be discovered by a scientific method combining mathematics with empiricism, the way was open for governments to become more concerned with improving conditions in this world. The additional belief that man was not hopelessly soiled with original sin but was a product of his environment[20] also encouraged activism.

As the concept of the state developed, the most conspicuous losers were the corporate bodies which had flourished during the Middle Ages, while the main beneficiary appeared to be the monarch. As we have seen, the apotheosis of absolute monarchy at Versailles lifted Louis XIV far above ordinary mortals into a realm of his own. But could *l'état* be *moi* (or rather *lui*)? Could an abstraction be mated with a person? Would not the issue of this union be as sterile as a mule? In understanding the contradiction which lay at the heart of Louis XIV's creation, the most helpful analytical tools are those supplied by Max Weber. In particular, Weber's tripartite categorization of political

[16] Quoted in Lothar Gall, 'Einleitung', in Lothar Gall (ed.), *Liberalismus*, 2nd edn. (Königstein im Taunus, 1980), p. 11.

[17] Marc Raeff, *The Well-ordered Police State: Social and Institutional Change through Law in the Germanies and Russia 1600–1800* (New Haven and London, 1983), p. 50.

[18] *Epitaph intended for Sir Isacc Newton.*

[19] A. Rupert Hall, 'On the historical singularity of the scientific revolution of the seventeenth century', in J. H. Elliott and H. G. Koenigsberger (eds.), *The Diversity of History: Essays in Honour of Sir Herbert Butterfield* (London, 1970), pp. 210–11.

[20] See above, p. 115.

legitimacy is enlightening. In answering the question 'why do men obey?' he identified three inner justifications: 'traditional' authority, which derives from simply existing for a very long time ('the eternal yesterday' in Weber's poetic formulation); 'legal' authority, which derives from 'the belief in the validity of legal statute and functional competence based on rationally created rules'; and 'charismatic' authority, which derives from a belief in the God-given superhuman qualities of a leader or prophet.[21]

Although they did not use Weberian language, Louis XIV's propagandists in effect proclaimed that the object of their veneration had combined all three sources of authority to form a package of unprecedented power. He could claim descent from Clovis (466–511), the first Merovingian king of the Franks. His restoration of order in his kingdom, together with Colbert's reform of the government apparatus, confirmed his status as law-giver and rational administrator. Most powerfully of all, his military success combined with the Versailles cult to make him the most charismatic king of all time, rivalled only by Charlemagne. But it turned out that each source of authority was flawed. No one doubted that he was the lawful King of France, but—as we have seen[22]—for all its ancient lineage, the Bourbon dynasty had ruled the country only since 1589. Moreover, the drive for absolutism had been accomplished at the cost of many traditional institutions, most notably the high nobility, the provincial Estates, and the Parlements. Closer inspection also revealed serious blemishes in his legal authority. If the duc de Saint-Simon was unusually outspoken in branding Louis a 'criminal' guilty of 'high treason' (for seeking to make his bastard sons eligible for the royal succession),[23] there was a growing number of critics who believed that 'absolutism' was nothing more than despotism.[24] Nor was 'functional competence based on rationally created rules' very apparent by 1715. The Colbertian reforms of the 1660s and 1670s had long succumbed to the pressures imposed by the paramount demands of war. Most fatally, perhaps, fiscal pressure had forced the abandoning of Colbert's plans to eradicate venality from the administration. The War of the League of Augsburg, which began in 1688, brought a massive expansion of offices for sale, from which the old regime never recovered.[25]

[21] 'Politics as a vocation' (a lecture given at Munich University 1918), in H. H. Gerth and C. Wright Mills (eds.), *From Max Weber: Essays in Sociology*, new edn. (London, 1991), pp. 78–9.

[22] See above, p. 39.

[23] W. H. Lewis (ed.), *The Memoirs of the Duc de Saint-Simon* (London, 1964), p. 114.

[24] Georges Pagès, *Les origines du XVIIIe siècle au temps de Louis XIV (1680–1715)* (Paris, 1961), p. 119.

[25] William Doyle, *Venality: The Sale of Offices in Eighteenth-century France* (Oxford, 1996), ch. 2, *passim*.

The most fragile source of authority, however, was Louis's charisma. That it existed is not in doubt. Although he did not use the word, this was the quality which the duc de Saint-Simon identified when he commented on the King's ability to command awe-struck obedience simply by his bearing, gesture, and tone of voice.[26] As another contemporary observed: 'no one possessed such a fine bearing as this sovereign, or a more noble appearance, or more assured manners. His rather theatrical way of moving would have seemed ridiculous in anyone else.'[27] In his prime, this special gift carried all before it. Perhaps its finest pictorial expression was provided by Pierre Mignard in *Louis XIV at Maastricht* of 1672. Dressed as a Roman emperor, Louis sits astride a rearing horse, controlling its strength without effort and radiating the regal confidence that comes from military victory, his Dutch conquests pictured in the background as Victory crowns him with a laurel wreath. Twenty-nine years later, Hyacinthe Rigaud painted an even more celebrated portrait. Swathed in an ermine cloak, the 63-year-old king stands on a dais against a background of swirling drapes and the attributes of kingship, as he looks down at the viewer with unsmiling *hauteur*. The pose he has struck is balletic, which shows off to good effect the young man's legs Rigaud has generously given him, their length accentuated by his red high-heeled shoes. But the face is the face of an old man, prematurely aged, with sunken eyes, puffy jowls, and a drooping lower lip implying the absence of teeth.

Heroes who rely on their charisma are best advised to die young, especially if youth forms part of their appeal. It was probably fortunate for his subsequent reputation that Alexander the Great died at the age of 32. As we shall see in the case of Frederick the Great, it is possible for a charismatic reputation to survive the ageing process, but only with the application of great intelligence and a good slice of luck. Louis XIV possessed neither in sufficient measure. The last twenty years or so of his reign were dogged with misfortune. There were good years as well as bad years, recoveries as well as slumps, but the overall trend was down—demographically, economically, fiscally, politically, and militarily. A run of defeats at the hands of the Austrians and the British in the War of the League of Augsburg (1689–97) and the War of the Spanish Succession (1701–14) made the bombastic triumphalism of Versailles seem hollow as well as outdated.[28] Events on the home front were equally dispiriting: the demographic catastrophe of 1693–4, when fewer than half the usual

[26] See above, p. 40.
[27] Quoted in C. Lenient, *La Poésie patriotique en France dans les temps modernes*, 2 vols. (Paris, 1894), vol. I, p. 377.
[28] See above, pp. 103–4.

number of children were born, or the devastating epidemic of 1700–1, or the great freeze of 1709–10 were among the great natural disasters of early modern Europe.[29]

Not surprisingly, the combination of dearth and defeat bred opposition. So grim were memories of the anarchy of the Frondes that Louis had enjoyed a prolonged honeymoon in their aftermath. Even dissident groups, such as Jansenists and Huguenots, accepted absolutism without question in the 1660s and 1670s. It was only after the revocation of the Edict of Nantes in 1685 and the 'Glorious Revolution' in England in 1688 that critical voices began to be heard. They certainly did not sing in unison. Some, such as Saint-Simon, looked back to an aristocratic golden age destroyed by Richelieu and his successors; some, such as Boulainvilliers, defended the nobility against the levelling policies of absolutism but also advocated political and social reform; some, such as Vauban, looked forward to a service nobility ruled by a king who was first servant of the state; some, such as Fénelon, called for moral renewal and religious revival; some, such as the Protestant exile Jurieu, concentrated on Louis's religious persecutions; some, such as Boisguillebert, wanted popular representation through the Estates General, fiscal control by the Parlements, and greater provincial autonomy; some, such as Saint-Pierre, looked beyond the *société d'ordres* to a meritocratic utopia.[30]

Certainly there was never any prospect of this discordant clamour posing a threat to the regime. The opposition's best hope lay in the reversionary interest that formed around the 'second Dauphin', Louis's grandson the duc de Bourgogne, but that was snuffed out with his untimely death in 1712. Nevertheless, the collapse of consensus among the French elite signalled the beginning of what was eventually to become a full-blown 'legitimacy crisis'.[31] It also revealed the shallow roots of the absolutist system Louis had created. In abandoning tradition and compromising legality, it placed too great a strain on royal charisma. As Weber was to observe, 'by its very nature, the existence of charismatic authority is specifically unstable,' because the leader can legitimate his authority only by performing appropriate deeds—if he is a prophet then he must perform miracles, if he is a war-lord, then he must win battles.[32]

[29] Pierre Goubert, *Louis XIV and Twenty Million Frenchmen* (1970), pp. 216, 257.

[30] Werner Gembruch, 'Reformforderungen in Frankreich um die Wende vom 17. zum 18. Jahrhundert: ein Beitrag zur Geschichte der Opposition gegen System und Politik Ludwigs XIV.', *Historische Zeitschrift*, 209 (1969), pp. 265–317. This is the best account and analysis of the opposition to Louis XIV available in any language.

[31] See below, pp. 374–405.

[32] 'The sociology of charismatic authority' [from *Wirtschaft und Gesellschaft*, pt. III, ch. 9], in Gerth and Mills (ed.), *From Max Weber*, pp. 248–9.

By the closing years of his life, Louis could manage neither. To guard against a loss of charisma or an inadequate successor, the quality must be institutionalized, that is to say, it must be associated with a value, an institution, or even an abstraction so that it can survive misfortune. In other words, a personalized political system such as Louis XIV's needs to be 'objectivized' (*versachlicht*) and thus made immortal. It was the failure of Louis and his successors to reinvigorate the political myth of absolutism that condemned the French old regime to early extinction. Yet it was not an impossible task, as we shall see in the next two sections.

THE PRUSSIAN WAY

Frederick II succeeded his father, Frederick William I, on 31 May 1740. Two days later he summoned his ministers and laid down the basic principles of his reign. Three independent eye-witness accounts agree that he announced a fundamental change of priorities: whereas his father had always drawn a distinction between the interests of the king and the interests of the country, 'I look upon the interests of the state as my own: I can have no interests which are not equally those of my people. If the two are incompatible, the preference is always to be given to the welfare and advantage of the country.'[33] This sounds very much like Louis XIV's declaration of 1679 quoted above,[34] but it was underpinned by quite a different political philosophy. Divine right meant nothing to Frederick: all religions, he opined, were 'more or less absurd' and none more so than Christianity, 'an old metaphysical fiction, stuffed with contradictions and nonsense, born in the fevered imagination of the Orientals and spread by them to Europe, where it was embraced by fanatics, exploited by opportunists, and believed by imbeciles.'[35] Nor did he employ arguments based on the 'eternal yesterday', perhaps because he was well aware that it had only been the day before yesterday that the Hohenzollerns had become margraves of Brandenburg (1415) and the previous evening that they had

[33] Leopold von Ranke, *Memoirs of the House of Brandenburg and History of Prussia during the Seventeenth and Eighteenth Centuries*, 3 vols. (London, 1849), II, p. 45.

[34] See p. 186.

[35] G. B. Volz (ed.), *Die Politischen Testamente Friedrichs des Großen* (Berlin, 1920), pp. 31, 185. Volz reprints the two political testaments in the original French. A German translation of the testament of 1752 can be found in Otto Bardong (ed.), *Friedrich der Große*, Ausgewählte Quellen zur deutschen Geschichte der Neuzeit. Freiherr vom Stein-Gedächtnisausgabe, vol. 22 (Darmstadt, 1982).

become kings in Prussia (1701). He had little or no dynastic sense, regarding other members of his family with deep mistrust and a loathing which was warmly if secretly reciprocated.[36] Legitimate political authority, Frederick argued in his numerous theoretical treatises, could be derived only from a contract between ruler and ruled. In the course of a discussion of religious toleration in his *Essay on the Forms of Government and the Duties of Sovereigns* (1777), he wrote:

One can compel by force some poor wretch to utter a certain form of words, yet he will deny to it his inner consent; thus the persecutor has gained nothing. But if one goes back to the origins of society it is completely clear that the sovereign has no right to dictate the way in which the citizens will think. Would one not have to be demented to suppose that men said to one of their number: we are raising you above us because we like being slaves, and so we are giving you the power to direct our thoughts as you like? On the contrary, what they said was: we need you to maintain the laws which we wish to obey, to govern us wisely, to defend us; for the rest, we require that you respect our liberty.[37]

That contract determined the nature of Frederick's kingship, which can be summed up in a single word: 'service'. It became the watchword of his regime and the essence of the political myth he created:

So that the prince never neglects his duties, he should often recall to mind that he is a man just like the least of his subjects. If he is the first judge, the first general, the first minister of society, it is not so that he can indulge himself but so that he can fulfil the duties. He is only the first servant of the state, obliged to act with honesty, wisdom, and with a complete lack of self-interest, as if at every moment he might be called upon to render an account of his stewardship to his fellow citizens.[38]

In the realm of political theory, notions of contract, obligation, and service were commonplace by 1740, but in the baroque world of the Holy Roman Empire, they represented a culture change of truly seismic proportions. Frederick's father had adopted as thoroughgoing a patrimonial attitude to his dominions as it is possible to imagine. In his own political testament of 1722 he listed his various bits and pieces of territory as if he were an English squire totting up his estates and—just like his English counterpart—sought to protect them from a wayward heir by means of an entail

[36] Gerhard Ritter, *Friedrich der Große. Ein historisches Profil*, 3rd edn. (Heidelberg, 1954), p. 202.

[37] 'Essai sur les formes de gouvernement et sur les devoirs des souverains', *Œuvres*, vol. IX (Berlin, 1848), p. 208.

[38] Ibid.

(*Fideikommiss*).[39] 'We are Lord and Master and can do as we please' pithily summed up his attitude to political responsibility. When he used the word 'state' (*Staat*) he did so only to designate his private domains (*Kammerstaat*) or to mean foreign policy (*Staatssachen*).[40] His semi-literate but trenchant advice to his son conveys well the flavour of pre-Frederickian political discourse in Prussia. Characteristically, Frederick William began with a prayer: he had always placed his trust in God, he was certain of salvation, and he repented of his sins. His successor must take no mistresses (or rather whores as they should properly be termed); he must lead a godly life and set an example to the country and army; he must not indulge in excessive eating or drinking; he must tolerate no theatre, opera, ballet, masquerades, or public dancing in his dominions, for they were all the work of the Devil—the house of Hohenzollern had always shunned such things, and that was why God had smiled on it; he must fear God and never start an unjust war, but must also stand up for Hohenzollern rights; and so on and so forth.[41]

One thing both Hohenzollerns could agree on, however, was the need for hard work. Both set a tireless example of devotion to public service which pulled both officers and officials along in their wake. Frederick William I's advice to make a personal inspection of each province annually was faithfully followed by his successor. No one knew where or when the King might pop up next, as he travelled around with just a few aides, asking awkward questions, issuing orders, criticizing, and (less often) praising, and above all setting an example. A good impression of what this could involve for a local official is Chief Bailiff Fromme's account of Frederick's visit to a village in the Mittelmark in 1779:

Towards eight in the morning His Majesty arrived in Seelenhorst. General Count von Görtz was also in the carriage. While the horses were being changed, the king talked to the officers of the Ziethen hussars, whose squadrons were put out to pasture in the surrounding villages...

Now the king reached Fehrbellin. There he spoke with Lieutenant Probst of the Ziethen hussars (his father had already served as squadron commander with the regiment) and with the local postmaster, Captain von Mosch...

[39] Fritz Hartung, 'Die politischen Testamente der Hohenzollern', in Otto Büsch and Wolfgang Neugebauer (eds.), *Moderne Preußische Geschichte*, vol. III (Berlin and New York, 1981), p. 1506.

[40] Ibid., p. 1505.

[41] 'Instruction König Friedrich Wilhelms I. für seinen Nachfolger', *Acta Borussica: Die Behördenorganisation und die allgemeine Staatsverwaltung Preussens im 18. Jahrhundert*, vol. III, ed. G. Schmoller, D. Krauske, and V. Loewe (Berlin, 1901), pp. 441–67.

KING List the estates on the right here.
FROMME Buskow, Radensleben, Sommerfeld, Beetz, Karwe.
KING That's it? Karwe. Who is the owner?
FROMME Herr von Knesebeck.
KING Was he in service?
FROMME Yes. Lieutenant or ensign in the guards.
KING In the guards? (Counting on his fingers.) You are right; he was lieutenant in the guards. I am very glad that the estate still belongs to the family...
KING What is the name of the village ahead?
FROMME Protzen.
KING Who is the owner?
FROMME Herr von Kleist.
KING Which Kleist?
FROMME A son of General von Kleist.
KING Which General von Kleist?
FROMME His brother was Your Majesty's adjutant, and is now lieutenant-colonel in the Regiment von Kalkstein, stationed in Magdeburg.
KING Oh, that Kleist! I know the family well. Was this Kleist also in service?
FROMME Yes, Your Majesty. He was ensign in the Regiment of Prince Ferdinand.
KING Why did he resign?
FROMME I don't know.

To keep his servants on their toes, Frederick William I had posted a number of spectacular warnings. In 1732, on the same day that he and his court knelt in prayer to greet Protestant refugees from Salzburg, he had an official found guilty of embezzlement garrotted in front of his office, with all other personnel obliged to watch.[42] Even more spectacular was the lesson he taught the Junkers of East Prussia when he visited the province on one of his tours of inspection. He told Councillor von Schlubhut, imprisoned for corruption, that he deserved to be hanged. 'One does not hang a Prussian nobleman' was the defiant reply. The councillor paid for his feeble grasp of his sovereign's psychology with his life: Frederick William promptly had a gallows built in the courtyard of Königsberg castle and had von Schlubhut hanged from it the following day, after first attending church and listening to a sermon on the text 'Blessed are the merciful, for they shall obtain mercy' (Matthew 5: 7). Frederick rejected both his father's religion and his criminology, partly out of conviction and partly because such brutality was no longer necessary: by 1740 the Prussian nobility was well broken in to state service, indeed, they

[42] Walther Hubatsch, 'Zum Preußenbild in der Geschichte', in *Das Preußenbild in der Geschichte*, ed. Otto Büsch (Berlin, 1981), p. 16.

had come to enjoy the enhanced income and status it brought. Frederick rather saw it as his duty to protect 'the finest jewel in his crown', as he described the nobility in his political testament of 1752, not only by preserving the status quo but by helping them to improve their material circumstances.[43] He was as insistent as his father, however, that service should be the only criterion of merit in the Prussian state:

Let me make it plain once and for all that I will not sell titles and still less noble estates for money to the debasement of the nobility. Noble status can only be gained by the sword, by bravery, and by other outstanding behaviour and services. I will tolerate as vassals only those who are at all times capable of rendering me useful service in the army, and those who because of exceptionally good conduct and exceptional service I choose to raise into the estate of the nobility.[44]

As this last comment suggests, social mobility was not impossible in Frederick's Prussia, for all his enthusiasm for defending the integrity of the Junkers. Indeed, it was in the course of his reign that a long-gestating development reached maturity with the formation of a new social group independent of both the nobility and the middle class, although consisting mainly of the latter. This was the *Beamtenstand* or 'estate of bureaucrats'. Its emergence, which was not confined to Prussia but was experienced in most German states, was of such importance that a word or two about its nature is needed. In Max Weber's classic analysis, a bureaucrat has five essential characteristics: he is governed by an abstract concept of duty, not personal fealty to an individual; he owes his appointment to his technical qualifications, not to purchase or nepotism; he has a tenured position and can be dismissed only with good cause; he is paid a regular salary and is not dependent on fees; and he enjoys a career structure based on promotion by merit and/or seniority.[45] In Prussia its origins are to be found in the exclusion from central government of the noble Estates by Frederick William, the Great Elector (1640–88) after the Thirty Years War. Faced with enhanced responsibilities in such fields as internal colonization, demographic expansion (*Peuplierungspolitik*), trade and industry, domains and forests—but determined not to fall back under the sway of the provincial

[43] Volz (ed.), *Die Politischen Testamente Friedrichs des Großen*, p. 26. For further discussion of Frederick's support of the nobility, see my article 'Frederick the Great and enlightened absolutism', in H. M. Scott (ed.), *Enlightened Absolutism: Reform and Reformers in Later Eighteenth-century Europe* (London, 1990), pp. 268–9.

[44] Quoted in C. B. A. Behrens, *Society, Government and the Enlightenment: The Experiences of Eighteenth-century France and Prussia* (London, 1985), p. 60.

[45] Anthony Giddens, *Capitalism and Modern Social Theory: An Analysis of the Writings of Marx, Durkheim and Weber* (Cambridge, 1971), p. 158.

Junkers—the Great Elector sought assistance from socially neutral technocrats.[46]

For all their very different approaches to government, both Frederick I (1688–1713) and Frederick William I (1713–40) continued the process. Of great symbolic importance was the introduction of examinations for admission to the upper reaches of the judicial system. In 1693 appointment to posts on the central court (*Hof- und Kammergericht*) was made conditional on oral and written examination, a requirement extended to the lower courts twenty years later. During the next half-century the principle was applied to other branches of the administration, culminating in 1770 with the establishment of a Civil Service Commission to supervise uniform training and examinations for all senior administrative grades (that is to say, eighty-five years before the establishment of its equivalent in Great Britain).[47] The Prussian rulers were helped by having at their disposal several universities which were theirs to command for secular purposes (not self-governing communities of scholars devoted to the study of the classics and mathematics like Oxford and Cambridge). At Frankfurt an der Oder (founded in 1506), Königsberg (1544), Duisburg (1655), and Halle (1691–4), the curricula were reorganized to allow aspiring Prussian bureaucrats to be trained in administrative techniques. These were not institutions where intellectual activity was cherished for its own sake. Frederick William I made no secret of his philistinism, as he demonstrated when he combined the post of President of the Academy of Sciences with that of Court Jester.[48] But he could see the advantages of having experts running his dominions, as he also demonstrated when he founded chairs for applied political science ('cameralism') at both Frankfurt an der Oder and Halle in 1727.[49]

Two aspects of these institutions and their role in constructing the Prussian bureaucracy command our attention. First, they were the main conduits through which the Enlightenment found its way into public life. Halle, in particular, became a major centre for progressive ideas. Christian Thomasius, the first German professor to lecture in the German language (rather than Latin) and especially Christian Wolff, who became professor of philosophy in 1706 at the age of 27, gave Halle the reputation of being the most progressive

[46] Christof Dipper, *Deutsche Geschichte 1648–1789* (Frankfurt am Main, 1991), p. 211.

[47] Wilhelm Bleek, *Von der Kameralausbildung zum Juristenprivileg. Studium, Prüfung und Ausbildung der höheren Beamten des allgemeinen Verwaltungsdienstes in Deutschland im 18. und 19. Jahrhundert* (Berlin, 1972), pp. 74–8.

[48] Helga Schultz, *Berlin 1650–1800. Sozialgeschichte einer Residenz* (Berlin, 1987), p. 158.

[49] Bleek, *Von der Kameralausbildung zum Juristenprivileg*, pp. 64–5.

university in Germany. Wolff's polymathy—he claimed to be a philosopher, theologian, political theorist, jurist, economist, sociologist, pedagogue, mathematician, and natural scientist (all branches)—now seems absurd, but his relentless application of rationalism to every branch of knowledge made an enduring impact.[50] Although he fell out with the Pietists in 1721 and was expelled by Frederick William I with characteristic brutality ('Leave Prussia within twenty-four hours or be hanged'), within a generation he had carried all before him at German universities, even in Catholic regions. According to one contemporary, writing in the mid-1730s, no fewer than 112 chairs (which included virtually all those of philosophy) were currently occupied by his supporters and 231 of his pupils had promoted his ideas in published form.[51]

Wolff's teaching and its extraordinary resonance, not only in Prussia but throughout the Holy Roman Empire, represented the victory of the idea of the impersonal state over traditional dynasticism in German political thought. Legitimacy he derived from contract:

> There is a contract between the authorities and the subjects, by which the former undertake to devote all their efforts and exertions to devising the most appropriate policies for promoting the common welfare and security and to establishing the institutions required for their implementation, and the subjects for their part undertake that they will willingly perform whatever the authorities see fit to command.[52]

In Wolff's ideal state the authorities would see fit to command a very great deal. In his numerous publications, he gave detailed instructions for almost every conceivable aspect of human life. Among many other things, the state was to provide free medical care, hospitals, antenatal clinics, and retirement homes, fix wages, hours, and conditions for the workforce, pay special attention to the regulation of the training, status, and pay of schoolteachers, control immigration and emigration, establish technical schools and apprentice schemes for artisans, and so on and so forth. As excessive drinking and womanizing prevented students from working properly, the university authorities were instructed to lay out attractive gardens and avenues to encourage their charges to engage in healthy walks and mutual instruction.[53]

50 Hanns Martin Bachmann, *Die naturrechtliche Staatslehre Christian Wolffs* (Berlin, 1977), p. 47.

51 Ibid., p. 14; Carl Justi, *Winckelmann und seine Zeitgenossen*, 2 vols. (Leipzig, 1943), I, p. 87.

52 Quoted in Horst Möller, *Vernunft und Kritik. Deutsche Aufklärung im 17. und 18. Jahrhundert* (Frankfurt am Main, 1986), p. 200.

53 Christian Freiherr von Wolff, *Vernünftige Gedanken von dem gesellschaftlichen Leben der Menschen und insonderheit dem gemeinen Wesen*, new edn. (Halle, 1756), pp. 212–14, 216–17, 238, 257, 345, 353, 357.

One of Wolff's most enthusiastic admirers was the youthful Frederick the Great. Just one week before he became king, Frederick wrote to Wolff to thank him for a copy of his latest work on natural law:

Every man who thinks and loves truth must take an interest in your book; every man of integrity and every good citizen must regard it as a jewel, which your generosity has given to the world and your acumen has discovered. I am all the more moved by it because you have dedicated it to me. Philosophers should be the teachers of the world and the teachers of princes. They must think logically and we must act logically. They must teach the world by their powers of judgement, we must teach the world by our example. They must discover, and we must translate their discoveries into practice. I have been reading and studying your works for a long time now and am convinced that all who have read them must esteem their author. That can be denied to you by no one.[54]

One of his first actions on ascending the throne was to recall Wolff from exile. By this gesture Frederick proclaimed that the Enlightenment was now Prussia's official ideology. In his own self-congratulatory but memorable phrase, this triumphant return of the most important philosopher of the German Enlightenment to the scene of his former persecution represented a 'conquest in the land of truth'.[55] That Frederick then increasingly turned his back on his earlier mentor in favour of Voltaire's scepticism and empiricism did not prevent the continuing close association between Wolff and the Prussian bureaucracy. It was not until a far greater and even more influential Prussian philosopher—Immanuel Kant—began to make his mark towards the end of Frederick's reign that Wolff's influence waned.[56]

The second aspect of the pivotal role played by the Prussian universities that needs to be emphasized is their contribution to the formation of an intelligentsia. Christian Wolff's biography demonstrates the opportunities which the development of the bureaucracy was opening up for gifted plebeians. The son of an artisan, he rose simply by dint of his talent. He was neither the first nor the last German intellectual to benefit from the political fragmentation of the Holy Roman Empire. In the first place it gave him access to one of about fifty universities, in his case Jena in Saxony-Weimar. It can be assumed with some confidence that if he had been born an Englishman, he would not have

[54] Bardong (ed.), *Friedrich der Große*, p. 76.

[55] Theodor Schieder, *Friedrich der Große. Ein Königtum der Widersprüche* (Frankfurt am Main, Berlin, and Vienna, 1983), p. 128.

[56] Eckhart Hellmuth, *Naturrechtsphilosophie und bürokratischer Werthorizont. Studien zur preußischen Geistes-und Sozialgeschichte des 18. Jahrhunderts* (Göttingen, 1985), p. 27.

gained access to Oxford or Cambridge.[57] Secondly, when he fell foul of Frederick William I, he quickly found comfortable and well-paid alternative employment at the university of Marburg in Hessen-Kassel. As we have seen already,[58] German princes without the resources for military activity satisfied their competitive instincts through cultural rivalry. Hiring the most fashionable academic of the day represented a coup just as prestigious as employing the most celebrated fresco painter. This market in intellectuals enhanced both their status and their value, so that Wolff ended his days fêted and prosperous, a baron of the Holy Roman Empire and the owner of a large house and a substantial estate.[59] The epochal significance of this rags-to-riches story has been well expressed by Nicholas Boyle:

> Wolff's career is a landmark in the development of German society. He is the first representative of a species which in the twentieth century is still under no threat of extinction: the professor, especially of philosophy, who establishes through his pupils an empire extending over many universities and who acquires in the eyes of the public something of the role of a secular preacher, a preceptor of the nation. After Wolff, the pattern is continuous from Kant to Habermas, for of all German institutions the universities in the last three hundred years have changed least. The phenomenal rise to fame and fortune of this son of a tanner announces a new, peculiarly German *modus vivendi* between the middle—that is, the mobile—class and the absolute State, the advent of an age in which the backbone of national culture is to be found not in the municipal councils but in the universities. Wolff's career proclaims that the German bourgeoisie has emerged from its cultural paralysis and has rediscovered itself—as a class of state officials.[60]

It was joined by significant numbers of the two other Estates. Indeed, the Lutheran clergy in Prussia had always been state officials, subject to the authority of their king, the *Summus Episcopus* of the state Church. As Frederick the Great derisively remarked to Voltaire, he was 'the Pope of Lutherans', despite his Calvinist upbringing and anti-Christian convictions. He was well aware, however, of how much he owed to his Church. It was the pastors who performed many of the most important government functions in their parishes, registering births and deaths, compiling statistics, recording tax payments, and, most important of all, keeping the conscript

[57] For a complete list of German universities, see H. Kiesel and P. Münch, *Gesellschaft und Literatur im 18. Jahrhundert* (Munich, 1977), pp. 207–8.

[58] See above, p. 59.

[59] Bachmann, *Die naturrechtliche Staatslehre Christian Wolffs*, p. 43.

[60] Nicholas Boyle, *Goethe: The Poet and the Age*. Vol. 1: *The Poetry of Desire* (Oxford, 1991), p. 18.

rosters.[61] Although most aspiring pastors had to eke out a living as schoolteachers or private tutors before gaining a parish, and even then could only look forward to modest material reward, it was a profession which offered security, status, and at least the opportunity for further advancement to positions at the centre. Its attractions were indicated by the very high level of self-recruitment: in the Prussian province of Pomerania, for example, 55 per cent of pastors were the sons of pastors and 64 per cent of their wives were the daughters of pastors.[62]

This tightly knit group was also united by 'Pietism', the special variety of Lutheranism which came to play an important part in the formation of a distinctively Prussian ethos. It provides us with such a good example of the ability of the 'Prussian way' to absorb, to neutralize, and then to exploit potentially disruptive ideologies that it merits further discussion. Pietism had begun in the middle of the seventeenth century as a movement for renewal within the Lutheran Church. The indiscriminate devastation of the Thirty Years War, which had afflicted Protestants just as much as Catholics, suggested that God had become exceedingly angry with the true believers. Led by Philipp Jakob Spener (1635–1705), who began his career as a pastor at Frankfurt am Main, a growing number of Lutherans came to believe that the failings of the Catholics identified and corrected by Luther had gradually returned to infect the Church he had founded. So they sought to get back to his pristine simplicity, by stressing the priesthood of all believers against the hierarchy, the inner light against doctrinal orthodoxy, the religion of the heart against the religion of the head, born-again conversion against mechanical observance, and practical acts of charity against scholastic disputation. Their preferred forum was not the church service but the *Collegia Pietatis*, a private group meeting to read the Bible and engage in mutual edification.[63] This programme touched a responsive chord in Lutheran communities throughout Germany, for Spener's manifesto—*Pia Desideria* (1675)—made a major impact. Needless to say, it made a less favourable impression on the orthodox hierarchy. When Spener moved to Saxony, the centre of Lutheranism, he encountered a combination of the doctrinal rancour and personal malice which are among the less appealing characteristics of clergymen. So in 1690 he was happy to accept the call to be Provost at the Nikolaikirche in Berlin and a Consistorial Councillor from the Elector of

[61] Hans-Ulrich Wehler, *Deutsche Gesellschaftsgeschichte*. Vol. I: *Vom Feudalismus des Alten Reiches bis zur defensiven Modernisierung der Reformära 1700–1815* (Munich, 1987), p. 272.

[62] Ibid., p. 274.

[63] C. M. Clark, *Pietism and the State in Prussia* (unpublished lecture, Cambridge, 1995).

Brandenburg, Frederick III (he did not become Frederick I, King in Prussia, until 1701).

Spener was now in a position to help his persecuted fellow Pietists, especially his most effective disciple, August Hermann Francke, who had been driven out of Leipzig in 1689 and from Erfurt in 1690. In the following year Spener secured him a position at the new university of Halle and the Pietist conquest of Prussia began.[64] Francke proved to be a truly superlative administrator. Not only did he play a major part in making the university of Halle one of the best in Germany, he also created a string of other institutions—first a school for the poor, then an orphanage, a grammar school, specialist schools for the nobility and for aspiring diplomats, a technical college, a college of education, a refuge for widows, a bookshop, a printing-press, a stocking factory, and a pharmacy.[65] Some of them were financed by private initiative—the orphanage was created on the strength of an anonymous donation of 500 thalers to the poor box, for example—but they could not have flourished without official protection. Francke was careful to stress the practical benefits of educating 'Christian artisans and merchants, good schoolteachers, and Christian preachers and councillors too, who will feel all the more obliged to devote their lives to serving others because they have experienced God's special care since childhood'.[66] He also drummed into his charges the importance of a work ethos: ceaseless activity is the best way of suppressing the temptations of the flesh and the Devil, hard work is a sacred duty, the lazy and the *rentiers* are destined for Hell, and poverty is a sign of failure, not of Grace.[67]

Frederick William I was believed to be much less sympathetic to Pietism than his father and it was widely expected that he would close Halle down when he succeeded in 1713. After a few anxious moments, however, the Pietists found that they did even better under the new regime. They helped their cause no end by the shrewd tactic of convincing their militarist king, when he made a personal inspection in the first year of his reign, that Pietist army chaplains were especially adept in making soldiers content with their lot

[64] The process is best followed in Carl Hinrichs, *Preußentum und Pietismus. Der Pietismus in Brandenburg-Preußen als religiös-soziale Reformbewegung* (Göttingen, 1971), *passim* but see especially ch. 2.

[65] Ibid., pp. 62–83.

[66] Ibid., p. 23. Cf. A similar observation is quoted in Mary Fulbrook, *Piety and Politics: Religion and the Rise of Absolutism in England, Württemberg and Prussia* (Cambridge, 1983), p. 165.

[67] Klaus Deppermann, *Der hallesche Pietismus und der preußische Staat unter Friedrich III. (I.)* (Göttingen, 1961), p. 174.

and amenable to discipline. Their triumph was sealed when they converted Prince Leopold von Anhalt-Dessau, the most important of Frederick William I's generals, whose regiment was stationed at Halle.[68] By the time Francke died in 1727, Pietism had become firmly established as the state religion.[69] Through the universities of Halle and Königsberg (which they colonized in the 1720s), the Pietists determined the education of all Prussian state servants, lay and ecclesiastical, military and civilian. In 1717 Frederick William I decreed that in future all candidates for the Lutheran ministry would have to study theology at Halle for at least two years.[70]

Like all durable partnerships, the alliance between the Prussian state and Pietism was mutually advantageous. Both could also flatter themselves that in promoting each other's advantage they were also doing God's work. In its harmony it was a relationship markedly different from that experienced by movements of religious dissent elsewhere in Europe. As Carl Hinrichs observed: 'In Prussia, Pietism became the standard-bearer of the power of the state, of "standardization" [*Gleichschaltung*], while in the Anglo-Saxon world, its equivalent—Puritanism—carried the flag of revolution.'[71] He might have added that the French equivalent—Jansenism—was to become one of the most corrosive of all the intellectual forces undermining the old regime.[72] For the stability of Prussia and indeed of all Germany, this was of great importance, given the number of intellectuals exposed to Pietist influence—of how many major figures of the Enlightenment, *Sturm und Drang*, and even Romanticism is it *not* said that they were influenced by Pietism? It must also be borne in mind just how many German intellectuals were the offspring of pastors: Pufendorf, Conring, Pütter, Schlözer, Lessing, Gellert, Gottsched, Wieland, Lenz, Schubart, Claudius, Bürger, Schelling, Schleiermacher, the Schlegel brothers, Schinkel—the list could be extended almost at will.[73]

Officials, clergy, and the children of clergy were joined in the Prussian intelligentsia by an appreciable number of nobles. Although education at Halle or Königsberg did not turn the Junkers *en bloc* into God-fearing, sober-living, deep-thinking intellectuals, there was clearly a cultural shift away from the 'Squire Western' model to something more urbane, sophisticated—and also pious. It was part of the Pietist message that social differences

[68] Hinrichs, *Preußentum und Pietismus*, p. 148.

[69] Ibid., p. 175.

[70] Winfried Ranke, *Preußen—Versuch einer Bilanz*, 5 vols. (Hamburg, 1981), I, p. 246.

[71] Hinrichs, *Preußentum und Pietismus*, p. 175. For a similar comment, see Oswald Hauser, 'Das geistige Preußen', *Jahrbuch der Stiftung Preußischer Kulturbesitz*, 10 (1972), p. 82.

[72] See below, p. 375.

[73] Wehler, *Deutsche Gesellschaftsgeschichte*, I, p. 274.

meant nothing in the eyes of God and that a born-again noble and a born-again peasant had more in common than the former and an unregenerate fellow aristocrat.[74] This was not a phenomenon confined to Prussia, for there is clear evidence that the proportion of nobles among students at German universities actually increased in the course of the eighteenth century.[75] Now that an academic qualification was required for an official post, any Prussian noble with ambitions for a career in public service was obliged to compete with commoners on equal intellectual terms. One result was significant noble participation in the literary output. It may have been mere chance that the first Prussian poet of any distinction was Ewald Count von Kleist, who died in 1759 of wounds sustained at the battle of Kunersdorf (one of twenty-three members of the Kleist clan to die during the Silesian wars, incidentally). However, a statistical study of the contributors to the *Berlinische Monatsschrift*, the most important enlightened periodical in Berlin, shows that he was not the exception that proved the rule. Of the 300 authors contributing:

45 (15%) were nobles
80 (26.7%) were professors and schoolteachers
60 (20%) were officials
50 (26.7%) were clergymen
10 (3.3%) were army officers
5 (1.7%) were merchants or bankers
2 (0.7%) were booksellers
1 (0.3%) was a craftsman[76]

It might also be observed in passing that only eight (2.7 per cent), can be termed independent of the government, although to this total should be added the ten to fifteen who had no profession whatsoever (3–5 per cent). The picture is confirmed by the analysis of the Berlin intelligentsia conducted by Friedrich Nicolai, the leading bookseller in Berlin, the editor of the *Allgemeine Deutsche Bibliothek* (the German equivalent of *The Times Literary Supplement*) and a prolific writer himself. In 1784 he listed 165 people who lived in or near Berlin and who had published something during the course of the year. Of these,

26 (15.75%) were nobles
32 (19.4%) were clergymen
33 (20%) were high officials

[74] Deppermann, *Der hallesche Pietismus*, p. 176.
[75] Möller, *Vernunft und Kritik*, pp. 242–3.
[76] Horst Möller, *Aufklärung in Preußen. Der Verleger, Publizist und Geschichtsschreiber Friedrich Nicolai* (Berlin, 1974), p. 252.

17 (10.3%) were medium-rank officials
18 (10.9%) were schoolteachers
30 (18.2%) were 'natural scientists' (mainly medical men)
2 (1.2%) were independent writers[77]

Consisting of nobles, clergy, and commoners, this group was socially disparate but united by common intellectual concerns and state service. Although not used at the time, 'intelligentsia' is the word best suited to describe it, even if 'of all the social strata, the intelligentsia is the most difficult to define.'[78] In the German-speaking lands in the eighteenth century, there was a significant move from using the words *die Gelehrten* (the learned) to *die Gebildeten* (the educated or cultivated).[79] In other words, there was a move from regarding professional academics with their specialized and narrowly focused expertise as the epitome of intellectual achievement to preferring the autodidact formed (*gebildet*) by a less formal but more wide-ranging and personal educational programme. It was a distinction well caught by Goethe in the dialogue between Faust and his pedantic colleague Wagner:

> WAGNER: My scholarly pursuits, how sore they weigh
> Upon my heart and mind! One ought
> To learn the means of mounting to the sources,
> Yet even this task almost passes my resources;
> For we poor devils, by the time we've got
> Less than halfway, we die, as like as not.
> FAUST: A manuscript—is that the sacred spring
> That stills one's thirst for evermore?
> Refreshment! It's your own soul that must pour
> It through you, if it's to be anything.[80]

As suggested by the two cognates already used—*die Gebildeten* and *gebildet*, the key word is *Bildung*, best if inadequately translated as 'self-cultivation' or 'self-formation'.[81] Although a neologism in the eighteenth century, it had its origin in the use of the word 'image', translated by Luther as *Bild* in two key biblical texts:

[77] Ibid., p. 266.

[78] Aleksander Gella, 'An introduction to the sociology of the intelligentsia', in Aleksander Gella (ed.), *The Intelligentsia and the Intellectuals: Theory, Method and Case Study* (London, 1976), p. 10.

[79] Ulrich Engelhardt, '*Bildungsbürgertum*'. *Begriffs- und Dogmengeschichte eines Etiketts* (Stuttgart, 1986), p. 64.

[80] Goethe, *Faust Part One*, ed. and trans. David Luke (Oxford, 1987), pp. 20–1.

[81] W. H. Bruford, *The German Tradition of Self-cultivation: 'Bildung' from Humboldt to Thomas Mann* (Cambridge, 1975), p. 1.

And God said, Let us make man in our own image, after our own likeness . . . So God created man in his *own* image, in the image of God created he him; male and female created he them. (Genesis 1: 26–7)

But we all, with open face beholding as in a glass the glory of the Lord, are changed unto the same image from glory to glory, *even* as by the Spirit of the Lord. (2 Corinthians 3: 18).[82]

Significantly, it was the Pietists who were mainly responsible for the transmission of the concept, although they used it in an exclusively religious sense. In the course of the eighteenth century it then became secularized, while retaining the strongly subjective element and ideal of personal perfection which betrayed its Pietist origins.[83] Even for those who rejected revealed religion and scriptural authority, *Bildung* offered a means of secular salvation through culture. It was not through the senses or through reason that man could discover what was good and true but through a third capacity: aesthetic feeling or the power of the imagination. It was this that brought together the emotional and rational sides of human nature and made it possible to combine the insights provided by both.[84]

Bildung was open to all. In a society with a rapidly expanding public sphere[85] and in a state with a rapidly growing need for public servants of various kinds, education opened the way for advancement. In the pithy formulation of Rudolf Vierhaus, 'the old adage "*Stadtluft macht frei*" [city air makes you free] made way for "*Bildung macht frei.*" '[86] The intellectuals who met in

[82] The German version in Luther's translation is: Genesis 1: 26–7 'Und Gott sprach: Lasset uns Menschen machen, ein Bild, das uns gleich sei, die da herrschen über die Fische im Meer und über die Vögel unter dem Himmel und über das Vieh und über die ganze Erde und über alles Gewürm, das auf Erden kriecht. Und Gott schuf den Menschen ihm zum Bilde, zum Bilde Gottes schuf er ihn; und schuf sie, einen Mann und ein Weib.' These texts also embody the concept of formation.

2 Corinthians 3: 18–19 'Nun aber spiegelt sich in uns allen des Herrn Klarheit mit aufgedecktem Angesicht, und wir werden verklärt in dasselbe Bild von einer Klarheit zu der andern, als vom Herrn, der der Geist ist.' On the origins of *Bildung*, see Franz Rauhut, 'Die Herkunft der Worte und Begriffe "Kultur", "Civilisation" und "Bildung" ', *Germanisch-romanische Monatsschrift*, II, 1 (1953), pp. 87, 89. Johann Christoph Adelung defined 'Bildung' as 'Giving the proper direction to abilities of the intellect and the will. Forming a heart and a nature'; Adelung, *Grammatisch-kritisches Wörterbuch*, I, p. 1015.

[83] David Sorkin, *The Transformation of German Jewry 1780–1840* (Oxford, 1987), pp. 15–17.

[84] Paul R. Sweet, *Wilhelm von Humboldt: A Biography*, 2 vols. (Columbus, Ohio, 1978–80), I, p. 52.

[85] See above, pp. 113–14.

[86] Rudolf Vierhaus, *Deutschland vor der französischen Revolution. Untersuchungen zur deutschen Sozialgeschichte im Zeitalter der Aufklärung* (unpublished Münster Habilitationsschrift, 1961), p. 226.

reading clubs, Masonic lodges, or coffee-houses, and who subscribed to the growing number of newspapers and periodicals, would have agreed with the claim of Friedrich Nicolai that 'rational and honest people belong together *without regard* for class [*Stand*], religion or any other considerations.'[87] This sense of being engaged in a common pursuit of truth and beauty did not, of course, create one big happy family. There were plenty of social, religious, ideological, and regional divisions, but it does seem that the special conditions of Prussia (and Germany as a whole) created a sufficient sense of identity to entitle one to speak of an intelligentsia.

It was a group that grew with the public sphere but it was also a group that grew with the state. Indeed, as we have seen,[88] the public sphere itself was in large measure the creation of the latter. This gave the German intelligentsia a special character which distinguished it sharply from other parts of Europe. In France, for reasons we shall discuss later in this chapter, the intelligentsia became divorced from the regime during the course of the eighteenth century and then helped to destroy it.[89] In Russia the reverse seems to apply, for the intelligentsia there was even more patently a creation of the state than in Germany; it was almost exclusively noble in origin and clung to its parent with the desperation of the new-born.[90] Yet it was just this degree of dependence that augured an unhappy adolescence: 'if the proletariat can be defined as a transient group between feudalism and automation, the intelligentsia can be considered, on much better grounds, just such a group between well-nigh total illiteracy and general literacy.'[91] By the time the word 'intelligentsia' actually came to be invented, first in Poland in 1844 and then in Russia two years later, it had acquired a connotation of alienation from the regime.[92] In Great Britain it is difficult to find any sense of there being an intelligentsia standing outside conventional social categories. It was a term not used until the twentieth century and even then applied only to

[87] Horst Möller, *Aufklärung in Preußen. Der Verleger, Publizist und Geschichtsschreiber Friedrich Nicolai* (Berlin, 1974), p. 246.

[88] See above, pp. 13–14.

[89] See below, pp. 380–4. See also Herbert Lüthy, 'The French intellectuals', in George B. Huszar (ed.), *The Intellectuals: A Controversial Portrait* (London, 1960), p. 444, who stresses that the concept of the intellectual in France has always been linked to the Left.

[90] Nicholas V. Riasanovsky, *A Parting of the Ways: Government and the Educated Public in Russia 1801–55* (Oxford, 1976), pp. 22–3; Marc Raeff, *Origins of the Russian Intelligentsia: The Eighteenth-century Nobility* (New York, 1966), p. 130.

[91] Riasanovsky, *A Parting of the Ways*, p. 286.

[92] Gella, 'An introduction to the sociology of the intelligentsia', p. 12. See also Martin Malia, 'What is the intelligentsia?', in Richard Pipes (ed.), *The Russian Intelligentsia* (New York and London, 1970), p. 6.

Russia.[93] A good example of the national suspicion of people too clever by half was the definition offered of the intelligentsia by the eponymous hero of H. G. Wells's *Mr Britling Sees It Through* (1916), who tells a first-time American visitor to England: 'I should have explained these young people. They're the sort of young people we are producing over here now in quite enormous quantity. They are the sort of equivalent of the Russian Intelligentsia, *an irresponsible middle class with ideas*.'[94]

The difference between the British and German experiences can be summed up in a single word: London. For there was no true metropolis in the German-speaking world before the middle of the nineteenth century. In 1800 London was five times bigger than the largest city in the Holy Roman Empire (Vienna) and ten times larger than most of the others. It therefore boasted a public sphere so much larger that British intellectuals could pursue their livelihoods on the open market. Moreover, it had no university until 1828 and no proper bureaucracy until even later. Together with relative social and political stability, this made the state in Great Britain peripheral to most branches of culture. A similar situation prevailed in the United States of America. Consequently, British and American sociologists have identified remoteness from the practical world of government and administration as one of the identifying characteristics of the intelligentsia, as in 'intellectuals are people who wield the power of the spoken and the written word and one of the touches that distinguish them from other people who do the same is the absence of direct responsibility for practical affairs' (Joseph Schumpeter) or '[an intellectual is distinguished by] a capacity for detachment from immediate experience, a moving beyond the pragmatic tasks of the moment' (Lewis Coser).[95]

Such generalizations would be singularly out of place in Germany in the eighteenth century. The belief that Germans have always been somehow 'unpolitical', seeking compensation for their practical impotence by metaphysical speculation, is a misconception as long-lived as it is erroneous. It was summed up in Lord Acton's *mot* that in the nineteenth century France ruled the land, Great Britain the seas, and Germany the air.[96] Only if one takes the

[93] *The Oxford English Dictionary*, 2nd edn., vol. II (Oxford, 1989)—'The part of the nation orig. in pre-revolutionary Russia, that aspires to intellectual activity; the class of society regarded as possessing cultural and political initiative'.

[94] H. G. Wells, *Mr Britling Sees It Through* (London, 1916), p. 62.

[95] Joseph A. Schumpeter, *Capitalism, Socialism and Democracy* (London, 1943), p. 147; Lewis A. Coser, *Men of Ideas: A Sociologist's View* (New York and London, 1965), p. viii.

[96] Hugh Tulloch, 'Lord Acton and German historiography', in Benedikt Stuchtey and Peter Wende (eds.), *Traditions, Perceptions and Transfers: British and German Historiography from the Eighteenth to the Twentieth Century* (Oxford, 2000), p. 159.

view that 'politics' is synonymous with 'party politics' can this be justified. If the term is understood in its proper sense of 'the science and art of government', then it will be seen that the intellectuals of Germany were more political than those of any other European country. No one would wish to deny the aeronautical skills displayed by German philosophers in soaring above the shadows in the cave, but usually they were also public servants, employed by the state and engaged in instructing the young. Wolff, Kant, Fichte, Hegel, and Schelling were all professors at Prussian universities at one stage or another during their careers. Of all the great German philosophers of the eighteenth and early nineteenth centuries, only Schopenhauer had the means and inclination to live the life of an independent scholar. If Wolff's successors did not share his concern with the minutiae of daily life,[97] they were certainly not indifferent to politics, nor was their work without political implications and influence. Moreover, these men constituted the very summit of intellectual rarefaction. Further down the slopes, most intellectuals were directly involved in conducting government business in one way or another as civil servants (Abbt, Hamann, Justus Möser, Friedrich Karl von Moser, Schlözer, Goethe, Sonnenfels, Martini, Brandes), as diplomats (Dohm, Müller, Humboldt), as professors (Gottsched, Wieland, Lichtenberg, Schiller), as clergymen (Gerbert, Herder, Hontheim, Dalberg, Schleiermacher), soldiers (Kleist, Mauvillon), or even as king (Frederick the Great, one of the most prolific and distinguished of German writers, even though he wrote in French). A list of independent writers would be short indeed: apart from Nicolai and Schubart, not many first-rank names spring readily to mind. Lessing looks like a particularly distinguished exception, for in 1764 he told his father that he was determined to avoid any form of employment which was not entirely to his liking. Four years later, however, he wrote to his brother Karl: 'Take my brotherly advice and abandon the notion of living from writing... see that you become a secretary or get a job as a civil servant. That is the only way to avoid ruin in the long run. For me it is just too late to change tack.'[98] In 1770 he himself succumbed to economic pressures and accepted employment as librarian to the Duke of Brunswick-Wolfenbüttel.

In describing the relationship between the German intelligentsia and the states of the Holy Roman Empire, for once that overworked metaphor 'symbiosis' ('the intimate living together of two dissimilar organisms in a mutually beneficial relationship') does seem appropriate. Of course, the intimacy and

[97] See above, p. 200.

[98] Quoted in H. Kiesel and P. Münch, *Gesellschaft und Literatur im 18. Jahrhundert* (Munich, 1977), p. 78.

harmony can be overdone. There was plenty of dissatisfaction in the system, for rare indeed was (or is) the intellectual who feels that he has been awarded his just deserts. Many had to spend demanding and demeaning years as private tutors to aristocratic households before gaining government or ecclesiastical appointments. Indeed, Jakob Michael Reinhold Lenz's play *The Private Tutor or the Advantages of a Private Education* (1774) might be thought to provide an excellent parable of the plight of the intellectual, for Läuffer, the eponymous hero of the work, castrates himself after seducing his nubile pupil. As the wise privy councillor tells Läuffer's father (a pastor): 'you didn't bring your son up to be a servant, but what else is he, if he sells his liberty to a private person for a handful of ducats?'[99] Lenz himself never found a niche in the system and died in poverty in Moscow in 1792.

Moreover, the experience of Russia in the nineteenth century suggested that, in some families, paternity can be the first step towards parricide. As Marc Raeff has written: 'dependency on the state helped to foster worship of the monarch, but sometimes became transmuted into complete rejection and hatred.'[100] Before this degree of alienation could be achieved, however, it needed the upheaval of the Napoleonic wars and the worst efforts of Alexander I and especially Nicholas I. Even the most celebrated of the eighteenth-century dissidents, Aleksandr Nikolayevich Radishchev, wrote the book which earned him a death sentence (commuted to ten years' exile in Siberia) not in order to criticize but to enlighten Catherine the Great.

In Germany it was the 'Metternich system' after 1815 that prised apart intelligentsia and state, although—as we shall see[101]—the rupture was half-hearted on both sides. And nowhere more so than in Prussia, to which we must now return. In the course of the eighteenth century, Prussia developed a political myth of impressive durability. Deftly exploiting his numerous assets, Frederick created a state which was not just concerned with power (*Machtstaat*) but was also a state governed by the rule of law (*Rechtsstaat*) and a state committed to the promotion of culture (*Kulturstaat*). This is a process which has been described and analysed many times, so only a brief summary is needed here.[102] The policy that appealed most to the intelligentsia was reli-

[99] Hans-G. Winter, 'Antiklassizismus: Sturm und Drang', in Viktor Zmegac (ed.), *Geschichte der deutschen Literatur vom 18. Jahrhundert bis zur Gegenwart*, vol 1, pt. 1, 2nd edn. (Königstein im Taunus, 1984), p. 223.

[100] Cf. Raeff, *Origins of the Russian Intelligentsia*, p. 120.

[101] See below, p. 432.

[102] I have dealt with this topic in greater detail in 'Frederick the Great and enlightened absolutism', in H. M. Scott (ed.), *Enlightened absolutism: Reform and Reformers in Later Eighteenth*

gious toleration. This was part of Frederick's inheritance, for ever since the Elector Johann Sigismund had converted to Calvinism in 1613 to strengthen his claim to the duchies of Jülich and Berg, Brandenburg had been a multi-denominational state. His successors had turned this necessity into a virtue by offering asylum to dissidents being persecuted elsewhere in Europe, notably Polish Socinians in 1667, French Huguenots in 1685, and Salzburg Protestants in 1732.[103] Frederick elevated this into a principle of government, deducing it from the social contract he used to legitimize his authority.[104] Less than a month after coming to the throne he issued two unequivocal instructions on the subject:

All religions must be tolerated and the sole concern of officials is to ensure that one denomination does not interfere with another, for here everyone can seek salvation in the manner that seems best to him [Plate 13].

All religions are just as good as each other, so long as the people who practise them are honest, and even if the Turks and heathens came and wanted to populate this country, then we would build mosques and temples for them.[105]

That second declaration was part of an affirmative reply to an inquiry from the General Directory as to whether a Roman Catholic should be allowed civic rights in Frankfurt an der Oder. For a sceptic of Protestant origins, the toleration of Catholics was the ultimate test and it was one which Frederick passed with flying colours. In 1747 he gave the land for the construction of a Catholic church in the centre of Berlin, next door to the royal opera house. The Church of St Hedwig, 'arguably the first Neo-classical building in Germany,'[106] caused a sensation in Europe and won for Frederick both the praise of the Pope and the criticism of Voltaire. In reply to the latter he wrote: 'you accuse me of excessive tolerance. I am proud of this failing. Would that it were the only failing of which princes could be accused.'[107] More telling was the approval he won for his toleration from the greatest philosopher of the day,

Century Europe (London, 1990), pp. 265–88 and in 'Frederick the Great and German culture', in *Royal and Republican Sovereignty in Early Modern Europe: Essays in Memory of Ragnhild Hatton*, ed. G. C. Gibbs, Robert Oresko, and Hamish Scott (Cambridge, 1996), pp. 527–50.

[103] For a good account and analysis of the toleration policies pursued by seventeenth-century Electors of Brandenburg, see Deppermann, *Der hallesche Pietismus*, pp. 23–4.

[104] See above, p. 195.

[105] Bardong (ed.), *Friedrich der Große*, p. 542.

[106] David Watkin and Tilman Mellinghoff, *German Architecture and the Classical Ideal 1740–1840* (London, 1987), p. 24.

[107] Walther Hubatsch, *Frederick the Great: Absolutism and Administration* (London, 1975), pp. 193–4.

Immanuel Kant, who wrote in his most accessible and most popular essay *What is Enlightenment?*:

A prince who does not regard it as beneath him to say that he considers it to be his duty, in religious matters, not to prescribe anything to his people, but to allow them complete freedom, a prince who thus even declines to accept the presumptuous title of *tolerant*, is himself enlightened. He deserves to be praised by a grateful present and posterity as the man who liberated mankind from immaturity (as far as government is concerned) and who left all men free to use their own reason in all matters of conscience.[108]

Reform of the law and the legal system was also something Frederick inherited, but again it was he who raised its profile and made it part of the Prussian political myth. It was he who laid down the principles and it was he who gave the necessary support to the minister responsible, Samuel von Cocceji, when vested interests obstructed them. The abolition of torture, the reduction of capital crimes, the reform of the judiciary, and the codification of civil law (which culminated in the posthumous publication of the General Code (*Allgemeines Landrecht*) in 1794) all helped to convey the image of a *Rechtsstaat* in the making. Frederick's claim in his will that he had established the rule of law and justice[109] was exaggerated when measured against absolute standards, but it could be sustained when the irrationality and barbarity of legal systems elsewhere in Europe were taken into account. Paradoxically, his most celebrated initiative in the field was also an abuse. In the 'Miller Arnold affair' of 1779 he interfered with the course of justice to punish judges he believed to have favoured Count Schmettau in his dispute with the miller, because of his noble status. By announcing that an example was being made of them 'because they must learn the lesson that the humblest peasant, yes and what is more even the beggar, is just as much a human being as His Majesty himself... and whether it is a prince accusing a peasant, or the other way round, the prince is equal to the peasant before the law,' Frederick achieved a public-relations coup which 'transfigured' him in the eyes of ordinary Prussians, according to a Berlin clergyman.[110] The message was spread to an admiring public across Europe through a number of media. For example, the

[108] Hans Reiss (ed.), *Kant's Political Writings* (Cambridge, 1970), pp. 58–9. Kant's definition of Enlightenment was, of course, 'man's emergence from self-incurred immaturity'.

[109] Bardong (ed.), *Friedrich der Große*, p. 454.

[110] Ingrid Mittenzwei, *Friedrich II von Preußen* (Cologne, 1980), p. 192; Daniel Jenisch, 'Denkschrift auf Friedrich den Großen', in Horst Steinmetz (ed.), *Friedrich II., König von Preußen und die deutsche Literatur des 18. Jahrhunderts. Texte und Dokumente* (Stuttgart, 1985), p. 244.

Paris-based Florentine engraver Vincenzo Vangelisti produced a magnificent pictorial account, which was copied several times, including an English version: *The Justice of Frederick*. The king sits on his throne, bearing perfectly balanced scales of justice, at his feet the supplicant Miller Arnold and his family, in the background the mill and its contested water supply. Themis, Goddess of Justice, carrying a sword and a shield bearing the Prussian device, is summoned by Frederick to chase away the corrupt judges, whose beneficent masks fall to reveal their evil features. Underneath the picture was printed a lengthy account of the affair, together with Frederick's judgement, part of which was quoted above.[111] It was also publicized in the form of an official poster, prefaced as follows: 'Extract from verdict pronounced by His Royal Majesty of Prussia on the three judges from Küstrin on 11 December 1779, in which the Solomon of the North expressed himself in the following terms'.[112]

Creating the image of Prussia as a *Kulturstaat* should have been straightforward, given that his reign coincided with a cultural surge in Germany comparable with the Italian Renaissance. His reign coincided with all or part of the careers of the following: Gluck (1714–87), C. P. E. Bach (1714–88), Winckelmann (1717–68), Kant (1724–1804), Klopstock (1724–1803), Lessing (1729–81), Hamann (1730–88), Haydn (1732–1809), Wieland (1733–1813), Herder (1744–1803), Goethe (1749–1832), Mozart (1756–91), and Schiller (1759–1805)—to mention only the undisputed stars. Yet his relationship with these great names was at best tangential and at worst hostile. He patronized only two: Kant through his chair at the Prussian university of Königsberg and C. P. E. Bach by employing him as a keyboard player. That meagre support might be deemed more than counterbalanced by the flight from Prussia of Winckelmann ('rather a Turkish eunuch than a Prussian') and Herder (as a clergyman more discreet in his choice of metaphor but no less negative).[113] Efforts by Wieland, Klopstock, and Lessing to ingratiate themselves were ignored or rejected with contempt, with predictably alienating effects. Turning in optimistic delusion to Joseph II after Frederick's rebuff, Klopstock

[111] There is an excellent reproduction in Hans Gerhard Hannesen (ed.), *Lovis Corinth 'Fridericus Rex'. Der Preußenkönig in Mythos und Geschichte* (Berlin, 1986), p. 61. This exhibition catalogue contains numerous other reproductions of engravings lauding Frederick in his various roles.

[112] The poster is reproduced in Hans Dollinger, *Preußen. Eine Kulturgeschichte in Bildern und Dokumenten* (Munich, 1980), p. 149.

[113] Rudolf Augstein, *Preußens Friedrich und die Deutschen*, new edn. (Frankfurt am Main, 1981), p. 71. See also Roy Pascal, *The German Sturm und Drang* (Manchester, 1953), p. 47. For more abusive comments by Winckelmann, see Hans Rosenberg, *Bureaucracy, Aristocracy and Autocracy: The Prussian experience 1660–1815* (Boston, 1966), p. 42.

exclaimed: 'The emperor loves his fatherland—but Frederick does not! And yet Germany is also his fatherland!' while Lessing notoriously apostrophized Prussia as 'the most slavish country in Europe'.[114]

Although a gifted musical performer and composer, Frederick could appreciate only composers who wrote in the Italian style, such as Hasse, Graun, and Agricola. He employed Carl Philipp Emanuel Bach for thirty years but was unwilling or unable to recognize his qualities as a composer. For contemporaries, it was C. P. E. not J. S. who was 'the great Bach', but for Frederick he was just a harpsichord-player.[115] Johann Friedrich Reichardt, Frederick's last *Kapellmeister*, was admittedly not in the class of either Bach, but he hardly deserved the derisive response, scribbled in the margin of his request for permission to compose an opera for the carnival season of 1782: 'He is not to compose an opera, because he doesn't know how to do it and does it all wrong.'[116] Frederick's inability to appreciate modern music was notorious. It seems that he simply had no knowledge of Mozart, although he heard enough of Haydn to feel able to dismiss his music as 'a shindy that flays the ears.'[117] This disparagement of contemporary music did not pass unnoticed in the rapidly expanding periodical press. The first musical journalist in Germany, Johann Mattheson, complained bitterly in 1740 about the new King of Prussia's despatch of his *Kapellmeister* to Italy to recruit singers, exclaiming: 'When will we give up our blind worship of foreigners and learn to judge our own countrymen fairly?!'[118]

Forty years later it was literature as much as music which fed German pride. Yet Frederick's attitude towards this genre was, if anything, even more hostile and ill-informed. The cultural revolution carried out during his long life by the great names listed earlier passed him by. While still Crown Prince, he had

[114] Robert Ergang, 'National sentiments in Klopstock's odes and *Bardiete*', in *Nationalism and Internationalism: Essays Inscribed to Carlton J. H. Hayes* (New York, 1950), p. 129; Steinmetz (ed.), *Friedrich II.*, p. 51. On Wieland's attempt to ingratiate himself by writing an epic in hexameters—*Cyrus*—see Sven Aage Jørgenson, Klaus Bohnen, and Per Øhrgaard, *Aufklärung, Sturm und Drang, frühe Klassik, 1740–1789* (Munich, 1990), p. 286. On Klopstock's plans for the promotion of German culture under the patronage of Joseph II, see Ernst Wangermann, 'Deutscher Patriotismus und österreichischer Reformabsolutismus im Zeitalter Josephs II.', in Heinrich Lutz and Helmut Rumpler (eds.), *Österreich und die deutsche Frage im 19. und 20. Jahrhundert* (Vienna, 1982), pp. 60–3.

[115] Thomas Bauman, 'Courts and municipalities in North Germany', in Neal Zaslaw, *The Classical Era: From the 1740s to the End of the Eighteenth Century* (London, 1989), p. 250.

[116] Walter Salmen, *Johann Friedrich Reichardt. Komponist, Schriftsteller, Kapellmeister und Verwaltungsbeamte der Goethezeit* (Freiburg in Breisgau and Zürich, 1963), p. 43

[117] E. E. Helm, *Music at the Court of Frederick the Great* (Norman, 1960), p. 71.

[118] Ibid., p. 92.

KING ALFRED'S COLLEGE
LIBRARY

written to Voltaire in 1737 that Germany could never expect to develop a vernacular culture of any value. He conceded that the Germans had some virtues—they did not lack intellect, they had ample good sense (being rather like the English in this regard), they were industrious and even profound. On the other hand, they were also ponderous, long-winded, and boring. The main—indeed, the insuperable—problem was linguistic: because Germany was divided into an infinity of territories, it would never be possible to reach agreement on which of the regional dialects should become the standard form.[119] This aversion to the German language became a recurrent theme of both his public works and his private correspondence, as in 'if we still retain some vestige of our ancient republican liberty, it consists of the worthless opportunity to murder at our leisure a language that is coarse and still virtually barbaric.'[120] He confirmed his own prejudice by using a form of German which, for all its characteristic vigour, was crude, misspelt, and ungrammatical.[121] The literature created in this primitive medium naturally attracted his corresponding contempt. As he wrote to Voltaire in 1775 (the year after the publication of Goethe's *Werther*), German literature was nothing more than a 'farrago of inflated phrases', German history was pedantic, and even German philosophy had died out since the days of Leibniz and Wolff. In short, he claimed, Germany's current cultural level was about two and a half centuries behind that of France.[122]

It was one thing to convey this abuse in private letters to Voltaire; it was quite another to broadcast it publicly in the form of a pamphlet, which is just what he did with *Concerning German Literature; the faults of which it can be accused; the causes of the same and the means of rectifying them*, published in 1780. As if to rub in his alienation from German culture, he wrote in French, leaving it to one of his officials (Christian Wilhelm von Dohm) to translate it into German.[123] He expressly denied that German literature was making progress: 'I do not believe that any writer can write well in a language which has not yet

[119] Reinhold Koser and Hans Droysen (eds.), *Briefwechsel Friedrichs des Großen mit Voltaire*, 3 vols, Publikationen aus den K. Preußischen Staatsarchiven, vols. 81, 82, 86 (Leipzig, 1908–9, 1911), I, pp. 71–2.

[120] *Des mœurs, des coutumes, de l'industrie, des progrès de l'esprit humain dans les arts et dans les sciences*, *Œuvres de Frédéric le Grand*, 30 vols (Berlin, 1846–56), I, p. 224.

[121] K. Biedermann, *Fredrich der Große und sein Verhältniß zur Entwicklung des deutschen Geisteslebens* (Brunswick, 1859) p. 5.

[122] Koser and Droysen, *Briefwechsel*, III, pp. 347–8.

[123] The French edition is in *Œuvres*, vol. VII. There is a good German edition in Steinmetz (ed.), *Friedrich II.*, which also includes much other relevant contemporary material. My references are to the latter edition.

been refined.' From that point the insults came thick and fast: 'The German language is still semi-barbaric and divided into as many dialects as Germany has provinces . . . The German language is confusing, difficult to use, does not sound pleasant and is not rich in metaphors . . . The endings sound so harsh in German and would be much improved by the addition of an "a", so that "*sagen*" would become "*sagena*", and so on . . .'[124] At least he had the good grace to concede that this last fatuous suggestion would not prove acceptable. As if he were seeking to cause maximum offence, Frederick then singled out the boy wonder of German letters—Goethe—for a special insult:

> To see just how bad contemporary taste in Germany is, just visit any theatre. There you will see the abominable plays of Shakespeare being performed in German translations and the audiences deriving great pleasure from these ridiculous farces which merit only to be performed in front of savages in Canada . . . Shakespeare can be forgiven because he lived at a time when English culture had developed but little. However, there is no excuse for our contemporaries making the same mistakes—as has been done, for example, in Goethe's *Götz von Berlichingen*, an abominable imitation of those bad English plays. Yet the public warmly applauds this rubbish and demands that it be repeated. I know one shouldn't argue about matters of taste, but I have to say that someone who can derive as much pleasure from a puppet-show as from the tragedies of Racine is just looking for a way of passing the time.[125]

Predictably, the pamphlet was greeted with outrage.[126] Yet there was no real surprise, for throughout his reign Frederick had flaunted his low opinion of German culture. When he revived the Academy in 1743, he gave it a French title (Académie Royale des Sciences et Belles-Lettres), French statutes, a French president (Maupertuis), a mainly French membership, and decreed that French should be the language of both oral and written communications.[127] This did not change: between the end of the Seven Years War and his death Frederick appointed only eighteen full members of his Academy, of whom only five were Germans.[128] No wonder that a German intelligentsia rapidly growing in numbers and self-confidence should take offence: as they saw it, he had the cream of a native culture both rich and fresh at his disposal,

[124] Ibid., pp. 61–2, 73, 77.

[125] Ibid., pp. 81–2.

[126] Several examples can be found in the *Œuvres*. A piece written by Goethe in reply was never published and has disappeared. For Goethe's own measured response, see ibid., pp. 141–2.

[127] Adolf von Harnack, *Geschichte der königlich preußischen Akademie der Wissenschaften zu Berlin*, 3 vols in 4 (Berlin, 1900), vol. I, pt. 1, pp. 266–7, 293–4.

[128] Ibid., I, 1, p. 362.

but preferred the sour and thin dregs of France. The fiasco of the appointment of Antoine Joseph Pernety as his librarian, mistaking him for Jacques Pernety, exemplified the problem.[129] In a similar fashion, the sculptor François Gaspard Balthasar Adam was brought to Berlin in mistake for his more famous elder brother Nicolas Sébastien.[130]

As *Concerning German Literature* revealed, Frederick was a living fossil, a relic of the generation before last. Baron von Grimm found the perfect simile: Frederick wrote of German literature like a blind man trying to describe colours.[131] Increasingly out of joint with the times, Frederick despised such new forms as the *comédie larmoyante* and the *drame bourgeois*, while he did not regard the novel as a literary genre at all, dismissing it as a mere 'diversion'.[132] A man who derided *the* great German epic—the *Nibelungenlied*—as 'not worth a shot of gunpowder' and dismissed the Middle Ages as 'twelve centuries of stupidity' was not likely to appreciate Herder or Goethe.[133] No more adventurous in the visual arts, his taste changed only by going backwards—from Watteau, Pater, and Lancret to Dutch, Flemish, and Italian old masters.[134] In all these ways Frederick can be made to look like the epitome of a culture which was absolutist, representational, courtly, and cosmopolitan, wholly at odds with the new German culture, which was liberal, critical, urban, and national. Frederick the Great and German culture, it seems, had nothing in common beyond geography. Yet the contemporary intelligentsia identified Frederick's Prussia as a *Kulturstaat*, and they were right to do so.

[129] Dieudonné Thiébault, *Mes Souvenirs de vingt ans de séjour à Berlin; ou Frédéric le Grand, sa famille, sa cour, son gouvernement, son académie, ses écoles, et ses amis littérateurs et philosophes*, 4th edn., 4 vols (Paris, 1813), IV, pp. 76–8.

[130] Eugen Paunel, *Die Staatsbibliothek zu Berlin. Ihre Geschichte und Organisation während der ersten zwei Jahrhunderten seit ihrer Eröffnung* (Berlin, 1965), p. 74.

[131] Harnack, *Geschichte der königlich preußischen Akademie der Wissenschaften zu Berlin*, I, 1, p. 464.

[132] Werner Langer, *Friedrich der Große und die geistige Welt Frankreichs*, Hamburger Studien zu Volkstum und Kultur der Romanen, vol. 11 (Hamburg, 1932), pp. 94–5, 185. See also Roland Vocke, 'Friedrich II. Verhältnis zur Literatur und zur deutschen Sprache', in Erhard Bethke (ed.) *Friedrich der Große* (Gütersloh, 1985), p. 175.

[133] Eckart Klessmann, *Die deutsche Romantik*, 2nd edn. (Cologne, 1981), p. 27; Pierre-Paul Sagave, 'Preußen und Frankreich', *Jahrbücher für die Geschichte Mittel und Ostdeutschlands*, 31 (1982), p. 69.

[134] Gerd Bartoschek, 'Friedrich II als Sammler von Gemälden', in Giersberg and Meckel (eds.), *Friedrich II. und die Kunst*, II, pp. 86–8; Paul Seidel, 'Friedrich der Große als Sammler von Gemälden und Skulpturen', *Jahrbuch der Königlich-Preußischen Kunstsammlungen*, 13 (1892), p. 188; Adolf Rosenberg, 'Fredrich der Große als Kunstsammler', *Zeitschrift für bildende Kunst*, NS 4 (1893), p. 210.

In the first place, Frederick was clearly aware of his German nationality. As his most distinguished modern biographer has observed, if he was torn between two national identities, it was not between a French and a German, but between a German and a Prussian.[135] In his correspondence with Voltaire, for example, where one might expect him to be at his most cosmopolitan, he refers repeatedly to his nationality, as in: 'I am only a good German and I do not blush to express myself with the candour which is an inseparable part of our national character' or 'I wager that you will think, when reading this: "that's just like a German, he shows all the phlegm of his bloodless nation". It's true we are vegetable-like when compared with the French; nor have we produced a *Jérusalem* or a *Henriade*. Since the Emperor Charlemagne took it into his head to turn us into Christians by slitting our throats, we have always been the same; and our cloudy skies and cold winters have done their bit too.'[136] As that last remark indicated, Frederick had not been a keen student of Montesquieu for nothing. In his own treatise on the subject—*Des mœurs*—he argued that the culture of every country had its own special flavour, as a result of 'the indelible character of each nation'. Books published in Padua, London, or Paris, for example, could easily be distinguished, even if written in the same language and on the same subject. Education could modify but never change fundamentally a national character.[137]

If Frederick was a merciless and (some might think) perceptive critic of German failings—pedantry, lack of humour, clumsiness, and '*le mal qu'on appelle logon diarrhœa*'[138]—he was no less severe on the French. It is a common but egregious error to suppose that Frederick admired all things French. On the contrary, he often subjected his alleged models to withering attacks, especially on account of their incorrigible taste for persecuting dissidents. 'The Englishman can think out loud,' he claimed, 'but a Frenchman hardly dares to betray an inkling of his ideas.'[139] It was for that reason that France could produce a Descartes or a Malebranche but never a really intrepid thinker such as a Leibniz, a Locke, or a Newton. Moreover, France's day was done.

[135] Theodor Schieder, 'Friedrich der Große—eine Integrationsfigur des deutschen Nationalbewußtseins im 18. Jahrhundert?', in Otto Dann (ed.), *Nationalismus in vorindustrieller Zeit* (Munich, 1986), p. 115.

[136] Letters of 19 April 1753 and 13 August 1766, in Koser and Droysen, *Briefwechsel*, III, 3, p. 127.

[137] *Des mœurs, des coutumes, de l'industrie, des progrès de l'esprit humain dans les arts et dans les sciences, Œuvres*, I, pp. 214–15.

[138] Harnack, *Geschichte der königlich preußischen Akademie der Wissenschaften zu Berlin*, I, 1, p. 388.

[139] *Histoire de mon temps, Œuvres*, II, p. 36.

There had been a few years during the ministry of Richelieu and during the reign of Louis XIV when its star had shone, but these were brief moments of wisdom in a long history of folly.[140] It was not just flattery that prompted him to tell Voltaire—often—that he was the last French writer of distinction.[141] Modern French literature, he told him, was a waste of time, fit only to be burned.[142] Rousseau he thought was 'mad', Diderot he seems not to have read at all—certainly there were none of his works in Frederick's personal library.[143] Special venom was reserved for the French avant-garde, for Holbach, against whom he wrote two counter-blasts, and for the 'Encyclopaedists', against whom he launched one of his 'conversations of the dead', in which he dismissed them as superficial and arrogant.[144] Far from advocating France as a model, he castigated its uncritical imitators in terms just as strong as anything employed by the *Sturm und Drang*:

> The taste for French drama was imported into Germany together with French fashions: enthused by the magnificence which Louis XIV impressed on all his actions, by the sophistication of his court and by the great names who were the ornaments of his reign, all Europe sought to imitate the France it admired. All Germany went there: a young man counted for a fool if he had not spent some time at the court of Versailles. French taste ruled our kitchens, our furniture, our clothes, and all those knick-knacks which are so much at the mercy of the tyranny of fashion. Carried to excess, this passion degenerated into a frenzy; women, who are often prey to exaggeration, pushed it to the point of extravagance.[145]

On the other hand, he had a clear sense that German culture was beginning at long last to develop in the right direction. As he rightly appreciated and recorded in *Concerning German Literature*, the devastations caused by the Thirty Years War, by religious conflict, and by the wars of Louis XIV had inflicted wounds on Germany which had taken a long time to heal. Recovery had not begun in earnest until after the War of the Spanish Succession and initially all effort had had to be concentrated on material reconstruction. But the process had been rapid, Germany was now flourishing again, everyone was getting richer, and eventually this would lead to cultural renewal too. Indeed, there were a few promising straws in the wind—German intellectuals were no

140 Koser and Droysen, *Briefwechsel*, III, p. 105.

141 Ibid., III, pp. 130, 135, 148.

142 Ibid., III, p. 105.

143 Thiébault, *Mes Souvenirs*, I, p. 9; Langer, *Friedrich der Große*, p. 191.

144 *Dialogue des morts entre le Prince Eugène, Mylord Marlborough et le Prince de Lichtenstein*, *Œuvres*, XIV, p. 253.

145 *Des mœurs*, p. 232.

longer ashamed to write in the vernacular, the first German dictionary had been published, and, more generally, there was a growing sense of excitement, reflected in the public discussion of Germany's national reputation. If sufficient patrons could be found, then Germany too would have its fair share of geniuses and would create its own classical literature. So he ended his pamphlet on the following wistful but optimistic note: 'These halcyon days of our literature have not yet arrived; but they are approaching and their arrival seems certain. I serve as their herald, although my advanced age robs me of the hope of seeing them myself. I am like Moses, I see the promised land from afar, but shall not enter it myself.'[146]

Many German intellectuals were convinced that it was Frederick's wresting of great-power status for Prussia which had given German culture the decisive impetus. The classic statement was provided by Goethe in his autobiography: 'The first true and really vital material of the higher order came into German literature through Frederick the Great and the deeds of the Seven Years War.'[147] Frederick's heroic feats, he argued further, gave Prussia—and with it all Protestant Germany—a priceless cultural advantage which Austria and the Catholics were never able to match.[148] Whether Goethe was right or not simply cannot be proved one way or the other. One could point to Quattrocento and Cinquecento Venice, to Elizabethan England, to the 'Golden Age' of Spain, to Louis XIV's France, to the baroque culture of late seventeenth-century Austria, or to twentieth-century America to support the hypothesis that power and culture march hand in hand. On the other hand, one might point to fifteenth-century Burgundy, eighteenth-century Venice, *fin-de-siècle* Vienna, or early twentieth-century Paris to support Hegel's aphorism that 'only in the twilight of history does the owl of Minerva begin her flight.' Either hypothesis is beyond the scope of this book. What *is* important is the fact that so many of Frederick's contemporaries echoed Goethe's assessment of the relationship. As the translator of his pamphlet *Concerning German literature*, Christian Wilhelm von Dohm, put it: 'Frederick's mighty deeds elevated the nation and inspired a patriotism of which previously there had been no inkling; and this had a beneficial effect on

[146] Steinmetz (ed.), *Friedrich der Große*, pp. 65–7, 97–9. This was a popular image among German sovereigns—Joseph II wrote to his mother from the Silesian frontier in 1766: 'Like Moses, we saw the promised land without being able to enter it'—quoted in Josef Karniel, *Die Toleranzpolitik Kaiser Josephs II.*, Schriftenreihe des Instituts für Deutsche Geschichte Universität Tel-Aviv, vol. 9 (Gerlingen, 1986), p. 129.

[147] *Goethes Werke*, hrsg. im Auftrage der Großherzogin Sophie von Sachsen, 133 vols (Weimar, 1887–1912), XXVII, p. 104.

[148] Ibid., p. 105.

literature too.'[149] Achim von Arnim was more concerned to stress the paradoxical nature of this process:

Frederick the Great belonged to that large number of German princes who were only prepared to support foreign drama with favour and funds. Yet because it was just during his reign that his victories over the French reawakened in Germans a sense of their own value, it was under his nose that a powerful reaction began—the development of mighty German dramatic talents which led to the expulsion of foreign influence, without Frederick himself or any of those entrusted with the implementation of his policies having the slightest inkling of it.

In other words, he concluded, Frederick had achieved by accident what Joseph II had set out to achieve by design: the foundation of a German national theatre.[150] One twist to this argument, stressing the contingent nature of the relationship between Frederick and German culture, found comfort even in the former's disdain for the latter. Goethe argued that the introduction of French culture to Prussia was 'highly beneficial' for Germans, because it spurred them on by provoking a reaction. He went on: 'Moreover, in the same way, Frederick's aversion to the German language as the medium for literature was a good thing for German writers. They did everything they could to make the King take notice of them.'[151] Frederick himself made the same point more pithily when he said to Mirabeau: 'What greater service could I have performed for German literature than that I didn't bother with it?'[152]

Although supported by the Olympian authority of Goethe, the link between Frederick's military achievements and the growth of German culture must remain rather speculative. More substantial are arguments based on his contributions to the formation of a public sphere. They were numerous. Firstly, he relaxed censorship. In June 1740 he gave a verbal order that censorship of

[149] Christian Wilhelm von Dohm, *Denkwürdigkeiten meiner Zeit, oder Beiträge zur Geschichte vom lezten Viertel des achtzehnten und vom Anfang des neunzehnten Jahrhunderts 1778 bis 1806*, 5 vols. (Lemgo and Hanover, 1814–1819), vol. IV, p. 615.

[150] Rudolf Payer von Thurn (ed.), *Joseph II als Theaterdirektor. Ungedruckte Briefe und Aktenstücke aus den Kinderjahren des Burgtheaters* (Vienna and Leipzig, 1920), p. 4.

[151] *Goethes Werke*, XXVII, p. 106. See also the similar passage in his *Maximen und Reflexionen*: 'The fact that Frederick the Great wanted to have absolutely nothing to do with them irked the German writers, and so they did their utmost to make themselves seem something in his eyes'; ibid., XLII, pt. 2, pp. 201–2. This passage is also quoted in Theodor Schieder, 'Friedrich der Große—eine Integrationsfigur des deutschen Nationalbewußtseins im 18. Jahrhundert', in Dann (ed.), *Nationalismus in vorindustrieller Zeit*, p. 127. A similar point was made by Prince August of Gotha in a letter to Herder of 25 December 1780; Bernhard Suphan, *Friedrichs des Großen Schrift über die Deutsche Literatur* (Berlin, 1888), p. 38.

[152] Biedermann, *Friedrich der Große*, p. 38.

newspapers in Berlin was to be abolished. When the official concerned—Baron Podewils—protested that foreign courts would be outraged, 'His Majesty replied that if newspapers were to be interesting they should not be inhibited.' In fact this order was just not obeyed and Frederick himself formally reimposed censorship in 1743, on the grounds that the journals had abused their freedom by publishing false reports offensive to Prussia's allies.[153] A new edict of 1749 then subjected all publications to pre-censorship.[154] Nevertheless, there was more scope for free expression on non-political matters than in most other European countries. When La Mettrie had to flee for his life from Holland in 1747 after the publication of *Homme machine*, or when d'Argens had to flee from France after the publication of *Philosophie du bon sens*, it was in Prussia that they sought refuge, which was a great source of self-congratulation among the Prussian intelligentsia.[155] Dramatic incidents such as these helped to create at least the image of a free country. That is certainly the inference to be drawn from an examination of essays written by Prussian school-leavers shortly after Frederick's death.[156] If that might seem a tainted source, the same cannot be said of the radical German Jacobin A. G. F. Rebmann, who wrote in 1793 of Frederick's detractors: 'It makes me cross that his critics usually forget the freedom to write and speak about everything which every scholar enjoyed in Prussia during Frederick's reign.'[157] The most judicious overall verdict is that of Horst Möller: 'Even if freedom of the press in the modern sense did not exist in Frederick's Prussia—and it hardly existed in the other states at this time—at least there did exist some freedoms of the press.'[158]

153 Ernst Consentius, 'Friedrich der Große und die Zeitungs-Zensur', *Preußische Jahrbücher*, 115 (1904), p. 220.

154 Wilhelm Dilthey, 'Der Streit Kants mit der Zensur über das Recht freier Religionsforschung', *Gesammelte Schriften*, vol. 4 (Leipzig and Berlin, 1921), p. 287.

155 Ann Thomson, *Materialism and Society in the Mid-eighteenth Century: La Mettrie's* Discours préliminaire (Geneva and Paris, 1981), p. 10. I am grateful to Prof. H. B. Nisbet for this reference. Friedrich Nicolai, *Andecdoten von Friedrich dem Großen und von einigen Personen die um ihn waren* (Berlin, 1788–92; reprint, Munich, n.d.), p. 33. See also Pierre-Paul Sagave, *Berlin und Frankreich 1685–1871* (Berlin, 1980), pp. 76–7.

156 Behrens, *Society, Government and the Enlightenment*, p. 182.

157 Horst Möller, *Vernunft und Kritik. Deutsche Aufklärung im 17. und 18. Jahrhundert* (Frankfurt am Main, 1986), p. 282.

158 Horst Möller, 'Königliche und bürgerliche Aufklärung', in *Preussen—Versuch einer Bilanz*, 5 vols. (Hamburg, 1981), vol. 2: Manfred Schlenke (ed.), *Preußen—Beiträge zu einer politischen Kultur*, p. 134. See also the observation of Leonard Krieger: 'Frederick fixed a permanent pattern of authoritarian alliance between aristocracy and monarch within the bureaucratic state, but he reformulated the traditional political values of the social hierarchy

For a world which has seen the politicization of every sphere of human activity and which views political values as supreme, it is difficult to conceive of an age in which religion and philosophy were the prime concerns. Yet such was Germany in the eighteenth century. That was why Kant devoted his celebrated article 'What is enlightenment?' to religious issues: 'I have portrayed *matters of religion* as the focal point of enlightenment, i.e. of man's emergence from his self-incurred immaturity.'[159] Of course, Lessing told Nicolai in his letter of 25 August 1769 'Don't talk to me about your Berlin freedom to think and write. It's just the freedom to market as many insults about religion as one likes,'[160] but this verdict owes its celebrity to its appeal to the twentieth century, not because it was representative of the eighteenth. Against Lessing must be set less lapidary but more numerous opinions such as that of the Berlin pastor Daniel Jenisch:

What chiefly elevates the eighteenth century above previous epochs is the degree and diffusion of intellectual endeavour [*Denkgeist*]: and it was the Prussian monarch who strove to arouse and invigorate it, with incalculable power; indeed, it can be said without exaggeration that he did more, and in more ways, than any other of the most notable men of the enlightenment.[161]

If a Lutheran pastor might be deemed too tame, the following echo from Moses Mendelssohn may be more persuasive:

I live in a state in which one of the wisest sovereigns who ever ruled mankind has made the arts and the sciences blossom and a sensible freedom of thought so widespread that their effects have reached down to the humblest inhabitant of his dominions. Under his glorious rule I have found both opportunity and inspiration to reflect on my own destiny and that of my fellow-citizens, and to present observations to the best of my ability on the fate of mankind and providence.[162]

What Mendelssohn is describing here is the formation of a public sphere. In view of the notorious inability of the British to find anything good to say about

into the ideal of freedom in the modern state'; *The German Idea of Freedom: History of a Political Tradition from the Reformation to 1871* (Chicago and London, 1972), p. 22.

159 Hans Reiss (ed.), *Kant's Political Writings* (Cambridge, 1970), p. 59.

160 Steinmetz (ed.), *Friedrich II.*, p. 50.

161 Ibid., pp. 234–5.

162 Quoted in Ludwig Geiger, *Die deutsche Literatur und die Juden* (Berlin, 1910), pp. 58–9. It is also quoted in Rudolf Vierhaus, *Deutschland vor der französischen Revolution. Untersuchungen zur deutschen Sozialgeschichte im Zeitalter der Aufklärung* (unpublished Münster Habilitationsschrift, 1961), p. 280, where more and similar tributes from other contemporary Prussians can be found. See also Mathys Jolles, *Das deutsche Nationalbewußtsein im Zeitalter Napoleons* (Frankfurt am Main, 1936), p. 63.

continental polities, especially when it was a question of civil liberties, the following tribute from John Moore is impressive:

Nothing surprised me more, when I first came to Berlin, than the freedom with which many people speak of the measures of government, and the conduct of the King. I have heard political topics, and others which I should have thought still more ticklish, discussed here with as little ceremony as at a London coffee-house. The same freedom appears in the booksellers' shops, where literary productions of all kinds are sold openly. The pamphlet lately published on the division of Poland, wherein the King is very roughly treated, is to be had without difficulty, as well as other performances, which attack some of the most conspicuous characters with all the bitterness of satire.

Anticipating Kant's famous remark, Moore concluded: 'A government supported by an army of 180,000 men may safely disregard the criticisms of a few speculative politicians and the pen of the satirist.'[163]

Secondly, Frederick identified himself with one of the major institutional forms of the public sphere—Freemasonry. Admitted to the order at Minden in 1738 while still Crown Prince, by the Count of Schaumburg Lippe, he founded his own lodge at Rheinsberg on his return.[164] On his accession to the throne two years later he was instrumental in founding a lodge at Berlin—'At the Three Globes'—and personally inducting his two brothers and other members of the Prussian aristocracy.[165] Although his active participation then waned, his continuing support for the movement was well advertised. In 1774, for example, he informed a Berlin lodge: 'His Majesty will always count it a special pleasure that he enjoys the opportunity to give his strong support to the promotion of the objectives of all true masonry, namely the intellectual elevation of men as members of society and making them more virtuous and more charitable.'[166] The masons returned the compliment by including the name of Frederick in a dozen of their lodges ('Frederick at the Golden Sceptre', for example) and by stressing the duty of their members to serve him and his state. In the year of his death a masonic address stated 'Whosoever fails to serve his king and his state loyally and honestly... is unworthy to be a mason.'[167]

[163] John Moore, *A View of Society and Manners in France, Switzerland and Germany*, 2 vols., 4th edn. (Dublin, 1789), II, p. 130.

[164] Rüdiger Hachtmann, 'Friedrich II. von Preußen und die Freimaurerei', *Historische Zeitschrift*, 264, 1 (1997), pp. 21–2.

[165] Ibid., p. 37. See also Karlheinz Gerlach, 'Die Berliner Freimaurerei 1783. Eine sozialgeschichtliche Untersuchung', in Helmut Reinalter and Karlheinz Gerlach (eds.), *Staat und Bürgertum im 18. und frühen 19. Jahrhundert* (Frankfurt am Main, 1996), p. 192.

[166] Hachtmann, 'Friedrich II. von Preußen und die Freimaurerei', p. 44.

[167] Ibid., p. 48.

Thirdly, Frederick was not only the 'first servant of the state', as he frequently claimed; he was also the first participant in the public sphere he did so much to create. It was crucial for future developments that his approach to culture was not that of the passive patron of representational art, but that of the active creator. That he was a genius certainly helped. As political theorist, historian, poet, dramatist, composer, and flautist, he would deserve his niche in any cultural history of the eighteenth century, even if he had not also been King of Prussia.[168] Whatever one might think about his regime or its impact on the subsequent course of German history, no one can read his works or listen to his music without realizing that he possessed extraordinary gifts. Although he did not call it such, the importance he attached to *Bildung*—individual self-cultivation—placed him squarely in the mainstream of German culture. A man who took Lucretius' *De Rerum natura* into battle and whiled away the intervals in the negotiations leading to the Peace of Hubertusburg by reading Rousseau's *Émile* was a man who gave a high priority to the intellect.[169] There is no reason to doubt the sincerity of his numerous declarations of faith, such as: 'Since my childhood I have loved the arts, literature and the sciences, and if I can contribute to their propagation, I dedicate myself with all the zeal at my disposal, because there can be no true happiness in this world without them.'[170] Moreover, the intellectualism he flaunted made him a role model, as Denina recorded: 'The enthusiasm generated by a king who was an author, by a king who was an academician in the fullest sense of the word ... by a king who kept the company of men of letters every day and everywhere, certainly gave a great momentum to every kind of intellectual endeavour.'[171]

[168] For a discussion of his numerous theoretical treatises on the nature of political power, see Friedrich Luckwaldt, 'Friedrichs des Großen Anschauungen von Staat und Fürstentum', *Historische Aufsätze Aloys Schulte zum 70. Geburtstag gewidmet* (Düsseldorf, 1927). The best modern account of his literary achievements is to be found in Theodor Schieder, *Friedrich der Große. Ein Königtum der Widersprüche* (Frankfurt am Main, Berlin, and Vienna, 1983), pp. 365–98. On Frederick as musician, see Helm, *Music at the Court of Frederick the Great*, *passim*, Helmuth Osthoff, 'Friedrich der Große als Komponist', *Zeitschrift für Musik*, 103, 2 (1936), and Helmuth Osthoff, 'Friedrich II. als Musikliebhaber und Komponist', in Bethke (ed.), *Friedrich der Große*, pp. 917–20.

[169] Peter Gay, *The Enlightenment: An Interpretation*. Vol. 1: *The Rise of Modern Paganism* (London, 1967), p. 100; Winfried Böhm, 'Bildungsideal, Bildungswesen, Wissenschaft und Akademien', in Bethke (ed.), *Friedrich der Große*, p. 186.

[170] Rosenberg, 'Fredrich der Große als Kunstsammler', 209.

[171] Abbé Denina, *La Prusse littéraire sous Frédéric II, ou histoire abrégée de la plupart des auteurs, des académiciens et des artistes qui sont nés ou qui ont vécu dans les États prussiens depuis MDCCXL jusqu'à MDCCLXXXVI. Par ordre alphabétique. Précédée d'une introduction, ou d'un tableau général des progrès qu'ont faits les arts et les sciences dans les pays qui constituent la Monarchie prussienne*, 3 vols. (Berlin, 1790–1), I, p. 43.

But Frederick was not only activist in his approach to culture, he was also critical—and it is this latter quality which Habermas deems the essential characteristic of the 'bourgeois public sphere'.[172] From his first major publication—*Antimachiavell*—which appeared on the eve of his accession to the throne, he entered the public arena repeatedly to engage in debate. As Goethe was sharp enough to spot, by simply publishing a pamphlet about German literature Frederick gave intellectual debate a momentum which no other living person could have matched. That his remarks were ill-informed, one-sided, and even at times absurd mattered not one jot. What was important was the fact that the King of Prussia had entered the public domain to take on all-comers. It was not his first appearance there, of course. He had already taken up his pen to attack Holbach's *Essai sur les préjugés* and *Le Système de la nature*, Rousseau's *Discours sur les sciences et les arts* and *Émile*, and the *philosophes* in general.[173] Moreover, he encouraged others to enter the public sphere in a critical spirit by having the Academy organize annual prize-essay competitions after 1744, setting such subjects as 'What has been the influence of governments on culture in nations where it has flourished?' (won by Herder), 'Can it be expedient to deceive the people?' and 'What has made French the universal language of Europe and does it deserve this supremacy?'[174]

As Horst Möller has justly observed, Frederick was more aware of the importance of the public sphere (*Öffentlichkeit*) than any other European monarch hitherto.[175] So aware was he indeed, that in 1784 he took the remarkable step of allowing extracts from a draft of the General Law Code (*Allgemeines Landrecht*) to be discussed in public. Only experts were to be involved and only certain aspects of the Code were affected, but it aroused much enthusiasm among the Prussian intelligentsia (as did, *mutatis mutandis*, Catherine the Great's exposure of her *Nakaz* to the Legislative Commission). The *Berlinische Monatsschrift* proudly claimed that one of the most impressive features of life in Prussia was the relative liberty with which political issues could be discussed.[176] For Leonard Meister, it was further evidence that Prussia was a *Rechtsstaat*, a state governed by the rule of law:

[172] Jürgen Habermas, *The Structural Transformation of the Public Sphere: An Inquiry into a Category of Bourgeois Society* (Cambridge, 1989), p. 54.

[173] Langer, *Friedrich der Große*, pp. 190–3.

[174] Harnack, *Geschichte der königlich preußischen Akademie der Wissenschaften zu Berlin*, I, 1, pp. 397–421. On the importance of the prize competition for Herder, see Robert E. Norton, *Herder's Aesthetics and the European Enlightenment* (Ithaca, NY, and London, 1991), p. 105. I am indebted to Professor H. B. Nisbet for this reference.

[175] Möller, *Vernunft und Kritik*, p. 203.

[176] Ibid., p. 303. See also Horst Möller, 'Wie aufgeklärt war Preußen?', in Hans-Jürgen Puhle and Hans-Ulrich Wehler (eds.), *Preußen im Rücklblick* (Göttingen, 1980), p. 195.

And this king unique among kings did still more. Not only did he promote order and security by introducing a wise legal code; when drawing it up, he sought the advice of all those who had advice to give, both Prussian citizens and foreigners, and he himself submitted himself to the laws. He proclaimed loudly and publicly that in matters of justice a peasant counted for as much as a prince . . . With views such as these and with a regime such as this, could the national spirit fail to be elevated? And this national spirit could take wing all the more boldly because nothing dazzled and nothing intimidated it, neither wanton display around the throne nor papal anathema from the altar. In this manner—and we cannot make the point often enough—Frederick gave the arts and the sciences the best possible wet-nurses: security, liberty, and toleration![177]

In conclusion, one final contribution by Frederick to German culture needs to be noted. It too was identified by Goethe in his autobiography. By his victories in the Seven Years War, Frederick not only gave German culture a Francophobe twist, he also turned it away from the Holy Roman Empire against which he was also fighting. As French historians are understandably eager to point out, it was not so much a French army as a Franco-Imperial army that was defeated at Rossbach on 5 November 1757. This was also made clear by Frederick himself in his own accounts of his reign, most notably in *The History of My Own Times* and *The History of the Seven Years War*. Goethe made the point with characteristic brilliance when he recounted the anecdote about Baron von Plotho, the Prussian envoy to the parliament of the Holy Roman Empire at Regensburg. When, early in 1757, an imperial notary came bearing the document which put Frederick to the ban of the Empire, Plotho seized hold of him, stuffed the writ into his shirt and then threw him downstairs. This defiant gesture acquired great symbolic significance and led to Plotho being lionized by the citizens of Frankfurt when he came to the city seven years later to attend the election of Joseph II as King of the Romans.[178]

There is a common, understandable but mistaken assumption that the German intellectuals who came to prominence in the second half of the eighteenth century were similar to their counterparts of today—gentle, pacific creatures, wholly at odds with the militaristic world of power politics. Some might be accurately described as such, but many more reacted like ordinary human beings to the events of the day. The surge of patriotic verse from Prussian poets such as Pyra, Lange, von Kleist, Ramler, and Gleim are well-known,[179] but the same spirit enthused many non-Prussian German writers as

177 Meister, *Friedrichs des Großen woltätige Rucksicht*, pp. 154–5.

178 *Goethes Werke*, XXVI, pp. 289–90.

179 Franz Muncker (ed.), *Anakreontiker und preußisch-patriotische Lyriker*, 2 vols. in 1 (Stuttgart, 1895), *passim*.

well. A good example is Christian Daniel Friedrich Schubart, a real radical by the standards of his times, who paid for his outspoken criticism of abuses in the duchy of Württemberg with ten years in prison. Quite rightly, he has been accorded a prominent place of honour in the pantheon of bourgeois emancipators. As one recent citation in what is probably the most widely used general history of German literature in the eighteenth century puts it: 'Schubart gave concrete expression to the idea of "liberty" by his struggle against feudal despotism and oppression, against clerical obscurantism, and against the exploitation of the peasantry.'[180]

Less often emphasized are Schubart's credentials as a nationalist, which are impressive. Moreover, he gloried not only in the superiority of German culture, he also gloried in German *power*. In the very first issue of his periodical *Deutsche Chronik* ('A German Chronicle') which became one of the most popular publications of the day, in an article simply entitled 'Germany', Schubart published what amounted to a manifesto. It can be summarized as follows:

> If we ever had reason to be proud of Germany, then today is that time. Foreigners now view with envy a nation which in the past they tried to reduce to submission by a combination of force and fashion. Once despised as imitators, we are now the imitated... Frederick the Great gives the law to Europe, and who can speak of him without enthusiasm? He is the cynosure of the world, the great original of present and future heroes, a German and still in the prime of life... It is no longer the French who dominate the continent of Europe, it is the German powers. Our martial arts have been brought to a peak of near-perfection and are now feared, admired, and copied by all the other nations.[181]

Schubart praised Frederick for his philanthropy, enlightenment, toleration, generous treatment of artists and their dependants, and for making Berlin 'the new Athens', but in almost the same breath he revelled in Prussia's military might, comparing Frederick with such legendary Teutonic heroes as Wotan and Hermann.[182] In a poem entitled 'A Hymn to Frederick the Great',

[180] Hans-G. Winter, 'Antiklassizismus: Sturm und Drang', in Viktor Zmegac (ed.), *Geschichte der deutschen Literatur vom 18. Jahrhundert bis zur Gegenwart*, vol 1, pt. 1, 2nd edn. (Königstein im Taunus, 1984), p. 213.

[181] Christian Daniel Schubart, *Deutsche Chronik* (Augsburg, 1774–7; reprinted in facsimile, Heidelberg, 1975), I, pp. 5–6. Even such an unmilitaristic figure as Goethe took pleasure in Prussia's military prowess: 'When we looked northwards, we were illuminated by Frederick, the polar star around which Germany, Europe, even the world seemed to revolve. His hegemony in everything revealed itself most forcefully when the French army adopted the Prussian drill manual and even the Prussian cane'—*Goethes Werke*, XXVIII, p. 56.

[182] Schubart, *Deutsche Chronik*, I, pp. 76–7, 533–4; II, pp. 45, 361–4; III, pp. 82, 260–1, 506; IV, pp. 309–10, 467–70. Cf. Schieder, *Friedrich der Große*, p. 483.

Schubart explicitly identified him with the legendary German heroes when eulogizing his military feats in the face of apparently impossible odds:

> Five times thundered Frederick Wotan,
> And Silesia was his,
> The most precious jewel in his crown.

Later, referring to Frederick's formation of the League of Princes in 1785 to counter Joseph II's expansionist schemes, Schubart extended his associational references:

> Teutonia's princes beat a path
> To Frederick's rocky fortress,
> Where this giant among men
> Lay brooding on his iron bed.
> They stretched out their hands to him, hailing him as
> The defender of their ancient rights, crying:
> 'Be our leader, Frederick Herman.'
> He hearkened to their cry, and created the German League.[183]

In an article entitled 'Monuments of the Germans', published in his *Patriotic Chronicle* for the revolutionary year of 1789, Schubart also provided the best example of the symbiosis of cultural and military achievement. He argued that what the Germans needed most was a truly national history which would inspire young people to emulate the great men of the past. Alas, he lamented, so much of German history had been devoid of incident: the mighty Herman had made a world-historical impact, with his wild heroism and rough virtues, but then Germany had fallen under the yoke of despotism and clericalism, the hapless prey of foreigners. The primeval liberty exemplified by Herman's defeat of the Roman legions had faded, reviving briefly under Luther but submerged again by the confessional strife which climaxed in the Thirty Years War. It was not until the wounds of that terrible conflict had begun to heal that a new epoch could begin, more glorious than anything the past had witnessed:

> It was Frederick the Great who now shone forth as the intellectual pillar supporting a whole new epoch in the history of mankind, and provided for the historian the richest stock of materials, namely the influence which the Germans now exert on almost all events in the world, their ascendancy in the arts and sciences, their profound search for truth, their reviving sense of liberty and their generosity of spirit.[184]

[183] C. F. D. Schubart, *Gesammelte Schriften und Schicksale*, 8 vols. in 4 (Stuttgart, 1839–40), IV, pp. 325, 327.

[184] Ibid., VII, pp. 185–7.

Of course, Schubart was well aware that his idol had negative features, seasoning his eulogies with criticisms of Frederick's miserliness, impiety, and ruthlessness.[185] But, as Goethe realized, it was just this grating mixture of attraction and aversion that made such a deeply etched impression on German culture. It also had momentous political consequences, for if the old regime in France collapsed because of its fatal combination of impotence and despotism, and if the secret of British stability lay in its ability to reconcile power with liberty, the Prussian way, initiated by Frederick the Great, combined power with culture.

THE BIRTH OF GERMAN NATIONALISM

In the introduction to this chapter it was argued that religious identity has been a potent and popular intensifier of national identity. The odd nation out appears to be the German. Reformation and then Counter-Reformation left the Holy Roman Empire divided between Catholics (about one-third of the population but controlling about two-thirds of the territories) and various forms of Protestantism. This confessional confusion certainly complicated political development, but such is the need for a nation to possess a sense of religious solidarity that an 'other' was found to provide it through reaction. This was France, of course, not the Catholic France of the old regime establishment, but the irreligious France of the *philosophes* and then the Antichrist of the Revolution. As responses to the French Revolution were to demonstrate, portraying Germany as the religious country *par excellence* was a particularly potent part of the German political myth which helped to unite civil society and state.

Although it proved to be a bonding agent after 1789, religion could have operated as a solvent, as it had done during the early sixteenth century. German humanism had created, as A. G. Dickens has put it, 'a legend of a nation resplendent in antiquity, valour and simple piety. Even before God took the empire from the less deserving Romans, here in the northern forests had flourished the obvious recipients of empire, the noblest Romans of them all.'[186] It was a myth with a strongly nationalist character, based partly on the virtues first described by Tacitus in *Germania* and partly on hostility to the foreigners who were bleeding the country dry. The rediscovery and publica-

185 Schubart, *Deutsche Chronik*, II, pp. 364–5.
186 A. G. Dickens, *The German Nation and Martin Luther* (London, 1974), p. 24.

tion of Tacitus' text in 1455 gave German self-awareness a tremendous fillip.[187] The main target of course was the papacy, associated with corruption and exploitation long before Luther spoke out. Conrad Celtis, for example, used his speech at the inaugural ceremonies of the university of Ingolstadt in 1492 to issue both a fierce indictment and a clarion call to arms. He complained that Germany's neighbours 'pursue our name with a kind of eternal hatred and calumny', even to the extent of using 'barbarians' as a synonym for 'Germans'.

Assume, O men of Germany, that ancient spirit of yours, with which you so often confounded and terrified the Romans, and turn your eyes to the frontiers of Germany; collect together her torn and broken territories. Let us be ashamed, ashamed, I say, to have placed upon our nation the yoke of slavery, and to be paying tributes and taxes to foreign and barbarian kings. O free and powerful people, O noble and valiant race, plainly worthy of the Roman empire, our famous harbour is held by the Pole and the gateway of our ocean by the Dane! In the east also powerful peoples live in slavery, the Bohemians, the Moravians, the Slovaks, and the Silesians, who all live as it were separated from the body of our Germany. And I may add the Transylvanian Saxons who also use our racial culture and speak our native language.[188]

Celtis was reasonably polite about the French, reserving his special venom for the Italians, the avaricious leeches sucking Germany's life-blood: 'Such has been the power of that long-standing and irreconcilable hatred between us and of that ancient strife between the protecting deities of our two nations, which would in view of the hostile spirits on both sides, inevitably have led to mutual slaughter, had not prudent Nature separated us by the Alps and by rocks towering to the stars.'[189] Other scholars preferred to use the French as the sounding-board for German virtues—Jakob Wimpfeling, for example, who in his *Epitome Germanorum* of 1505 claimed Charlemagne as a German who knew how to subjugate and rule over the French.[190]

In late fifteenth- and early sixteenth-century Germany there was a good deal of nationalism waiting to be exploited. It was at just this point, however, that the Habsburg dynasty, which had provided Holy Roman Emperors since the election of Frederick III in 1452, became more *inter*national than ever before.

[187] Hagen Schulze, *States, Nations and Nationalism from the Middle Ages to the Present* (Oxford, 1996), p. 127.

[188] Leonard Forster (ed.), *Selections from Conrad Celtis 1459–1508* (Cambridge, 1948), p. 47. Part of this quotation is also to be found in a different (and better) translation in Dickens, *The German Nation and Martin Luther*, p. 35.

[189] Forster (ed.), *Selections from Conrad Celtis*, p. 45.

[190] Schulze, *States, Nations and Nationalism*, p. 129.

The marriage of Maximilian I to the Burgundian heiress in 1477, his acquisition of the reversionary interest in the thrones of Hungary and Bohemia in 1491, and the marriage of his son Philip to the heiress of Castile and Aragon in 1496 created the greatest empire in Europe, not to mention the rapidly expanding possessions in the Americas. This international empire required an international outlook and an international religion. So the beneficiary of German nationalism proved to be Martin Luther and the German princes who supported him. In other words, in the Holy Roman Empire nationalism became a centrifugal force.

For most of the next two centuries, German fought against German, Protestant against Catholic, prince against emperor. Of all the many victims, perhaps the saddest were the Free Imperial Cities (*Reichsstädte*), the fifty or so self-governing republics subject only to the Emperor. In the early sixteenth century they boasted a civic culture second only to their Italian counterparts. Nuremberg, for example, was the home of Albrecht Dürer, Veit Stoss, Adam Krafft, Peter Vischer, and Hans Sachs. The collective achievement of Augsburg, Ulm, Frankfurt am Main, Worms, Speyer, Cologne, Hamburg, Bremen, and Lübeck outshone by far anything the princely courts could muster. A century and more of civil war reversed this relationship. Unable to compete economically or politically, the cities declined, together with the other weaker members of the Empire, such as the ecclesiastical states and the Imperial Knights. It was the greater princes who came out on top and it was to their courts that Germany's cultural leadership moved. As it did so, it changed character, ceasing to be civic, vernacular, and national and becoming representational, classical, and cosmopolitan, a process that reached a climax with the international baroque culture of courts such as that of Augustus the Strong of Saxony-Poland, which was examined in the second chapter.[191]

It was a culture devoid of any national character. With the advantage of hindsight, we may be able to say that Versailles looks French, Caserta looks Italian, and Castle Howard looks English, even though their visual vocabularies are similar, but can it be said that the Würzburg Residenz or Nymphenburg look German? This was not just a question of political disunity, for Italy was, if anything, more of a geographical expression in the seventeenth and eighteenth centuries, not having even the nominal unity provided by the 'Holy Roman Empire of the German Nation'. The special problem which made the latter's culture so bereft of nationality was the marginalization of its vernacular. In the High Middle Ages, the German language had dominated government, law,

[191] See above, pp. 60–72.

and secular culture; only in the Church did Latin prevail. So, for example, the two great legal codes—the *Sachsenspiegel* (Saxon Mirror) and the *Schwabenspiegel* (Swabian Mirror)—were composed in German. It was the reception of Roman law and Italian humanism in the fifteenth century that began a linguistic shift.[192] Despite the colossal contribution of Luther's translation of the Bible, by the end of the sixteenth century the German vernacular was in full retreat on all fronts. In 1520 Ulrich von Hutten, knight, nationalist, and humanist, felt obliged to apologize to his audience for having published previously in Latin—'But now I call to the fatherland / To the German nation, in its own language.' Alas, it was a call which ever fewer heeded.[193] As we have seen, by 1600 71 per cent of the books appearing in fair catalogues were in Latin.[194] The victory of the Counter-Reformation in north-western, central, and south-eastern Germany, and throughout the Habsburg monarchy, was also a victory for Latin culture, but even in Protestant regions Latin became the accepted medium for scholarly and legal discourse.

In Vienna it also survived in high society. A correspondent of the Parisian *Journal encyclopédique* reported in 1759 that Latin was spoken much more commonly and correctly there than in France.[195] By that time, however, it was Spanish, Italian, or French that served as the lingua franca of Austrian aristocrats. The Prussian envoy reported that the Chancellor of State, Prince Kaunitz, spoke the Romance languages perfectly but deliberately chose to butcher his German to demonstrate his distance from the common herd.[196] The capital of a multi-national empire, Vienna was of course exceptionally cosmopolitan, a quality well captured by the tri-lingual form adopted for his signature by Prince Eugene, the Monarchy's most distinguished military commander—'Eugenio von Savoie'.[197] Further north, the hegemony of French was undisputed. As we have seen, Frederick the Great was resolutely Francophone, reserving German for shouting at his soldiers and corresponding with his officials.[198] Two years before his death, his Académie Royale des Sciences et Belles-Lettres advertised a prize-essay competition on the subject 'What has made the French language the universal language of Europe? In

[192] Wolfgang Kunkel, 'The reception of Roman law in Germany', in Gerald Strauss (ed.), *Pre-Reformation Germany* (London, 1972), p. 263.

[193] Hauser, *Le Principe des nationalités*, p. 13.

[194] See above, p. 145.

[195] Bruce Alan Brown, *Gluck and the French Theatre in Vienna* (Oxford, 1991), p. 36.

[196] Ibid., p. 47.

[197] Louis Réau, *L'Europe française au siècle des lumières* (Paris, 1951), p. 290.

[198] See above, p. 52.

which respects does it merit this claim? Can one assume that it will maintain it?', dividing the prize between a professor from Stuttgart and Comte Rivarol of Paris.[199]

How far down the social scale did this preference for French reach? Just as what is incontestably the most celebrated novel in the Russian language—Tolstoy's *War and Peace*—begins with a French passage, so does what is probably the most celebrated novel in the German language—Thomas Mann's *Buddenbrooks*: '"And—and—what comes next?" "Oh, yes, yes, what the dickens does come next? *C'est la question, ma très chère demoiselle*!"'[200] At least old Johann Buddenbrook spoke mainly in German, just larding his speech with French phrases such as '*Mon vieux*', '*Tiens!*' and '*Excusez, mon cher!*' to show what a man of the world he was—or a '*chevalier à la mode*' as he put it himself. He had been born in 1760 and was still wearing the fashions of his youth—powdered hair, a pigtail, and knee-breeches—in 1835, which is when the action of *Buddenbrooks* begins.

Thomas Mann was a novelist, writing at the beginning of the twentieth century, so his evocation of early nineteenth-century Germany may be more *Dichtung* than *Wahrheit*. Nevertheless, as a symptom of the permeation of the German language by imported words (*Fremdwörter*), it will serve as well as any. It was a process which had long been recognized and long been resisted. Even in the darkest days of the seventeenth century, there had been efforts to maintain linguistic purity. What came to be known as 'language societies' (*Sprachgesellschaften*) were founded with the express purpose of keeping High German 'free from alien vocabulary, both in essence and in form', as the 'Fruitful Society' founded in 1617 put it.[201] The fantastic titles of these societies—'The Pegnesian Floral Order', 'The Order of the Swans of the Elbe', 'The Poetical Clover-Leaf', and so on—were more than matched by the orotund language of their statutes. The members of the 'Fruitful Society', for example, were to display 'sensibility and wisdom, virtue and courteousness, usefulness and delightfulness, and the geniality of moderation' and were to behave in a 'kind, genial, and friendly manner', avoiding 'improper address

[199] Harnack, *Geschichte der königlich preußischen Akademie der Wissenschaften zu Berlin*, vol. I, pt. 1, p. 421.

[200] In German the contrast is more striking because Consul Buddenbrook, who is conducting the catechism of little Antonia, is speaking Lübeck dialect: '"Was ist das,—Was—ist das..." "Je, den Düwel ook, *C'est la question, ma très chère demoiselle*!"' In the case of *War and Peace*, the contrast is heightened by the introduction of a Russian word which also juxtaposes Cyrillic with Latin script: 'Eh bien, mon prince. Gênes et Lucques ne sont plus que des apanages, des MomectbЯ, de la famille Buonaparte.'

[201] Richard van Dülmen, *The Society of the Enlightenment* (Cambridge, 1992), p. 14.

and crude raillery'.[202] As this suggests, the societies had a dual objective, to revive the old heroic virtues as well as to purify the language.[203]

As the courts of the princes embraced the culture associated with Latin Europe, one might have expected the supporters of the vernacular to be middle-class in origin. In fact, the 'Fruitful Society', the largest and most important of all the *Sprachgesellschaften*, was founded in 1617 as an aristocratic initiative, with Prince Ludwig of Anhalt-Köthen as chairman.[204] Although commoners were admitted, more than three-quarters of its membership consisted of nobles of varying degrees.[205] The membership of other societies, such as the 'Upright Society of the Fir' of Strassburg or the 'German-supporting [*Deutschgesinnte*] Society' of Hamburg was mainly middle-class, as befitted their location in Free Imperial Cities, but even so it is difficult to present this culture clash as part of a more general class conflict. Perhaps just because they lacked the cutting edge of class consciousness, the language societies failed miserably in their self-appointed task. By 1700 the stock of the German language had never been lower, as it appeared to be in its death throes as a medium of intellectual discourse.[206]

That was certainly the conclusion of the most eminent German philosopher of the day, Gottfried Wilhelm Leibniz (1646–1716). In 1679, at a time when Louis XIV and the French culture he personified seemed to be invincible, Leibniz wrote a pamphlet entitled *Exhortation to the Germans to exercise their Reason and their Language better*.[207] Unusually for him, he wrote this piece in the German language, all his major philosophical, political, and scientific treatises being in Latin or French. He also wrote, as he recorded, 'in a state of passion', fired by a wish to advertise the virtues of his fatherland: 'it is certain that next to the honour of God, it is the well-being of his fatherland which should be dearest to the heart of the virtuous man, not only because it promotes our own interest (both in giving security and promoting our

202 Ibid.

203 Karl F. Otto, *Die Sprachgesellschaften des 17. Jahrhunderts* (Stuttgart, 1972), p. 12.

204 Christoph Stoll, *Sprachgesellschaften im Deutschland des 17. Jahrhunderts* (Munich, 1973), p. 10.

205 Karl F. Otto, 'Soziologisches zu den Sprachgesellschaften: Die Deutschgesinnete Genossenschaft', in Martin Bircher and Ferdinand van Ingen (eds.), *Sprachgesellschaften, Sozietäten, Dichtergruppen* (Hamburg, 1978), p. 151.

206 Eric A. Blackall, *The Emergence of German as a Literary Language 1700–1775* (Cambridge, 1959), p. 1.

207 Gottfried Wilhelm Leibniz, 'Ermahnung an die Teutsche, ihren Verstand und Sprache beßer zu üben', *Sämtliche Schriften und Briefe*, 4th ser., vol. III (Berlin, 1986). The precise dating is uncertain, 1679 being the date preferred by the editors of this standard edition of his writings.

enjoyment) but because it is a general obligation.'[208] In his view, Germany was as perfect as any earthly paradise could be: it boasted a mild climate, an unequalled range of flora and fauna, rich deposits of minerals, inexhaustible stocks of salt, stone, and timber, a matchless network of navigable rivers, and a coastline indented with natural harbours. It was spared natural disasters such as earthquakes, volcanoes, and epidemic diseases: if orange trees were not indigenous, neither were scorpions. Germany might seem uncouth on the surface, he concluded, but it was healthy to the core, for its hills overflowed with wine and its valleys were replete with the fat of the land.

Moreover, the Germans, in Leibniz's view, possessed a national character to match these natural assets, for God had made them strong and courageous. They were naturally honest and their hearts and mouths spoke with the same voice: they said what they meant and they meant what they said. Their political and cultural institutions were correspondingly healthy: 'What is nobler than German liberty and was not that bold prince right who said that Germany is a free country, indeed the freest in the world?' The decentralization of power under the benign rule of the Habsburg Emperor enhanced both political participation and employment opportunities. Nowhere else in Europe were there so many self-governing city republics as in Germany, enjoying a merited reputation for flourishing trade and industry and sound government. Even the German peasants lived much better than was commonly supposed (and could live even better still if only they would learn to be a little more industrious and enterprising).

If Germany really were so well-placed to become a terrestrial paradise, what could be done to make reality fulfil potential? Optimistically, Leibniz decided to trust in God to find a solution to political and military problems. With divine assistance, such a wise Emperor as Leopold I would surely find a way to return Germany to its former glories. However, one area which was both vitally important and could be addressed by human agency was language. Never had the German language sunk so low, yet only a linguistic revival could secure Germany's future. As the history of Ancient Greece, Classical Rome, and Louis XIV's France demonstrated, the welfare of a nation was as surely determined by the welfare of a language as tides are governed by the moon. The Germans had shown they could do it, for a century or so ago they were writing an excellent form of their language. Yet in the terrible times which had followed, both their political and linguistic integrity had been cast aside, as German armies fought for foreigners against the fatherland and

[208] Ibid., pp. 796–7.

German blood was sacrificed to greed for territory. Leibniz believed that the chief culprit was France and so devoted the last part of his pamphlet to an attack on the French and their German imitators. There might be something to be said for the current craze for French fashions, he wrote, if they actually improved manners, although he himself would prefer to see an uncouth German talking and writing good sense in his own language than a sophisticate aping the French: 'better to be a German original than a French copy.' After this passionate diatribe—not the first or last time that a German was to combine a sense of national pride with a sense of national weakness—it is something of an anticlimax to find that the best solution Leibniz could think of was an association for the promotion of the German language.

It proved to be darkest before dawn. Within fifty years of Leibniz's death in 1716, the German language was flourishing as never before. In large measure this was the cumulative effect of the expanding public sphere examined in the previous chapter, for its preferred linguistic medium was the vernacular.[209] Of those who contributed to this development, the most important was Johann Christoph Gottsched (1700–66), yet another German intellectual who benefited from the cultural pluralism of the Holy Roman Empire. Born at Königsberg in East Prussia, his exceptional height made him a conspicuous target for Frederick William I's recruiting sergeants, so he fled to Leipzig in 1724, where he was appointed professor of poetry in 1730 and professor of philosophy in 1734. There he fulfilled Leibniz's instructions by founding a 'German Society', devoted to linguistic integrity: 'at all times the purity and correctness of the language shall be promoted; that is to say, not only all foreign words are to be avoided but also all incorrect German expressions and dialects; so that only High German will be written, not Silesian or Meissen, Franconian or Lower Saxon; so that it can be understood right across Germany.'[210] A prolific writer, Gottsched practised what he preached through polemics such as *The Critical Art of Poetry for the Germans* (1730) or the eight-volume *Critical History of German Language, Poetry and Speech* (1732–4). Similar German societies, often with statutes identical to those of Leipzig, were founded in Jena (1730), Göttingen (1738), Greifswald (1740), Königsberg (1741), Helmstedt (1742), Altdorf and Erlangen (1756), Vienna (1761), and Bremen (1762).[211]

[209] See above, p. 145.

[210] Blackall, *The Emergence of German as a Literary Language*, p. 107.

[211] Dülmen, *The Society of the Enlightenment* (Cambridge, 1992), p. 45; Paul Otto, *Die deutsche Gesellschaft in Göttingen (1738–1758)* (Munich, 1898), p. 9; Wolfgang Hardtwig, 'Wie deutsch war die deutsche Aufklärung?', in Wolfgang Hardtwig, *Nationalismus und Bürgerkultur in Deutschland 1500–1914. Ausgewählte Aufsätze* (Göttingen, 1994), p. 73.

Gottsched showed what a determined, energetic, and articulate intellectual could achieve in early-eighteenth century Germany.[212] He had something to say and he made himself heard. By the end of his life he had achieved such fame that Frederick the Great sought him out when campaigning in Saxony in the autumn of 1757. The two men met twice, spending several hours together discussing Aristotle, Cicero, Descartes, Leibniz, Wolff, Voltaire, and Rousseau. When Gottsched defended the ability of the German language to express delicate emotions and tender feelings, Frederick gave him a poem by Rousseau for translation. Whether Gottsched's response to this challenge was deemed satisfactory may be doubted, however, for Frederick sent in return a poem of his own composition, which stated that heaven had not been prodigal in dispensing gifts to the various nations, confining the French to being quick-witted, the English to being profound, and the Germans to being mighty warriors. He added that it was up to Gottsched, 'the swan of Saxony', to wrest from nature a further gift by civilizing a barbarous language.

As these exchanges took place just a couple of weeks before the epoch-making battle of Rossbach,[213] Frederick's remark about the Germans' martial prowess was soon confirmed. It was much less likely that it would be Gottsched who raised Germany's language and literature to a comparable level, for by this time he had come to seem very out of date. As a follower of Wolff and a firm believer in universal and immutable natural laws of aesthetics, he wished to emulate rather than reject French classicism: 'what the Greeks were for the Romans, the French are for us. They have given us the best models in all kinds of poetry.'[214] True to his word, his attempt to create a standard repertoire for the German theatre through anthologies such as the multi-volume *German Stage* (1741–5) consisted mainly of translations of works by Corneille, Racine, Molière, and Voltaire.[215] His pedantry and pomposity (which Frederick the Great had been quick to notice and lampoon) also helped to make him a figure of fun for the younger generation. A more charitable and perhaps further-sighted posterity has assigned him a key role in the development of German literature and the vernacular on which it was

[212] The following is based on Gottsched's own account 'Gespräch mit Friedrich II.', reprinted in Horst Steinmetz (ed.), *Friedrich II., König von Preußen und die deutsche Literatur des 18. Jahrhunderts. Texte und Dokumente* (Stuttgart, 1985), pp. 23–40.

[213] See above, p. 52.

[214] Quoted in Robert Ergang, 'National sentiments in Klopstock's odes and *Bardiete*', in *Nationalism and Internationalism: Essays Inscribed to Carlton J.H. Hayes* (New York, 1950), p. 123.

[215] Christoph Siegrist, 'Phasen der Aufklärung von der Didaktik bis zur Gefühlskultur', in Viktor Zmegac (ed.), *Geschichte der deutschen Literatur vom 18. Jahrhundert bis zur Gegenwart*, vol 1, pt. 1, 2nd edn. (Königstein im Taunus, 1984), p. 74.

1. The Palace of Versailles at the end of Louis XIV's reign by Jean-Baptiste Martin. The epitome of representational court culture, the Versailles system was beginning to atrophy by the time its creator died in 1715.

2. The Salon of War, Versailles. The bas-relief by Antoine Coysevox shows 'Louis XIV on horseback trampling on his enemies and crowned by glory', the fresco above, by Charles Lebrun, shows the Holy Roman Empire of the German Nation cowering in terror before the force of French arms, while in the bas-relief at the bottom Clio sets down the king's history for the benefit of posterity.

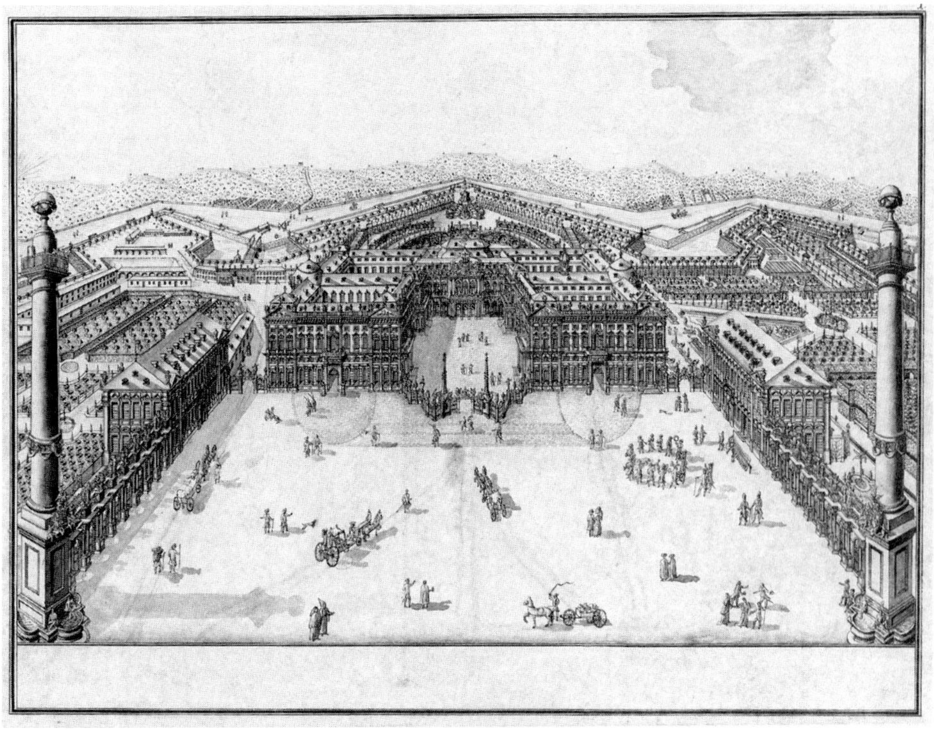

3. The Residenz at Würzburg. The greatest secular achievement of the German baroque, this great palace of a minor prince-bishop was compared favourably with Versailles by David Hume.

4. Giovanni Battista Tiepolo, *The Marriage of the Emperor Frederick Barbarossa to Beatrice of Burgundy in 1156*, Würzburg, Residenz. Painted in 1750, this fresco is one of a pair which adorns the Kaisersaal ('Emperor's Hall'), the main state-room of the palace. Tiepolo gave the features of his patron, Karl Philipp von Greiffenclau, to the bishop officiating.

5. Louis de Silvestre, *Augustus II, King of Poland and Elector of Saxony* (1718). This equestrian portrait was part of Augustus the Strong's campaign to establish his credentials as a major European monarch. In the following year he took a major step towards realising his goal when his eldest son was married to an Austrian Archduchess.

6. The Zwinger at Dresden. Designed by Matthias Daniel Pöppelmann for Augustus the Strong, this was an open space surrounded by pavilions, within which the Saxon court could play and display.

7. Ludwigsburg Palace (1704–34). Built, like its model Versailles, on what was essentially a green-field site, it was both residence and capital of the Duchy of Württemberg. It also became the centre of a substantial new town.

8. Joseph Vernet's painting of a French highway under construction in 1747 illustrates the major improvements made in communications during the course of the eighteenth century.

9. The lending library was an eighteenth century invention, allowing a new style of reading to develop: instead of reading a few texts repeatedly, the rapidly growing number of readers could read many books just once.

10. Daniel Chodowiecki's depiction of a German peasant reading shows not only that literacy filtered down to the labouring classes but also that contemporaries were aware of the fact.

11. The middle-class group in this charming study by Chodowiecki is listening with rapt attention to the latest novel being read out loud.

Vuë de la Place de l'Opéra,
et de la Nouvelle Bibliothèque ainsi que de l'Eglise Catholique.
Dedié à Son Altesse Royale, Monseigneur le Prince Frederic, Prince héréditaire de Prusse etc.

12. The 'Forum Fridericanum' in Berlin, comprising the opera-house on the left, St. Hedwig's (Catholic) Cathedral in the background and the royal library on the right, provide architectural evidence of Frederick the Great's transformation of Prussia into a state in which culture was cherished.

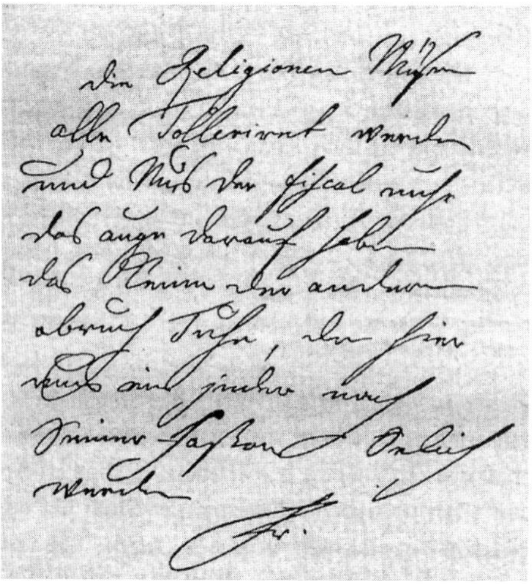

Die Religionen Müsen alle Tolleriret werden und Mus der fiscal nuhr das auge darauf haben das Keine der andern abruch Tuhe, den hier mus ein jeder nach Seiner Fasson Selich werden

Fr.

13. 'All religions must be tolerated and the sole concern of officials is to ensure that one denomination does not interfere with another, for here everyone can seek salvation in the manner that seems best to him' scribbled Frederick the Great in the margin of a document within a month of coming to the throne in 1740.

14. Louis François Roubiliac, *George Frederick Handel* (1738). This statue was erected at Vauxhall Pleasure Gardens by their owner, Edward Tyers, illustrating how a composer could find both fame and fortune in the public sphere.

15. William Hogarth, *O the Roast Beef of Old England, or The gate of Calais* (1748–9). The finest pictorial example of 'dietary nationalism' shows a fat friar and an incredulous French soldier slavering over the sirloin of English beef as it is brought ashore at Calais for delivery to Madam Grandsire's eating-house.

16. Antoine Watteau, *The shop Sign of Gersaint* (1721). Painted in the last year of Watteau's life, this captures the transition from the court culture of Versailles to the public sphere of Paris. As she steps into the shop, where the paintings are commodities, the lady on the left looks down at a portrait of Louis XIV being packed away.

17. Benjamin West, *The death of General Wolfe* (1770). As the mortally wounded hero expires, a messenger rushes from the battle, bearing the glad tidings of victory over the French. A truly world-historical moment, among other things it determined that eventually English would become the world-language.

18. Benjamin West, *Queen Charlotte* (1782). Piety, economy and fidelity were among the virtues which helped George III's consort to project the appropriate image of the British royal family. In the background can be seen twelve of the fourteen children she bore.

19. François Boucher, *Girl on a couch* (1752). Louise O'Murphy was one of Louis XV's many teenage mistresses and may have been as young as thirteen when she first caught the royal eye. That the king's official painter could depict her in such a pose indicates why many contemporaries believed that the monarchy was decadent.

20. The coronation of Louis XVI at Reims (1775). Turgot wanted the new king to begin his reign with a grand gesture by being crowned in a simple ceremony in Paris, but Louis XVI insisted on missing the first of many opportunities to retune the monarchy to catch the public ear.

frontispice.
Elle a beau méditer la perte des Francais,
Ses souhaits ne s'accompliront plus.
acte. 2me.
ah! gros coquin voila que tu débandes.
Voyez Page 38.
ah ma bonne amie ahi ahi je n'en puis plus
je me pa a ame.

21. In this scurrilous sequence, Marie Antoinette first plots the downfall of France and then seeks unsuccessfully to arouse Louis XVI's flaccid member before turning to a lesbian encounter with the Princesse de Lamballe.

based. In particular, it has been stressed that it was his insight that the peculiar social and political conditions dictated that drama rather than the novel would be the main genre.[216]

Although Gottsched's advocacy of the German language as a medium for a revived German literature was what his fellow intellectuals wanted to hear, the inferiority complex bred by a century and more of cultural eclipse proved tenacious. Even after the signs of a revival had become unmistakable, fear of a relapse combined with a secret envy of the much-derided French classicism to produce a nervous, almost neurotic sensitivity about the status of Germany and its culture. 'What are the Germans?' asked Friedrich Carl von Moser in 1766 and answered his own question with the following jeremiad:

We are what we have been for centuries; that is, a puzzle of a political constitution, a prey of our neighbours, an object of their scorn outstanding in the history of the world, disunited among ourselves, weak from our divisions, strong enough to harm ourselves, powerless to save ourselves, insensitive to the honour of our name, indifferent to the glory of our laws, envious of our rulers, distrusting one another, inconsistent about principles, coercive about enforcing them, a great but also a despised people; a potentially happy but actually a very lamentable people.[217]

Two years later Lessing wrote with equal bitterness about the lack of German national spirit after his attempt to create a national theatre at Hamburg had been frustrated by public indifference. He stressed that it was not his fatherland's political constitution he was criticizing but the 'moral character' of his fellow countrymen, especially their servile deference to anything French.[218]

This sensitivity was intensified by the belief that the French regarded Germany and the Germans with disdain. It was well justified: Voltaire's *Candide*, perhaps the most celebrated and most widely read work of the century, begins as follows:

[216] For a particularly sympathetic assessment of Gottsched's achievement see, Boyle, *Goethe*, vol. I, pp. 20–3.

[217] Quoted in Hagen Schulze, *The Course of German Nationalism: From Frederick the Great to Bismarck 1763–1867* (Cambridge, 1991), p. 43.

[218] 'Alas for the naïve idea of creating a National Theatre for the Germans when we Germans are not yet a nation! I do not speak of our political constitution but only of our moral character. One might almost say that this is not to have any. We are still the sworn imitators of everything foreign, in particular the humble admirers of the never sufficiently admired French'; George W. Brandt and Wiebe Hogendorn (eds.), *German and Dutch Theatre 1600–1848* (Cambridge, 1993), p. 10. See also Dieter Borchmeyer, 'Lessing und sein Umkreis' in Zmegac (ed.), *Geschichte der deutschen Literatur*, p. 138.

The most noble Baron of Thunder-ten-Tronckh was one of the most powerful lords in Westphalia; for his castle had not only a gate, but even windows; and his great hall was hung with tapestry. He used to hunt with mastiffs and spaniels instead of greyhounds; his groom served him for a huntsman; and the parson of the parish officiated as grand almoner. He was called 'My Lord' by all his people, and he never told a story but everyone laughed at it. My Lady Baroness weighed 350 pounds, consequently was a person of no small consideration.

Even after German literature had made an impact, the inability of the French even to spell the works of Goethe correctly, if indeed they mentioned them at all, caused particular offence.[219] Of the many chips that depressed German shoulders, the following sour complaint from Joseph von Sonnenfels, perhaps the most distinguished figure of the Austrian enlightenment, must suffice as an example: 'it is well-known how the French are accustomed to speaking and writing with unseemly contempt about German traditions, intellect, society, taste and everything else that blossoms under the German sun. Their adjectives "*tudesque*", "*germanique*" and "*allemand*" are for them synonyms for "coarse", "ponderous" and "uncultivated".'[220]

As we shall see, it was French disdain that was found most offensive, but there was also a gnawing awareness that other Europeans too were unappreciative of German merits. Schubart, for example, told his readers that the Italians were notoriously ignorant of true conditions north of the Alps, quoting the Roman who asked a musician in the service of the Elector of the Palatinate whether his master could afford a carriage and the Neapolitan lady who observed that 'Germany must be a large city.'[221] He was even more resentful of 'the proud Britons who believe they are a superior species and will not allow their King to travel among the subhuman Germans'.[222] Travellers to England both envied and resented the impregnable sense of superiority they encountered there. Even the Anglophile Justus Möser was exasperated by English insularity: 'looking abroad they see nothing but Hell itself... Their ignorance is so great that they view it as a fairytale whenever someone tells them that the same freedom exists in the best states

[219] Schubart, *Deutsche Chronik*, 'Revisionen', 30 (11 July 1774), p. 237.

[220] Joseph von Sonnenfels, *Betrachtungen eines österreichischen Staatsbürgers an seinen Freund, veranlaßt durch das Schreiben des Hrn. v. M** an Hrn. Abbé Sabatier über die französische Republik* (Vienna, 1793), p. 10. Cf. the almost identical sentiments expressed by Johann Georg Zimmermann in *Vom Nationalstolze*, 4th edn. (Karlsruhe, 1783), p. 42. For a very similar later example, see A. B. Marx, 'Eine Beobachtung über den heutigen Zustand der deutschen Oper, angeknüpft an Nurmahl von Spontini und Oberon von Weber', *Cäcilia*, VII (1827), p. 135.

[221] Schubart, *Deutsche Chronik*, 40 (18 May 1775), pp. 314–15.

[222] Ibid. Cf. *Deutsche Chronik*, 36 (14 July 1774), pp. 241–2.

of Germany.'[223] He would have been even more outraged if he had known that Jonathan Swift had called the Germans 'the most stupid people on earth.'[224]

As the eighteenth century progressed, however, the traditional image of the Germans as dim-witted clodhoppers, whose only culture was borrowed from abroad, began to make way for a more positive stereotype. Music led the way. It had always benefited from the pluralism of the Holy Roman Empire, but around 1700 the coincidence of numerous distinguished composers began to create a cultural tradition of special power. A simple list of the more prominent composers born before 1750 is as succinct as it is eloquent: Johann Pachelbel (1653–1706), Georg Philipp Telemann (1681–1767), Johann Sebastian Bach (1685–1750), Georg Friedrich Händel (1685–1759), Johann Joachim Quantz (1697–1773), Johann Adolf Hasse (1699–1783), Carl Heinrich Graun (1703–1759), Franz Benda (1709–86), Frederick the Great (1712–86), Carl Philipp Emmanuel Bach (1714–88), Johann Wenzel Anton Stamitz (1717–57), Johann Friedrich Agricola (1720–74), Georg Anton Benda (1722–95), Joseph Haydn (1732–1809), Johann Christian Bach (1735–82), Michael Haydn (1737–1806). No wonder that in 1741 a periodical published in Brunswick, entitled *Der musikalische Patriot* ('The Musical Patriot'), offered the following triumphant proclamation of the supremacy of German music:

> Must not the Italians, who previously were the tutors of the Germans, now envy Germany its estimable composers, and secretly seek to learn from them? Indeed, must not the high and mighty Parisians, who used to deride German talent as something provincial, now take lessons from Telemann of Hamburg? Indeed, I believe that we Germans can go on instructing foreigners in how music can be developed still further, in much the same way that our fellow countrymen, notably Leibniz and Wolff, have demonstrated how the philosophical and mathematical sciences can be raised to a still greater pitch of perfection.[225]

A hundred years later, musical supremacy would have been sufficient to generate national self-confidence among educated Germans, but in the middle of the eighteenth century music was too closely associated with the representational needs of court and Church to perform this function. As we have seen, throughout Europe the musical public sphere was still very much in its infancy outside the great metropolitan centres of London and Paris.[226] For the rapidly

[223] Quoted in Jonathan B. Knudsen, *Justus Moeser and the German Enlightenment* (Cambridge, 1986), p. 31.

[224] Albert Koester, *Die deutsche Literatur der Aufklärung* (Heidelberg, 1925), p. 5.

[225] *Der musikalische Patriot*, III (3 August 1741), p. 19.

[226] See above, p. 165.

growing educated middle class in Germany—the *Bildungsbürgertum*—it was literary achievement that really counted. If they made their mark later than their musical colleagues, German writers did so with comparable if not greater impact. The eruption of literary talent in the second half of the eighteenth century has been recounted so many times and in such depth and detail that only the barest outlines can be identified here. What follows is not intended even to be a summary of the 'German literary revival', as the phenomenon is usually if inadequately termed: attention will be paid only to those aspects which proved to be important in the development of nationalism and the creation of a national myth.

In seeking to make themselves heard above the cosmopolitan babble of French-dominated culture, German writers increasingly turned for inspiration to Great Britain, where they found a literary tradition with deep roots and a strong national identity. Not only was it quite different from the French model, it provided an alternative to the universal code of classicism which would allow emulation without imitation.[227] Of the many writers who found that a British model helped him to find his native voice, the most important during the middle years of the century was Friedrich Gottlieb Klopstock (1724–1803). In 1748 he published the first three books of his epic poem *The Messiah*, which bore the clear imprint of his enthusiasm for John Milton's *Paradise Lost* but had an unmistakable German character. Indeed, no less an authority than Herder later observed that 'next to Luther's translation of the Bible, *The Messiah* is the first classical work in our language.'[228] It was also Herder who identified a characteristic of Klopstock which was to become the watchword of the new German literary culture: individuality. Reviewing a collection of Klopstock's odes, he wrote:

> These poems have something unique, original, a spirit of their own; just as nature has given to every plant, shrub and animal its own shape, sense and character, which is individual and cannot be compared, so in each individual poem of Klopstock there floats a different fragrance and moves a spirit peculiar in its nature and passion.[229]

A strong influence on these odes was the British poet Edward Young (1683–1765), whose best-known work, *Night Thoughts* (1742–5), a long, didactic poem on death inspired by a string of bereavements, was even more popular and influential in Germany than in his native country. A third British influence

[227] There are many examples to be found in Michael Maurer, *Aufklärung und Anglophilie in Deutschland* (Göttingen, 1987).

[228] Siegrist, 'Phasen der Aufklärung', p. 97.

[229] Quoted in Pascal, *The German Sturm und Drang*, p. 255.

was 'Ossian', the alias of James Macpherson (1736–96), the Scottish poet who published *Fragments of Ancient Poetry, translated from the Gallic or Erse Language* (1760), *Fingal* (1762), and *Temora* (1763), claiming they were the work of the third-century Gaelic poet Ossian. As some sceptical contemporaries, notably David Hume and Dr Johnson, were quick to point out, they were written by Macpherson himself, but Klopstock was one of the great majority who believed in their authenticity. In 1767 he wrote to their translator, Michael Denis: 'If only we could find such a bard! The desire makes me quite excited.'[230]

Klopstock appointed himself to fill the vacancy. It was a long-cherished ambition: on leaving school in 1745 he had been stung by the claim of a French critic that there was not one truly creative German poet then living: 'Righteous indignation stirs my soul when I see the deep lethargy into which our nationality has sunk!'[231] To sound the clarion call he turned back to the earliest German history, to the legendary hero Hermann, chief of the Cherusci, who had defeated the legions of Publius Quinctilius Varus in the Teutoburg forest in AD 9. He was not the first. As Hermann had been fortunate enough to attract the attention of Tacitus in his *Germania*, he benefited from the German humanists' interest in Latin texts. Conrad Celtis, for example, who published an edition of *Germania* in 1500, used Tacitus' flattering account of Germany in general and Hermann in particular to attack foreign influences.[232] In 1529 the Lutheran patriot and humanist Ulrich von Hutten wrote a dialogue entitled *Arminius* (the Latin form of Hermann), in which the eponymous hero argues his case in the court of the dead, winning a place of honour as 'Brutus Germanicus', a freedom-fighter against foreign domination.[233] As we have seen, this patriotic initiative of the early sixteenth century proved to be short-winded. It was not until the middle of the eighteenth century that Hermann's exploits began to attract sustained attention. An early sign that he had not been entirely forgotten was his appearance in Johann Heinrich Zedler's *Universal Encyclopœdia* of 1732, in which a substantial article celebrated him as the 'liberator of Germany'.[234] Literary expression of the claim soon followed. Johann Elias Schlegel (1746), Justus Möser (1749), Otto Baron von Schönaich

[230] Quoted in Jørgenson, Bohnen, and Øhrgaard (eds.), *Aufklärung, Sturm und Drang, frühe Klassik*, p. 246.

[231] Quoted in Robert Ergang, 'National sentiments in Klopstock's odes and *Bardiete*', in *Nationalism and Internationalism: Essays Inscribed to Carlton J. H. Hayes* (New York, 1950), p. 124.

[232] See above, p. 233.

[233] Andreas Dörner, *Politischer Mythos und symbolische Politik. Sinnstiftung durch symbolische Formen am Beispiel des Hermannmythos* (Opladen, 1995), pp. 131–2.

[234] Ibid., p. 134.

(1751), and Christoph Martin Wieland (1751) had all produced their own versions before Klopstock wrote an ode entitled 'Hermann and Thusnelda' in 1752.[235] Inspired by the translation of Ossian's *Fingal*, which appeared in 1764, he expanded it into a major trilogy: *Hermann's Battle* (1769), *Hermann and the Princes* (1784), and *Hermann's Death* (1787).

Of course, next to nothing was known about the historical Hermann, whose very name was a later invention, for Tacitus' 'Arminius' was not given its improbable German form until the sixteenth century. That did not prevent the eighteenth-century authors from using him as a sounding-board for the projection of their own national identity. When the first-century Romans were presented as civilized but effete, sophisticated but treacherous, and their German conquerors as rough but virile, uncultured but honest, it was the contrast with contemporary France that was really being depicted. Other German virtues to which Klopstock gave poetic form were modesty, chastity, piety, humanity, morality and devotion to justice, duty, and self-sacrifice.[236] This combination of martial glory and ethical self-congratulation was irresistible, making Klopstock's version of the myth an immediate and durable influence. Extracts found their way into almost all anthologies of the late eighteenth century and were still being used to inspire enthusiasm for the patriotic cause in the War of Liberation of 1813.[237] This military aspect was not a later invention: writing *On German Language and Literature* in 1781, Justus Möser commended Klopstock's special literary form—the *Bardiet*, supposedly modelled on the lays of the ancient Teutonic bards: 'It is indisputably the best kind of song for our nation, because it is sung by our warriors going forth to battle for the defence of our fatherland, it is the best dance, because it takes them over the ramparts, and it is the best drama, because it inspires them with courage; but it is not a form which helps degenerates to while away their empty hours, nor does it pluck the heart-strings of a lady at court.'[238]

[235] Jørgenson, Bohnen, and Øhrgaard (eds.), *Aufklärung, Sturm und Drang, frühe Klassik*, p. 127; Richard Newald, *Von Klopstock bis zu Goethes Tod*. Vol. I: *Ende der Aufklärung und Vorbereitung der Klassik 1750–1786* (Munich, 1967), p. 32; R. Hamel (ed.), *Klopstocks Werke*. Vol.IV: Klopstocks 'Hermanns Schlacht' und das Bardenwesen des 18. Jahrhunderts, Deutsche National-Literatur. Historisch kritische Ausgabe, ed. Joseph Kürschner, vol. 48 (Berlin and Stuttgart, n.d.), p. 4. For reproductions of visual celebrations of Hermann, see Monika Wagner, 'Germania und ihre Freier. Zur Herausbildung einer deutschen nationalen Ikonographie' in Ulrich Herrmann (ed.), *Volk—Nation—Vaterland* (Hamburg, 1996), pp. 256–7.

[236] Ergang, 'National sentiments in Klopstock's odes and *Bardiete*'; Dörner, *Politischer Mythos*, p. 133.

[237] Ibid., p. 132.

[238] Justus Möser, 'Über die deutsche Sprache und Literatur', reprinted in Steinmetz (ed.), *Friedrich II.*, p. 127.

In October 1774, Christian Daniel Schubart told readers of his periodical *A German Chronicle*: 'It was with patriotic joy that I read the news that Germany's greatest genius—the immortal Klopstock—has received one proof after the other of the high esteem in which he is held by the great and the good.' He listed the jewel-encrusted portrait sent by Joseph II, the pensions granted by the King of Denmark and the Margrave of Baden, and the thousand roubles presented by the Grand Duke of Russia. How his heart beat with joy, he added, to learn that these princes had recognized 'the services rendered to our religion and Germany's honour' by 'the greatest man of his age.'[239] This apotheosis also represented the high-water mark of Klopstock's reputation. Although he lived for another thirty years and achieved a venerable status as the patriotic writer *par excellence*, he was already being overtaken when Schubart was writing his eulogy. At 50 he was deep into middle age by the standards of the time and ripe to be thrust aside by a younger generation.

It was led by Goethe, the uncontested genius of German letters of any age. While no theory of cultural development can predict the appearance of a phenomenon so unique, it is possible to appreciate why his arrival should have been so well-timed. Frederick the Great, in his notorious essay *Concerning German Literature; the faults of which it can be accused; the causes of the same and the means of rectifying them* of 1780, argued that in material terms Germany was flourishing, having recovered at long last from the devastation of the seventeenth-century wars, but that culture was still limping along behind. What was needed now, he observed, were geniuses, but unfortunately they could not be supplied to order. In the meantime, the Germans would have to go on relying on translations from the best classical and French authors (especially Montesquieu), in the hope that eventually native talent would emerge.[240] Although blind to the claims of Goethe, whose work he despised, Frederick did spot the paramount need for a figure of sufficient stature to give the Germans a sense of belonging to the first rank of European cultures. Despite their many merits, Klopstock, Lessing, Wieland, Herder, or any other of their contemporaries could not fill that role.

In the development of German nationalism, it was Goethe's achievement to make the Germans feel not just cultivated but different—and not just different but superior. For once, the over-worked phrase 'defining moment' does apply to his journey to Strassburg in March 1770, at the age of 21, to study law at the university. No city was better suited to awaken his sense of nationality. A

[239] Schubart, *Deutsche Chronik*, 54 (3 October 1774), pp. 430–1.

[240] *Über die deutsche Literatur; die Mängel, die man ihr vorwerfen kann; die Ursachen derselben und die Mittel, sie zu verbessern*, reprinted in Steinmetz (ed.), *Friedrich II.*, p. 76.

former Free Imperial City and an early champion of the Lutheran Reformation, it had been seized by Louis XIV in 1681 and formally incorporated into France at the Treaty of Ryswick in 1697. So it was on German-speaking but foreign-ruled soil that Goethe experienced a cultural conversion experience. The agent was the cathedral, the first great Gothic building he had seen. Like most educated Europeans, he had been taught to think of medieval architecture as the epitome of barbarism: 'Oh more than Gothic ignorance!' was the most dismissive insult Squire Western's metropolitan sister could find with which to brand her rustic brother. Representative of German opinion was the definition offered by Johann Georg Sulzer in his very popular encyclopaedia of the arts, first published in 1771: 'The epithet "Gothic" is frequently applied to the fine arts to designate a barbarous taste, although the meaning of the expression is seldom defined exactly. It seems to be used principally to indicate clumsiness and lack of beauty and good proportions, and originated in the clumsy imitations of ancient architecture perpetrated by the Goths who settled in Italy.'[241]

According to his autobiography, published in 1811, Goethe's first reaction to Strassburg Cathedral was to see its spire as the ideal vantage-point from which to view the surrounding countryside. Gradually, however, it began to arouse an aesthetic response which was as powerful as it was difficult to articulate. In thinking through the problems posed by the discrepancy between his anti-Gothic prejudices and the building's irresistible appeal, Goethe revolutionized his aesthetic code. All the classical canons were refuted by this irregular, asymmetric, idiosyncratic pile, which was not even finished, for one of the two projected spires had never been built, and which resembled an organism that had grown rather than a structure that had been built. What he had been taught to find offensive, he found just the reverse—it was nothing less than 'a new revelation'.[242]

It was a revelation he shared with the world in an essay entitled *Concerning German Architecture*, dedicated to Erwein von Steinbach, Strassburg Cathedral's main architect. Here he used his new enthusiasm for the Gothic to preach a new aesthetic *credo*. Any idea that beauty could be found by joining schools, adopting principles, or following rules was emphatically rejected: they were so many chains enslaving insight and energy. The ghastly good taste, harmony, and purity demanded by classical aesthetics did violence to nature's untamed spontaneity. With all the intolerance of youth, he poured

241 Quoted in W. D. Robson-Scott, *The Literary Background of the Gothic Revival in Germany* (Oxford, 1965), p. 12.

242 Johann Wolfgang von Goethe, *Aus meinem Leben. Dichtung und Wahrheit*, Part II, Book 9.

scorn on two representative targets—Johann Georg Sulzer and Marc-Antoine Laugier SJ. In the essay's key passage Goethe defined his alternative: 'The only true art is characteristic art. If its influence arises from deep, harmonious, independent feeling, from feeling peculiar to itself, oblivious, yes, ignorant of everything foreign, then it is whole and living, whether it be born from crude savagery or cultured sentiment.'[243] The crucial adjective is 'characteristic' (*karakteristische*), by which he meant art which grows naturally and spontaneously from the culture within which it is produced, not something that has been imitated. In the case of Strassburg Cathedral, it was not only characteristic art, it was also art that was characteristically German. It had been produced on German soil 'in authentically German times' (*in echter deutscher Zeit*) and only gained in stature by virtue of being treated with contempt by the Italians or the French.[244]

In 1771 Goethe gave creative expression to his revelation of the previous year in *The Dramatized History of Gottfried von Berlichingen of the Iron Hand*, which two years later was revised to become *Götz von Berlichingen with the Iron Hand*. Set at the time of the Lutheran Reformation, it chronicles the decline and fall of an Imperial Knight (a noble who acknowledged no other prince as his superior and was subject solely to the Holy Roman Emperor). For Götz, the times are seriously out of joint. Confronted by ambitious princes, greedy townspeople, and revolting peasants, not to mention a scheming *femme fatale*, his virtues of honesty, integrity, and loyalty prove hopelessly inadequate. As he laments to his wife, they live in degenerate times when the rule of deceit has begun. Outmanoeuvred and then betrayed, he dies gasping the word 'Liberty!'[245] The political world in which Götz moves so ineptly is wracked by civil conflict: the princes seek to obstruct the Emperor and expropriate the Knights, the Imperial Cities pursue their own selfish interests against everyone else, and the peasants murder, burn, and pillage. In as much as the play has an overt political message relevant to Goethe's own times, it is 'put not your trust in princes, but in the Emperor.' As the siege of his castle begins, Götz rouses his followers with a toast:

GÖTZ Long live the Emperor!
ALL Long live the Emperor!

[243] Johann Wolfgang von Goethe, 'Von deutscher Baukunst', reprinted in Johann Gottfried Herder (ed.), *Von deutscher Art und Kunst* (1773), ed. Edna Purdie (Oxford, 1924), p. 129.

[244] Ibid., p. 123.

[245] Johann Wolfgang von Goethe, *Götz von Berlichingen*, *Goethes Werke*, ed. Erich Trunz, 14 vols. (Munich, 1981), *Dramatische Dichtungen*, vol. II, p. 175.

GÖTZ And when we die, let those be our next-to-last words! I love him because he and I share the same fate. And I am better off than him. He has to catch the mice inside his Empire at the same time that the rats gnaw his lands from the outside. I know that he would rather die than have to be the soul of such a crippled body any longer—And what should our very last words be?

GEORGE Long live Liberty!

GÖTZ Long live Liberty!

ALL Long live Liberty![246]

If only liberty survives, Götz assures them, they can die in peace. Later in the same scene, he envisages a day when domestic order has been restored and they can devote themselves to eradicating wolves and entertaining their neighbours. And if that proves too boring, he adds, they can band together with their brother knights and venture forth 'like Cherubims with flaming swords' to smite Germany's enemies—the Turkish wolves in the east and the French foxes in the west.[247] Amidst this plethora of targets, it is the German princes who stand out as the main targets of Goethe's (and Götz's) wrath. Early on in the play, Götz is introduced to a friar called 'Brother Martin' (Luther, in other words), who exclaims: 'So you are Götz von Berlichingen! I give thanks to Thee, O God, that you have let me see this man, hated by the princes but the refuge of all who are oppressed!'[248]

But *Götz von Berlichingen* was not a political manifesto. Although Goethe played fast and loose with dates, he did not seek to simplify or distort the conflicts of the period to suit a contemporary agenda. His main concern was with liberty itself. In the most important single line of the play, the anti-hero Adelbert von Weislingen says: 'One thing is for certain: happy and great alone is the man who needs neither to command nor to obey to amount to something!'[249] Any kind of authority that was not self-generated but imposed from outside was to be rejected. For this reason, if no other, Goethe turned his back on classical drama with demonstrative radicalism. The unities of time, place, and action—the defining features of the dominant French model—were not so much abandoned as turned on their head. The action sprawls over several months, there are dozens of scene changes, and there are at least two main plots. Also calculated to grate on the classical ear was the language, for Goethe drew on two early sixteenth-century sources, Luther's Bible and the historical Götz's autobiography, as well as the Upper German dialect spoken in his home town of Frankfurt am Main.[250] The result was a wonderfully expressive idiom

[246] Ibid., p. 141. [247] Ibid., p. 142. [248] Ibid., p. 81. [249] Ibid., p. 101.

[250] Volker Neuhaus, *Götz von Berlichingen* (Stuttgart, 1973), p. 3.

but one that was also colloquial, ungrammatical, and generally rough-hewn. To move even from a contemporary play by Lessing to *Götz von Berlichingen* is to move into a completely new verbal world.

Reactions were commensurately extreme. Representative of the older generation was Frederick the Great's pamphlet mentioned earlier. The plays of Shakespeare he regarded as 'ludicrous farces', because they sinned against all the rules found in Aristotle's *Poetics*, and as for *Götz von Berlichingen*, it was nothing more than 'an abominable imitation of those bad English plays.'[251] Yet even he had to admit that this 'nauseating twaddle' had been greeted with great enthusiasm by the general public. Its more articulate members were quick to reprove the ageing King. In his influential pamphlet *On German Language and Literature*, Justus Möser told him that the Germans had no need to copy from the Greeks or Romans, let alone the French, but could produce everything they needed from their own resources. Home-grown German oaks were greatly to be preferred to ornamental French gardens: 'Although so disparaged by the King, *Götz von Berlichingen* is a noble and beautiful product of our own soil, it has appealed to the taste of a really large number of people, and I can see no reason why we should not see more of the same in future.'[252] Goethe's own later comment on what *Götz* represented was 'Germanness emerging' (*Deutschheit emergierend*),[253] which sounds a trifle pretentious but was justified by contemporary comments. After the premiere in Hamburg in 1774, a reviewer wrote that the play was 'imbued with the German spirit, glowing with patriotic fervour and a steely courage to triumph in the cause of liberty or to die,' while Gottfried Bürger wrote to the editor of the *Göttinger Musenalmanach*, 'What a totally German subject! What daring treatment! Noble and free like his hero, the writer treads the miserable rule-book beneath his feet.'[254]

Götz von Berlichingen lost—and loses—so much in translation that it could establish its author's reputation only within the German-speaking world. Just a year later, however, in 1774, Goethe caused another publishing sensation with *The Sufferings of Young Werther*. Already the leading German poet and playwright of his generation, he now added the novel to the genres he had conquered. With its contemporary setting and epistolary form, *Werther* had all

[251] Steinmetz (ed.), *Friedrich II.*, pp. 81–2.

[252] Möser, 'Über die deutsche Sprache und Literatur', reprinted in Steinmetz (ed.), *Friedrich II.*, p. 126.

[253] T. J. Reed, *The Classical Centre: Goethe and Weimar 1775–1832* (London, 1980), p. 12.

[254] Quoted in Winter, 'Antiklassizismus: Sturm und Drang', p. 218 and Boyle, *Goethe*, vol. I, pp. 143–4 respectively.

the apparent immediacy and spontaneity of a private correspondence. Into that realist frame, however, Goethe placed a hero whose morbid hypersensitivity could only find release in language of intense passion. Only about 40,000 words long, it was much shorter than such obvious predecessors as Richardson's *Clarissa* (1747) or Rousseau's *La Nouvelle Héloïse* (1761) but it also packed a much more intense punch. The plot is quickly recounted: Werther, a young man of middle-class but respectable station, meets and falls in love with a girl who returns his feelings but has already committed herself to another. Unable to come to terms with his frustrated passion, Werther shoots himself.

The Sufferings of Young Werther evoked a response like few novels before or since. The challenge it thrust in the face of cultural convention was so fierce that indifference was impossible. On the right, clerical conservatives found its glamorization of suicide repugnant; on the left, enlightened progressives found its disparagement of reason equally offensive.[255] But the book's admirers drowned the criticism with paeans of emotional praise worthy of Werther himself: Schubart told his readers: 'Here I sit, my heart melting, my breast pounding, my eyes weeping tears of ecstatic pain, and do I need to tell you, dear reader, that I have been reading *The Sufferings of Young Werther* by my beloved Goethe? Or should I rather say that I have been devouring it?'[256] Within a year there were eleven editions in print, most of them pirated; by 1790 there were thirty. Translated into French and English almost at once, by the end of the century it was available in almost every European language.[257]

The first truly international best-seller to be written by a German, *Werther* showed that German culture had at last come of age and no longer needed to feel inferior to its western or southern neighbours. Its national significance was clearly grasped by contemporaries—by Christian Stolberg, for example, who wrote in the year of its publication: 'It is a truly national book. No one but a German could have written it, and no one else could fully sympathize with it.'[258] Together with *Götz von Berlichingen*, Klopstock's *Messiah*, and all the other works produced by the great surge in German literary creativity, *Werther* set the seal on the emergence of nationalism. Although

[255] For a good sample of contemporary responses, see Kurt Rothmann, *Johann Wolfgang von Goethe, Die Leiden des jungen Werthers: Erläuterungen und Dokumente* (Stuttgart, 1987), pp. 130–50.

[256] Schubart, *Deutsche Chronik*, I (1774), p. 574.

[257] Boyle, *Goethe*, I, p. 175; Winter, 'Antiklassizismus: Sturm und Drang', p. 228.

[258] Quoted in Boyle, *Goethe*, p. 186.

he appears to have mainly England in mind, Adrian Hastings's insight is just as appropriate here:

Ethnicities naturally turn into nations or integral elements within nations at the point when their specific vernacular moves from an oral to written usage to the extent that it is being regularly employed for the production of a literature, and particularly for the translation of the Bible. Once an ethnicity's vernacular becomes a language with an extensive living literature of its own, the Rubicon on the road to nationhood appears to have been crossed.[259]

In the German case, it was crucial that the practice of Klopstock, Goethe, Schiller, and the rest was underpinned by a contemporary development of theory which made their individual achievements part of a nationalist narrative. This was largely the achievement of Johann Gottfried Herder (1744–1803), a writer as prolific as he was influential.[260] Yet another Prussian of humble origin who achieved fame through sheer intellectual talent (among his contemporary fellow countrymen were Hamann, Winckelmann, Kant, Nicolai, and Moses Mendelssohn), he achieved nothing less than a revolution in the way in which Germans viewed their culture. From his complex and often opaque prose, two main threads can be disentangled. The first was an emphasis on the individual's self-determination, derived partly from his Pietist upbringing, with its emphasis on the paramountcy of 'the inner light' and partly from the closely related but secular philosophy embodied in the slogan *sapere aude!* (dare to think for yourself) of his teacher Kant. It was on this that the expressive aesthetic of the *Sturm und Drang* (Storm and Stress) movement of the 1770s and later of Romanticism relied. No more kowtowing to the ancients, no more classical rules and proportions, no more mimesis—now it was the individual artist and his own special experience and emotions which were to take centre-stage. In effect, Herder was calling for the reorientation of culture from one centred on the work of art to one centred on the artist. No longer was harmonious, timeless, and universal beauty the objective; it was now the individual's originality, spontaneity, authenticity, and sincerity which were at a premium. This not only individualized aesthetics, it also aestheticized life, with clear implications for the way in which that life should be conducted. Summing up both the aesthetics and ethics of *Sturm und Drang*,

[259] Adrian Hastings, *The Construction of Nationhood: Ethnicity, Religion and Nationalism* (Cambridge, 1997), p. 12.

[260] The standard collected works run to thirty-three fat volumes of small print—*Sämmtliche Werke*, ed. Bernhard Suphan, (Berlin, 1877–1913).

Herder wrote to his fiancée Caroline Flachsland in 1773: 'All our actions should be self-determined, in accordance with our innermost character—we must be true to ourselves.'[261] It was also a position with activist implications, as Herder made clear in one of his best-known aphorisms: 'We live in a world we ourselves create.'[262]

But it is not a world in which we are alone. The obverse of Herder's individualism was his holism. His universe is a living organism, in which everything and everyone are interrelated and interacting.[263] For human beings, the vital link between part and whole, between one individual and another, between individual and community, between humans and the natural world, is language, the most important single concept in Herder's intellectual system. Without language there can be no knowledge, no self-consciousness, no awareness of others, no social existence. Language was not the invention of human reason, but its precondition, both the most natural and most necessary human function.[264] It was also the force which created the fundamental unit of human existence—the *Volk*. Of all German words difficult to translate into English, this is one of the most intractable. 'People' seems the most obvious choice, but *Volk* means much more than just an aggregate of individuals (for which the German equivalent is *Leute*). It also denotes a community bound by ethnic and cultural ties, as in 'the German people', together with a populist implication, as in 'the common people'. For that reason, the *Oxford-Duden German Dictionary*, for example, offers 'nation' as one possible translation of *Volk*. Especially when used as part of a composite word, it can be translated as 'folk', as in 'folk dancing' (*Volkstanz*) or 'folk songs' (*Volkslieder*). To avoid confusion, the original German word and its plural form (*Völker*) will be used in what follows.

[261] Quoted in Hans-G. Winter, 'Antiklassizismus: Sturm und Drang', in Viktor Zmegac (ed.), *Geschichte der deutschen Literatur vom 18. Jahrhundert bis zur Gegenwart*, vol 1, pt. 1, 2nd edn. (Königstein im Taunus, 1984), p. 204.

[262] Isaiah Berlin chose this as the epigraph for his lecture 'Herder and the Enlightenment', printed in Earl R. Wasserman (ed.), *Aspects of the Eighteenth Century* (Baltimore, Md., and London, 1965) and reprinted in a somewhat expanded form as the second part of *Vico and Herder: Two Studies in the History of Ideas* (London, 1976). Berlin states firmly: 'Herder is the true father of the doctrine that it is the artist's mission, above others, to testify in his works to the truth of his own inner experience'—*Vico and Herder*, p. 200. One art historian has gone further still, suggesting that in *Briefe zur Förderung der Humanität*, especially books 6–8, he 'lays out the whole programme of romanticism'; K. Andrews, *The Nazarenes: A Brotherhood of German Painters in Rome* (Oxford, 1964), p. 10.

[263] F. M. Barnard, *Herder's Social and Political Thought: From Enlightenment to Nationalism* (Oxford, 1965), pp. 36–7.

[264] Ibid., p. 56.

For Herder, the *Volk* is a natural community, formed by the physical environment in which it lives and with a character and culture peculiar to itself: 'There is a living organic force—I know not whence its origin, nor what is its essence; but that it exists, that it is a living force, that it fashions organic units from the chaos of homogeneous matter, that I see, that is indisputable.'[265] If the metaphysical location of this force (*Kraft*) had to remain mysterious, it is clear that physical geography and, in particular, climate, have a decisive influence on a *Volk*'s culture. Writing to his future wife in 1772 during a visit to the Teutoburg Forest, Herder linked geography, history, and national character:

I am now in the country, in the most beautiful, the most rugged, the most German, the most romantic region of the world. The very same field on which Herman fought and Varus was defeated; still an awful, rugged, romantic valley surrounded by singular mountains. However much of the German valour and of the Klopstockian ideal of morality and greatness may be lost, the soul is nevertheless disposed by the daring singular demeanour of this Germany to believe that there is a beautiful, rugged German nature.[266]

What gave Herman the German's people the necessary unity to resist and then defeat the incursions of the Romans (in AD 9), and then held their descendants together over the eighteen centuries that followed, was language. So, in Herder's view, the Germans of his day still had many of the characteristics of the inhabitants of *Germania libera* described by Tacitus.[267] The Germans were not special in this regard, for the essence of every culture is its language: 'Every *Volk* is one people having its own national culture as well as its language.'[268] Indeed, interpreters sympathetic to Herder have been at pains to stress his pluralism, that is, his belief that every culture has its own value which should be understood on its own terms, from the inside out, and not judged according to some allegedly objective scale of values.[269] To paraphrase Ranke's celebrated dictum, every culture for Herder was immediate to God.

[265] Quoted in Robert Reinhold Ergang, *Herder and the Foundations of German Nationalism* (New York, 1931), p. 86. This is a valuable study and one from which I have learned a great deal. However, Ergang's translations often leave a lot to be desired, so I have usually made my own. I shall cite the original as well as the page reference in Ergang's monograph. In this case it is from *Sämmtliche Werke*, ed. Suphan, vol. III, p. 269.

[266] Caroline Herder, *Erinnerungen aus dem Leben Johann Gottfried von Herders*, ed. J. G. Müller, 2 vols. (Tübingen, 1820), I, p. 221; quoted in Ergang, *Herder*, p. 71.

[267] Ergang, *Herder*, p. 95.

[268] Herder, *Sämmtliche Werke*, XIII, p. 258; Quoted in Ergang, *Herder*, p. 7.

[269] Isaiah Berlin, 'Herder and the Enlightenment', p. 54, where he defines pluralism as 'the belief not merely in the multiplicity but in the incommensurability of the values of different cultures and societies and, in addition, in the incompatibility of equally valid ideals, together

Herder did not, however, believe in multi-culturalism within a single community. He regarded the linguistic diversity of Livonia, for example, where Russian, German, Lithuanian, and Estonian all competed, as a handicap. It was a common language, in his view, which held a polity together, promoting social cohesion, a sense of identity and the formation of a 'patriotic public'.[270] Moreover, in practice Herder's pluralism proved to have definite limits. Like every other nationalist, Herder defined his own positive sense of identity mainly in terms of a negative reaction to 'the other'. In his case, as with most of his fellow countrymen, it was the French. In 1769, at the age of 25, he broke free from the restrictive life of a clergyman in Riga (a German city, albeit located in the Russian Empire) to travel west to the bright lights. What he found not only intensified his nascent nationalism, it also gave it a decidedly Francophobe twist. From Nantes, where he spent several months, he wrote to his friend and mentor Hamann: 'I am now in Nantes where I am getting to know the French language, French habits, and the French way of thinking—getting to know but not getting to embrace, for the closer my acquaintance with them, the greater my sense of alienation.'[271] Like so many other Germans, he was both awed and appalled by the size and splendour of Paris. An effort of the imagination is required to appreciate just what an impact a true metropolis made on someone for whom even a town of 10,000 was a great city. Given his Pietist mindset, Herder's reaction to the hedonism of Louis XV's Paris was predictable. In his 'Journal of my journey in the year 1769' he described it as a place 'festooned with luxury, vanity, and French nothingness', adding just before he left 'France can never satisfy me, and I am heartily sick of it.'[272] He also came away believing that the decadence of display was symptomatic of a more fundamental malaise: just as Germany's renaissance was dawning, dusk was gathering around France's much-vaunted cultural hegemony: 'her literary day is done, the century of Louis XIV is over; Montesquieu,

with the implied revolutionary corollary that the classical notions of an ideal man and of an ideal society are intrinsically incoherent and meaningless'.

[270] Heinrich Bosse, 'Patriotismus und Öffentlichkeit', in Herrmann, *Volk—Nation—Vaterland*, p. 69.

[271] Quoted in Rudolf Haym, *Herder nach seinem Leben und seinen Werken*, 2 vols. (Berlin, 1880–5), I, p. 338.

[272] Johann Gottfried Herder, 'Journal meiner Reise im Jahr 1769', *Sämmtliche Werke*, vol. IV, p. 435; Anthony J. La Vopa, 'Herder's *Publikum*: language, print and sociability in eighteenth century Germany', *Eighteenth Century Studies*, 29, 1 (1995), p. 14. On the context of this important work, see Richard Critchfield, 'Herder's *Journal meiner Reise*', in Wulf Koepke (ed.), *Johann Gottfried Herder. Language, History, and the Enlightenment* (Columbia, SC, 1990), pp. 98–107.

D'Alembert, Voltaire, and Rousseau are finished; the French live on their ruins . . . Their taste for encyclopaedias, dictionaries, anthologies, and digests advertises their lack of original works.'[273]

If Herder never abandoned pluralism in theory, he also retained his Francophobia in practice. As his most authoritative biographer observed, Herder's youthful experiences in France gave him an undying hatred for the French language, French literature, and French philosophy.[274] It was an aversion most pithily expressed when he apostrophized Voltaire, the embodiment of French enlightened culture, as 'a senile child'.[275] Foreign travel never did anything to broaden Herder's sympathy for other nations: during a visit to Italy in 1788–9 he wrote home that the more he got to know the local people and their ways, the more enthusiasm he felt for the Germans.[276] The outbreak of the French Revolution in the year he returned home left him torn between his attachment to liberty, especially the principle of self-determination, and his dislike of the French nation. He found refuge in non-intervention:

> No German need shed a tear over the cleaning of the French throne, when the French after a thousand years determine to give it the washing of which it was sorely in need. That nation has done our country nothing but harm for centuries, and has much to make good. We wish to learn from France, but not to resemble her or to interfere in her concerns.[277]

Hostility to the French was intensified by hostility to those Germans who imitated them. As a *Volk*'s only legitimate means of discourse was the language which lay at its heart, to borrow the language of another was a cultural crime (which we might call *lèse-nation* were it not a *Fremdwort*!):

> And you German, returning from abroad,
> Would you greet your mother in French?
> O spew it out before your door
> Spew out the ugly slime of the Seine,
> Speak German, O you German![278]

[273] Herder, 'Journal meiner Reise', p. 413.

[274] Haym, *Herder*, I, p. 414.

[275] Isaiah Berlin, 'The counter-enlightenment', in idem, *Against the Current: Essays in the History of Ideas* (London, 1979), p. 9.

[276] Ergang, *Herder*, p. 113.

[277] Quoted in G. P. Gooch, *Germany and the French Revolution* (London, 1920; reprinted 1965), p. 168.

[278] Quoted in Ergang, *Herder*, p. 154; 'An die Deutschen', *Sämmtliche Werke*, vol. XXVII, p. 128.

Old Johann Buddenbrook with his '*Mon vieux*' and '*Excusez, mon cher!*'[279] would certainly have both annoyed Herder and confirmed his view that it was the example set at the top which corrupted honest burghers' vocabularies. For his main target was the aristocrat, the sort of man who was educated as a Frenchman, dressed like a Frenchman, behaved like a Frenchman, and, worst of all, spoke like one too. For him, Germany's linguistic confusion was exemplified by Leibniz, who had written in French to nobles, in Latin to scholars, and in German to his relations. A generation later, the ability to speak French was still essential for admission to polite society: German was spoken only to servants, with the inevitable result that the sort of German spoken was crudely colloquial. It was a vicious circle which could be broken only by a refinement of the German language which would allow it to be used for civilized discourse.[280] In his proposal for a 'Patriotic Institute for the promotion of a sense of community [*Allgemeingeist*] for Germany' (1788) Herder argued that a standardized language would promote every aspect of the country's interest, *including its power*: 'the history of the human race shows that all dominant nations [*Völker*] have ruled not so much by the sword as by the exercise of reason, through the promotion of their culture and through the use of a more cultivated language, that often they have done so for millennia and even when their political power has decayed, their intellectual legacy and institutions have served as a model and an object of veneration for other nations.'[281] It was therefore a matter of urgency for German princes to demonstrate their respect for their native language by using it themselves and by encouraging their nobilities to follow suit. Two such princes were at hand—Karl Friedrich of Baden, who commissioned Herder's draft proposal, and Herder's employer, Karl August of Weimar, to whom it was addressed, but what little chance the planned Patriotic Institute might have had was scotched by the outbreak of the French Revolution.

Although Herder approved of the 'unity in diversity' represented by the Holy Roman Empire, the impossibility of persuading its hundreds of members to cooperate prompted him to dream on occasion of a Germany united politically as well as culturally. In 1780 he called on Joseph II to fulfil his imperial duty:

[279] See above, p. 236.

[280] Wolfgang Frühwald, 'Die Idee kultureller Nationbildung und die Entstehung der Literatursprache in Deutschland', in Otto Dann (ed.), *Nationalismus in vorindustrieller Zeit* (Munich, 1986), p. 136.

[281] Johann Gottfried Herder, 'Idee zum ersten patriotischen Institut für den Allgemeingeist Deutschlands', *Sämmtliche Werke*, vol. XVI, p. 604.

> O Emperor, the sovereign of the ninety-nine Princes and
> Territories which are as the sands of the seashore,
> Give us what we thirst for:
> A single German fatherland,
> And a single law and a single pure language
> And an honest religion.[282]

Joseph's decade as sole ruler, which followed, was a deeply dispiriting experience for a German patriot such as Herder. With characteristically brutal clarity, Joseph showed that all he cared about was the interest of his multinational monarchy and that when he promoted the German language, he did so only in the interests of greater administrative efficiency. Herder could not have been surprised. As his ideal state was decentralized and as invisible as possible, relying on the voluntary cooperation of its citizens, it was hardly likely that he would have had much in common with his relentlessly *étatist* emperor.[283] His belief in the *Volk* necessarily pushed him towards populism. True value in any nation resided not with the elite's classical culture—dismissed by Herder as a meretricious bird of paradise, all show and no substance and never touching the ground—but with the common people, whose roots were firmly planted in native soil and history. Folk art, folk dancing, and folk songs were not to be despised for their roughness but to be treasured for their authenticity. They were the 'archives of a nationality' or 'the living voice of the nationalities, even of humanity itself' and from them 'one can learn the mode of thought of a nationality and its language of feeling.'[284] Although Herder was careful to insist that by the *Volk* he did not mean the underclass—'*Volk* does not mean the rabble [*Pöbel*] of the streets, which never sings and creates, but roars and mutilates'[285]—he was equally insistent that the nation was one vertical community and that horizontal divisions into social classes were of a secondary order: 'There is only one class in the state, the *Volk* (not the rabble) and the king belongs to this class as well as the peasant.'[286]

That was not the least of Herder's achievements—to relocate cultural value. In Goethe's authoritative verdict: 'Herder taught us to think of poetry as the common property of all mankind, not as the private possession of a few refined, cultured individuals.'[287] But he did much more besides. More than

282 Quoted in Ergang, *Herder*, p. 246; *Sämmtliche Werke*, XXIX, 551.
283 Barnard, *Herder's Social and Political Thought*, pp. 63–7.
284 Quoted in Ergang, *Herder*, p. 198; *Sämmtliche Werke*, IX, 530, 532; III, 29; XXIV, 266.
285 Quoted in Ergang, *Herder*, p. 195; *Sämmtliche Werke*, XXV, 323.
286 Quoted in Ergang, *Herder*, p. 206; *Sämmtliche Werke*, XVIII, 308.
287 Peter Burke, *Popular Culture in Early Modern Europe* (London, 1978), p. 4.

any other thinker, with the possible exception of Rousseau, Herder was responsible for making nationalism intellectually respectable. In 1769, the year that Herder embarked on his journey to France, Lessing wrote to Gleim: 'I have no conception of love of the fatherland and, at best, it appears to me a heroic weakness with which I can gladly dispense.'[288] It was Herder's contrary view that the cosmopolitan citizen of the world 'belongs to every state and does nothing for any one of them.'[289] The power of Herder's mind, the profusion of his writings, his friendship with Goethe, and his location in Weimar after 1776 made the dominant cosmopolitanism of the Enlightenment come to seem increasingly out of date. One simple but highly effective means was the liturgical repetition of the word 'national', often as the prefix to one of the composite nouns of which the Germans are so fond, for example: national education (*Nationalerziehung*), national treasure (*-schatz*), national traditions (*-traditionen*), national products (*-produkte*), national work (*-werk*), national inclinations (*-neigungen*), national opinions (*-meinungen*), national prejudices (*-vorurteile*), national public (*-publicum*), national customs (*-sitten*), national sanctum (*-heiligtum*), national language (*-sprache*), national way of thinking (*-denkart*), national character (*-charakter*), national history (*-geschichte*), national virtues (*-tugenden*), national anthems (*-lieder*), and so on and so forth.[290] The importance of establishing the status of the word 'nation' and its cognates in the French Revolution, as in 'National Assembly' and 'National Guard', has long been recognized;[291] in Germany, its appearance may have been less dramatic but it had even more potent implications. When Herder coined the actual word 'nationalism' (*Nationalismus*) he was announcing the arrival of a new ideology which proved to have an explosive force.[292]

[288] Quoted in Ergang, *Herder*, p. 32.

[289] Quoted in Gooch, *Germany and the French Revolution*, p. 33.

[290] Ergang, Herder, pp. 110–11.

[291] See, for example, Jacques Godechot, 'Nation, patrie, nationalisme et patriotisme en France au XVIIIe siecle', *Annales historiques de la Révolution française*, 43 (1971), *passim* or Lynn Hunt, *Politics, Culture and Class in the French Revolution* (London, 1986), p. 123.

[292] It has been a matter of some debate as to whether Herder used the word 'nationalism' pejoratively or not. This is an issue of such importance that it needs to be sorted out here once and for all, even at the cost of a long footnote. In the first volume of his great work *Deutsche Gesellschaftsgeschichte*, Hans-Ulrich Wehler states firmly that the word 'nationalism' was first used by Herder in 1774 in a 'strictly pejorative sense' (p. 657 n. 1), but it turns out that he is simply following the Finnish historian Kemiläinen, who has misunderstood the passage in question in 'Auch eine Philosophie der Geschichte zur Bildung der Menschheit. Beytrag zu vielen Beyträgen des Jahrhunderts', which runs as follows: 'Alles was mit meiner Natur noch gleichartig ist, was in sie assimilirt werden kann, beneide ich, strebs an, mache mirs zu eigen; darüber hinaus hat mich die gütige Natur mit Fühllosigkeit, Kälte und Blindheit bewaffnet; sie

Herder's emphasis on the paramountcy of culture and language also allowed the great surge in creativity in German-speaking Europe to be woven into a nationalist narrative.[293] By the 1780s, at the latest, the cumulative effect of achievements in literature, philosophy, and music had created a confident belief among German intellectuals that their culture was becoming supreme in Europe. The furious reaction to Frederick the Great's pamphlet on the

kann gar Verachtung und Eckel werden—hat aber nur zum Zweck, mich auf mich selbst zurückzustossen, mir auf dem Mittelpunkt Genüge zu geben, der mich trägt. Der Grieche macht sich so viel vom Ägypter, der Römer vom Griechen zu eigen, als er für sich braucht: er ist gesättigt, das übrige fällt zu Boden und er strebts nicht an! Oder wenn in dieser Ausbildung eigener Nationalneigungen zu eigner Nationalglückseligkeit der Abstand zwischen Volk und Volk schon zu weit gediehen ist: siehe, wie der Ägypter den Hirten, den Landstreicher hasset! wie er den leichtsinnigen Griechen verachtet! So jede zwo Nationen, deren Neigungen und Kreise der Glückseligkeit sich stossen—man nennts Vorurtheil! Pöbelei! eingeschränkten Nationalism! Das Vorurtheil ist gut, zu seiner Zeit: denn es macht glücklich. Es drängt Völker zu ihrem Mittelpunkte zusammen, macht sie vester auf ihrem Stamme, blühender in ihrer Art, brünstiger und also auch glückseliger in ihren Neigungen und Zwecken. Die unwissendste, vorurtheilendste Nation ist in solchem Betracht oft die erste: das Zeitalter fremder Wunschwanderungen, und ausländischer Hoffnungsfahrten ist schon Krankheit, Blähung, ungesunde Fülle, Ahndung des Todes!' *Sämmtliche Werke*, V, 510. That should be translated as follows: 'Everything that is in harmony with my nature and can be assimilated by it, I envy, strive after, and make my own; beyond that, beneficent nature has armed me with insensibility, coldness, and blindness, which can even turn into contempt and disgust—but the sole purpose of this is to force me back on myself so that I find satisfaction in my own central point. The Greek takes as much as he needs from the Egyptian and the Roman from the Greek: then he is satiated, the rest of it is discarded, and he no longer strives for it! Or if in this development of particular national characteristics towards particular forms of national well-being, the distance between one nation and another grows too great, then see how the Egyptian detests the shepherd and the tramp, see how he despises the frivolous Greek! In the same way, when two nations with their own tastes and conceptions of happiness collide with each other, then it is called prejudice! vulgarity! blinkered nationalism! But prejudice is good at the right time, because it is conducive to happiness, it forces peoples back to their central point, secures them more firmly to their roots, makes them flourish in their own special way, makes them more ardent and therefore more content in their inclinations and ambitions. In this regard the most ignorant and the most prejudiced nation is often the best: the age when men harbour alien desires and hope for foreign things is an age of sickness, flatulence, decadent satiation, and a sense of impending death!' The crucial phrase here is 'then it is called' ('*man nennt's*'). Surely Herder is saying that some people call the attitude he is describing 'prejudice, vulgarity, and blinkered nationalism', but *he himself* regards it as beneficial, for the reasons he goes on to outline. The translation offered in F. M. Barnard (ed.), *Herder on Social and Political Culture* (Cambridge, 1969), pp. 186–7, is clearly defective. The crucial '*man nennt's*' is just omitted, as is the reference to 'the Egyptian'. The result of the latter omission is that the references to 'the shepherd' and 'the tramp'—i.e. the Greek and the Roman respectively—are misunderstood. The translation offered by Ergang, *Herder*, p. 111 reads rather oddly but does convey the central point accurately.

293 See the list of names above, p. 215.

alleged shortcomings of German literature[294] was symptomatic. The *Hamburgische Neue Zeitung*, for example, wrote:

Everyone knows that in all branches of intellectual activity our nation has achieved a great deal, and that in almost every branch we can boast of as many major figures as the proudest foreign nation. Foreigners use with gratitude the inventions and discoveries of the Germans. For a long time now foreigners have ceased to damn us with the faint praise that our industry has flourished at the expense of our creativity. Since the 1760's the French, British, Italians, Dutch, Danes and Russians have competed to translate our literature. This achievement has been all the more striking in that our innumerable princes for the most part have not understood, esteemed or encouraged our literature.[295]

This sort of boasting, both understandable and justified, could be replicated at will. More helpful is the following summary offered by Ernst Moritz Arndt in his *Spirit of the Age* in 1808:

In the 1780s, in the decade before the outbreak of the French Revolution, as Frederick the Great was taking his leave of his disconsolate fatherland, what was happening to the German *Volk*, what inspired it, what brought it together? It was a sense of a new and better epoch beginning that was being aroused by our better writers, a growing feeling of the *Volk*'s potential and of its value, which in turn led to a greater sense of community and common purpose, more perhaps than at any time in the past. People began to take a pride in the name 'German' and in German culture and the German way of life, and this pride would have cast invisible ties around the whole *Volk* and created a unity of consciousness if the French Revolution had not intervened.[296]

Both Arndt and Herder agreed that it was the intellectuals, especially the writers among them, who deserved the credit for regenerating the German nation. It was another indication of just how far their status had progressed, courtesy of the public sphere. Only a century earlier, many had been writing in Latin and most had been writing for a small academic public. Now they strode forwards as the creators of national identity. In Herder's words, 'the true writer is the creator of the nation around him, he gives his people a world to see and is a God on earth who holds the heart of the people in his hands.'[297] Although a

294 See above, pp. 218.

295 Steinmetz (ed.), *Friedrich II.*, p. 146.

296 Quoted in Mathys Jolles, *Das deutsche Nationalbewußtsein im Zeitalter Napoleons* (Frankfurt am Main, 1936), p. 70.

297 Hans-Jürgen Haferkorn, *Der freie Schriftsteller. Eine literatursoziologische Studie über seine Entstehung und Lage in Deutschland zwischen 1750 und 1800*, Archiv für Geschichte des Buchwesens, 5 (1964), p. 673.

Lutheran clergyman, Herder was opening the way for intellectuals to usurp his profession by sacralizing art and giving its creators a quasi-priestly function. This was a development with immense potential for the future, and not only in Germany. No one has expressed its essence better or more succinctly than Nicholas Boyle in his profound study of Goethe: 'Herder's theory of the creative individual linked by language to his national culture was a powerful counter-model to the Lutheran pattern of individual election and salvation within the Church.'[298]

Nationalism was articulated by the intellectuals, but was it confined to them? So axiomatic has been the belief that nationalism was a post-1789 phenomenon that few scholars have bothered to look for popular manifestations at an earlier date. A few straws in the wind suggest that there may be plenty to find. For example, Rudolf Zacharias Becker's best-selling *Peasants' Handbook* of 1788 included the following anecdote (the italicized passages are as in the original):

> An elderly peasant, who had been a soldier in his youth, recently gave the following advice to his sons: 'Children,' he said, 'you are now grown up and I shall die soon. There are too many of you for you all to live from your share of my holding. So you must go into service. Thomas, you are the tallest and the strongest: you shall become a soldier, and you too, Joseph, when you leave school. Serve your *Fatherland*: you owe it your blood and your life. And if an enemy should attack the *German Empire*, then your last drop of blood must be risked. For it is on the continuing security and liberty of the *Empire* that the welfare of the peasantry in *Germany* depends.'[299]

Whatever its social centre of gravity may have been, nationalism had a highly subversive potential. If the German princes had remained attached to foreign, and especially French, cultural models, a gulf would have opened up between them and the intelligentsia. In the event, enough of them made the necessary adjustment to allow the image of a common pursuit to be sustained. As we have seen, the first 'national theatre' in Germany was created in Hamburg, a self-governing city-republic, but it soon foundered. Subsequent creations were the work of the princes. It was particularly important that the next major initiative was taken by the Emperor Joseph II, who in 1776 turned the court theatre into a *Nationaltheater* with a repertoire devoted to works in the German language. Tobias von Gebler wrote to Nicolai: 'Every patriot must rejoice that our German *Joseph* has designated the national stage as his

[298] Boyle, *Goethe*, I, p. 99.

[299] Quoted in Ulrich Herrmann, 'Volk—Nation Vaterland: ein Grundproblem deutscher Geschichte', in Ulrich Herrmann (ed.), *Volk—Nation—Vaterland* (Hamburg, 1996), p. 12.

Court theatre. He will certainly employ no Frenchman until German plays are performed at Versailles.'[300] A periodical devoted to the theatre rejoiced: 'The Germans now have a national theatre, and it is their Emperor who has founded it. What a delightful, what a magnificent thought for everyone capable of feeling that he is a German! Everyone thanks the Emperor with a feeling of the deepest reverence for the great example he has given to the German princes.'[301] Showing his habitual surprisingly deft touch for gesture politics, Joseph symbolically elevated the status of German actors by having a series of portraits of leading actors in his theatres, dressed in the costumes of their most celebrated roles, painted by Hickel, and then displayed in a gallery established for the purpose.[302]

The imperial example was indeed followed, notably by the Elector Karl Theodor of the Palatinate, whose theatre at Mannheim, established in 1778, quickly became the leading German stage.[303] Of the other foundations, the most important was at Berlin, where Frederick William II began his reign in 1786 with a programmatic gesture worthy of his predecessor when he turned the previously French theatre on the Gendarmenmarkt into a national theatre, gave it a generous subsidy, and took a keen interest in its fortunes.[304] Many qualifications need to be made about these initiatives. They were sometimes short-lived; they were often undertaken for economic rather than cultural reasons, a native troupe costing less than the French; there was much uncertainty as to just what the 'national' in 'national theatre' might mean; and they invariably found that the German-language repertoire was not yet large or good enough to sustain public interest.[305] Nevertheless, they sent out a clear

[300] Quoted in Derek Beales, *Joseph II*, vol. I: *In the Shadow of Maria Theresa 1741–1780* (Cambridge, 1987), p. 233.

[301] Quoted in H. Kiesel and P. Münch, *Gesellschaft und Literatur im 18. Jahrhundert* (Munich, 1977) , p. 84.

[302] Roland Krebs, *L'Idée de 'Théâtre national' dans l'Allemagne des lumières. Théorie et réalisations*, Wolfenbütteler Forschungen, vol. 28 (Wiesbaden, 1985), p. 553.

[303] Eugen K. Wolf, 'The Mannheim court', in Neal Zaslaw (ed.), *The Classical Era: From the 1740s to the End of the Eighteenth Century* (London, 1989), pp. 222–3.

[304] Thomas Bauman, *North German Opera in the Age of Goethe* (Cambridge, 1985), p. 228; Marieluise Hübscher-Bitter, 'Preußens theatralische Sendung. Die königlichen Schauspiele zu Berlin unter der Intendanz des Grafen Brühl 1815 bis 1828', in Manfred Schlenke (ed.), *Preußen—Versuch einer Bilanz*, 5 vols. (Hamburg, 1981), 4, p. 190.

[305] Wolfgang Martens, 'Literatur und "Policey" im Aufklärungszeitalter', *Germanisch-romanische Monatsschrift*, 62 (1981), p. 412; Wolfgang Martens, 'Obrigkeitliche Sicht: Das Bühnenwesen in den Lehrbüchern der Policey und Cameralistik des 18. Jahrhunderts', *Internationales Archiv für Sozialgeschichte der deutschen Literatur*, 6 (1981) p. 43; T. J. Reed, 'Theatre, Enlightenment and nation: a German problem', *Forum for Modern Language Studies*, 14, 2 (1978), pp. 149–50; Horst Steinmetz, 'Idee und Wirklichkeit des Nationaltheaters. Enttäuschte

signal that the German princes had turned their back on foreign court culture, as one French troupe after another was closed down—at Hanover in 1757, Munich in 1758, Stuttgart in 1767, Dresden in 1769, Mannheim in 1770, Vienna and Bayreuth in 1772, and so on.[306] As the French Revolution began to unleash an ideological and military threat which made even Louis XIV's hegemony pale by comparison, princes and peoples in Germany found in their national culture a powerfully adhesive bond.

Hoffnungen und faslche Erwartungen', in Herrmann (ed.), *Volk—Nation—Vaterland*, p. 141. The last-named article overstates the limitations of the national theatres.

306 Krebs, *L'Idée de 'Théâtre national'*, p. 529.

7

The British Way

HANDEL, THE PUBLIC SPHERE, AND THE ENGLISH NATION

The year 1789 was as momentous for Great Britain as it was for France. Although less spectacular than the fall of the Bastille on 14 July or the removal of Louis XVI and his family from Versailles to Paris on 6 October, the 'Public Day of Thanksgiving' in London on 23 April, held to celebrate the recovery of George III from illness, revealed just how close was the alliance between king and country, state and society. Although frayed almost to the point of rupture by the king's two disreputable successors, it was a bond which was to hold for the best part of two centuries. When it had become common knowledge in November 1788 that George had succumbed to what appeared to be insanity, the general reaction had been despondency and sympathy rather than derision. The relief experienced four months later, when his recovery was signalled, was of corresponding intensity. Contemporary observers were unanimous:

> The demonstrations of national joy far exceeded any recorded in the English annals, and were probably more real and unfeigned than ever were offered on similar occasions... No efforts of despotism, or mandates of absolute power, could have produced the illuminations, which the capital exhibited in testimony of its loyalty; and these proofs of attachment were renewed, and even augmented, on the occasion of his Majesty's first appearance in public, and his solemn procession to St. Paul's, to return thanks to Heaven for his recovery.[1]

[1] *A Sketch of the Reign of George the Third from 1780 to the close of the year 1790*, 5th edn. (London, 1791), pp. 104–5. Cf. John Galt, *George III, his Court and his Family*, 2 vols. (London, 1820), II, p. 85.

If literary effusions of this kind might seem prejudiced, it is more difficult to doubt the authority of the following statistic: no fewer than 756 addresses congratulating the king on his recovery were submitted by various groups and corporations across the length and breadth of the country, or in other words, more than double the number generated by the seven most controversial issues of the previous generation (the Jewish Naturalization Act of 1753; the Cider Tax Bill of 1763; the Wilkes affair of 1769; the Catholic Relief Act of 1778; the campaigns for 'Economical Reform' in 1780 and for parliamentary reform in 1783; and the campaign in support of Pitt in 1784)—*put together*.[2]

Yet only seven years before George had suffered a series of shattering personal defeats, when obliged to recognize the independence of the American colonies and to accept two administrations in quick succession to which he was deeply opposed (the Rockingham Whigs in 1782 and the Fox–North coalition in 1783). So keenly felt were these humiliations that he even considered abdicating the English throne and moving to his electorate of Hanover to rule over his (supposedly) more pliable German subjects.[3] Indeed, some contemporaries talked of civil war, comparing Charles James Fox to Cromwell and—with casual disregard for chronology—George himself to James II.[4] With the advantage of hindsight, we can see that it was to be darkest before dawn. Pulling himself together, George now proceeded to turn the tables on his tormentors, turning them out of office in December 1783, installing the 24-year-old William Pitt as prime minister, and securing a working majority for him in the general election held in the spring of 1784. Pitt was to remain in office until 1801.

Against this background, the great Händel Commemoration organized in May 1784[5] takes on added significance. It may be said to have exemplified the consolidation of a national culture of great power and durability, here given physical expression by the king and his family, surrounded by his prelates, peers, and gentry, and attended by large numbers of the general public, celebrating a national cultural icon who was all the more British for being naturalized. The sense that the occasion was a demonstration of national unity was well captured by an eye-witness, Charles Burney, who produced a lavishly illustrated and luxuriously printed record of the occasion:

[2] Linda Colley, 'The apotheosis of George III: loyalty, royalty and the British nation 1760–1820', *Past and Present*, 102 (1984), p. 122.

[3] John Cannon, *The Fox–North Coalition: Crisis of the Constitution 1782–4* (Cambridge, 1969), p. 79.

[4] Ibid., p. xi.

[5] See above, p. 180.

> It was hardly possible for a Musical Historian not to imagine that an enterprise honoured with the patronage and presence of their Majesties; planned and personally directed by noblemen and gentlemen of the first rank; attended by the most numerous and polite audience that was ever assembled on a similar occasion, in any country; among whom, not only the King, Queen, Royal Family, nobility, and great officers of state appeared, but the archbishops, bishops, and other dignified clergy, with the heads of the law, form an æra in Music, as honourable to the art and to national gratitude, as to the great artist himself who has given occasion to the Festival.[6]

The same point was picked up by the *Whitehall Evening Post*, which took the view that the great success of the festival was due to nothing less than 'what may be called the Constitution', for it combined royal assent, aristocratic support, and 'last, not least in all Matters of Entertainment and Expence, by the Majesty of the People'.[7] The combination of the religious and the secular, both in the venues (Westminster Abbey and the concert hall at the Pantheon in Oxford Street) and the programme (*Messiah*, the Dettingen *Te Deum*, the Funeral Anthem for Queen Anne, and the Coronation Anthems written for George II) proclaimed that this was a sacral undertaking in a confessional state. The royalist tone was set with the first note of the first work—*Zadok the Priest*, first sung at the coronation of George II (and at every coronation since): '*Zadoc the priest, and Nathan the prophet, anointed Solomon king: and all the people rejoiced; and said, God save the king; long live the king: may the king live for ever. Amen*. (I Kings 1: 38). Burney reprinted this text, adding 'And from the first time that the first sound of this celebrated and well-known composition was heard, to the final close, every hearer seemed afraid of breathing, lest it should obstruct the stream of harmony in its passage to the ear.'[8]

Burney believed that the orchestra and chorus of 525 represented the largest music force ever assembled in England. Certainly it made a shattering impact on the amateur composer John Marsh when, after the long, quiet, almost teasing introduction by organ and violins, the full orchestra and chorus burst in: 'the force and effect almost took me off my legs, and caused the blood to forsake my cheeks.' As for the assembled company's response to 'God save the king, long live the king, may the king live for ever,' he wrote, 'it was all

[6] Charles Burney, *An Account of the Musical Perfomances in Westminster-Abbey, and the Pantheon, May 26th, 27th, 29th; and June the 3d, and 5th, 1784 in Commemoration of Handel* (London, 1785), pp. ii–iii.

[7] Quoted in Anna Verena Westermayr, *The 1784 Handel Commemoration: The Conduct and Interpretation of a Spectacle* (unpublished Cambridge M.Phil. dissertation, 1996), p. 17.

[8] Burney, *An Account of the Musical Perfomances in Westminster-Abbey*, p. 26.

ecstasy.'[9] Continental observers were particularly impressed by the popularity of the event. A German music journalist, Carl Friedrich Cramer, marvelled at the rush for tickets despite their cost (one guinea) and the huge capacity of Westminster Abbey (well over 4,000).[10] It was in response to this popular demand that the three performances originally intended by the festival organizers were increased to five.[11] This was done by royal command, the first extra performance being advertised 'By command of His Majesty' and the second 'By command of Her Majesty'.[12] George III also made his mark on the performance by asking for the Hallelujah Chorus to be encored. At the first performance this instruction was communicated to the conductor by the Earl of Sandwich, but at the second George gave the signal himself by waving his libretto.[13] The success of the Commemoration was also demonstrated in a way that every Englishman could understand: the five performances yielded the colossal sum of £12,736. Even after the expenses had been paid, there was plenty left to be distributed to charity, £6,000 to the Musicians' Fund and £1,000 to Westminster Hospital.[14]

As William Coxe observed, the Commemoration was 'the most splendid tribute ever paid to posthumous fame' and 'an honour to the profession, the nation and to the Sovereign'.[15] Handel's triumphant progress from humble origins in Halle (he was the son of a barber-surgeon) to this posthumous apotheosis reveals a good deal about the development of British culture in the eighteenth century. When he arrived in London in 1710 he was very much a product and a servant of representational culture. A good example of the milieu was provided by the contemporary chronicler Abel Boyer:

Tuesday, the 6th of February [1711], being the Queen's Birth-Day, the same was observed with great Solemnity, the Court was extream numerous and magnificent; the Officers of state, Foreign Ministers, Nobility and Gentry, and particularly

[9] H. Diack Johnstone, 'A ringside seat at the Handel Commemoration', *Musical Times*, 125 (November, 1984), p. 635.

[10] Carl Friedrich Cramer, *Magazin der Musik* (Hamburg, 1783–6; reprinted, Hildesheim and New York, 1971), quoted in Peter Schleuning, *Das 18. Jahrhundert. Der Bürger erhebt sich* (Hamburg, 1984), p. 409.

[11] William Weber, 'London: a city of unrivalled riches', in Neal Zaslaw (ed.), *The Classical Era: From the 1740s to the End of the Eighteenth Century* (London, 1989), p. 322.

[12] Burney, *An Account of the Musical Perfomances in Westminster-Abbey*, p. 92.

[13] Ibid., p. 112.

[14] 'The 1784 Handel Commemoration', in Jacob Simon (ed.), *Handel: A Celebration of his Life and Times* (London, 1985), p. 250.

[15] William Coxe, *Anecdotes of George Frederick Handel and John Christopher Smith* (London, 1799), p. 31.

the Ladies, vying with each other, who should most grace the Festival. Between One and Two in the Afternoon, was perform'd a fine Consort, being a Dialogue in Italian, in Her Majesty's Praise, set to excellent Musick by the famous Mr. Hendel, a Retainer to the Court of Hanover, in the Quality of Director of his Electoral Highness's Chapple, and sung by Cavaliero Nicolini Grimaldi, and the other Celebrated Voices of the Italian Opera: with which Her Majesty was extreamly well pleas'd.[16]

She demonstrated her pleasure by awarding Handel a pension of £200.[17] His other source of income during his early years in London was the recently established Italian Opera. Beginning with *Rinaldo* in 1711, he composed some forty *opere serie*, in the process confirming Frederick the Great's conviction that Italian music was best written by Germans.[18] He worked first for the company at the Queen's Theatre in the Haymarket and then for its successor, the grandly named 'Royal Academy of Musick' established in 1719. Despite its title, the latter was very different from Louis XIV's Académie Royale de Musique.[19] Although George I guaranteed an annual subsidy of £1,000 for five years, granted a royal charter, and made his Lord Chamberlain the Academy's governor, that was the limit of royal participation (and direction). It was a level of support which might reasonably be termed a necessary but not sufficient cause of the 'Academy's' existence. In a neat demonstration of the mixed nature of London's cultural scene, it was organized as a joint-stock company, with leading members drawn from the peerage (including seven dukes, thirteen earls, and three viscounts) and the gentry, and was meant to be run at a profit for its shareholders.[20]

Partly royal, partly aristocratic, partly commercial, the Italian Opera of the Royal Academy of Musick dominated London's cultural scene during the reign of George I and the first part of his successor's. It was at the first night of Handel's *Radamisto* in 1720 that a joint appearance in the royal box signalled the end of the rift between the King and the Prince of Wales. *Mutatis mutandis*, the rivalry between Handel's company and the 'Opera of the Nobility' founded in 1733 allowed George II and his own trying eldest son yet another opportunity to express their mutual hatred by patronizing one company and boycotting the other. So fierce did the opera war become that Lord Hervey

[16] Abel Boyer, *The History of the Reign of Queen Anne digested into Annals*, 11 vols. (London, 1703–13), IX, p. 315, quoted in Donald Burrows, *Handel* (London, 1994), p. 66.
[17] Ibid., p. 73.
[18] E. E. Helm, *Music at the Court of Frederick the Great* (Norman, Okla., 1960), p. 73.
[19] See above, p. 47.
[20] Burrows, *Handel*, pp. 102–3.

likened it to the struggle between the Green and Blue factions in the hippodrome at Constantinople, which nearly cost the Emperor Justinian his throne.[21] Given the cost of admission, the brevity of the season, and the limited capacity of the theatres, it may be doubted just how many people were affected by these operatic episodes.[22] There is good evidence, however, that they greatly exercised polite society. John Gay wrote to Jonathan Swift in 1723:

As for the reigning amusement of the town, it is entirely music . . . Everybody is grown now as great a judge of music, as they were in your time of poetry, and folks, that could not distinguish one tune from another, now daily dispute about the different styles of Handel, Bononcini, and Attilio. People have now forgot Homer and Virgil, and Cæsar, or at least, they have lost their ranks; for, in London and Westminster, in all polite conversations, Senesino [the leading Italian castrato] is daily voted to be the greatest man that ever lived.[23]

That was not everyone's opinion. In the same year that Handel's first opera was performed in London, no less a figure than Joseph Addison attacked the whole genre in the *Spectator*, remarking that later generations would find it difficult to believe that 'Persons of the greatest Politeness' were once prepared to sit through works performed in a language they did not understand—'one scarce knows how to be serious in the Confutation of an Absurdity that shews itself at the first Sight.'[24] It was sinister as well as absurd, for Italy was the home of popery, the Stuart Pretender, the baroque, and, it was believed, unnatural vice (which the English called *le goût florentine* and the continentals called *le vice anglais*). John Bull did not need a Jürgen Habermas to tell him that representational culture was associated with absolutism: 'wherever Operas have been a constant Entertainment, they have been attended with Slavery.'[25] It was even possible, Henry Carey suggested with an apparently straight face, that the words of the florid *da capo* arias sung by Italians were really those of the Catholic Mass:

[21] Ibid., pp. 107, 180.

[22] Michael Forsyth, *Buildings for Music: The Architect, the Musician, and the Listener from the Seventeenth Century to the Present Day* (Cambridge, Mass., 1985), p. 71—an annual subscription cost 20 guineas for 50 performances, almost four times that for a playhouse.

[23] Burrows, *Handel*, p. 113.

[24] *The Spectator*, new edn. (London, n.d.), no. 18, 21 March 1711.

[25] John Dennis, *Essay on the Opera's after the Italian Manner, which are about to be Establish'd on the English Stage: with some Reflections on the Damage which they May Bring to the Publick*, quoted in Ruth Smith, *Handel's Oratorio and Eighteenth Century Thought* (Cambridge, 1995), p. 73.

I curse the unintelligible Ass,
Who may, for ought I know, be singing Mass.[26]

Moreover, it was also feared that the siren sounds of the 'Warbling Eunuchs' and their effete music or rather 'Frothiness' ('a *Mio Caro* quavered and repeated half a Dozen times') threatened the moral fibre of English manhood, paving the way for national decadence. James Miller lamented in 1731:

In Days of Old, when Englishmen were—Men,
Their Musick, like themselves, was grave and plain...
Since Masquerades and Opera's made their Entry,
And Heydegger and Handell ruled our Gentry;
A hundred different Instruments combine,
And foreign Songsters in the Concerts join...
All league, melodious Nonsense to dispense,
And give us Sound, and Show, instead of Sense.[27]

Henry Carey warned of the primrose path which led to national decadence:

A false Politeness has possess'd the Isle,
And ev'ry Thing that's English is Old Stile...
Effeminate in Dress, in Manners grown,
We now despise whatever is our Own.
So Rome, when famous once for Arts and Arms,
(Betray'd by Luxury's enfeebling Charms)
Sunk into Softness, and its Empire lost.[28]

The most extreme statement came from R. Campbell Esq., a bluff, no-nonsense representative of the commercial interest of a type still only too familiar today. In *The London Tradesman* he expressed strong disapproval of *all* music, for it 'effeminates the Mind, enervates the more Manly Faculties, and erases from the Soul all manner of Martial Ardour'. For him, Italy provided the best possible illustration of this insight. While Italian music was mere noise, devoid of harmony, Rome ruled the world. It was only when the martial discords were sweetened that her decline and fall began and 'by degrees she has degenerated into what she is, a Nation of Priests, something less than Women; into a Race of mere effeminate Cowards'. The same process was under way closer to home, where the advance of music brought with it 'Luxury, Cowardice and Venality'. This was especially the case in the sybaritic

[26] Quoted in ibid., p. 72. Ruth Smith's highly original study, the worthy recipient of a British Academy prize in 1996, contains several more equally striking examples of this kind of prejudice.

[27] Quoted in ibid, p. 74. 'Heydegger' is John Jacob Heidegger.

[28] Quoted in ibid., p. 75.

south of England. The Scots and Irish, on the other hand, had succeeded in maintaining their own music, and with it their virility. So the lesson was clear: if there had to be music, then let it be English music:

> Refinement of our Taste into a Love of the soft *Italian* Music, is debasing the Martial Genius of the Nation; and may one Day be a Means to fiddle us out of our Liberties. I would chuse, if we are to be improved in Music, that the Composers would keep to the old *British* Key, and let us sing *English* as well as speak it.[29]

These examples of political, religious, and moral disapproval could be multiplied many times. By the late 1730s it was becoming apparent that the cultural environment in London was simply not conducive to Italian *opera seria*. It was not a question of resources, for London was both the largest and the richest city in Europe, but a lack of social will. It was a genre that could serve to entertain and represent the King and his most mighty subjects, but it could not express the country's national and nationalist aspirations. On the continent, a different structure allowed it to retain a measure of vitality until the French Revolution, when it began to metamorphose into grand opera. In 1791 the estates of Bohemia still thought it appropriate to commission Mozart to write an *opera seria* (*La Clemenza di Tito*) to mark the coronation of Leopold II. In the previous year a German visitor to England, Johann Wilhelm von Archenholz, recorded that most English people viewed Italian opera 'with the utmost contempt', adding that 'the nobility alone supports it; and they merely because—*it is the fashion*' [his emphasis].[30]

Handel was the perfect weather-vane to indicate the shift in the prevailing musical wind. He did very well from court and aristocracy, earning £600 per annum from the former by 1727 (a pension of £200 each from Queen Anne, George I, and George II) and living the life of an artist prince.[31] In the same year, the year in which he became a naturalized British subject by Act of Parliament, he demonstrated that he was worth every penny by writing *Zadok the Priest*, rightly described by his most recent biographer as 'one of the most dramatic gestures in the European music repertory'.[32] Its colossal impact

[29] R. Campbell, *The London Tradesman, being a compendious view of all the trades, professions, arts, both liberal and mechanic, now practised in the cities of London and Westminster, calculated for the information of parents and instruction of youth in their choice of business* (London, 1747), p. 89. Campbell added that he would rather raise his son as a blacksmith than a musician.

[30] Johann Wilhelm von Archenholz, *A Picture of England, containing a Description of the Laws, Customs and Manners of England* (Dublin, 1790), p. 234.

[31] Burrows, *Handel*, p. 117.

[32] Donald Burrows, 'George Frideric Handel. Coronation Anthems—Foundling Hospital Anthem', in the booklet accompanying the recording by the Choir of Winchester Cathedral, The Brandenburg Consort, conducted by David Hill, Argo 440 946–2.

pointed the way to a new source of fame and fortune, as the fashion for Italian *opera seria* waned. As we have seen,[33] in 1732 his 'Oratorio or Sacred Drama' *Esther* was performed as the first of its genre in London. For the next ten years Handel kept his options open, by presenting a mixture of opera and oratorio, but after 1741 he concentrated exclusively on the latter.

The immediate appeal of the new genre is not difficult to understand. Oratorio was respectable, because of its sacred subject-matter. Its structure was much more varied than formulaic *opera seria*. In particular, the major role assigned to choruses played to local strengths, for what the English musical tradition lacked in the production of solo voices, it made up for in the training of church choirs. Moreover, choral singing chimed in well with the congregational participation favoured by both Anglicans and Nonconformists. The demands made on the singers were modest in relation to the pyrotechnic displays of virtuosity required from the *castrati*, so that a competent church choir or even an amateur musical society could achieve a tolerable level of performance. The demands made on the audience were also less severe, an oratorio being usually about a third shorter in duration. Above all, oratorio was comprehensible to those without the benefit of a classical education: on the posters advertising the first performance of *Esther*, the fact that it was 'ORATORIO IN ENGLISH' was announced in letters almost as large as the title of the work itself.[34] In short, just as *opera seria* was the perfect medium for the representation of court culture, oratorio was ideally suited to the rapidly expanding public sphere of mid-eighteenth-century England.

It also lent itself to the propagation of ideology. In the secularized world of the late twentieth century, oratorios retain their appeal because of the quality of Handel's music. It may be doubted whether the texts of—say—*Athalia* or *Joshua* are now followed very closely. *Messiah* is perhaps the only exception. For Handel's contemporaries, however, 'the printed libretto—the word-book—was an indispensable part of attendance at the oratorio.'[35] It was sold in advance so that it could be studied, it was sold at the performance so that it could be followed then, and an accompanying commentary often set what was actually sung in a wider narrative context. It should be remembered that all members of an oratorio audience were fully versed in the Bible, including the Old Testament and the Apocrypha, and that their God was much more likely

[33] See above, pp. 179–80.
[34] Smith, *Handel's Oratorio and Eighteenth Century Thought*, p. 74.
[35] Ibid., p. 23.

to have been a wrathful Jehovah come to judgement than a remote first cause or a benign liberal.[36] For that reason alone, even the most austere present-day seeker after an 'authentic' performance of a Handel oratorio cannot possibly succeed.

More important still, Handel's audiences could see the relevance of Old Testament dramas to their own situation. Just as nineteenth-century Italians had no difficulty in casting themselves as the Hebrew slaves and their Austrian masters as the Babylonian tyrants at a performance of Verdi's *Nabucco*, so did English audiences of the 1740s identify the Old Testament characters of Handel's libretti with contemporary equivalents, notably Israel with Great Britain, King David with George II, and the Philistines with Catholic Europe.[37] One example must suffice: in 1746 Handel composed the music for *Judas Maccabæus* to a text by the Reverend Thomas Morell. It proved to be one of his most successful oratorios, not least because it fitted the context so well. In 1745 the Stuart Pretender Charles Edward ('Bonnie Prince Charlie') sought to take advantage of British involvement in the War of the Austrian Succession by raising his standard in Scotland and launching an invasion of England. The Hanoverian regime appeared to be vulnerable in the wake of a defeat at Fontenoy in Flanders in May 1745 at the hands of a French army commanded by the Maréchal de Saxe (an illegitimate son of Augustus the Strong of Saxony). Although the Pretender and his Jacobite army got as far south as Derby, the general lack of support and the inability of the French to come to their assistance forced a retreat. On 16 April 1746 they were crushed at Culloden by an English army commanded by the King's younger son, the Duke of Cumberland.

Judas Maccabæus was a tract for troubled times. From the second book of the Maccabees it tells the story of the Jewish hero who in the second century BC defended Judaea against the Seleucid king Antiochus IV Epiphanes, preserving the integrity of both the Jewish religion and the Jewish nation. When the oratorio begins, the Jews are in the depths of despair and have to be reminded by one of their more resolute number that:

[36] Handel himself responded tartly when told by the ecclesiastical authorities what to include in the coronation anthems in 1727 'I have read my Bible very well, and shall chuse for myself'; Burrows, *Handel*, p. 160.

[37] Ibid, p. 220. These associations were nothing new, of course. There had been a strong Protestant character to English imperialist discourse from the start, as in John Lyly's *Euphues Glasse for Europe* (1579), for example: 'So tender a care hath He alwaies had of that England, as of a new Israel and peculier people'; Friedrich Brie, 'Imperialistische Strömungen in der englischen Literatur', *Anglia. Zeitschrift für englische Philologie*, 40 (1916), pp. 13–14.

Distractful doubt and desperation
Ill become the Chosen Nation.[38]

They are given the encouraging promise that:

In defence of your nation, religion and laws,
The almighty Jehovah will strengthen your hands.

In his own pep-talk, Judas Maccabæus stresses that their cause is the cause of liberty:

Great is the glory of the conquering sword
That triumphs in sweet liberty restored.

and passes on an inspiring maxim from his late father:

'Resolve, my sons, on liberty, or death!'[39]

Judas Maccabæus and the Israelites duly triumph, but their rejoicing is short-lived, for a new invasion threatens, this time from Egypt. Nothing daunted, they sally forth again, singing:

We hear, we hear the pleasing dreadful call
And follow thee to conquest; if to fall
For laws, religion, liberty, we fall.

Once again, with God's help and in His name they triumph, this time decisively, and the oratorio ends amid general rejoicing and congratulation. It is inconceivable that many members of the audience failed to make the connection, especially as Morell included the following dedication in his libretto: 'To His Royal Highness Prince William, Duke of Cumberland, this faint portraiture of a Truly Wise, Valiant, and Virtuous Commander, As to the Possessor of like Noble Qualities.'[40] Yet if the work ended in triumph, it was far from being triumphalist. The Israelites (British) were indeed God's elect, and were especially virtuous by reason of their true religion, liberty, and laws, but they were also specially vulnerable to their idolatrous (Catholic) Seleucid

[38] There are many editions of *Judas Maccabæus* available. I have used the text adopted by Johannes Somary for his recording with the English Chamber Orchestra and the Amor Artis Chorale and included in the booklet accompanying the recording reissued as Brilliant Classics 99268.

[39] Morell thus anticipated Patrick Henry's cry of 'give me liberty or give me death!' to the Virginia Convention by some twenty years (if indeed Henry did say anything of the kind, his words being recorded only forty years later).

[40] Burrows, *Handel*, p. 291. Morell recorded later that the work was 'designed as a compliment to the Duke of Cumberland upon his returning victorious from Scotland'.

and Egyptian (French, Spanish, Jacobite) enemies. Constant vigilance and constant virtue would be the price of continuing liberty. If the Israelites (British) succumbed to idolatry or vice, God would punish them by allowing their enemies to triumph.[41]

Expounding the text of a work such as *Judas Maccabæus*, especially with such brevity, can give only a feeble impression of the work's impact. It was the power of Handel's music which turned a conventional message into an inspiring call to arms. On the printed page, the two following short verses, transferred from another 'Victory Oratorio' *Joshua*, mean little:

> See the conquering hero comes!
> Sound the trumpets, beat the drums;
> Sports prepare, the laurel bring,
> Songs of triumph to him sing.
>
> See the godlike youth advance!
> Breathe the flutes, and lead the dance;
> Myrtle wreaths, and roses twine,
> To deck the hero's brow divine.

But Handel wrote for them what was to become one of the most memorable melodies in music, giving it to trebles for the first verse and sopranos for the second, with minimal accompaniment. When both verses are reprised by the whole chorus and orchestra, the effect is electrifying.

Handel was a rich man when he turned to composing oratorios and he became even richer as a result. As Derek Beales has observed, he was 'the first composer and musical impresario who made a fortune from a paying public'.[42] For less outlay, less risk, and less effort, Handel found that he could make as much money from a seven-week oratorio season of twelve to fifteen performances as from a much longer opera season with four times that number of performances.[43] When he died in 1759, he left an estate valued at about £20,000, which made him a millionaire by present-day standards.[44] Riches were accompanied by high status. At a time when musicians on the continent were treated like liveried retainers,[45] Handel was fêted by king, aristocracy,

[41] The defensive and non-triumphalist character of *Judas Maccabæus* and the other Israel oratorios has been stressed by Ruth Smith in *Handel's Oratorio and Eighteenth Century Thought*; see, for example, pp. 271–5.

[42] Derek Beales, 'Religion and culture', in T. C. W. Blanning (ed.), *The Short Oxford History of Europe: The Eighteenth Century* (Oxford, 2000), p. 149.

[43] Burrows, *Handel*, p. 301.

[44] Ibid., p. 368.

[45] See above, pp. 81–2.

and country. Never dependent on any one, he benefited both materially and socially from all three. A private man who never married, he drew his few close friends from the upper ranks of society—the Earl of Gainsborough, Bernard Granville, the Earl of Shaftesbury, and James Harris.[46] In particular, his career was a fine illustration of the benefits a creative artist might draw from popular appeal to the public sphere. One highlight was the erection in 1738 of a full-length, life-size statue of Handel at Vauxhall, the largest pleasure-garden in London, by its entrepreneur, Jonathan Tyers (Plate 14). To pick the unknown immigrant sculptor Louis François Roubiliac was an inspired act of good luck or good judgement. His creation, which shows Handel in relaxed posture and dress, plucking a lyre in the role of Orpheus, became one of the most celebrated of all musical statues.[47] It was intended to be both an act of homage to a cultural hero and a reminder of the soothing power of music. As the *Daily Post* reported:

We are inform'd from very good Authority; that there is now finished a Statue of the justly celebrated Mr Handel, exquisitely done by the ingenious Mr Roubiliac of St. Martin's Lane, Statuary, out of one entire Block of white Marble, which is to be placed in a grand Nich, erected on purpose in the great Grove at Vaux-hall-Gardens, at the sole expense of Mr Tyers, Undertaker of the Entertainment there, who in Consideration of the real Merit of that inimitable Master, thought it proper, that his Effigies should preside there, where his Harmony has so often charm'd even the greatest Crouds into the profoundest Calm and most decent Behaviour; it is believed that the Expence of the Statue and Nich cannot cost less than Three hundred pounds.[48]

The Vauxhall statue was Roubiliac's first commission; his last was to be Handel's monument in Westminster Abbey, completed in 1761. This is much more formal, as befits the setting and occasion, showing an angel poised aloft, playing a harp, as Handel writes down the notes of 'I know that my Redeemer liveth' from *Messiah*.[49] By writing the Hallelujah Chorus in the same work, Handel has probably been responsible for more praise of his God than any other individual, so it may be hoped that his pious expectation has been fulfilled. That Handel should be honoured by such a prominent tomb in Westminster Abbey testifies to his personal status and the growing sacralization of his art. When he died, he was honoured at once by the first

46 Donald Burrows, 'Handel; his life and work', in Simon (ed.), *Handel*, p. 17.

47 The orignal is now to be found in the Victoria and Albert Museum.

48 Quoted in ibid., p. 112.

49 There is a reproduction in Joseph Burke, *English Art 1714–1800* (London, 1976), plate 50B.

book-length biography devoted to a musician.[50] Handel's success in so many different cultural spaces should guard against any temptation to postulate too sharp a division between the worlds of representation and the public.

THE RISE OF ENGLISH NATIONAL IDENTITY

The success of Handel's vernacular oratorios demonstrated that the growing public sphere in Great Britain was encouraging the development of a strong sense of national identity. Encouraging not inventing, for this was not a brand-new phenomenon. As was noted in the introduction, a sense of English identity was many centuries old. Indeed, Adrian Hastings has argued that all the elements of a nation were present as early as the reign of Alfred the Great (871–99), namely a national language, a national literature, national law, and a consultative corporate body, the Witan or Witenagemot.[51] For much of this present century, historians of medieval England, reacting against their Whig predecessors, denied that any nationalism could be found in the Middle Ages. Among other things, they pointed out that public life was dominated by a universal Church and a universal language.[52] The pendulum has now swung back the other way, as Patrick Wormald argues that the search for English national identity should begin in the age of Bede (c. 673–735), while James Campbell bluntly states that by 1066 England was 'a nation-state'.[53] The Norman Conquest and the imposition of a foreign culture could impede but not prevent further progress. By the middle of the thirteenth century, in the view of Thorlac Turville-Petre, a sense of English national identity expressed itself through a consciousness of having a distinct and charted territory, a common history, common cultural traditions, common law, a single economy with a common coinage and taxation, and finally some concept of shared rights.[54] All that was missing was a common language. That omission had

[50] John Mainwaring, *Memoirs of the Life of the late George Frederic Handel. To which is added, A Catalogue of his Works, and Observations upon them* (London, 1760).

[51] Adrian Hastings, *The Construction of Nationhood: Ethnicity, Religion and Nationalism* (Cambridge, 1997), p. 39.

[52] Barnaby C. Keeney, 'Military service and the development of nationalism in England, 1272–1327', *Speculum*, 22 (1947), p. 534.

[53] Patrick Wormald, '*Engla Lond*: the making of an allegiance', *Journal of Historical Sociology*, 7 (1994), p. 18. Hastings, *The Construction of Nationhood*, p. 36.

[54] Thorlac Turville-Petre, *England the Nation: Language, Literature, and National Identity, 1290–1340* (Oxford, 1996), p. 8.

been rectified a hundred years later, by which time the English language was clearly established as the national medium. In 1362 a statute ordered that English should henceforth be used in the law courts, and in the following year the Chancellor for the first time spoke in English when opening Parliament.[55]

Nationalism develops in a dialectical relationship between the imagined virtues of one's own nation and the imagined vices of another or others. An early victim of the xenophobia engendered by a developing sense of English identity was the Jewish community, expelled in 1290. In the following century, the Hundred Years War made the French the sounding-board for English virtues, as an anonymous clergyman demonstrated after the battle of Crecy (1346):

> Francia, foeminea, pharisea, vigoris idea
> Lynxea, viperea, vulpina, lupina, Medea...
> Anglia regna, mundi rosa, flos sine spina
> Mel sine sentina, vicisti bella marina.[56]

National stereotypes began to be established, for example, 'That frenche men synne yn lecherye, and englys men yn enuye'.[57] One possible reason for this contrast was that the French were not diverted from the sins of the flesh by the pleasures of the table. What might be called dietary nationalism has a long history. In *De laudibus legum Angliae*, written in 1471 after eight years of exile in France, Sir John Fortescue stressed the poverty of the mass of the French population as a result of the excessive fiscal burden:

> exasperated by these and other calamities, the people live in no little misery. They drink water daily, and they taste no other liquor unless at solemn feasts... the men and women eat no flesh, except bacon lard, with which they fatten their pottage in the smallest quantity. They do not taste other meats, roast or boiled, except occasionally the offal and heads of animals killed for the nobles and merchants.[58]

A hundred years later another exile, John Aylmer, exclaimed: 'Oh if thou knewest thou Englishe man in what welth thou liuest, and in how plentifull a Countrye: Thou wouldest times of the day fall flat on thy face before God, and geue him thanks, that thou wart born an English man, and not a french pezant,

[55] Hastings, *The Construction of Nationhood*, p. 46.

[56] Ibid., p. 49.

[57] Keeney, 'Military service and the development of nationalism', p. 536.

[58] Quoted in Orest Ranum, 'Counter-identities of western European nations in the early modern period: definitions and points of departure', in Peter Boerner (ed.), *Concepts of National Identity: An Interdisciplinary Dialogue* (Baden-Baden, 1986), p. 70.

nor an Italyan, nor Almane.'[59] It was a common boast among English beef-eaters that the French and Italians had to make do with 'grass' or 'herbs' (vegetables and salads).[60] As we shall see, this was to be a prejudice with a long history ahead of it. Within the British Isles too, the Celtic minorities were increasingly defined in negative terms and viewed with suspicion as a fifth column. It appears to have been in the twelfth century that the epithet *barbarus* was transferred from pagans to other—but Celtic—Christians. William of Newburgh described the Scots as 'a horde of barbarians ... to whom no food is too filthy to be devoured, even that which is fit only for dogs. It is a delight to that inhuman nation, more savage than wild beasts, to cut the throats of old men, to slaughter little children, to rip open the bowels of women.' His contemporary, John of Salisbury, had a similar view of the Welsh: 'rude and untamed; they live like beasts and though they nominally profess Christ, they deny him in their life and ways.' As for the Irish, another twelfth-century writer, Gerald of Wales, wrote: 'They are so barbarous that they cannot be said to have any culture ... they are a wild people, living like beasts.'[61] Attitudes do not appear to have changed as the centuries passed. Writing in the 1430s, the anonymous author of 'The Libel of English Policy', lamented that English control of 'the wylde Yrishe' was now confined to 'a lytelle cornere' of that strategically crucial island:

> ... if it be loste, as Christe Jhesu forbede,
> Ffarewelle Wales, than Englond cometh to drede
> Ffor alliaunce of Scotelonde and of Spayne.[62]

PROTESTANTISM

In short, both the positive and negative characteristics of English nationalism were in place by 1500. Medieval universalism had been elastic enough to allow the coexistence of national consciousness and national vernaculars. There can be no doubt, however, that the Protestant Reformation greatly intensified nationalism. By taking England out of communion with Rome and elevating

[59] J. C. D. Clark, *The Language of Liberty 1660–1832: Political Discourse and Social Dynamics in the Anglo-American World* (Cambridge, 1994), p. 49.

[60] G. R. Elton, 'English national self-consciousness and the Parliament in the sixteenth century', in Otto Dann (ed.), *Nationalismus in vorindustrieller Zeit* (Munich, 1986), p. 75.

[61] John Gillingham, 'The beginnings of English imperialism', *Journal of Historical Sociology*, 5 (1992), p. 397.

[62] Quoted in Hastings, *The Construction of Nationhood*, p. 55.

the king to be supreme head of the Church, and moreover a Church that was now *of* England not *in* England, as before, it made the country autarchic in its loyalties and began a surge of imperial literature: 'What Kingdom in the world is to be compared unto this our English Empire?' asked Thomas Becon (1512–67).[63] Although the Protestant Reformation might have appeared to be an international movement, the English laid a special claim to Christian primacy. As Timothy Bright put it in 1589, England was the first country to embrace the Gospel universally; Constantine, the first Christian emperor, was an Englishman; John Wycliffe, the first to challenge the authority of the Pope, was an Englishman; Henry VIII, the first king to renounce the Pope, was an Englishman; Edward VI, the first king to abolish 'popish superstition' was an Englishman; Elizabeth I, the hammer of the Pope, was an Englishwoman.[64] As the Reformation settlement was imposed through Parliament, it also helped to develop a central institution which would serve as a focus for the nation's interests and ambitions. As Sir Geoffrey Elton argued, king and Parliament were not opposing interests engaged in a running battle for supremacy but partners in the same enterprise. Just as the king was regarded as a member of the Parliament, so was the Parliament regarded as part of the king's government.[65] As other European countries were to discover much later, a representative assembly is certainly the best—and perhaps the only—way to galvanize national energies.

Religious independence was then underpinned by a surge of cultural nationalism. As Catherine Shrank has written, in her ground-breaking analysis of the contribution made by English humanism to the development of a national identity: 'In the wake of the split from Rome, Tudor culture is marked by a striking assertion of national autonomy.'[66] John Leland, for example, claimed in the *Newe Yeares Gyfte* he presented to Henry VIII in 1546, that Englishmen had been denied a sense of their history by foreign tyranny—'by ye space of a whole thousand yeares stopped vp'. It was his self-appointed task to restore 'the *old* glory' and to proclaim the fame of 'renoumed Britaine' throughout the world.[67] Angrily rejecting the arrogant claim of classical Rome and contemporary Italy to cultural superiority, he enumerated a great catalogue of native

[63] Brie, 'Imperialistische Strömungen', p. 12.

[64] Clark, *The Language of Liberty*, p. 48.

[65] Elton, 'English national self-consciousness', pp. 79–80.

[66] Catherine Lucy Shrank, *English Humanism and National Identity (1530–1570)* (unpublished Cambridge Ph.D. dissertation, 1999), p. 61.

[67] Ibid., p. 62.

English talent stretching back to the Druid bards. The death of Sir Thomas Wyatt moved him to make the following bathetic claim:

> Beautiful Florence of Dante justly boasts,
> And kingly Rome approves the excellence
> Of Petrarch's songs. In his own tongue as worthy,
> Our Wyatt bears the palm of eloquence.[68]

Dietary nationalism was also given added impetus by the break from Rome. With the authority of one who had spent three years in exile pining for wholesome English fare, the raffish William Thomas told the Italians: 'In that you exceede us in frutes, we exceede you both in the abundaunce and also the goodnes of flesh, foule and fysh.' The cool climate of the British Isles required their inhabitants to eat properly: 'whereof groweth the proverb, *Geve the Englyshman beoffe and mustarde.*'[69] Indeed Thomas expounded a form of dietary determinism (in an early version of '*Man ist was man isst*') by tracing a causal connection to forms of government and religion, as in 'what barbarowse people arr in other regions, what wante of goode foode they haue, what miserable lyves they leade, what servitude and subjection they endure, what extremities of heate and colde they suffer, what superstition they followe, and what a nombre of other inconveniences do hange vpon them.'[70]

More important was the virulent strain injected into traditional antipathies by sectarian hatreds. The Marian persecutions at home and the well-publicized (and often well-exaggerated) atrocities inflicted on Protestants abroad gave added urgency to the quest for national security. For a God-fearing Protestant who believed that the Pope was the seven-headed, ten-horned, scarlet-coloured beast number 666 'full of names of blasphemy' revealed to St John the Divine, it was not just a matter of life or death but of life and afterlife too. The attempt by Mary to reimpose Catholicism between 1553 and 1558, her marriage to Philip II of Spain, the lowering presence of the Catholic Pretender Mary Stuart until her execution in 1587, and the attempted Spanish invasion the following year, all conspired to keep the nerves of English Protestants taut. 'Fear and I were born together,' observed Thomas Hobbes (1588–1679) and he was not alone. So the triumphalism that followed the defeat of the Spanish Armada in 1588 and the other sea-faring exploits of the Elizabethan age was always shot through with anxiety. For example, there are no more celebrated lines in the English language singing

[68] Ibid., p. 65. [69] Ibid., pp. 101–2. [70] Ibid., p. 108.

the country's praises than those given to John of Gaunt by William Shakespeare in *Richard II* (1595):

> This royal throne of kings, this sceptered isle,
> This earth of majesty, this seat of Mars,
> This other Eden, demi-paradise,
> This fortress built by nature for herself
> Against infection and the hand of war,
> This happy breed of men, this little world,
> This precious stone set in the silver sea,
> Which serves it in the office of a wall,
> Or as a moat defensive to a house,
> Against the envy of less happier lands...
> This blessed plot, this earth, this realm, this England.

But Gaunt is on his deathbed, lamenting the decadence, civil strife, and threat of foreign invasion which has brought 'this dear, dear land' to the brink of ruin, for it

> Is now leased out—I die pronouncing it—
> Like to a tenement or pelting farm...
> England, bound in with the triumphant sea,
> Whose rocky shore beats back the envious siege
> Of wat'ry Neptune, is now bound in with shame,
> With inky blots, and rotten parchment bonds:
> That England, that was wont to conquer others,
> Hath made a shameful conquest of itself.

Significantly, in an earlier scene the Duke of York has identified for Gaunt the central malaise—the King's cultural treason:

> JOHN OF GAUNT Though Richard my life's counsel would not hear,
> My death's sad tale may yet undeaf his ear.
> DUKE OF YORK No, it is stopped with other flattering sounds,
> As praises, of whose taste the wise are fond,[71]
> Lascivious metres, to whose venom sound
> The open ear of youth doth always listen,
> Report of fashions in proud Italy,
> Whose manners still our tardy apish nation
> Limps after in base imitation:
> Where doth the world thrust forth a vanity—
> So it be new, there's no respect how vile—
> That is not quickly buzzed into his ears?

[71] 'fond' = made foolish by flattery.

Shakespeare was certainly not alone in fearing the enervating influence of foreign fashion. In his *Arte of Rhetorique* of 1553, Thomas Wilson had complained that travel abroad by the English elites led to linguistic contamination: 'like as thei loue to go in foreig[n] apparell, so thei wil pouder their talke with ouersea language.' Indeed, in extreme cases, 'I dare swere this, if some of their mothers were aliue, thei were not able to tell, what thei say.' So every effort should be made to guard against the further intrusion of *Fremdwörter* and to find good old English substitutes for those which had already gained access ('surgian' should be replaced by 'flesh clenser', 'barber' by 'bearder', for example).[72]

Pride and fear were intimate bedfellows, but their issue was venomous xenophobia. One obvious target was the Celtic fringe, especially 'the wylde Yrishe', now rendered all the more alien and threatening by their obstinate adherence to Catholicism. William Thomas divided Ireland into two zones: the English pale and lands of the wild Irish who were 'unreasonable beasts ... without knowledge of God or good manners'. In his view, the English had not conquered Ireland out of lust for conquest or for avarice but to introduce civilization to the 'wyld men' and to turn them 'from rude, beastly, ignorant, cruel, and unruly Infidels to the state of civil, reasonable, patient, humble and well governed Christians'.[73] He was not alone. There was no more sophisticated Elizabethan poet than Edmund Spenser, best known as the author of *The Faerie Queene* (1590–6), 'the celebration of the providential union of England and true religion under the sovereignty of Elizabeth'.[74] But Spenser was also secretary to the lord deputy of Ireland, the owner of an Irish plantation, and the author of *A View of the Present State of Ireland* (1595–6) and a *Brief Note on Ireland* (1598) in which he denounced the 'licentious barbarism' of the Irish and criticized the English government for not being harsh enough. His own remedy was certainly brutal: 'To subdue Ireland thoroughly, great force must be the instrument but famine must be the means for till Ireland be famished it cannot be subdued.'[75]

Under Elizabeth, resolutely Protestant and impeccably English, cultural achievement was married to political success to form a powerful source of legitimation. The Queen herself, aware that 'We princes ... are set on stages, in the sight and view of all the world duly observed,' proved from the start to

[72] Catherine Shrank, Rhetorical constructions of a national community: the role of the King's English in Mid-Tudor writing', Unpublished paper.

[73] Ibid.

[74] Hastings, *The Construction of Nationhood*, p. 83.

[75] Quoted in ibid., p. 84.

be an adept image-builder.[76] She was very much a sovereign on view, appearing regularly in public. The annual 'progresses' across England were self-conscious exercises in public relations, directed not only at the nobility and gentry but at the common people too. Pictures, pamphlets, ballads, and even amulets spread the image of the strong but caring Virgin Queen across the land.[77] As the quintessentially English queen, she was presented as the defender of Protestantism and English virtues against the various 'others' who lurked inside and outside the kingdom, as, for example, in a ballad of 1572, 'a godly ditty or prayer to be sung unto God for the preservation of his Church our queen, and realm, against all traitors, rebels and papistical enemies'.[78]

The Protestant nature of English national culture could only be intensified by the constitutional conflicts of the century that followed. This is no place even to summarize the debate on the causes of the Civil War and, more specifically, the causes of the regicide of 1649, except to note that not even the most thoroughgoing materialist can deny the importance of religious convictions. Elizabeth I had succeeded in defending both the nation and the faith; Charles I was deemed to have failed in both. The decision to marry him to Henrietta Maria, sister of King Louis XIII of France, in 1625, proved to be a choice even more unfortunate than that of Caroline of Brunswick for George IV or Lady Diana Spencer for the future Charles III (possibly). Part of the hard bargain driven by the French negotiators allowed Henrietta Maria to profess her faith openly, to establish a Catholic enclave in London, and to raise her children as Catholics.[79] Not only did this union bring no benefits to the conduct of foreign policy, it fatally compromised Charles I's Protestant credentials. 'Anti-popish hysteria'[80] was an obtrusive part of English public life throughout the century, regularly stoked by conspiracies real and imaginary, at home (the Gunpowder Plot, the Great Fire of London, the Popish Plot, etc.) and abroad (the Irish Rebellion of 1641, the

[76] Rudolf Braun and David Guggerli, *Macht des Tanzes—Tanz der Mächtigen. Hoffeste und Herrschaftszeremoniell 1550–1914* (Munich, 1993), p. 47.

[77] Kevin Sharpe, 'Representations and negotiations: texts, images and authority in early modern England', *Historical Journal*, 42 (1999), p. 871. 'As Elizabeth well knew, but so many of her successors apparently did not, the greatest single virtue of public thanksgivings and extended progresses was that they exposed the spectacle of the queen and her court to the widest possible audience'; R.O. Bucholz, '"Nothing but Ceremony": Queen Anne and the limitations of royal ritual', *Journal of British Studies*, 30 (1991), p. 297.

[78] Christopher Haigh, *Elizabeth I* (London, 1988), pp. 146–9.

[79] Mark Kishlansky, *A Monarchy Transformed: Britain 1603–1714* (London, 1996), pp. 106–7.

[80] Ibid., p. 252.

Revocation of the Edict of Nantes, etc.). The Vaudois Persecutions by the Duke of Savoy in 1655, for example, inspired one of John Milton's most powerful poems:

> Avenge, O Lord! Thy slaughter'd Saints, whose bones
> Lie scatter'd on the Alpine mountains cold;
> Even them who kept Thy truth so pure of old,
> When all our fathers worshipt stocks and stones.

If his genius was exceptional, Milton was typical of the English Puritans who identified the English Parliamentary cause with liberty and Protestantism, and the cause of their enemies with Catholicism and tyranny. In particular, Milton was deeply hostile to 'these murdrous Irish, the enemies of God and mankind', 'abhorred Irish Rebels ... inhumane Rebels and papists of Ireland ... those bloudy Rebels ... those Irish barbarians ... [and their] Murders, Massacres, Treasons, Pyracies ... a Crew of Rebells whose inhumanities are long since become the horrour and execration of all that heare them ... the irish, our most savage and inhuman enemies ... the villainous and savage scum of Ireland.'[81] Milton was one of many Commonwealth poets to glory in Cromwell's subjugation of the Celtic papists:

> Your drooping country, torn with civil hate,
> Restor'd by you, is made a glorious state;
> The seat of empire, where the IRISH come,
> And the unwilling SCOTS, to fetch their doom.[82]

The events of 1689–90, when the deposed Catholic James II sought to regain his kingdom by invading Ireland with French assistance, confirmed a rich web of associations which were not confined to Ulster Protestants. The constitutional convention, which met in London to discuss the state of the nation after the flight of James II, concluded unanimously that 'it hath been found by

[81] John Milton, *The Works of John Milton*, ed. F. A. Patterson, 17 vols. (New York, 1931–4), vol. III *The Reason of Church-government urg'd against Prelacy* (1641), p. 226; vol. VI *Observations upon the Articles of Peace with the Irish Rebels* (1649), pp. 243, 248; vol. VII *Pro Populo Anglicano Defensio*, p. 525; Willy Maley, 'The British problem in three tracts on Ireland by Spenser, Bacon and Milton', in Brendan Bradshaw and Peter Roberts (eds.), *British Consciousness and Identity: The Making of Britain 1533–1707* (Cambridge, 1998), p. 184.

[82] Edmund Waller, 'A Panegyric to my Lord Protector, of the present Greatness, and joint Interest of his Highness, and this Nation', *The Works of Edmund Waller Esq., in Verse and Prose* (Dublin, 1768), p. 107. For a recent argument that 'anxieties about nationhood were central to the English Civil War,' see Mark Stoyle, 'English "nationalism", Celtic particularism and the English Civil War', *Historical Journal*, 43, 4 (2000), *passim.*

experience, to be inconsistent with the safety and welfare of this Protestant Kingdom to be governed by a Popish Prince.'[83] At their coronation in 1689, in a deliberate departure from precedent designed to emphasize the Protestant nature of the ceremony, William and Mary swore to rule according to the 'true profession of the gospel, and the Protestant reformed religion established by law'. Lest they forgot, they were given a Bible each 'to put you in mind of this rule and that you may follow it'.[84] William's first task in his new role as *fidei defensor* was to cross to Ireland to smite the hosts of Antichrist. Defence of religion meant defence of the realm, and vice versa, against their joint enemies, the Irish and the French. As Steven Pincus has argued, the Glorious Revolution of 1688 was as much a nationalist revolution as a Dutch invasion.[85] As it turned out, when William of Orange landed at Brixham on 5 November 1688, which was the anniversary of the foiling of the Gunpowder Plot (an auspicious coincidence of dates), he was initiating a struggle with France that was to last until 18 June 1815 and the Battle of Waterloo. In the wake of the revocation of the Edict of Nantes in 1685 and the expulsion of the Huguenots from France, British Protestants were well aware that this was an international struggle for the true faith.[86] Incidents of Catholic persecution, such as the revolt of the Camisards (1702–10) or the expulsion of the Protestants from Salzburg in 1731, kept the image of a menacing Counter-Reformation alive. So the association between domestic and foreign enemies was sustained and even intensified.

The eighteenth century was the Protestant century in England, as the number of Catholics declined from about 115,000 in 1720 to about 69,000 in 1780, or in other words, from about 2 per cent of the total population to about 1 per cent.[87] Of the nineteen Catholic peers remaining in 1700, two

[83] Tony Claydon and Ian McBride, 'The trials of the chosen peoples: recent interpretations of Protestantism and national identity in Britain and Ireland', in Tony Claydon and Ian McBride (eds.), *Protestantism and National Identity: Britain and Ireland c. 1650–1850* (Cambridge, 1998), p. 3.

[84] Linda Colley, *Britons: Forging the Nation 1707–1837* (New Haven and London, 1992), p. 47. It should be noted that post-Reformation England took no notice of a new king's place of birth, so long as he was Protestant. This applied to James VI of Scotland (born at Edinburgh), William III, Prince of Orange (born at The Hague), and Georg Ludwig, Elector of Hanover (born at Osnabrück). I owe this insight, and many others, to Andrew Thompson of Queens' College, Cambridge.

[85] Steven Pincus, '"To protect English liberties": the English nationalist revolution of 1688–1689', in Claydon and McBride (eds.), *Protestantism and National Identity*, p. 87.

[86] Ibid., p. 75.

[87] Roy Porter, *English Society in the Eighteenth Century* (Harmondsworth, 1982), p. 194; Frank O'Gorman, *The long Eighteenth Century: British Political and Social History 1688–1832* (London, 1997), p. 312.

were attainted for treason, five became extinct, and seven converted to Anglicanism.[88] The alien character of Catholics in eighteenth-century England was thought to be demonstrated by the fact that their priests were educated abroad, that they themselves often attended foreign schools and universities, and that their services were conducted in Latin.[89] But it was also the Christian century. This realization has been one of the major gains of recent historiography. As Derek Beales has argued, the related notions that the eighteenth century was the 'Age of Enlightenment' and that the Enlightenment represented 'the rise of modern paganism' are contradicted by the intense—and intensifying—religiosity of the period. Better sobriquets would be 'the age of religion' and 'the Christian century', not least in England.[90] The deism of one such as John Toland, who found his way from Catholicism to freethinking via the decompression chamber of Anglicanism, never progressed beyond a small circle of intellectuals. By mid-century it had become apparent even to the latter that what little tide had once buoyed their hopes had turned and was now running strongly against them. David Hume remarked that the English were 'relapsing into the deepest Stupidity, Christianity and ignorance'.[91] As usual, he was right, although the objects of his disdain would have chosen other epithets to flank their faith. The Church of England recovered its confidence after the tribulations of the previous century, reformed its alliance with the state, and prospered mightily from agricultural advances. If its spiritual reinvigoration was less impressive, there were plenty of evangelical revivals inside and outside its ranks. The most important was Methodism, led by John Wesley, who demonstrated that the public sphere need not be left to the Devil. Fifty years of tireless travelling, preaching, and publishing created a movement with more than 70,000 hard-core adherents by the time of his death in 1791.[92]

The triumph of Protestant Christianity permeated English culture in the eighteenth century, however much freethinking contemporaries such as

[88] J. C. D. Clark (ed.), *The memoirs and speeches of James, 2nd Earl of Waldegrave 1742–1763* (Cambridge, 1988), p. 24.

[89] Colin Haydon, '"I love my King and my Country, but a Roman Catholic I hate": anti-Catholicism, xenophobia and national identity in eighteenth century England', in Claydon and McBride (eds.), *Protestantism and National Identity*, p. 34.

[90] Derek Beales, 'Religion and culture', in T. C. W. Blanning (ed.), *The Short Oxford History of Europe: The Eighteenth Century* (Oxford, 2000), p. 133.

[91] Paul Langford, *A Polite and Commercial People: England 1727–1783* (Oxford, 1989), p. 468.

[92] Beales, 'Religion and culture', p. 166. The best modern account of religion in eighteenth-century Britain is now W. R. Ward, *Christianity under the Ancien Régime 1648–1789* (Cambridge, 1999).

Hume and Voltaire chose to ignore it when discussing the English national character.[93] In France, the sensibility of Rousseau's *La Nouvelle Héloïse* was seen as a threat by both ecclesiastical and enlightened establishments; but in England, Richardson's mission 'to inculcate *religion* and *morality*', as he put it in the preface to *Pamela* with characteristic insistence, turned the same literary phenomenon 'into a tool of piety rather than paganism'.[94] The largest category of books published was on religion, the single most important literary form was the sermon.[95] The religious quality of English culture has been described with special cogency by Ruth Smith in her study of Handel's oratorios:

> This was still a culture in which . . . religious belief and the morality taught by religion informed prescriptions for the content of works of art and the works themselves. The pulpit was the major public-address system. Sermons addressed and influenced every aspect of private and public life (including art), religious debate was a major element of intellectual life, religious publications dominated book production, and people believed that God supervised their lives and could and would intervene with punishment on a personal or national scale if provoked by wrong-doing.[96]

THE SECOND HUNDRED YEARS WAR

Fortunately for the English, God was usually smiling on them in the eighteenth century. The structural problems eroding French hegemony, which we examined in the first chapter and shall return to in the next, created manifold opportunities for the expansion of British power. Charles II had been Louis XIV's satrap; William III was his hammer. The naval victory at La Hogue in May 1692 was the first of many over the French and, like many other exploits, found a permanent memorial in the shape of an inn-sign ('The Admiral Benbow', the setting for the beginning of Robert Louis Stevenson's *Treasure Island*). In the course of the War of the Spanish Succession (1701–13), England moved from being a junior partner in continental alliances to a major player. It

[93] Michael Maurer, 'Nationalcharakter und Nationalbewußtsein. England und Deutschland im Vergleich', in Ulrich Herrmann (ed.), *Volk—Nation—Vaterland* (Hamburg, 1996), p. 91.

[94] Langford, *A Polite and Commercial People*, p. 467. See also above, p. 148.

[95] John Brewer, *The Pleasures of the Imagination: English Culture in the Eighteenth Century* (London, 1997), p. 172.

[96] Smith, *Handel's Oratorio and Eighteenth Century Thought*, p. 8.

was a promotion sealed and symbolized by the Duke of Marlborough's victory at Blenheim in 1704, which also found a permanent memorial in the shape of the eponymous palace, the grandest of all English stately homes.

It was during the War of the Spanish Succession that it became clear that the struggle between the British and the Bourbon monarchies would be conducted as much outside Europe as within it. The cultural axioms which underpinned the British war effort were particularly well illustrated by *Liberty Asserted*, a play by John Dennis first staged in London in 1704. As this was the popular playwright's most successful work, regularly revived until mid-century, it clearly struck a chord with the contemporary public.[97] Set in 'Angie'[98] in contemporary Canada, it relates the trials and tribulations of Ulamar, the general of the five nations of the Iroquois, who with the assistance of the British general Beaufort has been beating off the attacks of the Hurons and their French allies. A strident anti-French message is conveyed throughout. After the first Anglo-Iroquois victory, Beaufort proclaims

> Impartial Heav'n has heard our just Appeal,
> And has supported Innocence and Faith,
> Against Injustice, Treason, Violence,
> Against Oppression, Perjury and Fraud,
> And all the Crimes of the perfidious French.[99]

He adds that the French possess no valour but always try to win by deceit. The noble Iroquois agrees, praising the English for their manifest virtues:

> The English always were a Gallant Nation,
> And Foes to Force, and Friends to Liberty.
> Those who without the Mind possess the Body,
> Possess by Force, and *Ravish, not Enjoy.*[100]

The national stereotypes duly act out their preordained roles: Beaufort declines the offer of the beautiful Iroquois maiden Irene because he can see that she prefers Ulamar. For their part, the French break a treaty as soon as it is

[97] On the popularity of the work, see Edward Niles Hooker (ed.), *The Critical Works of John Dennis*, 2 vols. (Baltimore, 1939–43), I, p. 505.

[98] In his preface to the printed version of the work, Dennis stated that it was set in 'Agnie', which he had changed to 'Angie' 'for the sake of a better sound'. I have used the modern edition of Dennis's critical works, which includes the prefaces to his plays, because this is more likely to be accessible to readers. There is no modern edition of the plays, however, so I have cited the originals.

[99] John Dennis, *Liberty Asserted. A Tragedy* (London, 1704), p. 6.

[100] Ibid., p. 25.

made and massacre their enemies in a treacherous ambush. Ulamar, sounding suspiciously like an English Whig (he turns out to be the son of a French aristocrat and a Huron woman), berates the French envoys:

> What have you taught the Nations after all?
> What have you taught them but Inglorious arts:
> To emascalate [*sic*] their minds? But cursed Luxury,
> Which makes them needy, venal, base, perfidious
> Black Traytors to their Country, Friends to you.

Beaufort then takes over the baton, helpfully adding the European context:

> For you win Provinces, as Hell gains Souls;
> 'Tis by corrupting them that you make them yours:
> They might defie your malice were they faithful:
> But first you enslave them to their own base Passions;
> And afterwards to yours.[101]

Although described on the title page as 'a tragedy', *Liberty Asserted* ends happily, with the French defeated and the cause of England and Liberty saved. Dennis was particularly anxious to present the French in his preface as both feeble and a threat. Personally contemptible, they could succeed only through pulling the wool over the eyes of the rest of Europe:

> That the Liberties of *Europe*, and of this Island particularly, are in no small Danger at present from the growing Power of *France*, will be easily granted by all but such who are either Fools or Knaves too incorrigible to be talked to. But this is plain, that they are not so much in danger, from what some call the Greatness of the *French*, as from the Baseness of the rest of *Europe*. If we were but as true to Liberty, as the *French* are to Tyranny, they would soon be as despicable in their Circumstances as they are now in their Principles.[102]

Liberty Asserted, in other words, was as good an example as one might wish of the accuracy of Dr Johnson's observation that 'In a time of war, the nation is always of one mind, eager to hear something good of themselves and ill of the enemy.'[103] As its name suggests, the War of the Spanish Succession was precipitated by the death of the last Habsburg King of Spain, Charles II, in 1700 and the accession of a Bourbon, the duc d'Anjou, Louis XIV's grandson.

[101] Ibid., p. 34.

[102] Dennis, Preface to *Liberty Asserted* (1704), in Hooker (ed.), *The Critical Works of John Dennis*, I, p. 320.

[103] Quoted in J. O. Bartley, *Teague, Shenkin and Sawney: Being an Historical Study of the Earliest Irish, Welsh and Scottish Characters in English Plays* (Cork, 1954), p. 1.

Although the succession was of course disputed, the fact that most of Spain rallied to Philip V, as Anjou styled himself, meant that the English were now confronted by a dynastic alliance between the two great Catholic powers of Europe. In the same measure that Spain was once more a threat, Hispanophobia was given a new lease of life. A year after *Liberty Asserted*, Dennis sought to repeat his success with an attack on the Spanish in *Gibraltar: or, The Spanish Adventure*. This did not pretend to be anything other than a farce, but the same sort of stereotypes reappear: the brave, honest Englishman is confronted by treacherous, feeble foreigners. Its flavour can be easily conveyed in one brief exchange between a French officer, Fourbe (a 'deceitful person', in other words) and his Spanish comrade Guzman. It has been ordered that the Spanish and French armies should amalgamate, even to the extent of exchanging uniforms. This, needless to say, is the occasion for some heavy-handed comic business, and also for a parade of national characteristics:

FOURBE Why look you, this is a Fighting Age, and Fighting is the chief Business of it. Now let us see what you must do to Fight like a *Frenchman*, and I to fight like a *Spaniard*.

GUZMAN What, pray?

FOURBE Why, in the First Place, supposing you cudgel me, why for you to act like a *Frenchman*, and me to suffer like a *Spaniard*, you must cringe, do you see, while you cudgel me, and I must swagger, and look big while I am beaten.[104]

Dennis also took the opportunity to point to the danger from the enemy within by introducing an episode when two English colonels are mistaken for Irishmen, complete with much incomprehensible Irish brogue and references to Ireland as 'Bog-Land'.[105] Contempt was also extended to sexual matters, as the English prove to have an irresistible appeal to Spanish ladies. Sexual and military prowess are then combined with the final 'Chorus of English Tars':

In the soft Field of Love; or the rough Field of War,
There's no resisting an English Tar,
When we're at Sea, we the Tempest out-roar,
And we can thunder too, when we're on Shoar,
There's no resisting an English Tar,
Witness impregnable Gibraltar.[106]

104 John Dennis, *Gibraltar: or, The Spanish Adventure* (London, 1705), p. 20.
105 Ibid., p. 55.
106 Ibid., p. 70.

More significant perhaps was the hope expressed by Dennis that England's military victories would soon be repeated in the realm of culture. He predicted in the Prologue:

> As all th' Efforts of France were forc'd to yield
> To English Fire, and thought at Blenheim's Field;
> The Hour will one Day come that shall advance
> The British Muse o'er Foreign Song and Dance.[107]

The confident triumphalism of Dennis was countered by a pessimistic isolationism which viewed *all* foreign powers as cheats, whether avowed enemies or alleged allies. In *Law is a Bottomless-Pitt*, John Arbuthnot presented the War of the Spanish Succession as an interminable lawsuit. Strutt (Charles II of Spain) is persuaded by a cunning parson and an attorney to leave his estate to his cousin Philip Baboon (Philip V), to the great disappointment of his other cousin (the Archduke Charles of Austria). As the Strutt family had failed to pay its bills for a very long time, John Bull the clothier (Great Britain) and Nicholas Frog the draper (the Dutch Republic) presented their accounts to Philip Baboon when he inherited. Unfortunately, Philip had a rascally old uncle Lewis (Louis XIV) who persuaded him not to honour his inherited debts. Afraid that Philip would switch all his custom to Uncle Lewis, John Bull and Nicholas Frog took him to court. Like so many cases, the legal proceedings lasted very much longer than any of the parties had expected and ended with the ruin of all of them. This rather clumsy fable is interesting less for the satire than for the self-image of the English which Arbuthnot presents: a decent, worthy, industrious people, but too generous for their own good and too vulnerable to the guile of treacherous foreigners:

> *Bull*, in the main, was an honest plain-dealing Fellow, Cholerick, Bold, and of a very unconstant Temper, he dreaded not Old *Lewis* either at Back-Sword, single Faulcion, or Cudgel-play... *John* was quick, and understood his business very well, but no Man alive was more careless, in looking into his Accounts or more cheated by Partners, Apprentices, and Servants: This was occasioned by his being a Boon-Companion, loving his Bottle and his Diversion; for to say Truth, no Man kept a better House than *John*, nor spent his Money more generously.[108]

[107] Ibid., unpaginated prologue.

[108] [John Arbuthnot], *Law is a Bottomless-Pit. Exemplify'd in the Case of The Lord Strutt, John Bull, Nicholas Frog, and Lewis Baboon, who spent all they had in a Law-Suit. Printed from a Manuscript found in the Cabinet of the famous Sir Humphry Poleworth* (London, 1712), p. 10. The monkey usually stood for the French and the frog for the Dutch until the nineteenth century, when the frog was transferred to the former; Michael Duffy, *The English Satirical Print 1600–1832: The Englishman and the Foreigner* (Cambridge, 1986), p. 36.

The Treaty of Utrecht which brought the War of the Spanish Succession to an end in 1713 marked the end of the first round in the struggle for the control of the world outside Europe between France and Great Britain by transferring from the former to the latter Acadia (Nova Scotia), Newfoundland, and the Caribbean island of St Kitts. The British now controlled the entire Atlantic seaboard of North America, with the exception of Florida, and also claimed a vast swathe of territory to the south of Hudson Bay. In between were the French, whose first expedition to the St Lawrence river had been made as early as 1534 and who now controlled the river valley to the Great Lakes and beyond. As Dennis told his readers in his preface to *Liberty Asserted*: '*Canada* is a vast Tract of Land in *Northern America*, on the Back of *New England* and *New York*, and the Country about them belong to the *English*, a considerable part of Canada is possess'd by the *French*; and as the *English* and *French* divide the Country, they divide the Natives.'[109] More recently, the French had also laid claim to territory far to the south, at the mouth of the Mississippi, naming their new possession 'Louisiana' after their king and founding New Orleans in 1718. Their obvious strategy was to link up these new acquisitions with their older colonies in the north via the Mississippi and Ohio River valleys. It was in the latter that increasingly they collided with settlers from the British seaboard colonies moving west across the Appalachians in search of new land. By the 1730s it was clear that armed struggle was inevitable.

So was a war between Britain and Spain. As the latter had been ruled since 1700 by a junior branch of the Bourbons, an axis between Madrid and Versailles was only to be expected. Its formation was delayed for a generation by the adventurous policies of Philip V's wife, Elizabeth Farnese—so adventurous, indeed, that France actually joined Britain in a war against Spain in 1719. Spanish hostility to Britain was determined by the loss of Gibraltar and Minorca at the Peace of Utrecht in 1713 and by the obligation to allow the British to supply Spanish colonies in America with African slaves (the *asiento*). In the course of the 1730s war became increasingly likely, as growing numbers of enterprising and unscrupulous British merchants flouted Spanish commercial restrictions. A more specific bone of contention was the formal settlement of Georgia, which intensified disputes about the northern limits of Spanish Florida.[110]

The war that broke out between Britain and Spain in 1739 was quickly subsumed in the War of the Austrian Succession. The name given to the

[109] Dennis, Preface to *Liberty Asserted*, p. 323.
[110] Langford, *A Polite and Commercial People*, p. 50.

Anglo-Spanish phase—'The War of Jenkins' Ear'—is less portentous but is certainly revealing. The owner of the ear was Captain Robert Jenkins of the merchant marine, who displayed it, pickled in a jar, to a committee of the House of Commons in 1738. He claimed that it had been amputated by a sword swipe from a Spanish coastguard, who had boarded and looted his ship off Havana. Three times he had been hoisted to the yard-arm and allowed to fall to the deck in an early display of bungee-jumping, albeit with a non-elastic rope.[111] No matter that the alleged incident had occurred seven years earlier; together with other horror stories it was enough to galvanize British public opinion by triggering all those powerful anti-Spanish, anti-Catholic associations, from the Inquisition to the Armada. Hispanophobia had been given a recent impetus by the assistance from Spain to an abortive Jacobite invasion in 1719. The war party inside and outside Parliament made the most of popular indignation, pressuring a reluctant Walpole to declare war. No doubt political intrigue against the ageing prime minister (in office since 1721) had much to do with the campaign, and no doubt some of the anger was simulated: it does not matter. What the campaign showed was that public opinion was powerful and that public opinion was nationalist and xenophobe. In the nature of things, it is difficult to find truly spontaneous evidence from the lower reaches of society of this kind of collective emotion, so the following extract from a letter written to his wife by a common sailor pressed into service is especially valuable:

> When I left you hevens noes it was an akin hart to be hauld from you by a gang of rufins but hover soon i soon ovecome that when I found that we were about to go in ernest to rite my natif contry and against a parcel of impodent Spaniards by whom I have often been ill treted and god nows my hearrt I have longed this fore years to cut of some of their Ears, and was in hopes I should have sent you one for a sample now, but our good Admiral God bless him was to merciful we have taken Port Belo with such coridge and bravery that i never saw before, for my own Part my heart was raised to the clouds and would ha scaled the Moon had a Spaniard been there to come at him, as We did the Batry.[112]

The sailor was referring to the capture of Porto Bello (now Portobelo) on the Atlantic coast of Panama by a squadron commanded by Admiral Vernon. A great feat of arms, it unleashed celebrations across the length and breadth of

[111] Jean O. McLachlan, *Trade and Peace with Old Spain 1667–1750* (Cambridge, 1940), p. 106.

[112] Quoted in Gerald Jordan and Nicholas Rogers, 'Admirals as heroes: patriotism and liberty in Hanoverian England', *Journal of British Studies*, 28 (1989), p. 206.

the country in at least fifty-four towns and twenty-five counties in England and Scotland. The *Norwich Gazette* reported that at Wymondham in Norfolk a grand procession was organized, including a man on a horse representing Vernon and another on an ass representing the Spanish commander Don Blass. The spontaneity of the event was emphasized: 'the whole was the general sense and free Act of the People, being in no way promoted by any leading Gentlemen.'[113] In triumphalist vein, one of several poetical panegyrics of the admiral celebrated the inevitable victory of free-born Britons over superstitious slaves:

> He deem'd Men groaning under TYRANT-SWAY,
> By *lying Priests* debas'd, and led astray,
> To BRITONS, nurtur'd in the Martial Field,
> To LIBERTY, to TRUTH, of course must yield.[114]

Vernon duly entered what was already a well-stocked Pantheon of British naval heroes. In 1779 a French visitor found him represented at Vauxhall Gardens, together with other naval and military heroes such as Anson, Boscawen, Hawke, Clive, Wolfe, and Amherst.[115]

The war against Spain of 1739 soon also became a war against France. If Spain could still trigger ancient animosities, there was no doubt that France was now seen as the more threatening and the more odious. That was revealed by much contemporary rhetoric, not least by *Alfred*, a masque cum opera first performed in 1740, with a libretto by James Thomson and David Mallet and music by Thomas Arne. Inasmuch as it has a plot, it recounts an episode from the reign of the ninth-century king of Wessex who successfully resisted the Danish invasions. But its main object was to provide an opportunity for a modern call to arms. In Act II, scene iii, for example, a hermit inspires the hard-pressed Alfred by conjuring up spirits from the future, including such hammers of the French as Edward III and the Black Prince. The greatest hero of the future, however, is William III, for it was he who banished that two-headed monster superstition and absolutism (James II) and his crony 'vile Servility, that crouch'd and kiss'd the whip he trembled at'. The hermit sees the Glorious Revolution as the turning-point in English history:

[113] Kathleen Wilson, *The Sense of the People: Politics, Culture and Imperialism in England, 1715–1785* (Cambridge, 1995), p. 143.
[114] *A Poem on the Glorious Achievements of Admiral Vernon in the Spanish West Indies* (London, 1740).
[115] G. F. Coyer, *Nouvelles observations sur l'Angleterre par un voyageur* (Paris, 1779), pp. 109–10.

From this great hour
Shall *Britain* date her rights and laws restor'd:
And one high purpose rule her sovereign's heart;
To scourge the pride of *France*, that foe profess'd
To *England* and to Freedom.[116]

The message of *Alfred* may have been conventional, but its impact was exceptional, for the good reason that the music Arne composed for the closing chorus proved to have unrivalled power. On this occasion, at least, there is no need for a musical quotation, for the words of the refrain alone will be sufficient reminder of the melody:

Rule, Britannia, Britannia rule the waves;
Britons never will be slaves.[117]

In the theatre it makes obvious sense to bring the curtain down at the close of the final *fortissimo* reprise, but in the published version, Thomson and Mallet brought the hermit back for a final vision of the future. Among other things, he saw the formation of a great British empire:

Shores, yet unfound, arise! In youthful prime,
With towering forests, mighty rivers crown'd:
These stoop to *Britain's* thunder. This new world,
Shook to its centre, trembles at her name:
And there her sons with aim exalted, sow
The seeds of rising empire, arts, and arms.

Britons proceed, the subject Deep command,
Awe with your navies every hostile land.
Vain are their threats, their armies all are vain:
They rule the balanc'd world, who rule the main.[118]

[116] *The Works of James Thomson, with his last corrections and improvements*, 4 vols. (London, 1766), III, p. 244.

[117] Ibid., p. 253. In the version of 'Rule Britannia' published separately, the second verse runs:

The nations not so blest as thee
Must in their turn to tyrants fall,
While thou shalt flourish great and free,
The dread and envy of them all.

[118] Ibid., p. 255. On the permeation of Hanoverian culture by imperialist concerns, see Kathleen Wilson, 'Empire of Virtue. The imperial process and Hanoverian culture *c.* 1720–1785', in Lawrence Stone (ed.), *An Imperial State at War: Britain from 1689 to 1815* (London and New York, 1994), pp. 130–43.

It took some time for the hermit's optimistic prophecies to be fulfilled. When the War of the Austrian Succession ended at the Peace of Aachen in 1748, the world-historical jury had not yet reached its verdict on the struggle between Britain and France for control of the world outside Europe. The British had taken control of the Atlantic, capturing Louisburg, the key to the St Lawrence, in 1745, but the French had taken Madras in 1746 and had defeated Britain's Austrian allies in the Low Countries.[119] It had all been a messy—and very expensive—draw and, like all inconclusive wars, it produced a short-lived peace. In 1752 a new French governor of Canada, Duquesne, arrived with instructions to reassert possession of the Ohio Valley and thus the geographical link with Louisiana.[120] In 1754 he built a fort at the confluence of the Allegheny and Monongahela Rivers, which together form the Ohio River, and named it after himself. By that time an undeclared war was under way between France and Great Britain, and it could only be a matter of time before it became official.

Just as the colonial conflict between Britain and Spain became subsumed in a larger European conflict, so did the Anglo-French struggle for control of North America become part of the Seven Years War, which began in 1756. This proved to be the decisive moment. After an uncertain start, losing Minorca to the French in 1756, the British were triumphant on all fronts, especially in the *annus mirabilis* 1759. It confirmed the belief of many that God was on their side. As the Revd Edward Clarke put it in his sermon at a service of thanksgiving for naval victory:

> What nation under heaven has ever received greater, or more frequent deliverances, than we have at the Almighty's hands? The history of this island is too full of such providential interpositions, either for the unlearned not to know, or the unbeliever to deny them. There is no occasion now to appeal to old records; the events of the present war, nay of this one memorable year, are sufficient to convince us.[121]

No victory in 1759 was more important than that gained by General James Wolfe at Quebec on 13 September. It was this which conquered Canada, destroyed any hope of a French empire in North America and arguably also determined that eventually English, not French, would become the world

119 There is an excellent account of the war, its conclusion, and its significance in Derek McKay and H. M. Scott, *The Rise of the Great Powers 1648–1815* (London, 1983), pp. 171–7.

120 Patrice Higonnet, 'The origins of the Seven Years War', *Journal of Modern History*, 40 (1968), p. 66.

121 Edward Clarke, *A Thanksgiving Sermon preached at the Rolls-Chapel, December. 9, 1759. Being the Day appointed to return Thanks to ALMIGHTY GOD, for the Victory gained over the* French *Fleet, on the 20th of* November *last* (London, 1759), pp. 17–18.

language. It was an episode that found its artist, or rather artists, for they vied with each other to depict the death of the hero at the moment of victory.[122] What became the most celebrated of these representations was also probably the most successful British painting of the century (Plate 17). Appropriately enough, in view of the consequences of Wolfe's victory, it was painted by an American, Benjamin West, born near Springfield, Pennsylvania (Cardinal Albani, who was blind, assumed him to be a Red Indian when introduced).[123] His picture may have been 'a splendid fraud',[124] because it included in the scene people and objects not actually present, but there was nothing counterfeit about the response it evoked. A brilliant combination of idealism (the composition is based on the Mourning of Christ, specifically Van Dyck's *Deposition*) and realism (the characters wear contemporary dress), it marries the triumphalism of victory to the pathos of a patriotic death: *dulce et decorum est pro patria mori* is the message.[125] In Simon Schama's graphic description, it is 'a stupendous piece of drama: brilliance and gloom, victory and death, saintly sacrifice and inconsolable sorrow set side by side, the sunlit sky of the imperial future banishing the grim clouds of past dissatisfactions'.[126] First exhibited at the Royal Academy in 1771, the painting was famous by rumour even before it was accessible to the public and queues formed down Pall Mall. Indeed, it attracted more spectators than any other in the history of British art.[127] If that success tells us something about the public mood of mid-eighteenth-century England, the manner of its exploitation is also informative. West sold the original to Lord Grosvenor for the huge sum (by contemporary standards) of between £400 and £600, but the man who really got rich was the entrepreneur John Boydell, who bought the engraving rights for a few hundred pounds but had made £15,000 by 1790.[128] In the process, of course, he had transported West's image of Wolfe's *Siegestod* into thousands of British homes. He also pointed the way for other painters with an eye for market appeal. In the years that followed, a host of British heroes were celebrated and

[122] Joseph Burke, *English Art 1714–1800* (London, 1976), p. 245. According to J. Steven Watson, 'No event has probably ever been more celebrated on canvas than Wolfe's capture of Quebec'—*The Reign of George III 1760–1815* (Oxford, 1960), p. 86.

[123] Ellis Waterhouse, *Painting in England 1530–1790* (London, 1953), p. 191.

[124] Colley, *Britons*, p. 178.

[125] Burke, *English Art*, p. 246.

[126] Simon Schama, *Dead Certainties (Unwarranted Speculations)* (London, 1991), pp. 21–2.

[127] Ibid. Klaus Lankheit, *Revolution und Restauration* (Baden-Baden, 1965), p. 251.

[128] Louise Lippincott, 'Expanding on portraiture. The market, the public, and the hierarchy of genres in eighteenth century Britain', in Ann Bermingham and John Brewer (eds.), *The Consumption of Culture 1600–1800: Image, Object, Text* (London and New York, 1995), p. 79.

commemorated, first in a massive canvas designed for public display and then in engraved reproductions of the original. Another enterprising American, John Singleton Copley, hired the Great Room at Spring Gardens for the display of his vast depiction of *The Death of Chatham* in 1781. Twenty thousand people paid for admission and 2,500 subscribed to the engraving.[129]

COMMERCE

As we have seen, the creation of an English national identity linked Protestantism to hatred of Catholic foreigners and to imperial expansion. Binding the two was the growing conviction that the country had been singled out by Divine Providence for material prosperity, but was ringed by envious enemies. Sir John Fortescue's patronizing comments on English wealth and continental poverty, cited earlier,[130] were often echoed in the centuries that followed. At the beginning of the seventeenth century, for example, William Camden wrote: 'Britaine ... is well knowne to be the most flourishing and excellent, most renowmed [*sic*] and famous Isle of the whole world: So rich in commodities, so beautifull in situation, so resplendent in all glorie, that if the most Omnipotent had fashioned the world round like a ring, as hee did a globe, it might have beene most worthily the onely gemme therein.'[131] If Camden had lived a century or so later, his encomium might well have been even more enthusiastic, for economic progress was plain for all to see. In the course of the eighteenth century, the population of England and Wales increased by about three-quarters, agricultural production increased by almost half, and the merchant marine trebled.[132] And if the pace and incidence of the expansion of manufacturing is no longer deemed to merit the tag 'industrial revolution', it was sufficiently visible to impress contemporaries.[133]

Of all the sources of wealth, it was the advance of commerce which made the strongest and most widespread impression. Edward Young, better known as the author of *Night Thoughts*, crowed in 1730 that the world conspired to make England rich:

[129] Burke, *English Art*, p. 250.

[130] See above, p. 280.

[131] William Camden, *Remaines of a Greater Worke, concerning Britaine, the inhabitants thereof, their Languages, Names, Surnames, Impreses, Wise Speeches, Poësies and Epitaphes* (London, 1605), p. 1.

[132] Porter, *English Society in the Eighteenth Century*, pp. 204, 229; O'Gorman, *The Long Eighteenth Century*, p. 322.

[133] Langford, *A Polite and Commercial People*, p. 666.

Luxuriant Isle! What Tide that flows,
Or Stream that glides, or Wind that blows,
Or genial Sun that shines, or Show'r that pours,
But flows, glides, breathes, shines, pours for Thee?
How every Heart dilates to see
Each Land's each Season blending on thy Shores?

Others may traffick as they please;
Britain, fair Daughter of the Seas,
Is born for *Trade*; to plough her field, the Wave;
And reap the growth of every Coast:
A Speck of Land! but let her boast,
Gods gave the *World*, when they the *Waters gave*.

Britain! behold the World's wide face;
Not cover'd half with *solid* space,
Three parts are *Fluid*; Empire of the Sea!
And why? for Commerce. *Ocean* streams
For *that*, thro' all his various *names*:
And, if for *Commerce*, *Ocean* flows for Thee.[134]

It was a vision shared ten years later, in 1740, by the hermit in Thomson's *Alfred* in his final exhortation to the beleaguered Saxon king:

I see thy commerce, *Britain*, grasp the world:
All nations serve thee; every foreign flood,
Subjected pays its tribute to the *Thames*.[135]

The colonial victories of mid-century and the continuing expansion of commerce, which accelerated despite the loss of the American colonies, could only intensify this nationalist pride. Significantly, it was explained not in terms of mere Providence but was tied to a set of social and cultural values. In *The Complete English Tradesman* of 1726, for example, Daniel Defoe advanced the following self-evident propositions: 'I. We are not only a trading country, but the greatest trading country in the world. II. Our climate is the most agreeable climate in the world to live in. III. Our *Englishmen* are the stoutest and best men . . . in the world . . . because strip them naked from the waist upwards, and give them no weapons at all but their Hands and Heels, and turn them into a

[134] Edward Young, *Imperium Pelagi. A Naval Lyrick: written in imitation of Pindar's Spirit. Occasion'd by His Majesty's Return, September, 1729 and the succeeding Peace* (London, 1730), pp. 10, 28–9.
[135] *The Works of James Thomson*, vol. III, p. 255.

room, or stage, and lock them in with the like number of other men of any nation, man for man, and they shall beat the best men you shall find in the world.'[136] These pugilists (who sound as though they would be more at home in the world of Bulldog Drummond than that of Robinson Crusoe) derived their virility from their egalitarian ethos. Not for them the effeminate foppery of Frenchified aristocrats; what made them and their nation great was their positive attitude to trade. It was trade that had raised the nation to its most powerful position in the world since the glory days of Edward III or Elizabeth I. Defoe observed with pride that this was a pre-eminence recognized by the social hierarchy, as the great houses and estates of the merchant princes around London demonstrated. On the other hand, many of the greatest families owed their fortunes to trade and did not disdain to return to it or to marry merchants' daughters. Status followed money: 'It was a smart, but just repartee of a *London* tradesman, when a gentleman, *who had a good estate too*, rudely reproached him in company, and bad him hold his tongue, for he was no Gentleman; *No, Sir*, says he, but I can buy a Gentleman, and therefore I claim a liberty to speak among Gentlemen.' '*In short*,' Defoe concluded, 'trade in *England* makes Gentlemen, and has peopled this nation with Gentlemen.'[137]

This was an opinion repeated too often to be wishful thinking. Four years before Defoe published his book, Richard Steele expressed an almost identical opinion through the character of Mr Sealand in his play *The Conscious Lovers*: 'I know the Town and the World—and give me leave to say, that we Merchants are a species of Gentry, that have grown into the World this last Century, and are as honourable, and almost as useful, as you landed Folks, that have always thought yourselves so much above us.'[138] John Gay was more forceful in *The Distress'd Wife*:

Is the name then [of merchant] of Reproach?—Where is the Profession that is so honourable?—What is it that supports every Individual of our Country?—'Tis Commerce—On what depends the Glory, the Credit, the Power of the Nation?—On Commerce.—To what does the Crown itself owe its Splendor and Dignity?—To Commerce.'[139]

[136] Daniel Defoe, *The Complete English Tradesman, in Familiar Letters; Directing him in all the several Parts and Progressions of Trade* (London, 1726), pp. 369–70.

[137] Ibid., pp. 371–6. For further examples of praise of commerce, see Bonamy Dobrée. 'The theme of patriotism in the poetry of the early eighteenth century', *Proceedings of the British Academy*, 35 (1949), pp. 62–3.

[138] Quoted in Bonamy Dobrée, *English Literature in the Early Eighteenth Century 1700–1740* (Oxford, 1959), p. 3.

[139] Ibid.

As the Seven Years War began, the actor and playwright Theophilus Cibber reminded his audience that it was the merchants who were the mainstay of the British nation:

> Ye lordly Merchants of the *British* Main!
> Well may your Influence mend, and raise their Station;
> Since *Europe* knows, 'Tis you support our Nation.
> Free Trade the vital Streams of State supplies,
> And when that Course is stopt, the Body dies.[140]

Pride in the commercial prosperity of England was accentuated by the belief that the country's enemies were consumed by malicious envy. As Jonas Hanway, a founder-member of both the Handel Commemoration and the Marine Society (established to encourage young men to join the Royal Navy) put it: 'It is beyond dispute that they [the French] ever behold with envious eyes the bounties which heaven bestows on this nation, and are watchful of opportunities to *ravish* them from us.'[141] It was an emotion which found especially memorable expression in another example of dietary nationalism, one of Hogarth's most successful engravings—*O The Roast Beef of Old England, or The Gate of Calais* (Plate 15).[142] Across the centre of the picture staggers a kitchen porter, bearing a massive sirloin labelled 'For Mrs Grandsire of Calais', the owner of the port's English eating-house. It is watched with slavering gluttony by a fat friar and with amazement by two emaciated and ragged French soldiers, whose own pot of thin gruel (*soupe maigre*) is carried past in the opposite direction by servants wearing wooden clogs. The association of Catholicism, France, poverty, and poor victuals is strengthened by three further images: by the group of hideous French nuns worshipping the likeness of Christ they think they have found in the dead skate; by the religious procession glimpsed through the gateway, with worshippers kneeling before the Host in what Hogarth believed was an idolatrous fashion and with the Holy Spirit represented on an inn-sign; and by the sun falling on the English coat of arms and the cross above the gate, a reminder of the days when the town was the home of the true (Protestant) faith. Lest English beef-eaters become complacent, Hogarth posted two warnings. First, he illustrated the treachery of the enemy within, by depicting Irish and Scottish soldiers serving

[140] Theophilus Cibber, *Two Dissertations on the Theatres. With an appendix in Three Parts*, 2 vols (London, 1756), II, pp. 11–12.

[141] Jonas Hanway, *A Letter from a Member of the Marine Society, shewing the Piety, Generosity, and Utility of the Design, with respect to the Sea-Service, at this important Crisis. Addressed to all True Friends of their Country*, 2nd edn. (London, 1757), p. 4.

[142] The oil painting on which the engraving was based is now in the Tate Gallery, London.

the Catholic Stuart Pretender, albeit with deep remorse in the case of the Scot reduced to living on garlic. Secondly, he introduced an autobiographical note to stress the tyranny that threatened if vigilance were relaxed. Visiting France at the end of the War of the Austrian Succession, Hogarth had been imprisoned on suspicion of being a spy. In the picture we are shown the moment of his arrest, as the hand of the agent of French absolutism grasps his shoulder.[143] In his *Autobiographical Notes*, Hogarth recorded his outrage that within sight of the English coast there should be 'a farcical pomp of war, parade of riligion [*sic*] and Bustle with little very little business . . . in short poverty slavery and Insolence with an affectation of politeness.'[144] The association of beef with English liberty and virility was clearly popular. A French visitor to London in the 1730s saw a play in which 'the excellence and virtues of English beef were cried up, and the author maintain'd, that it was owing to the qualities of its juice that the English were so courageous, and had such a solidity of understanding, which rais'd them above all the nations in Europe; he preferred the noble old English pudding beyond all the finest ragouts that were ever invented by the greatest geniusses that France has produced; and all these ingenious strokes were loudly clapp'd by the audience.'[145] It was well known to English audiences that the French ate roots and herbs, the Dutch ate frogs and butter, and the Scots ate oats and haggis.[146]

One final example of this potent nationalist cocktail must suffice. Ten years later, in 1757, Tobias Smollett published his play *The Reprisal: or the Tars of Old England*. Heartly, a young gentleman from Dorset, his fiancée Harriet, and his servant Brush, are taken prisoner by a French ship, commanded by the foppish Champignon, who speaks a weird Franglais. Although war had not been formally declared, the English captives are robbed of all their possessions, with Captain Champignon leading the plundering. The cast includes, of course, an Irish and a Scottish sailor in the service of the French, 'Oclabber' and 'Maclaymore'. At least these renegades are given some positive characteristics, but Captain Champignon is an unredeemed villain, who contrives to be

[143] For interpretations of this picture, see Colley, *Britons*, pp. 33–4; Joseph Burke and Colin Caldwell, *Hogarth: The Complete Engravings* (London, 1968), in the unpaginated 'Notes on the plates'; and Ronald Paulson, *Hogarth: His Life, Art and Times*, 2 vols. (New Haven, 1971), vol. II, 75–8.

[144] Quoted in David Bindman, *Hogarth and his Times* (London, 1997), p. 83. For a good account of Hogarth's journey to and from Paris, see Jenny Uglow, *Hogarth* (London, 1997), pp. 462–7.

[145] Quoted in Duffy, *The Englishman and the Foreigner*, p. 35.

[146] Daniel Statt, *Foreigners and Englishmen: The Controversy over Immigration and Population, 1660–1760* (Newark, NJ, London, and Toronto, 1995), p. 192.

both amorous and effeminate, a coward and a bully. For his first appearance in Act I, scene iii, Smollett provides stage directions which suggest he might have had the Hogarth engraving in mind: 'A Procession. First, the bag-pipe—then a ragged, dirty sheet for the French colours—a file of soldiers in tatters—the English prisoners—the plunder, in the midst of which is an English buttock of beef carried on the shoulders of four meagre Frenchmen. The drum followed by a crew of French sailors.' The captain of the English rescue ship, Lyon, proclaims in his final speech: 'While France uses us like friends, we will return her civilities: when she breaks her treaties and grows insolent, we will drub her over to her good behaviour.' It all ends happily, with a rousing chorus:

While British oak beneath us rolls,
And English courage fires our souls;
To crown our toils the fates decree
The wealth and empire of the sea.[147]

LIBERTY AND PATRIOTISM

Protestantism, power, and prosperity went together, but they would have counted for nothing in the eyes of contemporaries if they had not been underpinned by a fourth national asset: liberty. As Oliver Goldsmith proclaimed: 'Hail Britain, happiest of countries! happy in thy climate, fertility, situation and commerce; but still happier in the peculiar nature of thy laws and government.'[148] Not the least peculiar British characteristic was the link between power, prosperity, and liberty provided by Parliament. In the words of Carteret: 'The Security of our Liberties are [*sic*] not in the Laws but by the Purse being in the Hands of the People.'[149] Limitation of fiscal power might seem to militate against the extraction of revenue, but in reality it proved to be a great asset. To make a fiscal system work efficiently, a 'credible commitment' is needed to encourage taxpayers to pay willingly, and to achieve that, the state must generate trust by 'constraining Leviathan'.[150] The British taxation

[147] Tobias Smollett, *The Reprisal: or the Tars of Old England* (London, 1757).

[148] Oliver Goldsmith, 'A comparative view of races and nations', first published in the *Royal Magazine* (1760), reprinted in *The Collected works of Oliver Goldsmith*, ed. Arthur Friedman, vol. III (Oxford, 1966), here pp. 67–8.

[149] Quoted in John Brewer, *The Sinews of Power: War, Money and the English State 1688–1783* (New York, 1989), p. v.

[150] Martin Daunton, *The Ransom of Property: The Politics of Taxation in Britain, 1793–1914* (Cambridge, 2001), ch. 1.

system achieved this by being public, accountable, and transparent. (Significantly, the greatest failure of the state in the eighteenth century was its inability to convince the American colonists that the increased commitment called for after the Seven Years War was credible.) So the British state was able to extract large and growing amounts of money from its taxpayers without provoking political crises. As the French controller-general of finance, Jacques Necker, observed, it was not that the British were more timid, rather that taxation was viewed as a legitimate part of parliamentary government.[151] Both the new land tax, which grew out of the 'Aid' of 1692, and the increasingly important excise and customs revenues were subject to parliamentary approval and control.[152]

Parliament also made possible the other great fiscal asset of the British state—its ability to raise very large sums of money at moderate rates of interest. The Stuarts had found that a king's personal creditworthiness was strictly limited. In 1671, for example, an impecunious Charles II had repudiated unilaterally payments due on £1,300,000 worth of government securities, wrecking in the process the monarchy's credit rating.[153] What was needed was the depersonalizing of public credit. It was provided by the creation of the Bank of England in 1694, by which a City syndicate was incorporated by Act of Parliament to lend the government £1,200,000 raised from 1,268 investors. Crucially, the annual interest payments of 8 per cent were guaranteed by Parliament.[154] Thus began the creation of a properly managed national debt, whose collateral was nothing less than the landed and commercial wealth of the country itself, represented in Parliament. Gradually, the political nation came to lose its anxiety about the accumulating burden of debt and to see it as a safe and rewarding source of investment. By the middle of the eighteenth century there were some 60,000 public creditors, a number which had grown to around half a million by the end of the century.[155] Helped further by bureaucratization and the elimination of tax-farming and venality, the British military-fiscal state[156] was able to overcome its demographic inferiority

[151] Brewer, *Sinews of Power*, pp. 132–3.

[152] For the importance of the growing share of indirect revenue, see two very informative articles by Peter Mathias: 'Concepts of Revolution in England and France in the eighteenth century', *Studies in Eighteenth Century Culture*, XIV (1985), pp. 29–46, and (with P. K. O'Brien), 'Taxation in Britain and France 1715–1810', *Journal of European Economic History*, 5 (1976), pp. 601–50.

[153] Wilfrid Prest, *Albion Ascendant: English History 1660–1815* (Oxford, 1998), p. 85.

[154] Ibid.

[155] H. V. Bowen, *War and British Society 1699–1915* (Cambridge, 1998), p. 33.

[156] 'The creation of... "the fiscal-militarystate" was the most important transformation in English government between the domestic reforms of the Tudors and the major administrative

against France by raising a disproportionate percentage of its population for the armed forces. The participation rate of men of military age increased from 1 in 16 during the War of the Austrian Succession, to 1 in 10 in the Seven Years War, to 1 in 8 in the War of American Independence, to 1 in 5 or 6 during the French Revolutionary Wars.[157]

Yet this massive expansion in the power of the state was not accompanied by an erosion of personal or parliamentary freedom. On the contrary, the belief that liberty was a British monopoly was quite unshakeable, sustained by a pride in Parliamentary institutions that was matched only by an aversion to the absolutism believed to prevail on the continent. Even Justus Möser, an intelligent and well-informed German observer who knew England well, was exasperated by the majestic complacency of its people. They were 'prisoners of liberty', he observed, so insular in their attitudes and blinkered in their vision that foreign countries were viewed as so many circles of hell. The French were derided as 'slaves who dance in their chains', the Germans pitied as bovine beasts of burden.[158] So deeply imbedded was this conviction by the constitutional conflicts of the previous century that it could resist any amount of contrary information and opinion. Protestantism and liberty went hand in hand, supporting both imperial expansion and economic dynamism. Eighteenth-century literature at every level teems with examples, but one example of the importance attached to the right of public debate must suffice. In 1740, as another war against the 'continental despotisms' was getting under way, a pamphleteer wrote:

> The People of Britain in general have an undubitable Right to Canvass publick affairs, to express their sentiments freely, and to declare their sense of any grievances under which they labour, treating political subjects freely in print, and thereby submitting them to the view and censure of the Nation in general, is so far from being dangerous that it is really conducive to the Publick Peace. By this means, all Degrees of People, who have leisure and abilities, and a turn to this sort of reading, acquire rational ideas of liberty and submission, of the rights of the church, and of the power of the State, and of their duties as subjects, and of what they may justly claim as *Freemen*.[159]

changes in the first half of the nineteenth century'—Brewer, *Sinews of Power*, p. xvii. On the development of the bureaucracy, see also John Brewer, 'The eighteenth century British state. Contexts and issues', in Lawrence Stone (ed.), *An Imperial State at War: Britain from 1689 to 1815* (London and New York, 1994), pp. 59–69.

[157] Bowen, *War and British Society*, p. 14.

[158] Justus Möser, *Briefe*, ed. Ernst Beins and Werner Pleister (Hanover, 1939), p. 147. The letter in question was written to Thomas Abbt from London on 12 May 1764.

[159] Quoted in Wilson, *The Sense of the People*, p. 43.

A free state, it was held, was both supported by and helped to create a true culture. No eighteenth-century writer was more eloquent or influential on this point than Anthony Ashley Cooper, third Earl of Shaftesbury, whose collected essays—*Characteristicks of Men, Manners, Opinions, Times*—were published in 1711, two years before his death. His hugely influential project was nothing less than the legitimation of the post-1688 Whig regime.[160] Writing during the War of the Spanish Succession, when the world was once more threatened with 'a Universal Monarchy, and a new Abyss of Ignorance and Superstition',[161] Shaftesbury was especially sensitive to the interaction between political and cultural achievement. In particular, he was convinced that public virtue could not exist under an absolutist system:

A PUBLICK Spirit can come only from a social Feeling or *Sense of Partnership* with Human Kind. Now there are none so far from being *Partners* in this *Sense*, or Sharers in this *common Affection*, as they who scarcely know *an Equal*, nor consider themselves as subject to any Law of *Fellowship* or *Community*. And thus Morality and good Government go together. There is no real Love of Virtue, without Knowledge of *Publick Good*. And where Absolute Power is, there is no PUBLICK.[162]

In a later essay he went further, arguing that absolutism also precluded patriotism, of all emotions 'the noblest and most becoming human Nature'.[163] In a polity whose subjects were held together only by force, there could be no true sense of community, for 'Absolute Power annuls *the Publick*. And where there is no *Publick*, or *Constitution*, there is in reality no *Mother*-COUNTRY, or NATION.'[164] Although Shaftesbury was a Deist who had moved beyond Protestantism, he stressed that England's fortunes had only taken a turn for the better at the Reformation. Under Henry VII, in his opinion, England had been little better than Poland, wracked by civil strife and subject to the priests at home and the Pope abroad.[165] But there was still a long way to go. He was under no illusions about the current state of the creative arts in England, still very much in their infancy: 'They have hitherto scarce arriv'd to any thing of

160 Lawrence Klein, *Shaftesbury and the Culture of Politeness: Moral Discourse and Cultural Politics in Early Eighteenth Century England* (Cambridge, 1994), p. 1. This is by far the most lucid and cogent analysis of Shaftesbury's ideas.

161 Anthony Ashley Cooper, third Earl of Shaftesbury, *Soliloquy: or Advice to an Author* (London, 1710), p. 64.

162 Anthony Ashley Cooper, third Earl of Shaftesbury, '*Sensus communis*; an Essay on the Freedom of Wit and Humour', in *Characteristicks of Men, Manners, Opinions, Times*, 3 vols., 2nd edn. (London, 1724), vol. I, pp. 106–7.

163 'Miscellaneous Reflections', in ibid., vol. II, p. 143.

164 Ibid.

165 Ibid., pp. 150–1.

Shapeliness or [*sic*] Person. They lisp as in their Cradles: and their stammering Tongues, which nothing but their Youth and Rawness can excuse, have hitherto spoken in wretched Pun and Quibble.'[166] Indeed, Shaftesbury was too much the urban aristocrat to appreciate even the great names of Elizabethan and Jacobean drama. Shakespeare, Jonson, Fletcher, and Milton, he conceded, had asserted 'Poetick Liberty' by discarding 'the horrid Discord of jingling Rhyme', but they were very much diamonds in the rough.[167]

In this last respect, he anticipated Frederick the Great's notorious critique of German literature,[168] also feeling that, like Moses, he had been allowed to see the promised land from afar but was denied entry. For Shaftesbury had no time for the superior polish of Louis XIV's classicism. Certainly the French had taken far more trouble to seek correct proportions and stylistic grace and had been particularly successful in raising 'their Stage to as great Perfection, as the Genius of their Nation will permit'. But their best efforts were foiled inevitably by their fundamentally flawed political structure: 'the high Spirit of *Tragedy* can ill subsist where the *Spirit of Liberty* is wanting.'[169] That was the lesson taught by the fate of the Romans: no sooner had they emerged from barbarism under the tutelage of the Greeks than they began to subjugate the rest of the world, thus condemning their culture to decadence. Shaftesbury might well have used that cautionary tale to signal the dangers of British imperial expansion, but he trusted in liberty to serve as an antidote to overvaulting ambition:

> We are now in an Age when LIBERTY is once again in its Ascendant. And we are ourselves the happy Nation, who not only enjoy it at home, but by our Greatness and Power give Life and Vigour to it abroad; and are the Head and Chief of the EUROPEAN *League*, founded on this *common Cause*. Nor is it to be fear'd that we shou'd lose this noble Ardour, or faint under the glorious Toil; tho, like antient GREECE, we shou'd for successive Ages be contending with a foreign Power, and endeavouring to reduce the Exorbitancy of a *Grand Monarch*.[170]

Shakespeare may have been too 'rude' for Shaftesbury's sophisticated palate, but he proved to be very much to the taste of the next generation—and indeed every generation which followed. Significantly, the first writer to describe Shakespeare as a genius was John Dennis, the author of *Liberty Asserted*,[171] who in 1712 published a pamphlet entitled *Essay on the Genius and Writings of Shakespear*.[172] Lichtenberg observed on a visit to England in 1775: 'Shake-

[166] Shaftesbury, *Soliloquy*, p. 63.
[167] Ibid., p. 64.
[168] See above, p. 217.
[169] Shaftesbury, *Soliloquy*, p. 65.
[170] Ibid., p. 69.
[171] See above, p. 291.
[172] Jonathan Bate, *The Genius of Shakespeare* (London, 1997), p. 166.

speare is not only famous but sacred; his moral maxims are heard everywhere.'[173] As Michael Dobson has observed, it was no coincidence 'that Shakespeare was declared to rule world literature at the same time that Britannia was declared to rule the waves'.[174] In his choice of subject-matter, use of language, and flagrant disregard of the classical unities most recently codified by the French academician Nicolas Boileau, Shakespeare was held to personify the genius of England. Banished from the stage during the Commonwealth and derided as a primitive during the Restoration, it was not until the eighteenth century that Shakespeare achieved his due status as a national icon, symbolized by the erection of a monument in Westminster Abbey in 1737.[175] It was a process that owed much to a growing resentment of the imitation of foreign fashions. There was more than a touch of class envy here, for it was only the highest reaches of polite society who could afford to go on the Grand Tour. In *Lethe; or, Esop in the Shades*, first performed in 1740, a 'FINE GENTLEMAN' described his three-year sojourn on the continent as follows:

> Sir, I learnt drinking in Germany, music and painting in Italy, dancing, gaming, and some other amusements at Paris, and in Holland—faith, nothing at all. I brought over with me the best collection of Venetian ballads, two eunuchs, a French dancer, and a monkey, with toothpicks, pictures and burlettas. In short, I have skimmed the cream of every nation, and have the consolation to declare I never was in any country in my life but I have taste enough thoroughly to despise my own.[176]

Significantly, the author of this farce was Shakespeare's greatest champion, the actor and playwright David Garrick. Although in this extract he satirized several nationalities, his main target was the French. In the same play, a Frenchman wishing to drink the waters of Lethe is horrified to learn that Aesop does not speak French. Asked for his credentials, he replies:

> FRENCHMAN Sir, I am a marquis François, j'entens les Beaux Arts, Sir, I have been an avanturie all over the varld, and am à present en Angleterre, in Ingland, vere I am more honoré and caress den ever I was in my own countrie, or inteed any vere else.

173 Quoted in Francesca M. Wilson (ed.), *Strange Island: Britain through Foreign Eyes 1395–1940* (London, 1955), p. 111.

174 Michael Dobson, *The Making of a National Poet: Shakespeare, Adaptation, and Authorship, 1660–1769* (Oxford, 1992), p. 7.

175 Ibid., pp. 18, 138.

176 *The Plays of David Garrick*, ed. Harry William Pedicord and Frederick Louis Bergmann, vol. 1 (Carbondale and Edwardsville, Ill., 1980), p. 12.

AESOP And pray, Sir, what is your business in England?

FRENCHMAN I am arrivé dere, Sir, pour polir la nation. De Inglis, Sir, have too much a lead in deir head and too much a tought in deir head. So, Sir, if I can lighten bote, I shall make dem tout à fait Francois and quite anoder ting.

AESOP And pray, Sir, in what particular accomplishments does your merit consist?

FRENCHMAN Sir, I speak de French, j'ai bonne addresse, I dance un Minuet, I sing des littel chansons, and I have—une tolerable assurance. En fin, Sir, my merit consist in one vard. I am foreignere, and entre nous, vile de Englis be so great a fool to love de foreignere better dan themselves, de foreignere vould still be more great a fool did dey not leave deir own counterie vere dey have noting at all, and come to Inglande vere dey vant for noting at all, perdie. Cela, n'est il pas vrai, Monsieur Aesope?[177]

This provides as good an illustration as one could wish of how the English chose to view French culture. Yet Garrick's satire was directed as much against the cultural renegades among his fellow countrymen. To them he proclaimed the virtues of Shakespeare, 'this astonishing genius' who was 'the greatest dramatic poet in the world'.[178] Those lines are taken from the preface to the ode Garrick wrote for the great Shakespeare Jubilee, which he organized at Stratford-on-Avon in 1769. To give his panegyric more point, Garrick planted an actor in the audience to play the part of an aristocratic fop corrupted by the Grand Tour, who proceeded to denounce Shakespeare as crude, overrated, and in the worst of provincial taste. It was in reply to this onslaught that Garrick then declaimed his Ode in defence of the Bard.[179] The Jubilee was clearly not an unqualified success, as bad weather, a shortage of accommodation, and traditional English *Schadenfreude* took their toll, but Garrick's performance was acknowledged to be a triumph and the greatest performance of his career. In the words of the Jubilee's historian: 'The importance of the Jubilee in the history of Shakespeare's reputation can hardly be exaggerated. It marks the point at which Shakespeare stopped being regarded as an increasingly popular and admirable dramatist, and became a god.'[180] Garrick also adapted the proceedings for performance in the theatre, scoring a brilliant and sustained success.[181] Not the least interesting aspect of the stage version was his decision to present the events of the Stratford Jubilee through the eyes of an uncom-

[177] Ibid., p. 16.

[178] David Garrick, *An Ode upon Dedicating a Building and Erecting a Statue to Shakespeare, at Stratford upon Avon* (London, 1769), unpaginated preface.

[179] Dobson, *The Making of a National Poet*, p. 215.

[180] Christian Deelman, *The Great Shakespeare Jubilee* (London, 1964), pp. 6, 217.

[181] Brewer, *The Pleasures of the Imagination*, p. 328.

KING ALFRED'S COLLEGE
LIBRARY

prehending 'Captain O'Shoulder', described simply as 'Irishman', who cannot even pronounce the name of Shakespeare correctly.[182]

The apotheosis of Shakespeare marked the emergence of a more vigorous assertion of English cultural value, if not superiority. As Gerald Newman has pointed out, the third quarter of the century witnessed the creation of a number of national institutions and projects designed to consolidate this feeling: the Society of Antiquaries (1751), the Society for the Encouragement of Arts, Manufactures and Commerce of London (1754), Dr Johnson's *Dictionary of the English Language* (1755), the *Encyclopædia Britannica* (1768), the Royal Academy of Arts (1768), and the first histories of English poetry (1744–81), painting (1762–80), and music (1775–89).[183] The impetus was maintained by the confidence engendered by the victories of the Seven Years War, the resentment excited by the well-publicized French disdain for British culture (Voltaire's attack on the Shakespeare Jubilee, for example),[184] and the social edge injected by the cultural treason of the cosmopolitan elites. And perhaps a sneaking sense of continuing French influence lent added stridency to its rejection. As Martin Sherwood neatly put it in 1781:

> French follies, universally embrac'd,
> At once provoke our mirth, and form our taste.[185]

The admission of Shakespeare to the national pantheon provides an instructive example of the 'British way' of absorbing potentially disruptive forces into the establishment, for those who first took up his cause came from the opposition camp. It was Lord Cobham who began the process by installing Shakespeare in his 'Temple of British Worthies' at his Buckinghamshire seat at Stowe in 1733, together with fifteen other heroes of British liberty, including Alfred the Great, Elizabeth I, John Milton, John Hampden, and William of Orange. The plan to install a monument to Shakespeare in Westminster Abbey four years later was a continuation of this project, with the same architect (William Kent) and the same sculptor (Peter Scheemakers).[186] That this initiative came neither from the king nor his government was made explicit in a new prologue written for a benefit performance of *Julius Cæsar*, which spelt out the contemporary message:

[182] Dobson, *The Making of a National Poet*, p. 220.
[183] Gerald Newman, *The Rise of English Nationalism* (London, 1987), p. 112.
[184] [J. J. Rutledge] *The Englishman's Fortnight in Paris, or, The art of ruining himself there in a few days*. By an observer (London, 1777), pp. iii–x.
[185] Quoted in Newman, *The Rise of English Nationalism.*, p. 39.
[186] Dobson, *The Making of a National Poet*, pp. 136–8.

While Brutus bleeds for liberty and Rome
Let Britons crowd to deck his Poet's tomb.
To future times recorded let it stand,
This head was lawrel'd by the *publick* hand.[187]

For the first half of the eighteenth century, 'patriotism' and its cognates formed part of opposition rhetoric and ideology.[188] Of course it implied the assertion of national interests against hostile foreigners, but its domestic implications were just as, if not more important. A patriot at home placed the interests of the country above any selfish concern for political preferment and resisted the seductive wiles of government managers offering pensions or places. It was a 'country' programme which opposed an ideal of virtuous, clean-living independence to the corruption of the court and its absolutist tendencies.[189] More specifically, it meant opposition to Sir Robert Walpole, whose two decades in office (1721–42) were attributed by disappointed rivals to his corrupt exploitation of royal patronage. At a time when organized opposition was universally frowned on, the language of patriotism, with its heavy stress on selfless virtues, provided politicians excluded from power with a convenient source of legitimacy. So the plays, poems, and operas that proclaimed the majesty of the nation were often also directed against domestic enemies. In his five-part poem 'Liberty' of 1735–6 James Thomson identified the target:

Unblest by VIRTUE, Government a League
Becomes, a circling junto of the Great,
To rob by law…
By those THREE VIRTUES be the frame sustain'd
Of BRITISH FREEDOM: INDEPENDENT LIFE;
INTEGRITY IN OFFICE; and o'er all
Supreme, A PASSION FOR THE COMMON-WEAL.[190]

When he came to write *Alfred* five years later, he gave the hermit not only a vision of Britannia's bounds being ever wider set but also of a purer polity:

[187] Ibid., p. 138.

[188] It was not, however, anti-Hanoverian. This has been strongly argued by Christine Gerrard in *The Patriot Opposition to Walpole: Politics, Poetry, and National Myth 1725–1742* (Oxford, 1994), esp. pp.12–13, 117, 232.

[189] Marie Peters, *Pitt and Popularity: The Patriot Minister and London Opinion during the Seven Years War* (Oxford, 1980), pp. 25–7; Hugh Cunningham, 'The language of patriotism', in Raphael Samuel (ed.), *Patriotism: The Making and Unmaking of British National Identity.* Vol. 1: *History and Politics* (London and New York, 1989), p. 58.

[190] Ibid., vol. II, p. 153.

Led by these spirits friendly to this isle,
I liv'd thro' future ages; felt the virtue,
The great, the glorious passions that will fire
Distant posterity: when guardian laws
Are by the patriot in the glowing senate
Won from corruption; when th' impatient arm
Of liberty, invincible, shall scourge
The tyrants of mankind—and when the deep,
Thro all her swelling waves, shall proudly joy
Beneath the boundless empire of thy sons.[191]

So what the country needed was a king who would perform two interrelated tasks—cleanse the Augean Stables of 'Old Corruption' at home, and promote the national interest abroad. The latter was held to involve abandoning the partiality shown for their Hanoverian electorate by George I and George II in favour of the pursuit of a 'blue-water' strategy concentrating on the navy and colonial expansion.[192] As Bolingbroke, the most eloquent publicist of the group, expressed it in 1738, with a 'patriot king' Britain could increase her wealth and power at a rate faster than any of her rivals.[193] A year previously, the opposition had been given fresh hope after all their long years in the political wilderness by the spectacular breach between George II and his eldest son and heir, Frederick, Prince of Wales. The latter had been left behind in Hanover in 1714, not moving to England until 1728. He soon showed that he possessed the presentational skills so sorely lacking in his father and grandfather. Thomas Rundle noted approvingly:

> He is one universally beloved in town... He knows how to familiarise his greatness, and make it more amiable, without making it less awful. He is sprightly beyond all things; and is above the mean-spirited sullenness that often hath been mistaken for majesty; and he seems to think the way to be beloved is to shew in reality good qualities, instead of requiring people to believe that he hath them.[194]

He appreciated the importance of gesture politics, for example, throwing open the windows at Kensington to allow the public to enjoy his concerts, or demonstratively assisting in putting out a fire in the City, or erecting a statue

[191] *The Works of James Thomson*, vol. III, pp. 233–4.
[192] Peters, *Pitt and Popularity*, pp. 25–6.
[193] [Henry Saint John, first Viscount Bolingbroke], 'The Idea of a Patriot King', in *Letters on the Spirit of Patriotism; on the Idea of a Patriot King; and On the State of Parties at the Accession of George I* (London, 1749), p. 187. The introduction of 'The Idea of a Patriot King' is dated 1 December 1738.
[194] Quoted in Gerrard, *The Patriot Opposition to Walpole*, p. 195.

of Alfred the Great in the garden of his town house, and so on.[195] To woo the 'reversionary interest' was an obvious tactic, especially as the King was 54 years old in 1737. Lord Cobham had already made obeisance in this direction by including Edward the Black Prince [of Wales] in his patriotic Temple of British Worthies. Frederick returned the compliment by commissioning James Thomson and David Mallet to write *Alfred*, which was first performed at his country seat at Cliveden in 1740. Bolingbroke, who had dedicated *The Idea of a Patriot King* to the Prince, contributed a substantial ode to the closing scene.[196]

Alas, the optimistic visions of the hermit in *Alfred* were not fulfilled, or at least not those which related to the fortunes of the Prince of Wales. Ever obstinate, George II survived until 1760, outliving his son by nine years. Nor did the patriot programme make much progress. Walpole fell in 1742, but there was no major change of ministerial personnel or of measures. Bolingbroke never did regain public office and his idea for a patriot king stayed just that. A colonial war was fought against Spain and France after 1739, but George II had more than enough authority to give priority to the continental campaign. Indeed, it was his overriding concern to protect Hanover, through a convention of neutrality with France in October 1741, that helped to bring down Walpole.[197] As the War of Jenkins' Ear merged into the War of the Austrian Succession, it still seemed likely that patriotism would remain the ideology of opposition.

In contemporary France, as we shall see in the final chapter, that association was to erode the Bourbon monarchy's legitimacy. The Hanoverians escaped a similar fate, partly by luck and partly through their own efforts. Not the least of their assets was their ability to resist the temptation to indulge in the sort of baroque representational display which had made the Stuarts so unpopular. Although the court remained important as the interface between crown, government, and aristocracy, it never aspired to the pivotal status asserted by Versailles or the other continental courts.[198] George I was very much a private man, temperamentally averse to the bustle of court life, disliking fuss and ostentation and preferring a simple life alone or with a few intimates, tended

[195] Ibid.; Alan D. McKillop, 'The early history of Alfred', *Philological Quarterly*, 41, 1 (1962), p. 312.

[196] Jonathan Keates, 'Thomas Arne's *Alfred*: an opera born of patronage and patrotism', *BBC Music Magazine* (June 1997), pp. 9–10.

[197] O'Gorman, *The Long Eighteenth Century*, p. 84.

[198] R. O. Bucholz, *The Augustan Court: Queen Anne and the Decline of Court Culture* (Stanford, Calif., 1993), p. 35.

by his two Turkish servants, Mohammed and Mustapha.[199] Handicapped by his rudimentary knowledge of the English language, his ignorance of English conditions (he did not even know the ranks of the peerage when he arrived) and his lack of physical stature, he was both unable and unwilling to impose his personality on high society. As a result, the long-standing trend towards the strict separation of public and private in the life of the monarch was strengthened.[200]

In any event, the English court lacked an architectural framework comparable with even a middling continental state. The main London palace, Whitehall, had been destroyed by fire in 1697 and had not been rebuilt. Everyone recognized the need for a new royal palace and many plans were drawn up, but nothing was actually done. St James's Palace was not an adequate replacement, consisting of a maze of small rooms; as Daniel Defoe observed in 1734: 'so far from having one single beauty to recommend it, 'tis at once the contempt of foreign nations and the disgrace of our own.'[201] Although he commissioned important interior alterations at Kensington Palace, including a grand staircase hall decorated by William Kent, and major refurbishment at Hampton Court (the two residences visited by the court in spring and summer), George as a builder compared unfavourably with many minor German princes. In the crushing verdict of Sir John Plumb, he was 'very stupid and lacking interest in the arts, save music'.[202]

Even if he had possessed the same urge to display as his continental colleagues, George would have found it very difficult to find the necessary resources. After the unhappy experience of the Stuarts, the English Parliament was notoriously averse to financing anything that smacked of continental absolute monarchy. The long struggle against Louis XIV's France had completed the association in English minds between representational display and foreign tyranny, so there was little prospect that funds would be voted for anything remotely resembling Versailles. Sir Robert Walpole was of the opinion that rebuilding Whitehall would have pleased the British public,[203]

[199] John M. Beattie, in *The English Court in the Reign of George I* (Cambridge, 1967), p. 257, maintains that George I slipped in after dark when he first arrived in London on 20 September 1714, but this is directly contradicted by Christine Gerrard, who has written that the 'triumphal entry' lasted three hours, to allow due respects to be paid—*The Patriot Opposition to Walpole*, pp. 192–3.

[200] Ibid., pp. 11–12.

[201] Quoted in ibid., p. 9.

[202] J. H. Plumb, *The First Four Georges* (London, 1956), p. 59. For a kinder account of George I's activities as patron of the arts, see Ragnhild Hatton, *George I* (London, 1978), ch. 9.

[203] Ibid., p. 156.

but it may be doubted whether there would have been any enthusiasm for a great palace outside London on a green-field site. With public financing uncertain, any building scheme would have to be financed by the only funds directly under royal control—the Civil List. It had been only during the reign of William and Mary that a distinction had been recognized between public expenditure on such objects as the army and the fleet and the costs of the royal household. In 1697 the first Civil List Act had granted William III £700,000 a year 'for the service of his Household and family and for other his necessary expenses and occasions' [*sic*].[204] In the event, less than two-thirds of that sum had actually been paid. In 1715 George was granted the same amount, but steps were taken to ensure that it was paid in full. Even so, after £100,000 had been deducted for the separate establishment of the Prince of Wales, there was precious little left for ostentatious display. Although Sir Robert Walpole secured £800,000 per annum for George II, together with the surplus revenues from the allocated sources, no Hanoverian was ever in a position to emulate their continental colleagues.

This did not mean that there was no court at all.[205] It was always the centre of royal patronage, which remained considerable, whether it was peerages, promotions, or offices that were sought. The needy and the greedy flocked to St James's or Kensington Palace to pay their respects and to solicit favours. When the kings fell out with their eldest sons, as the Hanoverians invariably did, they found themselves confronted by a rival court centred around the 'reversionary interest', located at Leicester House under the first two Georges and Carlton House under the third. Then it became necessary for the king to try harder, to compete to hold the attention of the courtiers and prevent them migrating to the rival establishments, where they could wait for the next reign to bring them rewards. In the autumn of 1717, for example, following the Whig split and the spectacular rift with his son, George was obliged to make his court more welcoming, among other things holding three 'drawing-rooms' a week.[206] So a virtue was made out of necessity and a frugal but functional court emerged, which proved to be well suited to a parliamentary monarchy.

As the court played such a modest role in the social and cultural life of the capital, the peerage and gentry were obliged to organize their own

[204] Beattie, *The English Court in the Reign of George I*, p. 106.

[205] For a characteristically trenchant view that the court was the centre of the political world during the eighteenth century, see J. C. D. Clark (ed.), *The Memoirs and Speeches of James, 2nd Earl of Waldegrave 1742–1763* (Cambridge, 1988), pp. 2–4.

[206] Ibid., p. 267.

entertainment. Yet if they were denied the delights of Versailles, they benefited from the far greater variety of public pleasures on offer in London. This was partly a result of size: in absolute terms, London was a third more populous than Paris and relatively much more so, for while the latter's share of the national population held steady at around 2.5 per cent, London's grew from about 7 per cent in 1650 to 11 per cent a century later. It has been estimated that in the eighteenth century one in ten of the adult population of England lived in London and that one in six gained first-hand experience of the city at some point during their lives.[207] It was also due, however, to the far greater degree of political and cultural liberty which prevailed there. Unlike Paris, this great metropolis was home to numerous self-governing corporations and a correspondingly vigorous political public sphere. The City of London was a self-governing municipality with a franchise embracing all the 12,000–15,000 'freemen'.[208] The four parliamentary constituencies of Westminster, the City, Southwark, and Middlesex all had generous franchises (12,000, 7,000–8,000, 2,000, and 3,000–4,000 respectively) which allowed genuinely popular participation in the political process, albeit only every seven years.[209] Culturally, control of the theatres was tight, at least in theory, but there was none of the stultifying academic tyranny which characterized Paris.[210] As we have seen,[211] there was a vigorous musical life in which both upper and middle classes participated.

The first two Georges found this metropolitan environment impossible to master. Coming from a principality in which the economy was almost entirely agricultural and a tiny capital was dominated by the court, they had neither the skill nor the ambition to impose their will. Physically unimpressive and deficient in charisma, they lacked the personal assets to overcome the handicap of their audibly foreign nature. George II, in particular, seemed set on gratuitous alienation: for example, he alienated the City by refusing the Mayor and Aldermen permission to kiss his hand; he did not appear to the London crowds and declined to make royal progresses to the provinces. His habit of turning his large posterior to anyone incurring his displeasure inspired the celebrated satirical print of 1737: *The Festival of the Golden Rump*.[212] George I made no

[207] Neil McKendrick, 'The consumer revolution of eighteenth century England', in Neil McKendrick, John Brewer, and J. H. Plumb, *The Birth of a Consumer Society: The Commercialisation of Eighteenth Century England* (London, 1982), p. 21.

[208] George Rudé, *Wilkes and Liberty* (Oxford, 1962), pp. 150 ff.

[209] John Brooke, *The House of Commons, 1754–1790* (London, 1968), pp. 18, 30.

[210] On the control of theatre, see Brewer, *The Pleasures of the Imagination*, pp. 61, 384–9.

[211] See above, pp. 161–9, 171–2, 179–81.

[212] Gerrard, *The Patriot Opposition to Walpole*, p. 193.

secret of his reluctance to become King of England, nor of his hope that the personal union could soon be broken.[213] Both men showed their undimmed preference for the land of their birth by giving it as much priority in their decision-making as English ministers and English public opinion would allow. Despite the extreme physical toll exacted by eighteenth-century travel, they returned to Hanover repeatedly—George I six times in a reign of thirteen years, George II twelve times in a reign of twenty-seven years.[214]

That was not the way to win the affection of a people more than ever convinced that England was 'the Fairest Isle, all Isles Excelling' (Dryden). In 1714, and for a long time afterwards, there were many English people unimpressed by the Hanoverian claim to the throne (there were many other claimants—perhaps as many as fifty—more closely related to Queen Anne than George I, who was the grandson of a daughter of James I) and alienated by the patently foreign nature of the new arrival and his numerous German entourage. The failure of the Jacobite rebellion in 1715 was by no means a foregone conclusion and many a glass was still raised to James III as 'Best Born Briton'. He was, after all, Queen Anne's brother. As Nicholas Rogers has demonstrated, popular disorder was both widespread and violent under George I, fuelled by fear of another war, by the King's personal unpopularity, and the festering wounds of a legacy of confessional strife. The calendar of public celebrations became 'a calendar of sedition'.[215]

Yet slowly but surely, in fits and starts and more by luck than judgement, the Hanoverians adapted themselves to Britain's unique political culture. Their skills and virtues might have been of a minor order, but so were their vices. Their greatest asset was their Protestantism. When the Old Pretender decided that London was not worth a Mass, he also handed to his rivals a priceless advantage. Given the tiny size of the Catholic community in England and the confessional nature of the country's politics, the Stuarts could now only hope to make good their claim to the throne with the assistance of Spain or France. So the associations between Protestantism and patriotism and between Catholicism and treason were correspondingly intensified. A Stuart restoration now meant foreign invasion. When James III's second son, Henry, became a Catholic priest and a Cardinal to boot, the cost of a Stuart restor-

[213] Annette von Stieglitz, 'Personalunion und Kulturkontakt: der Hof als Schauplatz und Vermittler kultureller Wechselwirkungen', *The Personal Unions of Saxony-Poland and Hanover-England: A Comparison*, Dresden, 20–23 November 1997 (Warsaw, forthcoming).

[214] Ibid.

[215] Nicholas Rogers, *Whigs and Cities: Popular Politics in the Age of Walpole and Pitt* (Oxford, 1989), p. 372.

ation became too high for all but a small and diminishing number of Jacobite diehards.

The sea change in the public political scene was both advertised and consolidated by the events of 1745. A generation earlier the crowds had been mainly Tory, and often also Jacobite, but now they were Whig, and the chapels they vandalized and burned were Catholic, not Dissenting. Fewer than a hundred individuals in London and its surrounding counties were arraigned for expressed Jacobite opinions.[216] Even in Scotland, Hanoverian loyalism and anti-Jacobite demonstrations were widespread.[217] Sensing the loyalist potential, right across the country local elites organized anti-Jacobite pageants to ram home the dangers of the return of the Stuarts. At a parade through Deptford, for example, an impressive range of semiotic buttons were pressed: there was a Highlander carrying a pair of wooden shoes, neatly combining Celtic treachery with poverty (and anticipating Hogarth's depiction in *The Gate of Calais*); a Jesuit heralding the persecution of the Spanish Inquisition; two friars selling indulgences for murder, adultery, and rebellion; the Pope riding on a bullock and the Stuart Pretender riding on an ass, supported by a Frenchman on his right and a Spaniard on his left. Bringing up the rear was a band playing 'all sorts of rough musick'.[218] Although the Jacobite army got as far south as Derby, the episode served only to demonstrate the stability of the Hanoverian settlement. To paraphrase Karl Marx's paraphrase of Hegel, if the '15 was a comedy, the '45 was a farce. Only in Scotland, where something like a civil war broke out, was dissatisfaction with the regime sharp enough to be mobilized as armed force.

As Bonnie Prince Charlie fled back to France, George II had every reason to feel pleased with himself. In 1743 he had commanded in person the 'Pragmatic Army', which defeated the French at Dettingen near Frankfurt am Main (as it turned out, he was the last English sovereign to lead his troops in battle). In 1746 his son, the Duke of Cumberland, had defeated the Pretender's army at Culloden and then pacified the Highlands with exemplary rigour. The Hanoverian dynasty had come of age. At Newcastle-on-Tyne there had been a Jacobite demonstration in 1715, but in 1745 the church bells were rung all day to celebrate the King's birthday.[219] The second half of George II's reign

[216] H. T. Dickinson, *The Politics of the People in Eighteenth Century Britain* (London, 1995), p. 260.

[217] Bob Harris and Christopher A. Whatley, '"To solemnize His Majesty's birthday"', *History*, 83 (1998), pp. 397–9.

[218] Ibid., p. 380.

[219] Ibid., p. 382.

proved to be even more momentous, as economic expansion at home and imperial expansion abroad continued apace, reaching a climax with the great victories of 1759, the year before his death. It was said that George's funeral was 'not well attended by the peers nor even the king's old servants',[220] but there is plenty of diary evidence to suggest that the middling sort lamented the demise of a 'good old king'.[221]

GEORGE III: THE POLITICAL EDUCATION OF A PATRIOT KING

The accession in 1760 of George's grandson should have marked the final *rapprochement* between nation and dynasty, for the new king enjoyed several natural advantages denied to his Hanoverian predecessors. At 22 years of age he was adult but young; he had been born and brought up exclusively in England, was not only Protestant but Anglican (and not only Anglican but a devout Christian), and possessed a spotless personal reputation. Physically too, he was better equipped to command the respect of his subjects, being tall, well-built, and blessed with a good speaking voice.[222] Far from seeking to spend as much time as possible in Hanover, he expressed the greatest dislike for 'that horrid electorate, which has always lived upon the very vitals of this poor country'.[223] In his first speech from the throne, delivered on 18 November 1760, he proclaimed that 'born and educated in this country, I glory in the name of Britain.' The speech had been drafted by Lord Hardwicke, but it was George who had insisted that this sentence be included.[224] Moreover, this patriotism was entirely genuine: in a private letter signalling his acceptance that he could not marry Lady Sarah Lennox, for whom he nursed a strong passion, he wrote: 'the interest of my country must ever be my first care, my

[220] Colley, *Britons*, p. 230.

[221] I owe this information to Hannah Smith of Newnham College, Cambridge, who also saved me from a number of egregious errors in this chapter. It seems more than likely that the alleged unpopularity of the first two Georges has been greatly exaggerated; see Matthew Charles Kilburn, *Royalty and Public in Britain 1714–1789* (unpublished Oxford D.Phil. dissertation, 1997), chs. 1–5.

[222] John Brooke, *King George III* (London, 1972), p. 288.

[223] George to the Earl of Bute, 5 August 1759, Romney Sedgwick (ed.), *Letters from George III to Lord Bute, 1756–1766* (London, 1939), p. 28.

[224] Ibid., p. 88. There has been some confusion as to whether George said 'Britain' or 'Briton'. Brooke states firmly that the original draft quite clearly shows 'Britain' in the king's hand, but it was reported as 'Briton'; ibid., p. 390 n. 7.

own inclinations shall submit to it; I am born for the happiness or misery of a great nation, and must consequently often act contrary to my passions.'[225] Hanover was now demoted to peripheral status, as George explained in 1762: 'tho' I have subjects who will suffer immensely whenever this Kingdom withdraws its protection from thence [Hanover], yet so superior is my love for this my native country over any private interest of my own that I cannot help wishing that an end was put to that enormous expence by ordering our troops home.'[226]

Eventually, George would realize these various assets, but the road which led to political wisdom proved to be long and hard. That he came to the throne in the middle of a successful war, for which he could claim no credit, would have challenged even the most skilful and experienced of politicians. Yet George's pilgrimage to the Heavenly City was also hampered and prolonged by personal shortcomings, especially by the burden of fiercely held convictions he chose to bear with him. The first was his hatred and contempt—no weaker words will suffice—for his predecessor. Every male ruler from the House of Hanover, it seems, has been destined to be at odds with his parents. In the case of George III, the early death of his father in 1751 meant that his alienation had to be focused on his grandfather. Shortly before the latter's death, George wrote: 'The conduct of this old king makes me ashamed of being his grandson.' This aversion would not have been so serious if it had not been extended to the old king's ministers, especially the Duke of Newcastle ('his knave and counsellor') and William Pitt ('a true snake in the grass' and 'the blackest of hearts').[227] Unfortunately for George, both men exercised immense influence, both inside and outside Parliament. As the first decade of the new reign was to demonstrate, their cooperation was indispensable.

It was denied because George nursed a second and equally fervent belief, namely that the only man he could trust was his 'dearest friend', the Earl of Bute, whom he admired to distraction with puppy-like adoration. This proved to be a very serious error of judgement. Bute was 47 years old in 1760 but with very little experience of and even less aptitude for politics, 'a fine showy man, who would make an excellent ambassador in a court where there was no business'.[228] It was the death of the author of this withering epithet, Frederick, Prince of Wales, which gave Bute his opportunity. Already a member of the Leicester House set, he now rose high in the favour of the widowed Princess of

225 Quoted in Steven Watson, *The Reign of George III*, p. 6.
226 Sedgwick (ed.), *Letters from George III to Lord Bute*, p. 78.
227 Quoted in Brooke, *George III*, p. 62.
228 Ibid., p. 47.

Wales and her son. The secret of his success with the latter has been explained most convincingly by John Brooke: 'How shall we explain Bute's influence over King George III? It was simply that Bute was the first person to treat him with kindness and affection. He broke through the shell of loneliness with which the boy was surrounded.'[229]

Together, Bute and George spent the late 1750s planning for the next reign. It was an idealistic programme. They intended to wrest back liberty for both crown and country from the evil politicians, purge corruption, revive Christian piety, end the ruinously expensive war, eliminate the national debt, and generally usher in a reign of virtue.[230] When George II finally answered their prayers and died, they were ready to act with all the decisive certainty of moral conviction. That Bute was to be the new king's chief minister was made apparent from the start. Both the leaders of the current administration, Pitt and Newcastle, found that they had to see Bute before being admitted to an audience with their new master. A shocked Newcastle wrote to Hardwicke: 'His Majesty said these remarkable words: "My Lord Bute is your very good friend; he will tell you my thoughts at large", to which I only replied that I thought my Lord Bute was so.'[231] George also appointed a number of Tories to positions at court, thus signalling his determination not to succumb to what he believed to have been the fate of his two predecessors, and be a 'king in toils' at the mercy of the traditional Whig oligarchy. Less than six months after his accession, the Newcastle–Pitt administration became a Newcastle–Pitt–Bute administration when Bute was made Secretary of State for the Northern Department in March 1761. In October that year it became a Newcastle–Bute administration when Pitt resigned over the Cabinet's refusal to approve a pre-emptive declaration of war on Spain, and in May 1762 it became a purely Bute administration when Newcastle resigned over loss of control of financial policy.[232]

The most important task facing the new prime minister was negotiating an end to the war and steering the peace treaty through Parliament. Bute managed both, securing what was arguably the most favourable diplomatic settlement in English history and getting it through the House of Commons by 319 votes to just 65. It proved to be his one and only achievement in government, for he resigned in April 1763, so exhausted physically and emotionally by the hurly-burly of political life that he succumbed to something approaching a

229 Ibid., p. 53.
230 Sedgwick (ed.), *Letters from George III to Lord Bute*, p. lvi.
231 Brooke, *George III*, p. 74.
232 Watson, *The Reign of George III*, pp. 75, 79.

nervous breakdown.[233] If George had shown poor judgement in picking such a broken reed on which to lean, he had compounded the error by taking a scythe to the most obvious alternative. In the wake of the successful passage of the peace treaty through Parliament he had set about purging his patronage system of all those who had voted against it, together with their clients. This was very much a personal vendetta. Within half an hour of the end of the debate, he was at his desk working on the cull and was still hard at it five hours later.[234] This became known as the 'Massacre of the Pelhamite Innocents', after the family name of its main target, the Duke of Newcastle, and 'was to be almost fatal to the prospects of maintaining stable government'.[235] The victims included many 'King's Friends', Members of Parliament who normally supported any chief minister enjoying royal confidence.

There is no need to recount the instability which characterized the rest of the 1760s. Bute was succeeded by George Grenville, who was succeeded by the Marquess of Rockingham in 1765, who was succeeded by Pitt (now Earl of Chatham) in 1766, who was succeeded by the Duke of Grafton in 1768. None of these ministries was discrete, of course, there being a good deal of overlapping and continuity in personnel. A previous generation of historians debated long and fiercely whether or not George III was being unconstitutional in his attempt to break the mould of Hanoverian politics. The current consensus is that he was not—but that the Whigs had good reason to believe that he was.[236]

If the conflict had been confined to Westminster, George would have weathered the storm more easily. The monarch still had impressive resources of patronage at his disposal with which to create Parliamentary majorities for his chosen ministers. Almost from the start, however, his problems were greatly exacerbated by agitation in the public sphere, or 'without doors' in contemporary parlance. It was driven by that same combination of libertarianism, nationalism, and sleaze which was to destabilize the French monarchy.[237]

[233] Sedgwick (ed.), *Letters from George III to Lord Bute*, p. lxii. John Brewer, 'The misfortunes of Lord Bute: a case-study in eighteenth century political argument and public opinion', *Historical Journal*, 16 (1973), pp. 3–43.

[234] R. J. White recounted this in lectures on 'The reign of George III' given in Cambridge in 1961.

[235] O'Gorman, *The Long Eighteenth Century*, p. 203. For a hostile verdict on the 'pathetically naïve' George III, see John B. Owen, 'George II reconsidered', in Anne Whiteman, J. S. Bromley, and P. G. M. Dickson (eds.), *Statesmen, Scholars and Merchants: Essays in Eighteenth-century History presented to Dame Lucy Sutherland* (Oxford, 1973), pp. 118, 121–2, 127.

[236] The best concise modern discussion is to be found in O'Gorman, *The Long Eighteenth Century*, pp. 201–10.

[237] See below, Ch. 8.

The catalyst was John Wilkes, MP for Aylesbury since 1757 by courtesy of Earl Temple, the Whig magnate who dominated Buckinghamshire's political life from his seat at Stowe.[238] When Temple's brother-in-law, William Pitt, resigned from government in 1761, Wilkes was mobilized to lead a press campaign against Lord Bute. The latter could hardly complain about that, as he himself had set the example by subsidizing a number of newspapers and their journalists, including the redoubtable Dr Samuel Johnson. Indeed, it was as a direct riposte to Bute's paper, the *Briton* (edited by Tobias Smollett) that Wilkes launched the *North Briton* in 1761. However, Bute did complain—bitterly—to his royal master about the virulence and scurrility of the attack to which he was now subjected, especially about the persistent innuendo that he was conducting an affair with the Dowager Princess of Wales to further his ambitions. The belief that Bute was debauching the mother in order to corrupt the son became so widespread that the mere display of two simple symbols, the jackboot and the petticoat, were enough to constitute a political demonstration.[239] There was no more truth in the allegation than in the libels that circulated in France in the 1780s about Marie Antoinette's promiscuity, but the political journalism of the mid-eighteenth century was no more scrupulous than it is today. Asked whether he believed the story, Wilkes exclaimed: 'Not I, by God, but it will make excellent *North Briton*!'[240]

So it did, and a lot more besides, for the heavy-handed response of the King and Bute gave Wilkes all the publicity he craved. The last straw for them was the forty-fifth issue of the *North Briton*, which appeared on 23 April 1763, alleging that the King's Speech to Parliament had contained falsehoods. Wilkes was promptly arrested, charged with seditious libel, and imprisoned in the Tower of London. He was not there for long, for on 6 May his patron Lord Temple secured a writ of habeas corpus on the grounds that Wilkes enjoyed parliamentary immunity. Now he was able to pursue the government through the press and through the courts, concentrating his fire on the manner in which he had been arrested. The 'general warrant' had not named him, had not specified any offence, had authorized what was in effect an indiscriminate trawl for evidence, and generally bore too close a resemblance to the notorious

[238] The best concise account of the Wilkes affair remains Ian R. Christie, *Wilkes, Wyvill and Reform: The Parliamentary Reform Movement in British Politics 1760–1785* (London, 1962). Also helpful is George Rudé, *Wilkes and Liberty* (Oxford, 1962). The best biography of Wilkes is now Peter D. G. Thomas, *John Wilkes: A Friend to Liberty* (Oxford, 1996).

[239] They were to the early 1760s what a Mars bar was to the early 1960s—or a tampon or a cigar to the late 1990s.

[240] Quoted in Christie, *Wilkes*, p. 11.

French *lettres de cachet* for comfort. It says a good deal for the independence of the English judiciary that Wilkes was able to win his case against the Under-Secretary of State responsible for issuing the warrant and to obtain a very substantial sum in damages.

Significantly, Wilkes fared less well in Parliament than in the courts. In the autumn of 1763, the House of Commons voted that the offending issue of the *North Briton* was indeed a seditious libel and, moreover, that seditious libel was not covered by parliamentary privilege. The House of Lords concurred, adding for good measure that a pornographic parody of Alexander Pope's *Essay on Man*, which Wilkes had run off on his printing-press, was an obscene libel and a breach of parliamentary privilege.[241] Facing imprisonment, Wilkes escaped to France. By this time the contest was becoming more of a struggle between Parliament and Wilkes than between the king or Bute and Wilkes. That was even more the case during the second phase of the affair, which began early in 1768 when an impoverished Wilkes returned to England to seek his fortune again and was elected MP for Middlesex in the general election held in March. The authorities would have done well to have left him alone, for he posed little danger inside the system. As Horace Walpole observed on 31 March: 'the House of Commons is the place where he can do the least hurt, for he is a wretched speaker, and will sink to contempt.'[242]

Both ministers and Parliament, however, were determined to pursue Wilkes *à outrance*. In June 1768 he was prosecuted on the old charge of seditious libel, fined £1,000, and sentenced to twenty-two months in prison; in February 1769, after a delay caused by legal uncertainty, he was expelled from the House of Commons. When he was re-elected on 16 February by the voters of Middlesex, the election was annulled. When he was re-elected on 16 March, the election was once more annulled. When he was re-elected on 13 April, the election was annulled for the third time and the sequence brought to a close by the declaration that his opponent had been lawfully elected. Wilkes struck back through the courts, winning £4,000 in damages from the Earl of Halifax, who had been Secretary of State at the time of the issuing of the general warrant in 1763. He now switched his attention to the politics of the City of London, with such success that he was elected an alderman in 1769, sheriff in 1771, and Lord Mayor in 1774. In the same year he was elected as MP for Middlesex for the fifth time in four years. It was a clear indication that he was no longer regarded as a threat that this time he was allowed to take his seat.

[241] Rudé, *Wilkes*, pp. 31–4.

[242] Quoted in Langford, *A Polite and Commercial People*, p. 378. This chapter contains a particularly lucid account and acute analysis of this phase of the Wilkes affair.

More than a decade of Wilkite agitation yielded little in terms of concrete achievement beyond the recognition that general warrants were illegal. The House of Commons made belated amends for overruling the Middlesex electors when it voted in 1782 to expunge its resolution of 1769 from the official journal. Wilkes also certainly made an important contribution to the establishment of the *de facto* right of the press to report the proceedings of Parliament.[243] More important, however, was Wilkes's revelation—and realization—that there was now a public sphere to be exploited in London. With a population approaching three-quarters of a million, mass literacy, more than 200 printing-presses, and thousands of public places for social intercourse, the capital was ripe for an autonomous political movement. Its special character was revealed by its sprawling landscape: built by private money, with little contribution or control by ecclesiastical or royal authorities, it was 'the least authoritarian city in Europe'.[244]

Wilkes blazed the trail for extra-parliamentary campaigning. As we have seen, he began his political career in the retinue of a peer, but it was not long before he went into business on his own account. Although he made use of his aristocratic connections when it suited him, he was at pains to position himself outside the political establishment and to appear as the champion of the unrepresented masses. It was to the 'middling and inferior class of the people' or 'the lower and intermediate class of people' that he appealed, for it was this group, he claimed, 'which touches me more sensibly' and 'which stands most in need of protection'.[245] The former proposition was doubtful, the latter less so, for national political institutions were certainly under firm aristocratic control, with more than half the parliamentary boroughs controlled by peers and more than a hundred sons of peers or Irish peers sitting in the House of Commons.[246] Wilkes was not alone in challenging this hegemony. In 1761 one of the City MPs, the immensely rich merchant William Beckford, had found the perfect metaphor to express the resentment of the 'middling people' of England, when he told the House of Commons that 'the scum is as mean as the dregs.'[247]

243 Robert R. Rea, *The English Press in Politics 1760–1774* (Lincoln, Nebr., 1963), *passim*, esp. pp. 204–10.

244 John Summerson, *Georgian London*, rev. edn. (London, 1972), p. 25.

245 John Brewer, *Party Ideology and Popular Politics at the Accession of George III* (Cambridge, 1976), pp. 168, 305 n. 21.

246 Christie, *Wilkes*, p. 4; John Cannon, *Aristocratic Century: The Peerage of Eighteenth Century England* (Cambridge, 1984), p. 112.

247 Quoted in Christie, *Wilkes*, p. 9. On this great speech, see also Lucy Sutherland, 'The City of London in eighteenth-century politics', in Richard Pares and A. J. P. Taylor (eds.), *Essays presented to Sir Lewis Namier* (London, 1956), p. 66.

What made Wilkes stand out from the crowd of disgruntled commoners was his skill in catching and exploiting the popular mood. During the first phase of his agitation in 1761–3 he shook up a political cocktail of special potency, the three main ingredients being sleaze, xenophobia, and nationalism. They were concentrated in the person of Lord Bute, pilloried as the seducer of George III's mother, as a Scottish parasite, and as the architect of the traitorous peace of 1763. Of these, the most important was probably the second. Dr Johnson's notorious jibes ('the finest prospect for a Scotsman is the high road that leads to England' etc.) represented a prejudice held both widely and deeply. As the literary and pictorial examples already cited[248] have indicated, the Scottish stereotype was undernourished, unintelligible, uncouth, unwashed, and untrustworthy, with a dyed-in-the-tartan preference for all things Jacobite, papist, French, and despotic: 'their breath commonly stinks of Pottage, their linen of Piss, their hands of Pigs' turds, their body of sweat.'[249] Scottish visitors to London who were unwilling or unable to conceal their origin were subjected to public ridicule and abuse, so that long-term immigrants were obliged to take elocution lessons and Anglicize their names. Charles Burney, for example, was christened Charles Mackburney.[250] Horace Walpole was not inclined to be apologetic about his prejudices, telling Sir Horace Mann:

> What a nation is Scotland; in every reign engendering traitors to the State, and false and pernicious to the Kings that favour it most! National prejudices, I know, are very vulgar; but if there are national characteristics, can one but dislike the soils and climates that concur to produce them?[251]

There were few politicians in England more enlightened and cosmopolitan than the Earl of Shelburne, but even he dismissed the Scottish nation as 'a sad set of innate, cold-hearted, impudent rogues'.[252]

The obverse of Wilkes's lampooning of Bute's ancestry was an attack on his betrayal of the national interest by negotiating the Peace of Paris. No matter that this secured massive territorial gains in Africa, the Caribbean, and North America; there were plenty of armchair diplomats who believed that more could have been won and whispered that only corruption had managed to win

[248] See above, pp. 22, 281, 305.

[249] Michael Duffy, *The English Satirical Print 1600–1832: The Englishman and the Foreigner* (Cambridge, 1986), p. 19.

[250] Brewer, 'The misfortunes of Lord Bute', pp. 19–23; Kate Chisholm, *Fanny Burney: Her Life* (London, 1999), p. 4.

[251] *Horace Walpole's Correspondence*, ed. W. S. Lewis, 34 vols. (New Haven, 1937–65), vol. 25, p. 62.

[252] Quoted in Langford, *A Polite and Commercial People*, p. 328.

parliamentary approval. That William Pitt, to whom most accorded the laurels of victory, had resigned from the administration in protest against its feebleness, did nothing to enhance the peace treaty's popularity. In fact, opinion both inside and outside Parliament was eager for peace and objective enough to recognize the acceptability of the terms, but the myth of their unpopularity proved enduring.[253]

Although drawing on deep wells of national prejudice, Wilkes's campaign of 1761–3 owed too much to the exceptional circumstances of the new reign to be sustained for long. As Bute faded quickly from the scene, Wilkes looked for a more structured set of targets. The association of his personal struggle against the authorities with the central topos of English political culture was crucial in the slogan 'Wilkes and Liberty!' From the start, the *North Briton* proclaimed that 'the *liberty of the press* is the birthright of a BRITON, and is justly esteemed the firmest bulwark of the liberties of this country.'[254] Constant repetition and display ensured that 'Wilkes and liberty became synonymous terms,' as the radical publisher John Almon put it.[255] It was given memorable pictorial expression by Hogarth in his etching of 1763, which shows Wilkes holding a staff surmounted by a cap emblazoned by the word 'LIBERTY' in large letters.[256] A poor speaker, Wilkes reached his public through the written word and printed images, in pamphlets, periodicals, newspaper letters, handbills, ballads, verses, and political cartoons.[257] It was through these that he publicized his impressive gift for using court appearances to brand his persecutors as petty-minded tyrants, while broadcasting his own credentials as a principled liberator. Showing a remarkable attention to detail, he sent a card of thanks to anyone who voted for him in his various election campaigns and kept a careful register of all who could be identified as supporters.[258] Not that Wilkes confined his appeal to the enfranchised. A tireless self-publicist, he sought—and found—support in every part of society. In the short term, it proved very much to his advantage that the 1760s was such a troubled decade. Especially since the second phase of his campaign, beginning in 1768, took

[253] Ibid., pp. 349–51.

[254] Quoted in Thomas, *John Wilkes*, p. 19.

[255] Brewer, *Party Ideology and Popular Politics*, p. 169.

[256] The best reproduction is to be found in Burke and Caldwell, *Hogarth: The Complete Engravings*, p. 263. This was intended as a hostile caricature—on the table to the right of Wilkes stand two issues of *North Briton*; number 45, in which Wilkes had attacked the King, and number 17, in which he had attacked Hogarth.

[257] Brewer, *Party ideology and popular politics*, p. 171.

[258] John Brewer, *Political Argument and Propaganda in England, 1750–1770* (unpublished Cambridge Ph.D. dissertation, 1973), p. 295.

place against a backdrop of intense and prolonged social violence, including the 'Massacre of St. George's Fields' on 10 May, when the Guards fired into the crowd, inflicting numerous casualties.[259] In that month every ship in the Port of London was strike-bound and industrial unrest, generated by high grain prices, spread to many trades, from watermen to glass-grinders, from sawyers to weavers. So there were thousands of disaffected plebeians ready and eager to celebrate Wilkes's victories in the Middlesex elections, to intimidate his opponents, and to shout 'Wilkes and the coalheavers for ever!'[260]

The opportunism of the coalheavers was more than matched by the object of their admiration. Not the least important reason for the failure of two decades of agitation to do much more than irritate the established order was Wilkes's ruthless exploitation of the movement for his own ends. Even his initial assault appears to have stemmed from the belief that it was Bute who had prevented his appointment as envoy to Constantinople in 1761.[261] Time and again, his genius for taking the popular pulse and making it beat faster was marred by an act of selfish imprudence. After his release from the Tower of London in 1763, for example, he set up his own printing-press, not only to reprint the *North Briton* in volume form but also to run off the pornographic parody of Pope's *Essay on Man* referred to earlier.[262] The government could hardly believe its good fortune when it got wind of Wilkes's indiscretion and moved quickly to obtain a copy by bribing and intimidating the printer engaged to run the press. On 15 November the Earl of Sandwich read out the offending poem to a suitably shocked House of Lords, which unanimously condemned it as 'a most scandalous, obscene and impious libel'.[263] Wilkes had not helped his case by mischievously attributing the poem to William Warburton, the pious and scholarly Bishop of Gloucester. The episode did not destroy Wilkes's popularity but it did oblige many to distinguish sharply between the man and his cause. So William Pitt was prepared to defend Wilkes's entitlement to parliamentary privilege but also denounced him as 'the blasphemer of his God and the libeller of his King'.[264] Provincial opinion was also alienated by Wilkes's unsavoury reputation. A despondent William Dowdeswell reported from Worcestershire on the slow progress of the petitioning campaign of 1769:

[259] Rudé, *Wilkes and Liberty*, p. 51. This remains the best account of the social violence of the period.

[260] Ibid., p. 97.

[261] S. Maccoby, *English Radicalism 1762–1785* (London, 1955), p. 22.

[262] See above, p. 327.

[263] Rudé, *Wilkes and Liberty*, p. 33.

[264] Ibid.

Wilkes' character, of which men are inclined to think much worse than it deserves, and the advantage which he must necessarily receive from the restitution made to the public of its rights at present lost, have checkt this proceeding in most places.[265]

Nor did Wilkes's lack of scruple about courting plebeian support commend itself to many property-owners. With every act of social violence committed in the name of Wilkes, the government's task in holding the centre was made easier. At the height of the Middlesex election episode in 1769, for example, government supporters were able to mobilize a flood of addresses proclaiming the country's loyalty and attacking the seditious excesses of the mob.[266] On the left, growing disenchantment with Wilkes's cynical self-promotion prompted a major split in 1771, with John Horne Tooke and a number of other leading radicals seceding to form a separate organization. For his part, Wilkes soon nestled back inside the establishment, becoming Lord Mayor of London in 1774 and playing a leading role in the suppression of the Gordon Riots in 1780. As he himself once said contemptuously of a supporter: 'he was a Wilkite, I never was,' confessing that he had been 'a patriot by accident'.[267]

For all Wilkes's shortcomings, British politics had been transformed by the emergence of an autonomous extra-parliamentary movement. Moreover, it was increasingly an *anti*-parliamentary movement. If George III and Bute had been the focus of hostility in 1761–3, after 1768 it was the House of Commons which emerged as the villain of the piece, three times denying the wishes of the electors of Middlesex. So out of the Wilkite campaign emerged a programme for parliamentary reform, designed to make the lower house less prone to royal or oligarchic manipulation and more responsive to the needs and wishes of the electorate. By 1770 demands were being made for annual elections, a secret ballot, a widening of the franchise to include all householders of substance, the exclusion of place-holders, the increase of county members, and the abolition of rotten boroughs.[268] In addition, the aspiring reformers had created an organization, learned how to mobilize City interests and opinion, and how to make use of popular agitation, and discovered that there was support to be mustered in the provinces.

What they failed to address satisfactorily was the obstinate fact that the only body that could reform Parliament constitutionally was Parliament itself. Yet

[265] Quoted in John Norris, *Shelburne and Reform* (London, 1963), p. 70.

[266] Maccoby, *English Radicalism*, p. 112.

[267] Lucy Sutherland, *The City of London and the Opposition to Government 1768–1774: A Study in the Rise of Metropolitan Radicalism*, The Creighton Lecture 1958 (London, 1959), p. 13. Rudé, *Wilkes and Liberty*, p. 192.

[268] John Cannon, *Parliamentary Reform 1640–1832* (Cambridge, 1972), ch. 3, *passim*.

all Members of Parliament were necessarily beneficiaries of the existing order, with a vested interest in its continuation. So what was needed was a group with an ideology or a special interest strong enough to override this fundamental inhibition. The best candidate was the group of Whigs which came to be known after their nominal leader, the Marquis of Rockingham. They believed, not entirely without reason (thanks to their association with the Duke of Newcastle), that they stood in apostolic succession to the Whigs who had made the Revolution Settlement of 1688, and consequently had a natural right to dominate royal councils. When they found themselves excluded after 1760, especially after the 'Massacre of the Pelhamite Innocents', they concluded that the constitution had become unbalanced as a result of the evil machinations of Lord Bute. Their brief tenure of office in 1765–6 only served to feed their fears, although in truth their fall was due more to simple incompetence and a self-destructive refusal even to humour the King.[269] They were to pay for their folly by sixteen years in the wilderness.

To explain their failure, they embraced two myths: 'the minister behind the curtain', according to which Bute continued to dominate the councils of the King despite his formal resignation; and 'double cabinet', according to which an official body of puppets was shadowed by a secret cabal comprising Bute and his friends. To remedy this situation they adopted three tactics. First, they argued that when it came to rectifying the defective constitution, the formation of an organized party was not just legitimate but necessary.[270] They did not believe in a two- or multi-party system, only in the creation of the one true constitutional party of Old Whigs. Secondly, they advanced a legislative programme of 'Economical Reform', to reduce the amount of patronage at the disposal of the Crown and with it the means of corrupting Parliament.[271] Thirdly, they sought to construct an alliance with public opinion: in the words of Edmund Burke, Rockingham's secretary, 'we must strengthen the hands of the minority within doors by the accession of public opinion, strongly declared' and 'we know that all opposition is absolutely crippled if it can obtain no kind of support without doors.'[272] The high-water mark of this last-named policy was a great dinner held at the Thatched House Tavern on 9 May 1769,

[269] Paul Langford, *The First Rockingham Administration, 1765–1766* (Oxford, 1973), pp. 236–7.

[270] John Brewer, 'Party and Double Cabinet: two facets of Burke's *Thoughts*', *Historical Journal*, 14, 3 (1971), *passim*.

[271] Ian R. Christie, 'Economical reform and the influence of the Crown', in idem, *Myth and Reality in Late Eighteenth Century British Politics and other Papers* (London, 1970), pp. 297–310.

[272] Quoted in Sutherland, 'The City of London in the eighteenth century politics', p. 57.

attended by both the London radicals and the leaders of the opposition groups in Parliament.

This promising way forward to real constitutional change proved to be a cul-de-sac. The exit was soon barred by the realization that the objectives of reformers inside and outside Parliament were fundamentally different. The Rockingham Whigs included in their ranks some of the biggest borough-mongers in England, including their leader and his heir, Earl Fitzwilliam. Any measures aimed at eliminating rotten boroughs and redistributing seats would have cut at the roots of their power and were correspondingly unacceptable. Nor did these aristocrats feel comfortable with any kind of initiative stemming from below. As Rockingham himself put it: 'I *must say* that the thing which weighs most against adopting the mode of petitioning the King is, *where* the example was first set.'[273] Edmund Burke's articulation of the same reservation was even more condescending. He told the House of Commons: 'I cannot indeed take it upon me to say that I have the honour to *follow* the sense of the people. The truth is *I met it on my way*, while I was pursuing their interest according to my own ideas' and he added in a private letter to Rockingham, 'To bring the people to a feeling, such a feeling, I mean, as tends to amendment or alteration of system, there must be plan and management. All direction of public humour and opinion must originate in a few.'[274] For their part, the radicals found Economical Reform so pitifully inadequate as to be almost worse than nothing. John Jebb later found the perfect simile: 'moving the People of England to carry so small a Reform would be tempesting the Ocean to drown a fly.'[275] Moreover, neither group could speak with a single voice. The Marquis of Rockingham may well have believed that he was the natural head of the natural leaders of the country, but his paramountcy was not recognized by other opposition Whigs. Why should the Duke of Grafton, a descendant of Charles II, albeit under the bar sinister, or the Duke of Richmond, from another line of Caroline bastards, defer to their inferior in the peerage? As for the most prestigious and effective of the opposition

[273] Quoted in Sutherland, *The City of London and the Opposition to Government*, p. 29.

[274] Louis I. Bredvold and Ralph G. Ross, *The Philosophy of Edmund Burke* (Ann Arbor, Mich., 1960), p. 144. On the other hand, he wrote to a periodical in 1771 about his political associates: 'They respect public opinion; and, therefore, whenever they shall be called upon, they are ready to meet their adversaries, as soon as they please, before the tribunal of the public, and there to justify the constitutional nature and tendency, the propriety, the prudence, and the policy of their bill'; *The Correspondence of Edmund Burke*, ed. Lucy Sutherland. Vol. II : *July 1768–June 1774* (Cambridge, 1960), pp. 202–3.

[275] Eugene Charlton Black, *The Association: British Extraparliamentary Political Organization 1769–1793* (Cambridge, Mass., 1963), p. 74.

politicians, the Earl of Chatham (*né* William Pitt), it was his avowed ambition to 'pulverize parties'. Outside Parliament, the reformers were just as fissiparous, as they showed in 1770 when there was a major secession from the Wilkite Society of the Supporters of the Bill of Rights to form the Constitutional Society.[276]

Disunity was compounded by paucity of numbers. At no time during either phase of the Wilkes affair was the government majority in danger. Indeed, it was frustration at three years of fruitless opposition that had prompted the Rockingham Whigs to forge the short-lived Thatched House Tavern coalition in the first place. The petitioning campaign which followed was vigorously talked up by the opposition but was brushed aside by ministers with indifference. Only eighteen counties and twelve boroughs could be induced to participate and only in Yorkshire (Rockingham's home county) and Middlesex (Wilkes's stronghold) could large numbers of the electorate be induced to sign.[277] In other counties close to the capital— Essex, Kent, and Surrey—and in many other counties and boroughs, the meetings called to prepare a petition instead sent 'humble addresses' expressly supporting government actions. As William Dowdeswell, in the same letter quoted above,[278] lamented about Worcestershire: 'It is amazing how in most places People of rank and fortune shrink from this measure; and with what deference all orders below them wait for their leaders.' It is the view of Jonathan Clark that the number of radical intellectuals was small enough to allow them all to be fitted into a single London coffee-house, although that must surely be an exaggeration.[279]

It was also in 1770 that George III at last found safe haven after a decade of restless wandering from one chief minister to another. In Lord North he found a politician with the two crucial qualifications for a long and secure tenure of office: royal support and the ability to control the House of Commons.[280] Industrious, well-organized, intelligent, witty, and a good debater, North won respect inside and outside Parliament. As Burke ruefully conceded to Rockingham in the autumn of 1774: 'The character of the ministry either produces or perfectly coincides with the disposition of the publick.'[281] Yet Lord North

[276] Christie, *Wilkes*, p. 47.

[277] Ibid., p. 39.

[278] See above, p. 332.

[279] J. C. D. Clark, *English Society 1688–1832: Ideology, Social Structure and Political Practice during the Ancien Régime* (Cambridge, 1985), p. 320.

[280] Lord North enjoyed a courtesy title as eldest son of the Earl of Guilford and sat in the Commons as member for Banbury.

[281] John Cannon, *Lord North: The Noble Lord in the Blue Ribbon*, Historical Association Pamphlet, General Series no. 74 (London, 1970), p. 8. This excellent essay contains several

has suffered a worse press than any other British prime minister—'the worst prime minister since Lord North' was an epithet still in use in the late twentieth century.[282] The reason, of course, was the War of American Independence, which began in 1775 and ended in 1783, the year after North had finally been forced from office in ignominy. The crisis his departure precipitated was so intense that it might have ended in the abdication of the King, the elevation of the Prince of Wales, and a fundamental shift in the balance of the constitution. In the event, it led to the rout of the opposition and the apotheosis of George III.

The death agony of North's ministry was prolonged. The defeat of General Burgoyne at Saratoga in October 1777 not only ensured that there would be no quick victory over the American colonists but also encouraged France to enter the war the following year, seeking revenge for the defeats of the Seven Years War. The addition of Spain and her considerable naval forces in June 1779 gave the Bourbon alliance the opportunity at least to attempt an invasion of England. The knowledge that a Franco-Spanish fleet had been cruising unchallenged in the Channel, and had been dispersed only by bad weather, created an acute crisis of confidence in a nation accustomed to feeling impregnable. It was compounded by problems closer to home. Not for the first or last time, Irish dissidents exploited British embarrassment. By the summer of 1779 several thousand volunteers had formed themselves into military units, ostensibly to organize protection against foreign foes, in reality to wrest concessions from London. The economic recession which fuelled their sense of grievance also intensified political problems on the mainland. In November a by-election for one of the Middlesex seats was attended by mass meetings and calls for a national campaign against the ministry. On 29 November, the Yorkshire clergyman and landowner, Christopher Wyvill, issued a summons to his fellow country gentlemen, lamenting 'the present decline of trade and land-rents, and the apprehension of an additional land-tax' and calling for an end to corruption.[283]

examples of North's sardonic wit. One which is omitted but deserves wider currency is his comment on looking at the lists of admirals called up for active service on the outbreak of war with France in 1778: 'I know not what effect these names may have upon the enemy, but I know they make me trenble.' *Mutatis mutandis*, this remark is usually ascribed to the Duke of Wellington.

[282] My own father applied it without discrimination to each successive Labour prime minister.

[283] Herbert Butterfield, *George III, Lord North and the People, 1779–80* (London, 1949), p. 202. This odd but distinguished book remains the most detailed account of the crisis.

The response to Wyvill's appeal was massive and immediate, revealing just how deep and wide ran the disaffection with the government's conduct of affairs at home and abroad. The advertisement of the meeting of Yorkshire freeholders held on 30 December was signed by 209 major landowners. The petition calling for 'public economy' presented to that meeting was eventually signed by around 8,000 individuals.[284] Moreover, it was an initiative intended to be both continuous and national. An association was formed and links were established with similar organizations following Yorkshire's lead. Within a month, sixteen more counties and almost as many boroughs launched their own petitions, corresponding with each other to form a coordinated 'Association movement'. Where the sheriff of the county declined to convene a meeting to draw up a petition, private individuals did so on their own initiative.[285] Like the Wilkite movement, it was independent of parliamentary groupings; indeed, Wyvill insisted that no Member of Parliament could become a member of the Yorkshire Association's committee. Unlike the Wilkite petitions, those of the Association Movement were addressed not to the king but directly to Parliament.[286] Unlike raffish, opportunistic, populist Wilkes, the Reverend Mr Wyvill's movement was respectable, principled, and landed. It was also directed squarely against the excessive and abusive authority which accrued to the Crown from 'sinecure places and unmerited pensions', giving it 'a great and unconstitutional influence which, if not checked, may soon prove fatal to the liberties of this country'.[287]

During the winter of 1779–80, it looked very much as though a formidable coalition of disaffected interests was being assembled. In Parliament, the Rockingham Whigs took up the cause of Economical Reform with renewed vigour when Edmund Burke introduced his 'Establishment Bill' on 11 February. Outside Parliament, the Association Movement and the London radicals mobilized rural and urban public opinion in support. On 6 April, the opposition achieved what Horace Walpole called 'a codicil to Magna Carta', when John Dunning's motion that 'the influence of the crown has increased, is increasing, and ought to be diminished' passed a full house by 233 votes to 218.[288] Just as excited was Charles James Fox, rapidly emerging as the main bridge between the London radicals and the professional politicians, who exclaimed 'that if he died that night, he should think he had lived to good

[284] Black, *The Association*, p. 41; Christie, *Wilkes*, p. 77.
[285] Peter Fraser, 'Public petitioning and Parliament before 1832', *History*, 46 (1961), p. 202.
[286] Ibid.
[287] Ibid., p. 76.
[288] *Horace Walpole's Correspondence*, vol. 29, p. 211.

purpose in having contributed to bring about this second revolution'.[289] By that time, more than half the English counties had submitted petitions and about 20 per cent of the entire electorate had signed them.[290] A frantic Lord North took Dunning's motion to be a vote of no confidence in himself and pleaded once again with the king to be allowed to resign.[291]

There was no 'second revolution' in the offing. George III could see further than his prime minister, correctly observing that 'a little time will I am certain open the eyes of several who have been led on farther than they intended.'[292] He could see beyond the confident rhetoric to the reality of an opposition which was split at least four ways and quite incapable of joint action that went beyond high-sounding generalities. In part, this was a continuing struggle within the Whig opposition between the heirs of the Old Corps of Whigs and the heirs of William Pitt. The latter had died in 1778, but his interest was continued by the Earl of Shelburne, who had served in his administration in 1766 as Secretary of State. Shelburne had inherited from his mentor a strong antipathy to the Whig grandees.[293] But this was not just a familiar factional dispute within Parliament. It was also in part a re-run of the old conflict of interests between the Whigs and the radicals, which had surfaced in the 1760s.[294] Rockingham's position had not changed: he would promote Economical Reform but nothing more. Rejecting a compromise proposed by Wyvill, who offered to drop a demand for shorter Parliaments if only additional members were accepted, Rockingham pointed out that, while the petitioning campaign for Economical Reform had generated more than 60,000 signatures, he had seen no evidence of support for the other two demands.[295] Poor Wyvill was caught between a rock and a hard place—too radical for Rockingham but too conservative for the radicals. The latter had drafted a programme in March 1780 which called for nothing less than universal manhood suffrage, annual Parliaments, equal electoral districts, single-member constituencies, the removal of property qualification for MPs, and the payment of members.[296] In short, they were Chartists *avant la*

289 Langford, *A Polite and Commercial People*, p. 548.

290 Christie, *Wilkes*, p. 97.

291 Brooke, *George III*, p. 217.

292 Ibid.

293 Earl Stanhope, *Life of the Right Honourable William Pitt, with extracts from his MS, papers*, new edn., vol. I (London, 1879), pp. 80–1.

294 See above, pp. 333–4.

295 Christie, *Wilkes*, p. 122.

296 Carl B. Cone, *The English Jacobins: Reformers in Late Eighteenth Century England* (New York, 1968), p. 58.

lettre. Wyvill told one of their leaders, John Jebb, that their extremism would only drive provincial opinion back into apathy.[297]

The accuracy of George III's prediction was soon demonstrated, as specific measures for Economical Reform were emasculated or defeated, and a further motion by Dunning on 24 April that the House of Commons should not be prorogued or dissolved until the demands made by the petitioning campaign had been satisfied, and the balance of the constitution restored, was defeated by 254 to 203. The *coup de grâce* was then delivered by two events in June 1780. The first was the violent rioting which erupted when a petition was presented to Parliament by the 'Protestant Association' calling for the repeal of the Catholic Relief Act of 1778. Although led by an MP—and the younger son of a duke to boot—the 'Gordon riots' were anything but aristocratic. In their ferocity they were the most serious outbreak of urban violence of the entire century. For almost a week the capital was out of control as the mob pillaged and burned. By the time George III took control and ordered in the troops, hundreds had died, thousands had been injured, and countless buildings had been destroyed. It has been estimated that the rioters inflicted more damage to property than their French counterparts managed during the entire French Revolution.[298] By reminding the middle classes of the fragility of the social fabric, the Gordon riots crippled movements for political reform and may well also have inoculated middle-class English opinion against any wish to emulate events in France after 1789. One Londoner, J. Brasbridge, recalled:

> From that moment, trusting to the evidence of my own senses, I became a convert to loyalty and social order. I shut my ears against the voice of popular clamour, & have, I trust, ever since maintained the character of a true love of my king, and a well-wisher to my country.[299]

The second event to bring relief to a hard-pressed government was the news of Sir Henry Clinton's crushing victory over the American rebels at Charleston, South Carolina. The reaction showed once again that it was not the war that was unpopular, only military failure.

Unfortunately for George III and his prime minister, there was more military failure to come. On 25 November 1781 the terrible news reached London that on 19 October Lord Cornwallis had surrendered 8,000 men and 240 guns to a Franco-American army commanded by General George

[297] Ibid., pp. 133–4.

[298] R. R. Palmer, *The Age of the Democratic Revolution: A Political History of Europe and America, 1760–1800*, 2 vols. (Princeton, 1959, 1964), I, p. 299.

[299] Quoted in Black, *The Association*, p. 67.

Washington at Yorktown in Virginia. The failure of the Royal Navy to supply, reinforce, or evacuate Cornwallis's force, trapped on a coastal promontory for three weeks before its capitulation, completed the humiliating débâcle. Well might Lord North exclaim 'Oh God: it is all over!' on hearing the news.[300] Only the obdurate refusal of his royal master to concede defeat kept him in office during the winter. But George had now reached the limits of his authority. As John Brooke wrote, Yorktown 'broke the morale of the governing class and paralysed the national will to make war'.[301] On 27 February 1782, a motion against further prosecution of the war passed the House of Commons by 234 votes to 215. On 20 March North resigned, after learning that a substantial group of previously loyal independent members was no longer willing to support him. Twelve years of political stability were over and two years of intense instability were about to begin. It was to prove the final and most painful lesson in George III's political education.

The story of the crisis of 1782–4 has been recounted many times and need not delay us long here. At the end of March George was obliged to accept the detested Marquis of Rockingham as First Lord of the Treasury, although he was able to insist that Shelburne, who became Secretary of State for home and colonial affairs, should be regarded as a joint premier. Knowing that he and his supporters were indispensable, Rockingham exacted a heavy price. In a reverse 'Massacre of the Pelhamite Innocents', which he enjoyed with all the relish of a man entering into his kingdom after sixteen years out of office, he obliged the king to make a clean sweep of government and household.[302] Rockingham's enjoyment was short-lived, for on 1 July he died of influenza. George took immediate advantage by promoting Shelburne to the Treasury, a move which prompted Charles James Fox and the other Rockinghamites to resign. Among other vacancies thus created was the chancellorship of the exchequer, which went to the 23-year-old William Pitt. With only about 140 supporters in the House of Commons, Shelburne could not hope to survive for long without forming a coalition with another group. The obvious partner was Lord North, who still commanded a following of around 120 MPs, but North had fallen out with the King over financial irregularities. Moreover, William Pitt was adamant that he would not sit in a cabinet with him. In the event, North preferred Fox. On 14 February 1783 the two men formed a coalition, inflicted defeat on Shelburne on 18 February, and forced his resignation a week later. George twisted and turned this way and that for a fortnight, but on 12 March he bowed

[300] O'Gorman, *The Long Eighteenth Century*, p. 196.
[301] Brooke, *George III*, p. 219.
[302] Ibid., pp. 228–9.

to the inevitable and accepted the Fox–North coalition under the nominal leadership of the Duke of Portland.

This could have been a truly pivotal moment in the constitutional history of Great Britain, for both Fox and North intended that the new ministry would be marked by much more than just a change of personnel. It was Fox who had commissioned the proto-Chartist programme of the Westminster radicals of March 1780,[303] while North had declared, when forming his coalition with Fox: 'The King ought to be treated with all sort of respect and attention, but the appearance of power is all that a King of this country can have.'[304] To add personal insult to political injury, Fox had also taken up the cause of George's eldest son. Although only 20 years old, the Prince of Wales had already proved himself a true Hanoverian by falling out with his father. In his case, this traditional fracture was due to the young prince's compulsive self-indulgence in the pleasures of the flesh. By supporting an application to provide the Prince with a large annual income from the Civil List and to pay his enormous debts, Fox touched a particularly raw nerve. 'It is impossible for me to find words expressive enough of my indignation and astonishment,' was George's enraged reaction.[305] Before the year was out, he had his revenge. As soon as he secured William Pitt's agreement to lead a new administration, George engineered the defeat of the government's India Bill in the House of Lords by the simple expedient of instructing Lord Temple to pass the word to his fellow peers 'that whoever voted for the India Bill were not only not his friends but he should consider them as his enemies'. No one has described more graphically what happened next than Lord Rosebery in his biography of Pitt:

> The uneasy whisper circulated, and the joints of the lords became as water. The peers, who yearned for lieutenancies or regiments, for stars or strawberry leaves; the prelates who sought a larger sphere of usefulness; the minions of the bedchamber and the janissaries of the closet; all, temporal or spiritual, whose convictions were unequal to their appetite, rallied to the royal nod.[306]

Great was the anger of Fox and North at the 'treachery' of the King, but there was little they could do inside Parliament. 'Without doors' their plight was even more hopeless, as the general election held in the following spring demonstrated. Of course, the government hardly ever lost a general election

[303] See above, p. 338.
[304] Brooke, *George III*, p. 237.
[305] Ibid., p. 248.
[306] Lord Rosebery, *Pitt* (London, 1892), p. 44. This is only one of many eloquent passages in this short but brilliant book, a masterpiece of English prose.

held under the unreformed system; it was the manner in which it was won that was so revealing. The signs had long been there to be read, as more than 200 addresses of support for Pitt's appointment as prime minister poured in from every corner of the kingdom. That figure is put into perspective when compared with the thirty petitions mustered by the Society of the Supporters of the Bill of Rights in 1769, the thirty-eight supporting Economical Reform in 1780, or the forty-one supporting parliamentary reform in 1783.[307] Indeed, as noted earlier, Pitt attracted more petitions than the six previous most popular causes put together.[308] Moreover, the number of signatories of each petition was also striking: 8,000 in Westminster, 5,000 in Bristol, 4,000 in Glasgow, and so on. There could have been no better illustration of the strength of the royal hand than an incident on 25 February 1784. A delegation of opposition politicians visiting the king to present an address demanding Pitt's dismissal found that they could only 'with difficulty pass through the throng of delegates, crowding round the throne from Corporations, Counties and respectable bodies of men from all quarters, assuring their sovereign of their entire and unlimited confidence in and highest approbation of his new appointed ministers'.[309]

It was a famous and durable victory. Pitt was to be prime minister until 1801; North never again held office; Fox languished in the wilderness for twenty-three years, becoming foreign secretary again only during the last year of his life (1806). George achieved this astonishing reversal of fortune partly in spite of himself. He had placed himself in toils, by identifying himself too closely with a war that could not be won, prone to remarks such as 'the die is now cast, the colonies must either submit or triumph' (September, 1774), 'blows must decide' (November, 1774), or 'where violence is with resolution repelled, it commonly yields' (February, 1775).[310] Ironically, it was his tormenters in Parliament who saved him from himself. By forcing him to accept North's resignation and end the war, they destroyed the main source of his unpopularity.[311] Indeed, it might be added that all the tactical defeats George had suffered during the first twenty years of his reign worked to his strategic advantage. If John Wilkes had been left to languish in prison indefinitely, the cries of royal despotism would have gained some credibility. In the event, Wilkes was released on a writ of habeas corpus and was able to pursue

307 Cannon, *The Fox–North Coalition*, p. 187.

308 See above, p. 267.

309 *Leicester and Nottingham Journal*, 28 February, Quoted in Cannon, *The Fox–North Coalition*, p. 188.

310 Brooke, *George III*, p. 175.

311 L. G. Mitchell, *Charles James Fox and the Disintegration of the Whig Party 1782–1794* (Oxford, 1971), p. 5.

government agents through the courts, winning substantial sums in damages.[312] Wilkes was to show his gratitude by rallying to the royal cause in 1783–4, attacking the Fox–North coalition in the House of Commons.[313] More important, the events of 1782–3, and especially the resignations of North and Shelburne, showed that royal patronage was not enough by itself to keep in office a minister who had lost the confidence of the House of Commons. North himself made this point very well when opposing parliamentary reform in May 1783:

I was the creature of Parliament in my rise; when I fell I was its victim. I came among you without connection. It was here I was first known: you raised me up; you pulled me down. I have been the creature of your opinion and your power, and the history of my political life is one proof that will stand against and overturn a thousand wild assertions, that there is a corrupt influence in the Crown which destroys the independence of this House.[314]

North and his fellow opponents of reform won the day by the crushing majority of 293 votes to 149. A rejoicing Horace Walpole wrote: 'Were the House of Commons now existing the worst that ever was, still it must be acceptable to our Reformers: for which House of Commons since the Restoration, ever did more than tear two Prime Ministers from the Crown in one year?[315]

The sponsor of that motion for parliamentary reform was none other than William Pitt. Nor was it to be his last. Even when prime minister, he insisted on bringing forward a further measure, despite the misgivings of king and colleagues. It was indicative of one of his most potent assets: a reputation for being a man of principle, a sea-green incorruptible who had dedicated himself to a life of public service. Being his father's son helped, of course, but he worked hard to maximize the benefit. As his tutor at Pembroke College, Cambridge, observed, 'I never knew him spend an idle day, nor did he ever fail to attend me at the appointed hour.'[316] Moreover, Pitt demonstrated his aversion to anything that smacked of corruption in a way which even the most hardened cynic could appreciate. Shortly after he took office, he was in a position to award himself the Clerkship of the Pells, a sinecure which yielded

[312] See above, pp. 327–8.

[313] Thomas, *Wilkes*, p. 194. Thomas also reprints between pp. 182–3 a contemporary cartoon showing 'The New Coalition' as George III and Wilkes embrace, saying respectively 'Sure! The worthiest of Subjects & most virtuous of men' and 'I now find that you are the best of Princes.'

[314] Quoted in Christie, *Wilkes*, p. 183.

[315] *Horace Walpole's Correspondence*, vol. 25, p. 402.

[316] Stanhope, *Life of the Right Honourable William Pitt*, I, p. 15.

the princely sum of £3,000 *per annum* for life. Resisting temptation, he gave it instead to Isaac Barré, a veteran supporter of Shelburne.[317] This well-publicized gesture was in stark contrast to Charles James Fox's reputation for profligate debauchery. George Selwyn was representing popular perceptions when he compared the two rivals to 'The Idle and the Industrious Apprentice' of Hogarth's celebrated sequence of didactic engravings.

This contrast was mirrored by the relationship between the King and the Prince of Wales. The charges of corruption levelled against George were wholly political. Not one breath of scandal was to be heard about his personal morality. When Wilkes and the other gutter-journalists had sought to enlist sleaze in their service, the best they could do was to imply an improper relationship between George's mother and Bute.[318] George himself married Charlotte of Mecklenburg-Strelitz in 1761 and was impeccably faithful to her, the first English king to be completely free from sexual scandal since Charles I. Together they produced fifteen children in twenty-two years. It was a model marriage with a powerful appeal, enhanced further by the modest lifestyle the royal couple adopted (Plate 18). At Buckingham House, known as 'The Queen's House' because it had been a gift from George to his new bride, they created both the image and reality of domestic harmony, living 'in a retired manner, but easy of access' as one contemporary put it.[319] A German visitor, accustomed to the representational splendour of the imperial courts, was impressed by the contrast: 'the noble simplicity of the furnishings, the order and neatness, were marks of the character of the owner—marks of wise humility upon the throne.'[320] Indeed, the new owners had their home remodelled by Sir William Chambers to make it *less* ostentatious.[321] An eloquent and fine visual illustration of this informality was provided by Johann Zoffany in his celebrated painting of *Queen Charlotte and her two eldest sons*, which shows the two infants playfully interrupting their mother at her dressing-table.[322] In conveying an

[317] John Ehrman, *The Younger Pitt*. Vol. I: *The Years of Acclaim* (London, 1969), p. 152.

[318] See above, p. 326.

[319] John Watkins, *Memoirs of Her Most Excellent Majesty Sophia Charlotta* (London, 1819), p. 591. Quoted in Clarissa Campbell Orr, 'The Saxon Princess: Queen Charlotte and the English court 1760–1820' (unpublished paper presented to the Society for Court Studies, London, 19 March 1997).

[320] Edna Healey, *The Queen's House: A Social History of Buckingham Palace* (London, 1997), p. 52.

[321] Ibid., p. 39; Campbell Orr, 'The Saxon Princess'.

[322] Michael Levey, *Painting at Court* (New York, 1971), pp. 155–6. Simon Schama, 'The domestication of majesty: royal family portraiture 1500–1850', in Robert I. Rotberg and Theodore K. Rabb (eds.), *Art and history: Images and their Meaning* (Cambridge, 1988), p. 171.

appropriate image to the public sphere, it was especially helpful that both king and queen were pious Christians by conviction. In 1766 George composed a political testament for his son and heir which is none the less valuable for having had absolutely no impact on its intended beneficiary:

This has made me undertake to write down my own transactions which I call Heaven to witness I mean without partiality to myself fairly to state, that whenever God of his infinite goodness shall call me out of this world the tongue of malice may not paint my intentions in those colours she admires, nor the sycophant extoll me beyond what I deserve. I do not pretend to any superior abilitys, but will give place to no one in meaning to preserve the freedom, happiness, and glory of my dominions, and all their inhabitants, and to fulfill the duty to my God and my neighbour in the most extended sense. That I have erred is undoubted, otherwise I should not be human, but I flatter myself all unprejudiced persons will be convinced that whenever I have failed it has been from the head not the heart.[323]

For her part, the Queen banned the playing of cards for money at court, declined to set or follow extravagant fashions, devoted herself to improving her mind through close study of the natural sciences, and even dispensed with the services of her hairdresser on Sundays so that *he* might attend church.[324] Frugality, modesty, fidelity, and piety did not make for a lively court, but they were the sort of virtues many Britons liked to read about, see represented in prints, or witness at first hand. In 1781 the *Ladies' Poetical Magazine* published the following panegyric:

> Happy for England, were each female mind,
> To science more, and less to pomp inclin'd;
> If parents, by example, prudence taught,
> And from their QUEEN the flame of virtue caught!
> Skill'd in each art that serves to polish life,
> Behold in HER a scientifick wife![325]

The royal family's domestic bliss and the agricultural interests of 'Farmer George' were a constant theme of affectionate satires.[326] Of the many tributes which poured from the presses and were preached from the pulpits following

[323] Brooke, *George III*, p. 90.

[324] Campbell Orr, 'The Saxon Princess'.

[325] Clarissa Campbell Orr, 'Charlotte, scientific queen', in Clarissa Campbell Orr (ed.), *Queenship in Britain 1660–1837: Royal Patronage, Court Culture and Dynastic Politics* (Manchester University Press, forthcoming).

[326] M. Dorothy George, *Hogarth to Cruikshank: Social Change in Graphic Satire* (London, 1967), p. 59; Langford, *A Polite and Commercial People*, pp. 581–2.

George III's death, the following summarizes well the character popularly ascribed to him:

His virtues were those which soon reach the heart, and long remain there. Faithful in his conjugal relations—steady in his friendships—affectionate in his parental character—benevolent in his disposition—warm in his attachments—the glory of the *Monarch* was eclipsed by the goodness of the *Man*; and his Subjects loved to talk of him in his fireside enjoyments, rather than in his royal splendours.[327]

In keeping with this image was his judiciously careful patronage of the arts: enough to sustain a cultured reputation with the intelligentsia but without the representational excess associated with Stuart predecessors or continental contemporaries. On 10 December 1768 he issued the instrument which created the 'Royal Academy of Arts in London, for the Purpose of Cultivating and Improving the Arts of Painting, Sculpture and Architecture', paying its initial expenses and allocating it rooms in Somerset House.[328] Although his own tastes have not been franked by posterity, as he preferred Ramsay to Reynolds, he did allow the latter to become the Academy's first president and knighted him in 1769.[329] Reynolds responded with the following compliment, paid in his opening address to the first general meeting of the new academy, held on 2 January 1769: 'We are happy in having a prince who has conceived the design of such an institution, according to its true dignity, and who promotes the arts as the head of a great, a learned, a polite, and commercial nation.'[330] The next president was George's favourite, American-born Benjamin West, who made the hyperbolic claim in his annual discourse that 'in no age of the world have the arts been carried in any country to such a summit as they now hold among us.' The reason for British artistic supremacy, West continued, was plain:

As the source of that patronage, we look up with affectionate gratitude to the benign and flattering attention of our most gracious Sovereign, to whose regard for the

[327] Edward Holt, *The Public and Domestic Life of His late Most Gracious Majesty, George the Third; comprising the most eventful and important period in the Annals of British History*, 2 vols. (London, 1820), I, p. iv.

[328] Nikolaus Pevsner, *Academies of Art—Past and Present* (Cambridge, 1940), pp. 185–6.

[329] William T. Whitley, *Artists and their Friends in England 1700–1799* (London, 1928), pp. 254–6.

[330] John Pye, *Patronage of British art, an historical sketch: an account of the rise and progress of art and artists in London, from the beginning of the reign of George the Second; together with a history of the Society for the Management and Distribution of the Artists' Fund* (London, 1845), p. 171. This remains the fullest and best-documented account of patronage of the visual arts in England during the eighteenth century.

elegant arts, and munificent disposition to cherish every enlargement of science, and improvement of the human mind, his people are indebted for this public seminary, his own favoured Institution, and the first which this country has ever been so fortunate as to see established.[331]

Less spectacular but perhaps more beneficial was his devotion of very large sums from his private purse to the purchase of books to form the nucleus of a national library, designed for scholars and open to all. In 1783 the first American envoy to Britain, John Adams, described the library, which was housed in four large rooms at the Queen's House, as evincing 'the same taste, the same judgment, the same elegance, the same simplicity, without the smallest affectation, ostentation, profusion or meanness. I could not but compare it, in my own mind, with Versailles, and not at all to the advantage of the latter.'[332]

George's apotheosis was greatly assisted, and may indeed have been made possible, by a sharp improvement in the fortunes of war. If 1781 had been the worst year for the British, 1782 was the best. On land, they held on to New York and Charleston and went on the offensive in Connecticut. At sea, the combined forces of Rodney and Hood won a crushing victory over the French at the Saintes, winning back control of the Caribbean and the Atlantic. A triumphant Rodney told the Earl of Sandwich, the Secretary of State, that the French fleet had been given 'such a blow as they will not recover', concluding: 'you may now despise all your enemies.'[333] In the autumn of the same year, the final attempt by the combined Franco-Spanish force to capture Gibraltar failed comprehensively. In India, de Bussy's major expedition to achieve French control of the subcontinent, as part of a grand scheme for national economic regeneration, was delayed by British naval action and did not get going until after the peace preliminaries had been signed.[334] Fortified by this success, the British negotiators were able to extract a peace early in 1783 which was better than anything that could have been imagined even a year earlier. The independence of the United States of America was recognized, of course, but Canada, Newfoundland, and Nova Scotia remained British. The

[331] Quoted in John Galt, *The Life, Studies and Works of Benjamin West* (London, 1820; reprinted Gainesville, Fl., 1960), pp. 141–2. No wonder West was enthusiastic: between 1769 and 1801 he received from the king the colossal sum of £34,187 for pictures painted; Pye, *Patronage of British Art*, p. 230 n. 41.

[332] Brooke, *George III*, pp. 304–5.

[333] Stephen Conway, *The War of American Independence 1775–1783* (London, 1995), p. 140.

[334] Vincent T. Harlow, *The Founding of the Second British Empire*, 2 vols. (London, 1952–64), I, pp. 314–17.

French secured only Tobago, a share in the Newfoundland fishing, and a few trading stations in Senegal and India. The Spanish did rather better, regaining Minorca and Florida. In India the *status quo ante bellum* was restored. In short, the Bourbon allies signally failed to reverse the verdict of the Seven Years War.

Moreover, if the British had failed to win the war, they certainly won the peace. As Jonathan Dull concluded: 'ironically, the European state that ultimately benefited most from the war was Britain.'[335] Every passing year confirmed the accuracy of Shelburne's prediction that loss of political control over America would be followed by a compensating expansion of commerce between the two nations. Trade with the rest of the world, especially with the East, quickly regained, and then exceeded, prewar levels. Industrial output grew in proportion, benefiting especially from the resumption of uninterrupted supplies of raw cotton. With customs revenue booming, Pitt was able to bring under control the enormous rise in the national debt incurred by the war. He also put through a series of administrative reforms to the revenue service, which confirmed his growing reputation for prudence and efficiency.[336] Despite his youth and inexperience, he proved to be an adept manager of the House of Commons, which was just as well, given the quality of the opposition spokesmen. As William Eden observed: 'It is a very loose Parliament and Government has not a decisive hold of it upon any particular question.'[337] That Pitt failed to carry his private measure of parliamentary reform was not surprising; more serious was the defeat of his attempt to reform commercial relations with Ireland.

Careful husbandry was not the stuff of heroes. To catch the public imagination, a reassertion of British power was needed. The general opinion in Europe was that the American War had initiated the terminal decline of the British Empire, now expected to be even shorter-lived than the Dutch. In the spring of 1783, Joseph II told his ambassador at the court of Versailles: 'England's position beggars description; it shows just how much this nation has degenerated. If France had gained from the late war nothing beyond her demonstration to the rest of Europe of the desperate and pitiable condition of her rival she would have still achieved a great deal.' In his view, England was now to be regarded as a second-rate power on the level of Denmark or

[335] Jonathan R. Dull, *A Diplomatic History of the American Revolution* (New Haven and London, 1985), pp. 160–1.

[336] The best account of this very technical subject is to be found in Ehrman, *The Younger Pitt*, vol. I, ch. 10 *passim*.

[337] Rosebery, *Pitt*, p. 76.

Sweden.[338] Frederick the Great of Prussia was equally convinced of her 'exhaustion and weakness'.[339] So when the British came looking for a continental alliance with which to escape from their inglorious isolation, they were rebuffed. They were not helped by the vigorous policy pursued by their king in his capacity as Elector of Hanover. George's decision to join the Prussian-led 'League of Princes' (*Fürstenbund*) in 1785 cut straight across simultaneous efforts by his English ministers to negotiate an alliance with Austria.[340] Worse still, the treaty concluded between France and the Dutch Republic in the same year opened up the awful possibility that the loss of America would be followed quickly by the loss of India. Now that Dutch bases at the Cape of Good Hope and in Ceylon were at the disposal of the French, who already had a commanding position in the Indian Ocean, thanks to their possession of the Île de Bourbon (Réunion) and the Île de France (Mauritius), they had a decisive advantage in any future conflict. The British had no naval base between St Helena and India. An anxious Pitt wrote to the governor-general of India, Earl Cornwallis, in August 1787:

> From the maritime strength which it [the Dutch Republic] might at least be made capable of exerting (when acting under the direction of France, who would naturally turn everything to that object), from its local position, and particularly from that of its dependencies in India, I need not point out to your lordship how much this country would have to apprehend from such an event in any war in which we may be hereafter engaged.[341]

By the time Pitt wrote those gloomy words, a rapid train of events was already under way which would dispel the threat. Salvation was made possible by the descent of the Dutch Republic into something approaching civil war, as the traditional struggle between the maritime provinces, led by Amsterdam and supported by the French, and the landed interest, led by the Stadholder and supported by the British, reached a cyclical climax. In June 1787 the Princess of Orange, wife of the Stadholder William V, had been arrested by a paramilitary group of supporters of the dominant Patriot Party. Although she was soon released, her brother, Frederick William II of Prussia, sought but failed to extract satisfaction from the Dutch Estates General. Strengthened in his resolve by the outbreak of war in the Balkans, which was certain to

338 Quoted in T. C. W. Blanning, '"That horrid electorate" or "Ma patrie germanique"? George III, Hanover and the *Fürstenbund* of 1785', *Historical Journal*, 20, 2 (1977), pp. 314–15.

339 Ibid.

340 Ibid. *passim*.

341 Quoted in T. C. W. Blanning, *The Origins of the French Revolutionary Wars* (London, 1986), p. 49.

preoccupy the Austrians for the foreseeable future, in September Frederick William sent in the army. Within six weeks, the entire country was in Prussian hands. For the British, nothing could have been more welcome. With the Stadholder back under full control and his Francophile opponents in prison or exile, the way was clear to return the Dutch Republic to its traditional subordination to British interests. Edmund Burke was expressing a deeply held national prejudice when he told the House of Commons that 'Holland might justly be considered as necessary a part of this country as Kent'.[342] The sea-lanes to India, and with them the British Empire, were safe once more. Vital national interests had been asserted, the memory of America had been eclipsed if not expunged, and—just to put icing on the celebratory cake—the old enemy had been humiliated.

This was a great triumph, and was recognized as such.[343] Moreover, it signalled a radical transformation in the European states system very much to the benefit of Great Britain. With Russia, Austria, and the Ottoman Empire all tied down by the reopening of the Eastern Question; with the Dutch Republic and Prussia tied into a 'Triple Alliance'; and with France suffering from creeping paralysis, the British were in a position to give the law to Europe. And they did so. Their mediation between Prussia and Austria at Reichenbach in July 1790 raised British influence and prestige to unprecedented heights. As one diplomat crowed, Britain was 'now incontestably in possession of the balance of Europe'.[344] So the Temple of British Worthies was almost ready to receive the king under whose aegis this 'happy change' had occurred. He had prepared the way by a charm offensive following the American War, as he and his family increased their public exposure through tours and well-publicized attendance at military reviews and charitable events.[345] By now he was giving away to charity the huge sum of £14,000 a year, or about a quarter of his privy purse, thus earning the well-merited title of 'the most generous monarch in modern British history'.[346] In 1787 his 'Proc-

[342] Quoted in ibid., p. 47.

[343] Ehrman, *The Younger Pitt*, vol. I, p. 536.

[344] Alleyne Fitzherbert to the Duke of Leeds, quoted in ibid., p. 551.

[345] Frank Prochaska, *The Republic of Britain 1760 to 2000* (London, 2000), p. 9.

[346] Ibid, p. 10. See also the same author's *Royal Bounty: The Making of a Welfare Monarchy* (New Haven and London, 1995), ch. 1 *passim*. Like so many aspects of George III's kingship, this had its origins in the previous two reigns, during which the royal association with charity was secularized and objectivized (in the sense of being detached from the person of the monarch)—'the Hanoverian royal family was thus identified, slowly but effectively, with an emerging sector of British "national life"'; Matthew Charles Kilburn, *Royalty and Public in Britain 1714–1789* (unpublished Oxford D.Phil. dissertation, 1997), p. 56.

lamation against Vice and Immorality' was a well-timed gesture towards the growing Evangelical movement.

All that was needed now was a surge of public affection to give emotional zest to the respect and admiration which already existed. That a fund of good will did exist was demonstrated by the failure of an assassination attempt in August 1786, when a demented woman tried to stab him as he dismounted outside St James's Palace. George prevented her lynching by shouting to the crowd which had seized her: 'The creature is mad! Do not hurt her! She has not hurt me!' In the days that followed there were many demonstrations of public celebration at his escape. Fanny Burney reported on his visit to Kew:

> Kew Green was quite filled with all the inhabitants of the place—the lame, old, blind, sick, and infants, who all assembled, dressed in their Sunday garb, to line the sides of the roads through which their Majesties passed, attended by the band of musicians, arranged in the front, who began 'God save the King' the moment they came upon the Green and finished it with loud huzzas.[347]

Paradoxically, it was George's own descent into what appeared to be insanity, in the autumn of 1788, which set the seal on his popularity. The unseemly haste with which Charles James Fox and the opposition sought unlimited powers for the Prince of Wales as Regent, in blatant contradiction of their Whig principles, confirmed their reputation for unprincipled opportunism. That the Prince had now gone well and truly off the rails, aided and abetted by Fox and his hell-raising friends, only served to heighten the contrast between the purity of the afflicted father and the decadence of his enemies. Confident that the king would soon recover, Pitt fought a delaying action with a Bill to restrict the powers of the Prince Regent. By early February 1789 it was clear that George was on the mend. When his recovery was announced officially at the end of the month, there ensued 'the most brilliant, as well as the most universal exhibition of national loyalty and joy ever witnessed in England', as Nathaniel Wraxall put it.[348] Across the length and breadth of the country, services of thanksgiving were held and addresses of loyalty compiled. Of the latter, the following, from 'the Gentlemen, Clergy, Freeholders, Citizens and Principal Inhabitants of the City of Durham, and its Environs', provides a representative sample:

[347] Quoted in Brooke, *George III*, p. 315. On George's triumphal progress to Weymouth in June 1789, see Ida Macalpine and Richard Hunter, *George III and the Mad-business* (London, 1969), p. 96.

[348] Brooke, *George III*, p. 341.

Most Gracious and Potent Monarch,
Great Britain, the Queen of the Isles and Pride of Nations, Arbitress of Europe, perhaps of the World; the Nursery of the Arts, Freedom and Independence; the Terror of her Enemies, and Scourge of Tyrants, is once more raised from a depending, humbled Situation to its present glorious and resplendent Acme of Power, Opulence and Grandeur, by a Descendant of the great and illustrious Chatham, and his responsible Coadjutors in Administration, under the immediate Direction, benign and spirited Auspices of our most gracious, potent and much-beloved Sovereign, for whose happy Restoration to the inestimable Blessings of Health, Domestic Felicity, and for the Political Salvation and Comfort of these Realms, the humble and grateful Adorations to the Omnipotent be ever due. The Vallies may now again be justly said to laugh and sing, and the Mountains to leap for Joy, praising the One Eternal for His infinite Mercies.[349]

This address had been signed by 930 persons. The Prince of Wales, Fox, and their friends resumed their sulky opposition. The great majority of the political nation, however, rallied to their convalescent sovereign. Their enthusiasm greatly impressed the Austrian envoy, Count Reviczy, for example, not least because it contrasted so starkly with the aristocratic opposition to his own master, Joseph II. He reported that George returned to St James for the first time since his illness on 26 March. There was a tremendous press of peers at court, with almost all the ladies wearing ribbons on their hats proclaiming 'God Save the King!' He went on:

When one observes these manifestations of joy shining out everywhere on this occasion and in so extraordinary a fashion, one cannot help but be somewhat surprised that the King should possess the love and affection of the nation to such a high degree, indeed to an extent that has never been witnessed before, for in itself his reign has not achieved much to boast about but has suffered such calamities as the loss of a large overseas possession and the limitless expansion of the National Debt.

After observing that no one in England now regretted the loss of America, for trade had actually increased while the previous burden of defence had been lifted, he presented the following acute analysis of the reasons for George's success:

It is clear, therefore, that what has really counted in winning for the King the love of his people have been his good personal qualities, which allow them to live under his rule secure in their liberty and their rights, the judicious choice of ministers which the King has made, the economic way of life he follows, so that he can be as light a burden to the nation as possible, despite his numerous family which needs to be

[349] *London Gazette*, 13077, 14–17 March 1789.

provided for, and finally his morals, principles and piety make him more popular with each day that passes, so that for all time he can count on the most forceful demonstrations of devotion from his subjects.[350]

Among others moved to express their joy at the King's recovery in verse was the populist poet William Cowper (himself prone to bouts of instability and so naturally sympathetic), although it cannot be said that it inspired his best work:

The spring of eighty-nine shall be
An aera cherish'd long by me,
Which joyful I will oft record,
And thankful at my frugal board;
For then the clouds of eighty-eight,
That threaten'd England's trembling state
With loss of what she least could spare,
Her sov'reign's tutelary care.[351]

It was during the 1780s that 'public opinion' came of age as the ultimate political legitimator. It was Richard Pares's view that when George came to the throne in 1760 the concept 'meant so little as to be hardly worth using at all', but that twenty years later it had both established its position at the centre and had spread to the provinces.[352] The massive expansion of voluntary associations, public cultural institutions, and newspaper circulation combined to give 'the public' a status it has never since lost.[353] As we have seen, it was a development which did not necessarily favour opposition groups, especially not those led by peers with an aristocratic disdain for the masses. A sceptical Lord Shelburne queried: 'People talk of public opinion; and what creates or constitutes public opinion? Numbers certainly do not.' He complained that forty years of political experience had convinced him that 'the publick is

[350] Quoted in T. C. W. Blanning, 'George III, Hanover and the Regency Crisis', in Jeremy Black (ed.), *Knights Errant and True Englishmen: British Foreign Policy, 1660–1800* (Edinburgh, 1989), p. 147.

[351] *The Poetical Works of William Cowper*, ed. H. S. Milford (London, 1934), p. 386. This poem was entitled 'Annus Memorabilis, 1789. Written in commemoration of His Majesty's happy recovery'. See also 'On the Queen's visit to London the night of the 17th March 1789', p. 388.

[352] Richard Pares, *King George III and the Politicians* (Oxford, 1953), p. 198. On previous uses of the concept, see L. Hölscher, 'Meinung, öffentliche', in Joachim Ritter and Karlfried Gründer (eds.), *Historisches Wörterbuch der Philosophie*, vol. 5 (Darmstadt, 1980), p. 1024.

[353] On the importance of voluntary associations and cultural institutions, see Peter Clark, *Sociability and Urbanity: Clubs and Societies in the Eighteenth Century City*, The Eighth H. J. Dyos Lecture, 23 April 1986 (Leicester, 1986), *passim*.

incapable of embracing two objects at a time' and that it was better at demolition than construction.[354] However, by his actions after 1782 George III demonstrated an instinctive grasp that public opinion could be used as a powerful support for monarchical authority.

CONCLUSION

George's recovery early in 1789 came just in time. Six weeks after his return to court at the end of March 1789, the French Estates General met at Versailles. Most English people, including the intelligent and far-sighted William Pitt, believed that France had descended into irreversible anarchy, leaving Britain with a clear run. As late as February 1792 he was complacently predicting fifteen years of peace.[355] Almost exactly a year later, Great Britain embarked on a war which was to last for twenty-three years and make every previous conflict seem puny by comparison. It was to bring the 'Second Hundred Years War', which had begun in 1689 with James II's French-sponsored invasion of Ireland, to a triumphant conclusion. At the sharp end of proceedings, it was the naval victories at the Nile or Trafalgar, and the military victories at Salamanca and Waterloo, which determined the outcome. They were made possible, however, by the existence of a political culture which allowed the maximization of the country's resources to be combined with political and social stability. This chapter has sought to show how that culture came about.

If the strength of English national identity derived from the depth of its roots, the garish hues of its flowers have not been to everyone's taste. To modern eyes, obliged to be hypersensitive to anything smacking of national self-esteem (outside the world of sport), eighteenth-century boasting can seem comic, or offensive, or both. As a consequence, it is not always given the historical attention it deserves. Yet it was clearly obtrusive and powerful. The Abbé Le Blanc ironically thanked the English for denying the French the title of 'most ridiculously arrogant nation on earth':

> However good opinion one entertains of the English, he is still surprised at the excess of their prejudices: far from confining them to things which are peculiar to them, they extend them without bounds: they would be thought to excell all mankind in all

[354] Shelburne, 'A chapter of autobiography', in [Edmond George] Lord Fitzmaurice, *Life of William Earl of Shelburne afterwards Marquess of Lansdowne*, 2nd edn., 2 vols (London, 1912), I, pp. 24, 80–1.

[355] Blanning, *The Origins of the French Revolutionary Wars*, p. 134.

things... To take their words, all the efforts of the wit of man cannot imagine a wiser form of government than theirs; the English are the most industrious, brave and virtuous people of the whole earth; and the only one that has placed the treasure of liberty above the reach of destiny, both for the honour of human nature in general, and for their own in particular.[356]

A German visitor, Johannes Wilhelm von Archenholz was more generous—and also more understanding—when he linked English pride to English liberty, as in: 'it is with great reason that the English boast of the liberty of the press, and regard it as the *palladium* or safeguard of their civil liberty.' He concluded: 'The national pride of the English is a natural consequence of a political constitution, by which every citizen is exempted from any other dependence that that imposed by the laws. This pride is carried among them to a great length. Indeed, how is it possible to know and to feel all the merit of such a system of liberty, without attaching an uncommon value to it?'[357]

Both Le Blanc and Archenholz used the word 'English' rather than 'British'. They were right to do so. Undoubtedly there was a British identity in the making in the course of the eighteenth century, fuelled by a common Anglo-Scottish interest in preserving Protestantism, winning wars, and benefiting from an expanding empire.[358] Yet this was an exercise dominated by Englishmen and English interests, and was very much directed from London. Members of the Celtic fringe participated only at the cost of assimilating to English cultural models.[359] The emergence of France after 1688 as the great 'other', against whose Catholic despotism the English defined themselves, did not mean that more ancient antipathies closer to home were abandoned. Indeed, the simultaneous demonization of internal and external enemies accounts in large measure for the intensity of English nationalism. As Patrick Collinson has suggested: 'The question of the origins of English national

[356] [Jean François] Abbé Le Blanc, *Letters on the English and French Nations; containing curious and useful observations on their constitutions natural and political; nervous and humorous descriptions of the virtues, vices, ridicules and foibles of the inhabitants: critical remarks on their writers; together with moral reflections interspersed throughout the work*, 2 vols. (London, 1747), I, pp. 9–10. For a similar lament from Justus Möser, see above, p. 242.

[357] Johannes Wilhelm von Archenholz, *A Picture of England, containing a description of the laws, customs and manners of England* (Dublin, 1790), pp. 7, 32. He was enough of a German patriot, however, to add in a footnote: 'I must say, to the honour of our country, that, except England, there is no other kingdom in the world where an honest man may write so many bold truths, and discover so many abuses, as in Germany.'

[358] This is one of the central arguments in Linda Colley's trail-blazing *Britons*. See especially pp. 123–45.

[359] Murray G. H. Pittock, *Inventing and Resisting Britain: Cultural Identities in Britain and Ireland, 1685–1789* (London, 1997), pp. 131, 134–5, 173.

self-consciousness is ultimately one for the very early medievalist, the Anglo-Saxonist, since they evidently lay in confrontation with that "other" which was Celtic.'[360]

Collinson also pointed out, with his usual perspicacity, just how detachable was English nationalism from the person of the monarch or his dynasty. In 1641, as the struggle between Charles I and Parliament moved towards rupture, Edmund Calamy preached a sermon entitled 'England's Looking-Glasse', in which he told Parliament :

> You that are the representative Body of this Nation . . . You are the Nation representatively . . . you stand in the place of the whole Nation; and if you stand for Gods cause, the whole Nation doth it in you. As this is a *Nationall day*, and this Honourable Assembly a *Nationall Assembly*, so this Text is a *Nationall Text*, suitable for the occasion about which we are met, National Repentance will divert Nationall judgments and procure Nationall blessings.[361]

During the early modern period, at least, English nationalism was not dynastic. It could attach itself to an individual monarch if she or he appeared to be promoting English interests, but could as easily desert if the reverse were the case. It could even attach itself to a dynasty, as it did with the Hanoverians, if the alternative's identity was so manifestly anti-national as were the Catholic, French-sponsored Stuarts. And those interests were held to be Protestantism,[362] prosperity (especially commercial prosperity), imperial expansion, and liberty. It was George III's achievement, albeit after a long and painful political apprenticeship, to associate himself with those objectives so completely as to become their personification. The Patriot King had been found at last.[363] Under his aegis, the British appeared to have found the political equivalent of the philosopher's stone—the means of combining power with liberty. Among other things, it was to enable them to win the Second Hundred Years War.

360 Patrick Collinson, 'Biblical rhetoric: the English nation and national sentiment in the prophetic mode', in Claire McEachern and Debora Shuger (eds.), *Religion and Culture in Renaissance England* (Cambridge, 1997), p. 38 n. 14.

361 Ibid., p. 18. Collinson comments: 'All those repetitions of "national" were artful, not inadvertent. Is anyone still prepared to deny the potency of a kind of national consciousness in early modern England?'

362 I cannot agree with Jonathan Clark that it was Anglicanism rather than Protestantism which was crucial; J. C. D. Clark, 'Protestantism, nationalism and national identity', *Historical Journal*, 43, 1 (2000), p. 274. Certainly there were important divisions within and between the Protestant communities in England, but they were quick to combine when danger threatened from Catholic enemies within or without.

363 Gerrard, *The Patriot Opposition to Walpole*, p. 14.

8

The Cultural Origins of the French Revolution

THE MUSICAL ORIGINS

Jean-Jacques Rousseau died on 2 July 1778, so was denied the opportunity of analysing his contribution to the collapse of the old regime in France. However, he did insist, with his own special assertiveness, that he had once *prevented* a revolution. Writing in the *Confessions* about his pamphlet *Letters on French Music* of 1753, he claimed: 'Whoever reads that this pamphlet probably prevented a revolution in France will think that he is dreaming. Yet it is an actual fact, which all Paris can still bear witness to, for it is less than fifteen years since that singular incident.'[1] He was referring to one of his contributions to the *querelle des bouffons*, a controversy over the relative merits of French and Italian music, which raged during 1752–3. If his claim seems hyperbolic, it should be borne in mind that 'a passion for opera gripped Parisian high society' throughout the eighteenth century.[2] Contemporary observations confirming the accuracy of that assessment are not hard to find. Voltaire, for example, wrote in a letter in 1732: 'The opera is a public rendezvous where we assemble on certain days without knowing why. It is a place where everyone goes, although we all speak ill of the composer and even though he is boring. By contrast, a major effort is required to draw the multitude to the *Comédie*,

[1] Jean-Jacques Rousseau, *The Confessions*, ed. and trans. J. M. Cohen (London, 1953), p. 358.
[2] Jean-Marie Duhamel, *La Musique dans la ville de Lully à Rameau* (Lille, 1994), p. 47.

and I almost always find that the greatest success of a fine tragedy does not approach that of a mediocre opera.'[3] In Diderot's *novella* of the same name, Rameau's nephew asks the chevalier de Turcaret: '"Do you like music?" "Yes," is the reply, "worst luck, I am a subscriber at the Opéra." "It is the dominant passion of good society," observes Rameau's nephew. "It is certainly mine," agrees Turcaret.'[4] Charles Dufresny wrote in 1747: 'The clock strikes four in the afternoon, so it's time to go to the Opéra; we shall need at least an hour to get through the crowd which besieges the entrance.'[5] As the guidebooks instructed, for every visitor to Paris, from the provinces or from abroad, a regular visit to the Opéra was *de rigueur*. It was the public centre of fashionable Parisian cultural life.

The *querelle des bouffons* can be divided into three phases. On 14 January 1752, the Opéra revived *Omphale* by André Cardinal Destouches, a work first performed in 1701. A month later, Friedrich Melchior von Grimm published a pamphlet entitled *A Letter from M. Grimm on the Subject of Omphale*.[6] Grimm had been in Paris since 1748, seeking to carve out a niche in society, and this pamphlet was probably designed to establish his credentials as a music critic.[7] It was a judicious blend of criticism and flattery. On the one hand, he compared the French operatic tradition exemplified by *Omphale* most unfavourably with Italian music, which—he asserted—was preferred by every country in the world except France. On the other hand, he singled out for special praise the work of Rameau, currently the dominant figure in French music. A brief flurry of controversy followed the publication of Grimm's pamphlet, with replies and counter-replies from—among others—the Abbé Raynal and Jean-Jacques Rousseau.

This phase—centred on Grimm's pamphlet—had already come to an end by the time the second began in August of the same year, when an Italian entrepreneur, Eustachio Bambini, brought his *opera buffa* troupe to Paris to perform *intermezzi* at the Opéra (*intermezzi* being short comic operas staged between the acts or at the conclusion of the heavyweight lyric tragedies which provided the standard fare). The Italians opened their season with Pergolesi's *La Serva padrona* ('The servant as mistress'). It was hardly a topical work, for it

[3] Quoted in William Weber, 'Learned and general musical taste in eighteenth-century France', *Past and Present*, 89 (1980), p. 73.

[4] Quoted in Duhamel, *La musique dans la ville*, p. 47.

[5] Ibid.

[6] Reprinted in Denise Launay (ed.), *La Querelle des bouffons*, 3 vols. (Geneva, 1973), I, pp. 2 ff. Launay reprints 61 pamphlets, 2381 pages all told, but does not claim that this is a complete collection.

[7] Paul-Marie Masson, 'La *Lettre sur Omphale*', *Revue de Musicologie*, 24 (1945), p. 2.

had first been performed at Naples back in 1733 and the composer had died in 1736. It had made no impact when first performed at Paris in 1746, but in 1752 it proved to be a sensation.[8] News of their triumph reached even the gloomy duc de Luynes, who recorded in his journal that the *bouffons* had enjoyed '*le succès le plus grand et le plus brillant*'.[9] The popularity of the *bouffons* prompted another critic of German origin (and another baron, to boot)—d'Holbach—to publish a pamphlet in November 1752, which followed Grimm in praising Italian music at the expense of French. This began phase two, a more prolonged and much fiercer struggle, as response and counterblast kept the Parisian presses humming through the winter and into the new year. In the autumn of 1753, just as the controversy seemed to be running out of steam, it was given a new injection of life by none other than Rousseau, whose *Letter on French Music*, published in November, provoked a counter-attack of sustained intensity and volume. As he himself recorded with characteristic immodesty in *The Confessions*, 'A description of the incredible effect of this pamphlet would be worthy of the pen of Tacitus,' adding that the orchestra of the Opéra had planned to assassinate him and had been prevented only by an escort of musketeers thoughtfully provided by a military admirer.[10] During this third and final phase, Bambini's *bouffons* had been almost forgotten, leaving France in February 1754 after taking their farewell with the performance of a work appropriately entitled *I Viaggatori*.[11] Rousseau lived to fight another day, but the episode both fed his persecution complex and helped to alienate him further from the mainstream of *les lumières*.

If only because Rousseau was convinced of its importance, this is an episode to be taken seriously. A good place to start is with the music. As we have seen, a distinctively French musical genre was of relatively recent origin, being ironically the creation of an Italian, Jean-Baptiste Lully *né* Giovanni Battista Lulli, from 1660 the royal musical director. By the time he died in 1687 he had created the *tragédie lyrique*, a form of opera perfectly suited to the Versailles system.[12] The genre did not die with the old king, on the contrary it was to have a very long life, living on into the nineteenth century in the form of grand opera. In the eighteenth century it was kept going by the genius of

[8] For an excellent concise account of the affair, see Robert Wokler, '*La Querelle des Bouffons* and the Italian liberation of France: a study of revolutionary foreplay', *Eighteenth-Century Life*, 11 (1987), pp. 94–116.

[9] *Mémoires du duc de Luynes sur la cour de Louis XV (1735–1758)*, 17 vols. (Paris, 1861–5), XII, p. 195.

[10] Rousseau, *Confessions*. p. 359.

[11] Ibid., p. 96.

[12] See above, p. 44.

Jean-Philippe Rameau, who at the time of the *querelle des bouffons* was at the height of his career, fêted by both court and capital as 'the French Orpheus', celebrated not only as France's greatest living composer but also as the most authoritative musical theorist.[13]

For the audience at the Opéra in 1752, who experienced *La Serva padrona* as an intermezzo between two acts of Lully's *Acis et Galathée*, there could hardly have been a greater contrast between the lyric tragedy to which they were accustomed and the offerings of the *bouffons*. Both the plots and the scores of the former are long, complex, sophisticated, stately, and laden with symbolism. Those of *La Serva padrona* are short, crisp, fresh, simple, naïve, and direct, relying exclusively on the two foundations of Italian opera: melody and rhythm. Whereas to make sense of a lyric tragedy a classical education is essential, the plot of *La Serva padrona* makes no intellectual demands whatsoever. It has only three characters, one of whom is mute, and deals with simple people, taken from *la commedia dell'arte*, telling the story of Uberto, a silly old man, being tricked into marriage by his crafty female servant, Serpina. Sex is dealt with playfully and erotically, while in lyric tragedy it is part of a highly elaborate masque. Anyone who has sat through one of the periodic attempts to revive Rameau's work will appreciate why the *bouffons* seemed to have brought a rush of invigorating fresh air into the musty repertoire of the Opéra.[14] And that was the most important lesson taught by the *querelle*: that the court culture created by Louis XIV had lost its appeal and, more seriously, had lost its legitimacy. As we have seen, so far as music was concerned, at least, it had always been an artificial creation, in the sense that it had been invented for non-musical reasons to perform a political purpose. By the middle of the eighteenth century, the bombastic style this representational need engendered had come to seem over-elaborate, superannuated, boring. This was well put by Grimm in his second and more outspoken pamphlet, *Le Petit prophête de Boehmischbroda*, in which, in mock-biblical language, he described how a Bohemian musician was transported by magic to the Paris Opéra, where he found dancers constantly interrupting the music:

> For two and a half hours I was wearied by a collection of minuets, gavottes, rigaudons, tambourins and contredanses, interspersed with some scenes of plainsong that seemed to come straight from the evening service. I noted that in France this was called Opera.

[13] Masson, 'La *Lettre sur Omphale*', p. 16.

[14] William Christie and Les Arts Florissants made the best possible case for Rameau by presenting *Zorastre* in concert at the 1998 Promenade Concerts in London, but it was less than overwhelming.

It was not just a question of the passage of time. The whole genre of lyric tragedy, invented by Lully and continued by Rameau, was identified with the culture of Versailles. Indeed, the 'Royal Academy of Poetry and Music', which was the Opéra's full title, enjoyed a monopoly of all operatic performances in France, a monopoly which was jealously guarded. So the *philosophes* naturally lined up behind Grimm and the *bouffons* in their critical and artistic assaults on the Opéra, for—quite rightly—they saw it as the musical expression of the political establishment. In the voluminous pamphlet literature generated by the *querelle*, the cause of the *bouffons* was advanced as the cause of liberty per se against court, government, and establishment. No one put this better than d'Alembert, in a pamphlet entitled 'On the liberty of music':

I am amazed that in a century when all pens busy themselves with the liberty of trade, the liberty of marriage, the liberty of the press and even the liberty of printed linens, no one has yet written about THE LIBERTY OF MUSIC . . . Our great political figures reply: 'You are very short-sighted. All forms of liberty are linked and all are equally dangerous: liberty in music presupposes liberty to feel, and the liberty to feel involves liberty of thought, and liberty of thought involves liberty of action, and liberty of action is the ruin of states. So let us keep the Opéra as it is if we wish to preserve the kingdom, and so let us put a stop to the liberty to sing unless we want liberty to speak to follow' . . . It is difficult to credit, but the fact is that in the vocabulary of certain people, 'bouffoniste', 'republican', 'frondeur', 'atheist' (not forgetting 'materialist') are synonyms.[15]

With Diderot, d'Holbach, Grimm, Rousseau, Mably, not to mention d'Alembert himself, lining up on the side of the *bouffons*, that set of associations is not so difficult to understand. Moreover, the radical edge to the affair was sharpened by the triumphant success simultaneously achieved by Rousseau with the premiere of his comic opera *Le Devin du village* ('The village soothsayer') in the autumn of 1752. To appreciate the significance of this work, it needs to be borne in mind that three years earlier Rousseau had undergone a conversion experience which had altered fundamentally his attitude towards the modern world. In the summer of 1749, while walking to Vincennes to visit Diderot, currently languishing in prison there, he happened to read in the *Mercure de France* an advertisement for a prize-essay competition organized by the Dijon Academy. The subject specified was 'Has the progress of the sciences and arts done more to corrupt morals or improve them?' As Rousseau recorded in the *Confessions*: 'The moment I read this I beheld another universe

[15] Launay (ed.), *La Querelle des bouffons*, III, pp. 396–7.

and became another man.'[16] In a letter written later to Malesherbes, he expanded on this terse statement:

If ever anything resembled a sudden inspiration, it is what that advertisement stimulated in me: all at once I felt my mind dazzled by a thousand lights, a crowd of splendid ideas presented themselves to me with such force and in such confusion, that I was thrown into a state of indescribable bewilderment. I felt my head seized by a dizziness that resembled intoxication. A violent palpitation constricted me and made my chest heave. Unable to breathe and walk at the same time, I sank down under one of the trees in the avenue and passed the next half hour in such a state of agitation that when I got up I found that the front of my jacket was wet with tears, although I had no memory of shedding any.[17]

This epiphany marked not only the beginning of Rousseau's divorce from his fellow *philosophes* ('from that moment I was lost,' he recorded) but also, arguably, of Romanticism. Its first artistic fruit was *Le Devin du village*. The plot of this short work—it lasts only about an hour and a quarter—is simplicity itself. A shepherd, Colin, is seduced into neglecting his shepherdess, Colette, by the glamour of the lady of the manor. A despairing Colette enlists the help of the eponymous soothsayer. He tells Colin that Colette is cooling towards him, thus exciting Colin's jealousy and effecting a reconciliation. In the following extract, a suitably chastened Colin turns his back on the aristocratic world:

Je vais revoir ma charmante maîtresse.	I shall be seeing again the charming girl I love.
Adieu, châteaux, grandeurs, richesse,	Farewell, châteaux, pomp and riches,
Votre éclat ne me tente plus.	Your glamour tempts me no longer.
Si mes pleurs, mes soins assidus,	If only my tears and untiring attention
Peuvent toucher ce que j'adore,	can touch the heart of the one I adore,
Je vous verrai renaître encore,	then once again I shall see return
Doux moments que j'ai perdus.	those sweet moments I have lost.
Quand on sait aimer et plaire,	When one knows what it is to love and be loved,
A-t-on besoin d'autre bien?	does one need any other kind of riches?
Rends-moi ton cœur, ma bergère,	Give me back your heart, my shepherdess,
Colin t'a rendu le sien.	I, Colin, am giving you back mine.
Mon chalumeau, ma houlette,	Let my shepherd's pipes and my crook
Soyez mes seules grandeurs;	be my only badges of rank;
Ma parure est ma Colette,	my adornment is my Colette,
Mes trésors sont ses faveurs.	and my treasures are her favours.

[16] Rousseau, *Confessions*, p. 327.
[17] Quoted in Maurice Cranston, *Jean-Jacques: The Early Life and Works of Jean-Jacques Rousseau 1712–1754* (Harmondsworth, 1987), p. 228.

Que de seigneurs d'importance	If only the high and mighty
Voudroient avoir sa foi!	would share the trust she shows.
Malgré toute leur puissance,	For all their power,
Ils sont moins heureux que moi.	they are less happy than I am.

To drive home the gulf between the world of the aristocrat and the peasant, Rousseau wrote some incidental music for a ballet entitled 'Pantomime' to be choreographed according to the following scheme:

1. entry of the village girl
2. entry of the courtier
3. the courtier catches sight of the village girl; she dances while he observes her
4. he offers her money
5. she refuses it contemptuously
6. he gives her a necklace
7. she tries it on, gazing with delight at her image in the fountain
8. the villager enters
9. noticing the villager's distress, the girl returns the necklace
10. the courtier sees him; he threatens him
11. the girl tries to appease him and makes a sign to the villager to leave; he refuses and the courtier threatens to kill him
12. they both throw themselves at the feet of the courtier, who is moved and unites them
13. all three rejoice—the villagers in their union, the courtier in his good deed.

In other words, *Le Devin du village* looks very much like an exercise in social criticism, an exposé of the decadence of aristocratic mores. Yet it is both less and more than that. On the one hand, the work's message might be described as essentially conservative, for it is only the attempt by the peasants to leave their natural habitat which causes misery. Neither the lady of the manor in the opera nor the courtier in the ballet opposes the decision of Colin and Colette to return to their true world and true love. In that sense, the much older *La Serva padrona* is the more subversive, doubly so indeed, for in turning the tables on Uberto, Serpina is triumphing both as woman and as servant. Moreover, there was nothing in the reception of the work to suggest that it posed a threat to the social order. On the contrary: when the news leaked out from rehearsals that it was likely to be a success, the court intervened to claim the privilege of staging the première.[18] That took place on 18 October 1752 at Fontainebleau in the presence of Louis XV and his *maîtresse en titre*, Madame de Pompadour. It was a huge success, even with the notoriously unmusical

18 Ibid. p. 264.

king, who expressed a wish to meet the composer. Rousseau had condescended to put in an appearance at Fontainebleau, albeit 'dressed in my usual careless style, with a rough beard and an ill-combed wig, considering my unkempt state an act of courage'.[19] The first gentleman of the bedchamber, the duc d'Aumont, intimated to Rousseau that he would be rewarded at his royal audience with a pension. Never one to decline an opportunity to spurn good fortune, Rousseau at once returned to Paris, congratulating himself on rejecting the dependence that royal patronage would have entailed: 'so long as I took that pension, I should have to flatter or be silent' (adding more sensibly, 'besides, what assurance had I that it would be paid?').[20]

There was nothing feigned about Louis XV's enthusiasm. Pierre Jélyotte, the greatest singer of his day, who had created the role of Colin, wrote to Rousseau two days later to tell him that he had been a fool to turn his back on the greatest success the country had ever known. The whole court, he added, was enchanted with the work and the king went around all day long singing the arias 'with the worst voice in his kingdom'. The duc d'Aumont had assured Jélyotte that very morning that Rousseau would certainly have been given a pension if he had stayed for his audience.[21] Further evidence of royal approval came the following March, when *Le Devin du village* was performed again in the presence of the king at Madame de Pompadour's château of Bellevue, with the lady herself taking the part of Colin.[22] By that time, the work had also been given its first public performance at the Opéra, to great acclaim. It was to remain in the repertoire for the rest of the century and well into the next. Stendhal recorded going to see it in 1823, commenting acidly that it was 'a rather clumsy imitation of the sort of music which was fashionable in Italy around 1730. It was superseded a very long time ago, but the French will not give up their old ways. Europe is in state of upheaval in all regards, but the Opéra stands four-square unchanged.'[23] This one musical success made Rousseau famous overnight, confirming Voltaire's complaint noted earlier that it was opera which really counted in Paris. When the 18-year-old comtesse de Genlis arrived in Paris in 1764, she was very keen to meet Rousseau, not because of his books (she confessed that she had not read a word of them) but because he was the creator of *Le Devin du village*, 'a charming work which

[19] Rousseau, *The Confessions*, p. 352.

[20] Ibid., p. 354.

[21] Jean-Jacques Rousseau, *Correspondance complète*, ed. R. A. Leigh, vol. II (Geneva, 1965), p. 197.

[22] Ibid., pp. 212–13.

[23] Stendhal, *Life of Rossini*, trans. R. M. Coe (London, 1956), p. 292; first published in 1823.

pleased all those who liked natural things'.[24] Rousseau himself had mixed feelings, lamenting later that, although it had taken him only five or six weeks to write, it had earned him more money than *Émile*, which had cost him 'twenty years of meditation and three years of writing'.[25]

Although impossible to prove, it is at least very likely that Madame de Pompadour's motive in promoting *Le Devin du village* went beyond a desire to engage in amateur theatricals. She also wished to parade it as evidence that the French could write their own intermezzi, the equal if not the superior of anything the Italians could offer.[26] It was part of a two-pronged campaign, for she had already promoted a new lyric tragedy to advertise the undimmed superiority of French music. As Grimm put it in his *Correspondance littéraire* when commenting on the second phase of the *querelle des bouffons*: 'Patriotism revived. Madame de Pompadour believed that French music was in danger and quivered with indignation.'[27] She struck back with a gala performance of Mondonville's *Titon et Aurore* at the Opéra on 9 January 1753, spending even larger sums than usual on sets and costumes, enticing the great ballerina Camargo out of retirement for the occasion, ensuring that the two best singers of the day—Pierre Jélyotte and Marie Fel—were available, packing the stalls with her friends and—leaving absolutely nothing to chance—hiring a claque of musketeers to drown out the *bouffonistes* in the gallery. Grimm and his friends originally considered wearing mourning for the *bouffons* at this performance but thought better of it lest they found themselves in the Bastille.[28]

There the matter might have rested, but the most revealing episode in the saga was yet to come. In November 1753 Rousseau published a pamphlet entitled *A Letter on French Music*, a title which was something of a misnomer as it was his intention to demonstrate that the French had no music.[29] He began from first principles: all music consists of three elements, melody, harmony, and rhythm. As harmony is rooted in nature, it is the same for all nations, but melody does express national differences because its character is determined

[24] Madame de Genlis, *Mémoires inédits de Madame la Comtesse de Genlis, sur le dix-huitième siècle et la Révolution française, depuis 1756 à nos jours*, vol. II (Paris, 1825), p. 1. She added that she found him very uncouth, paying and receiving no visits.

[25] Cranston, *Rousseau*, p. 291.

[26] Louisette Reichenburg, *Contribution à l'histoire de la 'Querelle des Bouffons'* (Philadelphia, 1937), p. 69.

[27] Eve Kisch, 'Rameau and Rousseau', *Music and Letters*, 22 (1941), p. 102.

[28] Wokler, '*La Querelle des Bouffons*', *Eighteenth-Century Life*, 11, 1 (1987), p. 96.

[29] This is reprinted in Launay (ed.), *La Querelle des bouffons*, vol. I. An English translation of part of it can be found in Oliver Strunk (ed.), *Source Readings in Music History: From Classical Antiquity to the Romantic Era* (London, 1952), pp. 636–56.

mainly by language. It follows that there can be only one language in Europe suitable for music, and that is Italian, for it is especially sweet, harmonious, resonant (*sonore*), and stressed (*accentuée*). Consequently, 'any voice is good in Italian music, because the beauties of Italian singing are in the music itself, whereas those of French singing, if there are any, are all in the art of the singer.' French music, with its overemphasis on harmony, made a great deal of noise but had very little expression. He ended with the following crushing verdict:

I think that I have shown that there is neither measure nor melody in French music, because the language is not capable of them; that French singing is a continual squalling, insupportable to an unprejudiced ear; that its harmony is crude and devoid of expression and suggests only the padding of a pupil; that French 'airs' are not airs; that French recitative is not recitative. From this I conclude that the French have no music and cannot have any; or that if they ever have, it will be so much the worse for them.[30]

As Grimm observed, this was pretty rich, coming as it did from the composer of the most successful French comic opera of the century.[31] Rousseau had certainly introduced some 'Italian' elements into *Le Devin du village*, such as a three-part overture, the rapid recitative, and the brilliant violin piece, but they did not detract from its patently French character.[32] Rousseau stood condemned by his own arguments, for he had written his own libretto in the French language.

The pamphlet caused a sensation, greatly in excess of anything achieved by *Le Devin du village*, albeit the reaction was now as negative as it had been positive before. It also led to an immediate *renversement des alliances*. Whereas previously the battle-lines had been drawn between supporters of the *bouffons* and supporters of lyric tragedy, or more generally between the *philosophes* and the conservatives, it now became a confrontation between the defenders of French national honour and Rousseau. Many of those who liked Italian music, and were bored by Lully or Rameau, were deeply offended by the Swiss interloper's assertion that all French music was inevitably worthless—and rushed into print to say so. The very violence of their attacks suggested that they felt the ground moving beneath their feet, as French cultural hegemony began to crumble. The onslaught revealed one of the central dichotomies of modern politics: the essential divisibility of support for the cause of liberty and

[30] Ibid., p. 656.

[31] Maurice Tourneux (ed.), *Correspondance littéraire, philosophique et critique par Grimm, Diderot, Raynal, Meister, etc.*, vol. II (Paris, 1877), p. 307.

[32] Daniel Heartz, *Haydn, Mozart and the Viennese School 1740–1780* (New York and London, 1995), p. 525.

support for the cause of one's nation. These two ideals are not necessarily incompatible but are often likely to find themselves pulling in different directions. A commonplace of twentieth-century discourse, this was not so obvious even in the nineteenth century, or at least not until Bismarck showed what could be achieved by playing one off against the other.[33] Even during the first phase of the *querelle des bouffons* this had manifested itself, for example, in one of the anonymous replies to Grimm and his supporters. On the one hand, the author expressed impeccably libertarian principles:

> The land of taste is a land which is entirely free, and a land where no one can dictate or be dictated to. No one commands despotically there apart from Reason. Even kings are stripped of their rights there... When titled people write intellectual books, I praise their enthusiasm and their martial virtues, if they have any, but I pronounce their works to be bad, if they are bad; I respect them as barons, counts or marquises, but I deride them as authors... As soon as they set foot on Parnassus, we are equal; and I become their judge, just as they would be mine in a similar situation.[34]

On the other hand, he was very quick to defend French music against the other European nations. In his opinion, of the languages of Europe only Italian and French (and perhaps Turkish) were suitable for musical purposes. English was ruled out by its sibilant sounds which led to mumbling, as was Spanish by its solemnity and excessive slowness. Only the French had been able to cast off the Italian yoke and become self-sufficient culturally as well as materially. Turning to Grimm and Rousseau, he proclaimed: 'Whatever you Germans and Swiss may say, you will never succeed in taking away our vocal music, *which we cherish because it is our own* [his emphasis].'[35] Other pamphleteers during this first phase also stressed the superiority of French music over its Italian rival, on the ground of its greater virility and profundity.[36] A favourite epithet applied to Italian music was *coquette*, playful and pleasing but essentially trivial and superficial, best taken—if at all—as an hors d'œuvre before embarking on more solid French fare.[37]

Rousseau's *Letter on French Music* both multiplied the number and intensified the passion of these defences of French music. It was held to be in better

[33] Otto Pflanze, 'Bismarck and German nationalism', *American Historical Review*, 60, 3 (1955), pp. 548–66.

[34] Launay (ed.), *La Querelle des bouffons*, vol. I, p. 19.

[35] Ibid., pp. 9–10.

[36] See, for example, [Marin], *Ce qu'on a dit, ce qu'on a voulu dire. Lettre à Madame Folio, marchande de brochures dans la Place du vieux Louvre*; ibid., I, p. 13.

[37] *Réponse du Coin du Roi au Coin de la Reine*; ibid., I, pp. 1–2.

taste, more noble, more profound, better balanced, more expressive, more harmonious, more lucid, more sincere, and at the same time more substantial and more subtle.[38] Italian music, by contrast, was dismissed as over-elaborate, tedious, meretricious, volatile, superficial, platitudinous, formulaic, frivolous, puerile, over-emotional, pandering to base instincts, and constantly searching for effect at the expense of substance—just to give a sample of the abuse hurled.[39] Nor was this discrepancy confined to music. Most polemicists advanced French musical achievement as just one facet of a more general cultural supremacy. Following an argument expressed most famously by Voltaire, the age of Louis XIV was placed on an equal footing with classical Greece, Augustan Rome, and the Italian Renaissance. Yet while Greece had relapsed into barbarism, the Romans had disappeared in every sense and the Italians had been stripped of their glory, the French still flourished.[40] Indeed, not every writer was prepared to admit the Italian Renaissance to this cultural pantheon, for it had only been a geographical accident which brought Byzantine scholars to Italy first, following the Turkish capture of Constantinople. The feeble first draft of a revival of learning essayed there was very soon overtaken by the greater achievements of Francis I's France.[41]

How could one account for this French cultural hegemony? Significantly, the achievements of *le grand siècle* were not credited to Louis XIV, but were depicted as the culmination of a long historical process. France was unique because it was the oldest and best-preserved nation in Europe; because it had a Christian tradition stretching back almost to the days of the Apostles; and because its Salic laws had ensured that all kings of France had been native-born Frenchmen.[42] It was as a single united family that king and people had made their name feared throughout the world for their *goût militaire*, whether it was during the Crusades, the Hundred Years War, the conquest of Italy and Germany or, more recently, the War of the Spanish Succession, which had brought control of Spain and the Indies.[43] So culture and power had marched hand in hand to hegemony. How unlike their unhappy neighbours, whose

[38] Abbé Pellegrin, *Dissertation sur la musique françoise et italienne*; ibid., p. 33; [de Rochemont], *Réflexions d'un patriote sur l'opéra françois, et sur l'opéra italien, qui présentent le Parallele du goût des deux Nations dans les beaux Arts*; ibid., pp. 24, 81–2.

[39] Pellegrin, *Dissertation*, pp. 16, 19, 27, 47; [de Rochemont], *Reflexions*, pp. 42, 80–3.

[40] [Rousselet? or Fréron?], *Lettre sur la musique françoise. En réponse à celle de Jean-Jacques Rousseau*, ibid., I, pp. 5–6.

[41] [Le P. Castel], *Lettres d'un academicien de Bordeaux sur le fonds de la musique, à l'occasion de M. R*** contre la musique française*, ibid., pp. 9–11.

[42] Ibid., p. 29.

[43] Ibid., pp. 30–4.

disunity and discontinuity had condemned them to sterility and impotence! With majestic condescension, the English were allowed a certain aptitude for philosophy and mathematics, but were generally dismissed as materialists with no interest in the creative arts; the Germans were damned with faint praise for their ability to write more and bigger books than anyone else; if it was the Italians who had dug the precious stones from the mine, it had been the French who had polished them, cut them, set them, and made them sparkle; the Spanish had accomplished very little, especially in the arts.[44] As for music:

For more than 200 years now it has been said that 'the Spanish bark, the Germans bellow, the English whistle, the Italians quaver and the French sing.' Of all these attributes, only that of the French can apply to real music, for singing is music per se. How is it possible that we could have no music of our own today—we who had music at a time when no one else did, we who have the same music today as we did then? Indeed that proverb I have just quoted sometimes runs: '*only* the French sing.'[45]

It was a superiority which expressed itself most clearly in language. If Greek had been imprinted on Asia by Alexander, and Latin on the world by Augustus, French had been made the universal language of Europe by Louis XIV: 'it is since his reign that Europe has surrendered to our language, without mistrust and even with love.'[46]

This kind of boasting was not peculiar to the French, of course. As we have seen, the British and the Germans were equally fond of contrasting their special merits with the shortcomings of their neighbours.[47] Also familiar is the concern of the pamphleteers in the *querelle des bouffons* to strengthen their arguments by appeals to the allied concepts of 'public' and 'nation'. Indeed, two of the most powerful attacks on Rousseau were rooted in explicitly populist aesthetics. We have already noted, in a different context, the belief of one author that the verdict of the public 'is always governed by true feelings and rational opinions'.[48] Another lamented the subjectivism which necessarily marred individual judgements, especially in the arts, concluding: 'There is only one way of forming a judicious opinion, and that is never to rely on one's own feelings but to consult in silence the decision of the general public, for it is always imbued with mature principles, sincere feelings, and sound opinions.'[49]

[44] Ibid., p. 50.
[45] Ibid., p. 51.
[46] [P. Castel], *Réponse critique d'un académicien de Rouen, à l'académicien de Bordeaux, sur le plus profond de la musique*, ibid., pp. 10–11.
[47] See above, pp. 243, 294, 298, 301–15.
[48] See above, p. 108.
[49] [de Rochemont], *Réflexions d'un patriote*, p. vii.

He went on to argue that French opera had proved its superiority by keeping going throughout the year without a subsidy, despite its huge expense. Yet Italian opera, which only needed an orchestra and five or six singers, could survive only if sustained artificially by royal or aristocratic patronage. Even in the great and wealthy metropolis of London, he added, not all the enthusiasm of high society for Italian opera could prevent it from going bankrupt.[50] The inadequacy of this argument, which both ignored the endemic financial crisis of the Opéra and wilfully conflated *opera seria* with *opera buffa*, only serves to highlight the perceived need to enlist the public as an ally. Later in the same pamphlet, the author made a further appeal to the same authority: 'let us ask the public, that infallible oracle for everyone with the good sense to consult it and the ability to understand it.'[51] In his view, the French public was distinguished by feelings which were always sublime, always true, and so was always able to see through attempts to seduce it into following the siren sounds of foreign imports.[52]

The French public knew what was best for it, and that was French music. Long before Herder advanced his nationalist theories of language and culture, the contestants in the *querelle des bouffons* were anticipating his ideas. Peoples were different because their languages were different, argued one, so only Italians could compose in the true Italian style.[53] Not that anyone should wish to, added another, for the 'dominant taste of the [Italian] nation and the natural inclination of its people' had almost always been 'the mortal enemies of true feelings and sound reason'.[54] Superficially charming, the true character of their seductive wiles could be seen in the extraordinary indecency of the lascivious nude figures which defiled the religious paintings of Veronese and other Italian masters. That reflected their national character. *Mutatis mutandis*, French creative artists should respect their compatriots' concern for morality, decency, and propriety. There was nothing accidental about the artistic forms which had developed in France: 'it is the national character which has prescribed the laws for French opera, and which has required that music should express the sense of the libretto with the scrupulous accuracy.'[55] It was a view supported by another critic of Rousseau, who stated that what drama was for

[50] Ibid., pp. 1–10.

[51] Ibid., p. 72.

[52] Ibid., pp. 79–80.

[53] [V.T.H.S.V.], *Lettre de MM.... du Coin du Roi, à MM. du Coin de la Reine, sur la nouvelle Piece, intitulée... La Servante Maitresse*; ibid., pp. 12, 18.

[54] [de Rochemont], *Réflexions d'un patriote*; ibid., pp. 48–50.

[55] Ibid., pp. 50–1.

the English, opera was for the French: *un Spectacle Nationnal* [*sic*], adding that it was quite wrong for one nation to seek universal status for its particular brand of culture, as the Italians had done for their music.[56] This was indeed 'a dispute between nation and nation', added a third, and 'it is up to us, as true Frenchmen, as true patriots, as true subjects of the King, to make our voices heard.'[57]

As this sample demonstrates, the *querelle des bouffons* revealed the extent to which political discourse in France had become national. Legitimacy was no longer derived from the monarch but from abstractions such as state, public, *patrie*, and nation. Shortly after the conclusion of the episode, the Marquis d'Argenson recorded in his journal:

> It is striking how the words 'nation' and 'state' are used much more today than ever before: these two words were never uttered under Louis XIV, indeed no one had any idea of them. Never have we been so well informed about the rights of the nation and about liberty as we are today.[58]

The cause of the nation was the cause of liberty and vice versa, because liberty was held to be intrinsic to the French nation. As one of the protagonists in the *querelle des bouffons* put it: 'our language is a *living language*: but it is we ourselves who make it live and talk. Its great characteristic is *liberty, that freedom which is peculiarly French*. It is from the source of our language that this life, this liberty stems.'[59] (It might be worth reminding ourselves at this point that this was being written in 1753, not 1789.) It was ironic, but also revealing, that the great philosopher of liberty should excite such furious vilification for telling the French nation what he regarded as a few home truths about their music. But vilified Rousseau certainly was. In *The Confessions* he claimed, not without reason, that whereas the pamphlet by Grimm, which had started the *querelle des bouffons*, had been treated as something of a joke, his own *Letter on French Music* 'was treated seriously and raised the whole nation against me . . . immediately all other quarrels were forgotten; no one could think of anything except the threat to French music. The only revolt now was against me, and such was the outburst that the nation has never quite recovered from it. At Court they were merely deciding between the Bastille and

[56] [Cazotte], *Observations sur la lettre de J. J. Rousseau, au sujet de Musique Françoise*; ibid., II, p. 16.

[57] [Le P. Castel], *Lettres d'un academicien de Bordeaux*; ibid., pp. 3–4.

[58] *Journal et mémoires du marquis d'Argenson*, ed. E. J. B. Rathery, vol. VIII (Paris, 1867), p. 315, entry for 26 June 1754.

[59] [P. Castel], *Réponse critique d'un académicien de Rouen*, in Launay (ed.), *La Querelle des bouffons*, II, p. 10.

banishment.'[60] He was abused not only in pamphlets of the kind already cited but also in more demotic media, for example:

Les Lulli et les Rameaux
Sont des esprits opaques,
Des ignorants et des sots.
Ainsi l'a dit en deux mots
Jean-Jacques
Jean-Jacques
Jean-Jacques

De notre Hélicon les eaux
Ne sont que des cloaques,
Nos cygnes que des crapauds.
Ainsi l'a dit en deux mots
Jean-Jacques
Jean-Jacques
Jean-Jacques

Aux beaux arts, bien à crédit,
Peuple français, tu vagues.
Tout succès t'est interdit.
En deux mots ainsi l'a dit
Jean-Jacques
Jean-Jacques
Jean-Jacques[61]

The gutter press put around stories that Rousseau had been driven mad by venereal disease, that all the best bits in *Le Devin du village* had been plagiarized from music he had picked up during his stay in Venice, and so on.[62] On 1 January 1754, Grimm told subscribers to his *Correspondance littéraire*:

Rousseau's *Lettre sur la musique française* has gone into a second edition; a torrent of other pamphlets has been published in reply. The orchestra of the Opéra has burnt Rousseau in effigy. They claim to be the best orchestra in the world, whereas in reality they are just the best in Paris—there being only the one there. Rousseau is

[60] Rousseau, *The Confessions*, p. 358.

[61] Quoted in Jean Guéhenno, *Jean-Jacques Rousseau*, vol. I (London, 1966), pp. 286–7. (Lulli and Rameau have opaque minds; they are ignorant and stupid; Jean-Jacques has said so in a few words. Our Helicon is no spring, but a sewer; our swans are toads; Jean-Jacques has said so in a few words. Quite gratuitously do you cultivate the arts, O people of France; all success is denied to you; Jean-Jacques has said so in a few words.)

[62] Rousseau, *Correspondance complète*, II, p. 328.

afraid that he is going to be banished for his pamphlet and it would indeed be ironic if he were to get away with his political pamphlets but be banished for something on music. It is difficult to see how it will all turn out; the public takes more interest in it than in the Parlement imbroglio.[63]

That reference to the Parlement returns us to the claim made by Rousseau that he had 'probably prevented a revolution in France'.[64] There can be no doubt that the affair coincided with an exceptionally turbulent period in French politics. This particular episode had begun in March 1752, when the Parlement of Paris had taken action against a parish priest for refusing the last sacrament to a Jansenist.[65] On 9 May 1753 most of the Parlementaires had been exiled and in November the issuing of *lettres de cachet* against the Grand Chambre (the core of the Parlement) suggested that the Parlements were about to be abolished altogether. D'Argenson recorded in May that public opinion was entirely on the side of the Parlement and it would be mistaken to assume that exile would break the latter's spirit, 'for it is the whole nation which speaks through the organ of its magistrates, and it is not a trifling matter to anger a nation such as ours to this extent.'[66] By November he was reporting that Paris was *en combustion*, that the Parlements of France were developing into a 'national senate' and that the opinion was now general that the nation stood above the king, in the same way that a universal council of the Church outranked the Pope.[67] D'Argenson also provided support for Rousseau's claim to have been the inadvertent saviour of Louis XV. No one could have been more hostile than he was to the king, whom he regarded as a played-out, decadent voluptuary and a despot to boot, nor more favourable to the Parlements, which he saw as the representative of the nation, but he was also a stout defender of French music against the Italians and fiercely hostile to Rousseau—that *prétendu philosophe genevois*. He recorded with relish how Rousseau had been burned and hanged in effigy by the Opéra orchestra, how he had been jostled and kicked when he visited the theatre, and how he had been excluded from it even when his own work was being performed. D'Argenson also confirmed that the affair had become *une querelle nationale*.[68]

In the event, the political crisis was solved not by Rousseau but by Louis XV, who decided to appease his opponents at the expense of the clergy, whom he 'liked better but feared less'.[69] In September 1754 the Parlement of Paris returned from exile in triumph and was soon on the offensive once

[63] Tourneux (ed.), *Correspondance littéraire*, p. 312. [64] See above, p. 357.
[65] Michel Antoine, *Louis XV* (Paris, 1989), p. 653.
[66] *Journal et mémoires du marquis d'Argenson*, VIII, pp. 13, 20.
[67] Ibid., pp. 128, 152. [68] Ibid., pp. 179–80. [69] Antoine, *Louis XV*, p. 662.

again.[70] Yet although the *querelle des bouffons* did not justify Rousseau's grandiloquent description, it revealed a lot about the nature of French political culture in the middle of the eighteenth century. It showed how firmly the allied concepts of public, liberty, and nation had embedded themselves in political discourse. It also showed that the rapidly developing public sphere was a heterogeneous space that could accommodate a plurality of opinions. In particular, it demonstrated the force of nationalism, both as a positive pride in national identity and as negative disparagement of the claims of the other(s). It also hinted that this was a force which a nimble regime might utilize to deflect or negate other more subversive ideas. The inability of the French monarchy to appreciate the nature and extent of this opportunity, together with the consequences of the failure, will be the subject of the next section.

THE CRISIS OF LEGITIMATION

Within the maelstrom of events in 1789, three incidents stand out for their symbolic importance. The first was 17 June, when the deputies of the Third Estate declared that they constituted the 'National Assembly' of France. Thus they asserted the principle of national sovereignty, later to be enshrined in the Declaration of the Rights of Man and the Citizen as 'sovereignty resides essentially in the nation' (Article III). The second was 17 July, when Louis XVI went from Versailles to Paris, escorted by the new regime's paramilitary force, the National Guard. There he visited the Hôtel de Ville and donned a revolutionary cockade, signalling his acceptance of the transfer of sovereignty. The third was 5 October, when a Parisian crowd marched to Versailles, took the king and his family prisoner on the following day, and brought them back to the capital. They were followed a little later by the deputies of the National Assembly, who sent ahead six of their number to search for suitable premises to serve as their debating chamber. One of the six was Dr Joseph-Ignace Guillotin.[71] The separation of court from capital, begun by Louis XIV's departure from Paris, was now repaired.

Although it was within the power of the old regime to escape until the very moment its funeral bell began to toll, its predicament was of long standing. If there had been no linear descent into the abyss, hardly a year had passed in the

[70] Julian Swann, *Politics and the Parlement of Paris under Louis XV, 1754–1774* (Cambridge, 1995), ch. 4, *passim*.

[71] Armand Brette, *Histoires des édifices où ont siégé les assemblées parlementaires de la Révolution française et de la première république*, vol. I (Paris, 1902), p. 83.

previous century which had not been marked by another missed opportunity. Many were the failures of the monarchy, but the most serious was allowing the opposition to appropriate the national cause. In forging an alliance with the papacy to persecute the Jansenists, Louis XIV had turned his back on a centuries-old tradition of asserting French independence against interference from Rome. The bull *Unigenitus* ('Only Begotten') issued by Clement XI in 1713 proved to be the most contentious single document in the history of the Church in France. When the old king died two years later, the issue could have been consigned with his coffin to the burial vault at Saint-Denis, but it was allowed to survive by his infant successor's Regent and was then revived by Cardinal Fleury, chief minister from 1726 until 1743, and described by the Archbishop of Paris as 'a twenty-four-carat Molinist [i.e. ultra-orthodox]'.[72] In 1730 *Unigenitus* was declared to be a law of the state as well as a law of the Church.

There was nothing in the austere Augustinian theology of Jansenism to make it subversive. At its heart was an insistence on the depravity of humankind and the gratuitous nature of divine grace which, if anything, pointed towards unconditional submission to the powers ordained of God. It was the misfortune of the French monarchy that Cornelius Jansen's *Augustinus*, published posthumously in 1640 two years after the author's death, should have made such a powerful appeal to the kind of educated Frenchmen who became involved in the civil disorders later in the decade. Louis XIV never forgot or forgave the participation of Jansenists in the Frondes and for the rest of his life habitually referred to them as *républicains*.[73] Elsewhere in Europe, Jansenism was integrated into both Church and state, becoming in the process a powerful movement of reform from above.[74] Only in France was it forced outside both the ecclesiastical and the political establishment, eventually taking a terrible revenge on both.

It was able to do so because it found an institutional base in the Parlements. More royalist than the king, the *parlementaires* were quick to pick up the nationalist card discarded by their sovereign and to play it for all it was worth. Their hand was strengthened by the return in 1715 of their most powerful political weapon. In 1673 Louis XIV had announced unilaterally that in future the Parlements would be required to register royal edicts, and thus give them

[72] J. H. Shennan, *The Parlement of Paris* (London, 1968), p. 300.

[73] Durand Echeverria, *The Maupeou Revolution: A Study in the History of Libertarianism, France, 1770–1774* (Baton Rouge, La., 1985), p. 8.

[74] See, for example, Peter Hersche's important study *Der Spätjansenismus in Oesterreich* (Vienna, 1977), especially chs. 1–2.

the full force of law, before remonstrating against any aspect they might find objectionable. He was then basking in the full majesty of his youthful charisma and the Parlements had accepted his *diktat* without resistance. By the time he died, however, they were eager to reassert themselves. They were given the opportunity by Louis XIV's will, which specified a council of regency to act on behalf of his 5-year-old successor. In return for quashing this clause and allowing the duc d'Orléans to become sole regent, the Parlements regained their right of remonstrance before registration.[75] It was not long before they were making effective use of their restored weapon. In disputes over John Law's bank (1718–20) and new taxation (1725) they announced the return of an independent force to French politics.[76]

But it was the Jansenist issue which excited an intensity of contestation not seen in France since the Frondes. Beginning in 1727, Fleury's move against Jansenists high and low provoked a vigorous counter-offensive from the Parlements.[77] Yet when this episode petered out five years later, the *parlementaires* did not appear to have made much progress. For all their opposition, *Unigenitus* was now established as the law of the land, the Jansenist press had been muzzled, and Fleury was well on the way to purging the episcopate, the religious orders, and the theological faculties of their remaining Jansenist sympathisers. To guard against the natural tendency to highlight dissent, it should be noted that during the first thirty-five years of Louis XV's reign, the Parlement of Paris presented only thirty-seven remonstrances and deployed its most powerful weapon—the judicial strike—on only three occasions.[78] A second and more serious phase was touched off in the late 1740s by the appointment of the young, energetic, obstinate, and fiercely anti-Jansenist Christophe de Beaumont as Archbishop of Paris. Among other measures, he instructed that the sacraments should be administered only to those able to present a *billet de confession* certifying that they had been shriven by a non-Jansenist priest. The denial of extreme unction to the dying caused particular offence.

The bruising confrontations between king and Parlements that followed have been narrated and analysed many times.[79] What concerns us here is the

[75] J. H. Shennan, *Philippe Duke of Orléans: Regent of France 1715–1723* (London, 1979), pp. 30–1.

[76] Jean Égret, *Louis XV et l'opposition parlementaire* (Paris, 1970), pp. 36–7.

[77] For a good recent account, see the section 'Parlementary Jansenism, popular Jansenism: politics and miracles', in Daniel Roche, *France in the Enlightenment* (Cambridge, Mass., 1998), pp. 372–8.

[78] Égret, *Louis XV et l'opposition parlementaire*, p. 45.

[79] The best account in any language is now Swann, *Politics and the Parlement of Paris under Louis XV.* (Cambridge, 1995).

contribution they made to the development of a new political culture in France and the identification of a new source of legitimacy. Throughout this twenty-year conflict, the *parlementaires* enjoyed many advantages. Jansenism was more vibrant in a theological sense and, in the face of papal persecution, it could also draw on a strong Gallican tradition, which stressed the independence of the Church in France. There was nothing inevitable about this particular alliance; indeed, the eponymous founder of the movement had been ultramontane. If Louis XIV had continued the anti-Curial policies which had led to the regalian disputes of the 1680s, it would have been the monarchy that would have benefited. It was his enlisting of the support of the papacy in dealing with what he imagined to be a dangerously heterodox force which allowed the Jansenists to drape themselves in the Gallican flag. *Mutatis mutandis*, they also became associated with 'Richerism', an increasingly powerful movement in the French Church named after Edmond Richer (1560–1631), who had propagated the claims of the secular parish clergy against the prelates and the regulars. The denunciation of *Unigenitus* in 1727 by thirty Parisian *curés* and 120 other priests, in response to Fleury's campaign, signalled that both Jansenists and *parlementaires* had recruited another important group of allies.[80]

The Parlements drew comfort and confidence from the conviction that they were not separate institutions but just different *classes* forming one national body. As the Parlement of Paris claimed in 1755: 'the Parlement of Paris ... and the other Parlements form a single body and are only divisions of the royal Parlement.'[81] In the following year they went further, reminding the king that 'the metropolitan court and all its colonies are the diverse classes of a sole and unique Parlement, the diverse members of a sole and unique body, animated by the same spirit, nourished by the same principles and occupied by the same object.'[82] Nor were their functions confined to exercising appeal jurisdiction in individual cases. The Parlement of Rennes stated firmly in 1757:

> The functions which belong to the Parlement do not just consist in judging certain cases. One part of the parliament's activities cannot be detached and regarded as the totality of the rights and functions of the Parlement. To judge the equity and usefulness of new laws, to assess the interest of the state and of the public, to maintain law and order in the kingdom, to exercise sovereign justice and a general administrative control which extends to all matters, all topics, and all

[80] John McManners, 'The mid-century crisis', unpublished Trevelyan lectures, Cambridge, 1990.
[81] Shennan, *The Parlement of Paris*, p. 311.
[82] Swann, *Politics and the Parlement of Paris under Louis XV*, p. 163.

people—*these* are the original, exclusive and essential rights and functions of the Parlement.[83]

Moreover, this single national body claimed to represent the entire nation. From 1755 they were claiming to be the *tribunal de la nation*, the *conseil de la nation*, the *dépôt national*, and *le temple inviolable des lois nationales*.[84] The Parlement of Rennes also told Louis XV in 1757 that 'the Parlement never speaks to the nation except in the name of the king, and equally it never speaks to the king except in the name of the nation.' Seven years later it added, 'it is the consent of the nation that your Parlement represents and which gives support [*complément*] to the law.'[85] The repeated use of the word 'nation' and its cognates demonstrated that an alternative source of legitimation was emerging to challenge royal sovereignty—national sovereignty. It was one part, albeit the most important, of a general discursive shift from values and institutions specific to France to abstractions with universal application. Favourite expressions of the past, such as *monarchie légitime*, *lois fondamentales*, *dépôt des lois*, or *corps intermédiaires* increasingly made way for *droit*, *constitution* and *nation*.[86] The database of the American and French Research on the Treasury of the French Language (ARTFL) shows that between 1700 and 1710 the word '*nation*' was used 45 times in 7 different volumes, that during the next decade it was used 106 times in 12 volumes, and that by the 1750s the total had increased to 990 times in 43 volumes and was sustained at that level subsequently.[87]

So the Parlements paraded themselves as the defenders of the constitution and of the nation—acting with the king but, if necessary, against the king. It is some measure of the ineptitude of Louis XV and his advisers that they were allowed to get away with what was, at best, a very partial and very partisan account of their traditional role. They were also vulnerable to charges of oppression, as they enforced with enthusiasm even the more obscurantist laws, especially those aimed at minorities. It was the Parlement of Toulouse which supervised the judicial murder of the Protestant Jean Calas, perhaps the most celebrated single act of injustice committed under the old regime and, among other things, the inspiration for Voltaire's *Treatise on Toleration*. It was the Parlement of Paris which confirmed the sentence on the 18-year-old

[83] Antoine, *Louis XV*, p. 569.
[84] Roger Bickart, *Les Parlements et la notion de souveraineté nationale au dix-huitième siècle* (Paris, 1932), p. 110.
[85] Ibid., p. 114.
[86] Denis Richet, *La France moderne: l'esprit des institutions* (Paris, 1973), p. 157.
[87] Liah Greenfeld, *Nationalism: Five Roads to Modernity* (Cambridge, Mass., 1992), p. 160.

Chevalier de la Barre, convicted by a court at Abbeville of having sung impious songs and committed other trivial acts of blasphemy. After being tortured in the hope that he might reveal accomplices, he was paraded through the town in a tumbril with a placard round his neck announcing him to be a blasphemer until he reached the Church of Saint Wulfram. There he was obliged to dismount and to confess his crimes on his knees 'in an audible and intelligible manner'. Despite having made amends, the tongue which had uttered the offending blasphemies was then torn out. Next he was taken in the tumbril to the main square where he was beheaded. To complete the awful warning, his body was then burned at the stake and his ashes scattered to the four winds.[88] That happened in 1766. Voltaire told Frederick the Great that the sentence should have been commuted to the obligation to read St Thomas Aquinas's *Summa theologiæ* from start to finish, a fate worse than death, but Louis XV chose to confirm the original sentence.[89] As we have already seen, the Parlements also showed their conservative teeth when enforcing legislation governing the book trade.[90]

So the struggle between Parlements and Crown was hardly one between light and dark, enlightenment and reaction, but Louis XV contrived to make it seem so. Acutely aware of his royal dignity and fiercely jealous of his prerogatives, he was fond of making resounding statements about the personal nature of his authority. The most celebrated and uncompromising was his speech to the assembled chambers of the Parlement of Paris on 3 March 1766, a session which became known as the *séance de la flagellation*:

I shall not permit in my kingdom the formation of an association which allows the natural ties of reciprocal duties and obligations to degenerate into a conspiracy of resistance, nor one that introduces to the kingdom a fictitious corporation which can only disrupt harmony. The magistracy does not constitute a corporation, nor an order separate from the three legitimate orders of the kingdom. The magistrates are my officers charged with administering on my behalf my truly royal duty to dispense justice to my subjects . . . Sovereignty resides in my person alone . . . and my courts derive their existence and their authority from me alone. The plenitude of this authority remains with me. They exercise it only in my name and it may never be turned against me. I alone have the right to legislate. This power is indivisible. The

[88] The verdict is reprinted in full in John Lough, *An Introduction to Eighteenth-century France* (London, 1960), pp. 307–8.

[89] Reinhold Koser and Hans Droysen (eds.), *Briefwechsel Friedrichs des Großen mit Voltaire*, Publikationen aus den K. Preußischen Staatsarchiven, vols. 81, 82, 86 (Leipzig, 1908–11), vol. 86, p. 126.

[90] See above, p. 138.

officers of my courts do not make the law, they only register, publish, and enforce it. Public order emanates exclusively from me, and the rights and the interests of the nation, which it has dared to separate from the monarch, are necessarily united with mine and repose entirely in my hands.[91]

The constant repetition of the possessive pronoun—'*my* kingdom', '*my* subjects', '*my* courts'—projected a proprietorial vision of kingship increasingly at odds with the objective concepts of state, *patrie*, or nation. It is difficult to imagine a monarch less like an 'oriental despot' than good-natured, easy-going, indolent Louis XV (apart from his liking for a harem), but his political vocabulary allowed his enemies to depict him as such. He contrived to have the worst of all worlds. On the one hand, his regime was characterized by a signal lack of civil liberties. There was no liberty of association, as all assemblies not explicitly authorized were illegal; there was no freedom of the press, as the 941 booksellers, printers, journalists, and writers incarcerated in the Bastille between 1659 and 1789 bore witness; and there was no freedom from arbitrary arrest, as the countless victims of *lettres de cachet* would have confirmed.[92] On the other hand, the repression was so feebly applied that it served only to aggravate the problem it was supposed to solve. It could not stop Freemasonry, for example, spreading rapidly across the length and breadth of the country until every town of any size had at least one lodge. There were more than 700 Masonic lodges in France by 1789, including about 70 in Paris alone, with at least 50,000 members, representing perhaps as much as 5 per cent of the urban adult male population.[93] There were also several lodges at Versailles itself, one ominously named *Le patriotisme*, which, among other things, organized public concerts under the cover-name '*Société patriotique*.'[94]

Nor could the censors staunch the flow of illegal publications. As the comte de Ségur recalled in his memoirs, there were 'a thousand ways to evade the severity of the laws'.[95] One of the most remunerative was the importation of French-language pamphlets and periodicals from the crescent of enterprising

[91] Quoted in Antoine, *Louis XV*, p. 852.

[92] Dena Goodman, *The Republic of Letters: A Cultural History of the French Enlightenment* (Ithaca, NY, and London, 1994), p. 249; Roger Chartier, *The Cultural Origins of the French Revolution* (Durham, NC, and London, 1991), p. 63.

[93] Ibid., p. 162; D. Mornet, *La pensée française au XVIIIe siècle* (Paris, 1969), p. 192; R. B. Rose, *The Making of the Sans-culottes: Democratic Ideas and Institutions in Paris, 1789–92* (Manchester, 1983), p. 30.

[94] Bruno Brévan, *Les Changements de la vie musicale parisienne de 1774 à 1799* (Paris, 1980), p. 57.

[95] Louis-Philippe, comte de Ségur, *Mémoires ou souvenirs et anecdotes*, vols. 1–3 of *Oeuvres complètes* (Paris, 1824–6), vol. I, p. 18.

publishers that stretched from Amsterdam to Switzerland.[96] Inside France, it was not only those traditional friends of free expression—corruption and incompetence—which defeated government repression. By the 1750s the subverters were inside the gates of the citadel, invited in by guardians no longer convinced of the merits of the system they had been hired to protect. Indicative of how much had crumbled behind the façade was the appointment of Malesherbes (or Chrétien-Guillaume Lamoignon de Malesherbes, to give him his full name) as *directeur de la librairie* by his father Lamoignon (or Guillaume de Lamoignon de Blancmesnil, to avoid any confusion) on becoming chancellor in 1750.[97] Until his resignation in 1763, following his father's fall from royal favour, he intervened repeatedly to grant 'tacit permissions' for the publication of works which in the past would certainly have been banned. Not the least of his beneficiaries was the *Encyclopédie* of Diderot and d'Alembert, which survived a crisis in 1752 at the cost of an order in council denouncing the first two volumes for containing 'several maxims likely to destroy royal authority, to foster a spirit of independence and rebellion and, under cover of vague and equivocal terminology, to lay the foundations for error, the corruption of morals, irreligion and scepticism'.[98] It might well be conjectured that few people would have regarded the *Encyclopédie* as a threat to the regime—if the regime had not told them so. Yet even Malesherbes would not allow the publication of anything he deemed hostile to king or religion, and he could be as severe as the next censor. Indeed, it was during his tenure of office that the rate of imprisonment began to rise again.[99] He was especially concerned about the Francophone imports from the Dutch Republic, complaining that 'the gazettes of Amsterdam and Utrecht circulate all over Europe, set fire to the kingdom, and are constantly giving foreigners an impression of our difficulties that can only be disadvantageous to the state.' Yet he added despairingly that there was little point in trying to ban them, for 'there is not a single lackey fond of news in Paris who does not read them regularly.'[100]

[96] Elizabeth Eisenstein, *Grub Street Abroad: Aspects of the French Cosmopolitan Press from the Age of Louis XV to the French Revolution* (Oxford, 1992), *passim*.

[97] Chrétien-Guillaume Lamoignon de Malesherbes, *Mémoires sur la librairie et sur la liberté de la presse*, ed. Graham E. Rodwell, North Carolina Studies in the Romance Languages and Literatures, no. 213 (Chapel Hill, 1979), pp. 15–16. For a commentary, see Raymond Birn, 'Malesherbes and the call for a free press', in Robert Darnton (ed.), *Revolution in Print: The Press in France 1775–1800* (Berkeley, Los Angeles, and London, 1989), pp. 50–66.

[98] Robert Darnton, *The Business of Enlightenment: A Publishing History of the Encyclopédie 1775–1800* (Cambridge, Mass., 1979), p. 10.

[99] Chartier, *The Cultural Origins of the French Revolution*, p. 64.

[100] Jeremy D. Popkin, *News and Politics in the Age of revolution: Jean Luzac's Gazette de Leyde* (Ithaca, NY, and London, 1989), pp. 39, 42.

How many lackeys were fond of news? No one will ever know, although there is some fragmentary evidence that popular literacy was surprisingly high and growing all the while. Certainly there were plenty of contemporaries who believed that the reading revolution stretched down to the lower end of society. Louis-Sébastien Mercier, for example, wrote on the eve of the Revolution:

> Ten times more people are reading today than a hundred years ago. Today you can see a maid in a basement or a lackey in an ante-room reading a pamphlet. They are reading in almost every class of society, and so much the better. They should be reading even more. The nation that reads is a nation which carries in its breast a special and felicitous force, which can challenge and frustrate despotism.[101]

Although the plain people of Paris had far fewer opportunities to engage in politics than their British counterparts, their opinions did carry some weight. It was particularly important that the dispute between Crown and Parlements over *Unigenitus* acquired a popular dimension and was not confined to the elites. In 1727, just as Fleury was beginning his campaign, a popular cult began at the Parisian cemetery of Saint-Médard, centred on the grave of François de Pâris, a recently deceased Jansenist deacon of saintly reputation. As news spread of the posthumous cures his remains were effecting, crowds of pilgrims flocked to the site of the miracles. The supernatural aura was so strong that many of them experienced convulsions, as the dead man's intercessions attracted the presence of the Holy Ghost. Needless to say, the authorities were as hostile to this manifestation of Jansenism as to any other, but their persecution failed to halt the movement, which continued for the rest of the century. There was more at stake here than an outbreak of mass religious mania of a kind still endemic in the twenty-first century. Those who believed that the miracles performed by M. de Pâris were authentic—and that included a large number of Parisians—could not help but conclude that those who persecuted his followers were doing the Devil's work. As John Wesley later observed: 'if these miracles were real, they would strike at the root of the whole Papal authority, as having been wrought in direct opposition to the famous bull *Unigenitus*.' In an age of intensifying religiosity, governments meddled with popular forms of religion at their peril. As the episode's most recent historian has concluded: 'For all the force which the French state commanded, continued respect for its legitimacy depended in a large measure on general acceptance of shared myths and symbols; Saint-Médard showed this consen-

[101] Louis Sébastien Mercier, *Tableau de Paris*, new edn., 12 vols. (Amsterdam, 1783–88), XII, p. 151.

sus was wearing thin, and, two generations later, the Parisian districts where this kind of Jansenism was strong were stuffed with sans-culottes.'[102] The Jansenists themselves knew how important it was to marshal public opinion behind them. In 1727 they began publication of the *Nouvelles ecclésiastiques*, one of the great journalistic success stories of the eighteenth century and further proof (if it were needed) that the developing public sphere could serve religion as well as secular ideologies. On 1 January 1732 the editors paid tribute to the popular support they had received in their battle against the ungodly: 'the public is a judge they have been unable to corrupt.'[103]

So when the *parlementaires* confronted Fleury, de Beaumont, or Louis XV over the Jansenist issue, they did so secure in the knowledge that they enjoyed the support of ordinary Parisians. Of course this was not only due to the Saint-Médard incident: a sense of solidarity went back at least as far as the Frondes and had been strengthened by the abandoning of the capital by the king in favour of Versailles. Barbier noted in his diary in 1727 that 'the great majority of the bourgeois of Paris, the *noblesse de robe* and the Third Estate, and even—which is particularly pleasing—the women and the common people, are all incensed against the Jesuits and secretly denounce everything they do. That is why these critical writings circulate throughout the entire city and secretly pass from hand to hand.' The popularity of the Jansenist cause was a phenomenon he came back to repeatedly, as in the 'the bulk of the population of Paris—men, women and children—is Jansenist' and 'the good city of Paris is Jansenist from top to toe.'[104] This popular support for the Jansenists and the Parlement which defended them does not appear to have changed during the course of the century. During the major confrontation of the early 1750s, the marquis d'Argenson observed that the enthusiastic popular support for the Parlements' cause would oblige the ministry to come to terms.[105] Thirty years after that, Mercier observed that public opinion in Paris was naturally on the side of the *parlementaires* because the benefits they conferred were visible all around them, and in addition they were respected as popular representatives, the sole defenders of public liberty against a despotic regime.[106]

[102] W. R. Ward, *Christianity under the Ancien Régime 1648–1789* (Cambridge, 1999), pp. 31–2.

[103] Quoted in Peter R. Campbell, *Power and Politics in Old Regime France 1720–1745* (London, 1996), p. 303.

[104] Antoine, *Louis XV*, p. 599; Charles Aubertin, *L'Esprit public au XVIIIe siècle. Étude sur les mémoires et les correspondances politiques des contemporains 1715 à 1789* (Paris, 1873), p. 262.

[105] *Journal et mémoires du marquis d'Argenson*, ed. E. J. B. Rathery, vol. VIII (Paris, 1867), p. 128, entry for 23 September 1753.

[106] Mercier, *Tableau de Paris*, vol. VIII, pp. 281–4.

The Parlements were well aware of the importance of public opinion and took good care to cultivate it. As Louis XV often pointed out, communications between the king and his courts should be strictly confidential. In the course of their disputes, however, the *parlementaires* began to publish their remonstrances in printed form. Naturally, the medium influenced the message, and increasingly remonstrances were drafted with a view to maximizing public impact. D'Argenson noted in his journal on 24 May 1753, 'the great remonstrances of the Parlement appeared yesterday in printed form, and that makes a major impact on our French minds: it is a medium made for fixing and reversing the limits of royal authority.'[107] On the government side, ministers lamented the harm done by the publicity and the historian most sympathetic to their cause, Michel Antoine, has accused the Parlements of making a powerful contribution to the destabilization of the French state by means of incessant propaganda, disinformation, the manipulation of opinion in their assemblies, and the intimidation of government supporters among their number.[108]

Louis XV was not well placed to respond. His handicap was in part geographical. In 1722 the Regent had taken the decision to take the court back to Versailles; alienated from Paris by his unpopularity there, he believed that it would be a more suitable place for preparing the young king to take over. Louis himself did not resist, eager to return to the scene of happy childhood memories.[109] At a time when great palaces were going up all over Europe, the move was nothing out of the ordinary, but the advantage of hindsight suggests that it was a serious mistake. If there was always bound to be a certain tension between *la cour et la ville*, especially when the *ville* in question was as large and self-confident as Paris, there was no need to separate the two so radically. Moreover, the contrast between the two could only grow with the passage of time. When Versailles was constructed, it represented the last word in architectural design and all the other arts which made it the greatest palace in Europe. Already old-fashioned when taken out of mothballs in 1722, it became increasingly musty. The interior could be redecorated and remodelled periodically, but nothing could prevent the complex as a whole from losing its relevance. Voltaire's comment that 'the nation would rather that Louis XIV had preferred his Louvre and capital to the palace of Versailles' applied *a fortiori* to Louis XV (and even more so to Louis XVI).[110]

[107] *Journal et mémoires du marquis d'Argenson*, vol. VIII, p. 41.
[108] Antoine, *Louis XV*, pp. 592, 793. [109] Ibid., p. 102.
[110] Voltaire, *The Age of Louis XIV* (London, 1961), p. 319.

Isolated at Versailles and cocooned in court ritual, Louis XV was not likely to be sensitive or responsive to social and cultural change. He was helped neither by his upbringing nor by his personality. As his elder brother (duc de Bretagne), father (duc de Bourgogne), mother, grandfather (Monseigneur), and great-grandfather (Louis XIV) all died within four years of each other, he was the sole surviving male member of the main Bourbon line and so fell victim to a degree of cosseting unusual even by royal standards. Nor was it helpful that he was educated by the duc de Villeroy, described by Daniel Roche as 'a majestic cretin'.[111] It is idle to speculate whether a more normal childhood might have produced a more satisfactory monarch. No matter whether nature or nurture was responsible, by the time of his coronation in 1723, certain assets such as a quick intelligence and a prodigious memory were more than counterbalanced by an excessive timidity, which expressed itself in a dread of anyone or anything new, a reluctance to take decisions, an inability to stick to those decisions he did take, a preference for going at business in a roundabout, secretive way, and an extraordinary capacity for remaining silent.[112] The duc de Croÿ observed that 'the King possesses the quality of modesty to such an extent that it becomes a vice.'[113] He was also prone to periods of depression and indolence.

As a result of these personal deficiencies, Louis XV proved quite unable to make the representational court culture perfected by his predecessor work properly. In its complete version, Versailles provided a framework within which the person of the monarch was both distanced and made accessible. The multi-media iconography made it clear that the Sun King was elevated above mere mortals, but the everyday ritual made him visible to all. The palace was always open to the public; the royal festivals, especially weddings and baptisms, were public occasions; many daily functions, such as getting up and going to bed, were performed ceremonially and publicly; and the king always ate in public and alone. In short, the king denied himself a private life in the interests of his public persona. If the system were to work, it required application and charisma. Even Louis XIV came to find the routine too gruelling and towards the end of his life began to slip away to small châteaux such as Marly, seven kilometres away, where he could relax in private. His successor was disqualified by psychology from attempting even a pale imitation. He

[111] Roche, *France in the Enlightenment*, p. 259.

[112] Antoine, *Louis XV*, pp. 162, 411, 462–9. This remains the best biography available, although marred by a bias towards the subject and against the Parlements.

[113] William Ritchey Newton, *L'Espace du roi. La cour de France au château de Versailles 1682–1789* (Paris, 2000), p. 22.

performed some of the roles some of the time, but with neither conviction nor consistency. Under Louis XIV, for example, there were *appartements* four times a week, when the king and his court participated collectively in card-playing, music-making, and dancing; under Louis XV the number fell to one. He preferred the *petits appartements*, where he could see and entertain only those people he chose to see. Access to the king was now limited to a small inner circle of intimates (*particuliers*), with whom he spent three to four evenings a week and who accompanied him to the unofficial residences such as Choisy, La Muette, Saint-Hubert, Bellevue, or the Trianon, where he lived as a private citizen, albeit in great luxury, for longer and longer periods. In 1750 the king slept only fifty-two nights at Versailles and only sixty-three in the following year.[114]

But when the king was absent, the court was dead and the palace deserted. According to the Abbé de Véri, a rota system was introduced early in Louis XV's reign which allowed the ladies-in-waiting of the court to be absent for two-thirds of the time. As women provide the heart and soul of court society, he added, with the exception of the Court of Saint James, Versailles lost its appeal for the men too. Now, he lamented, people went to the palace only when they had business to transact or a duty to perform, with the result that the court had become a dismal and boring place.[115] Not the least problem was a growing shortage of space, as the expansion of the royal family and the families of the princes of the blood led to the eviction of aristocratic families further down the social hierarchy. It was a problem compounded by the conversion of residential blocks into public spaces, such as the opera house, which alone involved the loss of forty-four noble apartments.[116] As they moved back to Paris, the ex-courtiers took fashion with them. Gone were the days when Versailles set the cultural tone not just for France but for all Europe. In Mercier's words:

The word *court* no longer inspires respect among us, as it did during the reign of Louis XIV. The prevailing opinions are no longer supplied by the court; it is not the court which decides reputations these days, no matter in what branch of the arts; now it is only in a derisive way that one says: '*the court has decided thus*.' The verdicts handed down by the court are quashed and we simply say: 'the court understands nothing, is bereft of ideas, doesn't know how to find any and no longer has a point of view.'[117]

[114] See the important article by Jean de Viguerie, 'Le roi et le "public". L'exemple de Louis XV', *Revue Historique*, 563 (1987), pp. 23–34, on which this paragraph is based.

[115] Baron Jehan de Witte (ed.), *Journal de l'abbé de Véri* (Paris, n.d.), pp. 42–3.

[116] Newton, *L'Espace du roi*, pp. 24–8.

[117] Mercier, *Tableau de Paris*, vol. IV, p. 246.

His detection of a cultural shift was confirmed by several other observers, by Dr John Moore, for example, who recorded that 'the French disregard the decisions pronounced at Versailles in matters of taste. It very often happens that a dramatic piece, which has been acted before the royal family and the court, with the highest applause, is afterwards damned with every circumstance of ignominy at Paris. In all works of genius the Parisians lead the judgment of courtiers, and dictate to their monarch.'[118]

When an increasingly private monarch and an increasingly dysfunctional court rubbed up against a growing public sphere, the result was mutual alienation. It was particularly unfortunate that the private life Louis XV chose to lead was not such as to bear the public scrutiny it now inevitably attracted. In 1725 the 15-year-old king was married to Marie Leszczynska, the 22-year-old daughter of Stanislas Leszczynski, who had been the Franco-Swedish candidate for the Polish throne but had been defeated by Augustus of Saxony and his Russian supporters. Such a disadvantageous match attracted much derision both at court and in Paris, where the Poles were regarded as 'the Gascons of the north'. In one sense, however, it was an undoubted success. After the wedding night, a proud bridegroom was able to inform his first minister, the duc de Bourbon, that he had given his bride 'seven proofs of his affection'.[119] For eight years Louis exercised his potency exclusively in the marriage bed, but in 1733 he took his first mistress in the attractive shape of the married comtesse de Mailly, one of five daughters of the marquis de Nesle. She was then supplanted by her sister, the marquise de Vintimille, who died in childbirth. Louis promptly sought consolation in the arms of the youngest sister, the recently widowed marquise de La Tournelle, whom he made duchesse de Châteauroux, and may also have enjoyed the favours of a fourth sister. As the wags put it:

> To choose an entire family—
> Is that being unfaithful or constant?[120]

Adultery on this scale could not be kept secret. By 1737 rumours of royal debauchery had found their way into the diary of Edmond Barbier, for example.[121] Conveniently, Louis was a firm believer in the certainty of instant forgiveness, as the duc de Croÿ recorded: 'He had made a calculation on the

118 John Moore, *A View of Society and Manners in France, Switzerland and Germany*, 4th edn., vol. 1 (Dublin, 1789), pp. 87–8.

119 Antoine, *Louis XV*, p. 158.

120 Ibid, p. 490.

121 Ibid., p. 486.

matter and thought that, provided at death he repented and received the sacraments, these [sexual immoralities] were unimportant things... He counted always on the last minute, on a good *peccavi* to cover everything amiss'.[122] But ironically, Louis was also especially vulnerable because of his piety. Only if he knew himself to be in a state of grace would he touch sufferers for scrofula, so the announcement that he would not discharge this thaumaturgical function advertised that he was an unabsolved sinner. His refusal to take Easter Communion and touch the afflicted in 1739 caused a public scandal.[123] By this time, there was a public avid for news of the misconduct of the great and the good, real or imagined, and a growing number of booksellers willing to satisfy the demand. The rackety private life of the Regent had already inspired a rash of stories about orgies at the Palais-Royal, bawdy street songs, and political pornography in the shape of pamphlets such as *L'Histoire du prince Papyrus* and *Les Amusements de la princesse Amélie*.[124] Obscene publications and engravings were sold all over Paris, in cafés, on the streets, and especially wherever prostitutes gathered. Nor was the court spared. An inspection in 1749 showed that erotic books were available even at Versailles. In the same year, an intrepid kitchen-boy, Jean Lacasse, was sent to the Bastille for having placed a copy of the pornographic classic *Le Portier des Chartreux* in the royal chapel.[125] Significantly, while during the late 1720s all offences relating to the book trade concerned Jansenist tracts, in the following decades pornography was increasingly the target.[126] Of course, Bourbon kings had always taken mistresses, but they had not done so in the kind of publicity poor Louis XV had to endure. They had also been more discreet, confining their attention to one woman at a time and making their choice from the ladies of the court. That there was a less indulgent mood abroad, probably encouraged by Jansenist moral austerity, was demonstrated in 1744 when Louis XV suffered a serious bout of illness at Metz on his way to the war and believed that he was dying. Incited by the clergy, the townspeople ran the duchesse de Châteauroux and her sister, who of course were accompanying the king on campaign, out of town.[127]

[122] John McManners, *Church and Society in Eighteenth-century France*. Vol. I: *The Clerical Establishment and its Social Ramifications* (Oxford, 1998), p. 45.

[123] Ibid., p. 14. He never did touch for scrofula again.

[124] Roche, *France in the Enlightenment*, p. 455.

[125] Jean Marie Goulemot, *Forbidden Texts: Erotic Literature and its Readers in Eighteenth-century France* (Cambridge, 1994), pp. 17–18.

[126] Ibid., p. 19.

[127] Antoine, *Louis XV*, pp. 372–5. The episode produced a pornographic novel called *Tanastès*, written by Marie-Magdeleine Bonafon, a domestic servant of the Princesse de

The duchess died suddenly the same year, struck down by divine retribution, or so it was believed. Her replacement was to be perhaps the most famous courtesan in the history of France, if not of Europe, Jeanne Antoinette Poisson, who had married Charles-Guillaume Le Normant d'Étioles in 1740 but is better known by the title Louis created for her: marquise de Pompadour. The installation of a plebeian (and many were the unsavoury jokes made about her piscine maiden name) as *maîtresse en titre* caused outrage both to aristocrats, whose own womenfolk had been passed over, and to *bons bourgeois*, for whom this was one more sign of royal self-indulgence. Since the days of Louis XIV, there had been a sea change in public attitudes to royal adultery: 'Although historically the king's mistresses had been a symbol of regal potency and virility, eighteenth-century public opinion identified her with royal weakness and debauchery.'[128] Jansenists were also to the fore in denunciations, as in: 'Unclean monarch, your days are numbered! You will perish beneath your sceptre and both you and your courtesan will be struck down with tragic death!'[129] Madame de Pompadour's connections to the world of high finance through both her father and her husband only served to enhance the sleazy associations. Worse was to come. If she had been just another member of the Nesle family, recruited for temporary sexual gratification, the effects might not have been so serious. But Madame de Pompadour proved to be much more than a mere mistress. Her domination of the king's bed lasted only five years, but her mastery of his mind was to endure until her death from cancer in 1764. On the credit side, she proved to have good taste. Together with her brother, whom Louis made marquis de Marigny and Director of the King's Buildings, she played an important role in the construction of the École Militaire, the Place Louis XV (where Louis's grandson was to be guillotined in 1793, by which time it had been renamed Place de la Révolution), the Petit Trianon, and Château Bellevue.

Less constructive was the image she projected of profligate hedonism, not least through the numerous sumptuous portraits painted of her by François Boucher, broadcast to a disapproving public by engravings. Replicating the discourse of the *parlementaires*, La Font de Saint-Yenne blamed Madame de Pompadour and her coterie for the decadence of French art. Indeed, there was a close conjunction between aesthetic and political critiques. As Thomas

Montauban; Lisa Jane Graham, *If only the King knew: Seditious Speech in the Reign of Louis XV* (Charlottesville, Va., and London, 2000), ch. 2.

128 Ibid., pp. 58–9.

129 Arlette Farge and Jacques Revel, *The Vanishing Children of Paris: Rumor and Politics before the French Revolution* (Cambridge, Mass., 1991), p. 124.

Crow has written, 'Just as the Parlements presented themselves as the protectors of the nation against a king corrupted by *mauvais conseillers*, the early unofficial art critics presented themselves as preservers and defenders of a national artistic heritage corrupted by the ignorant and debased taste of the financiers and the court.'[130] In response there was a flood of *libelles*, which deftly married political criticism to pornography. Beginning in the 1740s, pamphlets began to appear, attacking the king and his mistress, not just for adultery but also for extravagance and corruption. Among others rounded up by the police was a volunteer in the cavalry and four women, imprisoned for having said that 'the king was an imbecile and a tyrant ... who allowed himself to be governed by his whore.'[131] Even after Louis XV's fickle eye had moved from Madame de Pompadour, she continued to live in her splendid Versailles apartment, continued to see the king on a regular basis, and—so it was rumoured—continued to have sex with him vicariously by procuring her successors. Stories began to spread of a private brothel at Versailles called the Parc aux Cerfs ('deer-park'), where the King sought to reinvigorate his flagging potency with ever younger girls and ever more bizarre stimulants, including bathing in the blood of virgins. The duc de Croÿ recorded in his journal that the King had had sexual relations with ninety different women there.[132]

It need hardly be added that these stories were much exaggerated. The Parc aux Cerfs did indeed exist, but it was not a single establishment but the name of a district of Versailles, where the king kept a number of his *petites maîtresses* under the supervision of his valet Lebel, who was in contact with the Paris brothels.[133] Nevertheless, the public claimed to know all about the comings and goings there and took a prurient interest in every reported detail. One of the most notorious of the inmates was Louise O'Murphy (variously spelled as Morfi, Morphise, etc.) who was immortalized by Boucher in one of the most frequently reproduced of all erotic images—*Girl on a Couch* (also known more graphically as *The sprawling O'Murphy*) (Plate 19). That the king's official painter should depict his master's teenage mistress in such a pose says a good deal about Louis XV's *insouciant* attitude towards the image he projected. There is some dispute as to just how old Louise O'Murphy was when procured

[130] Crow, *Painters and Public Life in Eighteenth-century Paris*, pp. 124–7.

[131] Margaret C. Jacob, 'The materialist world of pornography', in Lynn Hunt (ed.), *The Invention of Pornography: Obscenity and the Origins of Modernity, 1500–1800* (New York, 1993), pp. 187–8. See also n. 34 on p. 370.

[132] Antoine, *Louis XV*, pp. 503–6.

[133] G. P. Gooch, *Louis XV: The Monarchy in Decline* (London, 1956), p. 157.

for the king, estimates varying from 12 to 16, but her youth added a further *frisson* of excitement.[134] Some idea of the interest she and the other girls aroused can be gained from the following selection of entries from the diary of the marquis d'Argenson:

1 May 1753: The king is going to Bellevue to restore the reputation of Pompadour as his mistress, but he is very hot for his new love, the little Morfi girl. How can he possibly devote his time to such trivialities, to his buildings, his love-affairs, and his trips, at a time when the state is in such disorder and his authority is more undermined with every day that passes.

2 May 1753: in the event, the king did not go at all. The little Morfi knows how to pay pretty compliments to the king and it is said that she will be made his declared mistress.

7 May 1753: The public is entirely on the side of the Parlement. The background of little Morfi has been investigated; it is certain that her father is currently a cobbler and was a soldier in an Irish regiment.

14 May 1753: Madame de Pompadour is back in favour and Morfi has been sent off to a convent for eighteen months; her place at the Parc aux Cerfs has been taken by the niece of a hairdresser who is very pretty. The king needs these new titbits to sustain his virility for a little longer.

19 May 1753: everyone is thinking of leaving the capital. The expulsion of the Parlement is seen as the *coup de grâce* to what little national liberty remained... In several public places seditious placards have been posted saying 'Long live the Parlement! Death to the King and the Bishops.'

21 May 1753: the king has not given up Morfi, on the contrary he is infatuated with her more than ever.

18 December 1753: Morfi is 4 months pregnant.

20 January 1754: The king has taken a new mistress, even prettier than the little Morfi. She's a brand-new girl and from an even lower social rank, if that were possible, than the last two. The king is only 42 [*sic*] but he is already played out by excessive use of women, for he started too young, and now has to try to refresh his appetite by the variety of delicacies.[135]

The marquis d'Argenson's juxtaposition of references to the struggle of the Parlements with references to royal debauchery demonstrates that for a king obliged to operate in the public sphere, there can be no such thing as private

[134] The editor of E. J. F. Barbier, *Journal historique et anecdotique du règne de Louis XV*, ed. A. de la Villegille, 4 vols. (Paris, 1847–61), IV, p. 166 states firmly that she was only 12, while Michel Antoine (*Louis XV*, p. 504), ever anxious to present his subject's little weaknesses in the best possible light, states that she was 16. She probably did not know herself.

[135] *Journal et mémoires du marquis d'Argenson*, VIII, pp. 1–2, 13–14, 29, 35, 39, 183, 209. Louis XV was in fact 44 years old.

(im)morality. The symbiosis of despotism and debauchery, however, became even more damaging when Madame de Pompadour won a richly deserved reputation for meddling in politics. It was not enough to secure posts, pensions, and sinecures for her friends and relations, she also sought to influence the conduct of public policy. And she succeeded. Indeed, she had a part to play in what was the most fateful single decision of the reign: the 'diplomatic revolution' of 1756, known less dramatically in French as the *renversement des alliances*. It was at her Bellevue estate, and in her presence, that on 3 September 1755 the Abbé de Bernis began negotiations with the Austrian ambassador, Count Starhemberg, which would lead to the first treaty of Versailles the following April, described by Julian Swann as 'perhaps her greatest triumph'.[136] Moreover, it was thanks to Bernis's close friendship with her that he became first the negotiator and then, in 1757, foreign minister.[137]

There was good reason for France to abandon its traditional hostility to the Habsburgs, for the European states system had undergone a fundamental change since the days of Richelieu and Louis XIV. France's main enemy now was not Austria but Great Britain, while Austria's main enemy now was not France but Prussia. With an undeclared war with the British under way in North America,[138] it was imperative for the French to neutralize the continent, so that they could concentrate their resources on the all-important naval and colonial theatres. As Austria was the only continental power to pose a military threat to France, an alliance would bring security. But if the French conception of the alliance was essentially defensive, the Austrians intended to use it offensively, to win back Silesia and reduce Frederick the Great's Prussia to its old rank as just another middling German state. In that discrepancy lay the seeds of disaster. In August 1756 Frederick the Great upset everybody's calculations by launching a pre-emptive strike against Austria, thus activating the alliance with France. Even now the French were only obliged to make a modest military contribution to their ally, and it seemed only a matter of time before the Prussians succumbed to the most powerful coalition ever assembled in Europe (Austria, France, Russia, Sweden, and most of the Holy Roman Empire). So on 1 May 1757 the over-confident French signed a second treaty of Versailles, exactly one year after the first, which committed them to a major

[136] Swann, *Politics and the Parlement of Paris under Louis XV*, p. 55.

[137] Richard Waddington, *Louis XV et le renversement des alliances. Préliminaires de la Guerre de Sept Ans 1754–1756* (Paris, 1896), pp. 298–9. Waddington consistently misspells Starhemberg as 'Stahremberg'.

[138] See above, pp. 299–301.

military effort in Germany in return for control of the Austrian Netherlands (roughly equivalent to present-day Belgium).

So sudden a break with tradition was bound to cause misgivings, especially against the background of the struggle between king and Parlements. Ever since the armies of Charles VIII had entered Italy in 1494 to assert his claim to the throne of Naples, hostility to the Habsburgs had been the central axiom of French foreign policy. If the diplomatic revolution of 1756–7 had delivered what it promised, namely the acquisition of Belgium and the defeat of the British, it might well have gained acceptance—although it may be doubted whether by this time Louis XV was capable of doing anything right in the eyes of some. But in the event it ended in disaster. The war got off to a good start with the capture of Minorca, but then rapidly spiralled out of control. In North America, in the Caribbean, in India, and on the high seas, the British carried all before them. That was bad enough, but the worst humiliation came in Germany. On 5 November 1757 Frederick the Great and 22,000 Prussians inflicted a total rout on a French army almost twice as numerous. Prussian casualties amounted to 23 officers and 518 soldiers, of whom just 3 and 162 respectively were killed. Their opponents' losses comprised 700 dead, 2,000 wounded, and more than 5,000 prisoners of war, including 5 generals and 300 officers.[139] It is not certain that Louis XV exclaimed '*après nous le déluge*' on hearing the terrible news, but Voltaire did comment that Rossbach represented a greater humiliation for his country than Crécy, Poitiers, or Agincourt.[140]

Even before this defeat, there had been precious little enthusiasm for the war. Earlier in the year a government ordinance had sought to intimidate newspapers which had denounced royal foreign policy by threatening the death penalty for anyone convicted of writing seditous publications.[141] The duc d'Aiguillon reported from Brittany in October 1757 that the nobility of the province harboured 'insurmountable prejudices' against the war in Germany. In the following April Bernis lamented: 'Our nation is now more hostile than ever to the war. The King of Prussia is loved here to the point of madness, because those who organize their affairs effectively are always admired. The court of Vienna is detested, because it is regarded as a bloodsucker

[139] T. C. W. Blanning, *The French Revolutionary Wars 1787–1802* (London, 1996), p. 4.

[140] Theodor Schieder, *Friedrich der Große. Ein Königtum der Widersprüche* (Frankfurt am Main, Berlin, and Vienna, 1983), p. 455. See also his letter to Charles Augustin Feriol, comte d'Argentel, dated 19 November 1757; Theodor Besterman (ed.), *Voltaire's Correspondence*, vol. 32 (Geneva, 1958) , p. 177.

[141] Jean-Paul Bertaud, *La Presse et le pouvoir de Louis XIII à Napoléon* (Paris, 2000), p. 33.

battening on France and there is very little enthusiasm for seeing it—or indeed France—gaining territory'.[142] Nor could Louis XV take refuge behind the fiction of bad advice from wicked ministers. As he himself told the comte de Broglie, the head of his secret diplomatic service, the Austrian alliance was his personal achievement and he believed it to be a good move.[143] It was also well known that the French commander at Rossbach, the Prince de Soubise, was a close friend of both the king and Madame de Pompadour, and owed his command to the latter's influence. That was recorded by Barbier in a diary entry for 29 November 1757, together with the observation that there were lots of jibes against Soubise and Pompadour making the rounds in Paris.[144] The manifest unpopularity of the war and the Austrian alliance did not bring a change of policy. When Bernis was dismissed in 1758, he was replaced by the duc de Choiseul, an even closer associate of Madame de Pompadour and another warm supporter of the Austrian connection.

A good indicator of the public mood in the wake of the Seven Years War was the reception given to the play *The Siege of Calais*, by Pierre Laurent Buirette de Belloy, first performed in 1765, which proved to be 'one of the biggest dramatic successes of the century'.[145] This is such a revealing text that it merits a closer look. The eponymous siege took place in 1346, at a particularly low ebb in French fortunes, following defeat at the Battle of Crécy, a débâcle of Rossbach-like proportions. As the play begins, a last attempt to relieve the doomed city has failed, despite heroic French feats of arms, because the dastardly English have discovered the secret of gunpowder and have cheated by using artillery. Determined to resist *à outrance*, the surviving defenders decide to burn their city and themselves, rather than fall into the hands of the enemy. The victorious Edward III offers to allow the citizens safe passage, on condition that six of their number are handed over for execution. There is stiff competition for the honour of a martyr's death, of course, but it proves to be unnecessary. Aurelius, the son of Eustache de Saint Pierre, the mayor of Calais, asks Edward to be allowed to die first, out of sight of his father (who is also one of the magnificent six), asking rhetorically how Edward would have felt if he had been obliged to witness his father being put to death with red-hot pokers. This is all too much, even for an English king, who undergoes a sudden conversion experience:

[142] Antoine, *Louis XV*, p. 743.
[143] Ibid., p. 681.
[144] Barbier, *Journal*, vol. IV, p. 245.
[145] Richard Fargher, *Life and Letters in France: The Eighteenth Century* (London, 1970), p. 120.

Where am I? ah! what murmur!
What struggle in my breast?—what tender call!
It is the voice of nature.
ALIENORA Answer then That call.
Happy the world when kings will hear it.
EDWARD My wild ambition has misled me, glory,
Idol of kings! the people are thy victims![146]

In the wake of the defeats of the Seven Years War, it is easy to appreciate why the play found such a strong resonance. In its appeal to patriotism and celebration of the past greatness of the French nation, it conveyed a message of hope. Believing wrongly that his son has perished in battle, Saint Pierre exclaims:

My son is dead! he never could retreat.
O my poor boy!—lye still my heart; first let me
Save my country, and then I'll weep for him.
O patriot love! thou pure celestial flame!
Soul of my soul! and source of every virtue!
O in my bosom fan the generous fire,
And dry the tears paternal grief would shed.
It is my country, 'tis my king, 'tis France,
That calls, and not my son, who ought to die
In their defence.[147]

The military failure against the English is depicted as a temporary setback, which can soon be righted—if only a patriotic spirit of self-sacrifice is created. In his opening speech, Saint Pierre looked forward joyfully to laying down his life in the service of his nation:

I don't despair; my hopes are grounded on
The destiny of France. Woe to those states
Those coward states, who yielding to the storm
Forsake the helm, and give up all for lost;
And what is worst of all cease to esteem
Themselves! No, kind heav'n be praised, we are
Not yet reduced to that desponding state.
'Tis from th'abyss of woe resources spring.
Who knows? perhaps this very day my son
And I may perish for the state? should

[146] Pierre de Belloy, *The Siege of Calais* (London, 1765), p. 70. That the play was translated at once into English is some indication of its contemporary fame.
[147] Ibid., p. 5.

All our citizens have thoughts like these, t'would be
An omen of our country's preservation.[148]

Among other reasons for optimism, there is the contrast to be drawn between the excellence of traditional French institutions and the defects of those of their English enemies. Indeed, Belloy could not have supplied a better example of the definition of national identity in terms of the other. The difference between the two nations was also recognized by Edward III, who candidly admitted the failings of a parliamentary regime:

I left my stormy isle,
Country for ever wet with blood, that flows
From civil broils between the throne and liberty;
Where subjects are the tyrants of their masters,
Who roar for happiness, and yet refuse it.
In these disputes the senate and their king
Divide for a mistaken point of honour,
Their common interests; mistrust ensues,
The minister, to prop his wav'ring power,
Is forc'd, for his own safety, to collect
His friends, unmindful of the public welfare.
Have I not seen myself this daring senate
Precipitate my father from the throne?
Affront their king, load him with chains, and then
To a child's hand intrust the regal power?[149]

For Saint Pierre (and Belloy), 'despotism' was not a pejorative term, as Edward used it in a wholly favourable manner. He continues:

But shift the scene—what do I see in France
A king despotic, both rever'd and lov'd!
The nobles who derive their power from him
With grateful zeal establish his firm throne;
A people gentle, sensible, and true,
As if one loving family submit
By inclination to a father's will;
Assur'd he has at heart his children's good.
O fortunate Valois! Is there a king
On earth that does not envy thee such subjects?
How sweet the talk to render happy those
Whose love we have! 'tis in thy power to make
Thyself ador'd.[150]

[148] Ibid., pp. 2–3. [149] Ibid., pp. 30–1. [150] Ibid.

There was, however, a potential sting in that final line. Significantly, King Philip VI of France does not make an appearance in the play. He is presented as an essential component of the French nation but very much subordinate to it. Alienora, daughter of the governor of Calais, the comte de Vienne, explains patiently to King Edward that his claim to the French throne can never be recognized for the simple reason that he is not French. So anxious were the ancient French to be ruled only by one of their own number that they excluded women from succession, lest they marry a foreigner:

> To us our king and country are the same,
> Of whom our love and duty go together.
> This undivided zeal supports his throne,
> And makes him envied by all other kings.[151]

This fundamental law of the kingdom also commands the French to disobey their king if he should order something contrary to it. When King Philip offers to meet Edward III in single combat, with the French crown as the prize, the comte de Melun points out to Edward that this is unlawful:

> I know that Valois rates his subjects' blood
> Above the price of all your provinces.
> 'Tis ours, through love, to spill for him that blood
> He fain would save at hazard of his own;
> But, subject to the law that made him king,
> He may dispose of all except himself.
> What right has he then to transfer the crown,
> And to an alien too? could you extirpate
> Philip, and all the royal race of Capet,
> You would not be the nearer to the throne,
> The last of Frenchmen have a right before you,
> I speak our nation's voice—my duty's done.[152]

That should not have made comfortable listening for Louis XV, nor should Saint Pierre's vision of a charismatic hero:

> But O my countrymen! let but one brave,
> One steadfast hero rise above the frowns
> Of fate, one worthy of our glorious ancestors,
> He will recall those happy days when o'er
> The globe our lilies floated in the air;
> You'd see this now deject'd people rouz'd,

[151] Ibid., p. 40. [152] Ibid., pp. 64–5.

Admire and strive to rival him in fame.
His brave example will inflame their hearts,
And make them blush that ever they despair'd.
Their constancy shall force e'en fate to change,
And bring their country back its former glory.
All this will be the fruits reap'd by our death;
Whilst from our blood thousands like us shall spring.[153]

A tremor of unease should also have run up Louis's spine when he saw the faults of King Philip VI's court exposed. For it had been court intrigue and unjust imprisonment which had driven the mighty warrior, Godfrey of Harcourt, to leave France and enter the service of the King of England. Alienora muses on the lesson to be drawn:

Proud monarchs of the world be this your lesson,
To watch the welfare of your meanest people.
Sometimes a poor man by oppression dies,
That might, perhaps, have liv'd to save his country.[154]

Belloy's play used the rhetoric and semiology of patriotism, but of a kind that could be incorporated within traditional institutions and values. He explicitly took a stand against the cosmopolitanism of the *philosophes*, when he put the following words into the mouth of the 'good Englishman', Sir Walter Manny:

In England born, in England bred, I feel
I do prefer it to all other countries.
You have the same attachment to your own.
I hate those hearts that have no natal love,
That see without concern their country's woes,
And stile themselves compatriotes of the world,
Ungrateful children of their mother land!
Who do not merit to be claimed by any.[155]

Perhaps not surprisingly, the *philosophes* did not join in the applause for Belloy. Grimm, for example, found the subject 'fine and national' but the play so badly written as to 'humiliate the nation' by the 'imbecilic enthusiasm' it displayed.[156] Once again, as in the *querelle des bouffons*, here was a cultural opportunity for the court to exploit, by driving a wedge between enlightened opinion and nationalist public opinion—and once again the opportunity was

[153] Ibid., pp. 50–1. [154] Ibid., p. 51. [155] Ibid., p. 47.
[156] Quoted in Fargher, *Life and Letters in France*, p. 125.

spurned. Louis XV got off to a good start by awarding Belloy a gold medal, but then fell victim to thespian temperament. One of the great actresses of the day, Madame Clairon, who created the role of Alienora, incurred royal displeasure by refusing to act alongside the king's favourite actor, Dubois. She paid for her impertinence with five days in prison, but gained ample revenge when a public demonstration in her support was so riotous as to become known as the *Journée du Siège de Calais*. Unbroken, she resigned from the Comédie Française and went off to Ferney to enjoy a *fête champêtre* organized by Voltaire in her honour.[157] That seems to have marked the end of any official exploitation of the responsive chord sounded by Belloy. His contemporary biographer, who wrote a short account of his life as a preface to his collected works in 1779, recorded politely but reprovingly:

After writing *The Siege of Calais*, inclination and gratitude moved M. de Belloy to devote himself to French subjects. It was his ambition to win the honour of being exclusively the National Poet: his love of France was combined with admiration; he regarded the French as being incontestably superior to all other peoples: and if he allowed himself to be critical of the government (although he never complained on his own account, even when he was most suffering from neglect), it was to reproach it for not taking sufficient advantage of the national character, by always preferring honour to interest, for he believed that to be easier in France than anywhere else.

Yet, the biographer added, his two patriotic plays *Gaston et Bayard* and *Gabrielle de Vergy* were so shamefully neglected by the authorities that even his worst enemies were shocked.[158]

One potentially ominous aspect of Belloy's popularity was the special appeal *The Siege of Calais* made to army officers. According to the biographer, garrisons were especially active in staging performances and officers learned speeches off by heart. Certainly Belloy himself made a special appeal to the military in the prefaces to his plays. In the preface to *Gaston et Bayard*, for example, first performed in 1771, he wrote:

The nation likes to have the feats of its great men recounted . . . How happy I would be if love of the fatherland, that sublime passion, which has given France so many heroes, could inspire in my soul the ability to give them a poet worthy to celebrate them! Having expounded the general duties of the Citizen through the actions and feelings of Eustache de Saint-Pierre, I offer here to our young soldiers their own

[157] Ibid., p. 123.

[158] *Vie de M. de Belloy, écrite par un homme de lettres, son ami*, Pierre Laurent Buirette de Belloy, *Œuvres complètes*, 6 vols. (Paris, 1779), I, pp. 40–1.

models in the shape of two heroes, who I shall try to bring to life on the stage and who it would be glorious to see brought to life in our camps.[159]

For officers and gentlemen alike, there was little prospect of a latter-day Eustache de Saint Pierre, Gaston, Bayard, or even Joan of Arc appearing to rescue France in the hour of its need, so long as the Austrian alliance remained in place. As we have noted, the replacement of Bernis by Choiseul did not bring a change of policy, despite the military disasters. Indeed, it was Choiseul who implemented Louis XV's wish to see the new system survive his reign, by negotiating a marriage between the heir to the throne and the Archduchess Marie Antoinette, daughter of Maria Theresa of Austria. The wedding took place in May 1770. By the end of the year Choiseul had fallen from power, partly because his forward policies threatened to involve France in a new war with Great Britain, partly because he was thought to be too accommodating to the Parlements and partly because he fell victim to a court intrigue. Deeply implicated in the affair, at least in the eyes of the public, was Madame du Barry, the king's new *maîtresse en titre*. According to the Abbé de Véri, Choiseul and his friends had gone out of their way to humiliate her, even in the presence of the king, so she had not been slow to take revenge when the opportunity arose.[160] The exile of Choiseul to his estates at Chanteloup was turned into what one historian of the period has called a 'mini-Fronde', as more than 200 nobles demonstratively visited the disgraced minister to show their solidarity, having their names inscribed on a column especially erected for the purpose.[161] The young comte de Ségur wrote later in his memoirs that he would never forget the pleasure he experienced when seeing his name and that of his father enrolled on this *colonne d'opposition*.[162] Choiseul and his friends also resorted to vilifying Madame du Barry, and with her Louis XV, through pornographic *libelles*.[163] The new mistress certainly presented an easy target, for she represented a significant step down the social ladder from previous incumbents. She had been born Jeanne Bécu, the illegitimate daughter of a monk (or so it was alleged) and had been working as a prostitute in Paris before being brought to the king's attention in 1766. A combination of professional skill and physical beauty clearly made a powerful impression on the ageing

159 Ibid., vol. III, p. 95.

160 De Witte (ed.), *Journal de l'abbé de Véri*, p. 167.

161 Swann, *Politics and the Parlement of Paris under Louis XV*, p. 51.

162 Louis-Philippe, comte de Ségur, *Mémoires ou souvenirs et anecdotes*, vols. 1–3 of *Œuvres complètes* (Paris, 1824–6), vol. I, pp. 20–1.

163 Sarah Maza, *Private Lives and Public Affairs: The Causes Célèbres of pre-Revolutionary France* (Berkeley, Los Angeles, and London, 1993), p. 179.

KING ALFRED'S COLLEGE
LIBRARY

roué, for he had to show considerable determination in forcing her on his court as his *maîtresse en tître*. Madame de Genlis recorded that on Madame du Barry's first appearance there, all the women got up and moved away from her: 'nothing so scandalous had ever been seen there, not even under la Pompadour. It was simply disgraceful to present with so much pomp a street-walker to the royal family'.[164] It was also well-known that the king lavished huge sums on his new favourite: according to Werner Sombart, during her five years at court (1769–74) Madame du Barry got through 12,481,803 *livres*.[165]

The pamphlets circulating in Paris brought the monarchy down as far as it could go. Louis XV was depicted as a feeble decadent, so wasted by a life of debauchery that only a professional could tease an erection from him.[166] In the preface to a collection of what purported to be letters from Madame du Barry to her associates, he was described as weak, cretinous, idle, irresolute, devoted to the vilest debauchery, dishonoured in the eyes of his people and foreigners, despised and hated.[167] In *The Shade of Louis XV before Minos*, published shortly after his death, he finds himself in Hell and being interrogated about his conduct towards his army of mistresses, all of whom are also present. They complain that they experienced very little pleasure but a great deal of pain at his hands, although they concede that they were paid royally for their exertions. 'But not me!' complains a little village-girl covered in pustules, for she was already suffering from smallpox when raped by the king as his last victim and inadvertent killer. Minos tells Louis:

> All this lust, infamy, and prostitution would have mattered less, if at least you had concealed your filthy habits with the veil of secrecy and if you had shown respect for morality by not making public your criminal examples of incest, adultery, kidnap, and rape, and if you had not caused maximum outrage by choosing a mistress from the mire of debauchery, if you had not deluged her with the resources of the state so that she could wallow in luxury fit for a queen, if you had not multiplied taxes to indulge her crazy fancies and sacrificed your subjects' future to the whims of this madness.

But Louis is quite unabashed, replying: 'But I found her amusing, I needed her to keep me going—I would have died of boredom without her. It's absolutely

164 Madame de Genlis, *Mémoires inédits de Madame la Comtesse de Genlis, sur le dix-huitième siècle et la Révolution française, depuis 1756 à nos jours*, vol. II (Paris, 1825), pp. 109–10.

165 Werner Sombart, *Luxury and Capitalism* (Ann Arbor, Mich., 1967), p. 74.

166 Robert Darnton, *The Forbidden Best-sellers of Pre-revolutionary France* (London, 1996), pp. 212–13.

167 [Mathieu François Pidansat de Mairobert], *Lettres originales de Madame la comtesse du Barry; avec celles des Princes, Seigneurs, Ministres & autres, qui lui ont écrit, & Qu'on a pu recueillir* ('London', 1779), unpaginated preface.

necessary for my people to make sacrifices for me'.[168] As for the lady herself, she was depicted as an unprincipled whore of the lowest kind, who had sold her 'virginity' repeatedly to clergy and aristocrats, and who revelled in seeing princes of the blood grovel before her in the hope of securing favours from the king.[169] Typical of the visual pornography circulating was a depiction of her standing in a barrel, mending her underwear, while in the background we see her taking a client into her brothel and through an upstairs window starting to undress; meanwhile, a dog lifts his leg to urinate on the barrel. The destabilizing effects of this torrent of sleaze was undoubtedly intensified by its association with a sense of national decline. Back in 1749, following the disappointing end to the War of the Austrian Succession, which had given rise to a new simile—*bête comme la paix*—a policy spy had reported on a dissident moaning in a café:

Jules-Alexis Bernard, chevalier de Bellerive, esquire, former captain of dragoons: In the shop of the wigmaker Gaujoux, this individual read aloud . . . an attack on the king in which it was said that His Majesty let himself be governed by ignorant and incompetent ministers and had made a shameful, dishonourable peace, which gave up all the fortresses that had been captured . . . that the king, by his affair with the three sisters scandalized his people and would bring down all sorts of misfortune on himself if he did not change his conduct; that His Majesty scorned the Queen and was an adulterer; that he had not confessed for Easter communion and would bring down the curse of God upon the kingdom and that France would be overwhelmed with disasters. (Quoted in Robert Darnton, *The Forbidden Best-sellers of Pre-revolutionary France* (London, 1996), p. 235)

The much deeper wound inflicted on national pride by the Peace of Paris which brought the Seven Years War to an end, was correspondingly more damaging. Nor did the humiliation end there. In particular, the partition of one of France's oldest allies, Poland, in 1772 by the three eastern powers, including France's newest 'ally', Austria, seemed to signal that French power in Europe had collapsed altogether. Soulavie observed that it proved that the treaty of 1756 had been designed to turn France into an auxiliary of Austria, with the purpose of despoiling first Prussia and then Poland.[170]

168 [Pidansat de Mairobert], *L'Espion Anglois, ou correspondance secrète entre Milord All'eye et Milord Alle'ar [sic]*, 10 vols. ('à Londres', 1779), vol. II, letter 18 is a review of *L'Ombre de Louis XV devant Minos* but with extensive quotations.

169 [Pidansat de Mairobert], *Anecdotes sur M. la comtesse du Barri* ('à Londres', 1775), pp. 22–3.

170 J. L. Soulavie, *Mémoires historiques et anecdotes de la cour de France pendant la faveur de la marquise de Pompadour* (Paris, 1802), p. 6.

To sleaze and impotence was added a third leg—despotism—to form a monstrous tripod of political pejoratives. When Choiseul left office in 1770, the way was clear for the chancellor, Maupeou, the controller-general of finance, Terray, and the new foreign minister, the duc d'Aiguillon, to take charge. Their main task was to arrange a final showdown with the Parlements. Between 1762 and 1764 one Parlement after the other had taken action to exclude the Jesuits from their areas of jurisdiction. Although not as enthusiastic a supporter of the Jesuits as the more pious members of his family, notably the Dauphin, Louis XV did not wish to see them banished altogether. He was induced to give his consent by Choiseul, who was not a believer and was looking for a painless concession to the Parlements to win their support for new taxation.[171] Not for the first or last time, Louis XV contrived to have the worst of all worlds. On the one hand, he allowed the Parlements to claim a mighty symbolic triumph; on the other he failed to gain any kudos himself. On the contrary, he looked more like a weak-kneed cynic prepared to sacrifice his faithful supporters for the sake of expediency.[172]

Nor did this concession create a working relationship between Crown and opposition. Even before the final expulsion of the Jesuits had been agreed, another great confrontation was beginning to brew in Brittany. After 1763 a dispute developed between the Parlement of Rennes and the duc d'Aiguillon, *commandant en chef* in the province, which reached a climax in 1770, when he insisted that the accusations made against him should be tried in the court of peers.[173] In a move which appeared to be quintessentially despotic, the king intervened in the proceedings to declare the case against his minister null and void, thus apparently putting his executive officers beyond the reach of the law. He also took the opportunity to show that he had not changed his mind one jot about the location of sovereignty in his kingdom: 'We hold our Crown from God alone. The right to make laws ... belongs to us alone, independently and wholly.' The role of the Parlements, he added, was entirely advisory; they were

[171] The fullest account of the expulsion of the Jesuits is to be found in Dale Van Kley, *The Jansenists and the Expulsion of the Jesuits from France 1757–1765* (New Haven, 1975), *passim*. There is a good concise account in Emmanuel Le Roy Ladurie, *The Ancien Régime: A history of France 1610–1774* (Oxford, 1996), pp. 410–17.

[172] Conor Cruise O'Brien, 'Nationalism and the French Revolution', in Geoffrey Best (ed.), *The Permanent Revolution: The French Revolution and its Legacy 1789–1989* (London, 1988), p. 28. In the opinion of Dale Van Kley, one consequence of the episode was to make the words 'absolute', 'arbitrary', and 'despotic' seem like synonyms; Dale K. Van Kley, *The Damiens Affair and the Unravelling of the Ancien Régime* (Princeton, NJ, 1984), p. 201.

[173] This very complicated episode is best followed in Swann, *Politics and the Parlement of Paris under Louis XV*, chs. 9–11.

given the right of remonstrance only so as to be able to help their sovereign, not obstruct him.[174] A lifetime's exasperation with the Parlements' obduracy, together with the desire to pass on to his successor a stable system of authority, now prompted Louis XV to attempt a radical solution. Early in 1771, under the supervision of Chancellor Maupeou, the recalcitrant *parlementaires* were exiled and purged, and a new judicial structure was imposed which in effect emasculated the Parlements as a political force.

Contemporaries were in no doubt that an existential struggle had begun. Diderot wrote in April 1771: 'we are on the verge of a crisis which will end in slavery or liberty; if it is slavery, it will be a slavery like that which exists in Morocco or Constantinople. If all the Parlements are dissolved ... farewell to every privilege of the various estates constituting a corrective principle which prevents the monarchy from degenerating into despotism.'[175] It was indeed an episode of great significance, because it brought together in the public sphere the forces of public opinion and the Parlements' opposition over an issue which was wholly secular. After the expulsion of the Jesuits, the Jansenist issue had lost its immediacy. It was now a straightforward contest for sovereignty. In a very interesting article published on 20 January 1772, the *Journal Historique* wrote of this change:

> Jansenism having lost its great merit, its true interest, when the Jesuits were abolished in France, has transformed itself into the party of Patriotism. One must do justice to [the Jansenists]: they always had a strong bent towards independence, and they fought papal despotism with invincible courage. Political despotism is no less fearful a monster, and [the party] now directs all its forces towards this enemy, since they are no longer needed in the other combat.[176]

The importance of Jansenism in serving as midwife for a patriotic movement was also stressed by Pidansat de Mairobert in 1777, in the preface he wrote for Bachaumont's journal, which he published under the title *Secret Memoirs, a Contribution to the History of the Republic of Letters*.[177] He stated that the 'philosophic invasion' had brought about a revolution in the republic of letters in France. After the seeds had been sown by Montesquieu and Voltaire, three consecutive groups had tended the growing plant. The first were the Encylopædists, who had brought light to dissipate the dark clouds of theology,

[174] Echeverria, *The Maupeou Revolution*, p. 16.

[175] Quoted in William Doyle, *The Old European Order* (Oxford, 1978), p. 316.

[176] Jeremy Popkin, 'Pamphlet journalism at the end of the old regime', *Eighteenth Century Studies*, 22 (1989), p. 366.

[177] On the complex history of this publication, see Robert S. Tate, 'Petit de Bachaumont, his circle and the *Mémoires secrets*', *Studies on Voltaire and the Eighteenth Century*, 65 (1968), ch. 6.

destroying fanaticism and superstition. Then the Economists (physiocrats) had turned the emphasis to the practicalities of improving society and making people happier. Finally, the time of troubles and oppression brought forth the patriots, who went back to the origins of political authority to demonstrate the reciprocal obligations of subjects and sovereigns and established the great principles of government. He concluded: 'this band of *philosophes*, which took over leadership of the various literary groups, came into its own following the destruction of the Jesuits: that was the real moment when the revolution burst forth.'[178]

In the struggle for legitimacy, the king and his ministers were at a fatal disadvantage. All their attempts to influence the press and propagate their own side of the story were drowned by the clamour of opposition journalists. At least 167 pamphlets in support of the Parlements were published, with print runs of up to 5,000. Among those joining the throng was Beaumarchais, who had a personal axe to grind after losing an expensive court case under the new system. Although Voltaire was on the other side, he recognized the effect of Beaumarchais's polemics: 'I have never seen anything more singular, more brave, more comic, more interesting, more humiliating for his adversaries. He takes on ten or twelve people at a time, and knocks them to the ground just like an enraged Harlequin overturns a whole troop of guardsmen.'[179] As the scholar who has studied the episode most closely concludes: 'one may make the informed guess that a considerable majority of the literate and politically conscious portion of the population was pro-Patriot'.[180] According to Regnaud, there would have been a general rising in 1771 if the Parlement had offered physical resistance: 'if it had deviated in the slightest from obedience to the king's orders, the capital would have been plunged into the most terrible revolution . . . I can state that if a leader had been found at this critical moment, the revolution would have been most frightful.'[181] The popularity of the royal cause was not helped by the fact that at the same time that Maupeou was sorting out the Parlements, his colleague Terray was declaring what amounted to a partial bankruptcy and introducing some very unpopular fiscal measures, making the first *vingtième*, a theoretically temporary tax, first imposed in 1749, permanent and extending the second until 1781.

178 Eugène Hatin, *Histoire politique et littéraire de la presse en France*, (Paris, 1859), vol. III, p. 473.

179 Quoted in Crow, *Painters and Public Life*, p. 180.

180 Echeverria, *The Maupeou Revolution*, p. 25.

181 Aubertin, *L'Esprit public au XVIIIe siècle*, p. 416.

Opposition to the 'Maupeou Revolution' was intense and prolonged. It was also inclusive, embracing the duc de Chartres (heir to the duc d'Orléans), most of the other princes of the blood, a large section of the nobility, the Parlements, and public opinion. Yet it failed. Louis XV, d'Aiguillon, Maupeou, and Terray were too successful for the monarchy's own good. By establishing the new system of courts, recruiting enough lawyers to make them work, and repressing or ignoring opposition, they showed that a vigorous exercise of royal authority could ride roughshod over even the most determined opposition—at least in the short term. And that was the rub. We shall never know whether the new arrangement could have worked indefinitely, for Louis XV had only three more years to live. It might be conjectured that sooner or later a new financial crisis would have proved it to be unviable. A helpful analogy here is the fate suffered by the 'neo-absolutist' regime imposed on the Habsburg Empire after the revolutions of 1848–9, which had to be abandoned as unworkable after a decade. In both late eighteenth-century France and mid-nineteenth-century Austria, the old order had suffered such a haemorrhage of legitimacy, and the public sphere had expanded so far beyond government control, that fundamental constitutional change was inevitable. In the terse formulation of Durand Echeverria: 'France emerged from the experience of 1770–1774 a different nation.'[182]

LOUIS XVI, MARIE ANTOINETTE, AND THE FALL OF THE ABSOLUTE MONARCHY

Louis XV died on 10 May 1774, in a manner which only enhanced his sleazy reputation, for it was alleged that he had contracted the smallpox which killed him from a young peasant girl procured for him by Madame du Barry.[183] Apart from the latter, whose star now fell to earth, no one lamented his passing. When he had been dangerously ill back in 1747, 'all Paris' had rushed to Notre Dame to implore God to spare him, and every guild had commissioned a *Te Deum* when he was pronounced out of danger. In his final illness, the churches remained empty and not even the display of Saint Geneviève's relics could inspire prayers for intercession.[184] The new king, only 19 years old and

[182] Echeverria, *The Maupeou Revolution*, p. 297. Cf. the verdict of Monique Cottret: 'The end of the reign was marked by a process of detachment of the king from the nation'—*Jansénisme et lumières. Pur un autre XVIIIe siècle* (Paris, 1998), p. 144.

[183] Echeverria, *The Maupeou Revolution*, p. 29.

[184] McManners, *Church and Society in Eighteenth-century France*, p. 16.

separated from his grandfather by two generations, was in a position to reap all the popularity which a sharp break with the past made available. He got off to a good start by banishing Madame du Barry from the court, dismissing Maupeou and Terray, and appointing a ministry which combined experience in the shape of the comte de Maurepas, who had been languishing in exile on his estates since falling foul of Madame de Pompadour in 1749, with reforming vigour in the shape of Turgot, Intendant of Limoges and friend of the leading physiocrats. The recall of the Parlements announced that the reign of despotism was over.

Yet it soon transpired that very little had changed. A warning signal was hoisted early on by the new king's insistence that his coronation be conducted at Reims in the traditional fashion. With a keen eye for the importance of gesture politics, Turgot had wanted the ceremony to be simplified, modernized, and moved to Paris. He pointed out that a royal example of economy would be very popular, would be good for the tourist trade, and help to reconcile court and capital.[185] He also wanted a new coronation oath, considering that the traditional wording promised too much to the clergy but too little to the nation.[186] His new version stressed the king's secular obligations and in particular omitted the pledge 'to exterminate, in all lands subjected to my rule, the heretics declared to be so by the Church'.[187] Louis XVI had his way, of course. In June 1775 the royal retinue moved to Reims for six days of ceremonies costing an estimated 7,000,000 *livres*.[188] (Plate 20) The actual coronation ceremony included anointing with the oil originally brought from Heaven by the Holy Ghost at the behest of Saint Rémy when he baptized Clovis, the Merovingian King of the Franks, as a Christian about AD 493. (Aerial assistance in transporting the oil had been needed on that occasion because the crush of people prevented it being carried into the church by more conventional means.)[189]

As if to emphasize the traditional nature of the proceedings, Louis XVI also insisted on carrying out the ceremony of touching for the king's evil. Newly equipped with thaumaturgical powers, he laid hands on 2,400 suffering from

185 Hermann Weber, 'Das Sacre Ludwigs XVI. vom 11. Juni 1775 und die Krise des Ancien Régime', in Ernst Hinrichs, Eberhard Schmitt, and Rudolf Vierhaus (eds.), *Vom Ancien Régime zur Französischen Revolution. Forschungen und Ergebnisse* (Göttingen, 1978), p. 541; David Dakin, *Turgot and the ancien régime in France* (London, 1939), pp. 216–18.

186 [Condorcet], *Vie de Monsieur Turgot* (Berne, 1787), pp. 115–16.

187 McManners, *Church and Society in Eighteenth-century France*, p. 15.

188 Weber, 'Das Sacre Ludwigs XVI.', p. 540.

189 Anton Haueter, *Die Krönungen der französischen Könige im Zeitalter des Absolutismus und in der Restauration* (Zürich, 1975), p. 104.

scrofula. Unimpressed, Voltaire wrote to Frederick the Great that he had lost confidence in the King of France's miraculous power on learning that one of Louis XIV's mistresses had died of scrofula, despite being very well touched by the king.[190] However, in one important respect the ceremony was new in 1775, although the change did not point in the right direction. In the past, the Bishops of Laon and Beauvais had asked the congregation whether they accepted the king, whereupon the Archbishop of Reims had intoned '*quia populus acclamavit te, te sacro regem*' ('as the people have acclaimed you, I consecrate you king'), but on this occasion the whole episode was omitted. Whether this was due to an oversight or to a wish to stress the sacral nature of Louis's kingship is not clear, but it is certain that it was much criticized.[191] A pamphlet published later that year, entitled *The Royal Coronation, or the Rights of the French Nation Recognized and Confirmed by this Ceremony*, argued that a 'party of reaction' had conspired to change the ceremony to elevate the clerical interest. The anonymous author, together with others who wrote on the same theme, took the opportunity to argue that royal legitimacy rested not on divine right but on a social contract with the nation as a whole.[192]

The splendour of Louis XVI's coronation was matched only by those of Napoleon I and Charles X, both of whom also lost their thrones (although not their heads), so perhaps Turgot was right. His own tenure of office as controller-general was to be brief, as he was dismissed in May 1776. With him went his programme, designed to reform the fiscal system and to broaden the basis of monarchical support by means of a network of provincial assemblies. By that time he had alienated conservative opinion both inside the government, especially Maurepas and Vergennes, and outside, especially in the Parlements. As involvement in the War of American Independence loomed (and Turgot had advocated staying out), the chances for fundamental domestic restructuring diminished. The two most distinguished modern histories of France in the period both see the fall of Turgot as a watershed, whatever the rights or wrongs of the small print of his proposed reforms: 'thus, after the downfall of the triumvirate's [Maupeou, Terray, d'Aiguillon] neo-absolutist attempt, came the failure of the philosophical and reforming monarchy. In six years, the two paths of state arbitration had been explored in vain. At the end of this double shipwreck, there remained an ever more anti-absolutist public opinion and a monarchy which was falling apart' (François Furet) and 'Turgot's disgrace

[190] Ibid., p. 257.
[191] Weber, 'Das Sacre Ludwigs XVI', p. 558, favours the latter interpretation, John McManners prefers the former—*Church and Society in Eighteenth-century France*, p. 14.
[192] Ibid.

marked the failure of the alliance of philosophy with absolutism, the defeat of enlightened despotism in France, and the impossibility of overcoming entrenched privilege' (Daniel Roche).[193]

Ominous both substantively and in terms of perception was the role alleged to have been played in Turgot's fall by the queen.[194] It was not to be the last time that she interfered with matters that should not have concerned her. So much has been written about Marie Antoinette that any analysis of her role in the unravelling of the French monarchy can be concise. In a single sentence it can be said that, for public opinion and its minders, she assumed the role vacated by Louis XV. Three main groups of charges were laid against her. First, she was accused of wild extravagance. There was some substance to this, for she did spend large sums on clothes, horse-racing, and gambling. Most conspicuous was her expenditure on buildings after 1783, despite the monarchy's financial straits in the aftermath of the American War. The hamlet of twelve houses constructed on the banks of the Great Pond of Trianon at Versailles appeared to be particularly self-indulgent, although her apologists have justified it as an exercise in progressive agriculture.[195] Her most damaging architectural project was the purchase of the Palace of Saint Cloud from the duc d'Orléans in 1784, which attracted a great deal of hostile publicity. It was unprecedented for a queen to buy a château on her own account, even more so to staff it with servants wearing her own special livery, and more so still to issue orders signed *de par la reine*. Madame Campan recalled:

> This livery of the queen at the gates of a palace where one only expected that of the king: those words *de par la reine* at the head of notices posted on the railings caused a sensation and had a very bad effect, not only among the common people but among their social superiors; all this was seen as undermining the customs of the monarchy, and customs are closely linked to laws.[196]

Also unpopular were the huge sums believed to be squandered on Marie Antoinette's entourage. Although the stories grew with the telling, many

[193] François Furet, *Revolutionary France 1770–1880* (Oxford and Cambridge, Mass., 1992), pp. 26–7; Roche, *France in the Enlightenment*, p. 475.

[194] Munro Price, *Preserving the Monarchy: the comte de Vergennes, 1774–1787* (Cambridge, 1995), pp. 50–1. John Hardman, in *French Politics 1774–1789: From the Accession of Louis XVI to the Fall of the Bastille* (London, 1995), p. 206, argues that in reality it was the king not the queen who brought down Turgot.

[195] Vincent Cronin, *Louis and Antoinette* (London, 1974), p. 194. Despite the overblown style and excessively exculpatory tone, this is a well-researched and informative study.

[196] Quoted in Price, *Preserving the Monarchy*, pp. 147–8.

millions of *livres* did indeed find their way into the pockets of friends such as the Princesse de Lamballe, who drew 170,000 *livres* as superintendent of the queen's household and many hundreds of thousands more in gifts and loans. The most rapacious was the impoverished Polignac clan, which won a ducal title and pensions totalling 700,000 *livres* a year, thanks to the friendship of the queen with Gabrielle de Polignac.[197] Among those most horrified by her dissipation were her Austrian relations. Virtually from the time she arrived in France, but especially from the accession to the throne in 1774, the Austrian ambassador, Count Mercy, the Austrian foreign minister, Prince Kaunitz, and her brother, Joseph II, joined in a chorus of criticism about her extravagance, her gambling, and her raids on the treasury for the benefit of her friends. In November 1777 Mercy reported to Joseph that his sister's conduct during the court's sojourn at Fontainebleau had been marked by 'a dissipation as complete in its variety as in its excess'.[198] Constant stern warnings from her mother and brother had no effect. Nine years later Mercy was still complaining that 'dissipation exercises a pernicious influence on her.'[199]

The gossips at court—and the pamphleteers in the capital—alleged that Marie Antoinette's intense friendships with her female friends were consummated physically. This was the second kind of charge levelled against her, namely that she was promiscuously and rampantly bisexual. Although this was almost certainly not true, it is not difficult to see why it might have been believed. In his reply to Voltaire's mocking letter about the coronation cited above,[200] Frederick the Great sneered that Louis XVI had never committed a mortal sin in his life, adding that this must be a great comfort to patients touched by him.[201] Certainly it seems likely that Louis was never guilty of sins of the flesh. In 1771 another monarch, George III of England, was told that Louis XV had said of his grandson, 'the Dauphin is well made and perfectly well formed yet has hitherto shown no desire for women, nay rather seems to loathe them.'[202] Although the future Louis XVI was in fact neither a eunuch nor a misogynist, he was as muted in his sexual activity as his predecessor had been priapic. Indeed, he was the only Bourbon monarch never to commit adultery. As we have seen, in the case of George III marital fidelity was a

[197] Furet, *Revolutionary France*, p. 33.

[198] Alfred Ritter von Arneth and J. Flammermont (eds.), *Correspondance secrète du comte de Mercy-Argenteau avec l'empereur Joseph II et le prince de Kaunitz*, 2 vols. (Paris, 1889–91), vol. I, p. 514.

[199] Ibid., vol. II, p. 56.

[200] See above, p. 408.

[201] Haueter, *Die Krönungen der französischen Könige*, p. 257.

[202] Cronin, *Louis and Antoinette*, p. 407.

desirable, if not an essential qualification for a monarch wishing to endear himself to public opinion in the second half of the eighteenth century. Unfortunately, Louis XVI turned a virtue into a vice by acquiring the reputation of impotence. Although there remains some uncertainty about the exact nature of his sexual relations, seven years passed before he was able to consummate his marriage. According to many accounts, the problem was mainly physiological, namely a phimosis, that is to say, a contraction of the foreskin which makes sexual intercourse very painful or even impossible. It was only when Louis's brother-in-law, Joseph II, persuaded him to have a painful but necessary operation that consummation could be achieved. However, Derek Beales's careful examination of all the evidence has established that there was almost certainly no operation and that the problem was simple ignorance, cured when Joseph gave Louis some basic lessons in sexual technique.[203]

The happy couple now made up for lost time. Marie Antoinette produced a daughter in 1778, a son in 1781, another son in 1785, and a second daughter in 1786. This fecundity was too late to save the reputation of either king or queen. Indeed, it was when it became known that the queen was pregnant for the first time that the real flood of pornographic *libelles* began. When the Dauphin was born, many names were canvassed as the possible sire, but all the pamphleteers agreed that it could not have been the king:

All Paris is delighted
With the birth of a Dauphin;
But his sudden appearance
Bewilders Heaven:
'Who the Devil has produced it?'
Says the Word angrily;
'It must be some trick by the Holy Spirit
For no one claims
That the King is the father.'
'Excuse me, O Master'
Cries the dove,
'It was not I who breathed life
Into this dear little newborn babe,
From what one can tell,
He clearly takes after the Queen,

[203] Derek Beales, *Joseph II*. Vol. I: *In the shadow of Maria Theresa 1741–1780* (Cambridge, 1987), pp. 371–5. John Hardman, *Louis XVI*, p. 24 states firmly that 'Louis needed a minor operation' but does not cite Beales's book in his bibliography.

While Coigny, burning with love,
Didn't spare his candle
When lighting the flame.[204]

Rumours of Marie Antoinette's immorality had been circulating long before that. As early as 1774, the Abbé Baudeau recorded in his diary: 'The Queen is said to sleep with the duc de Chartres and M. de Lamballe: with the former after putting up stiff resistance, with the latter willingly; also with Madame de Lamballe, Madame de Pecquigny, etc. etc. The underhand cabal of the Chancellor [Maupeou] and the old bigoted aunts spread these stories, to try to ruin this poor princess, and retain sole control of the Court.'[205] It was also in 1774 that Louis XV authorized the expenditure of large sums to buy up copies of a pamphlet circulating in London and Amsterdam which cast aspersions on the Dauphin's potency.[206] The psychopathology of the torrent of filth which now poured over the public reputation of the hapless queen and her spouse lies beyond the scope of this study and the understanding of its author, but certain characteristics are obtrusive and important. First, there was a clear link with the pornographic *libelles* of the previous reign, with Marie Antoinette often equated to Madame du Barry. Indeed, she was even cast as a female version of Louis XV, with her own version of the Parc aux Cerfs in which she prostituted herself to the leading clergymen and nobles of the kingdom.[207] Secondly, there was an obsessive interest in unorthodox forms of sexual behaviour, especially in incest, lesbianism, and sodomy: Marie Antoinette is said to have lost her virginity to her brother, Joseph II; in almost every pamphlet she is depicted consorting with women; and her male lovers often spend as much time copulating with each other as with her (Plate 21).[208] This was part of a wider scenario presented by the *libellistes*, who directed 'a barrage of anti-social smut', as Robert Darnton has put it, against every aspect of the commanding

[204] Cronin, *Louis and Antoinette*, p. 198. I have altered the translation given by Cronin, I hope for the better.

[205] Quoted in ibid., p. 402.

[206] Sarah Maza, 'The diamond necklace affair revisited (1785–1786): the case of the missing queen', in Lynn Hunt (ed.), *Eroticism and the Body Politic* (Baltimore, Md., and London, 1991), p. 116.

[207] Lynn Hunt, 'Obscenity and the origins of modernity', in idem (ed.), *The Invention of Pornography*, p. 40.

[208] See for example, *Vie de Marie Antoinette d'Autriche, reine de France, femme de Louis XVI, roi des Français; L'Autrichienne en goguettes ou l'orgie royale. Opéra proverbe. Composé par un Garde-du-Corps et publié depuis la Liberté de la Presse et mis en musique par la Reine; Le Godmiché royal*; and *Bordel royal. Suivi d'un entretien secret entre la Reine et le Cardinal de Rohan après son entré aux États-généraux*, all reprinted in Chantal Thomas, *La Reine scélérate. Marie Antoinette dans les pamphlets* (Paris, 1989).

heights of the old regime—courtiers, nobles, clergy, academicians, as well as the king and queen. The aristocratic elites appear as impotent or deviant, leaving their wives to be serviced by their more virile servants.[209] Thirdly, the sexual voracity of the queen was contrasted with the impotence of the king, invariably presented as a dim, lazy, complaisant, drunken sot. In *L'Autrichienne en goguettes* ('The Austrian Bitch on a Spree'), for example, Marie Antoinette uses his recumbent form as a mattress on which to fornicate with his younger brother, the comte d'Artois.[210]

All these sleazy threads came together in 1785 in the Diamond Necklace Affair, the greatest *cause célèbre* of the old regime. The Cardinal-Archbishop of Strasbourg, Louis de Rohan, was induced to buy a diamond necklace worth 1,600,000 *livres*, believing that he was acting on behalf of Marie Antoinette and hoping thus to ingratiate himself with her. In reality, she knew nothing about it, for the whole scheme was a swindle organized by a gang of confidence tricksters. When the scandal finally broke, Louis XVI behaved with amazing ineptitude, choosing to have the naïve and foolish but essentially innocent Rohan prosecuted and thus allowing the affair to gain maximum publicity. Everything that could go wrong did go wrong: Rohan was acquitted but the name of the queen was well and truly dragged through the mire. A flood of *libelles* followed, alleging among many other things that for all her feigned indignation, the queen had been the Cardinal's lover, had contracted venereal disease from him, and had proceeded to infect the whole court.[211] Public interest in the affair was colossal, with even the legal documents in the case being devoured avidly. The briefs written for Rohan by his barrister, for example, reached a print run of 20,000 copies.[212] Against all likelihood and against what evidence there was, the public chose to believe that the affair had shown the king being cuckolded by a cardinal.[213] In the view of John Hardman, 'if any one incident may be said to have begun the "unravelling" of the ancien régime', it was the Diamond Necklace

[209] Robert Darnton, 'The high enlightenment and the low-life of literature in pre-revolutionary France', *Past and Present*, 51 (1971), pp. 105–6. For some particularly unpleasant examples of this genre, see Antoine de Baecque, 'Pamphlets: libel and political mythology', in Robert Darnton (ed.), *Revolution in Print: The Press in France 1775–1800* (Berkeley, Los Angeles, and London, 1989), pp. 167–72.

[210] Thomas, *La Reine scélérate*, p. 118.

[211] Hardman, *Louis XVI*, p. 84. This chapter contains the best detailed account of the affair.

[212] Sarah Maza, *Private Lives and Public Affairs: The Causes célèbres of Pre-Revolutionary France* (Berkeley, Los Angeles, and London, 1993), pp. 193–4.

[213] Robert Darnton, *The Forbidden Best-sellers of Pre-revolutionary France* (London, 1996), p. 226.

Affair.[214] It was also the occasion for one of Goethe's rare but penetrating political insights: recalling his play based on the affair—*The Grand Cophta*—he observed much later that it had been a good subject because in one sense it had been the cause of the French Revolution. By being exposed to public ridicule, he explained, the royal family had lost public respect, and that proved fatal, 'for it is not hatred but contempt which destroys regimes.' It was a view shared by William Eden, the British diplomat, who after 1789 wrote a memoir on the effects of the affair, which he had observed at first hand when negotiating the Anglo-French commercial treaty which bears his name. He absolved Marie Antoinette of any fraudulent conduct (although even he believed that she had seen the necklace and had wished to have it) 'but the calumnies of the Parisians were directed against her with much malignity, and were circulated in printed libels and letters through the provinces, and became a symptom, and in some degree a cause, of the catastrophe that was preparing.'[215]

As the title of *L'Autrichienne en goguettes* indicated, the attacks on Marie Antoinette arraigned her as a foreigner, an enemy to France. This was the third set of charges laid against her. Indeed, the first hostile pamphlet—*Antoinette ou la nouvelle Pandore*—was not obscene at all, but concentrated on her Austrian origins.[216] Particularly frequent was the accusation that she had diverted millions of *livres* in gold from the French treasury to her Austrian brother, an indictment which reached a climax at her trial in 1793, when the public prosecutor, Fouquier-Tinville, used sexual imagery to describe her relations with foreign powers.[217] Although Marie Antoinette was in no position to arrange for financial subsidies to Austria, there was real substance to the charge that she viewed herself as an Austrian agent first and Queen of France second. The Austrian ambassador, Count Mercy, saw her on a regular basis, received what intelligence she had been able to muster, and gave her instructions about what to do next. If she failed to exercise a decisive influence on the conduct of French policy, it was not through want of trying. In October 1784, for example, she lectured Vergennes on the importance of the Austrian alliance and the need to maintain it by supporting her brother Joseph in his dispute with the Dutch.[218] In the event, Louis did not do as he was

214 Hardman, *French Politics 1774–1789*, p. 209.

215 William, Lord Auckland, *Journal and Correspondence*, 4 vols. (London, 1861–2), I, pp. 131–2.

216 Cronin, *Louis and Antoinette*, p. 402.

217 Lynn Hunt, 'The many bodies of Marie Antoinette: political pornography and the problem of the feminine in the French Revolution', in idem (ed.), *Eroticism and the Body Politic* (Baltimore, Md., and London, 1991), p. 110.

218 Arneth and Flammermont (eds.), *Correspondance secrète du comte de Mercy-Argenteau*, vol. I, p. 318 n 1. These two volumes teem with similar examples.

told, indeed he told his brother-in-law that, if forced to choose between his existing ally (Austria) and his prospective ally (the Dutch), he would opt for the latter. However, he did eventually broker a settlement, but only by agreeing to pay the 10,000,000 gulden Joseph was demanding as compensation.[219] This represented a very good deal for France, but the fact that money had changed from French to Austrian hands only served to alienate public opinion further.[220]

One final feature of the attacks on Marie Antoinette needs to be noted. As the Abbé Baudeau indicated in the diary entry quoted above,[221] they originated inside the establishment, where her enemies were rife. One of the most powerful was the duc d'Orléans (styled duc de Chartres until the death of his father in 1785), head of the junior Bourbon branch descended from Louis XIV's brother. Blaming Marie Antoinette for the humiliating end to his naval career in 1779, Orléans took revenge by financing attacks on her. His headquarters in Paris, the Palais-Royal, became a centre of opposition journalism, a space where the scum of the court and the dregs of the capital could meet in conspiratorial synergy.[222] *Pace* Robert Darnton, the *libellistes* were not all or even mainly embittered outsiders but were the paid hacks of court factions: 'rather than representing a counter-culture with revolutionary aspirations, the milieu of the Parisian pamphleteers in the 1770s and 1780s represented the diversity of elements within France's elites willing to appeal to the growing force of public opinion to settle their disputes'.[223]

As this suggests, the court was even more dysfunctional after 1774 than it had been under Louis XV. What had once worked for Louis XIV was now a drag on the monarchy. In the crushing verdict of François Bluche: 'Louis XV and Louis XVI were to be the curators of a museum where paintings were no longer restored and objects never moved, and which was no longer replenished with new acquisitions.'[224] An insuperable problem was geographical isolation.

219 There is a brief account of the episode in T. C. W. Blanning, *Joseph II* (London, 1994), pp. 138–42.

220 Ségur, *Mémoires*, vol. II, p. 94.

221 See above, p. 412.

222 E. S. Scudder, *Prince of the Blood* (London, 1937), pp. 76–80.

223 Popkin, 'Pamphlet journalism at the end of the old regime', p. 363. Darnton's thesis was first advanced in two articles published in 1971—'The High Enlightenment and low life of literature' and 'Reading, writing and publishing in eighteenth-century France: a case-study in the sociology of literature', *Daedalus*, 100 (1971). He has repeated it at regular intervals since, most recently in *The Forbidden Best-sellers of Pre-revolutionary France* (London, 1996). For critiques of Darnton's work, see the articles by Jeremy Popkin, Elizabeth Eisenstein, and Daniel Gordon in Haydn T. Mason (ed.), *The Darnton Debate: Books and Revolution in the Eighteenth Century*, Studies on Voltaire and the Eighteenth Century, 359 (1998).

224 François Bluche, *Louis XIV* (Oxford, 1990), p. 619.

The new king was no more enthusiastic about Paris than his predecessors; indeed, given his passion for hunting (the only activity to quicken his slow pulse-rate) he showed even greater preference for the country retreats. In an article entitled 'The king at Paris' of 1787, Mercier lodged the following complaints: the Louvre remained empty and would never be finished; Louis XVI had shown what he thought of his capital by never spending more than twenty-four hours there; the first Bourbon, Henry IV, had also been the last of his dynasty to make Paris his residence; and his successors had been the only monarchs in Europe to cut themselves off from their subjects. Mercier invited his readers to compare the King of France with his British counterpart. On the rare occasions the former left Versailles, he did so surrounded by a swarm of courtiers, and with an escort of Household Cavalry and French and Swiss Guards to clear the way. But George III went out on the streets of London in a sedan-chair and with no more than three escorts—yet this was a man who could send 150 ships of the line to sea and commanded a world empire.[225] Perhaps the contrast was a little stark, but Mercier had a point. Louis XVI was even more sluggish than his grandfather when it came to showing himself to his people. He left the châteaux and hunting-lodges of the Versailles region on only three occasions: in 1775, when he went to be crowned at Reims; in 1786, when he went to inspect new fortifications at Cherbourg; and in 1791, when he tried to run away from the Revolution.

Despite periodic efforts to rehabilitate him, Louis XVI still cuts a poor figure. Hesitant, timid, lacking in confidence, prone to long periods of silence like his grandfather, evasive, and hopelessly irresolute, the new king proved quite unable to make the court work to his advantage. The comte de Provence chose the following graphic metaphor to describe his spinelessness: 'the weakness and indecision of the king are beyond description. Imagine balls of oiled ivory you try in vain to hold together.'[226] Louis was strong-willed enough to stop Marie Antoinette running foreign policy in the interests of Austria, but he could not stop her exercising enormous and well-publicized influence on government and household appointments. In the scramble for spoils, it was her influence which counted most.[227] As Munro Price has written: 'By 1781 she combined the emotional ascendancy of a mistress with the permanence of a queen: a formidable obstacle to any first minister who was

225 Mercier, *Tableau de Paris*, vol. X, pp. 122–5.

226 Albert Sorel, *Europe and the French Revolution*, vol. I (London, 1969), p. 244. Alas, this was the only volume of Sorel's great work to be translated.

227 The struggle for power and influence between the groups is a very complex story and need not delay us here. It is best followed in Price, *Preserving the Monarchy*, *passim*.

not her creature. The emergence of the queen as a powerful political figure in her own right was the most significant development at Versailles in the reign of Louis XVI.'[228] Quite unable to stand above factions and to play one off against the other, never able to dissimulate when meeting people she disliked or was bored by, she managed to alienate a growing section of high society. As Mercy complained in 1776, she found Versailles 'sad and barren' and spent as little time as possible playing her representational role there, preferring to relax in the company of a few close friends in the informal surroundings of the Petit Trianon or one of the other *petits châteaux*. The duc de Lévis recorded in his memoirs that royal favour was granted to only a few capriciously selected intimates. Most of the nobility, however high their rank, ancient their lineage, or distinguished their services, were excluded, being admitted to the royal presence only for a brief period on Sundays. So they soon found travelling out to Versailles a pointless waste of time and stayed in their *hôtels* in Paris. 'And so,' he concluded, 'Versailles, this theatre of magnificence created by Louis XIV, to which all Europe came with such a sense of urgency to take lessons in good taste and manners, became nothing more than a little provincial town, to which one only went with reluctance and from which one fled as soon as possible.'[229]

The French nobility may have found Versailles 'sad and barren', but that was not how public opinion chose to view the court. Decades of exposés had implanted the image of a self-indulgent pleasure palace, in which decadent sybarites wallowed in excess. The periodic attempts at economies were soon overtaken by some fresh act of well-publicized extravagance. Hard on the heels of Necker's retrenchment, for example, came the high-profile expenditure of Calonne, including the purchase of Rambouillet for 18,000,000 *livres* from the duc de Penthièvre, Saint Cloud for the queen, and a fresh shower of pensions to the insatiable Polignacs. Compared with the sums required to maintain the armed forces and service the debt, the court was relatively unimportant in terms of objective cost, which amounted to about 42,000,000 *livres* in 1788 or 6.63 per cent of total expenditure.[230] Its most detrimental effect was to prevent that 'credible commitment' which is a prerequisite of an efficient fiscal system.[231] That was revealed to an

[228] Ibid., p. 25.

[229] Lough, *An Introduction to Eighteenth-century France*, pp. 198–9. On this atrophy of the court, see also William Ritchey Newton, *L'Espace du roi. La cour de France au château de Versailles 1682–1789* (Paris, 2000), pp. 22–3.

[230] Jean-François Solnon, *La Cour de France* (Paris, 1987), p. 518.

[231] On the 'credible commitment', see above pp. 3, 306–7.

incredulous Louis XVI on 19 July 1787 by his ministers, as bankruptcy stared them in the face:

Duc de Nivernais: '. . . we cannot hide from Your Majesty that the public mood is bad.' 'But why so?' said the King. No one replied. [Castries] spoke up: 'Because the public views with some surprise, Sire, that whilst Your Majesty prepares to place new burdens of taxation on the people, he makes no personal sacrifice; that whereas he has made a bad choice [Calonne] which has led to the ruin of his finances, he seems disposed to make his subjects pay the price; that his building continues on all sides etc.'[232]

In François Furet's shrewd judgement: 'Had he attacked court wastefulness, Louis XVI would not have saved his finances, but he might perhaps have salvaged even more—the monarchy itself.'[233]

This was no exaggeration. It was impending bankruptcy that sent Calonne to see Louis XVI on 20 August 1786 for an interview which set in train the events leading to the Revolution. The situation was desperate, as the monarchy was locked in an interest-deficit spiral—the cost of servicing the debt had grown to the point at which it could only be financed by raising more loans, which increased the deficit, which increased the need for more loans, and so on. The annual deficit was thought to be currently in excess of 100,000,000 *livres* on what was thought to be a total revenue of about 475,000,000 *livres*—although no one could be sure about any of these figures—and debt repayments were consuming about half the income. The third *vingtième*, which had been imposed with so much difficulty in 1782, was due to expire in 1787. Over a billion *livres* had been borrowed since 1776 and loans could now be filled only slowly and at escalating rates of interest.[234]

This was not a problem of exemption, as was once assumed. Although the clergy made only a modest contribution to the state, the nobility was taxed hard—harder indeed than in Great Britain, where peers and commoners paid at the same rate.[235] The real problem was structural. This was due in part to the centuries-old practice of leasing the right to collect royal taxes to private corporations and individuals.[236] Among many other things, the private, con-

232 Quoted in Hardman, *Louis XVI*, p. 129.

233 Furet, *Revolutionary France*, p. 33.

234 Jean Égret, *Louis XV et l'opposition parlementaire* (Paris, 1970), pp. 5–6.

235 C. B. A. Behrens, 'Nobles, privileges and taxes at the end of the Ancien Régime', *Economic History Review*, XV (1962–3), pp. 29–45.

236 This is the central argument of J. F. Bosher, *French Finances 1775–1795: From Business to Bureaucracy* (Cambridge, 1970), whose main conclusions have been accepted even by the notoriously autarchic French historiography.

tractual, non-bureaucratic nature of the system made an accurate annual budget impossible. The result was private affluence and public squalor. It was also due in part to the centuries-old practice of selling offices. By the end of the old regime, there were about 70,000 of these in France, or in other words, about 1 per cent of adult Frenchmen with about a third of a million dependants held venal offices. It was a system so extensive and expensive that it could not be abolished (except by revolution).[237] Part of the fiscal problems of the old regime derived from an excessive reliance on direct taxation. As the British and the Prussians demonstrated, the most efficient way to raise money was to tax consumption, through excise and customs duties. Although such taxes were socially regressive, in the sense that they bore heaviest on the poor, they had the advantage of being relatively invisible because they were included in the price of a commodity.[238] Other fiscal problems were due to the difficulty of raising loans at moderate rates of interest in the absence of a central bank. Following the ignominious failure of John Law's scheme in 1720, there was no new attempt to create one until 1800. Moreover, lending money to the King of France was a risky business, as Terray's partial bankruptcy of 1770 had shown. What was needed was something similar to the system in Britain, where a Parliamentary guarantee meant in effect that the entire landed wealth of the country was offered as collateral to potential lenders. In short, the financial problems of the French monarchy derived essentially from its failure to adjust to the developing public sphere and the political discourse which developed inside it. Expedients such as leasing tax collection or selling offices had been preferred to devising ways of integrating social and cultural change. A credible commitment could not be inspired by the dead hand of representational culture, nor could the country's resources be tapped effectively by a monarch whose ideology denied him the status of patriot-king or first servant of the state. Why should anyone wish to pay taxes or lend money to the king, only to see it squandered by his queen?

The fiscal consequences of cultural failure lay behind the final crisis. On the face of it, it looked like a case of 'brightest before nightfall', for French involvement in the American War had enjoyed some success. Unfortunately, it had ended on a sombre note, with naval defeat at the Saintes and the failure

[237] William Doyle, *Venality: The Sale of Offices in Eighteenth-century France* (Oxford, 1996), pp. 59, 100.

[238] On this point see the important articles by Peter Mathias and Patrick O'Brien, 'Concepts of Revolution in England and France in the eighteenth century', *Studies in Eighteenth Century Culture*, XIV (1985), pp. 29–46, and 'Taxation in Britain and France 1715–1810', *Journal of European Economic History*, 5 (1976), pp. 601–50.

of the siege of Gibraltar in 1782, which obliged them to settle for much less than public opinion had come to expect in the aftermath of the great victory at Yorktown the previous year. A share in the Newfoundland fishing, a couple of West Indian islands, and a few trading stations in Senegal and India represented a meagre return for more than four years of ruinously expensive fighting. Their Spanish allies, on the other hand, whose war effort had been markedly inferior, emerged with two plums: Minorca and Florida. Once again, it seemed to contemporaries, the French had done all the dirty work but had ended up with next to nothing for themselves. Louis XVI's wonderful ability to pass up even the most inviting prospect of a public relations coup was demonstrated by his treatment of the marquis de Lafayette, 'the hero of two worlds', on his return to France after distinguished service in Washington's army. Given an ecstatic welcome by the public and lionized by court society, Lafayette was placed under house arrest by the king for having gone to America without royal permission.[239] The economic benefits of the American War also proved to be illusory, for as we have seen in an earlier chapter, it was not long before Anglo-American trade returned to normal.[240]

In the same year as the peace—1783—came a sharp reminder of the decline of French influence on the continent, when Catherine the Great of Russia unilaterally annexed the Crimea, previously under the suzerainty of the Ottoman Turks. This despoliation of France's oldest ally caused outrage at Versailles, outrage which was all the greater because it was known to be impotent. Worse was to come. Instead of agreeing to cooperate with the French to bring pressure to bear on Russia, Joseph II coolly announced that he had been allied to the latter since 1781 and expected *France* to cooperate with *him* to bring pressure to bear on the *Turks* to make them accept Catherine's *démarche*.[241] Nothing could have advertised better the one-sided nature of the Franco-Austrian alliance, especially as there were now fears abroad that Joseph was contemplating a total partition of the Ottoman Empire with his new Russian ally. Joseph's dispute with the Dutch in 1783–5, referred to above,[242] also seemed to demonstrate that the Austrian alliance was fundamentally inimical

[239] Simon Schama, *Citizens: A Chronicle of the French Revolution* (New York, 1989), p. 40.
[240] See above, pp. 348–9.
[241] The episode is best followed through the correspondence between Mercy and Kaunitz in the Arneth collection, which also includes copies of the most important French missive; Arneth and Flammermont (eds.), *Correspondance secrète du comte de Mercy-Argenteau*, vol. I, pp. 185–200.
[242] See above, p. 414.

to the national interest of France. The comte de Ségur recorded the prevailing mood as follows:

'What would become of our old hegemony, our dignity, the balance of power in Europe and our own security if we ceased to be regarded as the protector of the weaker states against the three predators [Austria, Prussia, Russia]? Had a decision been taken to step down from the rank to which we had been raised by Henry IV, Louis XIII, Cardinal Richelieu, the celebrated Treaty of Westphalia, and the glory of Louis XIV?'—Those were the comments made everywhere, in all classes of the population, from the galleries of Versailles to the cafés of the Palais-Royal, that new political rendezvous. The *Parlementaires* and the *philosophes*, motivated by their spirit of opposition, spoke out against the negligence of the ministers; and young people passionately embraced the cause of the Dutch, that is to say in favour of war.[243]

Joseph II's simultaneous attempt to secure Bavaria in exchange for the Austrian Netherlands provided yet another cause of grievance, and yet another demonstration of French weakness. When a number of German princes formed a league in 1785 to prevent Habsburg expansion, it was under the auspices of Prussia, not France.[244]

But the French still had an ace in the hole. In the secular struggle for control of the world outside Europe, they had succeeded in ejecting the British from their American colonies. After October 1785 they also seemed to be in a strong position to repeat that achievement in India, for it was then that they secured an alliance with the Dutch Republic. Although fallen on increasingly hard times since the glory days of the previous century, that little state could still punch well above its weight in global terms. This was partly due to its geographical position, partly to its still considerable naval forces, but mainly to its colonial possessions at the Cape of Good Hope and in Ceylon. Combined with French possessions in the Indian Ocean, the new alliance would be in a strong position to take the place of the British on the Indian subcontinent. We have already examined from the British perspective how this scenario failed to materialize and how a sudden rush of events in 1787 saw the Dutch Republic invaded by Prussia, forcibly extracted from its existing alliance with France, and tied into a new relationship with Prussia and Great Britain.[245] From the French point of view, the crucial moment came in the summer and autumn of 1787, when the Dutch patriots asked for the help so often promised

243 Ségur, *Mémoires*, vol. II, p. 85.

244 These episodes are explained in Blanning, *Joseph II*, ch. 5.

245 See above, pp. 349–50.

in the past. The French talked about forming an armed camp at Givet, ready to intercept any Prussian attempt at invasion, but actually did nothing. On 22 September Louis XVI informed the Dutch patriots that France would not be able to help them.[246]

They did nothing because the new prime minister, Loménie de Brienne, Archbishop of Toulouse, decided that the country could not afford a military intervention. He was probably right, although there is some evidence that enough money could have been scraped together.[247] On the other hand, the advocates of forward action were even more right when they argued that the monarchy could not afford *not* to intervene. The Secretary of State for the Navy, the marquis de Castries, told Louis XVI: 'present the idea of *la gloire* to Frenchmen, and you will effect the most useful... diversion from the present turmoil. Give the appearance of necessity to taxation, and the mood will calm and perhaps you will see government recapture a part of what it is ready to lose.'[248] When Louis XVI opted for Brienne's financial prudence, Castries resigned, as did the Secretary of State for War, the comte de Ségur, whose son later wrote in his memoirs:

> Our situation was critical: this was the time when our court should have taken bold action; a vigorous and decisive initiative would probably have thrown our enemies into confusion, reassured the Dutch, checked the Prussians, made the Turks see reason, and so would have diverted abroad that turbulence of opinion which was convulsing France and which urgently required occupation outside the country if it were not to provoke an explosion at home.[249]

Speculation on what might have happened, if only this or that had been done, can sometimes be helpful, especially when the exercise is conducted by contemporaries. The military men among the latter were agreed that a golden opportunity had been lost. Lameth, for example, recorded the 'general opinion' that stopping the Prussians would have been easy, especially as the Dutch opposition party had offered an immediate grant of 12,000,000 *livres*. The political benefits of intervention, he argued, would have far outweighed any cost, for whereas a successful campaign would have restored the loyalty of the army, the actual betrayal of France's allies by the supine ministry

[246] Orville T. Murphy, *The Diplomatic Retreat of France and Public Opinion on the Eve of the French Revolution, 1783–1789* (Washington, DC, 1998), p. 90.

[247] J. F. X. Droz, *Histoire du règne de Louis XVI pendant les années où l'on pouvait prévenir la Révolution française* (Brussels, 1839), p. 19.

[248] Quoted in Hardman, *Louis XVI*, pp. 128–9.

[249] Ségur, *Mémoires*, vol. II, p. 263.

had completed its demoralization.[250] Lameth was almost certainly right. The naturally timid Frederick William II was reluctant to intervene, finally agreeing only when intelligence reports about the true nature of the non-existent camp at Givet assured him that the French would take no action.[251]

When the young comte de Ségur learned that no action was going to be taken to honour French promises to the Dutch patriots, he realized that the end had come (or so he claimed in his memoirs).[252] However wise he was being after the event, there is a great deal to be said for his insight. To be proved impotent over Poland, the Crimea, or even the league of German princes was one thing, but to be unable to act in one's own backyard to defend a vital national interest was quite another. And Ségur was not the only contemporary to realize that a watershed had been reached: 'France has collapsed,' recorded Joseph II, 'and I doubt whether it will rise again.'[253] It is no exaggeration to say that the Dutch fiasco represented the terminal humiliation of the old regime. It demonstrated as well as anything could the intimate relationship between culture and power, and culture and impotence, which has been at the centre of this book.

Moreover, the Dutch did not appear to be the only victims of the regime's paralysis. The belief also spread that the Turks, France's oldest allies, would be the next to be sacrificed. It was enough for them to be involved in a war with the queen's brother for their popularity to soar. The bookseller Simeon-Prosper Hardy recorded in his journal in 1788: 'Everyone has become, so to speak, Turkish in our capital, so much do people now show interest in the cause of the Ottomans, so much do they seem to wish them success.'[254] The commercial treaty with Russia, concluded the previous year, confirmed fears that France would look on with indifference as the eastern powers inflicted on the Turks what they had done to the Poles fifteen years earlier. Opposition

[250] Alexandre, comte de Lameth, *Histoire de l'Assemblée Constituante*, 2 vols. (Paris, 1828), I, p. lxxviii. See also Charles de Peyssonnel, *Situation politique de la France et ses rapports actuels avec toutes les puissances de l'Europe*, 2 vols. (Neuchâtel and Paris, 1789), I, pp. 229–32. For support for Lameth's view, see Ghislain de Diesbach (ed.), *Mémoires du Baron de Besenval sur la cour de France* (Paris, 1987), pp. 436–42.

[251] Felix Salomon, *Wilhelm Pitt der jüngere*. Vol. I, pt. 2: *Bis zum Ausgang der Friedensperiode (Februar 1793)* (Leipzig and Berlin, 1906), p. 329.

[252] Ségur, *Mémoires*, vol. II, p. 307.

[253] Quoted in Munro Price, 'The Dutch affair and the fall of the *ancien régime*, 1784–1787', *Historical Journal*, 38, 4 (1995), p. 904.

[254] Quoted in Thomas Kaiser, 'The evil empire? The debate of Turkish despotism in eighteenth-century French political culture', *Journal of Modern History*, 72, 1 (2000), p. 31.

pamphlets stoked the fires of public indignation, reporting that the French ambassador in Constantinople had been summoned by the Grand Vizier to be denounced for 'French perfidy', that Joseph II had asked his sister's favourite, the Baron de Breteuil, to secure 50,000,000 *livres* from the French treasury 'to accomplish my project against the Turks', and so on.[255] Together with the continuing—and intensifying—unpopularity of the commercial treaty negotiated with the British in 1786, which was blamed for the recession in the French textile industry, the foreign situation interacted with domestic problems to produce a crisis. Although it was out of fashion for most of the twentieth century, there is still much to be said for Ranke's insight: 'Much has been said about the causes of the [French] Revolution . . . One of the most important, in my opinion, is the change in the international position of France, which brought the government into deep discredit.'[256]

To the sleaze of the Diamond Necklace Affair of 1785–6 and the impotence of the Dutch episode of 1787 was now added despotism. Between February and May of 1787 Calonne had tried to secure support for his fiscal and political reform programme from the 'Assembly of Notables', an ad hoc body drawn from the great and the good. The hope that this body would prove less obstructive than the Parlements was soon proved to be sadly mistaken. The chief victim of the episode was Calonne himself, dismissed on 8 April. He was followed by Brienne, who had been one of the opposition leaders at the Assembly of Notables. Changes in personnel were no longer enough. Such was the alienation between monarchy and civil society that nothing less than a fundamental change in the constitution would satisfy the latter. It was now that the success of Louis XV and Maupeou in creating a judicial system back in 1771 came back to plague their successors, for it reminded the opposition of how vulnerable the Parlements were. Moreover, the day of the *parlementaires* was almost done. Since that earlier crisis, public opinion had grown to full maturity, and the groups calling themselves variously *patriotes* or *nationaux* no longer saw themselves as subordinate auxiliaries.[257] So calls for the summoning of the Estates General, as a truly national body, first heard during the earlier crisis, now became increasingly frequent and strident. It was also ominous that pamphleteers were now referring to the Estates General as the 'National Assembly'.[258]

[255] Ibid., pp. 31–2.

[256] Quoted in Murphy, *The Diplomatic Retreat of France*, p. 1.

[257] Richet, *La France moderne*, p. 172.

[258] Boyd C. Shafer, 'Bourgeois nationalism in the pamphlets on the eve of the French Revolution', *Journal of Modern History*, 10 (1938), p. 40.

A first crisis occurred in the autumn in the wake of the Dutch fiasco. On 10 October 1787 Amsterdam had fallen to the Prussians; on 19 November Louis XVI went in person to the Parlement of Paris to enforce the registration of new loans. His cousin, the duc d'Orléans, rose to tell him that what he was attempting was illegal, to which Louis replied: 'Think what you like, I don't care... Yes, it is legal because I want it.'[259] 'What the king wills is lawful'—there could not have been a better definition of despotism. That was followed in the spring of 1788 by a last attempt by the monarchy to save itself by executive action from above. Brienne's 'May Edicts' sought, in effect, to repeat Maupeou's *coup d'état* by imposing a radical restructuring of the judicial system. This time it failed, foiled by a credit strike, a collapse in taxation revenue, and vigorous resistance from the Parlements, supported by public opinion often expressed through physical violence. Bankrupt both literally and figuratively, the regime capitulated: on 8 August 1788 it was announced that the Estates General would meet at Versailles on 1 May the following year.

When Ségur *père* heard that Louis XVI had convened the Assembly of Notables, he exclaimed, 'The King has just resigned!'[260] That verdict proved to be premature, as he showed an unusual degree of determination in trying to push Brienne's reform programme through the Parlements. It would certainly have been appropriate, however, if applied to the convocation of the Estates General. There were three stages in the royal abdication. The first was reached on 19 November 1787, when coercive action against the Parlements was accompanied by the announcement that the Estates General would meet in 1792. More important was the decision of 5 July 1788 to consult public opinion on how the Estates General should conduct its business when it eventually met. As Tocqueville observed, this was tantamount to setting the French constitution as the topic for a national prize-essay competition. Such was the authority of this new source of legitimacy that it had eroded the confidence of the very heart of the old regime: '"Public opinion" had become the articulating concept of a new political space with a legitimacy and authority apart from that of the crown: a public space in which the nation could reclaim its rights against the crown. Within this space, the French Revolution became thinkable.'[261] The third stage was reached just over a month later when the date for the convocation of the Estates General was brought forward to 1 May 1789.

259 Quoted in Hardman, *Louis XVI*, p. 132.

260 Quoted in Schama, *Citizens*, p. 238.

261 Keith Michael Baker, 'Public opinion as political invention', in idem, *Inventing the French Revolution* (Cambridge, 1990), p. 199.

Perhaps with a sigh of relief, Louis XVI now left everything to Necker: 'I was forced to recall Necker; I didn't want to, but they'll soon regret it. I'll do everything he tells me and we'll see what happens.'[262] But Necker saw himself as simply a receiver in bankruptcy, keeping the ruined firm going until a purchaser could be found and a new management team installed in the boardroom. The initiative now passed completely to the public sphere, which was enjoying an explosive process of politicization following the effective abolition of censorship. Louis XVI's inactivity during 1788–9 contrasts both sharply and unfavourably with George III's very different response to his own existential crisis of 1782–4. Of course, he had a stronger hand to play, but, as we have seen, he did so with skill, energy, and determination.[263] His French colleague simply folded every hand, even when dealt a royal straight flush. It was not long before even the images of kings and queens were to be banned from French playing-cards.

With the revolutionary crisis well and truly under way, it is time to leave the hapless Louis XVI and his queen to their oft-recounted fate. One final point needs to be made. This chapter has been concerned with the haemorrhage of legitimacy from the representational culture of the old regime and the development of a new concept of national sovereignty legitimized by public opinion. To revert to Max Weber's tripartite definition of legitimacy, the French monarchy had lost its claim to legal and traditional authority by its despotism and had lost its claim to charismatic authority by a combination of sleaze and impotence. But, as Weber pointed out, a state has a dual nature, as a centre not only of legitimacy but also of force—if its force has to be legitimate, its legitimacy has to be backed by force.[264] In the context of the revolutionary crisis of 1789, it was particularly important that the group most alienated by the forces discussed earlier was the officer corps. When Louis XVI reached for his weapon of last resort, following the unilateral declaration of the Third Estate on 17 June 1789 that it now regarded itself as the 'National Assembly', the army fell apart in his hands. He was told by his senior commanders that the troops would mutiny if ordered to impose order on Paris.[265] Characteristically, he chose to believe them, although there is good evidence that enough German-speaking regiments could have been mustered to do the job.

[262] Quoted in Hardman, *Louis XVI*, p. 136.

[263] See above, pp. 341–2.

[264] See above, pp. 33, 191.

[265] Samuel F. Scott, *The Response of the Royal Army to the French Revolution: The Role and Development of the Line Army 1787–1793* (Oxford, 1978), p. 60.

It was not the rank and file that was the main problem. During 1788–9 many disaffected officers had demonstrated their sympathy for the political opposition, by declining to order their troops to disperse rioters or by resigning their commissions in protest when the government took action against the Parlements. When the marquis de la Tour du Pin arrived to take charge of his new regiment, the Royal-Vaisseaux, he found 'that this body of troops was in a state of great indiscipline, not by the conduct of the soldiers and the non-commissioned officers, which was excellent, by the attitude of the officers'. His attempt to restore order was greeted by 'a perfect storm of discontent, and punishment, arrests, prison—no measures could determine the officers to fulfill their duties'.[266] Their chance to organize resistance on a national basis came with the calling of the Estates General. In one electoral assembly of the Second Estate after another, it was army officers who took the lead. Of the 278 noble deputies who went to Versailles in May 1789, no fewer than 221 were serving or retired officers and 11 more sat with the Third Estate.[267] Emile Léonard has pointed out the striking number of liberal nobles who were army officers, citing in particular the comte de Clermont-Tonnerre, the marquis de Lally, the comte de Virieu, the duc de La Rochefoucauld-Liancourt, the duc de La Rochefoucauld-d'Enville, the marquis de Lafayette, the vicomte de Noailles, the duc de Biron, the comtes de Lameth, the marquis de Custine, the duc de Montmorency-Laval, Victor, Prince de Broglie, the duc d'Aiguillon, the comte de Montesquiou-Fezensac, the comte de Dillon, the vicomte de Mirabeau, and the marquis de Laborde-Méréville.[268] In part at least, the French Revolution was a military coup. As one of the most clear-sighted observers of the Revolution, Antoine Rivarol, wrote: 'the defection of the army is not one of the causes of the Revolution, it is the Revolution itself.'[269] All revolutions are like that.

[266] Walter Geer (ed.), *Recollections of the Revolution and Empire by la marquise de La Tour du Pin* (London, 1933), p. 62.

[267] Gilbert Bodinier, 'La Révolution et l'armée', in Jean Delmas (ed.), *De 1715 à 1871*, vol. II of André Corvisier (ed.), *Histoire militaire de la France* (Paris, 1992), p. 200.

[268] Émile G. Léonard, *L'Armée et ses problèmes au XVIIIe siècle* (Paris, 1958), pp. 305–6.

[269] Jean Chagniot, 'Les rapports entre l'armée et la société à la fin de l'anciem régime', in Delmas (ed.), *De 1715 à 1871*, p. 128.

9

Conclusion: The Power of Culture

1789 was a very eventful year in Europe. In the Balkans, the Turkish war effort began to falter as the Russians and Austrians went on the offensive. Inside the Habsburg monarchy, Hungarian dissidents threatened to move from protest to rebellion, aided and abetted by the Prussians and the Poles. In the south, the Sardinians and Spanish laid plans to partition Habsburg possessions in Italy. In the far north, the war between Russia and Sweden continued. In the west, insurgents in the Austrian Netherlands overthrew Austrian authority and proclaimed the independence of the 'United States of Belgium'. In France the absolute monarchy collapsed. Only the British periphery appeared to be unaffected by this maelstrom of foreign and domestic upheaval, although an incident at Nootka Sound on the west coast of Canada would almost lead to war with Spain in 1790.

Of all these crises, only the French Revolution proved to be existential. Two contrasting vignettes from the autumn of 1789 help to explain the difference between an earthquake and a tremor. On 5 October, a crowd about 7,000 strong, mainly women, marched from Paris to Versailles on a mission to frustrate what they believed to be a plot to deprive them of food and to destroy the revolution. As with the storming of the Bastille, this injection of popular violence had a decisive effect on the course of events. At six in the evening, an intimidated Louis XVI overcame his scruples and gave his long-withheld consent to the National Assembly's two great measures of the summer—the abolition of the 'feudal regime' (4–5 August) and the Declaration of the Rights of Man and the Citizen (26 August). On the following morning, the Parisians increased the stakes by storming into the palace in search of the queen, shouting their intention to 'tear out the heart of the *coquine*, cut off her head, *fricasser* her liver!'.[1] Although they managed to lynch the guards who barred their way, they failed to catch their quarry, who fled via a secret staircase to the king's apartments.[2] By this time the insurgents were demanding that the king and his family return with them to Paris. Pressured further by Lafayette, the commander of the National Guard, Louis XVI agreed. Together with the royal family, the National Assembly was also taken prisoner, for the deputies felt obliged to follow their notional master (the king) and their real masters (the crowd). One of the six commissioners they charged with the task of finding suitable premises in Paris was Dr Joseph-Ignace Guillotin, the eponymous inventor of the instrument of execution.[3] This mass transfer to Paris proved to be a massive step down the road leading to a republic and regicide. So long as the French Revolution had two centres, the National Assembly out at Versailles could maintain a certain detachment from street violence. Once installed in the capital, the deputies were exposed to all the pressures of popular political culture and responded accordingly: the same personnel in a different space became a new body.

A week after the women of Paris marched on Versailles, General von Kleebeck rode into Vienna, bearing the glad tidings that the great Turkish fortress of Belgrade had fallen to an Austrian assault four days earlier. In the words of one observer: 'now began a victory celebration which lasted for three days and which I now describe to show foreigners how such things ought to be done, for three days like these we had never witnessed before.' By the time the travel-weary general made a second ceremonial entry at twelve noon, the whole city knew about it, so the streets and squares were lined by cheering crowds. All work stopped, houses were illuminated, and the dancing and singing at street parties went on throughout the night. Indeed they were still going two days later, when a *Te Deum* was celebrated in St Stephen's cathedral: 'The Emperor [Joseph II] was accompanied by full court ceremonial, by the gentlemen of the bedchamber, by the great court dignitaries, and by the noble life-guard. Every window and every street was filled to bursting-point with spectators. When the Sovereign reached the Kohlmarkt, a hundred thousand hands applauded him, and when he reached the Graben, the joyful applause

[1] Simon Schama, *Citizens. A chronicle of the French Revolution* (New York, 1989), p. 467.

[2] There is a particularly vivid account of the episode in Antonia Fraser, *Marie Antoinette: The Journey* (London, 2001), ch. 18.

[3] Armand Brette, *Histoire des édifices où ont siégé les assemblées parlementaires de la Révolution française et de la première république*, vol. 1 (Paris, 1902), p. 83.

rang out towards him with redoubled force.' At midnight, as the celebrations reached their climax, a procession of 900 students marched from the university to the imperial palace to honour the Emperor with 'a majestic serenade'.[4] Joseph II was already dying from the tuberculosis that would kill him the following February, yet his dynasty survived for another century and more, until the most destructive conflict in European history polished off the Habsburgs along with the Romanovs, Hohenzollerns, Wittelsbachs, Wettins, etc. His French brother-in-law was suspended from office on 10 August 1792, deposed on 22 September, and guillotined on 21 January 1793. The fate of his two younger brothers, Louis XVIII (restored by the allies in 1814, deposed by Napoleon in 1815, only to be restored yet again by the allies later in the year) and Charles X (deposed by the Revolution of 1830) demonstrated that the Bourbons could return only as farcical reprises of Louis XVI's original tragedy.[5]

The contrasting fates of the Bourbons and Habsburgs, revealed by the contrasting episodes of October 1789, are instructive about the culture of power and the power of culture in the late eighteenth century. Joseph II had modernized the ideological bases of his rule with even greater clarity than had Frederick the Great.[6] In his very first political memorandum, written in 1761 shortly after his twentieth birthday, he proclaimed: 'Everything exists for the state; this word contains everything, so all who live in it should come together to promote its interests.'[7] It was to be the lodestar of his existence. Twenty years later, on assuming sole control of the Habsburg monarchy, he recorded his proudest boast that he had 'lived as a servant of the state'.[8] Like his Prussian rival, Joseph was tireless in his pursuit of what can truly be called his vocation, constantly travelling the length and breadth of his dominions and eventually working himself into an early grave. Yet in the process he showed that he had grasped the need to reinvent the monarch as a public servant. The great palace of Schönbrunn, built by his great-uncle Joseph I as an Austrian Versailles, was closed and mothballed. The Hofburg, the palace which dominated the old city of Vienna, was turned into offices. He himself preferred to live in a house he

[4] T. C. W. Blanning, *Joseph II* (London, 1994), pp. 186–7.

[5] 'Hegel says somewhere that all great events and personalities in world history reappear in one fashion or another. He forgot to add: the first time as tragedy, the second as farce'—Karl Marx, *The Eighteenth Brumaire of Louis Bonaparte* (1852).

[6] See above, pp. 194–8.

[7] Alfred, Ritter von Arneth, *Maria Theresia und Joseph II. Ihre Correspondenz sammt Briefen Josephs an seinen Bruder Leopold*, 3 vols. (Vienna, 1867–8), I, p. 10.

[8] Quoted in Lorenz Mikoletzky, *Joseph II. Herrscher zwischen den Zeiten* (Göttingen, 1979), p. 94.

built for himself in the Augarten, described by his biographer as 'no bigger, and much plainer and less ostentatious than a Victorian suburban villa'.[9] He was also well aware that a public sphere had formed and that its members needed to be taken seriously. After ordering the abolition of elaborate court etiquette, he added that it was to be publicized in all parts of the monarchy, 'together with the supplementary order that no one, no matter who he might be, who wishes to petition for something or to submit anything, shall kneel down, because this is not a fitting form of behaviour from one human being to another and should be reserved for God alone . . . all this is to be published in the newspapers'.[10] He also showed himself the master of 'gesture politics', turning the Glacis, the open space protecting the old city of Vienna, into a public recreation area and throwing open to the public the Prater in 1766 and the Augarten in 1775. Over the gate of the latter a sign was erected reading 'This place of recreation has been dedicated to the People by one who esteems them.'[11]

Joseph was still working for the state and the public when death finally claimed him at 5.30 a.m. on 20 February 1790. His passing was welcomed by the innumerable vested interests and privileged groups he had enraged by his levelling reforms, many of which he had been forced to abandon or were to be revoked by his successors. Yet he had dragged the Habsburg monarchy kicking and screaming into the culture of the public sphere and had given it sufficient progressive momentum to carry it through what was to prove a very taxing period during the French Revolutionary and Napoleonic wars. The *parvenu* Emperor Napoleon sneered that the Habsburgs were always one idea and one army behind the rest of Europe—that may well have been true, commented Albert Sorel, who recounted the jibe, but at least they always had an idea and they always had an army. It was Napoleon who ran out of both.[12] As this combination suggests, Joseph grasped the intimate relationship between culture and power. It was his army that saved him in 1789, when the implosion of his monarchy seemed imminent, by winning a series of decisive battles against

[9] Derek Beales, *Joseph II*, Vol. I: *In the shadow of Maria Theresa 1741–1780* (Cambridge, 1987), p. 197.

[10] Blanning, *Joseph II*, p. 64.

[11] Günter Düriegl, 'Wien—eine Residenzstadt im Uebergang von der adeligen Metropole zur bürgerlichen Urbanität', in Richard Georg Plaschka and Grete Klingenstein (eds.), *Österreich im Europa der Aufklärung. Kontinuität und Zäsur in Europa zur Zeit Maria Theresias und Josephs II. Internationales Symposion in Wien 20.–23. Oktober 1980*, 2 vols (Vienna, 1985), vol. I, pp. 313–14.

[12] Quoted in T. C. W. Blanning, *The French Revolutionary Wars 1787–1802* (London, 1996), p. 273.

the Turks, including the hugely symbolic prize of Belgrade. However ramshackle the Habsburg monarchy might appear to historians accustomed to mock its idiosyncrasies, to Joseph's subjects it appeared as a great and vibrant power, dominating Central Europe and thrusting the infidel back towards Asia. So in the monarchy's heartlands there was no disaffected aristocrat seeking to play the role of Lafayette and there were no Austrian versions of the mutinous French Guards sallying forth to storm an Austrian Bastille.

Nor was there in Great Britain or in Prussia, or in any other of the German states. As we have seen, in their various ways, and with varying degrees of success, their rulers had come to terms with changing conditions. Only in France was the failure almost total. Two episodes in the last decade of the old regime demonstrated the monarchy's chronic inability to make culture work in its cause. The first was 'one of the three or four great dates in the history of the French theatre'[13]—the much-delayed performance of Pierre-Augustin Caron de Beaumarchais's *The Marriage of Figaro* on 27 April 1784. Completed six years earlier, the text had fallen victim to the capricious censorship system. No fewer than six separate censors scrutinized the play before publication was eventually authorized. Particularly serious for Louis XVI's reputation was the common knowledge that it had been his personal decision to hold up its staging. Lobbied hard by Beaumarchais's supporters at court, eventually the king relented to the extent of asking Lenoir, the chief of police in Paris, to obtain one of the many manuscript copies that were making the rounds. Madame Campan recorded in her memoirs how she was summoned to the royal presence to read the play secretly to an audience consisting of just the king and the queen. When she reached Figaro's celebrated monologue at the beginning of Act V, there was an explosion of royal wrath. Figaro is recounting how he was thrown into prison for writing an innocuous pamphlet on the nature of wealth:

> I'd like to get my hands on one of those fly-by-night tyrants. I'd tell him . . . that insults in print are of no importance to anyone except to those who are trying to suppress them: that without the liberty to criticise no praise has any value: and that only little men are scared of little jokes.
>
> *(He sits down again)*
>
> Tired of feeding a prisoner they've never heard of—they throw me back into the street. And since a man has to have his dinner, even when he's not in prison, I sharpen my pen again and ask everybody what the great debate is now. They tell me that during my period of economic restraint a new free system's been established in

[13] Frédéric Grendel, *Beaumarchais: The Man who was Figaro* (London, 1977), p. 218.

Madrid, governing the sale of products, including products of the printing press: and that providing I don't write about the authorities, or the church, or politics, or morals, or anybody holding public office, or influential corporations, or the Opera, or the other theatres, or mention anyone with any opinion at all, I am at liberty to print anything subject to it being inspected by two or three censors. Wishing to take advantage of this glorious liberty, I advertise that I am starting a new paper. I call it *The Useless News*, thinking I'm not trespassing on anyone else's preserves—whew!—thousands of poor miserable hacks all up in arms against me for plagiarism. I'm suppressed and there I am, once more without employment.[14]

At this point, Louis XVI jumped to his feet with uncharacteristic animation and exclaimed: 'This is odious, this will never be staged, we would have to demolish the Bastille before putting on a play like this could be anything other than an act of dangerous irresponsibility. This man derides everything that ought to be respected in a government.' To his consort's enquiry: 'so, it's never going to be performed?' he replied: 'No, certainly not, of that you can be sure.'[15] News of royal disapproval only made the forbidden fruit more appealing. In June 1783 a group of nobles sought to stage a performance in Paris on the stage of the Hôtel des Menus-Plaisirs, normally used by the Opéra for rehearsals. The king found out only on the day of the performance, and at once sent off the duc de Villequier with a *lettre de cachet* to put a stop to it. The emissary found the theatre already half-full, the doors besieged, and the street full of carriages, so news of the ban met a very hostile reaction. Madame Campan recorded: 'the anger excited by this disappointment was so intense that never before the fall of the throne were the words *oppression* and *tyranny* articulated with such passion and vehemence. Beaumarchais was so enraged that he exclaimed: *Very well then! He doesn't want us to put the play on here, but I tell you that it will be performed eventually, perhaps even in the choir of Notre Dame!*'[16]

This represented a dangerous personalization of the dispute, for it was obvious that Beaumarchais identified himself with Figaro and used the character as his mouthpiece. That meant that Louis XVI had assigned himself the role of Count Almaviva, as a symbol of privileged tyranny (although he was less convincing as a lecher). Yet he was also a weak tyrant, for in 1784 Louis finally agreed to allow public performances. Public anticipation by this time was so

[14] John Leigh (ed.), *Beaumarchais: The Figaro Plays* (London, 1997), p. 135.

[15] [Jeanne Louise Henriette Genet Campan], *Mémoires sur la vie privée de Marie Antoinette, Reine de France et de Navarre, suivis de souvenirs et d'anecdotes historiques sur les règnes de Louis XIV, de Louis XV et de Louis XVI*, 2 vols. (London, 1824), I, pp. 261–2.

[16] Ibid., p. 263.

intense that a *succès fou* was guaranteed. The theatre was besieged from early morning, a massive traffic-jam was caused by an unbroken line of carriages stretching from the Odéon to the Seine, three people in the pit were crushed to death, and every last seat was taken long before curtain up.[17] The play ran for sixty-eight performances in a row, a quite unprecedented sequence, and grossed 350,000 *livres*—'for the first time in French history, a play had made its author rich'.[18] It was also a play with an obvious political agenda. Even if Beaumarchais had not already made his name with attacks on the Maupeou Parlements, the play's radicalism could not be missed. This was how La Harpe reviewed it:

> I shall never forget my astonishment at the fifth-act soliloquy, which lasted at least a quarter of an hour. But the focus of my astonishment soon changed, for this speech was astounding in more than one sense. A good half of it was nothing more than a satirical attack on the government; I knew it already, since I had heard it before. But I was far from expecting that a government could possibly agree to such attacks being uttered on a public stage. The more they applauded, the more I was amazed and perplexed. At last I came to the decision that it wasn't the playwright who was at fault; for although the speech, in its context, was incomprehensible to the point of absurdity, the tolerance of a government which allowed itself to be humiliated like this in the theatre was even more so—so that Beaumarchais had a perfect right to speak like this on stage, on any subject whatsoever, if the authorities saw fit to allow it.[19]

The subversive association was sealed the following year when Beaumarchais published a polemic in the *Journal de Paris*, in the course of which he referred to the 'lions and tigers' who had tried to prevent the performance of *Figaro*. The elder of the king's two brothers, the comte de Provence, persuaded him that he was Beaumarchais's 'lion' ('the king of the Beasts') and that Marie Antoinette was the 'tiger'. The king agreed, scribbling the following order: 'To the Chief of Police: as soon as you receive this letter, you will arrange for the imprisonment of M. de Beaumarchais at Saint-Lazare. This man has become too insolent; he has been badly brought up and his education needs attention.'[20] Sending Beaumarchais to Saint-Lazare, rather than the

[17] Claude Petitfrère, *Le scandale du Mariage de Figaro: prèlude à la Révolution française?* (Paris, 1989), pp. 7–9.

[18] Grendel, *Beaumarchais*, pp. 219–20.

[19] Quoted in William D. Howarth, *Beaumarchais and the Theatre* (London and New York, 1995), p. 187.

[20] René Dalsème, *La Vie de Beaumarchais*, 11th edn. (Paris, 1928), p. 290. This seems almost too good to be true, but Dalsème's biography is a serious work of scholarship, based on extensive use of archival sources.

Bastille, was adding insult to injury, for it was normally reserved for profligate noblemen and juvenile delinquents.[21] A storm of public protest, a carefully composed petition from Beaumarchais, and the intervention of the king's younger brother, the comte d'Artois, secured the prisoner's release after only five days, but the damage had been done. Arnault, although secretary of the comte de Provence, Beaumarchais's main opponent at court, recorded: 'Everyone saw this action as a threat not only to the liberty but also to the dignity of all.'[22] Beaumarchais's release from prison was turned into a political demonstration as well-wishers queued to sign a book of congratulation. This all happened, of course, in 1785, the year of the Diamond Necklace Affair.[23]

1785 was also the year that saw the exhibition of the most enthusiastically received painting of the eighteenth century—Jacques-Louis David's *The Oath of the Horatii*. The critics gushed: 'Finally I have seen this *Oath of the Horatii*, so longed-for, so praised, so admirable. I owe my readers a confession of the keen pleasure it awakened in me' (Carmontelle) or 'The composition is the work of a new genius; it announces a brilliant and courageous imagination . . . we regard it as the most distinguished production to come from a French brush in many a year' (*Mercure de France*).[24] The thousands who flocked to the Salon to view the painting were entirely familiar with the episode depicted—among other things, it had provided the subject-material for Corneille's *Horaces*—but a summary may be helpful to twenty-first-century readers. The eponymous Horatii were the triplet sons of Horatius, chosen as champions to fight for Rome in about 650 BC against a rival group of triplets, the Curiatii, representing the kingdom of Alban. In David's picture we see the Horatii taking an oath to their father to conquer or die. The situation was complicated, however, by the fact that a sister of one of the Curiatii was married to one of the Horatii, and that a sister of the Horatii, Camilla, was betrothed to one of the Curiatii. It is these two ladies we see united in apprehensive grief on the right of David's painting. The battle itself at first went the way of the Curiatii, who slew two of

[21] Jacques Guicharnaud, '1784, 27 April: Pierre Caron de Beaumarchais's *Le mariage de Figaro* triumphs at last at the Comédie-Française', in Denis Hollier (ed.), *A New History of French Literature* (Cambridge, Mass., 1989), p. 550.

[22] Quoted in Félix Gaiffe, *Le Mariage de Figaro* (Paris, 1942), p. 114.

[23] See above, pp. 413–14.

[24] Thomas E. Crow, *Painters and Public Life in Eighteenth-century Paris* (New Haven and London, 1985), p. 214. On the previous page, Crow reproduced Martini's engraving of the salon of 1785 which shows the prominent place accorded to the *Oath of the Horatii*. There are several other supporting illustrations in Crow's later work *Emulation: Making Artists for Revolutionary France* (New Haven and London, 1995), ch. 2.

their opponents, but the sole surviving Roman craftily feigned flight and was able to pick off his pursuers one by one. When the survivor arrived home in triumph, he was cursed by Camilla for killing her intended, whereupon he slew her with the cry: 'So perish any Roman woman who mourns the enemy.' Although condemned to death for sororicide, he was saved by an appeal to the Roman people by his father, Horatius, who argued for the primacy of patriotism.

Conceived in 1781, painted in Paris and Rome in 1783–4, *The Oath of the Horatii* is by no means a straightforward political manifesto, despite the late Kenneth Clark's confident opinion that it is 'a perfectly conscious piece of propaganda, which was planned like a political campaign'.[25] Although David consorted with members of the opposition nobility, such as the duc d'Orléans and the comtes de Lameth, in the years before 1789, he left no evidence that he was making a contemporary political statement. His only authentic statement on the picture in his correspondence refers to his unilateral decision to increase the dimensions of the picture. In a letter to the marquis de Bièvre, he wrote: 'I have abandoned the picture I was doing for the King and have done one for myself instead. No-one will ever make me do anything detrimental to my reputation, and it now measures thirteen by ten feet.' If that might have sounded a touch defiant, he added immediately, 'You need not doubt my desire to please the King, as I do not know whether I shall ever paint another picture like it.'[26] If the painting really was intended as a republican call to arms, David had made an odd choice of period, for Rome was still a kingdom in the mid-seventh century BC and was to remain so for another century and a half.[27] Nor is it clear from either the painting or anything David wrote that he followed Horatius in privileging fatherland over family. Both here and in David's other great pre-revolutionary success—*The Lictors returning to Brutus the bodies of his sons* (1789)—there is a good case to be made for the superiority

[25] Kenneth Clark, *The Romantic Rebellion: Romantic versus Classical Art* (London, 1973), p. 23. See also David L. Dowd's view that David's canvas was imbued with 'the political and social reformist philosophy of the rising middle classes'; David L. Dowd, *Pageant-master of the Republic; Jacques Louis David and the French Revolution*, University of Nebraska Studies, NS 3 (Lincoln, Nebraska, 1948), p. 6. For some even crasser views along the same lines, see Jack Lindsay, *Death of a Hero: French painting from David to Delacroix* (London, 1960), p. 47, Arnold Hauser, *The Social History of Art*. Vol. 3: *Rococo, Classicism and Romanticism* (London, 1962), pp. 134–6, and Albert Boime, *Art in an Age of Revolution 1750–1800* (Chicago and London, 1987), pp. 392–405.

[26] Quoted in Anita Brookner, *Jacques-Louis David* (London, 1980), p. 76.

[27] That has not stopped Matthew Craske referring to 'the early republic celebrated in David's *Oath of the Horatii*'; *Art in Europe 1700–1830* (Oxford, 1997), p. 272. The early republic did not begin until 509 BC.

of the grieving women over the homicidal men.[28] Equally uncertain is the source of David's inspiration—Rome? Herculaneum? Winckelmann? Mengs? Corneille? Poussin? Noverre?

Nevertheless, even if no satisfactory direct link can be established between David's paintings and the decline and fall of the old regime, there is no need to throw out the baby with the bath-water. In Anita Brookner's judgement: 'The affair of the Queen's necklace; the revolt of Britain's American colonies; the inspired insubordination of Beaumarchais' Figaro: to these factors which were to influence the formation of public opinion on the eve of the Revolution of 1789 must be added the hypnotic appearance of the *Oath of the Horatii* with its mysteriously defensible air of resolution and unity. Beaumarchais and David were the Parisian answer to Versailles.'[29] Thomas Crow has also conjectured that the hostile reaction to the painting from conservative critics was fuelled by 'a perception that David has made an unholy alliance with a public whose desires and interests are alien to their own'.[30] If these verdicts seem a little speculative, it certainly seems to have been the case that the regime had lost control of the Salons. In 1771 Louis XV's *maîtresse en titre*, Madame du Barry, had herself painted by Drouais, surrounded by the attributes of the arts she patronized and showing a good deal of her voluptuous figure. The exhibition of the large canvas at the Salon of 1771 was turned into a political demonstration, as spectators noisily registered their disapproval, a scene witnessed by the subject herself. The painting had to be withdrawn.[31] Memories of that episode were still fresh in 1787, when Elisabeth Vigée-Lebrun's portrait of Marie Antoinette was withheld from the Salon for fear of public protests. The association of Madame du Barry with Marie Antoinette, as the archetypal royal whores, was of course often made by this time. Henry Swinburne recorded that 'the anti-court people say of the Queen that the only difference between her and Madame du Barri [*sic*] is that the latter "*quitta le public pour le roi, et la reine quitte le roi pour le public*".'[32] For the critic of the *Mémoires secrets*, the decision not to exhibit the Queen's portrait was a defining moment in the fall of the regime: 'I recognized in these trivialities the true character of

[28] Norman Bryson, *Word and Image: French Painting of the Old Regime* (Cambridge, 1981), ch. 8.

[29] Brookner, *Jacques-Louis David*, p. 81.

[30] Crow, *Painters and Public Life in Eighteenth-century Paris*, p.220. See also Thomas Crow, 'The *Oath of the Horatii* in 1785: painting and pre-revolutionary politics in France', *Art History*, 1 (1978), pp. 424–71.

[31] Crow, *Painters and Public Life in Eighteenth-century Paris*, p. 176.

[32] Henry Swinburne, *The Courts of Europe at the Close of the Last Century*, 2 vols. (London, 1841), II, p. 45.

despotism, which on one hand takes the harshest official measures against its magistrates, the defenders of the nation, defying the nation itself and grinding the most sacred rights under its heel; and on the other, displays a miserable weakness, a puerile faint-heartedness.'[33]

The success of the *Horatii* and David's subsequent career as a revolutionary exemplified the failure of the French establishment to adjust the previous century's cultural institutions to modern requirements. As we have seen, the biennial Salons came to form an important part of the public sphere, and were celebrated as a prime example of the force of public opinion.[34] Although when writing about the Salon of 1777, the critic Pidansat de Mairobert complained about the heat, dust, noise, and smell created by the press of so many people, he added:

> But here nevertheless is a thing to delight the eye of an Englishman: the mixing, men and women together, of all orders and all ranks of the state... This is perhaps the only public place in France where he could find that precious liberty visible everywhere in London. This enchanting spectacle pleases me even more than the works displayed in this temple of the arts. Here the Savoyard odd-job man rubs shoulders with the great noble in his *cordon bleu*; the fishwife trades her perfumes with those of a lady of quality, making the latter resort to holding her nose to combat the strong odour of cheap brandy drifting her way; the rough artisan, guided only by natural feeling, comes out with a just observation, at which an inept wit nearby bursts out laughing only because of the comical accent in which it was expressed; while an artist hiding in the crowd unravels the meaning of it all and turns it to his profit.[35]

That there was a strong demand for the opportunity to view paintings was confirmed by other observers, by the journalist Mercier, for example, who reported on the Salon of 1783, 'the crowds flock there; the waves of people do not subside from morning until night during six whole weeks; there are times when one is choked.'[36] Yet the regime did next to nothing to satisfy, guide, least of all to manipulate this potential asset. It was not so much a case of providing the public with pictures of appropriate subjects, for that might well have backfired; what was needed was a demonstration that the monarchy was taking the lead in creating a state in which culture was cherished and promoted—a *Kulturstaat*. In 1750 a major step in this direction was taken when the Luxembourg Palace was opened as the first public art gallery in

[33] Quoted in Crow, *Painters and Public Life in Eighteenth-century Paris*, p. 229.
[34] See above, pp. 106–7.
[35] Quoted in Crow, *Painters and Public Life in Eighteenth-century Paris*, p. 4.
[36] Ibid., p. 21.

France, displaying ninety-nine paintings and twenty drawings from the royal collection. This initiative may have been a response to complaints that the greatest works of art in the country were being squirrelled away at Versailles, where the general public could never view them.[37] It was a good start, but that was all it ever became. Open for only three hours on Wednesdays and Saturdays, its constituency was confined to connoisseurs. In 1779 it was closed altogether, for the palace was reassigned to the comte de Provence as his principal Paris residence, a change of use of symbolic as well as practical significance. By that time the government had grand schemes for a major new museum at the Louvre. During the next decade the Director-General of the King's Buildings, the comte d'Angiviller, worked very hard on plans for opening up the old palace as a national monument to the fame and glory of king and country. He also bought over 200 new paintings and commissioned a series of history paintings and statues of great men to adorn it.[38] Yet it all came to nothing. 1779, the year after France joined the American War, was not a good year for launching expensive projects of this kind, and conditions did not improve in the next decade. It was left to the Revolution to create the Louvre as we know it today—and to Napoleon to fill it with booty looted from the rest of Europe. It is difficult to avoid the temptation to be judgemental and to observe that the money Louis XVI spent on buying Saint-Cloud for his queen would have been better spent on refurbishing the Louvre for the nation. That opinion is less anachronistic than it might sound, for at least one contemporary took the same view. Jacques-Henri Meister, Grimm's successor as editor of the *Correspondance littéraire* wrote in 1795: 'Who knows if this museum, completed to perfection, might not have saved the monarchy, by providing a more imposing idea of its power and vision, by calming anxious spirits, and by dramatizing the benefits of the Old Regime.'[39]

Its anachronism is diminished further by a comparison with a contemporary initiative undertaken by Joseph II. In 1777 he opened the Belvedere, the great summer palace built by Lukas von Hildebrandt for Prince Eugene, as a public gallery, appointing the Swiss Christian von Mechel as its first director, assembling 'the finest pieces of painting' from the various Habsburg palaces, and providing 70,000 florins for new frames. The pick of the paintings yielded by the dissolution of the monasteries in the 1780s were also assigned to the new gallery. Characteristically, Joseph 'superintended in person' and directed what

[37] F. W. J. Hemmings, *Culture and Society in France 1789–1848* (Leicester, 1987), p. 73.

[38] Andrew McLelland, *Inventing the Louvre: Art, Politics and the Origins of the Modern Museum in Eighteenth-century Paris* (Cambridge, 1994), ch. 2.

[39] Ibid., p. 8.

should be shown where.[40] It was open to the public on Tuesdays, Thursdays, and Saturdays from nine until noon and from three until six in summer as well.[41] The court library was also opened to the public on a daily basis from eight until noon in summer and from nine until noon in winter.[42] Not even Joseph's most fervent admirer claimed that his interest in culture went much beyond the utilitarian, but equally no one could deny his concern for promoting the public good. Autocratic by nature, he too banned performances of Beaumarchais's *The Marriage of Figaro* because it contained 'much that is offensive'. However, it was only his direct intervention that made the staging of Mozart's opera of the same name possible. He attended it both in rehearsal and in performance, gave special permission for dances to be included, and obliged his niece, the Archduchess Maria Theresa, to accept the opera as part of her nuptial celebrations (given the opera's subject-matter, it was hardly the most obvious choice).[43] Yet his reputation as a cultural liberator remained intact, because his regime did mark a significant relaxation of censorship and because he knew how to catch the eye of progressive opinion. In 1783, for example, an anonymous pamphlet was published attacking his policies of religious toleration. Among other things, he was accused of being a disciple of Luther and a notorious iconoclast. Joseph had the pamphlet reprinted at his expense, sold at six kreuzers a copy, and the proceeds sent to the Protestant community. Particularly memorable was his dismissal of attacks on his person:

> If anyone should be so shamelessly impertinent as to attack us with frivolous and arrogant slanders, or should seek to denigrate our policies, then such impropriety should be countered not by punishment but by disdain. If the slanders derive from arrogance, the author deserves contempt; if they derive from mental deficiency, he deserves pity; and if simple ill-will is the cause—then we forgive the idiot.[44]

Many are the qualifications that need to be made about Joseph II's progressive policies—about their motivation, about their impact, about their popularity, and about their durability. Yet when they have all been sorted and weighed,

[40] N. W. Wraxall, *Memoirs of the Courts of Berlin, Dresden, Warsaw, and Vienna, in the years 1777, 1778, and 1779*, 2 vols., 2nd edn. (London, 1800), p. 432.

[41] Johann Pezzl, *Beschreibung und Grundria der Haupt- und Residenzstadt Wien* (Vienna, 1802), pp. 150–5.

[42] Ignaz de Luca, *Beschreibung der kaiserlichen königlichen Residenzstadt Wien. Ein Versuch*, 2 vols. (Vienna, 1785–7), II, p. 20.

[43] Rudolf Payer von Thurn (ed.), *Joseph II als Theaterdirektor. Ungedruckte Briefe und Aktenstücke aus den Kinderjahren des Burgtheaters* (Vienna and Leipzig, 1920), p. 60; Derek Beales, *Mozart and the Habsburgs* (The Stenton Lecture, University of Reading, 1993), p. 11.

[44] Blanning, *Joseph II*, p. 162.

there remains on the other side of the scales a countervailing sense of a common pursuit of the public good by both sovereign and people.

This concluding comparison of a regime which survived and a regime which failed has been designed to reprise the central arguments of this book. Joseph II and the Habsburg monarchy have been chosen because they had perhaps suffered from relative neglect elsewhere. Yet the same sort of points could have been advanced about Frederick the Great and Prussia, or about George III and Great Britain. Across Europe in the eighteenth century, the cultural landscape changed. Different regimes did not start from the same place, nor did they travel by the same route or arrive at the same destination. What worked in insular England could not be attempted in Prussia ('a collection of frontiers', as Frederick the Great put it); what worked in militarized Prussia would have been unacceptable in civilian Britain. What these regimes had in common was a realization—however late, unplanned, or imperfect—that new circumstances required a new political culture. Their most important discovery was that the rise of the public sphere was both an opportunity and a challenge. It was some measure of the inability of the regime in France to follow their example that it was apostrophized as the quintessentially 'old regime' by its executioners.

The British, Prussians, and even Austrians viewed the Revolution of 1789 with majestic complacency, as a belated and bloody attempt to emulate their own achievements. Little did they suspect that it would very quickly create an alliance between regime and public, which would unleash a combination of culture and power far more potent than anything Europe had yet seen. The revolutionaries expanded and politicized the public sphere to an extent undreamed of in the past. They depersonalized, objectivized, and nationalized the state to the point of regicide and terror. They exploited and maximized the nation's resources to such effect that they were able to conquer western, central, and southern Europe. And in doing so, they tested the monarchies to the very brink of destruction. It was a school of very hard knocks, as all the lessons of the eighteenth century were taught again and with much greater intensity. Why it ended with the collapse of the Revolution and the apparent triumph of the old regimes must await a further volume.

SELECT BIBLIOGRAPHY

This volume's credentials are listed in the footnotes. I have listed here only those titles which are of special distinction or might be especially helpful to readers wishing to pursue the topics discussed further.

Adamson, John, *The Princely Courts of Europe: Ritual, Politics and Culture under the Ancien Régime 1500–1750* (London, 1999).

Alewyn, R., *Das große Welttheater, die Epoche der höfischen Feste* (Hamburg, 1959).

Anderson, Benedict, *Imagined Communities: Reflections on the Origins and Spread of Nationalism*, rev. edn. (London, and New York, 1991).

Anthony, James R., 'Jean-Baptiste Lully', in Stanley Sadie (ed.), *The New Grove Dictionary of Music and Musicians*, 20 vols. (London, 1980), vol. 11, pp. 314–29.

Antoine, Michel, *Louis XV* (Paris, 1989).

Aubertin, Charles, *L'Esprit public au XVIIIe siècle. Étude sur les mémoires et les correspondances politiques des contemporains 1715 à 1789* (Paris, 1873).

Auerbach, Erich, 'La cour et la ville', in his collected essays, *Scenes from the Drama of European Literature* (Manchester, 1984), pp. 133–82.

Aulard, Alphonse, *Le Patriotisme français de la Renaissance à la Révolution* (Paris, 1921).

Bagwell, Philip S., *The Transport Revolution from 1770* (London, 1974).

Bahr, Ehrhard (ed.), *Was ist Aufklärung?* (Stuttgart, 1974).

Baker, Keith Michael, 'Defining the public sphere in eighteenth-century France: variations on a theme by Habermas', in Craig Calhoun (ed.), *Habermas and the Public Sphere* (Cambridge, Mass., and London, 1992), pp. 181–211.

—— 'French political thought at the accession of Louis XVI', *Journal of Modern History*, 50/2 (June, 1978), 279–303, reprinted in T. C. W. Blanning, *The Rise and Fall of the French Revolution* (Chicago, 1996), pp. 65–89.

—— 'On the problem of the ideological origins of the French Revolution' and 'Public opinion as political invention', in K. M. Baker, *Inventing the French Revolution* (Cambridge, 1990), pp. 12–27.

Balet, Leo, and Gerhard, E., *Die Verbürgerlichung der deutschen Kunst, Literatur und Musik im 18. Jahrhundert* (Strassburg, 1936).

Barber, Giles, and Fabian, Bernhard (eds.), *Buch und Buchhandel in Europa im achtzehnten Jahrhundert* (Hamburg, 1981).

Bardong, Otto (ed.), *Friedrich der Große* (Darmstadt, 1982).

Barnard, F. M., *Herder's Social and Political Thought: From Enlightenment to Nationalism* (Oxford, 1965).

Bartley, J. O., *Teague, Shenkin and Sawney. Being an historical study of the earliest Irish, Welsh and Scottish characters in English plays* (Cork, 1954).

BAUMAN, THOMAS, *North German Opera in the Age of Goethe* (Cambridge, 1985).

—— 'Courts and municipalities in North Germany', in Neal Zaslaw, *The Classical Era. From the 1740s to the end of the eighteenth century* (London, 1989), pp. 240–67.

BEALES, DEREK, 'The false Joseph II', *Historical Journal*, 18 (1975), 467–95.

—— *Joseph II*. Vol. I: *In the shadow of Maria Theresa 1741–1780* (Cambridge, 1987).

—— *Mozart and the Habsburgs* (The Stenton Lecture, University of Reading, 1993).

—— 'Religion and culture', in T. C. W. Blanning (ed.), *The Short Oxford History of Europe: The Eighteenth Century* (Oxford, 2000), pp. 131–77.

—— 'Was Joseph II an enlightened despot?', in *The Austrian Enlightenment and its Aftermath*, Austrian Studies 2, ed. Ritchie Robertson and Edward Timms (Edinburgh, 1991), pp. 1–21.

BEATTIE, JOHN M., *The English court in the reign of George I* (Cambridge, 1967).

BECKER, HEINZ, 'Friedrich II.', in *Die Musik in Geschichte und Gegenwart*, ed. Friedrich Blume, vol. 4 (Kassel and Basle, 1955), pp. 955–62.

BEETHAM, DAVID, *The Legitimation of Power* (London, 1991).

BEHRENS, C. B. A., *Society, Government and the Enlightenment: The Experiences of Eighteenth-century France and Prussia* (London, 1985).

BELLANGER, CLAUDE, GODECHOT, JACQUES, GUIRAL, PIERRE, and TERROU, FERNAND (eds.), *Histoire générale de la presse française*. Vol. I: *Des origines à 1814* (Paris, 1969).

BENDA, KALMAN, 'Probleme des Josephinismus und des Jakobinertums in der Habsburgischen Monarchie', *Südostforschungen*, 25 (1966), 271–90.

BENDIX, REINHARD, *Max Weber: An Intellectual Portrait* (Berkeley and Los Angeles, 1977).

BENOIT, MARCELLE, *Versailles et les musiciens du roi 1661–1733. Étude institutionelle et sociale* (Paris, 1971).

BERKOV, P. N., *Istoriya russkoy zhurnalistiki XVIII veka* (Moscow and Leningrad, 1952).

BERLIN, ISAIAH, 'The bent twig: on the rise of nationalism', in Isaiah Berlin, *The Crooked Timber of Humanity: Chapters in the History of Ideas* (London, 1990), pp. 238–61.

—— 'The counter-enlightenment', in Isaiah Berlin, *Against the Current: Essays in the History of Ideas* (London, 1979), pp. 1–24.

—— 'Herder and the Enlightenment', in Earl R. Wasserman (ed.), *Aspects of the Eighteenth Century* (Baltimore and London, 1965), pp. 47–104.

BERMINGHAM, ANN, and BREWER, JOHN (eds.), *The Consumption of Culture 1600–1800: Image, Object, Text* (London and New York, 1995).

BERTRAND, LOUIS, *La Fin du classicisme et le retour à l'antique dans la seconde moitié du XVIIIe siècle et les premières années du XIXe siècle en France* (Paris, 1897).

BICKART, ROGER, *Les Parlements et la notion de souveraineté nationale au dix-huitième siècle* (Paris, 1932).

BIEDERMANN, K., *Friedrich der Große und sein Verhältniß zur Entwicklung des deutschen Geisteslebens* (Brunswick, 1859).

BINDMAN, DAVID, *Hogarth and his Times* (London, 1997).

BLACK, EUGENE CHARLTON, *The Association: British Extraparliamentary Political Organization 1769–1793* (Cambridge, Mass., 1963).

BLACK, JEREMY, *The English Press in the Eighteenth Century* (London, 1987).

BLANNING, T. C. W., 'The commercialization and sacralization of culture', in T. C. W. Blanning (ed.), *The Oxford Illustrated History of Modern Europe* (Oxford, 1996), pp. 120–47.

—— 'The Enlightenment in Catholic Germany', in Roy Porter and Mikulas Teich (eds.), *The Enlightenment in National Context* (Cambridge, 1981), pp. 118–26.

—— 'Frederick the Great and enlightened absolutism', in H. M. Scott (ed.), *Enlightened Absolutism: Reform and Reformers in Later Eighteenth-century Europe* (London, 1990), pp. 265–88.

—— 'Frederick the Great and German culture', in *Royal and Republican Sovereignty in Early Modern Europe: Essays in Memory of Ragnhild Hatton* ed. G. C. Gibbs, Robert Oresko, and Hamish Scott (Cambridge, 1996), pp. 527–50.

—— *The French Revolution: Class War or Culture Clash?* (London, 1998).

—— *The French Revolutionary Wars 1787–1802* (London, 1996).

—— *The Origins of the French Revolutionary Wars* (London, 1986).

—— *Joseph II* (London, 1994).

—— *Reform and Revolution in Mainz 1743–1803* (Cambridge, 1974).

BLAUKOPF, KURT, *Musik im Wandel der Gesellschaft. Grundzüge der Musiksoziologie* (Munich and Zürich, 1982).

BLEEK, WILHELM, *Von der Kameralausbildung zum Juristenprivileg. Studium, Prüfung und Ausbildung der höheren Beamten des allgemeinen Verwaltungsdienstes in Deutschland im 18. und 19. Jahrhundert* (Berlin, 1972).

BLESSINGER, KARL, 'Die Kunstpolitik Friedrichs des Großen', *Die Musik*, 32 (1940), pp. 295–305.

BLUCHE, FRANÇOIS, *Louis XIV* (Oxford, 1990).

BLUNT, ANTHONY, *Art and Architecture in France 1500–1700* (Harmondsworth, 1973).

BODI, LESLIE, *Tauwetter in Wien. Zur Prosa der österreichischen Aufklärung 1781–1795* (Frankfurt am Main, 1977).

BÖHM, WINFRIED, 'Bildungsideal, Bildungswesen, Wissenschaft und Akademien', in Erhard Bethke (ed.), *Friedrich der Große* (Gütersloh, 1985), pp. 186–201.

BOERNER, PETER (ed.), *Concepts of National Identity: An Interdisciplinary Dialogue* (Baden-Baden, 1986).

BOSHER, J. F., *French Finances 1775–1795: From Business to Bureaucracy* (Cambridge, 1970).

BOUCHER, THIERRY-G., 'Rameau et les théâtres de la cour (1745–1764)', in Jérome de la Gorce (ed.), *Jean-Philippe Rameau. Colloque international organisé par la Société Rameau, Dijon 21–24 septembre 1983* (Paris and Geneva, 1987), pp. 565–77.

BOYLE, NICHOLAS, *Goethe: The Poet and the Age*. Vol. 1: *The Poetry of Desire* (Oxford, 1991).

BRAUBACH, MAX, 'Die katholischen Universitäten Deutschlands und die französische Revolution', in Max Braubach, *Diplomatie und geistiges Leben im 17. und 18. Jahrhundert. Gesammelte Abhandlungen*, Bonner Historische Forschungen, 33 (Bonn, 1969), pp. 660–94.

BRAUN, RUDOLF, and GUGGERLI, DAVID, *Macht des Tanzes—Tanz der Mächtigen. Hoffeste und Herrschaftszeremoniell 1550–1914* (Munich, 1993).

BRAUNBEHRENS, VOLKMAR, *Mozart in Vienna* (Oxford, 1991).

BRENET, MICHEL, *Les Concerts en France sous l'ancien régime* (Paris, 1900; reprinted New York, 1970).

BRÉVAN, BRUNO, *Les Changements de la vie musicale parisienne de 1774 à 1799* (Paris, 1980).

BREWER, JOHN, 'The eighteenth-century British state: contexts and issues', in Lawrence Stone (ed.), *An Imperial State at War: Britain from 1689 to 1815* (London and New York, 1994), pp. 52–71.

—— 'The misfortunes of Lord Bute: a case-study in eighteenth-century political argument and public opinion', *Historical Journal*, 16 (1973), 3–43.

—— '"The most polite age and the most vicious". Attitudes towards culture as a commodity 1660–1800', in Ann Bermingham and John Brewer (eds.), *The Consumption of Culture 1600–1800: Image, Object, Text* (London and New York, 1995), pp. 341–61.

—— 'Party and Double Cabinet: two facets of Burke's *Thoughts*', *Historical Journal*, 14 (1971), 479–501.

—— *Party Ideology and Popular Politics at the Accession of George III* (Cambridge, 1976).

—— *The Pleasures of the Imagination: English Culture in the Eighteenth Century* (London, 1997).

—— *The Sinews of Power: War, Money and the English State 1688–1783* (New York, 1989).

—— 'This, that and the other: public, social and private in the seventeenth and eighteenth centuries', in Lesley Sharpe and Dario Castiglione (eds.), *Shifting the Boundaries: Transformation of the Languages of Public and Private in the Eighteenth Century* (Exeter, 1995), pp. 1–21.

BROMLEY, J. S., 'The decline of absolute monarchy', in J. Wallace-Hadrill and J. McManners (ed.), *France: Government and Society*, 2nd edn. (London, 1970), pp. 134–60.

BROOKE, J., *The House of Commons, 1754–1790* (London, 1968).

BROOKE, JOHN, *King George III* (London, 1972).

BROOKNER, ANITA, 'Aspects of neo-classicism in French painting', *Apollo*, (September, 1958), pp. 67–73.

—— *Greuze: The Rise and Fall of an Eighteenth-century Phenomenon* (London, 1972).

—— 'Jean-Baptiste Greuze', *Burlington Magazine*, 98, (May–June, 1956), 157–62 and 192–9.

—— 'J. L. David—a sentimental classicist', in *Stil und Überlieferung in der Kunst des Abendlandes. Akten des 21. Internationalen Kongresses für Kunstgeschichte in Bonn 1964*, vol. I (Berlin, 1967), pp. 184–9.

—— *Jacques-Louis David* (London, 1980).

BROWN, BRUCE ALAN, *Gluck and the French Theatre in Vienna* (Oxford, 1991).

—— 'Maria Theresa's Vienna', in Neal Zaslaw, *The Classical Era: From the 1740s to the End of the Eighteenth Century* (London, 1989), pp. 99–215.

BRUFORD, W. H., *Deutsche Kultur der Goethezeit* (Konstanz, 1965).

—— *The German Tradition of Self-cultivation: 'Bildung' from Humboldt to Thomas Mann* (Cambridge, 1975).

BUCHOLZ, R. O., *The Augustan Court: Queen Anne and the Decline of Court Culture* (Stanford, Calif., 1993).

BUCK, AUGUST, KAUFFMANN, GEORG, SPAHR, BLAKE LEE, and WIEDEMANN, CONRAD (eds.), *Europäische Hofkultur im 16. und 17. Jahrhundert. Vorträge und Referate gehalten anläßlich des Kongresses des Wolfenbütteler Arbeitskreises für Renaissance-forschung und des Internationalen Arbeitskreises für Barockliteratur in der Herzog August Bibliothek Wolfenbüttel vom 4. bis 8. September 1979*, 3 vols. (Hamburg, 1981).

BURKE, JOSEPH, *English Art 1714–1800* (London, 1976).

—— and CALDWELL, COLIN, *Hogarth: The Complete Engravings* (London, 1968).

BURKE, PETER, *The Fabrication of Louis XIV* (New Haven, 1992).

BURROWS, DONALD, *Handel* (London, 1994).

BURTT, SHELLEY, *Virtue Transformed: Political Argument in England 1688–1740* (Cambridge, 1992).

BUTTERFIELD, HERBERT, *George III, Lord North and the People, 1779–80* (London, 1949).

CANNON, JOHN, *Aristocratic Century: The Peerage of Eighteenth-century England* (Cambridge, 1984).

—— *The Fox–North Coalition: Crisis of the Constitution 1782–4* (Cambridge, 1969).

—— *Lord North: The Noble Lord in the Blue Ribbon*. Historical Association Pamphlet, General Series no. 74 (London, 1970).

—— *Parliamentary Reform 1640–1832* (Cambridge, 1972).

—— 'The survival of the British monarchy', *Transactions of the Royal Historical Society*, 5th ser., 36 (1986), 143–64.

CENSER, JACK R., 'The coming of a new interpretation of the French Revolution?', *Journal of Social History*, 21 (1987), 295–309.

—— *The French Press in the age of Enlightenment* (London, 1994).

CHARTIER, ROGER, *The Cultural Origins of the French Revolution* (Durham, NC, and London, 1991).

—— 'Print culture', in Roger Chartier (ed.), *The Culture of Print: Power and the Uses of Print in Early Modern Europe* (Cambridge, 1989), pp. 1–10.

Chartier, Roger, and Julia, Dominique, 'L'école: traditions et modernisation', in *Seventh International Congress on the Enlightenment: Introductory Papers. Budapest 26 July–2 August 1987* (Oxford, 1987), pp. 107–17.

—— and Roche, Daniel, 'Livre et presse: véhicules des idées', in *Seventh International Congress on the Enlightenment: Introductory Papers. Budapest 26 July–2 August 1987* (Oxford, 1987), pp. 93–106.

Christie, Ian R., *Myth and Reality in Late Eighteenth-century British Politics and other Papers* (London, 1970).

—— *Stress and Stability in Late Eighteenth-century Britain: Reflections on the British Avoidance of Revolution* (Oxford, 1984).

—— *Wars and Revolutions: Britain 1760–1815* (London, 1982).

Christout, Marie-Françoise, *Le Ballet de Cour au XVIIe siècle* (Geneva, 1987).

Clark, J. C. D., *English Society 1688–1832: Ideology, Social Structure and Political Practice during the Ancien Régime* (Cambridge, 1985).

—— *The Language of Liberty 1660–1832: Political Discourse and Social Dynamics in the Anglo-American World* (Cambridge, 1994).

—— 'Protestantism, nationalism and national identity', *Historical Journal*, 43 (2000), pp. 249–76.

Clark, Peter, *Sociability and Urbanity: Clubs and Societies in the Eighteenth-century City*. The Eighth H. J. Dyos Lecture, 23 April 1986 (Leicester, 1986).

Claydon, Tony, and McBride, Ian (eds.), *Protestantism and National Identity: Britain and Ireland c.1650–1850* (Cambridge, 1998).

Colley, Linda, 'The apotheosis of George III: loyalty, royalty and the British nation 1760–1820', *Past and Present*, 102 (1984), 94–129.

—— 'Britishness and otherness: an argument', *Journal of British Studies*, 31(1992).

—— *Britons: Forging the nation 1707–1837* (New Haven and London, 1992). pp. 309–29.

Collins, James, *The State in Early Modern France* (Cambridge, 1995).

Collinson, Patrick, 'Biblical rhetoric: the English nation and national sentiment in the prophetic mode', in Claire McEachern and Debora Shuger (eds.), *Religion and Culture in Renaissance England* (Cambridge, 1997), pp. 15–27.

Comninel, George C., *Rethinking the French Revolution: Marxism and the Revisionist Challenge* (London and New York, 1987).

Conisbee, Philip, *Painting in Eighteenth-century France* (Oxford, 1981).

Consentius, Ernst, 'Friedrich der Große und die Zeitungs-Zensur', *Preußische Jahrbücher*, 115 (1904), pp. 220–49.

Coulet, Henri, *Le Roman jusquà la Révolution*, 2 vols. (Paris, 1967).

Crook, J. Mordaunt, *The Greek Revival: Neo-classical Attitudes in British Architecture 1760–1870* (London, 1972).

Crow, Thomas, 'The *Oath of the Horatii* in 1785: painting and pre-revolutionary politics in France', *Art History*, 1 (1978), 424–71.

—— *Painters and Public Life in Eighteenth-century Paris* (New Haven and London, 1985).

Cunningham, Hugh, 'The language of patriotism', in Raphael Samuel (ed.), *Patriotism: The Making and Unmaking of British National Identity.* Vol. 1: *History and Politics* (London and New York, 1989), pp. 57–89.

Curtius, Ernst, 'Friedrich II. und die bildenden Künste', *Alterthum und Gegenwart. Gesammelte Reden und Vorträge*, vol. 2 (Berlin, 1882), pp. 63–77.

—— 'Friedrich II. und die deutsche Litteratur', *Alterthum und Gegernwart. Gesammelte Reden und Vorträge*, vol. 3 (Berlin, 1889), pp. 41–7.

Cust, Lionel, and Colvin, Sidney, *History of the Society of Dilettanti* (London, 1898).

Czok, Karl, *Am Hofe Augusts des Starken* (Leipzig, 1989).

—— 'Zur Leipziger Kulturgeschichte des 18. Jahrhunderts', in Reinhard Szekus (ed.), *Johann Sebastian Bach und die Aufklärung* (Leipzig, 1982), pp. 20–35.

Dann, Otto, 'Die Lesegesellschaften und die Herausbildung einer modernen bürgerlichen Gesellschaft in Europa', in Otto Dann (ed.), *Lesegesellschaften und bürgerliche Emanzipation* (Munich, 1981), pp. 9–28.

—— *Nation und Nationalismus in Deutschland 1770–1990* (Munich, 1993).

Darnton, Robert, 'An enlightened revolution?', *New York Review of Books*, 38 (24 October 1991), 33–6.

—— 'First steps towards a history of reading', *Australian Journal of French Studies*, 23 (1986), 5–30.

—— *The Forbidden Best-sellers of Pre-revolutionary France* (London, 1996).

—— *The Great Cat Massacre and other Episodes in French Cultural History* (Harmondsworth, 1985).

—— 'The high enlightenment and the low-life of literature in pre-revolutionary France', *Past and Present*, 51 (1971), 81–115.

—— 'Reading, writing and publishing in eighteenth century France: a case-study in the sociology of literature', *Daedalus*, 100 (1971), 214–56.

Deelman, Christian, *The Great Shakespeare Jubilee* (London, 1964).

Deutsch, Otto Erich, *Mozart—a documentary biography*, 2nd edn. (London, 1969).

Dickens, A. G. (ed.), *The Courts of Europe: Politics, Patronage and Royalty 1400–1800* (London, 1977).

Didier, Béatrice, *La Musique des lumières. Diderot—L'Encyclopédie—Rousseau* (Paris, 1985).

Dietz, Mary, G., 'Patriotism', in Terence Ball, James Farr, and Russell L. Hanson (eds.), *Political Innovation and Conceptual Change* (Cambridge, 1989), pp. 177–93.

Doane, J., 'The Academy of Ancient Music', *Musical Directory* (London, 1794).

Dobrée, Bonamy, *English Literature in the Early Eighteenth Century 1700–1740* (Oxford, 1959).

—— 'The theme of patriotism in the poetry of the early eighteenth century', *Proceedings of the British Academy*, 35 (1949), 49–65.

DOBSON, MICHAEL, *The Making of a National Poet: Shakespeare, Adaptation, and Authorship, 1660–1769* (Oxford, 1992).

DÖRNER, ANDREAS, *Politischer Mythos und symbolische Politik. Sinnstiftung durch symbolische Formen am Beispiel des Hermannmythos* (Opladen, 1995).

DOYLE, WILLIAM, *The Old European Order* (Oxford, 1978).

—— *Origins of the French Revolution*, 2nd edn. (Oxford, 1988).

—— *The Oxford History of the French Revolution* (Oxford, 1989).

—— 'The Parlements', in K. M. Baker (ed.), *The French Revolution and the Creation of Modern Political Culture*. Vol. II *The Political Culture of the French Revolution*, ed. Colin Lucas (Oxford, 1988), pp. 157–67.

DUDEK, LOUIS, *Literature and the Press: A History of Printing, Printed Media, and their Relation to Literature* (Toronto, 1960).

DÜLMEN, RICHARD VAN, 'Antijesuitismus und katholische Aufklärung in Deutschland', *Historisches Jahrbuch*, 89 (1969), 52–80.

—— *Der Geheimbund der Illuminaten* (Stuttgart, 1975).

—— *Die Gesellschaft der Aufklärung. Zur bürgerlichen Emanzipation und aufklärerischen Kultur in Deutschland* (Frankfurt am Main, 1986).

—— *The Society of the Enlightenment* (Cambridge, 1992).

DÜRIEGL, GÜNTER, 'Wien—eine Residenzstadt im Uebergang von der adeligen Metropole zur bürgerlichen Urbanität', in Richard Georg Plaschka and Grete Klingenstein (eds.), *Österreich im Europa der Aufklärung. Kontinuität und Zäsur in Europa zur Zeit Maria Theresias und Josephs II. Internationales Symposion in Wien 20.–23. Oktober 1980*, 2 vols. (Vienna, 1985), vol. I, pp. 305–18.

DUFFY, MICHAEL, *The English Satirical Print 1600–1832: The Englishman and the Foreigner* (Cambridge, 1986).

ECHEVERRIA, DURAND, *The Maupeou Revolution: A Study in the History of Libertarianism, France, 1770–1774* (Baton Rouge, La., 1985).

ECKARDT, HANS WILHELM, *Herrschaftliche Jagd, bäuerliche Not und bürgerliche Kritik. Zur Geschichte der fürstlichen und adligen Jagdprivilegien vornehmlich im südwestdeutschen Raum* (Göttingen, 1976).

EGRET, JEAN, *The French Pre-revolution* (1977).

—— *Louis XV et l'opposition parlementaire* (Paris, 1970).

EHRLICH, CYRIL, *The Music Profession in Britain since the Eighteenth Century: A Social History* (Oxford, 1985).

EINEM, HERBERT VON, *Deutsche Malerei des Klassizismus und der Romantik 1760–1840* (Munich, 1978).

EISENSTEIN, ELIZABETH, *Grub Street Abroad: Aspects of the French Cosmopolitan Press from the Age of Louis XV to the French Revolution* (Oxford, 1992).

EITNER, LORENZ, *Neoclassicisim and Romanticism 1750–1850*. Vol. I: *Enlightenment/Revolution* (London, 1971).

ELIAS, NORBERT, *The Court Society* (Oxford, 1983).

ELKIN, ROBERT, *The Old Concert Rooms of London* (London, 1955).

ELOESSER, ARTHUR, *Das bürgerliche Drama. Seine Geschichte im 18. und 19. Jahrhundert* (Berlin, 1898).

ELTON, G. R., 'English national self-consciousness and the Parliament in the sixteenth century', in Otto Dann (ed.), *Nationalismus in vorindustrieller Zeit* (Munich, 1986), pp. 73–82.

ENGELHARDT, ULRICH, *'Bildungsbürgertum'. Begriffs- und Dogmengeschichte eines Etiketts* (Stuttgart, 1986).

ENGELSING, ROLF, *Analphabetentum und Lektüre. Zur Sozialgeschichte des Lesens in Deutschland zwischen feudaler und industrieller Gesellschaft* (Stuttgart, 1973).

ETTLINGER, L. D., 'The role of the artist in society', in *The Eighteenth Century*, ed. Alfred Cobban (London, 1969), pp. 217–58.

FARGE, ARLETTE, and REVEL, JACQUES, *The Vanishing Children of Paris: Rumor and Politics before the French Revolution* (Cambridge, Mass., 1991).

FARGHER, RICHARD, *Life and Letters in France: The Eighteenth Century* (London, 1970).

FEATHER, JOHN, *A History of British Publishing* (London, 1988).

FEBVRE, LUCIEN, and MARTIN, HENRI-JEAN, *The Coming of the Book: The Impact of Printing 1450–1800*, trans. David Gerard (London, 1976).

FEIST, PETER H., HÄNTZSCHE, THOMAS, KRENZLIN, ULRIKE, and LAMMEL, GISOLD, *Geschichte der deutschen Kunst 1760–1848* (Leipzig, 1986).

FERNÁNDEZ DE PINEDO, EMILIANO, GIL NOVALES, ALBERTO, and DÉROZIER, ALBERT, *Centralismo, ilustración y agonía del antiguo régimen (1715–1833)*, Historia de España, ed. Manuel Tuñón de Lara, vol. 6 (Barcelona, 1981).

FERRIER-CAVERIVIÈRE, NICOLE, *L'Image de Louis XIV dans la littérature française de 1660 à 1715* (Paris,1981).

FEUCHTMÜLLER, RUPERT, and KOVÁCS, ELIZABETH (eds.), *Welt des Barock*, 2 vols. (Linz, 1986).

FEULNER, ADOLF, *Skulptur und Malerei des 18. Jahrhunderts in Deutschland* (Potsdam, 1929).

FLEISCHAUER, WERNER, *Barock im Herzogtum Württemberg*, 2nd edn. (Stuttgart, 1981).

FLORISOONE, MICHEL, 'Romantisme et néo-classicisme', in *Histoire de l'Art*, vol. III, ed. Jean Babelon (Paris, 1965), pp. 799–1035.

FOERSTER, ROLF HELLMUT, *Das Barock-Schloß. Geschichte und Architektur* (Cologne, 1981).

FORSYTH, MICHAEL, *Buildings for Music: The Architect, the Musician, and the Listener from the Seventeenth Century to the Present Day* (Cambridge, Mass., 1985).

FRÜHWALD, WOLFGANG, 'Die Idee kultureller Nationbildung und die Entstehung der Literatursprache in Deutschland', in Otto Dann (ed.), *Nationalismus in vorindustrieller Zeit* (Munich, 1986), pp. 129–41.

FULBROOK, MARY, *Piety and Politics: Religion and the Rise of Absolutism in England, Württemberg and Prussia* (Cambridge, 1983).
FURET, FRANÇOIS, *Interpreting the French Revolution* (Cambridge, 1981).
—— *Revolutionary France 1770–1880* (Oxford and Cambridge, Mass., 1992).
FURET, FRANÇOIS, and RICHET, DENIS, *The French Revolution* (London, 1970).
GAGLIARDO, JOHN, *Germany under the Old Regime 1600–1790* (London, 1991).
GALBRAITH, V. H., 'Nationality and language in medieval England', *Transactions of the Royal Historical Society*, 4th ser. 23 (1941), 113–28.
GAY, PETER, *The Enlightenment: An Interpretation*. Vol. 1: *The Rise of Modern Paganism* (London, 1967) and vol. 2: *The Science of Freedom* (New York, 1969).
—— *Voltaire's Politics* (New York, n.d.).
GEIRINGER, KARL, *Haydn: A Creative Life in Music* (London, 1982).
GELBART, NINA R., '"Frondeur" journalism in the 1770s: theater criticism and radical politics in the prerevolutionary French press', *Eighteenth Century Studies*, 17 (1984), 493–514.
GEMBRUCH, WERNER, 'Reformforderungen in Frankreich um die Wende vom 17. zum 18. Jahrhundert: ein Beitrag zur Geschichte der Opposition gegen System und Politik Ludwigs XIV.', *Historische Zeitschrift*, 209 (1969), 265–317.
GEORGE, M. DOROTHY, *Hogarth to Cruikshank: Social Change in Graphic Satire* (London, 1967).
GERTEIS, KLAUS, 'Das "Postkutschenzeitalter". Bedingungen der Kommunikation im 18. Jahrhundert', in Karl Eibl, *Entwicklungsschwellen im 18. Jahrhundert, Aufklärung*, 4, 1 (1989), pp. 49–71.
GESTRICH, ANDREAS, *Absolutismus und Öffentlichkeit. Politische Kommunikation in Deutschland zu Beginn des 18. Jahrhunderts* (Göttingen, 1994).
GIDDENS, ANTHONY, 'Jürgen Habermas', in Quentin Skinner (ed.), *The Return of Grand Theory in the Human Sciences* (Cambridge, 1990), pp. 121–39.
GIERSBERG, HANS-JOACHIM, *Friedrich als Bauherr. Studien zur Architektur des 18. Jahrhunderts in Berlin und Potsdam* (Berlin, 1986).
GIRAUD, MARCEL, 'Crise de conscience et d'autorité à la fin du règne de Louis XIV', *Annales. Économies, Sociétes, Civilisations*, 7 (1952), 172–90 and 293–302.
GIRDLESTONE, CUTHBERT, *Jean-Philippe Rameau: His Life and Work* (London, 1957).
GODECHOT, JACQUES, 'Nation, patrie, nationalisme et patriotisme en France au XVIIIe siecle', *Annales historiques de la Révolution française*, 43 (1971), pp. 481–501.
GOLDFRIEDRICH, JOHANN, *Geschichte des deutschen Buchhandels vom Beginn der klassischen Literaturperiode bis zum Beginn der Fremdherrschaft (1740–1804)* (Leipzig, 1909).
GOMBRICH, E. H., 'The social history of art', in *Meditations on a Hobby Horse and other Essays on the Theory of Art*, 2nd edn. (London, New York, 1971).
GOOCH, G. P., *Louis XV: The Monarchy in Decline* (London, 1956).

GOODMAN, DENA, 'Enlightenment salons: the convergence of female and philosophic ambitions', *Eighteenth-Century Studies*, 22 (1989), 329–50.

—— 'The public and the nation', *Eighteenth Century Studies*, 29 (1995), pp. 1–4.

—— *The Republic of Letters: A Cultural History of the French Enlightenment* (Ithaca, NY, and London, 1994).

GÖPFERT, HERBERT G., 'Lesegesellschaften im 18. Jahrhundert', in Franklin Kopitzsch (ed.), *Aufklärung, Absolutismus und Bürgertum in Deutschland* (Munich, 1976), pp. 403–10.

GORDON, DANIEL, '"Public opinion" and the civilising process in France: the example of Morellet', *Eighteenth-Century Studies*, 22 (1989), 302–28.

GOUBERT, PIERRE, 'La force du nombre', in Fernand Braudel and Ernest Labrousse (eds.), *Histoire économique et sociale de la France*, vol. II: *Des derniers temps de l'âge seigneurial aux préludes de l'âge industriel (1660–1789)* (Paris, 1970), pp. 9–86.

GREENFELD, LIAH, *Nationalism: Five Roads to Modernity* (Cambridge, Mass., 1992).

GRUNDY, ISOBEL, 'Restoration and eighteenth century', in Pat Rogers (ed.), *The Oxford Illustrated History of English Literature* (Oxford, 1987), pp. 214–73.

GUIET, RENÉ, 'La question de la langue française dans les querelles musicales au XVIIIe siècle', in Caroline. B. Bourland et al. (eds.), *Essays contributed in Honor of President William Allan Neilson*, Smith College Studies in Modern Languages (Northampton, Mass., 1940), pp. 89–102.

GUINARD, PAUL-JACQUES, *La Presse espagnole de 1737 à 1791. Formation et signification d'un genre* (Paris, 1973).

GUMBRECHT, HANS ULRICH, REICHARDT, ROLF, and SCHLEICH, THOMAS (eds.), *Sozialgeschichte der Aufklärung in Frankreich*, 2 vols. (Munich and Vienna, 1981).

GUNN, J. A. W., 'Public opinion', in Terence Ball, James Farr, and Russell L. Hanson (eds.), *Political Innovation and Conceptual Change* (Cambridge, 1989), pp. 247–65.

GURLITT, CORNELIUS, *August der Starke. Ein Fürstenleben aus der Zeit des deutschen Barock*, 2 vols. (Dresden, 1924).

HAASS, ROBERT, *Die geistige Haltung der katholischen Universitäten Deutschlands im 18. Jahrhundert* (Freiburg, 1952).

HABERMAS, JÜRGEN, *The Structural Transformation of the Public Sphere: An Inquiry into a Category of Bourgeois Society*, trans. Thomas Burger, (Cambridge, 1989).

HACHTMANN, RÜDIGER, 'Friedrich II. von Preußen und die Freimaurerei', *Historische Zeitschrift*, 264 (1997), pp. 21–54.

HAFERKORN, HANS-JÜRGEN, *Der freie Schriftsteller. Eine literatursoziologische Studie über seine Entstehung und Lage in Deutschland zwischen 1750 und 1800*, Archiv für Geschichte des Buchwesens, 5 (1964), pp. 523–711.

HAMMERSTEIN, NOTKER, *Aufklärung und katholisches Reich. Untersuchungen zur Universitätsreform und Politik katholischer Territorien des Heiligen Römischen Reichs deutscher Nation im 18. Jahrhundert*, Historische Forschungen, vol. 12 (Berlin, 1977).

HAMPSON, NORMAN, 'The Enlightenment in France', in R. Porter (ed.), *The Enlightenment in National Context* (Cambridge, 1981), pp. 41–53.
——'Grub Street revolutionaries', *New York Review of Books* (7 October 1982), 43–4.
HANÁK, PETER, 'Österreichischer Staatspatriotismus im Zeitalter des aufsteigenden Nationalismus', in Reinhard Urbach (ed.), *Wien und Europa zwischen den Revolutionen (1789–1848)* (Vienna and Munich, 1978), pp. 317–28.
HANSLICK, EDUARD, *Geschichte des Concertwesens in Wien*, 2 vols. (Vienna, 1869).
HARDMAN, JOHN, *French Politics 1774–1789: From the Accession of Louis XVI to the Fall of the Bastille* (London, 1995).
——*Louis XVI* (New Haven, 1993).
HARDTWIG, WOLFGANG, 'Wie deutsch war die deutsche Aufklärung?', in Wolfgang Hardtwig, *Nationalismus und Bürgerkultur in Deutschland 1500–1914. Ausgewählte Aufsätze* (Göttingen, 1994), pp. 55–78.
HARRIS, MICHAEL, 'The structure, ownership and control of the press, 1620–1780', in George Boyce, James Curran, and Pauline Wingate (eds.), *Newspaper History from the Seventeenth Century to the Present Day* (London, 1978), pp. 82–97.
HARRIS-WARRICK, REBECCA, 'Ballroom dancing at the court of Louis XIV', *Early Music*, 14 (1986), 41–9.
HARTUNG, FRITZ, *Enlightened Despotism*. Historical Association, General Series, no. 36 (London, n.d.).
——'L'état c'est moi', *Historische Zeitschrift*, 169 (1949), 1–30.
——'Die politischen Testamente der Hohenzollern', in Otto Büsch and Wolfgang Neugebauer (eds.), *Moderne Preußische Geschichte*, vol. III (Berlin and New York, 1981), pp. 1481–1513.
HASKELL, FRANCIS, 'Art and the language of politics', *Journal of European Studies*, 4 (1977), 215–32.
HAUG-MORITZ, GABRIELE, *Württembergischer Ständekonflikt und deutscher Dualismus. Ein Beitrag zur Geschichte des Reichsverbands in der Mitte des 18. Jahrhunderts*, Veröffentlichungen der Kommission für geschichtliche Landeskunde in Baden-Württemberg, series B (Stuttgart, 1992).
HAUTECŒUR, LOUIS, *Histoire de l'architecture classique en France*. Vol. IV: *Seconde moitié du XVIIIe siècle. Le style Louis XV (1750–1792)* (Paris, 1952).
——*Littérature et peinture en France du XVIIe au XXe siècle*, 2nd edn. (Paris, 1963).
——*Rome et la renaissance de l'antiquité à la fin du XVIIIe siècle*, Bibliothéque des écoles françaises d'Athènes et de Rome, vol. 105 (Paris, 1912).
HEARTZ DANIEL, *Haydn, Mozart and the Viennese School 1740–1780* (New York and London, 1995).
——'Opera and the periodisation of eighteenth century music', paper given to the symposium *Critical Years in European Musical History 1740–1760*, Report of the Tenth Congress of the International Musicological Society Ljubljana 1967, ed. Dragotin Cvetko (Kassel, Basle, Paris, London, 1970), pp. 161–9.

HEISTER, HANNS-WERNER, 'Konzertwesen', in *Die Musik in Geschichte und Gegenwart*, ed. Ludwig Finscher, vol. 5 (Kassel, Basle, London, New York, Prague, and Weimar, 1996), pp. 686–710.

HELM, E. E., *Music at the Court of Frederick the Great* (Norman, Okla., 1960).

HINRICHS, CARL, *Preußentum und Pietismus. Der Pietismus in Brandenburg-Preußen als religiös-soziale Reformbewegung* (Göttingen, 1971).

—— 'Zur Selbstauffassung Ludwigs XIV. in seinen *Mémoires*', in Gerhard Oestreich (ed.), *Preußen als historisches Problem* (Berlin, 1964), pp. 299–315.

HINTZE, OTTO, *Die Hohenzollern und ihr Werk*, 8th edn. (Berlin, 1916).

—— 'Das Politische Testament Friedrichs des Großen von 1752', in Otto Hintze, *Regierung und Verwaltung*, 2nd edn. (Göttingen, 1967), pp. 429–47.

HOBSBAWM, ERIC, *Nations and Nationalism since 1780: Programme, Myth, Reality* (Cambridge, 1990).

HOCHEDLINGER, MICHAEL, '"La cause de tous les maux de la France". Die "Austrophobie" im revolutionären Frankreich und der Sturz des Königtums 1789–1792', *Francia. Forschungen zur westeuropäischen Geschichte*, 24 (1997), 73–120.

HOLLIER, DENIS (ed.), *A New History of French Literature* (Cambridge, Mass., 1989).

HÖLSCHER, L., 'Meinung, öffentliche', in Joachim Ritter and Karlfried Gründer (eds.), *Historisches Wörterbuch der Philosophie*, vol. 5 (Darmstadt, 1980), pp. 1023–33.

HUNT, LYNN, 'Introduction', in Lynn Hunt (ed.), *The New Cultural History* (Berkeley, Los Angeles, and London, 1989), pp. 1–15.

—— 'The many bodies of Marie Antoinette: political pornography and the problem of the feminine in the French Revolution', in Lynn Hunt (ed.), *Eroticism and the Body Politic* (Baltimore, Md., and London, 1991), pp. 108–30.

—— *Politics, Culture and Class in the French Revolution* (London, 1986).

—— (ed.), *The Invention of Pornography: Obscenity and the Origins of Modernity, 1500–1800* (New York, 1993).

HYSLOP, B. F., *French Nationalism in 1789 according to the General Cahiers* (New York, 1934).

INGRAO, CHARLES, *The Habsburg Monarchy 1618–1815* (Cambridge, 1994).

IRWIN, DAVID, *English Neo-classical Art: Studies in Inspiration and Taste* (London, 1966).

ISHERWOOD, ROBERT M., *Music in the Service of the King: France in the Seventeenth Century* (Ithaca, NY, and London, 1973).

JÄGER, GEORG, and SCHÖNERT, JÖRG, 'Die Leihbibliothek als literarische Institution des 18. und 19. Jahrhunderts—ein Problemaufriß', in Georg Jäger and Jörg Schönert (eds.), *Die Leihbibliothek als Institution des literarischen Lebens im 18. und 19. Jahrhundert* (Hamburg, 1980), pp. 7–60.

JÄGER, WOLFGANG, *Öffentlichkeit und Parlamentarismus. Eine Kritik an Jürgen Habermas* (Stuttgart, Berlin, Cologne, and Mainz, 1973).

Jørgensen, Sven Aage, Bohnen, Klaus, and Øhrgaard, Per, *Aufklärung, Sturm und Drang, frühe Klassik 1740–1789* (Munich, 1990).

Kaiser, Gerhard, *Pietismus und Patriotismus im literarischen Deutschland* (Wiesbaden, 1961).

Kalnein, Wend Graf, and Levey, Michael, *Art and Architecture of the Eighteenth Century in France* (London, 1972).

Kantorowicz, Ernst H., '*Oriens Augusti—Lever du Roi*', *Dumbarton Oaks Papers*, 17 (1963), pp. 117–78.

Keldysh, Yu. V., *Russkaya muzyka XVIII veka* (Moscow, 1965).

Keller, H., *Die Kunst des 18. Jahrhunderts* (Berlin, 1971).

Kemp, Betty, 'Patriotism, pledges and the people', in Martin Gilbert (ed.), *A Century of Conflict 1850–1950: Essays for A. J. P. Taylor* (London, 1966), pp. 35–46.

Kidd, Colin, *British Identities before Nationalism: Ethnicity and Nationhood in the Atlantic World, 1600–1800* (Cambridge, 1999).

—— 'Protestantism, constitutionalism and British identity under the later Stuarts', in Brendan Bradshaw and Peter Roberts (eds.), *British Consciousness and Identity: The Making of Britain, 1533–1707* (Cambridge, 1998), pp. 321–42.

Kimbell, David, *Italian Opera* (Cambridge, 1991).

Kishlansky, Mark, *A Monarchy Transformed: Britain 1603–1714* (London, 1996).

Kohn, Hans, 'The genesis and character of English nationalism', *Journal of the History of Ideas*, 1 (1940), 69–94.

Koht, Halvdan, 'The dawn of nationalism in Europe', *American Historical Review*, 52 (1947), 265–80.

Kopitzsch, Franklin, 'Aufklärung und Bürgerlichkeit', in Klaus Bohnen, Sven-Aage Jørgensen, and Friedrich Schomöe (eds.), *Kultur und Gesellschaft in Deutschland von der Reformation bis zur Gegenwart* (Copenhagen and Munich, 1981), pp. 57–82.

Koselleck, Reinhart, *Critique and Crisis: Enlightenment and the Pathogenesis of Modern Society* (Leamington Spa, 1987).

Kossok, Manfred, *Am Hofe Ludwigs XIV.* (Stuttgart, 1990).

Krome, Ferdinand, *Die Anfänge des musikalischen Journalismus in Deutschland* (Leipzig, 1896).

Krückmann, Peter O. (ed.), *Der Himmel auf Erden. Tiepolo in Würzburg*, 2 vols. (Munich and New York, 1996).

Krüdener, Jürgen, Freiherr von, *Die Rolle des Hofes im Absolutismus* (Stuttgart, 1973).

Krummel, D. W., and Sadie, Stanley (eds.), *Music Printing and Publishing* (London, 1990).

Kunze, Stefan, 'Die *opera seria* und ihr Zeitalter', in Friedrich Lippmann (ed.), *Colloquium 'Johann Adolf Hasse und die Musik seiner Zeit'* (Siena, 1983), Veröffentlichungen der musikgeschichtlichen Abteilung des Deutschen Historischen Instituts in Rom (n.p., 1987), pp. 1–11.

LANDES, JOAN B., *Women and the Public Sphere in the Age of the French Revolution* (Ithaca, NY, and London, 1988).

LANDON, H. C. ROBBINS, and JONES, DAVID WYN, *Haydn: His Life and Music* (London, 1988).

LANG, PAUL HENRY, 'Music and the court in the eighteenth century', in Paul Fritz and David Williams (eds.), *City and Society in the Eighteenth Century* (Toronto, 1973), 147–63.

LANGFORD, PAUL, *A Polite and Commercial People: England 1727–1783* (Oxford, 1989).

LEITH, JAMES A., *The Idea of Art as Propaganda in France 1750–1799* (Toronto, 1965).

LENIENT, C., *La Poésie patriotique en France dans les temps modernes*, 2 vols. (Paris, 1894).

LEVEY, MICHAEL, *Painting at Court* (New York, 1971).

—— *Rococo to Revolution: Major Trends in Eighteenth-century Painting* (London, 1966).

LOUGH, JOHN, *An Introduction to Eighteenth-century France* (London, 1960).

—— *Paris Theatre Audiences in the Seventeenth and Eighteenth Centuries* (Oxford, 1957).

LOWINSKY, EDWARD, 'Taste, style and ideology in eighteenth century music' in Earl J. Wasserman (ed.), *Aspects of the Eighteenth Century* (Baltimore, Md., and London, 1965), pp. 163–206.

LUCAS, COLIN (ed.), *The Political Culture of the French Revolution* (Oxford, 1988).

MCKAY, DEREK, and SCOTT, H. M., *The Rise of the Great Powers 1648–1815* (London, 1983).

MCKENDRICK, NEIL, BREWER, JOHN, and PLUMB, J. H., *The Birth of a Consumer Society: The Commercialisation of Eighteenth-century England* (London, 1982).

MCLELLAND, CHARLES E., 'German universities in the eighteenth century: crisis and renewal', in James A. Leith (ed.), *Facets of Education in the Eighteenth Century, Studies on Voltaire and the Eighteenth Century*, 167 (Oxford, 1977), pp. 169–89.

MCVEIGH, SIMON, *Concert Life in London from Mozart to Haydn* (Cambridge, 1993).

MARTIN, HENRI-JEAN, and CHARTIER, ROGER, (eds.), *Histoire de l'édition française*. Vol. II: *Le livre triomphant 1660–1830* (Paris, 1984).

MATHIAS, PETER, 'Concepts of Revolution in England and France in the eighteenth century', *Studies in Eighteenth Century Culture*, XIV (1985), pp. 29–46.

MATHIAS, PETER, and O'BRIEN, P. K., 'Taxation in Britain and France 1715–1810', *Journal of European Economic History*, 5 (1976), 601–50.

MAZA, SARAH, 'The diamond necklace affair revisited (1785–1786): the case of the missing queen', in Lynn Hunt (ed.), *Eroticism and the Body Politic* (Baltimore, Md., and London, 1991), pp. 63–89.

—— *Private Lives and Public Affairs: The causes célèbres of Pre-Revolutionary France* (Berkeley, Los Angeles, and London, 1993).

MELTON, JAMES VAN HORN, *Absolutism and the Eighteenth-century Origins of Compulsory Schooling in Prussia and Austria* (Cambridge, 1988).

—— 'The emergence of "society" in eighteenth- and nineteenth-century Germany', in Penelope J. Corfield (ed.), *Language, History, and Class* (Oxford, 1991), pp. 131–49.

—— *Politics, Culture and the Public Sphere in Enlightenment Europe* (Cambridge, 2000).

Middleton, Robin, and Watkin, David, *Neo-classical and Nineteenth-century Architecture* (New York, 1980).

Mikoletzky, Hanns Leo, *Oesterreich—Das große Jahrhundert. Von Leopold I. bis Leopold II.* (Vienna, 1967).

Milligan, Thomas B., *The Concerto and London's Musical Culture in the Late Eighteenth Century* (Epping, 1983).

Millner, Frederick L., *The Operas of Johann Adolf Hasse* (n.p., 1979).

Minogue, Kenneth, *Nationalism* (London, 1967).

Mittenzwei, Ingrid, *Friedrich II. von Preußen* (Cologne, 1980).

Möller, Horst, *Aufklärung in Preußen. Der Verleger, Publizist und Geschichtsschreiber Friedrich Nicolai* (Berlin, 1974).

—— *Fürstenstaat oder Bürgernation: Deutschland 1763–1815* (Berlin, 1989).

—— 'Königliche und bürgerliche Aufklärung', in Manfred Schlenke (ed.), *Preußen—Versuch einer Bilanz*, 5 vols. (Hamburg, 1981). Vol. 2: *Preußen—Beiträge zu einer politischen Kultur*, pp. 120–35.

—— *Vernunft und Kritik. Deutsche Aufklärung im 17. und 18. Jahrhundert* (Frankfurt am Main, 1986).

—— 'Wie aufgeklärt war Preußen?', in Hans-Jürgen Puhle and Hans-Ulrich Wehler (eds.), *Preußen im Rückblick* (Göttingen, 1980), pp. 176–201.

Morrow, Mary Sue, *Concert Life in Haydn's Vienna: Aspects of a Developing Musical and Social Institution* (Stuyvesant, NY, 1988).

Nathans, Benjamin, 'Habermas's "Public sphere" in the era of the French Revolution', *French Historical Studies*, 16 (1990), 620–44.

Newman, Gerald, *The Rise of English Nationalism* (London, 1987).

Nichols, David J., and Hansell, Sven, 'Johann Adolf [Adolph] Hasse', in Stanley Sadie (ed.), *The New Grove Dictionary of Music and Musicians*, vol. 8 (London, 1980), pp. 279–93.

Nipperdey, Thomas, *The Rise of the Arts in Modern Society* (London, 1990).

Nisbet, H. B., '*Was ist Aufklärung?* The concept of enlightenment in eighteenth century Germany', *Journal of European Studies*, 12 (1982), 77–95.

Nora, Pierre (ed.), *Les Lieux de mémoire*, 7 vols. (Paris, 1984).

Novotny, Fritz, *Painting and Sculpture in Europe 1780–1880* (Harmondsworth, 1958).

Ogilvie, Sheilagh, 'The European economy in the eighteenth century', in T. C. W. Blanning (ed.), *The Short Oxford History of Europe: The Eighteenth Century* (Oxford, 1999), pp. 91–130.

O'Gorman, Frank, *The Long Eighteenth Century. British Political and Social History 1688–1832* (London, 1997).

OSTHOFF, HELMUTH, 'Friedrich II. als Musikliebhaber und Komponist', in Erhard Bethke (ed.), *Friedrich der Große* (Gütersloh, 1985), pp. 179–87.

OUTRAM, DORINDA, *The Enlightenment* (Cambridge, 1995).

OWEN, JOHN B., 'George II reconsidered', in Anne Whiteman, J. S. Bromley, and P. G. M. Dickson (eds.), *Statesmen, Scholars and Merchants: Essays in Eighteenth-century History presented to Dame Lucy Sutherland* (Oxford, 1973), pp. 113–34.

OZOUF, MONA, 'Public opinion at the end of the old regime', *Journal of Modern History*, 60 (Supplement, September 1988), 1–21.

PALMER, ROBERT R., 'The national idea in France before the Revolution', *Journal of the History of Ideas*, 1 (1940), 89–111.

PARES, RICHARD, *King George III and the Politicians* (Oxford, 1953).

PASCAL, ROY, *The German Sturm und Drang* (Manchester, 1953).

PAULSON, RONALD, *Hogarth: His Life, his Art, and Times* (New Haven and London, 1974).

PLACE, ADELAÏDE DE, *La Vie musicale en France au temps de la Révolution* (Paris, 1989).

PLUMB, J. H., 'The public, literature and the arts in the eighteenth century', in Michael R. Marrus (ed.), *The Emergence of Leisure* (New York, 1974), pp. 11–37.

POLLEROSS, FRIEDRICH B., 'Sonnenkönig und österreichische Sonne. Kunst und Wissenschaft als Fortsetzung des Krieges mit anderen Mitteln', *Wiener Jahrbuch für Kunstsgeschichte*, 40 (1987), 239–56.

POPKIN, JEREMY D., *News and Politics in the Age of Revolution: Jean Luzac's Gazette de Leyde* (Ithaca, NY, and London, 1989).

—— 'Pamphlet journalism at the end of the old regime' *Eighteenth Century Studies*, 22 (1989), 351–67.

—— 'The royalist press in the reign of terror', *Journal of Modern History*, 51 (December 1979), 685–700.

PORTER, ROY, *English Society in the Eighteenth Century* (Harmondsworth, 1982).

PRESS, VOLKER, *Kriege und Krisen. Deutschland 1600–1715* (Munich, 1991).

PRICE, MUNRO, 'The Dutch affair and the fall of the *ancien régime*, 1784–1787', *Historical Journal*, 38 (1995), 875–905.

—— *Preserving the Monarchy: the comte de Vergennes, 1774–1787* (Cambridge, 1995).

PROCHASKA, FRANK, *The Republic of Britain 1760 to 2000* (London, 2000).

PYE, JOHN, *Patronage of British Art, an historical sketch: an account of the rise and progress of art and artists in London, from the beginning of the reign of George the Second; together with a history of the Society for the Management and Distribution of the Artists' Fund* (London, 1845).

RAABE, PAUL, *Bücherlust und Lesefreuden. Beiträge zur Geschichte des Buchwesens im 18. und frühen 19. Jahrhundert* (Stuttgart, 1984).

RAVEN, JAMES, *Judging New Wealth: Popular Publishing and Responses to Commerce in England, 1750–1800* (Oxford, 1992).

RAYNOR, HENRY, *A Social History of Music from the Middle Ages to Beethoven* (London, 1972).

Réau, Louis, *L'Art au XVIIIe siècle en France. Style Louis XVI 1760–1789* (Paris, 1952).
——*L'Europe française au siècle des lumières* (Paris, 1951).
——*Histoire de la peinture française au XVIIIe siècle*, vol. 2 (Paris and Brussels, 1926).
Reed, T. J., *The Classical Centre: Goethe and Weimar 1775–1832* (London, 1980).
——*Schiller* (Oxford, 1991).
Rivers, Isabel (ed.), *Books and their Readers in Eighteenth-century England* (Leicester, 1982).
Robson-Scott, W. D., *The Literary Background of the Gothic Revival in Germany* (Oxford, 1965).
Rosenblum, Robert, *Transformations in Late Eighteenth-century Art* (Princeton, NJ, 1967).
Rubin, David Lee (ed.), *Sun King: The Ascendancy of French Culture during the Reign of Louis XIV* (Washington, DC, 1992).
Savage, Gary, 'Favier's heirs: the French Revolution and the secret du roi', *Historical Journal*, 41 (1998), 225–58.
Schama, Simon, *Citizens: A Chronicle of the French Revolution* (New York, 1989).
——'The domestication of majesty: royal family portraiture 1500–1850', in Robert I. Rotberg and Theodore K. Rabb (eds.), *Art and History: Images and their Meaning* (Cambridge, 1988), pp. 155–81.
Schieder, Theodor, *Friedrich der Große. Ein Königtum der Widersprüche* (Frankfurt am Main, Berlin, and Vienna, 1983).
——'Friedrich der Große—eine Integrationsfigur des deutschen Nationalbewußtseins im 18. Jahrhundert', in Otto Dann (ed.), *Nationalismus in vorindustrieller Zeit* (Munich, 1986), pp. 109–27.
Schleuning, Peter, *Das 18. Jahrhundert. Der Bürger erhebt sich* (Hamburg, 1984).
Schnapper, Antoine, 'The King of France as collector in the seventeenth century', in Robert I. Rotberg and Theodore K. Rabb (eds.), *Art and History: Images and their Meaning* (Cambridge, 1988), pp. 183–207.
Schulze, Hagen, and Stürmer, Michael, *Mitten in Europa. Deutsche Geschichte* (Berlin, 1987).
Schultz, Helga, *Berlin 1650–1800. Sozialgeschichte einer Residenz* (Berlin, 1987).
——'Mythos und Aufklärung. Frühformen des Nationalismus in Deutschland', *Historische Zeitschrift*, 263 (1996), 31–67.
Schulze, Hagen, *The Course of German Nationalism: From Frederick the Great to Bismarck 1763–1867* (Cambridge, 1991).
——*States, Nations and Nationalism from the Middle Ages to the present* (Oxford, 1996).
Sedlymayr, Hans, 'Die politische Bedeutung des deutschen Barock. Der "Reichsstil"', in idem, *Epochen und Werke. Gesammelte Schriften zur Kunstgeschichte*, vol. II (Vienna and Munich, 1960), pp. 139–55.

SHARPE, KEVIN, 'Representations and negotiations: texts, images and authority in early modern England', *Historical Journal*, 42 (1999), 853–81.
SKINNER, QUENTIN, *The foundations of modern political thought*, 2 vols. (Cambridge, 1978).
—— 'The state', in Terence Ball, James Farr, and Russell L. Hanson (eds.), *Political Innovation and Conceptual Change* (Cambridge, 1989), pp. 90–131.
SMITH, ANTHONY D., *The Ethnic Origins of Nations* (Oxford, 1986).
—— 'Gastronomy or geology? The role of nationalism in the reconstruction of nations', *Nations and Nationalism*, 1 (1995), 3–23.
—— 'Memory and modernity: reflections on Ernest Gellner's theory of nationalism', *Nations and Nationalism*, 2 (1996), 371–88.
—— 'Nations and their pasts', *Nations and Nationalism*, 2 (1996), 358–70.
—— *The Newspaper: An International History* (London, 1979).
—— *Theories of Nationalism* (London, 1983).
SMITH, RUTH, *Handel's Oratorio and Eighteenth-century thought* (Cambridge, 1995).
SOLNON, JEAN FRANÇOIS, *La Cour de France* (Paris, 1987).
SOLOMON, MAYNARD, *Mozart: A Life* (London, 1995).
SOMBART, WERNER, *Luxury and Capitalism* (Ann Arbor, Mich., 1967).
SOREL, ALBERT, *Europe and the French Revolution*. Vol. I (1969).
SPIELMAN, JOHN P., *Leopold I of Austria* (London, 1977).
STAUBER, REINHARD, 'Nationalismus vor dem Nationalismus?', *Geschichte in Wissenschaft und Unterricht*, 47 (1996), 139–65.
STEINBERG, S. H., *Five Hundred Years of printing*, new edn., revised by John Trevitt (London, 1996).
STEINMETZ, HORST (ed.), *Friedrich II., König von Preußen und die deutsche Literatur des 18. Jahrhunderts. Texte und Dokumente* (Stutgart, 1985).
SUMMERSON, JOHN, *Architecture in Britain 1530–1830* (Harmondsworth, 1970).
—— *Georgian London*, rev. edn. (London, 1972).
SWANN, JULIAN, *Politics and the Parlement of Paris under Louis XV, 1754–1774* (Cambridge, 1995).
THOMAS, KEITH, 'The meaning of literacy in early modern England', in Gerd Baumann (ed.), *The Written Word: Literacy in Transition* (Oxford, 1986), pp. 97–131.
VAN KLEY, DALE K., *The Damiens Affair and the Unravelling of the Ancien Régime* (Princeton, NJ, 1984).
—— 'In search of eighteenth century Parisian public opinion', *French Historical Studies*, 19 (1995), 215–26.
VANN, JAMES ALLEN, *The Making of a State: Württemberg 1593–1793* (Ithaca, NY, and London, 1984).
VERBA, CYNTHIA, *Music and the French Enlightenment: Reconstruction of a Dialogue 1750–1764* (Oxford, 1993).

VIGUERIE, JEAN DE, 'Le roi et le "public". L'exemple de Louis XV', *Revue Historique*, 563 (1987), pp. 23–34.

VIROLI, MAURIZIO, *For Love of Country: An Essay on Patriotism and Nationalism* (Oxford, 1995).

WANGERMANN, ERNST, 'Deutscher Patriotismus und österreichischer Reformabsolutismus im Zeitalter Josephs II.', in Heinrich Lutz and Helmut Rumpler (eds.), *Österreich und die deutsche Frage im 19. und 20. Jahrhundert* (Vienna, 1982), pp. 60–72.

WARD, W. R., *Christianity under the Ancien Régime 1648–1789* (Cambridge, 1999).

WARD, ALBERT, *Book Production, Fiction and the German Reading Public 1740–1800* (Oxford, 1974).

WARNING, RAINER (ed.), *Das Fest* (Munich, 1989).

WEBER, HERMANN, 'Das Sacre Ludwigs XVI. vom 11. Juni 1775 und die Krise des Ancien Régime', in Ernst Hinrichs, Eberhard Schmitt, and Rudolf Vierhaus (eds.), *Vom Ancien Régime zur Französischen Revolution. Forschungen und Ergebnisse* (Göttingen, 1978), pp. 539–65.

WEHLER, HANS-ULRICH, *Deutsche Gesellschaftsgeschichte*. Vol. I: *Vom Feudalismus des Alten Reiches bis zur Defensiven Modernisierung der Reformära 1700–1815* (Munich, 1987).

WELLESZ, EGON, and STERNFELD, FREDERICK, *The Age of Enlightenment 1745–1790*. The New Oxford History of Music, vol. VII (Oxford, 1973).

WILENTZ, SEAN (ed.), *Rites of Power: Symbolism, Ritual and Politics since the Middle Ages* (Philadelphia, 1985).

WILLIAMS, RAYMOND, *Keywords: A Vocabulary of Culture and Society* (London, 1983).

WILSON, KATHLEEN, *The Sense of the People: Politics, Culture and Imperialism in England, 1715–1785* (Cambridge, 1995).

WILSON, PETER H., *War, State and Society in Württemberg, 1677–1793* (Cambridge, 1995).

WITTMANN, REINHARD, 'Was there a reading revolution at the end of the eighteenth century?', in Guglielmo Cavallo and Roger Chartier (eds.), *A History of Reading in the West* (Amherst, Mass., 1999), pp. 284–312.

WOODMANSEE, MARTHA, 'The genius and the copyright: economic and legal conditions of the emergence of the "author"', *Eighteenth Century Studies*, 17 (1983–4), 425–48.

WORMALD, PATRICK, '*Engla Lond*: the making of an allegiance', *Journal of Historical Sociology*, 7 (1994), 1–24.

ZASLAW, NEAL, *The Classical Era: From the 1740s to the End of the Eighteenth Century* (London, 1989).

INDEX

KING ALFRED'S COLLEGE
LIBRARY